ANCIENT J1

Gideon Bohak gives a pioneering account of the broad history of ancient Jewish magic, from the Second Temple to the rabbinic period. It is based both on ancient magicians' own compositions and products in Aramaic, Hebrew and Greek, and on the descriptions and prescriptions of non-magicians, to reconstruct a historical picture that is as balanced and nuanced as possible.

The main focus is on the cultural make-up of ancient Jewish magic, and special attention is paid to the processes of cross-cultural contacts and borrowings between Jews and non-Jews, as well as to inner-Jewish creativity. Other major issues explored include the place of magic within Jewish society, contemporary Jewish attitudes to magic, and the identity of its practitioners. Throughout, the book seeks to explain the methodological underpinnings of all sound research in this demanding field, and to highlight areas where further research is likely to prove fruitful.

GIDEON BOHAK teaches in the Department of Jewish Culture, University of Tel Aviv. He is author of *Joseph and Aseneth and the Jewish Temple in Heliopolis* (1996).

ANCIENT JEWISH MAGIC

A History

GIDEON BOHAK

CAMBRIDGE
UNIVERSITY PRESS

University Printing House, Cambridge CB2 8BS, United Kingdom

Published in the United States of America by Cambridge University Press, New York

Cambridge University Press is part of the University of Cambridge.

It furthers the University's mission by disseminating knowledge in the pursuit of education, learning and research at the highest international levels of excellence.

www.cambridge.org
Information on this title: www.cambridge.org/9780521180986

© Gideon Bohak 2008

This publication is in copyright. Subject to statutory exception and to the provisions of relevant collective licensing agreements, no reproduction of any part may take place without the written permission of Cambridge University Press.

First published 2008
First paperback edition 2011

A catalogue record for this publication is available from the British Library

Library of Congress Cataloguing in Publication data
Bohak, Gideon, 1961–
Ancient Jewish magic: a history / Gideon Bohak.
p. cm.
Includes bibliographical references and index.
ISBN 978-0-521-87457-1 (hardback)
1. Magic, Jewish – History. 2. Magic in rabbinical literature. I. Title.
BF1622.J45B64 2007
133.4′3089924–dc22   2007046052

ISBN 978-0-521-87457-1 Hardback
ISBN 978-0-521-18098-6 Paperback

Cambridge University Press has no responsibility for the persistence or accuracy of URLs for external or third-party internet websites referred to in this publication, and does not guarantee that any content on such websites is, or will remain, accurate or appropriate.

Contents

List of figures	page	vi
Acknowledgments		vii
Introduction		1
1 Jewish magic: a contradiction in terms?		8
2 Jewish magic in the Second Temple period		70
3 Jewish magic in late antiquity – the "insider" evidence		143
4 Non-Jewish elements in late-antique Jewish magic		227
5 How "Jewish" was ancient Jewish magic?		291
6 Magic and magicians in rabbinic literature		351
Epilogue		426
Bibliography		435
Index		480

Figures

3.1 A bronze amulet from Sepphoris. IAA negative no. 331414. Courtesy of the Israel Antiquities Authority. *page* 151

3.2 Amulets found in Ḥorvat Maʿon. IAA negative no. 19171. Courtesy of the Israel Antiquities Authority. 152

3.3 Inscribed clay sherds from Ḥorvat Rimmon. IAA negative no. 138528. Courtesy of the Israel Antiquities Authority. 157

3.4 A magical gem showing Daniel feeding the Babylonian snake-god. KM 26125, Kelsey Museum of Archaeology, the University of Michigan. 160

3.5 An amuletic bronze ring with a holy rider. KM 26165, Kelsey Museum of Archaeology, the University of Michigan. 163

3.6 A Babylonian incantation bowl with two bound male demons. KM 33756, Kelsey Museum of Archaeology, the University of Michigan. 186

3.7 A magical gem with hybrid deities. KM 26054, Kelsey Museum of Archaeology, the University of Michigan. 188

3.8 A magical gem with King Solomon. KM 26092, Kelsey Museum of Archaeology, the University of Michigan. 213

3.9 A Genizah fragment of a magical recipe book, Cambridge University Library, Taylor-Schechter AS 142.146. Courtesy of the Syndics of Cambridge University Library. 218

4.1 A Genizah amulet, Cambridge University Library, Or. 1080.14.13. Courtesy of the Syndics of Cambridge University Library. 273

4.2 A Genizah magical fragment, Cambridge University Library, Taylor-Schechter K 12.60. Courtesy of the Syndics of Cambridge University Library. 275

Acknowledgments

Scholarship is an eminently social thing, and the present study is no exception. Its ultimate origins lie in my Princeton days, when John Gager initiated me into the study of ancient magic. Its initial growth took place in Ann Arbor, when I was allowed to teach several courses on ancient magic and to curate an exhibition of ancient magical artifacts from the University of Michigan's rich archeological and papyrological collections (see Bohak 1996). But the book itself began to take shape here, at Tel-Aviv University, while teaching at the Department of Jewish Philosophy and the Program in Religious Studies and enjoying constant feedback from colleagues and students alike.

Many people have helped me along the way, with criticism and advice, and it is both a duty and a pleasure to thank them here. Ithamar Gruenwald, Yuval Harari, Reimund Leicht, and Dan Levene have been arguing with me on different aspects of ancient Jewish magic for many years now, and have commented on several chapters of this book when still in draft form. Shaul Shaked shared with me his unpublished work on the Genizah magical texts, without which this study would have been much the poorer, and provided helpful advice on numerous other occasions. And the anonymous readers of the original manuscript, who have left no stone unturned in their searching criticism, have surely helped me build a sounder scholarly structure. Finally, my students Ortal-Paz Saar and Bar Belinitzkey read the entire manuscript and improved it with many useful comments and suggestions, and my colleague Meir Shahar read it and assured me that some of it would make sense even to a Sinologist.

Many other scholars have helped me with specific advice, and shared some of their extensive knowledge with me. I am especially grateful to Tzvi Abusch, Avriel Bar-Levav, Jeffrey Chajes, Jacco Dieleman, Edna Engel, Esther and Hanan Eshel, Chris Faraone, Alexander Fodor, Mark Geller, David Jordan, Hagai Misgav, Matthew Morgenstern, Michael Morony, Shlomo Naeh, Arpád Nagy, Joseph Naveh, Bill Rebiger, Stefan Reif, Robert

Ritner, Ishai Rosen-Zvi, Peter Schäfer, Jeffrey Spier, Jacques van der Vliet, and Ada Yardeni. And if I have forgotten anyone, it was with no malice in mind, for I am forever grateful to all those who helped me in word or deed.

During the many years in which this book has been growing, I also had the occasion to present parts of my work on ancient Jewish magic in lectures, seminars, and conferences in Israel, Europe, and the USA. Listing all the places and occasions where I presented my work would make for a very tedious reading, but I would like to thank all these audiences for their helpful comments, criticism, and additional references, most of which have been incorporated into the present study. I would also like to thank the staff of the Tel-Aviv University Library and of the Institute of Microfilmed Hebrew Manuscripts in Jerusalem, for permission to study the microfilm copies of many Genizah fragments, and to the staffs of Cambridge University Library, the Library of the Jewish Theological Seminary, the Bodleian Library, and the British Library for granting me access to the actual fragments.

Finally, four institutions deserve special thanks. The Israel Science Foundation funded my research project on "Jewish Magical Recipe Books From the Cairo Genizah" (Grant no. 725/03). With this money, and the help of dedicated research assistants (Irena Lerman, Shani Levy (who also compiled the index for the present volume), and Karina Shalem), I have been able to survey hundreds of unpublished Genizah magical texts, and while the full results of this project shall be published elsewhere, they have done much to enrich my understanding of ancient and medieval Jewish magic, as shall be seen from the many references to unpublished Genizah fragments throughout the present study. The German Academic Exchange Service (DAAD) funded a month-long stay with Peter Schäfer and his research team at the Freie Universität, Berlin (September 2002), which enabled me to coordinate my research efforts with theirs. And the Institute for Advanced Study, at the Hebrew University, sponsored a research group on ancient magic (headed by Shaul Shaked, Yuval Harari, and myself) from March to August 2006. It was during that half year, among magic-oriented colleagues and friends, that the final version of this study was revised for publication.

Last, but by no means least, I wish to thank the Rothschild Foundation (Yad ha-Nadiv) for that fateful phone-call on 13 May 2001, informing me that I had won the Michael Bruno Award (sometimes seen as the Israeli version of the MacArthur Fellowship). This prize enabled me to take a leave of absence from all my university obligations for eighteen months, during which much of the research that went into this book was conducted. It also gave me that confidence which only comes with recognition and with financial security, and enabled me to write the kind of book I have always had in mind. At a time when young academics are often forced to prostitute their half-baked wares to the goddess of productivity, I have been blessed with the challenge to produce the kind of monograph that would justify a prize I have already won, and with the opportunity to do so. I will always cherish the experience, but whether the final product indeed justifies the initial investment is only for you, the reader, to decide.

Introduction

> There are many different tunnels in historiography. Among the narrowest and darkest are the ethnic tunnels. And of all the ethnic tunnels, none is quite so dark and narrow as that which is called "Jewish History."[1]

A book on ancient Jewish magic calls for no apologies. The last good book on this fascinating topic appeared in 1898, and much has changed in the intervening century – not only the perspectives from which we examine "magic," but also the evidential basis on which such an examination must be based. When Ludwig Blau wrote his authoritative study, the only available sources were the rabbinic writings and a few documents of Greek magic which display strong Jewish influences. In our own times, we are almost too blessed with new sources – not just a few rabbinic passages unknown to or unnoticed by Blau and many more Greek magical texts of which he was still unaware, but also thousands of Aramaic, Hebrew, and Judeo-Arabic magical texts of whose very existence he was entirely ignorant. Much of this material has not yet been published, but by reading all the published sources and many of the unpublished ones one may gain a wide enough view of this large field to allow a broad sketch of some of its main features, as shall be done in the present study. And in order to clarify its scope and limitations, we may begin by explaining the three words which make up its title.

"Ancient" is perhaps the easiest term to define. The present book covers the development of Jewish magic from the Second Temple period to the early Middle Ages, or – to be slightly more specific – from about the third century BCE to the seventh century CE. Its heart, however, lies in the period which is nowadays known as "late antiquity" – from about the third century to about the seventh century CE. As shall become clear in Chapter 2, the coverage of the earlier period is beset by the relative dearth of evidence, the reasons for which shall be discussed there. The late-antique evidence, on

---

[1] Fischer 1970, p. 144.

the other hand, and that evidence whose origins go back to late antiquity, is both abundant and varied, and thus allows a reliable reconstruction of at least some aspects of late-antique Jewish magic. It is to this reconstruction, especially of the western branch of late-antique Jewish magic, as practiced mainly by the Jews of Palestine and Egypt (as against the eastern branch of late-antique Jewish magic, as practiced by the Jews of Babylonia), that most of the present book shall be devoted (Chapters 3 to 6). Occasionally, we shall add a word or two about the "afterlife" of ancient Jewish magic in the Jewish magic of later periods, but a full survey of this issue is beyond the scope of the present study.

"Jewish" is a more tricky adjective. In speaking of "Jewish magic," we shall be looking for magic as practiced by Jews, for Jewish or non-Jewish clients, and as borrowed from them by non-Jews. This does, of course, raise both theoretical and practical difficulties. On the theoretical level, one may ask whether everything done by ancient Jews is indeed "Jewish," and whether the practitioners' ethnic origins, or religious affiliation, are at all relevant in the study of magical practices. On the more practical level, one must always recall that when we look at a specific magical document, especially one written in such a universal language as Greek was in late antiquity, it sometimes becomes quite difficult to decide whether the person who composed it was a Jew or not. This, however, is an issue to which we shall repeatedly return, and which need not detain us here. Moreover, we shall devote some attention to the question of how "Jewish" ancient Jewish magic really was, and see how in spite of many borrowings of non-Jewish magical technology, ancient Jewish magic was in fact distinctly Jewish. It is for this reason that one is justified in devoting a separate study to ancient Jewish magic, rather than studying it as one side-branch of ancient magic as a whole.

As was already hinted above, and as we shall note at greater length in Chapter 3, ancient Jewish magic seems to fall into two distinct traditions, a western branch and an eastern one. But as our knowledge of the eastern branch of ancient Jewish magic is destined to be transformed in the very near future by the publication of hundreds of new incantations bowls, we shall focus here mainly on the western branch, and on the Jewish magical texts of Palestine and its closest neighbors, from present-day Egypt to Syria and Turkey. Thus, we could easily add the word "Palestinian" to the title of this book, were it not a loaded adjective which might be misconstrued by its potential readers.[2]

---

[2] Let me also stress that by referring to the area between the Jordan river and the Mediterranean as "Palestine" – rather than "Eretz Israel," "the Land of Israel," or "the Holy Land" – I am making no

"Magic." When Blau wrote about ancient Jewish magic, the meaning of that term was hardly in doubt. But the century which separates his work from ours has seen a tectonic shift in the way scholars use many of their favorite terms, and "magic" has seen perhaps the greatest changes of them all. Much ink has been spilled in an attempt to define, or eliminate, this term, and while a full survey of all the definitions of magic offered and rejected over the years seems quite unnecessary here, several points should be made clear at the outset. First, we may follow Evans-Pritchard and the cultural anthropologists and insist that the most difficult issue in the study of foreign cultures (including those of our distant forefathers) is the problem of translation. In studying such a culture, we must try to understand its own terms (what anthropologists now call an "emic" interpretation), for if we merely impose upon it our terms (an "etic" interpretation), we are bound to distort the picture that emerges from the evidence pertaining to that culture. Thus, in the study of another culture's magic, we would be better off first trying to understand whether the culture we are studying has such a category at all (apparently, not all cultures do), and what that category entails – which practices are included under it, which attitudes are displayed towards it, and whether and how its mechanisms and rituals are explained by members of that society. All these variables vary enormously from one culture to the next and even from one period to another, and any study of ancient Jewish magic, as of the magical activities of any other human group in any period in its history, must take account of such considerations.

So much for the theory. Unfortunately, when it comes to practicing it, things are not that simple. As we shall see throughout the present study, ancient Jews did indeed use a whole set of terms and adjectives which often seem to be closely related to our own concept of "magic," but never offered any clear-cut definition of what was meant by these terms. Moreover, unlike some ancient Greek or Roman writers and rulers, and some Christian religious and political leaders, ancient Jews rarely labeled people as "magicians," or punished them for practicing "magic." Thus, an "emic" definition of ancient Jewish magic that is based on the Jewish literary sources is simply not available. Even more disturbing, the hints provided by some of the relevant sources are not necessarily valid when it comes to a different period or a different social group within the Jewish world. Thus, while rabbinic literature does provide us with a good sense of the *rabbis'* conception of "magic" (as we shall see in Chapter 6), their views hardly help us elucidate the concepts of "magic" of the different religious groups within the Jewish

political statement about the current dispute between Israelis and Palestinians, but merely adhering to what seems like standard English usage.

society of the Second Temple period (see Chapter 2). And when we move to the later Geonic period, and to the Karaite attacks on Rabbanite magic, or to the earlier biblical period, and the Torah's discussions of magicians and diviners (see Chapter 1), we find ourselves again in very different historical and social contexts, each with its own definitions of magic – or the lack thereof.

This being the case, we must resort to an etic definition of magic, at least as a heuristic device for setting aside those phenomena in our sources which we would like to study in the present book. Unfortunately, the decision to adopt an etic definition does not yet solve our problem, for a quick glance at the relevant literature will reveal that scholars and lay-persons alike can hardly agree on what *we* mean by "magic," that is, on the emic definition of this term within our own culture. In the present study, we shall take our cue from those scholars who have wisely decided to focus less on the identification of magical *practices* and more on the identification of magical *texts and artifacts*, whose classification as such often proves much easier. The implications of this choice for the study of ancient Jewish magic will be explained in Chapter 1, but we must also note that the focus on "Jewish magic" comes at the expense of texts and practices which sometimes were related to it, but were not an integral part thereof. In what follows, we shall mostly ignore all the highly technical disciplines which usually go under the name of "occult sciences," including such divinatory techniques as astrology, physiognomy, chiromancy (=palmistry), palmomancy (=twitch-divination), *gorallot* (=*sortes*, the use of divinatory lots), geomancy, calendology, hemerology, bibliomancy, divination from natural phenomena (thunders, earthquakes, etc.), or the interpretation of dreams, and such transformative techniques as alchemy. Some of these specialized disciplines had already been in use by Jews from very early times, as a few Qumran fragments eloquently demonstrate and as may be gathered from stray remarks in Josephus or in rabbinic literature, while others are first attested in the Cairo Genizah. In the present study, however, we shall leave them all aside and focus only on the magical technologies utilized by ancient Jews. This is not to deny the possibility that in some instances the practitioners of the magical technologies and those of the occult sciences were the very same people, or that these different disciplines occasionally influenced and cross-fertilized each other. But when we examine the manuscripts in which they were inscribed, both at Qumran and in the (much more extensive, and much better preserved) Cairo Genizah, we repeatedly find the magical spells and recipes and the occult sciences inscribed in different manuscripts, or in different sections thereof. Thus, it would seem more advisable for the different disciplines to be studied separately, or in clusters of closely related disciplines, and by scholars who have mastered the required expertise, which often is not only arcane, but also highly technical.

"Ancient Jewish Magic" is a large topic, which could, and should, be studied from many different disciplinary perspectives – be it philology (which would include the description or publication of as many ancient Jewish magical texts as possible, the identification of textual parallels and sources, and the analysis of their textual transmission), phenomenology (what kinds of magical techniques were used in ancient Jewish magic? for which aims? using which *materia magica*?), sociology (who practiced magic? who were the clients? what were the economic aspects of these transactions?), comparative religion (how does ancient Jewish magic resemble, or differ from, the magical beliefs and practices of other cultures and other historical periods?), or ritual studies (what mechanisms are operated by the magical procedures, and what kinds of changes could they bring about?). In the present study, however, we shall focus mainly on one aspect of ancient Jewish magic, its cultural make-up, and what it tells us about its origins and transformations and about the people who practiced it. To approach such questions correctly, we must study both the Jewish and the non-Jewish magical traditions of antiquity, and we must approach them historically, beginning with the earliest evidence and tracing its gradual development. We must also develop tools which would enable us to trace at least the broader contours of the different stages of ancient Jewish magic, from the Second Temple period to the Muslim conquest, and separate earlier phenomena from later ones. And it is here, in the historical approach, that the present book differs most from all previous treatments of Jewish magic. For, as was rightly noted by Moshe Idel, most of the earlier treatments of Jewish magic – whether ancient or medieval – were written by practicing rabbis, not by historians.[3] Sound as their scholarship might be – and in some cases it was very sound – it was often characterized by an ahistoric approach which confused early and late, mixed ancient phenomena with modern phantoms and apologetics, and misused some of the basic tools of philological enquiry. And the great interest in things Jewish evinced by many scholars of ancient magic as a whole has only made things worse, for it often led to fanciful hypotheses on "Jewish" magical words, symbols, and practices, unfettered by an intimate familiarity with ancient Jewish culture as a whole. Thus, the present book seeks to provide both an outline of the development of

---

[3] See Idel's Foreword to the new reprint of Trachtenberg 1939, p. ix.

the Jewish magical tradition in antiquity and an example of how the Jewish magical texts and artifacts could be analyzed and contextualized within the wider frameworks of ancient Jewish society and culture, and of ancient magic as a whole. It also seeks to point to areas where there is need for further research, and to the types of research which might prove most productive for the future study of ancient Jewish magic. Needless to add, the discovery and publication of new sources, and further analysis of the existing sources, are bound to make the present study obsolete, but when this happens, it will have achieved its goal. We come to praise a topic, not to bury it.

One final note. When Blau wrote his pioneering work, it was still customary to begin a study on magic – if one chose to write one at all – by apologizing for the choice of such an "unseemly" topic and for dealing with "superstitious" and "irrational" practices. Moreover, both before and after his time, any study on Jewish magic was written within the framework of two all-encompassing cleavages which generated much polemics and apologetics. The first was the ongoing debate, not to say *Kulturkampf*, within the Jewish people, between the rationalist reformers and modernizers on the one hand, and the tradition-bound conservatives on the other. This cleavage is especially apparent in many of the earlier scholarly discussions of how "contaminated" the Jewish tradition (and especially the Talmud) really was by magic and superstition, with the ancient sources used as ammunition in modern debates, and the modern debates shaping the reading of the ancient sources. The second major cleavage was the Christian–Jewish schism, and the recurrent use of the medieval stereotype of Jews as magicians, the Devil's own henchmen, as a central pillar of some of the most virulent forms of medieval anti-semitism. Thus, any data pertaining to Jewish magic, and especially "black" magic, was often apologetically handled, or instinctively ignored, by Jewish scholars. In more recent times, however, the post-Holocaust decline of Christian anti-semitism, and the post-modern realization that "rationality" is not the only – and certainly not the best – yardstick with which to measure cultures, created an intellectual climate which is far more open to the study of Jewish magic. Perhaps the best sign of these new attitudes, and of this newly found ability to approach Jewish magic *sine ira et studio*, is that a full century after the discovery of the Cairo Genizah, and long after the study of almost all other types of Genizah texts, the Genizah magical texts are finally being scrutinized by scholars in Jerusalem, New York, Berlin, Princeton, and Tel-Aviv. Slow as this process may seem, its direction is plain to see; the bridge has been crossed, and the road ahead is clear. If anything, one might begin to worry lest the pendulum might swing too far and create an academic vogue which would ultimately lead to too much stress being laid on Jewish magic, a process that is well known to anyone who has followed the place of Kabbalah within the academic study of Judaism in the wake of Gershom Scholem's pioneering studies. Hopefully, the rise of interest in Jewish magic, after such a long period of neglect, will not lead to a disproportionate estimation of its importance within the history of Jewish culture as a whole, but to its incorporation as one more aspect of Jewish cultural creativity, and fully deserving of a critical historical analysis.

CHAPTER I

Jewish magic: a contradiction in terms?

INTRODUCTION

In their reaction to Jewish magic, students of Jewish culture and history often reenact the famous joke about the man who goes to the zoo for the first time in his life. Staring for a long time at the giraffe, and noting all its peculiar features, he finally turns around, mutters to himself "There is no such animal," and leaves the zoo. Perhaps the best example of this attitude to the Jewish magical tradition is provided by the works of Solomon Schechter and Shlomo Dov Goitein, the founding father and the re-founding father of Genizah scholarship. Going over the vast hoard of fragments found in the used-texts-storage-room of a medieval synagogue in Cairo in search of those texts they found interesting, these brilliant scholars had to sift through the thousands of magical texts strewn there; in their voluminous works, however, hardly a trace of such encounters will be found. Combining the works of both scholars, with Schechter's preference for literary texts, Goitein's for the documentary, we would arrive at a reasonably comprehensive coverage of most types of Genizah materials – with the glaring exception of its numerous fragments which deal with magic, divination, and the occult sciences, fragments which both scholars simply treated as if they did not exist.[1] In fact, it took a complete outsider – an Indian anthropologist and novelist – to admit that "a very large number of the documents in the Geniza . . . consist of magical formulae, and treatises related to esoteric rites."[2]

While the deliberate neglect of Jewish magic might be characteristic especially of older scholarship, still constrained by age-old Jewish apologetics and the Enlightenment's disdain for all forms of magic and superstition, it

---

[1] For Schechter's view of Jewish magic, see his famous reference to "the fool by his amulet," quoted by Wasserstrom 1992, p. 160, and by Reif 2000, p. 85. For Goitein's views of magic, see Goitein 1967–93, vol. I, pp. 323–24 and 346, and esp. vol. V, pp. 336–77; see also Frenkel 2002, pp. 52–55; Cohen 2006.
[2] Ghosh 1992, p. 263.

8

is in no way uncommon in contemporary scholarship as well. Thus, to give just one example, a recent encyclopedia of medieval Jewish civilization has useful entries on many aspects of Jewish culture in the Middle Ages – and not a word on magic.[3] It is, moreover, quite symptomatic that the serious study of the Genizah magical texts began when a talmudic expert in search of rabbinic manuscripts in the Cambridge Genizah collections ran into a recipe, written in excellent Mishnaic Hebrew, for winning the chariot races by harming the other competitors and felt he could not ignore it even if he found it utterly revolting.[4] Another impetus for the study of Genizah magical texts was the desire to find new texts in Palestinian and Babylonian Jewish Aramaic, and yet another was provided by the hope that these texts might shed some light on the history of Jewish mysticism, which is now very much in vogue. The study of Jewish magic as an independent, and important, component of Jewish culture is only in its infancy, although the need for such a study has often been recognized.[5]

Given the almost total neglect of Jewish magic in previous scholarship – with Blau's book on rabbinic magic and Trachtenberg's on medieval Jewish magic as the major exceptions – one might begin a book on ancient Jewish magic with a detailed analysis of what earlier students of Jewish history and culture have said about Jewish magic, and especially what they have not. Such a survey would try to understand why the general outlook of most Jewish scholars was so hostile to the Jewish magical tradition that it mostly denied its very existence and ignored its abundant remains, and why even non-Jewish scholars showed so little interest in these remains. This survey, however, will not be undertaken here, both because several such studies have already been written and because it would be more conducive for the present study to examine only the main arguments adduced or assumed by previous scholars to support their conviction that "Jewish magic" is a contradiction in terms.[6] Since this conviction never was based on the analysis of Jewish magical texts and the claim that they were not magical at all, but on the a priori assumption that Jewish magic simply *could* not exist and the benign neglect of the relevant sources, it would perhaps be

---

[3] Roth 2003. Other recent encyclopedias do not ignore Jewish magic – see, e.g., Chajes 1999; Alexander 2000.
[4] Margalioth 1966, p. xvi.
[5] For the desirability of such a study, see, e.g., Gruenwald 1980, pp. 225–26 and Hengel 1984, p. 23, end of n. 38: "Eine neue grundlegende Untersuchung der jüdischen Magie im Vergleich mit dem gemeinantiken Phänomen ist ein dringendes Desiderat." For the growing attention granted to Jewish magic in recent scholarship, see *Pe'amim* 85 (2000) (Heb.) and *Mahanaim* 14 (2002) (Heb.) – two collections of studies entirely devoted to this topic.
[6] For previous surveys of the scholarship, see Harari 1998, pp. 59–98; Gruenwald 1996. See also Lorberbaum 2004, pp. 27–82.

best to dismantle that barrier before turning to the Jewish magical texts themselves. Thus, the aim of the present chapter is not to demonstrate the existence of Jewish magic as a distinct sphere of Jewish culture, at least from late antiquity onwards; the following chapters will provide enough evidence of that to convince even the most ardent skeptics. Our task here is to try to understand why so many intelligent people, scholars and laymen alike, have so vehemently insisted that no such animal could even exist.

Adopting a bird's eye view, we may note five different reasons for this common assumption. The first and most important is that the practice of magic is supposed to be explicitly forbidden by the Hebrew Bible, which might mean that Torah-observant Jews would shun it altogether. If so, the Jewish magical texts and practices we do find must be attributed to antinomian heretics, peddling their illicit wares on the margins of Jewish society and forcefully persecuted, or, at most, barely tolerated, by the Jewish establishment. A second reason is that magic is conceived as superstitious and irrational, and therefore presumably limited to the lowest and least-educated classes of Jewish society, and only grudgingly tolerated by the enlightened establishment. And a third reason is that magic is seen as intrinsically un-monotheistic, since it tries either to appeal to forces other than God or to force God to act against His Will. If some Jews tried to walk down that road, they must have been stopped and punished once their offence was discovered, for it was a road not to be taken by Jews.

To these three types of arguments, each of which has a long history in the study of Judaism, two more may be added, which have only been raised quite recently. On the one extreme we find those scholars who, adopting the view that "magic" is not a definable set of beliefs and practices, but a derogatory label one affixes to other people's religion, are now claiming that in Jewish culture too there is no such thing as magic, and that here too "magic" is just a derogatory label, always reserved for the religious activities of "the other." On the opposite extreme, we find those scholars who, reacting against the age-old claim that Judaism knows no magic, are now insisting that Judaism of all periods was shot through with magical beliefs and practices, so that one cannot even talk about Jewish religion without immediately talking about Jewish magic. In spite of the great differences between these two claims, and between them and the first three, they all share one thing in common, in that they deny the existence of a specifically magical tradition as one distinct expression of Jewish culture. It is this bottom line – and the ensuing neglect of the Jewish magical texts and artifacts – which is common to all five types of claim. Thus, if we are to understand why scholars are wrong in assuming that Jewish magic does not and could not exist, we had better spend some time looking at each of these claims and assumptions. It must be stressed, however, that while embarking upon philosophical, theological, and phenomenological issues, our interest here is less in a theoretical analysis of all the different manners in which the existence of Jewish magic could perhaps be explained, but rather in those explanations which are of relevance for the study of ancient Jewish magic. In later periods of Jewish history, and in Christian, Muslim, or other cultural traditions where magic plays an important role, both the formulation of the problem and the nature of the solutions might prove quite different, but such issues will have to be dealt with elsewhere.

BIBLICAL PROHIBITIONS AND BIBLICAL PARADIGMS

Given the repeated, and well-known, biblical prohibitions against dabbling in magic, sorcery, witchcraft, augury, and all related arts, one might expect magic to be practiced, if at all, only by Jewish deviants and heretics.[7] And yet, as the present study will amply demonstrate, magic was widely practiced by Jews at least from late antiquity onwards, and was in no way limited to apostate Jews, or to some religiously lax strata of Jewish society. How, then, are we to explain the enormous gap between the letter of the law and the spirit of the people?

One possible explanation would be that the Jewish readers of the Hebrew Bible found creative ways to overcome its prohibition of magic. Religious systems, and especially the so-called "book religions," often are forced to deal with the gap between their changing norms and those ordained by their sacred Scriptures, and can display amazing ingenuity in the process.[8] In the Jewish case, we may note how the biblical demands for "an eye for an eye" justice were reinterpreted by the rabbis of late antiquity and turned into a system of monetary fines and compensations, or how the prohibition against lending money on interest to other Jews, and the injunction to annul all such debts every seven years, were creatively subverted from the Second Temple period onwards by social and religious leaders who realized how impractical they were. We may also note how the prohibition against the fashioning of any images was interpreted very literally in some periods of Jewish history and in certain circles of Jewish society, and very liberally

---

[7] This, for example, is how Margalioth viewed *Sepher ha-Razim* (Margalioth 1966, p. xv).
[8] For such processes, see Smith 1993, esp. chapter 5, and Halbertal 1997, pp. 11–44.

in others. In the sphere of magic, too, we shall see some such ingenuity – as when we discuss (in Chapter 6) the rabbinic injunction that one may not *practice* magic, but one may *study* it, and even *teach* it to others (including, of course, some hands-on demonstrations!) – but such examples can hardly explain the pervasiveness of Jewish magic in antiquity. Nowhere in the ancient Jewish discussions of *halakha* (the Jewish legal system, which encompasses every aspect of the traditional Jewish way of life) will we find a systematic and concerted effort to legalize magic, as it were; if we are to understand how magical practices could become so popular within Jewish society of all periods, we must look for a different type of explanation.

Another possible line of reasoning would take the opposite route. If magic was pervasive, perhaps this was due to the willingness of a large number of Jews to ignore the biblical prohibitions on this score, and if so, perhaps these Jews ignored other biblical injunctions as well.[9] Here, however, we are sliding down a very slippery slope, for one of the greatest difficulties in the study of ancient Jewish society is to know which Jews – and especially how many Jews – observed which types of *halakha*, and which Jews ignored it altogether. As we shall see in Chapter 4, ancient Jewish magicians often were quite willing to borrow powerful names, signs, and practices from their non-Jewish neighbors, including some which were not strictly "kosher." And yet, we shall also see (especially in Chapter 5) that the same magicians often went to great lengths to avoid transgressing the basic biblical commandments, and that almost all of their activities lay well within the borders of the normative Jewish behavior of their time. Thus, while we have some evidence of Jews who completely abandoned the Jewish way of life (what the ancient Jewish writers who mention them call "apostates"), or of Jews who went so far in allegorizing the biblical legislation that they no longer observed its literal precepts, such Jews hardly are suitable candidates on which to peg the magical activities we shall examine in subsequent chapters, much of which is entirely Jewish.[10] Similarly, while rabbinic literature often speaks of *minim* (a blanket term covering different types of "Bible-reading heretics") as dabbling in magic, and even describes magical duels between rabbis and such *minim* (see Chapter 6), when we read the actual Jewish magical texts we find nothing in them that would support reading them as connected with such *minim*. In fact, as we shall see in Chapter 5, the Jewish magical texts of late antiquity are very Jewish, and in some ways even more conservative than other strands of Jewish culture

---

[9] This, for example, is the view of Goodenough 1953–68, esp. vol. I, pp. 3–33.
[10] For apostate Jews in antiquity, see Barclay 1998 and Bohak 2002, both with further bibliography.

at the time. Thus, the question of the gap between the biblical legislation and the actual behavior of Torah-abiding Jews remains.

If the difference between what the Bible seems to say and what Bible-bound Jews seem to do lies neither in their deliberate attempts to legalize magic nor in their conscious decision to ignore the biblical injunctions on this score, its roots may be sought in the Hebrew Bible itself, and especially in two different aspects of the biblical dealings with magic. First, in the nature of the prohibitions against magic, which upon a closer examination turn out to be much more complex and less straightforward than is commonly acknowledged. Second, in the biblical stories about men of God and the miracles they performed, and in some of the rituals whose practice the Hebrew Bible describes, tolerates, and even prescribes, both of which could serve as powerful paradigms for post-biblical Jewish magicians. It is to a brief survey of these issues that the present section is devoted.[11]

One final point of introduction. Given our interest in post-biblical Jewish magic, the following discussion does not seek to offer a survey of all passages in the Hebrew Bible which have something to say about magic, or to study the magical practices of the Jews of the First Temple period. Its object is much more modest – to show how post-biblical Jews could dabble in magic without seeing themselves as transgressing the laws of the Torah. It is also for this reason that the following analysis will ignore such issues as the textual criticism of the Hebrew Bible, or the sources of the biblical laws and stories, as well as most of the voluminous output of modern biblical scholarship. Rather than search for what the biblical writers may have written and what they may have had in mind, we focus here on how the texts found in the Hebrew Bible may have been read by those post-biblical Jews who saw it as sacred and binding.

Some biblical prohibitions

Reading the laws of the Torah (=the Pentateuch), one is struck by its recurrent condemnation of a wide range of magical and divinatory practices and practitioners. And yet, looking more closely at these prohibitions, one also discovers how ambiguous their overall effect must have been for some of their post-biblical readers. To begin assessing this issue, let us first focus on the most detailed and comprehensive set of biblical prohibitions of magic and divination. It is found in the Book of Deuteronomy, which purports to consist of Moses' first-person farewell speech to the sons of Israel as

---

[11] For what follows, see also the important study of Kuemmerlin-McLean 1986.

his death was approaching, and is embedded in a set of laws concerning legitimate types of religious and political leadership for the future Jewish polity. Following some descriptions of the nomination and roles of judges, inspectors, levites, and priests, and even a king (Dt 16.18–18.8), we find out whom the Israelites may not appoint or consult:

> When you come to the land which YHWH your God is granting you, you shall not learn to do like the abominations of those Gentile nations. There shall not be found among you one who passes his son and his daughter through the fire, a *qosem* of *qesamim*, a *me'onen*, a *menahesh*, and a *mekhasheph*. And a *hover* of *hever*, and one who asks an *'ov* and a *yide'oni*, and one who seeks of the dead. For whoever does these is an abomination to YHWH, and it is because of these abominations that YHWH your God uproots them from before you. Innocent shall you be with YHWH your God. For these Gentile nations whom you shall supplant listen to *me'onenim* and *qosmim*, whereas you, not thus has YHWH your God granted you. A prophet from among you, from your brothers, like myself (i.e., Moses) shall YHWH your God raise up for you; to him shall you listen. (Dt 18.9–15)

The passage goes on to describe the roles and functions of God's prophets, and especially the touchy issue of how to distinguish between God-appointed and self-appointed ones, but such issues are of less interest for the present inquiry. For our study of the biblical attitudes towards magic and divination we must note that the prohibitions here are not so much on certain *practices* as on certain *practitioners*, who are presented as the exact opposite of the God-sent prophet. To him one may listen, to them one may not. This is an extremely important observation, for it seems quite clear that neither magic nor divination are forbidden *per se*, and that one might even expect God's legitimate priests and prophets (or other Jewish leaders) to provide God's followers with many of the services that these forbidden practitioners provide for the Gentile nations whom the Jews are about to supplant. Elsewhere in the Hebrew Bible, this implicit distinction is made patently clear, as, for example, in the story of Saul, whose attempts to consult YHWH through dreams, the *Urim and Thumim*, and the prophets is considered legitimate, while his turning to a *ba'alat 'ov* is not (1 Sm 28.6, 15), or in the story of King Ahaziah, who is rebuked not for trying to foretell the future, but for consulting "Baal Zebub the god of Ekron" rather than the Jewish God (2 Kgs 1.2–6, 16).[12] As we shall see many more such examples below, we may now stress that the formulation of the biblical prohibitions as against practitioners and not against practices is the norm in other parts of the Pentateuch as well, even in contexts which

---

[12] See also Fishbane 1971, pp. 30–37, and Lust 1974.

have nothing to do with legitimate or illegitimate types of leadership. In Ex 22.17, the terse injunction that "a *mekhashepha* you shall not let live" (which takes only three words in biblical Hebrew!) is embedded in a miscellany of laws on entirely unrelated subjects. And in Lv 19.31 and 20.6, the prohibition against turning to the *'ovot* and the *yide'onim* is inserted in a long set of laws designed to preserve the Israelites' ritual and moral purity. Within that unit, one also finds the prohibition, "you shall not *tenaḥashu* and you shall not *te'onenu* (Lv 19.26)," a rare example of a Torah passage in which the actual practices are prohibited, and not just those who practice them. Finally, in Nm 23.23, Balaam testifies that "there is no *naḥash* in Jacob, and no *qesem* in Israel," an emphatic statement which some readers happily seized upon as the ultimate proof that there is no such thing as Jewish magic. Here, as in many other cases, Yahwistic wishful thinking was turned by the biblical narrators into a statement of fact (and put in the mouth of the greatest non-Jewish expert in the art of magic!) and was adopted as such not only by some medieval Jewish philosophers, but even by some modern scholars.

A second striking feature of the long list of forbidden practitioners in Deuteronomy 18, and one which is of even greater importance for the study of post-biblical Jewish magic, is that it consists mostly of technical terms whose meaning is far from clear. Modern scholars, equipped with all the tools of philological and historical inquiry, and with an ever-growing corpus of Ancient Near Eastern magical texts with which to compare the biblical injunctions, are far from agreeing on the exact meaning of each of these biblical terms, or on how to translate them (soothsayers, wizards, augurs, sorcerers, magicians, diviners, fortune-tellers – English too has an extensive, and quite vague, vocabulary for such professionals!).[13] It is for this reason that we are better served by transliterating these technical terms than by translating them, for most of these terms admit of no certain translation. Needless to add, they would have been much more puzzling to their ancient readers, who had no access to the lexical, textual, and archeological evidence accumulated by modern scholarship, and very little awareness of its possible uses.[14] And when such readers turned to the other passages in the Hebrew Bible in which these terms appear, in order to learn more about their exact meanings, they learned very little about the

---

[13] See, for example, Robertson Smith 1884–85; Davies 1898, pp. 40–59 and 78–90; Jeffers 1996; Seidel 1996, pp. 15–66; Schmitt 2004, pp. 107–16; see also Kuemmerlin-McLean 1986, pp. 60–106 and 114–33.

[14] And see, for example, Sifre Dt 171–72 (pp. 218–19 Finkelstein) and Midrash Tannaim to Dt 18.9–11 (pp. 109–10 Hoffmann), for the rabbis' divergent identifications of many of these technical terms.

practices involved (the one exception being the *ba'alat 'ov* of Endor, in 1 Sm 28, whose activities are described in some detail). In many instances, they found further insistence that these were evil customs, practiced by non-Israelites and by "bad Israelites," and highly displeasing to God.[15] But in other cases they found the very same terms in textual contexts which only made their meaning even harder to fathom. Thus, to give just one example, the prophet Isaiah warns his audience that God would soon remove from Jerusalem and Judea all its leaders, and lists them in detail as "a hero and a man of war, a judge and a prophet and a *qosem* and an elder; a commander of fifty soldiers and a man of noble status, and a counselor and a man wise in *ḥarashim*, and an expert in *laḥash*."[16] How is it that a *qosem*, who certainly is one of the "bad guys" in Deuteronomy 18, here appears side by side with the judge, the prophet, and all the other legitimate Jewish leaders?[17] And what about a man wise in *ḥarashim* or an expert in *laḥash* – what exactly is it that they do, and, if it is an activity relating to magic or divination, why are they listed here, and why are they never even mentioned in the Torah's legislation on these issues? Post-biblical readers of the Hebrew Bible certainly were puzzled by such exegetical conundrums, as can be deduced from their very different renderings of and commentaries on this and similar passages in the Hebrew Bible.[18]

And this brings us to the third and final problem with the list of magical and divinatory practitioners provided by Deuteronomy 18, namely, that it is neither consistent nor complete. The first item on the list, "one who passes his son and his daughter through the fire," has generated much scholarly discussion, but it is commonly agreed that the religious custom to which it refers has little to do with magic or divination. Thus, it seems as if the underlying connection between these prohibitions is not that they deal with magic and divination, but that they are religious customs common to the pre-Israelite dwellers of the Land of Canaan. This might also explain the absence from this list of other types of magicians and diviners who happen to be mentioned elsewhere in the Hebrew Bible, such as *ḥarṭumim*, *gazrin*,

---

[15] Non-Israelites: See, e.g., Nm 22.7; Jos 13.22; 2 Kgs 9.22; Is 47.9, 12; Na 3.4. "Bad Israelites": 2 Kgs 17.17, 21.6; Is 2.6; Mi 5.11; Mal 3.5; 2 Chr 33.6, etc.

[16] Is 3.2–3.

[17] See also Jer 27.9 or Prv 16.10. Of course, readers of the Hebrew Bible would have known that some of the technical terms may have undergone semantic changes during the biblical period itself, as is made clear by 1 Sm 9.9.

[18] For other ambiguous passages, see, e.g., Ez 21.26 (are belomancy, divination by the *teraphim* and hepatoscopy all subcategories of *qesem*, or independent parallel practices?); Jer 27.9 (why are prophecy and divination by dreams included in the list? Are all the practices mentioned here forbidden, or is it just the answers they provided which irritated Jeremiah?); Neh 3.12 (*Ben ha-Loḥesh* as a personal name); etc.

Jewish magic: a contradiction in terms?

ashaphim, or *casdim* (Chaldaeans), who are always associated with the courts of the Egyptian or Babylonian kings.[19] But while the absence of such practitioners from this specific passage may be clear enough, their absence from the other biblical prohibitions of various practitioners of magic and divination is far more striking. Were we to adopt the intuitive assumption that what is not explicitly forbidden by the law might in fact be permitted, we could even conclude that the Hebrew Bible forbids consulting a *qosem* but permits the consulting of a *casdi* or an *ashaph*. This would, of course, be the wrong conclusion to reach, but it does highlight the incomplete nature of the biblical legislation on this score. Equally defensible, and much more important for the study of post-biblical Jewish culture, would be the claim that the use of *laḥash* – which literally means "whisper" and which is used, for example, to charm snakes – is permitted, since it is never forbidden by the Torah and is actually referred to quite favorably in other books of the Bible.[20] As we shall see in the subsequent chapters, the whispering of secret curses, biblical verses, and magical incantations was a favorite pastime of many ancient Jews, including some of the leading religious authorities of their time.

The lacunose nature of the biblical legislation concerning magic may be highlighted by looking at one more example. In Leviticus 24, a story is told of a man of mixed parentage (his mother was an Israelite but his father an Egyptian) who, in a fight with an Israelite person, "*naqav*ed the Name ... and cursed." He was immediately brought to Moses and put in confinement, until God would instruct Moses as to what must be done in this case. The verdict was sharp and clear – the culprit was to be stoned to death by the entire community. To this verdict, God appends a more general ruling:

And to the sons of Israel you shall say thus: Whichever man curses his God will bear responsibility for his sin. And he who *noqev*s the Name (of) YHWH will surely die, the whole community will surely stone him; whether a *ger* or an Israelite – if he *noqev*s the Name, he should die.[21]

The story is striking in three major ways. First, here is an interesting attestation of what is perhaps the oldest continuous practice in the history of Jewish magic, namely, the use of God's Name to achieve beneficial or aggressive results. We shall have much more to say about the development

---

[19] *Ḥarṭumim*: Gn 41.8; Ex 7.22 etc.; Dn 1.20 etc. *Gazrin*: Dn 2.27 etc. *Ashaphim*: Dn 1.20; 2.2. etc. *Casdim*: Dn 2.2 etc.
[20] For *laḥash*, see Ps 58.6; Is 3.3; Jer 8.17; Eccl 10.11; and cf. Is 3.20; Neh 3.12.
[21] Lv 24.10–16.

and offshoots of this practice in subsequent chapters of the present study. Second, that although the prohibition formulated here is not against consulting a certain practitioner but against a specific practice, the exact nature of this practice (which seems to require no special knowledge and may be known even to a half-Israelite) is not entirely clear. The verb used here, *naqav*, usually means "to perforate, make a hole in" but is also used for the marking of names on a list and even for saying or expressing a single name.[22] It may also be connected with the root QB(B) "to curse," but the prohibition against cursing God is made clear by many other biblical passages, and our culprit does not seem to have cursed God, but his rival.[23] Once again, we are left wondering what post-biblical readers of this passage had to make of it, especially when elsewhere in the Hebrew Bible they found numerous protagonists uttering YHWH's Name, and in at least one case – that of Elisha, to which we shall return below – they found an eminent man of God cursing his rivals "in the Name (of) YHWH" (2 Kgs 2.24). In this case too, it would seem, the Bible was sending its readers some very mixed messages about what was forbidden and what was not.

But the third and most surprising point about this story is that the praxis mentioned here – which we would readily identify as the magical use of God's powerful Name – is conspicuously absent from the prohibitions of magic and divination in Deuteronomy 18, Exodus 22, or Leviticus 19 and 20. Once again, we are forced to admit that the laws there dealt not with "magic" and "divination" as such, but with foreign practitioners and practices which the Jews may not follow, and for which God's prophets would provide proper and acceptable substitutes. The misuse of God's Name apparently fell under a very different rubric.[24]

This, then, is the heart of the matter. Unlike the biblical prohibitions of murder, of homosexual relations between males, of lighting a fire on the Sabbath, and of numerous other activities, which are phrased in ways that leave no room for doubt about what exactly is forbidden, there is no clear-cut biblical prohibition of magic or divination. What the Pentateuch did provide its readers was a partial list of magical and divinatory practitioners to whom one may not turn, or whom one should not even let live, and occasional references to such practices which are forbidden to Jews and

---

[22] Marking names on a list: e.g., Nm 1.17; expressing a single name: see esp. Is 62.2.

[23] For the possible connection between NQB and QBB see Fishbane 1971, pp. 277–8. For the prohibition of cursing God, see Ex 22.27, and cf. 1 Sm 3.13 (with the *tiqqun sophrim*); 1 Kgs 21.10, 13; Is 8.12; Jb 2.9, etc.

[24] And cf. the prohibition, in Ex 20.7 and Dt 5.11, against "raising" God's Name in vain, which may or may not have had some magical connotations.

which (if we may take Balaam's words for it) they indeed do not practice. But the Torah never provides clear indications as to what exactly to include under each of the many rubrics it mentions, and no overarching explanation of why it is that these practices are forbidden, except for the fact that they were foreign and caused defilement, and that they might pose a threatening alternative to the legitimate leadership which God had provided for His people Israel. The misuse of God's Name to gain immediate benefits also was forbidden, but apparently was classified under a different category. Thus, when post-biblical Jews wanted to know whether a specific practice common in their own times was forbidden by the biblical legislation, they had a very hard time finding it there. Are exorcisms forbidden by the Torah? Is the use of amulets forbidden? Does the adjuration of demons and angels contravene any biblical injunction? And what about the use of spells and incantations, of *materia magica*, *abracadabra* words, or arcane magical signs and symbols? Of course, those Jews who wanted to prohibit all such activities could easily subsume them under a blanket term such as *qosem* or *mekhasheph*, and thus "prove" that they were forbidden by Torah.[25] All other Jews, however, could go on practicing their magical and divinatory activities and honestly insist that these were not forbidden by the biblical legislation. If we charge such Jews with duplicity, it only testifies to our inability to understand the complex relations between a religious community and its sacred texts.

Some biblical paradigms

When post-biblical Jews read the Hebrew Bible, they found in it not only the disjointed and vague set of prohibitions which we have just surveyed. They also found in it a large set of stories, descriptions, and injunctions from which they could deduce that certain types of practitioners and certain types of practices actually were accepted, and even applauded, by the biblical legislator and narrators. Such descriptions could therefore serve as powerful paradigms upon which these readers could model their own behavior without any fear lest this would somehow involve them in actions displeasing to God. Let us therefore first focus on what is by far the most important paradigm for the study of later Jewish (and Christian!) magic – that of the holy man and his activities; we shall then turn to another set of

---

[25] As was done, for example, by Maimonides in his *Mishneh Torah*, Hilkhot 'Avodah Zarah 11.4–16. Well aware of the *lacunae* in the biblical legislation, Maimonides provides an extensive list of *practices* forbidden (according to his view!) by the Torah.

powerful paradigms, that of the use of the great powers inherent in God's sacred objects and those who handle them.

The man of God

Certainly the most striking biblical stories relating to the actual practice of what by most modern definitions of magic would fall under that rubric are those dealing with the wonder-working men of God, and especially Elijah and Elisha.[26] Unlike such prophets as Isaiah, Jeremiah, or Ezekiel, Elijah and Elisha were not great orators and preachers who sometimes accompanied their verbal messages with striking symbolic actions. Unlike Moses, they were not great military or political leaders and legislators who also worked many miracles on the way. For these two, wandering around and bending the laws of nature to their own will seems to have been both a hobby and a vocation. How exactly Elijah became such a holy man we are never told, but from his first appearance in the biblical text – declaring to King Ahab that "there will be no dew or rain throughout these years except according to my own command" (1 Kgs 17.1), his self-confidence is quite astounding. The biblical narrator does not record Ahab's response to this impertinent threat, but does describe Elijah's immediate flight to the regions by the Jordan river, where, at God's command, some ravens provide him with fresh bread and meat (1 Kgs 17.6). And when the drought he had ordained makes living in Palestine impossible, and presumably quite dangerous for the man who had brought this hardship upon the helpless peasants, he leaves the Israelite territories and temporarily settles in Zarphath, a village in the hinterland of Sidon, where he performs two impressive miracles. First he produces *ex nihilo* a seemingly endless supply of flour and oil for the poor widow with whom he is staying (1 Kgs 17.14–16), and next he resuscitates her dead boy by praying to YHWH and stretching himself three times over the fresh corpse (1 Kgs 17.19–24). Two years later he is back in drought-stricken Samaria and in King Ahab's court, where the king's chief servant is convinced that his long absence had been due to some marvelous vanishing act (1 Kgs 18.10–12). He then beats Baal's priests in a competition for the production of instantaneous fire by merely praying to God (1 Kgs 18.30–39), and finally produces the rain which he had stopped two years earlier by sitting on the ground, placing his head between his knees, and repeatedly sending his servant-boy to look for the approaching rain clouds (1 Kgs 18.41–45). In spite of the heavy rain which begins to fall,

---

[26] For an intelligent reading of the Elijah and Elisha stories from a Central African perspective, see Wendland 1992.

he manages to outrun the mounted Ahab (1 Kgs 18.46), and then marches for forty days and forty nights after eating one small cake and drinking a cup of water (1 Kgs 19.6–8). Several years later, he is back at it again, producing two more instantaneous fires, each of which consumes fifty armed men and their commanders (2 Kgs 1.9–12), and cleaving the Jordan river in twain by merely beating the water with his garment, so that he and Elisha can cross it on dry land (2 Kgs 2.8). Finally, he caps his achievements by mounting a chariot of fire and vanishing high in the sky (2 Kgs 2.11).

With Elijah gone, Elisha – who had been chosen by God to succeed him (1 Kgs 19.16), was "ordained" when Elijah threw his garment upon him without any prior warning or training (1 Kgs 19.19–21), and is now in possession of Elijah's garment (2 Kgs 2.13) – is immediately revealed as a worthy successor. Stuck on the farther side of the Jordan river, his first feat is to re-cleave it in twain by consciously imitating his vanished master (2 Kgs 2.14). He then settles in Jericho, and is soon approached by the locals with a request worthy of his rising reputation – to sweeten the city's water-source, which currently is undrinkable (just as Moses had done at Marah (Ex 15.25)). He does this by taking a new dish with some salt, throwing the salt into the water-source, and emphatically stating that "Thus says YHWH: I have cured these waters, there shall be no more death and miscarriage from there" (2 Kgs 2.20–22). Nine centuries later, we may add, the water was still drinkable, and was even used to bring fertility to barren women – all as a result of Elisha's ancient miracle. This, however, is a point to which we shall return in the following chapter.

Having just helped the people of Jericho, Elisha soon reveals the darker side of the man of God's great thaumaturgical powers:

And he went up from there (towards) Bet El, and as he was going up the road little boys came out of the town and made fun of him and said to him, Up you go, baldy; up you go, baldy! And he turned around and saw them, and he cursed them in the Name (of) YHWH; and two female bears came out of the forest and mangled forty-two of these children. And he went from there to Mt. Carmel, and thence returned to Samaria.[27]

This gruesome story is an extremely important corrective for our rosy perception of the man of God as a kind and righteous precursor of Robin Hood, helping the widows, producing rain for the poor farmers, and punishing the wicked priests of Baal. In thinking of such holy men, we must always remember that it was Elijah himself who had sent the drought upon the poor farmers in the first place, and recall how the quick-tempered and

---

[27] 2 Kgs 2.23–25.

vindictive Elisha sent the bears upon the children who had teased him, and did not even stop to tend to the wounded.[28] When all is said and done, the most characteristic feature of the man of God is not his community services, or even his divine message or exceeding piety, but his great powers. And when the power is there, the abuse of that power is never far behind.

Arresting as this scene might be, Elisha's feats do not end here. First, he produces *ex nihilo* an abundant supply of oil (2 Kgs 4.2–6), just as Elijah once did, but outshines his master's example by foretelling to his hostess that she would soon bear a child (2 Kgs 4.16–17). A few years later, the boy whose birth fulfilled the prophecy duly dies of a sunstroke, enabling Elisha to retrace Elijah's footsteps once again. Apparently bent on accomplishing a feat never performed by his master, he first sends his servant to place his staff on the boy's face, in an attempt to heal him telepathically. Only when this procedure fails (an interesting demonstration of the limits of Elisha's powers!) does he resuscitate the boy in person, by praying to God and lying upon the corpse (2 Kgs 4.29–35). He then cures a stew into which some poisonous bulbs were mistakenly thrown, a feat he performs by merely throwing some flour into the cauldron (2 Kgs 4.38–41). Some time later, he is asked by the king of Israel to heal Naaman, the great military commander of the kingdom of Aram (Syria), of his leprosy. The wretched colonel comes in person to Elisha's own home, expecting him to "come out and stand, and call by the Name (of) YHWH his God and raise his hands over the (afflicted) part and gather the leprosy away," (2 Kgs 5.11) and is quite insulted when Elisha sends him to bathe seven times in the Jordan river. But his servants convince him to follow Elisha's advice, and when he bathes in the river his leprosy immediately vanishes (2 Kgs 5.13–14). When he wishes to pay Elisha for this service, the man of God emphatically refuses (2 Kgs 5.16), and when his servant surreptitiously charges a fee from the Syrian general, Elisha telepathically discovers the crime and vengefully sends Naaman's leprosy upon him and his descendants (2 Kgs 5.25–27). Once again, we are reminded not to fool around with a man of God.

Elisha's subsequent feats include making a sunken iron axe float by merely throwing a piece of wood on the water's surface (2 Kgs 6.6), and telepathically discovering all the war-plans devised in the council of the Syrian king (2 Kgs 6.8–12). Incensed, the king orders his arrest, but Elisha is undisturbed by the forces besieging his home. When his servant panics, he prays

---

[28] For the rabbis' displeasure with this repugnant behavior, see bt Sot 46b–47a. And note how, in 1 Kgs 17.18, the widow is convinced that it is Elijah's presence which has brought death upon her son, and castigates him accordingly.

to God to open the servant's eyes until he realizes that Elisha in fact is protected by a cohort of invisible fiery chariots – an interesting hint of the presumed sources of his great powers (2 Kgs 6.16–17). Elisha now prays to God to strike the besiegers with a temporary blindness, and then leads them, like the Pied Piper of Hamelin, into the hands of the king of Israel (2 Kgs 6.18–20). After one more feat of telepathic eavesdropping (2 Kgs 6.32), and two accurate predictions of future events (2 Kgs 7.1–2, 16–20), he removes himself to Damascus and correctly foretells the sad fate of its current king and the future actions of the king's successor (2 Kgs 8.10, 12).[29] This is almost his last great feat, for we next hear of his illness (2 Kgs 13.14), and – after one more clash with the king of Israel and one more accurate foretelling of future events (2 Kgs 13.19, 25) – of his death. This all too human finale, so different from the glorious vanishing act performed by his master Elijah, sealed his future history – he would never follow his master in becoming a wandering mediator between the Jews and their Maker and a herald of the coming Messiah. It did, however, have one small advantage, in that it enabled him to demonstrate the magical powers of his dry bones, something Elijah could never do. For when a year passed and Elisha's corpse had already decomposed, a funeral procession surprised by an enemy ambush dumped the corpse it was leading to burial into Elisha's tomb and fled the scene, "and the (dead) man touched the bones of Elisha and came back to life and stood up on his feet" (2 Kgs 13.21).[30]

Elijah and Elisha are, of course, not the only biblical protagonists to perform miracles and wonders, and one could easily adduce a long set of amazing feats performed by prophets, men of God, and political and military leaders, including Joshua's successful stopping of the movement of the sun and moon, and the many wondrous feats performed by Moses, the great leader and lawgiver himself.[31] But rather than rehearsing all these examples here, we may merely stress some of their wider implications for post-biblical Jewish (and Christian) readers of these stories and for the development of post-biblical Jewish magic. First, we must note the long and variegated list of supernatural feats performed by such men of God. They can cure one patient of an illness or send it upon another, bring the dead to life or kill whomever they will, hear faraway voices, divine future

---

[29] In this case, however, one might claim that it was Elisha's prediction that triggered Ben Hadad's murder (2 Kgs 8.15), which is how the prediction was fulfilled.
[30] That later Jewish readers were impressed with this feat may be seen, for example, from Ben Sira 48.14.
[31] Men of God: see, e.g., 1 Kgs 13.1–6; 1 Kgs 20.35–36, etc. Joshua: Jos 10.12–14; Moses: numerous examples, including Ex 14.21, 27; 15.25; 17.6, 11–12, etc.

events, and stop the rain or restart it, stop the sun and the moon in their courses, make iron float, cure poisonous substances, resuscitate the dead and do away with the living, and so on. With such a strong thaumaturgical paradigm embedded so deeply into sacred Scriptures, later readers of the Hebrew Bible would have a very hard time accepting any claim that such feats are intrinsically impossible, because of some philosophers' insistence on the fixed laws of nature which cannot easily be bent.[32] If Moses, Joshua, Elijah, and Elisha could bend the laws of nature to their will, there was no real reason to cast doubt on the claims of latter-day holy men and magicians who insisted that they too could perform similar feats. Some of the claimants may be lying, but the claim itself was in no way deemed implausible by all but the most extreme rationalists.

A second point of some importance has to do with gender. In the Hebrew Bible, the men of God are always men, and while females sometimes perform great deeds – be it Deborah's leadership in times of war or Yael's courageous murder of an enemy general – no biblical woman is ever portrayed as reviving the dead, curing the sick, or performing any of the other feats performed by the men of God. As we shall see throughout the present study, this would remain an important paradigm in later Jewish history (in contrast, for example, with later Christian history), with only a few hints in ancient Jewish literature that women too could sometimes perform miracles. From its very beginning, Jewish thaumaturgy was a deeply engendered affair.

A third point which bears stressing is the recurrent emergence of a close connection between holy men and politics. In the case of Elijah or Elisha, this can be seen from their frequent encounters with kings and commanders, both Israelites and foreigners, who wish to tap their powers, and from their frequent clashes with the political establishment. But the involvement of such men with politics can take other shapes too. In the case of Joshua, we see how a military leader not otherwise identified as a man of God can stop the sun and moon in their course when the exigencies of a battle so demand. And in the case of Moses, we see how a man of God who also is the supreme secular leader of his people – a status that no other biblical man of God ever achieved – uses his miraculous powers to strengthen his social control over the lost sheep of Israel. Time after time we find the great leader confronted with the hardships of life in Egyptian bondage or in the desert wilderness and challenged by his flock to improve their situation or make way for other leaders, and each time he rises to the occasion by

---

[32] See, e.g., Robinson 1983 and Kreisel 1984.

performing a great miracle on their behalf or annihilating the opposition. As we shall see in subsequent chapters, the use of miracles and magic to gain public influence or social control was well known to later Jewish leaders as well.

A fourth point to be stressed here is that in the many stories of the men of God and their miracles the Hebrew Bible complements its anti-magical legislation by ensuring us that while turning to non-Israelite practitioners is not to be tolerated, there are adequate substitutes for such practitioners within Jewish society itself. If you lost some property, you could go to the Israelite seer or prophet or man of God (1 Sm 9.6ff) who would help you find it, and if your child died, or your food got poisoned, or you needed an accurate prediction of future events, you could turn to a prophet or a man of God, and he would solve your problem in a way that was entirely acceptable to the biblical narrators. Thus, there is no real need to turn to any of the forbidden practitioners, for anything they can do the man of God can do better. In light of such precedents, the fact that later readers of these stories had no qualms about turning to Jewish holy men and magicians in their own society should hardly raise an eyebrow. Moreover, the Hebrew Bible makes it clear that when Aaron and Moses were confronted by actual magicians (something which never happened to Elijah or Elisha), they beat them at their own game with a striking series of signs and miracles (Ex 7.8ff). As we shall see throughout the present study, this too could serve as a powerful paradigm for subsequent readers of the Hebrew Bible, who had to devise their own attitudes towards troublesome magicians and their boastful challenges.

And here we come to the most important issue, namely, the clues provided by these biblical narratives for a possible distinction between holy men and magicians in a Jewish context, a distinction which is necessary in light of the fact that these two types of wonder-workers often appeared in similar social settings and performed similar feats. This distinction is of great importance, if only for the fact that the label "magician" has often been used – both in ancient literature and in modern scholarship – as a pejorative appellation affixed to people who saw themselves, and were seen by others, as men of God, a polemical bias which has done much harm to the study of Jewish magic.[33]

Looking at the biblical men of God, we find that some of their actions are in the service of God and nation, but others are motivated by purely personal reasons, be it Elijah's desire to help the widow who had helped him

---

[33] For a pertinent example, see Smith 1978, rightly criticized by, e.g., Garrett 1989.

or Elisha's rage at the puerile pranksters who made fun of his receding hairline. In most cases they help their Israelite brethren, but they also cater to non-Israelite admirers and clients, be it a poor widow from the Phoenician hinterland or the Chief of Staff from Damascus. Some of their actions are noble and moral, some – like Elisha's posthumous resuscitation of a corpse – are unintentional, and some are vindictive and downright reprehensible. Finally, and perhaps most significantly, the range of techniques they employ to perform their feats is itself quite impressive: in some cases, a simple verbal command or a short prayer is all it takes; in others, they use bodily movements and gestures, and perhaps also certain acts of supreme concentration (1 Kgs 18.42); and in many cases they use various implements, devices and materials, be it a garment, a staff, a plate with some salt, a piece of wood, a pinch of flour, or the water of the Jordan river. In most cases, these are readily available, daily objects and substances, ones which would take no effort to procure, and yet the very fact that such objects are needed at all is noteworthy, for no attempt is made by the biblical narrators to claim that holy men could work their miracles by their will, or by their word, alone. More surprising, perhaps, in some cases it is God Himself who instructs Moses on which ingredients to use to perform his miracles, be it some soot from a furnace to get a plague going (Ex 9.8–10) or a piece of wood to cure a bitter water-source (Ex 15.25).

What all this adds up to, in other words, is an extremely useful set of paradigms for post-biblical Jewish practitioners to choose from. Both the holy men who were so common in later Jewish (and Christian) history and the magicians, who were no less common, and in some periods and places much more so, could easily justify most of their claims, aims, techniques, and social aspirations by appealing to the biblical precedents provided by Elijah, Elisha, Moses, and their like. Viewed from this perspective, it would seem that the magicians of post-biblical Judaism differed little from the holy men of their time or of the biblical past. Like them, they too practiced their rituals for the sake of themselves and of others (both Jews and non-Jews), aimed both for morally commendable and for reprehensible results, and used a wide range of techniques and implements. Unlike the holy men, they probably charged a per-service fee, but even this is far from certain,[34] and holy men too often relied on their clients for accommodation and provisions, as Elijah and Elisha used to do, or expected some kind of compensation for their efforts, as the young Saul took for granted

---

[34] As we shall note in subsequent chapters, the sources at our disposal are such that we know much more about what the Jewish magicians of antiquity did than about how they were paid for their services.

(1 Sm 9.7–8). Unlike the holy men, who would often describe themselves, and be described by some of their followers, as on a mission from God, the magicians would usually make no claims of an ulterior mission behind their praxis. And unlike the holy men, who catered only to some of the needs of the wider population, the magicians responded to more of their clients' needs, and especially their personal needs – including, for example, erotic magic, in which the men of God never (or rarely) engaged. On the other hand, there were some activities, such as resuscitating the dead or producing rain, in which the holy men frequently engaged but which the magicians tended to avoid.

These distinctions notwithstanding, the biggest difference between the Jewish holy men and the magicians seems to have been that the former relied on their own innate powers, and on readily available paraphernalia, to perform their miraculous deeds. The magicians, on the other hand, relied on an *acquired body of technical knowledge* – whose changing contents are the main focus of the present study – and often also on specifically magical implements, materials, words, and symbols, to perform their own miracles. Thus, the manner by which Elisha became a man of God, when Elijah merely threw his garment upon him (1 Kgs 19.19–21), is extremely instructive, precisely because it involved election, not instruction. The garment with which Elijah had performed some of his miracles has now been passed on to his heir, who will use it in a similar fashion, but no technical advice on how to use it, or how to perform miracles, was passed along with it. As we shall see in the following chapters, it is the exorcistic manuals of the Second Temple period and the magical recipe books of late antiquity which provide us with the best clues that their Jewish owners and users were not holy men, but technical experts, that is, professional exorcists and magicians.

As we shall see throughout the present study, there were many people in ancient Jewish society who could work miracles (or, at least, saw themselves and were seen by others as performing miracles) by their innate powers, which they viewed as God's gift. There were many others, however, who could perform similar feats (or, at least, saw themselves and were seen by others as performing similar feats), but did so by virtue of techniques and spells which were transmitted to them, either orally or in writing, from their masters and colleagues, or devised by themselves for those purposes. Had they had the power to perform such deeds without this special technology, they would probably never have bothered to learn it at all. But as not all of us are holy men, some of us must learn how to do what to others comes naturally – or by the grace of God.

The uses of the sacred

While the man of God had it within him to bend the laws of nature to his will, this was not the only manner by which, according to the biblical narrators, the Israelites could achieve supernatural feats. One other mode of access to great powers involved the manipulation of sacred objects, that is, objects connected with the cult of YHWH. That such objects had great powers is demonstrated by the sad fate of Nadab and Abihu, the sons of Aaron and nephews of Moses, who were burnt alive for approaching God's altar in the desert Tabernacle in the wrong manner (Lv 10.1–2, etc.). It is made even clearer by the similar fate of Uzza, whose sole sin was his desire to prevent the Ark of the Covenant from falling down and being crushed to the ground; as he sent his hand to touch it, God became furious and killed him on the spot, a numinous behavior which King David found both infuriating and frightening (2 Sm 6.2–9).[35] Such passages provide ample evidence of the immense power associated with God's holiest objects, and certainly explain why not everyone was allowed to handle such objects, and why even authorized personnel had to take extreme precautions and observe strict rules of purity and propriety in order to approach any space or artifact connected with God (see, e.g., Ex 3.5, Jos 10.14). But like nuclear energy, quite dangerous to use but too useful not to, this power made such objects and spaces not only frightening, but also potentially useful in many ways, and some of these uses were already made clear both by the biblical legislation and by some biblical stories. Even the passage immediately following the Uzza story tells us that when the Ark had to spend a few months in the home of Oved Edom, his house was greatly blessed by the presence of the sacred object (2 Sm 6.11–12), a blessing which many others probably coveted. And as we shall soon see, the use of the power inherent in such objects often entailed a recourse to the priests who were in charge of guarding and handling them.

Beginning with the legislation, we may focus on the *soṭah* ritual of Numbers 5.11–31, by far the clearest example of the close connections between the sacred objects, God's priests, and rituals that we would readily identify as "magic," were it not for their presence deep within the Judaic religion of the time. In this specific case, a wife suspected by her husband of adultery (but not caught *in flagrante* by himself or by others) is brought to the Tabernacle (or, in later periods, to the Temple) so that God would decide her guilt or innocence. She is brought by her husband, who brings

---

[35] For other examples, see, e.g., 1 Sm 6.19, where God kills 50,070 people in Beth Shemesh because "they saw the Ark of YHWH." For Uzza's sin, cf. 1 Sm 5.1–6.14, which makes it very clear that the Ark can manage on its own.

along an appropriate offering, and is placed by the priest before YHWH (11–16). The priest then takes holy water in a clay vessel, adds some dust from the Tabernacle floor, dishevels the woman's hair, places the offering in her hands and adjures her with two elaborate formulae, whose exact wording is provided, and to which she responds Amen, Amen (17–22). The priest then writes these curses down, washes the text into the water, and makes the woman drink the resulting brew (23–24). He then takes the offering from her hands and places it on the altar, after which he makes the woman drink the water (once again?). If she is guilty, the water would make her belly swell and her thigh fall, thus proving her guilt. And if she is not guilty, no such effect would be discernible, and she shall be declared innocent and have sex with her husband (as his way of confirming the verdict) (25–31). This is, of course, a typical ordeal, and one for which many parallels have been adduced by modern scholars, from many different cultures worldwide.[36]

For a modern reader, such a ritual immediately provokes a psychological analysis – it is the guilty woman's great fear, in such awesome surroundings and with such a frightful ritual centered around her – that would make her guilt so physically manifest, while an innocent woman would remain calm throughout. Such readings were not unknown in antiquity as well, but they were dwarfed by the far commoner assumption, that it was the sacred location, the power of the holy water, of the dust from the Tabernacle or Temple, of the priest, and especially of the sacred oath (including YHWH's powerful Name) which made the ritual so effective. It worked, if we may borrow a phrase coined only much later and in a non-Jewish context, *ex opere operato*, for it tapped into great reservoirs of numinous power. In the same vein, we may note that when the Israelites sinned and made themselves a Golden Calf, one of Moses' first actions was to grind the Calf to dust and make them drink it in their water.[37] Apparently, the power of sacred objects extended even to such "anti-sacred" objects, which had to be consumed by their suspected producers as an effective ordeal, proving their guilt and punishing them at the same time.

The biblical *soṭah* ritual may be the most striking example of the use of the innate powers of sacred objects and God's priests for rituals which have little to do with the service of God and much to do with the service of men, but many other instances show that such powers were employed

---

[36] For Babylonian parallels, see Fishbane 1971, pp. 231–60, and Fishbane 1974. For other parallels, see the extensive collection in Frazer 1918, vol. III, pp. 304–414.
[37] Ex 32.20, but note the different account in Dt 9.21. For the comparison between Moses' behavior and the *soṭah* ceremony, see already t AZ 3.19 (p. 465 Zuckermandel); pt AZ 3.3 (42d); bt AZ 44a.

in other contexts as well. Still focusing on the biblical legislation, we may note how Aaron, or the high priest, confesses all the sins of the entire nation and then "places" or "transfers" them upon the head of a hapless goat which carries all the sins of the Israelites into the desert (Lv 16.7–22).[38] Or we may focus on the ritual of the priestly blessings, in which God's priests bless God's people that God will bless them, guard them, and bring them peace (Nm 6.22–27). This passage is of some importance, since we now possess even archeological evidence confirming the popularity of these verses, and perhaps also of the ritual they describe, in the form of two silver amulets, found in a First Temple period tomb at Ketef Hinnom, Jerusalem, and dated to the late seventh or early sixth century BCE.[39] This is, we may note, the only evidence we have of the Jewish use of written amulets in the First or Second Temple periods, an issue to which we shall return in Chapter 2. It is also the first attested use of the Priestly Blessing for magical and apotropaic purposes, a practice to which we shall return in Chapter 5.

Thus far, we have limited our survey to the uses of the sacred in the biblical legislation, but when we turn from the legal sections to the more historical narratives of the Hebrew Bible, we find many more examples of the practical uses of the sacred, especially in times of war. In the war against the Midianites, for example, Moses sends 12,000 warriors into battle, as well as a priest and some sacred vessels which presumably help clinch the victory (Nm 31.6–12). And when confronted with the need to cross the Jordan with the entire people, Joshua sends the priests and the Ark first, and once the priests' feet touch the water the Jordan is cloven in twain, and the whole nation crosses on dry land, with the priests and the Ark standing in the dry river-bed. Only when the last persons have passed, do the priests carry the Ark to the other bank, and the blocked-up river returns to its normal flow (Jos 3.5–17, cf. 4.7). Not long after, God instructs Joshua how to conquer Jericho, and the latter then commands his army to wheel around the besieged city in a peculiar formation – first come some military forces, in dead silence, then seven priests blowing the sacred trumpets, then more priests carrying the sacred Ark, and then more military units, they too observing a complete silence. This colorful parade circumambulates the city walls once a day for six days, and on the seventh it completes seven more circumambulations. Only then are the forces ordered to sound

---

[38] For this ritual, see Gruenwald 2003, pp. 202–30.
[39] See Barkay 1992; Yardeni 1991; Barkay *et al.* 2004.

the battle cry and mount a concentrated attack, which proves remarkably successful – the walls of Jericho crumble, and the city is captured (Jos 6.2–20). But while the narrators' insistence that the miracle indeed took place is hardly unusual – most biblical stories assume that, *Deo volente*, anything can happen – the need for such an elaborate ritual is quite telling. Rather than waiting for God to fulfill His promise to Abraham and give them the Holy Land on a silver platter, or standing around the walls of Jericho and begging God to destroy them, Joshua and his men embark upon a stylized ritual procession. And while their actions could be interpreted in a psychologizing mode – as something akin to a war-dance, encouraging the besiegers and disheartening the besieged – its effects are not described as psychological, but as entirely physical. Thus, no reader would fail to note how the ritual use of sacred objects, at least when performed by the right people, in the right manner, and for the right cause, could have highly beneficial effects, including the complete subversion of the ordinary laws of nature. And, perhaps most interesting, no reader of this story would have failed to note that it was God Himself who had come up with the elaborate plan.

As we noted in the previous section, biblical men of God could work miracles, but their powers were not without limits, and sometimes they failed to achieve the results they had aimed for. Thus, when Elisha tried to heal a boy by merely sending his staff and performing the feat telepathically, the procedure proved an abject failure. The same, we may now add, holds true for the sacred appurtenances, whose power also has its limits. In one case, after losing a battle against the Philistines, the Israelites decided to take the Ark of the Covenant from the Shiloh sanctuary and bring it, together with the two priests – Eli's sons, Ḥophni and Pinḥas – who were in charge of it, to the battlefield. The Ark's arrival had a dramatic effect in boosting the spirits of the Israelite warriors and depressing those of their opponents – a sure sign of the psychological effects of the presence of powerful sacred objects. But after the initial shock, the Philistines decided to redouble their efforts, and their enthusiasm brought them a glorious victory. The Ark's priestly handlers were slain, along with 30,000 Israelite soldiers, and the Ark itself was captured by the Philistines (1 Sm 4.1–11). From the narrators' perspective, the failure was preordained, the result of the priestly transgressions of Eli's two sons (1 Sm 2.11–17, 22–37; 3.11–14). From a reader's perspective, however, it was an important reminder that powerful as God's holy objects might be, their effect was in no way automatic, and depended in part on the status in the eyes of God of those who were about to use them. Clearly, this was a Doomsday weapon, to be used only in extreme emergencies, and only as a last resort.[40] Moreover, this was not the only object which possessed great power by virtue of its contact with the divine, and we may note such items as Samson's flowing hair, which he let grow as a result of a nazirite vow, and which gave him superhuman powers, or God's different temples, where a prayer would be more efficacious, or God's very Name, not really a material object at all, but a source of great power in its own right.[41] We have already noted above how the Bible forbids the *naqav*ing of the Name in order to harm an opponent, or for any other purpose; we also noted Elisha's use of the Name in cursing the children who offended him. In later periods, the power of the Name and of its many substitutes will become a mainstay of Jewish religious belief and magical praxis, as we shall see in the following chapters.

To all these paradigmatic examples of the power of God's sacred objects, one more example must be added, one which even some ancient Israelites, or at least some biblical narrators, apparently found quite disturbing. For when the Israelites encamped in a desert full of vipers, it was God Himself who told Moses to make a bronze serpent and place it on a flagpole, so that anyone bitten by a viper may see it and live – a solution which proved remarkably successful (Nm 21.6–9). What is unusual here is not the magical use of a sacred object, but the fact that this was not one of the regular paraphernalia of God's cult, or an existing instrument such as Moses' staff, but a purpose-built implement which had no existence prior to this incident and no cultic uses after it. It thus comes as no surprise when we read that many years later, King Ḥezekiah annihilated the bronze serpent which Moses had made, "for until those days the sons of Israel would make incense-offering to it" (2 Kgs 18.4). The powerful implement had become a cultic object in its own right, one not sanctioned by Torah and lacking a fixed position in the Temple cult, and therefore had to be destroyed. Here, in other words, the biblical narrative provides an interesting example of an object which tries to move from the realm of "magic" into that of "religion" and is eventually rejected, even if it was originally produced at God's own behest. As we shall see below, and throughout the present study, such movements, and the attempts to stop them, were quite common in the history of later Jewish magic and religion as well.

---

[40] And note how the Philistines, marking the Ark's arrival on the battlefield, insist that "this has never happened before" (1 Sm 4.7). On the other hand, the Ark seems to have been used in more than one military campaign – see 1 Sm 14.18 and 2 Sm 11.11.

[41] For Samson, see Jgs 13.4–5; 16.17–22. For God's temples, see 1 Sm 1.9 and 1 Kgs 8.27–49. See also Ez 40.9, 12, for the healing properties of the stream that would one day flow from the Temple.

Surveying all these powerful objects and the people who used them, we may note how the Hebrew Bible displays a deep-seated conviction that many striking feats – from the cleaving of rivers to the destruction of mighty walls – could be achieved not only by men of God, but also by the correct manipulation of God's sacred objects. But while holy men could come from any segment of Israelite society and rise to prominence by means of their innate powers, the use of sacred objects to achieve supernatural feats also granted a monopoly on such powers to the Israelite priests, who had regular access to the divine objects and knew how to approach and manipulate them without endangering themselves or others.[42] And here too, just as in the case of the men of God, it is only men, and not women, who are involved in such thaumaturgy, since women were a priori precluded from access to God's holiest objects. Moreover, here too we find persistent links between magic and politics or magic and social control, be it the uses of the Ark and other sacred vessels in times of war, or Moses' use of the bronze serpent to solve an urgent problem which made his flock restive to the point of rebellion. Finally, here too we find the flip-side of the Torah's legislation against magic and divination, for while turning to a long list of magical and divinatory practitioners is forbidden, using the power inherent in God's holy object is quite acceptable. Sometimes it is even very clear that God's sacred objects and priests are used as a *substitute* for non-Jewish practices and practitioners – as when the Bible condones and encourages divination by means of the *Urim and Thumim* while utterly forbidding any contact with non-Israelite diviners.[43] In all these cases, we may note how the insistence on the powers of such objects would create an enormous temptation to use them even for aims not specifically sanctioned by the biblical legislation. In this regard, it is interesting to compare the crossing of the Jordan by Elijah and Elisha with the crossing of the same river by the entire people, led by the priests and the holy Ark. The action is the same, but the means are different, and whereas the Ark and its priests can cleave the Jordan for a whole nation to pass through, the holy men's efforts suffice only for their own crossing. Here, then, we have one more powerful paradigm that would shape the growth of later Jewish (and Christian) magic, and some of the inner-Jewish debates about the borderlines between the permitted and the forbidden

---

[42] The priests' monopoly over such knowledge may be seen in other cases too, such as 2 Kgs 17.24–28.
[43] For this divination technique, and the different attempts to ascertain its exact nature, see Van Dam 1997, pp. 9–103, 215–32. For the priests' great powers, see also the manner by which Aaron stops the plague by using some incense in Nm 17.11–15.

uses of the power of the sacred. This, however, is an issue to which we shall return in subsequent chapters.

Summary

Incomplete and sketchy as they might be, our surveys of the biblical passages pertaining to magic should suffice to highlight the two main features of the biblical handling of this topic. First, that the legislation against magic and divination is far from precise when it comes to what exactly is forbidden and what is not. Second, that other sections of the Hebrew Bible make it clear that many magical activities are permitted, and even encouraged, as long as they are conducted by the right people and in the right manner. The paradox inherent in the possible contradiction between the prohibitions and the paradigms is, of course, not unique in the history of religions; it is not even unique in the Hebrew Bible itself. As an instructive analogue, we may note how the Pentateuch places the prohibition of murder as one of its central commandments, and how in this case, at least, the plain sense of the law hardly is in doubt (Ex 20.13; Dt 5.17). And yet, while the Pentateuch forbids murder, it also describes, and quite approvingly, several interesting cases of judicial and extra-judicial killings. When Moses kills an Egyptian who was roughing up a Jewish slave-laborer (Ex 2.11–12), we may perhaps speak of self-defense; when he orchestrates the execution of religious offenders (Lv 24.23; Nm 15.36), we may perhaps quote all the arguments adduced by the modern defenders of the death penalty as the ultimate barrier against social anarchy. But when the same Moses orders the murder of women and children war-captives (Nm 31.14–18) or the summary and random execution of 3,000 members of his own community (Ex 32.26–29), or instigates and approves of the cold-blooded murder of an amorous couple bent on the pursuit of happiness (Nm 25.5–8), we can only conclude that from the perspective of the biblical narrators, murder in the Name of the Lord is permitted, and even desirable.[44] And as any student of Jewish history would readily concede, some post-biblical Jews insisted on following the biblical legislation on this score, while others – and not only in the days of Josephus, but in our own days as well – took their cue from the biblical paradigms, whose implicit message is very different from that of the explicit prohibition of murder in the Ten Commandments.

---

[44] There are, of course, many more examples outside the Pentateuch, be it Samuel's cold-blooded murder of a war-captive (1 Sm 15.33), David's genocide in Edom (1 Kgs 18.40), Elijah's slaughter of Baal's priests (1 Kgs 11.15–16), and numerous other instances.

Jewish magic: a contradiction in terms?

This complex Jewish attitude to murder is a useful analogue with which to think about the relationship between post-biblical Jewish magic and the Hebrew Bible. Those Jews – be it Philo, the Karaites, Maimonides, or the modern *Maskilim* – who sought to ban all or most magical activities from the Jewish polity could easily adduce the biblical legislation as a proof that this indeed is what God had ordained. They did so, however, not because this is what a careful reading of the Torah convinced them to be true, but because other aspects of their religiosity and theology (which, in many cases, boils down to direct or indirect contact with Greek philosophy and its consequences) convinced them that magic was unacceptable. And those Jews who were unaware of this line of thought, or knew it and consciously rejected it, could easily insist that the biblical prohibitions did not refer to the beliefs and practices in which they indulged, and also point to the many biblical paradigms with regard to similar beliefs and practices as a proof that they were in no way "un-Jewish." It is not for us to judge which of the two camps was more faithful to the actual letter of the law; what we can say, however, and with some degree of certainty, is that the latter camp attracted a much larger following, and had a far greater impact on the development of Jewish magic, and of Jewish culture as a whole, throughout most periods of Jewish history.

MAGIC AND RATIONALITY

One of the oldest and most pernicious hurdles confronting the academic study of magic is the question of the complex relations between magic and rationality.[45] More than with any other noun, "magic" seems to go hand-in-hand with "superstition" and all its derogatory connotations in Western discourse from antiquity to the present. And regardless of whether we subscribe to Frazer's understanding of magic as a misguided form of primitive science, to Lévy-Bruhl's elaborate reconstructions of the savage mind and its pre-logical thinking, to Freud's view of magic as the most infantile stage in human development, or to the cultural anthropologists' stress on the meaning of magical rituals in terms of the cultural frameworks in which they are embedded and the symbols they manipulate, they all have one thing in common, namely, the insistence that magic is inherently irrational, or, at best, non-rational. This is less of a problem when dealing with a pre-literate tribal society in some remote corner of the world, but is quite discomfiting when dealing with cultures which lie at the heart of

---

[45] For what follows, see esp. Glucklich 1997, pp. 3–96. See also Vyse 1997.

Western civilization. In the study of Judaism, the assumption that magic has nothing rational about it had one obvious implication – magic is an intrinsically un-Jewish activity. If some Jews dabbled in it, they must have been of the lower classes, the uneducated masses, those Jews whose unseemly practices the enlightened religious establishment was grudgingly forced to endure.[46]

As we shall see in subsequent chapters of this book, it is often hard to tell who exactly were the practitioners behind the Jewish magical practices in antiquity. But the preservation, at least from late antiquity onwards, of so many *written* Jewish magical texts tells us that quite a few practitioners were far from illiterate, and some of these magical texts even display the scribal hands, writing styles, and modes of textual production which come only with many years of scribal learning and practice.[47] Moreover, when we do find evidence outside the actual magical texts as to who practiced such magical rituals, that evidence repeatedly demonstrates the acceptance, and even practice, of magic by members of the Jewish elite, including the religious establishment itself. In subsequent chapters, we shall encounter Josephus' glowing descriptions of the praxis of exorcism, the exorcistic hymns recited by the overseer(s) of the Qumran community, and the favorite magical recipes of some of the foremost talmudic authorities – to name but a few striking examples. Thus, while the analysis of Jewish magic as a form of "popular" or "folk" religion is not without value – as can be seen from Trachtenberg's book on medieval Jewish magic, subtitled *A Study in Folk Religion*[48] – there is no doubt that such an analysis hardly applies to most of the "insider" sources which we shall analyze throughout our study. Most of these sources were not the product of Jewish "folk magic," but of "intellectual magic," produced by learned experts who mastered a specialized body of knowledge and consulted many different sources, sometimes in more than one language.[49] How, then, can we explain this recurrent recourse, by intelligent Jews, to practices which seem utterly irrational?

Looking at Jewish culture as a whole, one cannot help noting that the issue of rationality seldom comes up in the ancient Jewish discourse on magic and magicians. In Classical Greek and Roman literature, one can find a rational critique of magic, and an occasional mockery of the magicians'

---

[46] For a classic formulation of this view, see Rubin 1887, p. 12. Trachtenberg 1939 often follows this line of reasoning (e.g., on pp. 107–08).
[47] For this point, see esp. Swartz 1990.
[48] And see also Sharot 1982, pp. 9–11 and 27–44, for a similar approach.
[49] For similar conclusions regarding later periods, see Barel 1991; Etkes 1995. See also Hansen 1978, for some non-Jewish parallels.

claims and practices.⁵⁰ This is, however, part of a much wider Greek discourse of rationality, one in which the Jews began taking part in a serious and lasting manner only after the second Jewish encounter with Greek philosophy – the one that took place in the Middle Ages and involved reading Greek philosophy through its Arabic translations and Muslim interpretations. From the Geonic period onwards, we find in Jewish writings too the claim that some of the magicians' claims are just impossible, and that the magicians' practices achieve none of their purported aims. This critique reaches its climax in the writings of Maimonides, whose extensive reading of magical texts, and recurrent fulminations against "the madness of amulet writers" have often been studied.⁵¹ Even then, however, the claim that magic does not work was based on a general assumption that magic *could* not work, since it would subvert the fixed laws of nature, and not on an empirical demonstration that magic *does* not work. In fact, as we shall soon see, Maimonides was quite ready to admit that some amulets, for example, might actually work, and that some magical practices do not work, but have a positive psychological effect. Whether the rationalistic critique of the magicians' art had any impact on the development of medieval Jewish magic is a question which has never even been asked, but which lies outside the chronological framework of the present study.⁵²

The question as to why the first Jewish encounter with Greek culture, in the Second Temple and rabbinic periods, failed to produce any substantial Jewish grappling with Greek philosophy (with the partial exception of Philo, to whom we shall turn in the next chapter), has already attracted some scholarly attention, and will surely attract much more in the future.⁵³ For the present enquiry, however, we need look not at its postulated causes but at its apparent results. In ancient Jewish culture, religious claims were not subjected to the systematic questioning of their plausibility, reliability, or efficacy, and the basic premise of Greek philosophers from the sixth-century BCE Hecataeus of Miletus onwards – that the Greek myths contained much that was implausible, or downright silly – was not adopted by ancient Jewish thinkers with regards to the biblical stories. Similarly, the Greek distinction

---

⁵⁰ For the rational critique of magic in Classical antiquity, see Edelstein 1937; Lloyd 1979, pp. 15–29; Martin 2004, pp. 38–40.
⁵¹ For disparaging remarks on the efficacy of magic, see, e.g., Hai Gaon's words in Emanuel 1995, p. 131: "A fool will believe anything"; Maimonides, *Commentary to the Mishnah*, Sot. 7.4; *Mishneh Torah*, Hilkhot 'Avodah Zarah 11.16, etc.; *Guide* 1.61; 3.37. For Maimonides' critique of magic, see Lewis 1905; Schwartz 1999, pp. 92–110; Ravitzky 2002.
⁵² For the possible influence of Maimonides' rationalistic reinterpretation of the Jewish tradition on the rise of Kabbalah see Idel 1990b.
⁵³ For a useful starting-point, see Harvey 1992.

between "true piety" and "superstition," that is, religious behavior which simply made no sense to a rational (Greek) observer, was quite meaningless to most ancient Jews.[54] Some Jews developed a rationalistic critique of other people's religious beliefs and customs, but their own myths and rituals remained immune to such critique.[55] For a typical example of this immunity, we may look at the biblical story of the "witch" of Endor and its ancient Jewish amplifications and interpretations.[56] For the biblical narrators, the fact that the non-Israelite *ba'alat 'ov* could raise Samuel's ghost, so that he would accurately foretell to her client the unfolding future, was virtually taken for granted. The same is true, however, of the story's many post-biblical readers in antiquity, all of whom accepted the possibility of necromancy and even offered learned explanations of how it was possible at all. Only in the late Geonic period (tenth–eleventh centuries) do we find, and only among some biblical commentators, an insistence that the story as told in the biblical narrative is simply impossible, and the claim that any story in the Hebrew Bible which contradicts our reason or our senses should not be taken literally.[57] But even then, and throughout later Jewish history, this claim aroused much controversy, and was far from unanimously accepted by all Jewish thinkers, many of whom went on taking the Endor story at face value and insisting that necromancy indeed is possible.

This, then, is the first answer to the question of Jewish magic and Jewish rationality in antiquity. There never was a clash between the two, for the simple reason that the second phenomenon did not yet exist. And yet, while this answer is true on one level, it is quite unsatisfactory on another. If Jews had no discourse of rationality, and if Jews did practice magic, does it mean that they were simply irrational? This would be a disturbing conclusion not only for apologetic reasons (no one enjoys thinking of his forefathers as stupid), but for historical reasons as well. No student of ancient Jewish history and culture, and no reader of ancient Jewish literature, can fail to note the presence there of some highly intelligent figures, and of some impressive examples of rational thinking and action.[58] Thus, to give just one concrete

---

[54] For the Greek concept of *deisidaimonia*, often defined as "excessive fear of the gods," see Theophrastus, *Char.* 16; Plutarch, *Superst.*; Martin 2004.
[55] See, for example, Daniel's exploits in the Greek Additions to the Book of Daniel, or (Pseudo?-) Hecataeus' story of Mosollamos, as quoted by Josephus, *Ap.* 1.200–04, which will be mentioned again in the following chapter.
[56] The "witch" of Endor: 1 Sm 28.6–20 with Cogan 1995 and Smelik 1977. For a later period, see Barzilay 1974, pp. 262–65.
[57] See Brody 1998, pp. 296–99, 304–12.
[58] For a recent attempt to struggle with this issue, see Fisch 1997.

example, the Jews' refusal to defend themselves on the Sabbath – a refusal which was derided as "superstition" by some of their Greek observers – was overturned by the Hasmoneans when they realized that not fighting on the Sabbath meant not fighting at all, since all the enemy had to do was to wait for the next Sabbath and attack.[59] In this case, then, we see Jews who are not only aware of what actually works and what does not, but are even able to modify their own religious legislation in a rational way, so as to fit the lofty religious ideal to the exigencies of life in this world. Not all Jews, we must add, accepted this Hasmonean reform, and some seem to have refused to fight on the Sabbath both in the second century BCE and in the first century CE.[60] And yet, this example of Jewish rational behavior is far from an isolated example, and the question must therefore be asked – how could intelligent Jews believe that magic actually works?

Before beginning to unpack the complex issue of the rationality of ancient Jewish magic, one possible set of explanations must be ruled out. Ever since antiquity, it has been popular among religious polemicists to argue that various magical practices or traditions were based on conscious fraud, that is, on the deliberate manipulation of the ignorant masses by quacks and charlatans who used various ruses to dupe their followers.[61] Reading Lucian's descriptions of the tricks supposedly used by Alexander of Abonuteichos in founding the oracular shrine of the snake-god Glykon and enhancing its reputation, Hippolytus' long list of tricks used by magicians and heretics to deceive their followers, or the rabbis' descriptions of how the priests of Baal had tried to dupe the spectators during their celebrated contest with Elijah, we come into contact with an impressive set of quite sophisticated techniques intended to fraudulently create the impression of magical and miraculous feats. To make a statue or an image speak, you drill a hole through it, insert the windpipe of a crane or some other long-necked creature through the cavity, and have someone speak into the pipe from an invisible spot behind the "speaking" statue.[62] To create a fearful apparition of a fiery Hecate flying through the air, you choose a moonless night and tell your audience to watch out for the deity and to cover their faces and bow down once she appears. You then have your assistant wrap a hapless

---

[59] For the Greek mockery of this Jewish *deisidaimonia*, see Agatharchides FGrH 86 F20a–b in Josephus, *Ap.* 1.205–11 (GLAJJ 30a) and *Ant.* 12.5–6 (GLAJJ 30b), and Plutarch, *Supers.* 8 (GLAJJ 256). For the Hasmonean decision to drop this impossible limitation, see 1 Macc. 2.32–41 and Josephus, *Ant.* 12.276–77.
[60] See Frontinus, *Str.* 2.1.17 (GLAJJ 229), with Stern's commentary.
[61] For some of the Renaissance and modern examples of this discourse, see Smith 2002, pp. 79–83.
[62] Lucian, *Alex.* 26; Hippolytus, *Ref.* 4.28.9 and 4.41.2.

bird in flammable fibers, set it alight, and release it for all to see.[63] To make an altar blaze with "miraculous" fire, you hide an accomplice inside it with the appropriate equipment and the right instructions, and he will light the fire at the agreed-upon moment.[64] In a few cases, we even find claims that some Jews used such tricks to dupe their followers or for other reasons, such as the claim that Bar Kokhba could breathe fire by blowing on a smoldering straw he hid in his mouth, or the story of Rav Naḥman's daughters, who could stir a boiling pot with their bare hands.[65] But when we turn to the Jewish magicians' own handbooks, including those that probably were hidden from the sight of all but their owners, we rarely find any references to this type of trick; the same, we may add, is true of the Greek magical papyri.[66] Thus, we must generally forego the assumption of conscious fraud on their part, and assume that both practitioners and clients took these recipes and practices very seriously and copied and performed them in order to achieve the goals for which they were intended. The question, then, cannot be avoided or evaded – how could they take all this seriously? Why did they think it would work?

The question of the rationality of magic has, of course, often been asked before, especially in the anthropological study of "primitive" societies. Not content with the old interpretations (of Tylor, Frazer, Lévy-Bruhl, or Freud), which saw members of technologically backward societies as intellectually deficient and as possessing a "pre-logical" or "savage" mind all of their own (or quite like that of little children in a modern society!), several prominent anthropologists have tried to offer more charitable explanations of why "primitive" people practice their magic. Applying their insights to the study of ancient Jews, we may offer several different explanations of the extensive recourse to magic by these Jews, including some of their most prominent and intelligent thinkers. Delving into the numerous discussions of magic and rationality over the last century and a half, one finds many different lines of reasoning which might be adopted here, each with its own advantages and

---

[63] Hippolytus, *Ref.* 4.35.4–4.36.2, with Ganschinietz 1913, p. 69. For other nightly apparitions, see, e.g., Hai Gaon's description in Emanuel 1995, p. 139.

[64] For this story, known both to the rabbis and to some early Christian writers (and so nicely reproduced in a fresco from the Dura Europus synagogue!), see Ginzberg 1909–38, vol. IV, p. 198 and vol. VI, p. 319, n. 15.

[65] Bar Kokhba: Hieronymus, *Adv. Ruf.* 3.31 (PL 23.480; CC 79, p. 102 Lardet), with Dickie 2001, p. 113, and p. 338, n. 78. Rav Naḥman's daughters: bt Gitt 45a; for this trick and how to do it, see Hippolytus, *Ref.* 4.33.2, with Ganschinietz 1913, p. 49.

[66] For the few exceptions which only prove the general rule, see, e.g., PGM VII.167–86 (the *paignia* of Democritus), and T-S Ar. 44.7, briefly described by Golb 1967, p. 13. For an early modern example, see Bos 1994, pp. 65–66 and 111. Although a category of "sleight of hand" magic did exist in ancient Jewish thought, it was seen as a separate category, as we shall see in Chapter 6.

Jewish magic: a contradiction in terms?

limitations. But in order not to discuss the issue on an entirely theoretical level, which may then prove inapplicable to the study of ancient Jewish magic, let us focus our attention on some specific examples of magical rituals known to have been used by Jews at the time, including exorcisms, healing the sick with unusual substances, incantations and rituals, magical techniques aimed at bringing a recalcitrant man or woman to the magician's client for marital, amorous or sexual purposes, amulets to aid in conception, prevent abortions, or protect a newborn baby, and magical rituals to keep evil creatures away, quell a storm at sea, or destroy the walls of a city.[67] How are we to assess the magicians' recurrent claims that their recipes were "tested" and that they had the technology necessary to perform such feats? To unpack this issue, let us begin with those practices which may actually have worked, at least in some cases, and then turn to different types of explanations for the persistence of magical practices – even those that are not likely to have worked under any circumstances.

When magic works

In recent years, it has become quite fashionable in some academic circles to entertain the possibility that magic actually works. Some anthropologists and ethnographers, for example, insist that having tried the magicians' techniques, or having spent some time observing them in action, they have become quite convinced that these magicians can in fact harm their opponents, transform nature, or perform other feats which are entirely inexplicable in our rational-scientific terms.[68] The present writer does not share these convictions, and yet, even the most rationalist or scientifically minded observers of all ages have occasionally had to concede that some of the magicians' practices do, in fact, work. Galen, for example, conducted a celebrated experiment which convinced him that peony root, when worn around the neck as an amulet, is indeed effective in keeping epileptic seizures at bay. And Maimonides, a whole millennium later, followed in Galen's footsteps and accepted the efficacy of this specific amulet, as well as other "occult" medicines of whose effectiveness he became convinced.[69] He also followed in the rabbis' footsteps and accepted the concept of a "tested amulet," i.e., as he put it, "an amulet which has cured three persons or

---

[67] For my choice of these examples, cf. Glucklich 1997, pp. 83–96.
[68] For pertinent examples, see, e.g., Favret-Saada 1980; Stoller and Olkes 1987.
[69] Galen: *De simp. med.* 6.3.10 (vol. XI, p. 859 Kühn); Maimonides: *Guide* 3.37; *Pirkei Moshe* (=*Aphorisms*) 22.18 (p. 270 Muntner), and the entire twenty-second chapter of that work (pp. 268–79 Muntner).

which has been made by a person who has cured three persons by means of other amulets."⁷⁰ In short, even the staunchest warriors against magic and superstition could not help admitting that some amulets do, in fact, work.

The claim that magic sometimes works is supported even by modern science, where it is again especially in the realm of medicine that we find magical practices which might actually have some positive effects on those who try them.⁷¹ We have all learned not to dismiss the native medicine man as a witch doctor, as our intellectual forefathers used to do, but to examine some of the substances used by him or her and test their possible efficacy in our laboratories and hospitals, sometimes leading to the development of new (to us) and effective medicines.⁷² Moreover, here too we may revert to Maimonides, who concedes that whispering an incantation over a snake- or scorpion-bite is permitted, including on the Sabbath, "even though it is (medicinally) useless," since it has a positive psychological effect upon the patient.⁷³ What we now know as the placebo effect was not lost on earlier generations, and is certainly one way of explaining how some magical recipes may have worked in at least some cases. And we may even go a step further and suggest that in some cases the sheer power of a society's belief in the efficacy of certain healing or aggressive rituals might ensure the success of these very rituals.⁷⁴ Thus, while the waters of the fountain of Jericho can hardly have contained any active ingredients that would increase a woman's chances of successful conception, the belief that they did – and the practices and rituals which probably accompanied their perusal – may have helped some Jewish women of Josephus' time conceive their long-desired babies. A few centuries later, the extensive production of written amulets to help women conceive children, prevent premature abortions, and facilitate childbirth is a sure testimony to their soothing effect on the women who carried them, a psychological boost which may even have had tangible physiological effects. Even more obviously, a belief in the pernicious effects of malevolent demons and in the exorcists' abilities to drive them away could certainly explain the exorcists' successes in healing some psychosomatic disorders, as even modern psychiatry is slowly learning to admit.⁷⁵ And some Jewish magic rituals – such as

---

⁷⁰ Maimonides, *Mishneh Torah*, Hilkhot Shabbat, 19.14, based on bt Shab 61a–b.
⁷¹ See, e.g., Sagan 1996, pp. 231–34.   ⁷² See, e.g., Plotkin 1993, and the studies in Holland 1996.
⁷³ Maimonides, *Mishneh Torah*, Hilkhot 'Avodah Zarah, 11.11, echoing such ancient views as Soranus 3.42.3. For the placebo effect, see also Vyse 1997, pp. 135–37.
⁷⁴ For a celebrated defense of this last point, see Lévi-Strauss 1963.
⁷⁵ For the employment of such techniques side by side with modern psychiatry, see Bilu and Witztum 1994.

Jewish magic: a contradiction in terms? 43

those for "dream requests" or for summoning up various angels or demons, certainly could lend themselves to psychological explanations of how they might actually work, since the results they promise (the appearance of a dream or a vision) could be construed by us as purely subjective and self-induced.[76]

But magic could sometimes work not only on the psychological level, since the magicians' own formularies occasionally contained recipes which we would actually see as quite in line with the claims of modern science. Looking at a four-page sequence of a Jewish recipe book from medieval Cairo, we find numerous rituals and incantations which could only be classified as "magic," and which are not likely to have had any of the effects they were intended to achieve. In their midst, however, we find a recipe to expel mice from the house, which involves placing in their holes a mixture of three ingredients, including arsenic.[77] As arsenic is a known toxicant, what we have here is a recipe which was used by Jewish magicians but which certainly could have worked, even according to our strictest scientific criteria. Its users apparently saw no difference between this recipe and the next one, which enjoins placing rooster(?)-feathers behind one's ears in order to transfix a person to the floor in the bathhouse, but from our perspective these are two very different recipes. This is a medieval example (arsenic was not used as a toxicant before Jabir bin Ḥayyan's experiments in the eighth century), but it is quite likely that late-antique Jewish magicians also used some magical recipes whose potential efficacy even we would not doubt.[78]

To these psychological and scientific explanations of why a handful of magical practices could have worked we may add a third factor, that of mere chance. It does not take a believer in the power of magic to admit that sometimes the performance of an erotic ritual would be followed by the victim's falling in love with, or coming into the sexual submission of, the client on whose behalf the ritual had been performed. Even rationalists like Maimonides could not help noting that magic sometimes seems to work, if only by sheer coincidence, so that even a magician whose rituals have no bearing whatsoever on the processes they are supposed to influence could

---

[76] For (medieval) Jewish dream requests, see now Idel 2005 (who covers only a fraction of the available evidence).
[77] MTKG III, 69 (T-S AS 142.13 and NS 317.18), 1b/4–7, with the editors' notes (for the correct page order, see Bohak 2005, pp. 15–16). For the use of arsenic as mouse-poison in later periods, see Bos 1994, p. 90, and Buchman 2001, pp. 57–58. I am also grateful to Raz Dekel for comments on the history of arsenic.
[78] For an example from Pliny's *Natural History*, see Green 2004, p. 268.

have a few accidental successes.[79] And yet, even when we make room for those practices of ancient Jewish magicians which may have worked, and for the coincidental success of a few others, we shall be left with numerous spells and recipes which simply could not have worked, and yet were assiduously practiced, and apparently trusted, by practitioners and clients alike. It is this great gap between what may actually have worked and what was commonly practiced that we must try to understand.

The manipulation of emotions

One possible approach to magical rituals which make no sense from our scientific-empirical perspective would be to admit their irrational nature, but limit the scope of their application and stress their psychological significance. Ancient seafarers, for example, had no effective means for handling sea-storms, or even foretelling their arrival. Needless to add, neither they nor their rickety vessel or its cargo were insured, and no mechanism existed to compensate them, or their partners or heirs, for their losses. In such a situation, there is little doubt that amulets and other rituals intended to protect the seafarer from the dangers of the sea could have provided their users with some sense of security in a sea of danger. In medieval literature, at least, the seafarer who takes storms lightly because of the special protection he had procured in the form of a spell or an amulet even became a literary *topos*.[80] Thus, one possible approach to the question of the rationality of magical rituals to quell a storm would be to adopt Malinowski's famous observation that in the technologically backward societies he had studied, the "natives" employed very rational solutions to all the problems that the knowledge and technology available to them enabled them to solve. They turned to more magical means only when challenged with threatening situations for which they had no practical solutions.[81] This general claim, that "primitive" people display their rationality by not turning to magic when other means are available, certainly is applicable for some members of ancient Jewish society. Josephus, for example, had no doubts about the existence and pernicious effects of malevolent demons, or of the existence of effective means of driving them out. But when he fell off his horse and fractured the palm of his hand, he had some physicians, and not an

---

[79] For Maimonides' admission that the magicians' promises sometimes are fulfilled, but only through sheer coincidence, see *Guide* 3.37; *Commentary* on m AZ 4.7.
[80] See the brief but brilliant analysis by Goitein 1967–93, vol. I, pp. 323–24. But note also the entirely non-magical nature of the Jewish skipper's behavior in Synesius, *Epist.* 5 (GLAJJ, vol. III, pp. 48–58).
[81] See, e.g., Malinowski 1925.

exorcist, treat the injury.[82] Presumably, the same was true for many other Jews, who never turned to exorcists for the solution of medical problems whose origins certainly were not demonic, or turned to them only when all other physicians failed to solve their problem.[83] It is also quite possible that erotic, aggressive, and other magical rituals were the clients' last resort, after all non-magical modes of attaining their goal had failed to produce the desired effect. When John Hyrcanus II and his followers asked Ḥoni the Circle Maker to curse their own brethren, who were besieged in the Jerusalem Temple, it was mainly because the Temple was very hard to capture by purely military means.[84] Moreover, in all these cases we may follow Malinowski's lead and stress the positive psychological effects of the magical rituals upon those who perform them, be it the terrified sailor, the sick patient, the disgruntled lover, or the besieger of mighty walls. In some of these cases, we might even suggest that the magical ritual would surely fail to achieve the desired result, but would at least let the practitioner or client vent their aggressive emotions by means of the magical ritual they performed.[85]

Such examples could be multiplied, but their significance should not be exaggerated in the service of apologetic scholarship. The abundance of Jewish magical texts and practices makes it clear that many Jews took this kind of activity very seriously, and placed much faith in its effectiveness. Claiming that they used such practices only as a stop-gap for their technological deficiencies would hardly suffice to explain the pervasiveness of Jewish magic. Thus, one cannot help thinking that the sailor who drowned after meticulously following the instructions of a magical recipe to quell a storm probably did not go down with a smile, and that disgruntled lovers and warriors probably were quite vexed when the magical rites they employed failed to secure the triumphs they desired. Even more to the point, when reading a magical recipe for "path jumping," that is, the instantaneous teleportation to a distant land, one cannot help thinking that the practitioners who tried such recipes were disappointed on each and every occasion, as they realized that they were still deeply embedded in their

---

[82] For Josephus on demons and exorcisms, see Chapter 2. For his injured wrist, see *Vita* 403–04. And cf. Green 2004, p. 271.
[83] For turning to physicians first, see, e.g., Tb 2.10; Mk 5.26; Josephus, *Ant.* 6.166; Diodorus Siculus 31.43.1 and the other examples adduced by Green 2004, pp. 269–70. For modern examples, see Varol 2002.
[84] See Josephus, *Ant.* 14.19–24, discussed in Chapter 2.
[85] For this line of thought as applied to ancient erotic magic, see, for example, Winkler 1991, pp. 225–28, with Graf 1997, pp. 146–47 and Faraone 1999, pp. 81–83.

pre-ritual location.[86] Thus, while emotionalist explanations might help explain the recourse to magic in some cases and contexts, they certainly cannot serve as the sole basis from which to understand why ancient Jews were so convinced that magic really works, and thus feel much relieved in the face of adversity.

The manipulation of symbols and culture-specific assumptions

A very different line of reasoning from that based upon the works of the "emotionalist" anthropologists is based upon the fruits of cultural anthropology, and insists that the rationality of rituals must be sought in culture-specific terms. Given a certain set of premises, axioms, or symbols, some practices are, in fact, entirely rational within the cultural framework in which they occur.[87] This is also why in some periods and cultures, be it late-antique Neoplatonism, medieval Islam, or Renaissance Europe, elaborate theories could be developed which sought to explain why magic actually works, theories based on invisible forces of nature (such as sympathy and antipathy, or the emanation of astral powers, or the doctrine of signatures, or the cosmic powers of words and sounds), invisible entities (such as angels and demons), or the special psychic powers of some individuals. Focusing on ancient Jewish magic, we may note, for example, the recurrence of rituals aimed to adjure angels and other heavenly powers to fulfill the desires of practitioners and their clients. As the assumption that various forces of nature have an angel "ministering" over them was common enough in late-antique Jewish culture, and given an additional axiom that angels can be adjured by humans (esp. by an appeal to the power of God, who created them and whom they greatly fear), the adjuration of angels to quell a storm, bring back a recalcitrant lover, or perform other great deeds would be a perfectly rational action. And yet, while pointing to the "specific rationality" of ancient Jewish magic might make us conclude that the adjuration of angels was in no way irrational, it would fail to explain why such adjurations were almost always accompanied by elaborate rituals which had little to do with the adjuration itself. Faced with such data, we could, of course, opt to follow the symbolic-cultural line of interpretation, as practiced most extensively by Victor Turner, and try to explain the meaning of every ritual practice

---

[86] For such recipes, see Verman and Adler 1993/94.
[87] For this line of reasoning, see, e.g., Tambiah 1990 and Kieckhefer 1994 (whose analysis, however, is based on medieval discussions of magic, and not on the magical handbooks themselves). For its application to ancient Jewish magic, see esp. Janowitz 2002. See also Swartz 1990 and HAITCG, pp. 60–62.

performed by Jewish magicians, and of every symbol they manipulated, within the framework of ancient Jewish culture as a whole. Developing this line of reasoning to its logical conclusion, we would arrive at what Clifford Geertz has called a "thick" description of the ritual in question, that is, a description which pays attention to every little detail of the practice being studied, and interprets its meanings within the intricate web of explicit and implicit signposts provided by the cultural matrix of its performer(s) and primary observers.[88]

However, valuable as such an approach might be for the study of Jewish magic, it soon runs into three specific problems. First, the quest for the meaning of every little detail risks over-interpreting the data, and even the basic assumption – that the individual components of a cultic activity have specific meanings – cannot be taken for granted.[89] Second, and most important for the study of magical rituals, the Jewish magical practices (like those of many other societies) are very eclectic, and stem from several different cultural milieus (as we shall see in Chapters 4 and 5); thus, looking for their meaning within the Jewish cultural framework, when their origins may lie outside it, might lead to some very misleading results.[90] Third, and most important for the present discussion, it must be stressed that the symbolic-cultural interpretation of magical rituals actually bypasses the issue of their rationality. The "thick" description of ritual seeks to show how the details of a given ritual might fit within the framework of the culture which produced it, but it does not help explain the gap between their cultural premises and nature's refusal to play by their rules. In other words, it shows us how a ritual might "work" in the cultural sense of the word, but not how it might actually work in achieving the results it proclaims.[91] One may, of course, choose to follow that approach and even change one's concept of rationality and practicality, from "that which makes sense" and "that which works" to "that which makes sense and is supposed to work within a given culture," but this is just one more way of evading the issue.[92] By relativizing our convictions of which practices may bring down a mighty wall and which may not we are not dismantling the barriers separating us from our forefathers, we are only erecting new ones. If their view of the universe differed greatly from ours, it is our duty to try and understand it,

---

[88] For an interesting application of this interpretive scheme to a medieval Jewish ritual, which amply demonstrates the method's merits and limitations, see Marcus 1996.
[89] For trenchant criticisms of this assumption, see Staal 1989; Gruenwald 2003.
[90] For a preliminary discussion of some of these issues (as relating to the use of Jewish myths by non-Jewish magicians), see also Bohak 2004.
[91] This point was forcefully raised by Jarvie and Agassi 1970.
[92] For this line of reasoning, see Penner 1989.

but we need not give up our own views in the process, or even pretend to do so.

Statistics and excuses

While the anthropological literature of the twentieth century provides us with some interesting tools for analyzing magical rituals, it seems ill-equipped to explain why ancient Jews were so convinced that magic actually works. Thus, unless we are willing to adopt some more extreme theories of how magic might work – such as Jung's notion of "synchronicity" or New Age conceptions of a mutable reality whose true nature lies beyond our grasp – we must again face the question of why, if magic generally does not work, ancient Jews failed to discover this fact and kick the habit.[93] A useful starting-point is provided by the story of Diagoras, one of the most famous atheists of Greek antiquity. When shown all the votive offerings set up by people saved by the gods from storms at sea, and asked how he could still deny that the gods exist and care for humanity, he responded that those persons who were not saved from the storms set up no votive offerings.[94] Taking our cue from this story, we could quite sarcastically note that a magical ritual to quell a storm at sea would have left no disappointed clients, and that warriors who relied on the efficacy of magical rituals to destroy a city's walls probably were the first to fall in battle.[95] Even more important, the few people who tried these recipes and happened to survive or be victorious would have reported this with some embellishments, and a few successes go a long way to establish a magician's reputation.[96] Thus, it would hardly surprise us if many people in antiquity insisted that magic does work, especially when we recall that even those medieval Jewish thinkers who insisted that it did not had no way of proving their bold claim, and – unlike modern critics of magic – no demonstrably superior technology with which to outdo the magicians' own promises. Moreover, once we admit that some of the magicians' recipes could indeed have worked, as we already did in our earlier discussion, we can begin to see why a magician could expect

---

[93] For what follows, see also Goldin 1976.
[94] Cicero, *ND* 3.37.89. For the same anecdote told about Diogenes of Sinope, see Diogenes Laertius 6.59.
[95] And note Luther's famous story of the Jew who invented a magical protection against all weapons (Trachtenberg 1943, p. 75), or the case of the Jewish soldiers who relied on their amulets and perished in battle, which we shall examine in the following chapter.
[96] See the apt formulation of Dodds 1951, p. 115: "As we see in the case of Lourdes, a healing shrine can maintain its reputation on a very low percentage of successes, provided a few of them are sensational." For the psychological powers of coincidence, see also Vyse 1997, pp. 106–10.

a few successes even in the midst of repeated failure. And when we read Philostratus' description of how many people reverted to magical practices and then attributed every minor success to the art of magic, even if they would have achieved the very same results without any resort to magic, we begin to realize that such "successes" must have been quite common.[97] Thus, when the rituals were carried out and the clients' wishes happened to be fulfilled, all was well. But when they did not, some explaining must have been needed. And it is here, in the need to explain what went wrong, that we can best understand the ancient magicians' professional attitude, since it greatly resembles that of many modern professionals. Like modern taxi drivers, software engineers and stockbrokers, they showered upon their clients a large stock of promises which they could not always keep and predictions which did not always come true. And like these modern professionals, they must have had an even larger stock of excuses and explanations, always in retrospect, of what went wrong and why. Like plumbers or car-mechanics explaining why a leak persistently returns, they could always claim that the praxis they had recommended or performed had not been carried out correctly, and thus perhaps get a second chance (as Elisha once did, when he failed to resuscitate a dead boy from a distance), or a good excuse for not taking one.[98] Like insurance agents, they could claim that the events which did transpire actually were not covered by the original policy (read the fine print!), or that their failure was due to a *force majeure*, perhaps even God Himself (and even the Ark of the Covenant once failed to secure victory over the Philistines!).[99] Like psychologists and psychiatrists, they could insist that their methods are not suitable for all patients and occasions, and that what works extremely well in one case may not work in another (otherwise, all lepers would be healed by dipping seven times in the Jordan river, as Naaman once was!).[100] They could even claim that it was lack of faith on the patient's part which explains the ritual's failure to do good on that patient's behalf.[101] And like well-trained and well-paid

---

[97] Philostratus, *VAT* 7.39.
[98] For a wonderful list of such excuses (not even offered by the magicians, but by the clients themselves!), see Philostratus, *VAT* 7.39. Note also the story in bt Pes 111b, of the rabbis' disciple who wrote the wrong amulet, discussed in Chapter 6.
[99] And note the story of how the Egyptian king Nectanebo, divining that it was the gods themselves who were leading the Persian invasion of Egypt, did not even apply his magical technology and fled to Macedonia instead (Ps.-Callisthenes, *Alexander Romance* 1.3).
[100] For a typical example, see Pliny, *NH* 30.6.16: The Magi say that people with freckles cannot force the gods to do their will, and cannot even see them. See also Bos 1994, p. 85, for Ḥayyim Vital's explanation of failure, Etkes 1995, p. 84, for Katzenelbogen's, and Petrovsky-Shtern 2004, p. 237, for Hillel Baʿal Shem's.
[101] For a medieval example, see Schwartz 1999, p. 178.

modern physicians telling a dying patient that there is nothing to be done in his or her specific case, ancient magicians could perhaps even admit to their clients the shortcomings of their currently available technology and assure them that "We are still working on it." In fact, they could, and did, use failure as a mean to further elaborate and "improve" upon those recipes and techniques which seem to have failed, while simultaneously explaining the failure away.[102] Finally, and perhaps most importantly, like any religious or political leader from time immemorial, magicians too could insist that they have in fact delivered on their promises, even in the face of contradictory evidence, or that their promises will soon be fulfilled, if only the patients are patient enough. And when all else failed, they could always move to another town or village and start all over again, or simply choose another vocation.[103]

This, then, seems to be the most commonsensical approach to the problem of the rationality of ancient Jewish magic. On the one hand, we may ask whether the actions taken by the magicians indeed would have contributed to the achievement of the goals towards which they were performed. In a few cases, the answer would be, Yes; in a few more, Maybe; but in most cases, there would be no way – direct or indirect – in which the magicians' actions could be conceived as helpful towards generating the changes in the natural or the social order which they were intended to achieve. But having reached that conclusion, we must now raise our eyes from the ancient texts, look all around us, and honestly ask ourselves how many promise-mongers in our own world would pass such a rigorous test. Some certainly would, but many others – including most academics – would find themselves protesting that the question itself is unfair. We should also think of all those instances in which we too turn to specialists who possess a distinct body of knowledge and who insist upon their ability to solve our problems and better our lives. In some cases, their claims can be rationally defended and empirically verified, but in many others, both the rationalization and the verification are either entirely absent, or performed by people whose methods and manners of demonstration are utterly inaccessible to the average layman. In fact, our own times have seen such a proliferation of quick-fix solutions to the problems faced by ordinary people in their daily lives – be it depression, obesity, substance abuse, job insecurity, real or perceived poverty, or a terminal illness of oneself or a loved one – and such a difficulty in distinguishing those solutions which may work from those

---

[102] For this important point, as demonstrated by Thessalus' explanation of the failure of Nechepso's recipes, see Gordon 1997, p. 77. The story in bt Pes 111b is again instructive.
[103] For a nice illustration, see Apuleius, *Met.* 2.12–14.

which never did and never will, that we should not be too smug about the quick-fix solutions of antiquity. Moreover, as we shall see throughout the present book, there are many more interesting questions to ask when studying ancient Jewish magic than the banal question, "But did it work?" Even if we could offer a reliable analysis of the efficacy of each magical ritual employed by ancient Jews, the answer would probably not be worth the effort invested in reaching it. And even if our answer would be mostly negative, as suggested above, this would not make the study of ancient Jewish magic any less interesting – and perhaps even more so. For it is precisely when human convictions are demonstrably false yet stubbornly persistent that their study becomes most rewarding.

MAGIC AND MONOTHEISM

Omnipotent gods are immune to magic, and the history of monotheism entails the gradual elimination of magic from the sphere of religion. Coming from a founding father of sociology, and the founding father of the sociology of religion, such emphatic convictions certainly deserve our careful attention, even if they fly in the face of all the evidence at our disposal.[104] Both Islam and Judaism, whose monotheistic nature Max Weber himself often conceded, are shot through with magical practices and display extremely developed magical traditions, and even the Protestant sects, his favorite example of a magic-free religion, turn out to be quite far from that.[105] Leaving aside the Muslim and Christian examples, we may note how these and similar insights are applied to the study of Jewish monotheism, and give rise to the claim that biblical religion knows neither myth nor magic, only a single God who created the entire world and who rules it by His Will, and by His Will alone.[106] But if monotheism indeed knows no magic, then we must conclude that the Jews whose magical practices will occupy us in the present book were not monotheists, quite a substantial charge to lay at their door.[107] And when we find little damning evidence to substantiate that accusation, we must explain how it is that some Jews in antiquity could accept the monotheistic principle and dabble in magic at the same time.

[104] For Weber's view of magic, see Weber 1952, pp. 222–23, 244–46, 400.
[105] For magic and monotheism in Islam, see Fahd 1987. For magic in the Protestant sects, see Thomas 1971, pp. 133–78.
[106] For the classic formulation of this claim, see Kaufmann 1938, vol. I, pt 2, pp. 286–303, esp. 302–03; see also pp. 458–85. See also von Rad 1962, vol. I, pp. 34–35.
[107] I leave aside the claim – raised by Hayman 1991 – that no Jews in antiquity were truly monotheistic, since they all believed in a plurality of heavenly beings besides God.

The evidence for the entry into the Jewish magical texts of late antiquity of some pagan beliefs and practices will be assembled in Chapter 4. We can already state, however, that nowhere in the ancient Jewish magical texts will we find any divine being which would rival the Jewish God, or even challenge Him, or even influence His actions in any major way. Thus, there is nothing that would show that the Jews behind these texts abandoned the basic monotheistic principle of worshiping One God only, or even of acknowledging the existence of just One God, and there is some evidence that they excised from their pagan sources most of the potentially offensive elements (see Chapter 5). Similarly, while the Jewish magical texts (just like the non-magical ones) evince a firm belief in the existence of numerous malevolent powers, such as demons, these powers are not ranged against God Himself and evince no dualistic aspirations. In other words, while the magical texts are not much bothered by theological questions, their monotheistic credentials are virtually impeccable.

How, then, is it possible to be a monotheist and a magician at the same time? To answer this question, we must note that the main issues at stake are not so much God's uniqueness as His Omnipotence and His Providence. On the one hand, His Omnipotence, or the absolute supremacy of His Will, seems to make magic impossible within a monotheistic framework, since no magician can perform a ritual more powerful than God's decrees. On the other hand, the practice of magic might endanger God's providential rule of the universe, since if the power of magic is strong enough, it might even achieve things which are contrary to God's own plans. We shall therefore take a closer look at each of these issues, and then examine the possible, and perhaps surprising, contribution of Jewish monotheism to the development of Jewish magic.

Coercing God?

If omnipotent gods are immune to magic, one possible explanation of the ubiquity of Jewish magic in antiquity would be to stress that at least in some strands of late-antique Jewish religious thought, including rabbinic Judaism, God is not always conceived of as omnipotent. In quite a few rabbinic sayings and stories, God is described as crying over the Temple which He had let the Romans destroy, as repeatedly going into exile with His people Israel, as letting His right arm remain tied behind His back, as conceding His defeat in arguments with rabbinic sages and even as having needed Moses to strengthen Him when things got rough on Mount Sinai, and as gaining in strength whenever the Jews fulfill His commandments.

The rabbis even boast that in many cases, what God Himself has decreed a righteous person – not to mention a rabbi – may annul.[108] Thus, one could perhaps claim that with God so busy moaning, wandering, and conceding to the rabbis' every whim, some late-antique Jews concluded that with the appropriate use of magical technology He could be coerced, or at least encouraged, to place His powers at their service. This is a danger of which the Jewish leadership at the time was fully aware, and to which it seems to have reacted with some force. The paradigmatic story for this phenomenon has often been quoted, but it is worth quoting once again:

> Once, the people said to Ḥoni the Circle-Maker, "Pray that it would rain." He said to them, "Go out and bring your Passover ovens indoors, so they would not rot." He prayed, but there was no rain. What did he do? He drew a circle and stood inside it, and said before Him, "Master of the Universe! Your children turned their faces to me, since I am like a son of the household before you. I swear by your great Name that I will not move from here until you have mercy on your children." Rain drops began falling. He said, "That is not what I asked for, but for rain (that fills) wells, cisterns and caves!" The rain became violent. He said, "That is not what I asked for, but for rain of goodwill, blessing and charity." The rain became moderate . . . Shimeon son of Sheṭaḥ sent him (a message): "Were you not Ḥoni, I would decree an excommunication upon you. But what can I do to you if you cajole God for something and He does what you want, like a son who cajoles his father and his father does his will?"[109]

Asking God to send rain, or asking God for any other legitimate favor, was, of course, entirely normative in ancient Jewish culture. But the acceptable way to do so was to put on a sackcloth, sprinkle one's head with some ashes, and – most important – *beg* God for mercy.[110] It is not Ḥoni's request which Shimeon found offensive, but the impudent manner in which he forced God to obey. Viewed from the perspective of comparative religion, Ḥoni's action and words seem relatively mild; in other cultures, one might easily threaten a god that if s/he does not perform a certain deed its statue will be flogged, its shrine harmed, and its holy objects desecrated or destroyed. But within a monotheistic framework, Ḥoni's behavior was entirely unacceptable, even if his ultimate goal was saving God's people from starvation. However, as we shall note at greater length in Chapter 5, one of the striking features of the Jewish magical texts of late antiquity and the early Middle Ages is their apparent avoidance of any attempt to coerce or influence God.

---

[108] For such rabbinic materials, see, e.g., Liebes 1993 and Fishbane 2003. See also Chapter 6, n. 164.
[109] m Taan 3.8, and cf. Josephus, *Ant.* 14.22, who only says that "Ḥoni prayed to God to end (λῦσαι) the drought, and God heard (γενόμενος ἐπήκοος) and sent down rain."
[110] See, for example, Josephus, *Ant.* 12.300, on the Jewish custom of putting on sackcloth when supplicating God.

The Jewish practitioners were remarkably willing to adjure an endless host of angels and demons, but God Himself was left alone. This was a line in the sand that they never tried to cross.

Here, then, is where Max Weber's intuition that monotheistic magic is a contradiction in terms breaks down, at least in the case of ancient Jewish magic. Contrary to his implicit assumption, the magicians felt no need to coerce God, and thus did not have to face the problem of God's Omnipotence. Like a great king (to use the rabbis' favorite metaphor!), God was the supreme and absolute ruler, but the actual running of the daily affairs of the kingdom was the domain of a highly complex heavenly bureaucracy, consisting of an endless variety of underlings who could be cajoled, and even coerced, into accomplishing their specific task in a way that would suit the magician's needs – or those of his clients. Often, the means used to frighten these underlings into submission consisted of adjurations in the Name of the great king himself, a practice to which He apparently did not object. And, as we shall see in Chapter 6, while the rabbis of late antiquity were not entirely happy with this procedure, they did not really try to fight it either – and occasionally used it themselves.

The implications of this peculiar feature of Jewish magic, which indeed makes it different from the magical practices of the polytheistic religions, shall be examined in greater detail in Chapter 5. For the time being, we must ask two more theoretical questions; first, how would ancient Jews have conceived of the relations between the powers of magic and God's Providence? Second, how should we conceive of the relations between Jewish monotheism and the development of Jewish magic?

Magic and providence

As we already noted, Jewish magicians never tried to coerce God into a certain action; they did, however, try to bring about many changes in the natural and social world – to quell a storm, to heal a sick patient, to make one person love or marry another, to maim or kill an adversary, and so on. Which raises the question, How would all these changes fit within God's plan and His providential handling of the universe? Was the storm or the disease not sent by God, who also determined whom one would marry, when one would die, and all other natural and human affairs? If so, could the Jewish magician save a sinner from punishment, harm a righteous person, or derail God's providential plans and actions in any other way? As might be expected, the magical handbooks and other magical texts at our disposal hardly busy themselves with such questions; being practical and goal-oriented, they have little use for theoretical speculations about abstruse theological issues. Occasionally, one sees in these texts the claim that the person asking for the punishment of his opponent is indeed righteous and is only seeking to redress an evil done him by his would-be victim (not to mention rituals for catching thieves or returning a stolen object), but such cases certainly are but a small minority of the magical texts at our disposal. In most other magical texts, the issues of right and wrong, of human morality and divine justice, simply do not come up at all. In the non-magical literature, however, such questions do surface. In the Torah, they are at least implied in those stories which make it very clear that no magician – not Pharaoh's wizards, not even the great Balaam himself – can stop God's plans from unfolding; elsewhere in the Hebrew Bible, it is again made clear that while magic works, God's power is much greater than that of any magician.[111] In later Jewish literature, the focus is less on the fate of the nation and more on that of the individual, but the issue of Providence versus magic is explicitly discussed. Perhaps the most famous, and most commonly misquoted, discussion of this issue is found in the following story from the Babylonian Talmud, embedded in an extensive discussion of magic and magicians:

A certain woman came to take dust from underneath R. Hanina's feet. He said to her, If it works out for you, go ahead and do it, for it says "There is no one but Him." (Dt 4.35)[112]

The scene is instructive: R. Hanina is sitting there, and sees the woman coming to gather the dust from underneath him, dust which she would use in an aggressive magical ritual aimed against him (what Frazer would call "contagious magic"). The expected reaction to such an action can be seen from a parallel scene in Apuleius' *Metamorphoses* (= *The Golden Ass*), when the crafty witch sends her servant Photis to gather some hair-clippings of the handsome object of her desire from the barber-shop, in order to use them for her aggressive erotic spell. But the barber – fully aware of the woman's reputation – immediately kicks poor Photis out of his shop, and she is forced to find other hair-clippings instead, with some hilarious consequences.[113] Thus, Rabbi Hanina's decision not to do so, but to let the woman gather dust from under him, is highly unusual; and the verse he quotes, "You have been shown to know that YHWH is the God; there

---

[111] See, for example, Is 44.25, on God confounding the diviners and *qosmim*.
[112] bt San 67b, and bt Hull 7b, with minor differences. For the wide diffusion of the claim that even *keshaphim* are subjected to God's rule cf. Yahalom 1999, p. 202.
[113] Apuleius, *Met.* 3.16.

is no one but Him," certainly testifies to his unswerving faith in God's Providence. Since the Lord is all alone up there, and since His Will governs the world and all that is in it, there is nothing for me to fear, says R. Ḥanina. If I am righteous before God, He would protect me against any adversity, including the magic spells and rituals of a miserly witch, and if I am not, He would punish me in any case. Thus, if her wicked plans materialize, it is only because this too is a part of God's plan. This reaction, so different from that of most people at the time, and so much in line with Max Weber's ideal type of monotheistic faith, has often been quoted by modern scholars.[114] Less often quoted, however, is the Talmud's own reaction to this story, which comes immediately after it:

Is that so? Since Rabbi Yoḥanan said, Why are they called "magicians" – because they contradict the heavenly host!? Indeed, R. Ḥanina is a special case, for he has many merits.[115]

Not only Apuleius would have found R. Ḥanina's equanimity unusual; the Talmudic editors too found it unusual, and quoted R. Yoḥanan's playful etymology, explaining the Hebrew word MEKHASHPHIM ("magicians") as a composite amalgam of MAKḤISHIM ("they contradict", or "they weaken") and PAMALIA (the Latin word, *familia* [*Caesaris*], which is the standard rabbinic designation for God's angelic host), that is, stressing the magicians' ability to force God's angels to follow their orders.[116] If this is so, asks the Talmud, how could Rabbi Ḥanina be so complacent about the dangers of the magical praxis about to be practiced upon him? The answer, says the Talmud, is that R. Ḥanina is a man of so many merits, a man who has so many good points in God's logbooks, that he need not fear the witch's sorceries at all. Like his contemporary Plotinus, and like other pagan philosophers and Christian bishops, R. Ḥanina, too, was entirely immune to magic.[117] But if R. Ḥanina is a special case, ordinary Jews cannot blindly trust God's Providence to make them magic-proof, and when they see a witch collecting the dust from underneath them they better react just like Apuleius' barber. Magic works, and it can cause great harm even to decent people, and only a fool, or an exceptionally meritorious person (or one

---

[114] See, e.g., Lieberman 1942, p. 113. For a view similar to Ḥanina's, see Quran 2.102 (the magicians can hurt none, unless by God's permission).
[115] bt San 67b; Hull 7b.
[116] And cf. Rashi to San 67b: "that they (the magicians) kill those who were decreed to go on living."
[117] For Plotinus' immunity to aggressive magic, see Porphyry, *Vita Plot.* 10. For its theoretical underpinnings, see Plotinus, *Enn.* 4.4.43–44. For philosophers' immunity to magic see also Celsus in Origen, *CC* 6.41, and for Origen's insistence (*ibid.*) that true Christians are immune to magic, cf. Ambrose's immunity, described by Paulinus, *Vita Ambrosii* 20 (PL 14.33–34).

who is both), can afford to trust God's Providence in the face of a magical attack. No wonder that the rabbis often recommended many precautions, and some powerful spells and rituals, against magic and witchcraft!

If there is one thing which the pervasiveness of Jewish magic can teach us about its practitioners' attitudes to their religious system, it is that they refused to accept some of the more simplistic biblical models of Providence and its consequences for their daily lives. When facing a storm in the midst of the sea, a sick child, or a person who refused to submit to their will, some ancient Jews turned to magical practices and rituals which, they hoped, would solve their specific problem. In and of itself, such behavior may not be un-monotheistic, but it is interesting to note how it replaces, or at least supplements, the behavior which the Jewish religious establishment did try to encourage. Rather than trusting divine Providence, or searching deep within one's soul for the possibility that one's troubles were sent by God as a punishment for one's sins, and then repenting of these sins and praying to God for His mercy, these Jews turned to magical short-cuts aimed at achieving the same effect. As one example out of many, we may note how a verse like Exodus 15.26, which promises the Jews that *if* they do what is pleasing to God, and fulfill all of His commandments, He would keep them healthy, has itself become a spell to be recited over sick patients or inscribed on amulets to be worn by them (see Chapters 5 and 6). One may only assume that at least in some cases the verse was used by and for people who had not always met the conditions it so clearly laid out, but were hoping that it would do the job just the same.[118] This is, of course, part of a much wider pattern to which the Jewish magical texts testify, namely, the dissolution of the claim – repeatedly hammered home by the biblical legislators – that if only the Jews would observe God's commandments God would assure them longevity, prosperity, peace, fertility, and everything else they may hope for.[119] It must be stressed, however, that rabbinic literature too testifies to a wide range of perceptions concerning the possible correlation – or the lack thereof – between a person's sins and merits and the events of his or her life.[120] Here, as in many other issues, the assumptions implicit in the ancient Jewish magical texts do not differ greatly from the explicit claims of other strands of late-antique Jewish literature. Like many other Jews, our magicians and their clients consciously refused to "leave it all to

---

[118] This point was not lost on the rabbis, as may be seen, for example, from Rabbi Yoḥanan's words in bt San 101a.
[119] For such biblical promises, see, e.g., Ex 23.25–26; Lv 26.3ff; Dt 28. That the issue was much debated already in the biblical period may be seen, for example, in the books of Job and Ecclesiastes.
[120] For rabbinic views of divine rewards and punishments, see Urbach 1975, pp. 255–85, 420–523.

God" and risk calamity, or accept their sad fate and then complain about it, as Job once did. And once again, the same is true of the rabbis of late-antique Palestine and Babylonia, who had their own healing and aggressive magical recipes and techniques, and sometimes used them as supplements to, or as substitutes for, a pious prayer or the meticulous observance of God's commandments. Faced with the instability of fortune and the inscrutability of God's ways (which often amount to one and the same thing) the Jews of late antiquity tried all the methods they could think of, and some of those devised by their non-Jewish neighbors, to gain control over processes which were, in fact, beyond their control.

Jewish monotheism and the growth of Jewish magic

Having seen that Jewish magic need not spell a compromise of Jewish monotheism, we also noted that its development in fact was at least partly shaped by that monotheism, which left little room for other divinities besides God, or for magical operations to be conducted upon God Himself. We shall briefly return to both issues in Chapter 5, but must now raise the opposite question: was there something about Jewish monotheism which actually encouraged the development of Jewish magic? This question is not as bizarre as it might first seem, for it has in fact been suggested that Jewish magic is one by-product of the theological implications of Jewish monotheism, and it might also be suggested that it is one by-product of its sociological implications.

On the theological level, it has recently been suggested that one outcome of Jewish monotheism, and of the growing transcendence of the Jewish God, was a widening gap between the ordinary Jew and his God, and that the proliferation of angelic and demonic powers, and the growth of Jewish magic, served to bridge that gap.[121] In passing, we may note that this argument echoes many nineteenth-century Christian reconstructions of the history of Judaism, with the ever-more-distant God giving rise (or should we say, giving birth?) to one or more mediators. In its older formulation, the argument was not free of anti-semitic overtones, since it implied, or insisted, that when the Jews did receive the best mediator they could have hoped for, they brutally rejected him.[122] That a similar argument could now be raised even by an Israeli scholar is a fine testimony to the liberating powers of the Zionist revolution, as interpretations which would have been

---

[121] For this argument, see Fernandez Marcos 1985, p. 105, and Stein 2004, pp. 184–85.

[122] For an exposition and a trenchant critique of these nineteenth-century perceptions, see Moore 1921, esp. pp. 233–36, 242–54.

apologetically rejected by Jewish scholars only a few generations ago are now being re-formulated and re-examined by Jewish scholars in the Jewish state itself.[123] The argument's validity is, of course, an entirely different matter, and one to which we shall soon return.

The possible contribution of Jewish monotheism to the development of Jewish magic may also be examined from a sociological perspective. One corollary of Jewish monotheism in the First, and especially in the Second Temple period was the unification of the cult in one place, and at the hands of a single, closed, priestly caste. That this process was related to the biblical legislators' rulings concerning magic and divination seems quite obvious, since we already noted how in Deuteronomy 18 a sharp dichotomy is posited between legitimate and illegitimate religious experts. Judges and inspectors, levites and priests, prophets and even kings were all legitimate leaders, and one could turn to them – but not to a *qosem*, or a *mekhasheph*, or a *yide'oni*, and so on – for guidance and assistance. Thus, when one needed some extra help in saving a sick child or foretelling the future of the agricultural season, one could turn to the nearest prophets and priests, who probably catered to the population's special needs, as did their non-Jewish colleagues throughout the Ancient Near East. This type of process may have encouraged the development of Jewish substitutes to pagan magic, some of which – such as priestly ways of crossing rivers, winning battles, foretelling the future, or detecting adulteresses – are attested already in the biblical period itself, as we already saw. In the Second Temple period, and with the gradual elimination of "idolatry" from Jewish society, the process may have been intensified. When the Hasmonean priests, for example, prevented their followers from wearing the gods of Iamneia under their garments when setting off to battle (as we shall see in the following chapter), they may have offered them more "kosher" substitutes instead. Thus, the unification of the cult and the clergy and the prohibition against turning to any foreign ritual experts may in fact have encouraged the development of indigenous Jewish forms of magic and divination – just as it did in the Christian world a few centuries later. And following this line of thought to its logical conclusion, we might even suggest that with the destruction of the Jewish Temple in 70 CE, and the creation of many new cult centers (such as the local synagogues) instead of a single shrine, and an alternative religious leadership (such as the rabbinic class) instead of the hereditary priestly caste, the road was open for the rise of a large group of Jewish magicians and diviners, who offered their Jewish clients a set of "kosher"

---

[123] For another example of this intriguing process, see Yuval 2006.

solutions for their everyday needs (while not neglecting their non-Jewish clients as well). This too is a process that is well documented in the Christian world.[124]

These two explanations of the possible connections between Jewish monotheism and Jewish magic have one thing in common, namely, the claim that the consolidation of the Jewish belief in one God and one God only, and the concomitant unification of the cult and the clergy, may have encouraged the development of a home-grown type of Jewish magic, one that would fill the gap between what a monotheistic system can provide and what its followers actually need. Thus, we might expect a gradual growth of the Jewish magical tradition, a deep involvement of the priestly class in magical activities during the Second Temple period, and an exponential growth of Jewish magic in the post-destruction period. It must be stressed, however, that while such historical reconstructions could easily be defended on a theoretical level, and could even be supported with some specific data, they are very hard to substantiate in a satisfying manner. As we shall see in the following chapters, the most important factor determining our ability to study ancient Jewish magic is the apparent move from a mostly oral to a mostly scribal mode of transmitting and executing magical knowledge and magical practices, and this move may be quite unrelated to the processes postulated here. Thus, while there is some evidence that the priests of the Second Temple period did dabble in magic (as we shall see in the following chapter), assessing the scope of their activities is made quite impossible by the absence of substantial remains to testify to these activities. And while there is a marked growth of the evidence for Jewish magic from late antiquity onwards (see Chapter 3), this mainly reflects the growing production of written artifacts as part of the magical rituals and the growing tendency to transmit the magical know-how in written recipe-books, and does not necessarily reflect a growth in the quantity or frequency of magical rituals practiced by Jews at the time. Similarly, any attempt to compare the quantity of magical activities of Jews and non-Jews in any given period, to see whether Jews indeed were more prone to practice magic than some of their non-monotheistic neighbors, is bound to run into the same methodological difficulties, which seem quite insurmountable. Thus, while we may ask whether and how Jewish monotheism assured Jewish magic a flavor distinct from that of Egyptian or Greek magic, for example (and we shall do so in Chapter 5), asking whether Jews practiced

---

[124] For the forces shaping the growth of Christian magic, see Thomas 1971, pp. 27–57, and especially Flint 1991.

more magic or less magic than pagans probably would lead us nowhere. But we may at least stress that there is no need to see Jewish magic and Jewish monotheism as incompatible, and that the exact opposite may in fact be true.

THERE IS NO SUCH THING AS MAGIC...

One more way of denying the existence of Jewish magic is to follow the claim of those scholars who insist that there is no such thing as magic, since "magic" is just a label one affixes to the religious practices of one's opponents.[125] The origins of this line of thought lie in Evans-Pritchard's focus on the way the Azande whom he had studied utilized the concepts of "magic" and "sorcery" as an explanation of unexpected misfortunes. Aware of the fact that huts sometimes collapse and people sometimes fall ill, his Azande informants nevertheless insisted that the fact that the mishap occurred to one specific person is to be explained as the result of some outside intervention in these "natural" processes. They therefore turned to look for the witch or magician who set these forces in motion. Developing this insight, and coupling it with the difficulty of finding an essentialist definition of magic, numerous historians have taught us to think of "magic" not as a definable set of beliefs and practices, but as a personal accusation or a pejorative label affixed to other people's religions.[126] And given the tainted history of the term "magic" in Western culture, many scholars took Evans-Pritchard's suggested moratorium on the use of this word *ad absurdum*, and developed a wide range of politically correct circumlocutions – such as "ritual acts to gain power" – to replace the contaminated term.[127] In most cases, this led merely to the substitution of one term for another, a process which closely parallels the recent scholarly shift from BC (Before Christ) and AD (*Anno Domini*) to BCE (Before the Common Era) and CE (Common Era) – a shift which replaced problematic terms with terms deemed less offensive, but left the older (and admittedly Christianocentric!) dating system intact. In other cases, however, the excision or deconstruction of the term "magic" brought about a complete confusion as to what it is that we are trying to study and how we should go about studying

---

[125] See, e.g., Gager 1992, pp. 24–25: "But it is our conviction that magic, as a definable and consistent category of human experience, simply does not exist . . . the beliefs and practices of 'the other' will always be dubbed as 'magic,' 'superstition' and the like."
[126] For a classic application of this model, see Brown 1970; see also Aune 1980 and Segal 1981.
[127] For spirited defenses of this practice, see Meyer and Smith 1994, pp. 1–6; Smith 1995; Lesses 1998, pp. 55–61. For an equally spirited deconstruction, see Hoffman 2002.

it.[128] What has often been forgotten is the fact that while "magic" may mean different things in different cultures (and even mean nothing in some), and is or has been used as a pejorative slur in some contexts, this should not prevent us from using this term ourselves, as long as we do it in a self-reflective manner. On the one hand, we must remember that we are using "magic" only as a heuristic device – a means to gather together a group of related cultural phenomena, texts, and artifacts – and not as an explanatory category. By classifying certain Jewish texts and practices as "magic," we are saying nothing about their truth-value, their significance, or their origins; we are only saying that they deserve to be studied as a group, because they resemble each other more than their resemblance with other types of Jewish texts and practices. On the other hand, we must constantly recall that we are using "magic" in our own sense of the term, and that ancient Jews had very different views and definitions of *keshaphim* and related terms, views which deserve our attention as part of the study of ancient Jewish magic. And once we embark on this enquiry, we shall realize that the basic assumption of much of contemporary scholarship on ancient Jewish magic – that "magic" is used as a label affixed to one's opponents ("What I do is miracle; what you do is magic") – is mostly irrelevant for ancient Jewish society.[129] There are, to be sure, a few instances in which this perspective makes sense, as in the rabbinic discussions of magic and women and magic and *minim*, but – as we shall note at greater length in Chapters 2 and 6 – such cases are far less common than we might expect.

Even more important than the Jewish discourse of magic, a glance at the ancient and medieval Jewish texts available to us clearly shows that while it indeed is difficult to define "magic" in a way that will cut across cultures, or that will be accepted even by all students of a given culture, it often turns out to be surprisingly easy to identify actual texts and artifacts as belonging in the realm of magic.[130] In many cases, it is not only the subject matter and contents of the text which disclose its magical nature, but even the very material on which the text is written or the layout of the written materials on the writing surface – not to mention the proliferation of special signs, symbols, and word-shapes which only occur in this type of text. We shall return to this issue below, but for the time being must note that the presence

---

[128] See, e.g., Janowitz 2001, where magic, alchemy, and apotheosis are arbitrarily studied together, with no explanation as to why such ritual activities are included and others are not, and with little benefit to the study of any of these mostly unrelated fields.

[129] For such studies, see esp. Neusner 1989; Seidel 1996; Janowitz 2001.

[130] See also Shaked 1995, esp. p. 197.

of so many Jewish texts which could only be classified as "magic" makes the claim that magic is not a valid category of academic discourse seem woefully inadequate. In fact, the only way to sustain such a claim is to ignore the Jewish magical texts altogether – a procedure which unfortunately remains quite common among scholars in spite of its detrimental effect on the study of Jewish magic.

"RELIGION" AND "MAGIC" IN JEWISH CULTURE

In the first three sections of the present chapter, we examined three types of assumptions that have made earlier interpreters of Jewish culture insist or imply that "Jewish magic" is a contradiction in terms. The overall effect of these three assumptions has been to downplay the significance of many magical aspects of Jewish culture, and to prevent most students of Jewish history and culture from devoting any attention to the Jewish magical tradition. In more recent scholarship, however, one also sees an opposite trend, which strongly reacts to the denial of the very possibility of Jewish magic, and insists that magic is, and has always been, a central aspect of Jewish culture.[131] And whereas in the previous section we examined the claim that magic simply does not exist, we now turn to the opposite extreme, and to the claim that magic is everywhere, at least in Jewish culture.

The starting-point for this claim is the definition of magic as a set of beliefs and practices which aims to change reality by means which defy scientific explanation, or any similarly intuitive definition of magic.[132] Equipped with such a definition, we find the road to claiming that much in Jewish religiosity falls under this category wide open. A public fast in times of drought certainly is magic, since it tries to procure rain in a way that has nothing to do with the natural processes which generate precipitation, and the same is true for the water-libation ritual on the last day of the Sukkoth (Tabernacles) holiday. The wearing of *tephillin* (known in English as "phylacteries," the Greek word for "amulets" which was used by the Septuagint to translate this Hebrew term) on one's arm and forehead

---

[131] For different formulations of this claim, see Gruenwald 1996; Idel 1997. See also Schäfer 1997, who sees Jewish magic as a part of the Jewish religion, but one which the religious authorities often try to ward off, and Bar-Levav 2002, who sees a continuum between magic and religion in Jewish culture.

[132] See Idel 1997, p. 195: "By Jewish magic I mean a system of practices and beliefs that presupposes the possibility to achieve material gains by means of techniques that cannot be explained experimentally; these topics are part of Jewish traditions that were conceived of as transmitted and as relying on the authority or the experiments of others." This definition is adopted, for example, by Bar-Levav 2003.

as a means to ward off all evil is equally magical, as is the affixing of a *mezuzah* to one's doorpost, or the reciting of the *shema'* prayer on one's bed – all of which often were credited with great apotropaic value. The same is true for the offering of a sacrifice, or the recital of a prayer, as a means to secure God's grace, or the observance of any of the biblical laws in the hope of getting something in return.[133] Unfortunately, even that memorable biblical commandment, "Honor thy father and thy mother," turns out to be nothing but magic, since the reason provided by the biblical legislator is not that this is the right thing to do, or that this is what God expects of pious people, or even that this would increase the likelihood that your own children would one day honor you. As the biblical legislator put it, you should honor your parents, "in order that you will achieve longevity upon the land which YHWH your God is giving you."[134] Until a detailed statistical study would demonstrate that people who honor their parents indeed live longer than those who do not, even the Ten Commandments would have to be taken as full of magic.

The view that the performance of any religious ritual or precept in order to achieve material gains is tantamount to magic is, of course, not new. In the study of religions, it has often served as the basic starting-point for the study of magic and for the separation of "magic" from "religion." More recent studies, however, tend to stress that the origins of this perception of "magic" are deeply rooted in the Protestant critique of all efficacious rituals as "papist magic" (including, notoriously, the Catholic Mass and its efficacious transubstantiations).[135] The Jewish world, however, had no need for the Protestant Reformation for the formulation of such a discourse of magic, since it was already well established – and much debated – several centuries earlier. Its origins lie in the failed Maimonidean attempt to purify Jewish religiosity of any form of "magic" and "superstition," an attempt which led Maimonides to insist that the commandments must be fulfilled only because they were given by God, and that any expectation of material gains ensuing from merely fulfilling God's orders was sheer blasphemy. Thus, whereas earlier scholars have taken Maimonides' view of Judaism as a yardstick, and simply ignored whatever did not measure up to his standards, the current trend takes the Maimonidean perspective to the other extreme. Other than Maimonides and a small group of his followers, all other strands of Jewish culture are shot through with the assumption

---

[133] See Idel 1997, p. 203: "The belief that the performance of the Biblical ritual has dramatic repercussions on the course of nature, which is basic for the biblical thought, is imanently and emanently magical."

[134] Ex 20.12; cf. Dt 5.16.   [135] See, e.g., Thomas 1971, pp. 58–65; Styers 2004, pp. 9–12, 36–44.

that fulfilling God's commandments would bring about perceptible gains on the personal or on the community level, or even on both. Judaism, in short, is full of magic.

This view of magic as an endemic and systemic constituent of Jewish religion is not without value, for it helps highlight the fact that Judaism, like all other religious systems, has a strong *do ut des* component; the believer gives something to the powers that be, or follows their instructions, but he or she also expects to receive something in return, be it health, peace, prosperity, protection from evil, or any other benefit. It also has its value in the current debate raging within Israeli society over the place of religion, or of its deliberate dismantling, in a modern Jewish state. It must be stressed, however, that such a perspective is no less detrimental to the study of the Jewish magical tradition than that which would deny the very possibility of Jewish magic, for it too downplays the very significance of that tradition. If much in Judaism is magic, then there is little reason to devote much attention to the Jewish magical texts, which would presumably not teach us anything that we did not already know from all the other Jewish texts at our disposal. Rather than pretending that the giraffe does not exist, some scholars now insist that most animals in the zoo are quite like giraffes anyway; a close examination of the actual giraffe is once again unnecessary.

Here, then, we must decide what it is that we wish to study. If we decide to focus on the magical dimensions of Jewish religion, we may certainly adopt any intuitive definition of magic and search for all aspects of Jewish culture which fall under that definition.[136] But if we wish to study *Jewish magic*, we must adopt a somewhat different strategy, in order to separate Jewish magic from Jewish religion. Luckily, this is not so difficult, for there exists an extensive body of ancient Jewish texts which would fall under our intuitive category of "magic," and which certainly were not a part of the standard (or "normative") Jewish religion at the time, or even that of some specific inner-Jewish group or sect. No reader of the Palestinian amulets or the Babylonian incantation bowls would fail to note their "magical" contents, including many signs, words, and themes which were borrowed from non-Jewish magicians and are found – even in the pagan and Christian worlds – only in specifically magical texts. And no reader of a book like

---

[136] For a good starting-point, see the definition offered by Flint 1991, p. 3: "Magic may be said to be the exercise of a preternatural control over nature by human beings, with the assistance of forces more powerful than they." And note the use of this definition by Idel 1995, pp. 29–30. For another starting-point, note Apuleius, *Apol.* 26, who claims that *magus*, popularly defined, is "one who, through immediate communication with the immortal gods, commands incredibly powerful charms to achieve anything he wants." Replace "the immortal gods" with "God, and/or angels and demons," and you have a useful definition of the ancient Jewish magician.

Sepher ha-Razim would dispute its classification under that rubric (even if it contains some non-magical elements and passages as well), and this is equally true of the numerous magical recipe-books from the Cairo Genizah, whose generic classification poses no difficulty. At least from late antiquity onwards, such texts were a major vehicle for the transmission and dissemination of Jewish magical technology; they may now serve as the main point of entry into that tradition. They may even provide a point of departure for a more essentialist definition of the major characteristics of "Jewish magic," which could then be compared with those of the Babylonian, Greco-Egyptian, Coptic, Syriac, Muslim, or any other culture-specific magical tradition.[137] It must be stressed, however, that such an effort – to arrive at a definition of "Jewish magic" which is based on the Jewish magical texts themselves – will have to take into account the fact that many of the relevant written sources have disappeared long ago, and that many relevant "sources" have never been written down to begin with, since much of the magical activity was conducted orally. Moreover, it will have to take count of the fact that the main characteristics of "Jewish magic" in fact saw some major shifts from one period of Jewish history to the next, as we shall note in the following chapters.

Seen from this perspective, "Jewish magic" cannot be described in rigid essentialist terms, since the contents of what we might label "magic" could change from one period to the next, and even from one Jewish group or community to another at one and the same time. The best example for such processes is the recurrent debates within Jewish society itself over whether certain practices were "magic," and therefore forbidden, or a legitimate part of Jewish religiosity.[138] Moreover, while some Jewish texts may easily be classified as "magical," the borderline between "religion" and "magic" is sometimes blurred, and some texts and practices can move from one side of the dividing line to the other, just as the bronze serpent fashioned by Moses at God's behest was considered legitimate in one period, illegitimate in another. The rabbinic prayers, for example, certainly were a part of the "religion" of the Talmudic sages and their followers; but when the very same prayers were quoted and recycled within magical texts, they became a part of the magicians' arsenal, side by side with the biblical verses or divine and angelic names which they were so fond of using.[139] And when medieval

---

[137] For this method, see Versnel 1991b; for its application to Jewish magic, see Harari 1998, pp. 111–22 and Harari 2005b.

[138] For this line of reasoning, cf. Phillips 1986, esp. p. 2731: "In conclusion, the antithesis of magic and religion has value only if qualified by an understanding of the ways a particular social group employed the distinction. Magic should never represent an absolute contemporary category."

[139] For the magical uses of the rabbinic liturgy, see Schäfer 1996.

Jews added both angelic names and magical signs to the customary text of their doorpost *mezuzah* in order to enhance its apotropaic powers, we may clearly classify such *mezuzah*s as "magic," while keeping in mind that quite a few medieval rabbis insisted that they were completely acceptable, and thus a legitimate part of Jewish "religion."[140]

To sum up. Rather than looking into the phenomenology of Jewish ritual and praxis and classifying parts thereof as "magical," we should focus on those bodies of non-normative Jewish texts which could only be classified as "magical," and use them as the starting-point for any study of the Jewish magical tradition. This does not entirely solve the problem, since it is not always easy to know which texts to classify as normative, and among which social groups, especially when dealing with such texts as the exorcistic hymns from Qumran or some of the magical recipes found in rabbinic literature. In each of these specific cases, however, we shall have the opportunity to examine the validity of our classification at greater length, while in most other cases we will be dealing with texts and artifacts whose classification as "magic" could hardly be disputed.

SUMMARY

It is time to wrap up our analysis of the supposed impossibility of Jewish magic. As we noted throughout the present chapter, rather than insist that Jewish magic simply could not exist and then ignore its abundant remains, we should learn to examine these remains and ask what elements within the Jewish cultural matrix had made them possible, and perhaps even inevitable. Looking at the biblical legislation, we noted that while the Hebrew Bible repeatedly forbids the consultation of a long range of magicians and diviners and the use of some of their techniques, it does so in ways that are both vague and inconsistent, while at the same time insisting that there are acceptable substitutes for most of these practitioners and practices. We also noted two fundamental paradigms of legitimate miracle-working and divination in the biblical legislation and the biblical narratives – that performed by the "man of God" and that which relied on the innate powers of God's sacred objects and the priests who handled them. Thus, not only is the Hebrew Bible far from systematically outlawing all forms of magic, it even lays the foundations for the development of some specifically Jewish magical technology. Turning to the complex relations

---

[140] See the condemnations of all these "additions" by Maimonides, *Mishneh Torah*, Hilkhot Mezuzah 5.4 and 6.13; and cf. his *Commentary* on m Sot. 7.4; *Guide* 1.61. For the opposite view and the rabbis who expressed it, see especially Aptowitzer 1910–13 and Trachtenberg 1939, pp. 148–52.

between magic and rationality, we saw that while most of the magical practices utilized by ancient Jews certainly did not produce the hoped-for results, insisting that this makes them "un-Jewish" involves a gross misapprehension of ancient Jewish culture. Rather than assuming the Jews of antiquity to have read Maimonides (and to have been convinced by what they read!) a whole millennium before he ever wrote, we should try to see how their magical practices fit the wider framework of their culture and its explicit and implicit assumptions about God, the universe, and humanity. Rather than castigating them for appealing to rituals which never worked, we should learn to ask what effect those rituals could have had within their cultural premises, and to note that we too employ a whole range of beliefs and activities which often cannot fulfill the hopes pegged upon them. We all share the all-too-human tendency to face the hardships of life with solutions that do not really work rather than admit that there are, in fact, no solutions.

From legality and rationality we turned to theology, and noted that the supposed incompatibility between magic and monotheism is nothing but a hoax. Rather than insisting that monotheism knows no magic when each of the monotheistic religions evinces a lively magical tradition, we should ask whether their magical traditions differ from those of polytheistic societies. Thus, in studying Jewish magic we should always look for evidence of polytheistic tendencies, but when we fail to find it we should ask ourselves how a specifically Jewish cultural trait made Jewish magic different from that of some of the Jews' closest neighbors.

Our fourth section dealt with a broader claim, that "magic" simply does not exist, a claim which may prove useful in the study of some magical traditions, but does a great disservice to the study of Jewish magic. The claim that "magic" sometimes was used by Jews too as a negative label affixed to the beliefs and practices of one's opponents certainly is correct, and we should keep our eyes open for such usage of the term. But this should not blind us to the fact that a whole range of Jewish texts, at least from late antiquity onwards, can only be classified as "magic," and that these texts deserve to be studied as evidence for one more type of Jewish cultural activity, in order to examine the internal consistency and inter-relatedness of this distinct body of sources. It should be clear, however, that such a study should not lead to the complete isolation of these texts in their own little ghetto, detached from other Jewish sources. On the contrary, we should study them as a group in order to re-integrate them into the wider frameworks of Jewish cultural creativity, Jewish social relations, and Jewish history. And we should, as we noted in the final section of the present chapter, highlight the differences between this cultural activity and Jewish religion as a whole, for by insisting that all Jewish religiosity is somehow "magical" we would once again miss the opportunity to see what is unique about the Jewish magical texts themselves.

With all this in mind, we are now ready to confront ancient Jewish magic. To do so, we must focus not on theoretical potentialities but on what real Jews actually did in the millennium and more separating the reconstruction of the Jerusalem Temple in the late sixth century BCE from the conquest of the entire Near East by the Muslim armies in the early seventh century CE. To do so, we must turn to the sources available for the study of Jewish history and culture at the time and see what they can teach us about Jewish magic.

CHAPTER 2

Jewish magic in the Second Temple period

INTRODUCTION

Perhaps the most important distinction to be made in the study of any magical tradition, and especially those of the distant past, is between "outsider" accounts and "insider" evidence, or, to phrase it more accurately, between the representation of magicians and references to them by people who are not themselves involved in magic and the picture which emerges from the texts and artifacts manufactured and utilized by the magicians themselves.[1] When we study the world of Greco-Roman magic, for example, we are faced with an almost endless series of witches, sorcerers, magicians, and enchanters, both male and female, who make an appearance in hundreds of literary pieces from Homer to the Christian saint lives and beyond. Against these literary representations, which often are excruciatingly detailed, we may place thousands of objects and documents which were the work of actual practitioners, be these magical recipes and recipe-books, amulets, curses, voodoo dolls, divination boards, or other ritual accessories. Thus, one of the main features of the study of Greco-Roman magic is the constant comparison between the two corpora: does Theocritus' account of Simaetha's desperate attempts to bring back her lover tally with what we know of the magical practices of the time, and does Vergil's adaptation of that poem reflect changes in the magical technology itself over the two centuries and more that separate the two poets? Is Lucan's witch Erichto the figment of his gory imagination, or the result of a thorough study of contemporary necromantic rituals? And how does the extensive knowledge of magical practices displayed by Apuleius in his "I am not a magician" speech match what we know from the "insider" sources about the practices of the real magicians of his day? Classicists have spent many an hour pondering such questions, and complementing the evidence provided by one corpus

[1] Some scholars prefer to call the "insider" evidence "primary" and the "outsider" evidence "secondary," but the distinction remains the same.

of texts (the literary) with that found in another (the magical), in order to arrive at a reconstruction of Greco-Roman magic that is as nuanced and multi-faceted as possible.[2]

As we shall see in subsequent chapters of the present study, this method of confronting the "outsider" accounts with the "insider" evidence may fruitfully be applied to the Jewish magical tradition from late antiquity onwards, when both bodies of evidence become sufficiently large and variegated. But when we turn to the Second Temple period, from the late sixth century BCE to the first or early second century CE, we must first note the heart-wrenching paucity of the available evidence. Looking for "insider" evidence for the Jewish magical tradition at the time, we find almost none. One could, of course, note that in the Classical case too the quantity and quality of the "insider" evidence grows exponentially with the rise of Greco-Egyptian magic in the Roman period (as we shall note in the next chapter), but whereas the number and length of pagan magical texts begins to rise from about the first century CE, in the Jewish case a similar process seems to have taken place only a few centuries later. As we shall see in the next chapter, only from the fourth or fifth century CE do we find the variegated and abundant "insider" evidence for Jewish magic which is so conspicuously absent from the records of earlier periods. Such an absence might be due in part to the magical texts of the Second Temple period having been written solely on perishable materials, but as we shall see throughout the present chapter, this certainly is not a sufficient explanation for the dearth of "insider" evidence for Jewish magic at the time.

Not only is the "insider" evidence scanty, the "outsider" evidence for Jewish magic in the Second Temple period is equally hard to find. For the period from c. 500 BCE to c. 200 BCE, this hardly is surprising, given the general dearth of Jewish texts that describe this period or can securely be dated to it. The subsequent three centuries, however, from c. 200 BCE to c. 100 CE, are relatively rich in source materials for the study of various aspects of Jewish history and culture, and yet the sources for the study of Jewish magic are sorely lacking. Reading the Jewish literature of the time – from Daniel and Ben Sira through the Books of the Maccabees and the many apocalypses or para-biblical narratives that can securely be dated to this period, to the hefty oeuvres of Philo and Josephus and the enormous literary deposits of the caves of Qumran (the Dead Sea Scrolls) – one is struck by how little these numerous texts tell us about Jewish magic or the Jews' recourse to magical activities. In this, ancient Jewish literature stands

---

[2] For recent examples of this approach, see, e.g., Graf 1997 and Faraone 1999.

in marked contrast with Greco-Roman literature, where discussions of the magicians' art and descriptions of magicians in action abound. Moreover, when we look for evidence of *Jewish* magic and magicians in Greco-Roman literature, we are once again greatly disappointed – apart from a few vague references to the contributions to the world of magic made by Moses and the Jews, we find only one real description of a Jewish magician (or, to be precise, a Jewish exorcist) at work.[3] Only in the Christian literature, first in the New Testament, and then much more so in the writings of the Church Fathers, do we find extensive references to Jewish exorcists, magicians, and miracle-workers.

Surprisingly, students of Second Temple period Jewish magic tend to ignore the paucity of the available evidence and rarely stop to ponder its possible causes or implications.[4] In part, this is because this topic, so relevant for the study of the New Testament and early Christianity (as well as that of Jewish history and culture), attracts a disproportionate amount of scholarly activity; with too many scholars chasing a limited number of sources, the resulting inflationary pressures lead to an unwarranted rise in the perceived value of any single source (not to mention the steep decline in the value of the scholarly currency). Thus, the basic inadequacy of the sources at our disposal often goes unmentioned. Worse still, most students of ancient Jewish magic simply extrapolate from the later evidence (which, as we already noted, is far more abundant) backwards into the earlier period. This is, of course, a very risky procedure, for it assumes that the Jewish magical tradition changed little from the days of Josephus at the end of the first century CE to those of the Palestinian amulets and Babylonian demon bowls of the fifth or sixth century. But given what we know about the great transformation of Jewish culture between the Second Temple period and its late-antique sequel, including the destruction of the Jerusalem Temple and the social structures it supported, the decline of Jewish sectarianism, apocalypticism, and iconophobia, the rise of rabbinic Judaism and the emergence of the synagogue and its liturgy as the main form of Jewish communal worship, the assumption that Jewish magic somehow remained static and unchanged is a priori unlikely. Moreover, as we shall

---

[3] For pagan references to Jewish magic, see Posidonius, FGrH 87 F70 = F 279 Edelstein-Kidd, in Strabo, *Geog.* 16.2.43 (GLAJJ 45 = GLAJJ 115) (who may not be referring to Jews); Pliny, *NH* 30.2.11 (GLAJJ 221) (and see *NH* 30.1.1–3.13, for the place of Jewish magic within Pliny's history of magic as a whole); Apuleius, *Apol.* 90 (GLAJJ 361) (who clearly relied on Pliny). For Jewish exorcists, see Lucian, *Trag.* 171–73 (GLAJJ 374), and esp. his *Philops.* 16 (GLAJJ 372), discussed below. See also Bloch 1999, pp. 145–47 and 2003, pp. 247–49.

[4] For previous discussions of Jewish magic in the Second Temple period, see Yamauchi 1983; Lightstone 1984, pp. 17–56; Alexander 1986; Seidel 1996, pp. 67–156. Many more studies will be mentioned below.

see throughout the present study, once the sources are studied in proper chronological order, both the similarities *and* the differences between late-antique Jewish magic and its Second Temple predecessors emerge more vividly, and the latter often outweigh the former.[5]

Given the apparent danger of historical anachronism, any study of Jewish magic in the Second Temple period must focus on those magic-related texts and traditions that can securely be dated to the period up to the first or early second century CE. This choice, however, has some important implications for the manner in which the available sources may be analyzed and the results one might expect to obtain from this analysis, and these implications should first be made clear. When we turn to the abundant evidence for late-antique magic, in the next four chapters, we shall divide our sources into "insider" evidence and "outsider" accounts, and study the latter in light of the former. We shall also try to distinguish between different but contemporary branches of the Jewish magical tradition: that practiced by the Jews of Palestine and Egypt and that practiced by the Jews of Babylonia. Finally, we shall try to identify within the western branch of late-antique Jewish magic some elements and practices whose origins lie in the Greco-Egyptian magic of late antiquity and some which are of Jewish origins. Unfortunately, such divisions and analyses of the source materials are a luxury we simply cannot afford when the amount of available sources is as meager as the evidence for Jewish magic in the Second Temple period. It is for this reason that we shall have to adopt a different strategy here, by limiting our discussion to a single chapter, and by focusing on two related questions: (1) What was the Jewish attitude to magic and magicians in the Second Temple period, and (2) What types of magical rituals were practiced by Jews at the time? In each case, we shall survey both the "insider" and the "outsider" evidence, and see what it might tell us about the Jewish recourse to specific magical practices and about ancient Jewish magic as a whole. We shall end with more general remarks about the overall nature of Jewish magic in the Second Temple period, focusing on the nature of the available sources, on the identity of the practitioners involved, and on the "magical technologies" utilized by them.

THE JEWISH DISCOURSE OF "MAGIC" IN THE SECOND TEMPLE PERIOD

Undoubtedly the most important characteristic of Jewish history in the six and a half centuries separating the reconstruction of the Jerusalem Temple

[5] See esp. Swartz 2001, and cf. Alexander 1999a, pp. 351–52.

in the late sixth century BCE and the quelling of the Bar Kokhba Revolt in 135 CE is the constant external upheavals and internal turmoil faced by Jewish society at the time. The period in question saw the rise and fall of the Babylonian and the Persian empires, the creation of Alexander's huge empire and its rapid disintegration, the emergence of several smaller empires which often fought each other, and finally the slow but steady conquest of the entire region by the Roman empire. For the Jews, this spelled many centuries of almost constant unrest, including numerous wars in which the Jews were not directly involved but from which they greatly suffered, a brief period of political independence between the successful Hasmonean revolt against Seleucid rule in the 160s BCE and Pompey's conquest of the Eastern Mediterranean in 63 BCE, and a long period of constant anti-Roman unrest. This culminated in the failed revolt of 66 CE which led to the destruction of the Jerusalem Temple four years later, and in the equally disastrous revolt of Bar Kokhba, crushed in 135 CE and bringing to a close this tumultuous chapter in Jewish history.

A second feature of Jewish history in the Second Temple period, and one which was in some ways the result of the political upheavals, but in some ways also among their causes, was the enormous diversity and division within Jewish society and culture throughout much of this period. Though the roots of this social fragmentation may lie in an earlier period, it is from the second century BCE – when our sources become more numerous and more adequate for historical analysis, and when Jewish independence under the Hasmoneans brought many inner divisions to their boiling point – that we can trace the enormous diversity of Jewish culture and its dire implications for the stability of Jewish society as a whole. Josephus, writing in Rome in the last three decades of the first century CE, neatly divided Jewish society into three "schools" – the Pharisees, the Sadducees, and the Essenes – to which he added a fourth wheel, the Zealots, who were like the Pharisees in all else but were fanatic in their rejection of Roman rule. Modern scholars, however, often find themselves unable to follow Josephus' basic trichotomy when classifying the many and multifarious literary and archeological remains of the period. Far too many persons, groups, and religious texts of the Second Temple period seem not to fall neatly into his tripartite scheme, but such is the nature of the evidence that it precludes the possibility of offering an alternative scheme, beyond noting the existence of many different "packages" of beliefs and practices available to Second Temple Jews from which to choose – or not to.

These two main features add up to a picture which is characterized by complexity, diversity, and fluidity. Perhaps more than any other period in pre-modern Jewish history, the period from the second century BCE to the second century CE was a period of constant instability, change, and development. It saw the rise of new institutions (a non-Davidic kingship, the synagogue, a non-priestly class of Torah-interpreters), groups (Sadducees, Pharisees, Essenes, Therapeutai, followers of Jesus, and so on), beliefs (in an afterlife, in an approaching *eschaton*, in the Messiah, in elaborate demonologies and angelologies), attitudes (extreme iconophobia, avoidance of intermarriage with non-Jews, sectarian and dualistic mindsets, and so on), practices (fighting on the Sabbath, the acceptance of Gentile converts, and the forced conversion of the Jews' neighbors), and modes of biblical exegesis (allegorism, *pesher*, etc.), some of which were short-lived, while others are still with us today. More important, it saw an amazing willingness – unparalleled in subsequent Jewish history until our own times – of Jews not only to die for their religious convictions, but also to kill their own brethren in the name of God. Only the destruction of the Temple in 70 CE, and the complete de-Judaization of Jerusalem and much of Judea in the aftermath of the Bar Kokhba revolt, put an end to the social and religious upheaval of Jewish society at the time, by physically eliminating many of the groups which were responsible for the turmoil together with their power-bases, and by making many of the older disputes – especially those focused on the Temple and the proper manner of worship there – quite obsolete.

Given this explosive combination of diversity and intolerance, and given what we have learned from anthropologists, from Evans-Pritchard onwards, concerning the use of accusations of magic against one's social and political opponents, we might expect "magic" – which is explicitly and repeatedly condemned in the Hebrew Bible – to have been a term of abuse often hurled by members of one group against those of another. This, however, apparently was not the case.[6] In Josephus' descriptions of the major differences between the Sadducees, Pharisees, and Essenes the issue of magic is never mentioned, and even in his nasty remarks about the Samaritans the issue of magic never comes up. The same is true of the Dead Sea Scrolls, which have some interesting things to say about magic, and many nasty things to say about the "Sons of Darkness," but never use "magic" as a label to affix to their Jewish opponents to their discredit.[7] And even the Gospels, by far

---

[6] In this context, we may also add that "magic" does not seem to appear in Second Temple Jewish literature as an explanation for misfortune, even in contexts where we might expect it to. When a tower fell on some people (Lk 13.1–5), the question asked was not whether there was magic involved, but whether they were sinners who deserved it. This, of course, is the major difference between ancient Jewish society and the Azande studied by Evans-Pritchard.

[7] Especially noteworthy is 4Qp Nah 3–4.2.7–10 (discussed, e.g., by Brooke 2003, pp. 76–77), where Babylon and her *keshaphim* (Nah 3.4) are interpreted as referring to "Ephraim" (probably, the

the most polemical Jewish texts of the Second Temple period, display little interest in magic accusations. Unlike later Jewish texts, such as the Babylonian Talmud or the *Toledoth Yeshu* traditions, which gleefully describe Jesus as a magician, in the Gospels Jesus' Jewish opponents only accuse him of being possessed by a demon or expelling demons with the aid of Beelzebub ("Satan casting out Satan"). And when the Gospels themselves vilify the scribes, Pharisees, and other Jewish opponents of Jesus, they pile up many nasty accusations, but never accuse their Jewish opponents of practicing magic (a constant anti-Jewish accusation in later Christian polemics), or of trying to harm Jesus with magic rituals (as the Jews were later accused of trying to bewitch Muhammad, or medieval bishops, or the pope).[8]

The "failure" of Second Temple Jews to use magic as a label which can be thrown in an opponent's face is quite striking, especially when seen in the perspective of later periods in Jewish history, be these the recurrent Karaite railings against Rabbanite magic, the anti-Kabbalistic polemics from the Middle Ages onwards which equated the Kabbalah (or at least some of it) with magic, or the extensive anti-Hasidic literature of both *Mitnagdim* and Maskilim in the eighteenth and nineteenth centuries, in which the accusation of magic looms large. All these accusations find few precedents in the Second Temple period, and this, we may note, is one reason for the relative dearth of "outsider" sources on the magical praxis of the time. When magic becomes a bone of contention, much more attention is devoted by the contending parties to defining, excluding, condemning, or defending the practices it entails. Moreover, one by-product of this silence is that we have almost no access to "emic" definitions of Jewish magic at the time; this is in marked contrast to what we shall see in Chapter 6, when we discuss the rabbinic attitudes to magic.

What, then, did Second Temple Jews have to say about magic? Given the recurrent biblical condemnation of different types of magical practitioners and practices, it hardly comes as a surprise that different strands of Second Temple Jewish literature evince a general animosity towards the world of magic. But unlike other spheres of knowledge and action, magic seems to have aroused very few debates. When we look at contemporary Jewish attitudes to professional medicine, we find some attempts to claim that healing comes only from God, and some powerful demonstrations

---

Pharisees) misleading their hapless followers, but not a word on *keshaphim*. Note also CD 5.17–19, where the vague analogy between the sect's opponents and "Jannes and his brother" who had opposed Moses and Aaron in Egypt is left undeveloped.

[8] For the medieval stereotype of the Jew as magician, see Trachtenberg 1939, pp. 1–10 and 1943, pp. 57–155, with Cohn 1970. For bewitching Muhammad, see Lecker 1992. For bewitching bishops, and even the pope, see Trachtenberg 1943, pp. 122–23.

that if the doctors can heal the sick it means that God wants them to and approves of their craft.[9] And astrology seems to have aroused an even greater debate, with some Jews condemning it outright and others praising it, and even insisting that it had been invented, or at least developed, by Abraham himself.[10] But when we look at Jewish attitudes to magic, we see that it found no defenders within Jewish society at the time, and whereas rabbinic literature sometimes evinces lax attitudes towards magic, and even encourages the study, teaching, and occasional use of this technology, earlier Jewish literature merely condemns the entire field. The Septuagint, the Greek translation of the Torah made in the third century BCE, translates the biblical prohibitions against consulting various magicians and diviners – which we discussed in the previous chapter – into the Greek terms of its own time. We thus learn that not only necromancy, augury from birds, and other divinatory techniques are entirely forbidden, but also the dabbling in *pharmaka* (plural of *pharmakon*, which means both "poison" and "magical procedure," not to mention the meaning "medicine," whence the English word "pharmacy") and the reciting of incantations.[11] The *Third Sibylline Oracle*, a Jewish work written in Greek (probably in Egypt, probably in the second century BCE), provides a similar list of practices, and insists that Jews indeed shun all of them, including *pharmaka* and incantations.[12] And the Jewish writer who now goes under the name of Ps.-Phocylides, and who probably lived in the first century BCE or CE, instructs his readers to "Make no *pharmaka* and keep away from books of magic" – unfortunately, without telling us what such books might look like.[13] In a similar vein, some of the para-biblical narratives whose production was a favorite pastime of ancient Jewish writers include references to the magic practiced by such figures as Queen Jezebel or King Manasseh, both of whom had been charged with this offense in the biblical narrative itself, or the destruction of idolatry and magic by King Josiah, again in line with the biblical stories.[14]

---

[9] See, for example, the defense of medicine by Ben Sira (38.1–15), with Hogan 1992, pp. 38–48. See also Kottek 2000 and Stuckenbruck 2002.

[10] For the condemnation/acceptance of astrology in the Second Temple period, see Charlesworth 1987, pp. 933–38; Reed 2004, pp. 125–26, 142–45.

[11] See, e.g., LXX Dt 18.10–11: οὐχ εὑρεθήσεται ἐν σοὶ φαρμακός, ἐπαείδων ἐπαοιδήν . . . ; LXX Ex 22.17: φαρμακοὺς οὐ περιποιήσετε. Note also how Pharaoh's *ḥarṭumim* are consistently rendered by οἱ ἐπαοιδοί (LXX Ex 7.11, 22; 8.3, etc.).

[12] *Sib. Or.* 3.218–34. The condemnation of magical practices recurs in the later (and non-Jewish) sections of the *Sibylline Oracles* as well (e.g., *Sib. Or.* 1.95–96; 2.283).

[13] Ps.-Phoc. 149: Φάρμακα μὴ τεύχειν, μαγικῶν βίβλων ἀπέχεσθαι. See also van der Horst 1978, pp. 212–13.

[14] *Mart. Isaiah* 2.5: Among the iniquities of Manasseh were "sorcery and magic, augury and divination, fornication and adultery . . ." (see 2 Chr 33.6); Josephus, *Ant.* 9.118: Jehu calls Jezebel a φαρμακόν and a whore (see 2 Kgs 9.22). 2 Bar. 66.2: Josiah destroyed all idolatry, and the magicians, enchanters, and diviners (see 2 Kgs 23, esp. 23.24).

And some of the Jewish apocalypses of the time, when recounting the gory details of the sinners' punishment in Hell and its many equivalents, do not forget to count among them those who dabbled in witchcraft and incantations.[15] Unfortunately, all these statements tell us relatively little about Jewish magic, or even about Jewish attitudes towards magic, beyond the expected conventional condemnations.[16] It is only rarely that we can reconstruct in greater detail some Jewish authors' or groups' attitudes towards magic. In analyzing such texts, we shall begin with two extreme views, those of Philo on the one hand, and those of the Dead Sea Scrolls on the other, and then turn to the views espoused by Josephus, which probably were closer to the mainstream of Jewish culture at the time. We shall end with the rabbis' reminiscences about Jewish magic in the Second Temple period, which may or may not reflect some Second Temple views of Jewish magic.

Magic in Philo

Living in Alexandria from c. 20 BCE to c. 45 CE, the Jewish exegete and community leader Philo presents us with a relatively clear statement of his views of magic. In his detailed survey of the Mosaic legislation, *On the Special Laws*, he explains that Moses, knowing how addicted the masses are to all form of divination, expelled all these practitioners – including the reciters of incantations – out of his polity, while offering the Jews legitimate substitutes instead.[17] In a subsequent section, which deals with the treatment of murderers in the Mosaic legislation, he offers a detailed explanation of why Moses ordered the summary execution of "magicians and those who deal with *pharmaka*."[18] The ensuing discussion makes it clear that by the latter term he here refers to poisons, especially those placed in people's foods, but he soon returns to the former category, that of magicians, and explains that there are two types of magic. On the one hand, there is true magic, which is a scientific endeavor by which the facts of nature are revealed, a revered and much sought-after discipline which is of interest even to the greatest kings, and especially those of Persia, who cannot even become kings unless they first joined the race of the Magi. On the other hand,

---

[15] E.g., 2 Enoch 10.
[16] The same is true of such condemnations of magic and its practitioners as are found in *Wisd. Sol.* 12.4; *Didache* 2.2; 3.4, etc.
[17] Philo, *Spec. Leg.* 1.60–65, esp. 60. Cf. also 4.48–52, on the false prophet.
[18] Philo, *Spec. Leg.* 3.93–103. For οἱ μάγοι καὶ φαρμακευταί, see esp. 3.93.

there is a counterfeit of this, most properly called an evil art, pursued by mendicant priests and altar parasites and by the basest of the women and slave population, who make it their profession to deal in purifications and disenchantments and promise with some sort of philters and incantations to turn men's love into deadly enmity and their hatred into profound affection ... All these things our lawgiver had in view, I think, when he prohibited any postponement in bringing those who deal with *pharmaka* to justice, and ordered that the punishment should be exacted at once.[19]

Philo goes on and on, but for our own purpose the most important aspect of his distinction between good magic and bad is that its roots lie not in the Hebrew Bible, which knows of no such dichotomy, but in the history of the Greek word *mageia*, whence our English word, "magic." It was the fifth-century encounter between Greeks and Persians – before, during, and after the Persian invasions of the Greek peninsula – that gave rise to the term *mageia*, "that which the (Zoroastrian) Persian Magi do" and to its negative connotations in Greek eyes. These negative connotations, however, and the inclusion of more and more ritual practices which the Greeks and Romans found unacceptable under this rubric, never completely stripped the word of its original meaning, having to do with the arcane, but often admired, Zoroastrian practices. To the very end of antiquity, in Greek and in Latin alike, the term *magos* (Gr.) / *magus* (Lat.) retained its dual meaning, referring both to a nefarious or exotic "magician" and to a legitimate and equally exotic Persian priest.[20] We shall return to this issue, and its significance for the Greek discourse of magic, in subsequent chapters of the present study. For the time being, suffice it to note that Philo is well aware of both meanings of *mageia*, and wants to assure his readers that while the divine knowledge of the Persians is fully acceptable to the Mosaic legislation, practitioners of the base art which sometimes goes by the same name are liable to summary execution.

Philo's adoration of the Magi, which is equally visible in his other writings, was in no way unusual in Second Temple Jewish society.[21] In his *Jewish Antiquities*, Josephus tells an illuminating story of how Felix, the Roman procurator of Judea in the 50s CE, fell in love with Drusilla, the daughter of King Agrippa I and sister of King Agrippa II. As she was married to

---

[19] Philo, *Spec. Leg.* 3.101–02 (LCL tr., with minor modifications). For Philo's discussions of magic and *pharmaka* see Heinemann 1932, pp. 386–89, and Seland 2006.
[20] Note, for example, Dio Chrys., *Or.* 36.41, or Apuleius' crafty play upon this dual meaning in *Apol.* 26. For the positive use of *magos/mageia*, see also Chapter 5, n. 134. For recent surveys of this issue, see de Jong 1997; Graf 1997, pp. 20–29; Bremmer 1999. See also Heliodorus, *Aeth.* 3.16, whose dependence on the Philonic passage (or its source) has often been noted.
[21] For Philo, see also *Quod Omn. Prob.* 74.

Azizus, the king of Emesa – who had even circumcized himself in order to marry the Jewish princess – Felix sent a friend of his, a Cypriote Jew (and therefore unknown to her or to those around her), who pretended to be a Magus, to persuade her to leave her husband and marry her new admirer. The scheme worked, and she soon married Felix even though he was not circumcised. This scene, which would fit so well in any of the Greek novels, is a sure sign of the high repute which real Magi enjoyed among the Jews, as among other peoples, in the first century CE.[22] Perhaps most telling of all, the inclusion of a story of three Magi who came to greet the baby Jesus by the author of the Gospel of Matthew eloquently demonstrates its Jewish author's assumptions about the significance of the admiring approval of these wise men from the East. In the Gospels' world, as in that of other contemporary Jews, the Persian Magi were the carriers of a hoary oriental wisdom, not the teachers of forbidden witchcraft and sorcery.

The Jewish admiration for the Magi is, of course, of little help for the study of Philo's views of magic, for which only his description of the "counterfeit" variety of *mageia* is of interest. Here, we may note how he is thinking both of professional practitioners, who wander around from place to place and sell their services (and elsewhere he refers both to Balaam and to Pharaoh's *ḥartumim* as *magoi*) and of a more popular magic, as practiced by women and slaves (some of whom, however, may also have become professionals).[23] We may also note how he singles out aggressive, and especially erotic magic – to separate lovers and unite haters – apparently because he saw this as the most socially destructive form of magic, and how he refers to some of the rituals involved, such as purifications, potions, and incantations.[24] First-century Alexandria was an excellent place in which to watch the growth, and perhaps even the fusion, of both Greek and Egyptian magic, and presumably of Jewish magic as well. Unfortunately, Philo's agenda did not encourage a detailed description of any of the phenomena and processes which are the focus of the present study, and he never even hints at the existence of exorcisms, amulets, and magical cursing rituals. Thus, while he provides us with what is perhaps the clearest "emic" definition of magic we shall find in any ancient Jewish text, his discourse also is the most "magic free" Jewish mindset we shall encounter in the present chapter, and in the present study as a whole.

---

[22] Josephus, *Ant.* 20.142–43 (the important phrase is μάγον εἶναι σκηπτόμενον). For Felix and Drusilla, cf. *Acts* 24.24. For the historical context, see Schürer 1973–87, vol. I, pp. 460–63.

[23] For Balaam the *magos* and his μαγικὴ σοφιστεία, see *Vita Mosis* 1.276–77. For Pharaoh's *magoi*, see *Vita Mosis* 1.92; *De Migr. Abr.* 83.

[24] Philo's infatuation with erotic philters may also be seen from his frequent metaphorical use of φίλτρον/α, an issue which lies outside the scope of the present study.

Magic in 1 Enoch, Jubilees, and the Dead Sea Scrolls

If in Philo's world "magic" is divided into the "true" magic of the Magi and a counterfeit, "false" magic of cheats, women, and slaves, for some Jews in the Second Temple period "magic" was an evil affair of demonic origins. We first encounter this view in the *Book of the Watchers*, one of the textual units which make up what is known today as 1 Enoch. This short apocalypse (1 Enoch 1–36), which may be dated in the third century BCE, tells the story of the Fallen Angels, those "sons of God" who lusted after the "daughters of man" (see Gn 6.1–4).[25] Leaving their heavenly abodes, the rebellious angels came down to earth and mated with human females, thus producing a multitude of giants and other "bastard" offspring. They also used this opportunity to teach the human race various arts, including teaching its female members magic, incantations, the loosening of *keshaphim*, the cutting of roots, and the use of plants.[26] These arts are just a small part of what the Fallen Angels had taught humanity, but for the purpose of the current enquiry we may ignore the claims that astrology, cosmetics, the making of weapons, and many other human sciences and technologies sprang from this dubious source, and focus only on the claims made here with regards to magic. These clearly show that by the third century BCE some Jews were very much aware of many types of magical practices, and saw them as demonic in origins and nature. Their claim struck root, and it reappears not only in other sections of 1 Enoch, but also in other Jewish texts, in Christian ones, and even in the Quran and later Muslim texts.[27] And the other element embedded in this claim – that magic is mostly a female affair – is an aspect of the non-Jewish and Jewish discourse of magic to which we shall repeatedly return, not least in our discussion of the rabbis' use of the very same stereotype.

If magic was demonic and evil in origins, we might expect all Second Temple Jews, or at least all those who read the *Book of the Watchers* and took it seriously, to avoid magic at all cost. And yet, the blanket condemnation of all types of magical practice was not without its problems, since it implicitly entailed a decision to forego many types of healings which were considered highly beneficial at the time. It thus comes as no surprise to find the

---

[25] For recent studies of this story and its transmission history, see Eshel 1999, pp. 10–76; Reed 2005; Wright 2005.
[26] 1 Enoch 7.1 and 8.3. For an English tr. of the Ethiopic version, see Isaac in Charlesworth 1983, p. 16; for the extant Aramaic fragments, see Milik 1976, pp. 150, 157, 166, 170.
[27] E.g., 1 Enoch 65.6; 3 Enoch 5 (=*Synopse* §8); *Sib. Or.* 1.96; Justin, *2 Apol.* 5.4; Tertullian, *Apol.* 35.12; Quran 2.102.

Book of Jubilees, written in the second century BCE and relying heavily on the Enochic literature, expounding a somewhat different view of the issues involved. There, we read that when Noah's children were oppressed by evil demons which caused many afflictions, Noah prayed to God (and we shall cite this prayer below), and God sent his angels to bind the demons. When the demons' leader, Mastema ("Hatred"), begged for some clemency, God let one demon out of ten remain free and roam the earth, but also ordered one of the angels "to teach Noah all their healing," and, as the angelic narrator of *Jubilees* so nicely puts it,

And the healing of all their illnesses together with their seductions we told Noah so that he might heal by means of herbs of the earth. And Noah wrote everything in a book just as we taught him according to every kind of healing. And the evil spirits were restrained from following the sons of Noah. And he gave everything which he wrote to Shem, his oldest son, because he loved him much more than all of his sons.[28]

What we see here is a new twist to an old story. Magic and illness indeed are the work of the evil demons, but to fight these demons one must use special means, such as the use of special herbs, means which are divine or angelic in origin, and therefore entirely acceptable. Thus, a whole new category is opened up, a category of licit magic and medicine, or, to be more precise, of apotropaic activities which could not and should not be classified under the rubric of *keshaphim* or any other activity forbidden by the Hebrew Bible. Unfortunately, the author of *Jubilees* does not see fit to elaborate further on this category, but it seems clear that with the door open for some practices, many others were bound to follow, as long as they could be justified as anti-demonic, apotropaic, and beneficial in nature.

To see the further development of this process, we must turn to the Dead Sea Scrolls, written by sectarian Jews who were avid readers of both the Enochic literature and the *Book of Jubilees*.[29] Reading the Scrolls, we find the expected prohibition of *keshaphim* and all the other activities listed in Deuteronomy 18, as rehearsed, for example, in the famous *Temple Scroll*.[30] We also find two interesting addenda to magic-related legislation. The first, and quite expected, is a complete prohibition on cursing by the Name or uttering it in any other context, which we find in the *Rule of the Community*,

---

[28] *Jub.* 10.10–14 (tr. Wintermute, in Charlesworth 1985, p. 76). Note the use of this passage in *Sepher Asaph ha-Rophe* (see Muntner 1957, pp. 147–49), and cf. Jellinek 1853–78, vol. III, pp. 155–56.

[29] For the discourse of magic in the Dead Sea Scrolls, see esp. Alexander 1997; Lange 1997; Lyons and Reimer 1998; Brooke 2003.

[30] 11QT^a 60.16–21.

the punishment for such an offence being expulsion from the sect for life.[31] The second, and less expected, is the injunction that "whoever is ruled by the spirits of Belial and speaks apostasy is to be judged in accordance with the law of the *'ov* and the *yide'oni*."[32] The attribution of deviant words and behavior to the demons' success in leading one of the group's members astray probably was not unique to the Qumran sectarians.[33] But given the Qumranites' rigid *halakhic* and social norms, and the great danger that any expression of doubts and objections by some of the sect's members would lead to its ultimate collapse, they had some compelling reasons to subsume such behavior under the biblical prohibition of *'ov* and *yide'oni*, thus enabling the summary punishment of those found guilty. Thus, the classification of any type of social deviance under the rubric of "magic and divination" is an aspect of the Qumranites' discourse which fit well with their dualistic view of humanity, and of their own place in the process of cosmic salvation.

To the Qumranites' explicit discourse of magic, we must also add the implicit one. As we shall see below, the Qumran library included quite a few very interesting exorcistic texts, and it also included some divinatory texts (physiognomy, brontology, astrology) of the kind not covered by the present study. Nowhere in the Qumran texts will we find a clear statement on how such practices should be classified or why they are permitted, but there is no doubt that permitted they were, and that some of them were part of the sect's communal practices, and were carried out by its accepted leaders in normative ritual contexts. This, however, is an issue to which we shall return below.

Magic in Josephus

While Philo and the Dead Sea sectarians evince some interest in magic and in its status within Jewish law, Josephus (37/8 – c. 100 CE) is surprisingly elusive on this score.[34] Nowhere is this more apparent than in his long summary of the Mosaic legislation (*Ant*. 4.199–301), where all the biblical laws and prohibitions which we have surveyed in the previous chapter are neatly summarized, or subverted, in a single sentence:

---

[31] *Serekh ha-Yahad* 6.27–7.2.
[32] CD 12.2–3: כל איש אשר ימשלו בו רוחות בליעל ודבר סרה, כמשפט האוב והידעוני ישפט.
[33] And note Jn 7.20; 8.48, 52; 10.20, where socially deviant statements are understood as a sign of demonic possession, or the rabbis' claim (bt Sot 3a) that "a man does not transgress the laws unless a spirit of madness entered into him."
[34] There is no systematic study of Josephus' discourse of magic, but see Smith 1987 and Deines 2003, and esp. Bloch 2003.

Let no Israelite whatsoever possess a *pharmakon*, neither a deadly one nor one which causes other harms. And if an Israelite is caught owning one, he should be put to death, suffering that which he would have inflicted on those against whom the *pharmakon* was intended.[35]

Reading this statement, we cannot help noting how Josephus condenses the biblical prohibition of a long range of practitioners and practices to the use of harmful *pharmaka*. As has often been noted, to his Roman audience this would have sounded quite like their own *Lex Cornelia de sicariis et veneficiis* of 81 BCE, which ordered severe punishments for all types of *veneficia* (the Latin equivalent of the Greek *pharmaka*). A historian of Jewish magic, on the other hand, would find it very hard to know from this passage how Josephus viewed the place of magic in Jewish law and Jewish society. Moreover, in his entire *oeuvre* there is not even a hint that magic is somehow forbidden to Jews. When he tells the story of the Jew who pretended to be a Magus, to which we alluded above, he stresses that Drusilla's marriage to an uncircumcised non-Jew was against the Jews' ancestral customs, but has nothing to say about a Jew playing the Magus.[36] And when he castigates the fanatic rabble-rousers whom he blames for the disastrous revolt which had ruined his country, his Temple, and his life, he often refers to them as *goêtes*, a Greek word whose semantic field includes the meaning of "sorcerers," but which he seems to use in the sense of "impostors" and "charlatans." In spite of the obvious opportunity to do so, he never even implies that these *goêtes* dealt in sorcery and witchcraft (or even in *pharmaka*), or that they should have been put to death in line with the biblical legislation on *keshaphim*.[37] And when countering the claims by non-Jews that Moses himself was a *goês*, and even a magician, he stresses (a) that Moses did not invent his own laws, but received them directly from God, and thus was no impostor, and (b) that the miracles performed by Moses were far greater than those performed by Pharaoh's Egyptian magicians, which proves their divine origins, and disproves the charge of magic.[38] Beyond this, however, Josephus shows no interest in magicians, except for the Persian / Babylonian Magi whom he discusses at some length in his paraphrase of Daniel in book 10 of his *Antiquities*.[39]

Josephus' disinterest in magic, or his reluctance to talk about it, is something we shall encounter again and again throughout the present chapter.

---

[35] *Ant.* 4.279. [36] Josephus, *Ant.* 20.142–43.
[37] See *War* 2.261, 264; 4.85; 5.317; *Ant.* 20.97, 161, 167, 188; see also *Life* 40. For this and the following note, see the excellent analysis by Bloch 1999.
[38] Moses was no impostor: *Ap.* 2.145ff, and especially 160–62. Moses practiced no magic: *Ant.* 2.284–86.
[39] See *Ant.* 10.195, 198 (twice), 199, 203, 216, 234, 235, 236; see also 11.31 on the Persian Magi.

For the time being, we may note the intriguing story in his autobiography of the two Gentile noblemen from the court of Agrippa II who took refuge with him during the Great Revolt. At first, the Jewish mob demanded that they be circumcised if they wished to receive asylum, but Josephus vehemently rejected this demand.[40] Next, the mob insisted that the two strangers were *pharmaka*-mongers who made it impossible for the Jewish rebels to destroy the Roman army. Josephus says that he laughed at this silly accusation about *pharmaka*, and explained that the Romans would not have kept so many myriads of soldiers if it were possible to win wars with the help of *pharmaka* and those who employed them. Apparently, his audience remained unconvinced, for they soon tried to lynch the unwelcome guests, whom Josephus eventually had to smuggle across the Sea of Galilee.[41] In this case, Josephus clearly depicts himself as the rationalist, who does not believe in the reality of military magic, but in many other instances (for example, in discussing the feats of Pharaoh's magicians), he clearly assumes that magic does work. More important, in this case we can see how the Jewish population, especially in times of crisis, was quite willing to label newly arrived foreigners as magicians and kill them on the spot. Unfortunately, Josephus usually prefers to discuss other things.

Given Josephus' general disinterest in magic, it seems quite clear that we cannot arrive at any clear sense of his (emic) definition of this term. As we shall see below, he clearly viewed exorcisms – both by means of demon-repellent substances and by means of Solomonic adjurations – as entirely acceptable, and was very proud of the Jews' achievements in this field. He also was proud of the fact that water from the spring of Jericho – "cured" nine centuries earlier by the prophet Elisha of every "death and miscarriage" – kept on bringing fecundity to barren women in his own times.[42] And when he repeatedly described the Essenes' interest in occult lore and divination he nowhere implied that their expertise was in any way connected with *pharmaka*, or forbidden by the Hebrew Bible. In fact, he was quite proud of his own achievements in such fields as dream-interpretation and divination, and often saw them as a part of his priestly vocation.[43] On the other hand, when we read his account of the philters and *pharmaka* in Herod's court, his great displeasure with such practices is quite evident; aggressive magic was disruptive and evil, but apotropaic and medicinal magic apparently were not seen by Josephus as incompatible with the Mosaic legislation.

[40] *Life* 113.   [41] *Life* 149–53.   [42] Josephus, *War* 4.459–67.
[43] See, e.g., *War* 3.8.351–52, where he boasts of his abilities as a dream-interpreter; *War* 3.399–408, where he boasts of his abilities as a prophet.

Second Temple period magic in rabbinic literature

As we shall see in Chapter 6, the rabbis of late-antique Palestine and Babylonia had much to say about magic and its practitioners. One aspect of this issue which they gleefully rehearsed was the supposed pervasiveness of *keshaphim* in the Second Temple period. Unfortunately, it is very hard to tell whether this reflects the view of some Second Temple Jews, or the *realia* of the rabbis' own times, or even their fertile imagination or hidden agendas.[44] When the rabbis tell us that certain towns and villages were destroyed (in 70 or in 135 CE) because of inner-Jewish contention, others because of fornication, and yet others because of *keshaphim*, we might feel that this is a moralizing retroactive interpretation of a great historical catastrophe.[45] And when they repeatedly insist that Shimeon ben Shetah (c. 100 BCE) once hung eighty *mekhashphot* in Ashkelon (and we shall cite their colorful description of that event in Chapter 6), we may note that there is no other ancient evidence to support this claim, even though the Jewish lynching of suspected witches is not a priori impossible. But when we encounter the recurrent rabbinic claims that Second Temple priests dabbled in *keshaphim*, including the most aggressive types, we are less sure about the significance of such claims. On the one hand, it was easy to present priestly ritual as magic (and need we recall the Protestant fulminations against "papist magic"?), and the rabbis had all the reasons in the world to portray the priests of old as practicing magic and thus present themselves as more legitimate substitutes in Jewish leadership roles. On the other hand, we already noted in Chapter 1 the connections between priests and powerful magical rituals, and shall examine below some evidence, even outside rabbinic literature, pointing to the priests' involvement in magical practices in the Second Temple period. Thus, dismissing the rabbinic claims as late and therefore irrelevant certainly will not do, and we must figure their reports too into our reconstruction of the discourse of magic in the Second Temple period, as shall be done below. For while the rabbis shared neither Philo's distinction between good Magi and bad perversions of their art nor the demonic view of magic of 1 Enoch, they also seem to be far less reticent on this score than Josephus was, and therefore potentially quite useful for the study of Jewish magic even in the Second Temple period.

---

[44] Elsewhere, the rabbis sometimes paint a very rosy picture of the Second Temple period, as if as long as the Temple was standing miracles and prodigies were a matter of course (at least in Jerusalem) – see, e.g., m Avot 5.5; AdRN A 35, B 39 (pp. 103–06 Schechter).

[45] See pt Taan. 4.6 (69a) and Lam.R. 2.106 (p. 106 Buber): Shihin (was destroyed) because (they practiced) *keshaphim*. See also m Sot 9.13: fornication and *keshaphim* ruined everything.

Summary

Having noted the general absence of magic from the public discourse of Second Temple Jews, including its most contentious and divisive manifestations, we turned to a detailed analysis of the concept of "magic" as used in four textual corpora. On the one extreme, we noted Philo's very Greek concept of magic, which distinguishes between the noble art of the Persian Magi and the base counterfeit of that art as practiced by women and slaves. On the other hand, we saw the literary trajectory leading from 1 Enoch to *Jubilees* and to the Dead Sea Scrolls, with an elaborate demonological awareness, a conviction that magic is one of the evil things taught to humanity by the Fallen Angels, and a willingness in the Qumran sect to condemn any deviant member under the biblical rubric of the *'ov* and the *yide'oni*, as well as a willingness to use many techniques that we might see as "magic" in the daily fight against the forces of evil. We also noted, between these two extremes, Josephus' general disinterest in "magic" as a concept, his downplaying of the relevant biblical legislation, and his pride in such ancient Jewish practices as the exorcism of demons. Finally, we noted how the rabbis, living and transmitting their traditions in the post-destruction period, recall the Second Temple period as a time rife with magical activity. What all these broken images add up to is a multiplicity of views of magic and an absence of any real emic definition of magic as a legal or social concept. Of the rabbinic discourse of licit and illicit magic, the medieval polemics about magic, religion, and rationality, and the modern discourse of magic and empirical science there is hardly a trace, nor is there a sign that "magic" was as central a concept in the minds of Second Temple period Jews as it would become in later periods. Thus, when setting out to map the magical activities practiced by Jews in the Second Temple period, we already know that there is only this much we can expect to learn from the "outsider" sources, since their authors did not really care much for such issues. Unfortunately, we shall soon see that the "insider" sources for this period are often equally disappointing, and even more so.

JEWISH MAGICAL TECHNOLOGY IN THE SECOND TEMPLE PERIOD

As noted at the beginning of this chapter, our aim in the following survey is to examine the available evidence for the Jewish recourse to different magical practices in the Second Temple period. To do so, and to avoid cataloging all the available evidence in a way that would be both tedious and necessarily fragmentizing, we shall focus on three specific spheres of magical activity, examine which "insider" and "outsider" evidence we have for each, and see what this evidence reveals.[46] We shall first focus on Jewish exorcisms, certainly the best-documented Jewish magical practice of the time, and then move to the Jewish use of amulets, for which our evidence is surprisingly meager. We shall end with the Jewish uses of aggressive and erotic magic, for which our evidence is, once again, surprisingly meager, but quite instructive when it comes to the nature of Jewish magic at the time. Only after surveying these three types of magical praxis shall we turn to a broader examination of the general contours of Jewish magic in the Second Temple period.

Exorcism

Of all the Jewish magical practices of the Second Temple period, exorcism – by which we refer both to driving a demon or a group of demons out of a certain physical space and to driving it or them out of a human being – is the best attested. It is, moreover, the only Jewish magical practice of the time for which we have "insider" evidence and "outsider" accounts which display a remarkable degree of congruence, and may therefore be combined in reconstructing the mechanics of ancient Jewish exorcisms in some detail.[47] These mechanics seem to fall into three distinct types: the first involves the use of animal, vegetal, or mineral substances whose manipulation or fumigation automatically drives demons away. The second depends less on the exorcistic technique than on the personality and innate powers of the exorcist himself. And the third type involves the use of elaborate incantations, as well as specific implements and rituals, by a professional exorcist who has mastered the right technique and uses the appropriate texts.[48] (A fourth type, exorcisms "in the name of Jesus," is one of the earliest signs of the parting of the ways between Judaism and nascent Christianity, and will not be dealt with here.) Let us examine each of these types of techniques in greater detail, by analyzing the evidence for its use in the different sources in which it appears. We must stress, however, that in addition to the evidence concerning exorcisms, there is a much larger body

---

[46] For a useful phenomenological survey of the aims of the magical practices of late-antique and early-medieval Jewish magic, see Harari 1998, pp. 136–228.

[47] For useful analyses of Jewish exorcisms in the Second Temple period, see Twelftree 1993; Eshel 1999, pp. 194–320; Sorensen 2002, pp. 47–74. See also Kotansky 1995. Further studies will be cited below.

[48] There may have been other types too, such as exorcisms at ancestors' tombs or with their bodily remains, but the evidence for such practices is late and mostly Christian; for some examples, see Jeremias 1958, p. 132 with van der Horst 2002.

of evidence documenting the pervasive belief in the existence of demons by most Second Temple period Jews, and of numerous traditions about their origins, their ancient and recent history, and their appearance, behavior, and other salient features.[49] In what follows, we shall ignore most of the theoretical aspects of ancient Jewish demonology, and focus only on the practical aspects, and the magical techniques employed to expel or thwart dangerous demons.

Exorcism by means of vegetal, animal (and mineral) substances
Certainly the most popular method for exorcizing demons in the Jewish world of the Second Temple period was the use of a long list of vegetal, animal, and mineral substances which were seen as exorcistic in nature. It first appears in the book of *Tobit*, probably written in the fourth or third century BCE, perhaps by a Babylonian Jew and probably in Aramaic, which relates how the Jewish maiden Sarah had lost seven husbands, each of whom was killed by the evil demon Asmodaeus (better known under his Hebrew name, Ashmedai) on the night of the wedding (3.8). The problem is only solved when Tobias, the son of Tobit, drives Ashmedai away with the help of a technique he had learnt on the road from a young Jewish man, who – as the narrator assures us – was none other than the angel Raphael appearing in disguise. The technique itself consists of fumigating the heart and liver of a certain fish from the Tigris river (the fish's gall also serves to heal Tobit's eyes, but not by way of exorcism),[50] and Raphael promises the young Tobias that this will drive away any demon or evil spirit and keep them away forever (6.8, 16–17). Before the consummation of his marriage with Sarah, Tobias indeed places the fish's liver and heart on an incense-burner, and the resulting odors drive the evil Ashmedai all the way from Persian Ecbatana to Upper Egypt, where Raphael quickly binds him up (8.2–3).[51]

In analyzing this passage, we may note that this is the earliest appearance of Ashmedai in Jewish literature; this demon, whose name is probably derived from the Iranian *Aêšma daeva*, "the demon of wrath," will be one of the "stars" of Jewish demonology for many centuries to come.[52] More

---

[49] For a useful survey, see Eshel 1999.
[50] For Babylonian precedents, see von Soden 1966; for Classical parallels and an ophthalmological analysis, see Papayannopoulos *et al.* 1985, and cf. Kollmann 1994, pp. 293–97.
[51] See Moore 1996, pp. 146–47, 201, 207, 211–15, 236–37; Fitzmyer 2003, pp. 150–51, 217, 242–43; Hogan 1992, pp. 27–37; Stuckenbruck 2002. And cf. Dion 1976, for the possible Babylonian precedents to *Tobit*'s exorcism.
[52] For his earlier history, see Shaked 1994, and de Jong 1997, p. 316, n. 17. For Zoroastrian demonology, see also Ahn 2003.

significant for our purpose here, the means to drive him away consist solely of a physical act of fumigating certain animal substances; as the text makes abundantly clear, it is the *smell* which drives the demon away, and no further actions – neither verbal nor written incantations, nor any additional implements or rituals – are needed to perform this task. The exorcism, in this case, is assumed to work according to the laws of nature, not unlike those little electric "fumigators" which are used today to drive mosquitoes away by slowly burning a chemical substance whose effects they would rather avoid. And although in this case the origin of the special knowledge is described as angelic – a sure sign of its legitimacy, and a *topos* to which we shall immediately return – such knowledge circulated widely in the ancient world, and was available even to the likes of Tobias, who certainly was not a skilled exorcist or magician. And as this mode of exorcism is not likely to leave any traces in our archeological records, the lack of any "insider" evidence for its use is hardly surprising. But while "insider" sources are unavailable, "outsider" reports provide much information on the pervasive use of this kind of exorcism by ancient Jews. A rabbinic story, for example, recounts how a Gentile once asked the first-century CE Rabban Yoḥanan ben Zakai about the Red Heifer ritual, and the Jewish rabbi asked him if he had ever seen a demoniac. The man said he had, and then described how the demon must be exorcised – you bring roots and fumigate them under the person, and you pour water over the demon, and it runs away.[53] While this story is found only in late sources and need not be taken as an accurate transcription of a conversation held by the first-century rabbi, the ritual described here certainly was common, among non-Jews as well as Jews, throughout antiquity. This is also made clear by Justin Martyr's reference to the use by Jewish exorcists, as by the Gentile ones, of "fumigations and adjurations."[54] And in the *Jewish War*, written c. 75 CE, Josephus describes a certain plant which grows in a valley near the Transjordanian fort of Machaerus. The description is so colorful and so informative as to be worth quoting in its entirety:

In the ravine which encloses the town (Machaerus) on the north, there is a place called Baaras, which produces a root bearing the same name. The root has a flame-like color and towards evening it emits a brilliant light; it eludes the grasp of persons who approach with the intention of plucking it, as it shrinks up and can only be made to stand still by pouring upon it a woman's urine or menstrual blood. Yet even then to touch it is fatal, unless one brings the very same root, suspended from

[53] PRK Parah, Mandelbaum p. 74 and parallels.
[54] Justin, *Dial. w. Trypho* 85.3: θυμιάμασι καὶ καταδέσμοις χρῶνται. I assume that by *katadesmoi* he is referring to "adjurations" and not to "*defixiones*," which is what the word usually means.

one's hand. Another innocuous mode of capturing it is as follows. They dig all around it, leaving but a minute portion of the root covered; they then tie a dog to it, and the animal rushing to follow the person who tied it easily pulls it up, but instantly dies – a substitute, as it were, for the one who intended to remove the plant, since after this, the root poses no danger to those who handle it. With all these attendant risks, it possesses one virtue for which it is prized; for the so-called demons – that is, the spirits of wicked men which enter the living and kill them unless aid is forthcoming – are promptly expelled by this root, if merely applied to the patients.[55]

This juicy passage certainly is worthy of a detailed analysis, but for our own purposes the following points are the most crucial. First, it must be stressed that there was absolutely no narrative necessity for Josephus to enter this entire subject here; writing on the fall of Machaerus and the sad fate of the Jewish rebels who had fled there, he had no need to delve into the wonderful properties of a root which is found there or the exotic manner by which it is extracted. If he chose to include this description, it is because he was proud of the *mirabilia* of his homeland and the ingenuity of its inhabitants.[56] A generation earlier, the Alexandrian grammarian Apion had told – in a public lecture attended by the young Pliny (the Elder) – of the plant Cynocephalia ("Dog-Head"), also called Osiritis, which kills whoever tries to uproot it, but which also has divine powers and is useful against all poisons and witchcraft.[57] To us, the story of the dog which dies while pulling out the root might seem quite amusing, and eminently worthy of its many medieval narrators and illuminators.[58] Josephus, however, just like Apion before him, saw nothing wrong with this kind of story, but rather took it as a source of ethnic pride; below, we shall see further evidence of his pride in his compatriots' exorcistic expertise.

The second point of importance for our enquiry involves the *ba'aras* root itself.[59] The name provided by Josephus seems like a transliteration of the Aramaic word for "flame," which probably was first attached to the red-hot root – not unlike the Greek name, *aglaophôtis*, "wonder-shine," which was attached to this or a similar plant in Greek botanical lore – and only then to

---

[55] Josephus, *War* 7.180–85 (LCL tr., with minor modifications).
[56] For other local *mirabilia* see, e.g., *War* 2.189–91; 3.420, 509–13; 4.459–85, 530–33; 7.96–99.
[57] Apion, FGrH 616 F15 in Pliny, *NH* 30.6.18.
[58] For the medieval transformations of the *mandragoras* legends, see, e.g., Ullmann 1978, p. 110 and Kottek 1993, p. 101, n. 128.
[59] For previous studies, and different identifications of this root, see Löw 1881, no. 142 (pp. 188–89); Hopfner 1921–24, no. 507; Herrmann 1954–55, p. 308; Kottek 1993, pp. 100–01. See also Rosenthal 1991, who shows that while the place Ba'aras is mentioned in the Maddaba Map and patristic writings, it does not appear in the rabbinic sources.

the ravine in which it grew.[60] And as Josephus' description makes patently clear, this is a "soul-drawing" root, which will "draw out" the soul and thus kill whoever tries to pluck it without taking the right precautions. Once plucked from the ground, however, this root loses much of its power, and it will therefore "draw out" only the alien souls that have crept into demon-struck patients without harming the patients themselves. It is, in other words, quite like the fish-parts used by Tobias, in that its powers are "built in"; no special ritual will be needed in order to use it (in this case, not even a fumigation), and while extracting the root calls for some expertise, using it probably does not; it does its work by merely being brought next to the demon-afflicted patient. For all we know, *ba'aras* roots, as well as false *ba'aras* roots, were being sold throughout the markets of Palestine, side by side with numerous other substances whose magical potencies were vouched for by their vendors and accepted even by a well-educated Jewish priest like Josephus. In other regions of the ancient world, similar roots and other substances – or even the same materials, but with different local names – were credited with similar powers. In addition to Apion's Osiritis plant, we may cite the claim, attributed to one Thrasyllus of Mendes, that the Nile produces a bean-shaped stone which makes dogs stop barking when they see it, and also works wonders for the demon-possessed, "for the minute it is brought to their nostrils, the demon flees away."[61] Such naturally exorcistic substances must have been extremely common in antiquity, and commonly used by Jews and non-Jews alike.

One final note. In his description of how the root helps fight demons, Josephus feels obliged to provide his readers with a definition of the "so-called demons" (*ta kaloumena daimonia*), for fear lest his non-Jewish audience may not know what he is talking about.[62] And the explanation itself also is interesting, since he ignores the claim that the demons were the bastard offspring of the Fallen Angels and the daughters of men, and instead describes them as the ghosts of evil people (what in later Jewish parlance would be called a *dybbuk*), perhaps because this would make more sense to a non-Jewish audience, well aware of the existence of nefarious ghosts.[63]

In summing up this section, we may note that the pervasive belief, common among ancient Jews but in no way unique to them, that some

---

[60] For the *aglaophôtis* and its uprooting with a dog which then dies see Aelian, *NA* 14.27.
[61] Thrasyllus of Mendes (FGrH 622 F1) in Ps.-Plutarch, *De fluv.* 16. The same stone is described in Ps.-Aristotle, *Mir. Ausc.* 166.
[62] And cf., for a somewhat different example, Philo, *Somn.* 1.141, who explains that what the Greek philosophers call *daimones*, the Torah calls "angels."
[63] For a non-Jewish parallel, see, e.g., Pausanias 6.6.6, on the δαίμων of a stoned rapist. For ghost-possessions in later Jewish magic, see Nigal 1994 and Chajes 2003.

substances have an innate power to drive demons away probably encouraged the growth of ever-expanding catalogues of the properties of different substances. And while such manuals are still unattested among the literary or archeological remains of the Second Temple period, their existence at the time seems virtually certain. Above, we quoted *Jubilees*' reference to the book of anti-demonic treatments supposedly written by Noah, and Josephus, for his part, tells us that Solomon's great wisdom included much philosophical and scientific inquiry, so that "there was no form of nature with which he was not acquainted or which he passed over without examining, but he studied them all philosophically and revealed the most complete knowledge of their several properties."[64] And in the *Wisdom of Solomon*, probably composed in the first century BCE or the early first century CE, "Solomon" boasts of all the knowledge he had received from God, including not only the make-up of the universe and the potencies of the elements, but also "the forces of the spirits and the thoughts of humans, the varieties of plants and the powers of roots."[65] Unfortunately, he does not explicitly state that he wrote all this knowledge in books, for future generations to use, but the circulation of such books in the Second Temple period seems quite certain. Returning to Josephus, we may note his claim that the Essenes

> display an extraordinary interest in the writings of the ancients, singling out in particular those which make for the welfare of soul and body; with the help of these, and with a view to the treatment of diseases, they make investigations into medicinal roots and the properties of stones.[66]

While such descriptions do not specify whether the roots and stones discussed in these "writings of the ancients" were used for exorcisms or for other types of healing, they make it quite clear that books about the occult medical properties of various substances, pseudepigraphically attributed to angels or biblical ancestors and presumably written in Hebrew, were in circulation in the Second Temple period. Such books, and their study, also imply a degree of professionalization far removed from Tobit's accidental acquisition of knowledge about the potent powers of a single fish. And while no such works are known to have survived, it is not unlikely that fragments thereof would one day surface among some Second Temple period texts, or among the many late-antique and medieval herbaria, lapidaria, and

---

[64] *Jub.* 10.10–14; Josephus, *Ant.* 8.44 (LCL tr.).
[65] *Wisd. Sol.* 7.17–21. See Winston 1979, pp. 175–76 and Hogan 1992, pp. 49–60. While *pneumata* could easily be translated as "winds," and was thus translated by *Wisdom*'s Latin translator, the order within the passage argues for a demonological context, and not a meteorological one.
[66] Josephus, *War* 2.136 (LCL tr.).

related texts, extant in so many manuscripts in half a dozen languages and more.[67]

Exorcisms performed by holy men
If *Tobit*'s exorcism is simple and somewhat mechanical, as are all exorcisms which rely on the innate natural powers of various substances to drive demons away, those performed by holy men, the distant heirs of such biblical figures as Elijah, Elisha, and Moses, tend to be just as simple, but to involve a different type of technique. Looking at these holy men – whose deeds are recounted especially in the New Testament and in rabbinic literature, but occasionally also by Josephus and other Second Temple period writers – we find them performing most of the miracles performed by their paradigmatic heroes, including healing the sick, controlling the rain, crossing rivers or lakes, and in some cases even bringing the dead back to life. We also find them employing the same kind of simple techniques and quotidian implements employed by their biblical forerunners, and even working miracles unintentionally, as when someone merely touched their garments or their shadow. Where they differ from their models is in the extension of their powers to spheres not covered by Elijah, Elisha, and Moses, and most notably to the exorcising of demons.

Of all the types of exorcisms performed by ancient Jews, those performed by holy men are the most difficult to study. In part, this stems from the fact that a "holy man" is a very idiosyncratic phenomenon, and there is no reason to believe that they all behaved in the same manner. Also, with Jesus of Nazareth as the best example of this type of exorcist, we run into the trouble of separating the "historical Jesus" from later accretions and deciding how typical the exorcisms attributed to Jesus may have been; presumably, not all demons addressed their would-be exorcists with "What have I to do with you, NN, son of the Most High God? I adjure you by God not to torment me" (Mk 5.7). But the main problem is that in such exorcisms, the major issue at stake was the exorcist's innate powers, which enabled him to command the demons to depart (and also gained him many of his followers) and so it was likely to raise some intensive debates about the identity of the exorcist and the authority by which he was exorcizing. Thus, whereas both "natural" and "technical" exorcisms might be described by third parties, and in books which otherwise show little interest in magic or exorcisms (such as *Tobit*, or Josephus' *Jewish Antiquities*), exorcisms

---

[67] Note, for example, the possibility that the highly technical plant descriptions adduced by Josephus as illustrations for the high priest's head-gear (*Ant.* 3.172–77) were excerpted from some such treatise (and cf. his reference to the Greek *rhizotomoi* in 3.172).

performed by holy men are likely to be described mainly by the exorcists' own followers, and objective reporting is not even to be expected. Moreover, as holy men used no manuals of technical instructions, and hardly used any implements for their exorcisms, we are not likely to find any archeological remains confirming their activities.

To see what such exorcisms looked like we may examine several references in the Jewish literature of the Second Temple period to such exorcisms, and one reference penned by a pagan author.[68] One example of a successful exorcism without recourse to any special exorcistic substances or texts is found in the so-called *Genesis Apocryphon*, found at Qumran, but likely to be of a non-sectarian origin. The text of this idiosyncratic retelling of the biblical stories of the Patriarchs unfortunately is badly mutilated, but among the few well-preserved columns one also finds an interesting story of Abraham's exploits in Egypt, an amplification of the Genesis account of Pharaoh's affliction. Whereas the biblical story merely says that "YHWH plagued Pharaoh and his house with great plagues because of Sarai, Abraham's wife" (Gn 12.17), the *Genesis Apocryphon* explains that "the Most High God sent an afflicter to afflict him and all his household, an evil spirit, and it afflicted him and all his household."[69] Since Pharaoh's physicians, wizards, and wise men could find no cure, Pharaoh sent a messenger to Abraham, asking him to pray for the king and to lay his hands upon him (just as Naaman had once expected Elisha to do), that he may live. Abraham indeed prayed and laid his hands on Pharaoh's head, and the plague and the evil spirit departed from him.[70] While the contents of Abraham's prayer are not recorded here, there is no indication that it was a specifically exorcistic text; rather, the power of the exorcism seems to derive from Abraham's personality, and from his close proximity to God. It is also possible, however, that in this case Abraham's prayer was so efficacious because it was against him that Pharaoh's sin was committed, so it was he who could best forgive it. Elsewhere in Second Temple Jewish literature, there are no depictions of Abraham as an exorcist, or as working any other miracles.

While the evidence of the *Genesis Apocryphon* is both textually corrupt and contextually problematic, there is much other evidence for exorcisms

---

[68] After some hesitation, I chose to leave out 4Q242, the "Prayer of Nabonidus," since it is not clear there whether it was the Jewish *gzar* who healed Nabonidus, or God who healed him as a result of his repentance of his sins – a common *topos* in ancient Jewish literature; for the text and its different reconstructions, see Dupont-Sommer 1960; Hogan 1992, pp. 149–57, and Collins 1996, with an extensive bibliography.
[69] 1QapGen 20.16–17.
[70] See 1QapGen 20.28–29, with Flusser 1957; see also Dupont-Sommer 1960 and Fitzmyer 2004, pp. 212–13.

performed by holy men in the Second Temple period. Looking at the exorcisms performed by Jesus, we may note him exorcizing the demoniacs wherever he encounters them – in a synagogue, in the countryside, and among his disciples and other crowds.[71] The exorcism itself consists of a simple command or rebuke, such as "be muzzled and come out (of the demoniac)" or "dumb and deaf spirit, I command you to come out of (the demoniac) and no longer enter him."[72] That this is what was expected in such situations is made clear by a rabbinic story of Rabbi Shimeon bar Yoḥai and his exorcism of the demon Ben Themelion by calling him "Ben Themelion, come out! Ben Themelion, come out!"[73] And the exorcisms of Jesus sometimes involve a certain amount of dialogue between exorcist and demon, or some haggling over the terms of departure, but this seems to have varied according to circumstances.[74] And here, too, some confirmation is afforded by rabbinic literature, such as the story of how Ḥanina ben Dosa, the famous miracle-worker, met the female demon Agrath bat Maḥlath and negotiated with her that from that moment on she would have permission to harm people only on two nights a week.[75]

To see how such exorcisms may have appeared to a complete outsider, we need only look at the mocking account penned by Lucian of Samosata, in the second half of the second century CE, of a Jewish or Christian exorcist at work.[76] The demoniac falls down, eyes rolling, and foam coming out of his or her mouth, and the exorcist interrogates the demon, who answers in its own native language, sometimes different from that of the demoniac. The exorcist then drives the demon out with adjurations and threats (and the onlookers even see the demon depart, all black and sooty!), and sends the demoniac home, safe and sound, after charging a large fee. Interestingly, Lucian says nothing about the use of written, or oral, spells and incantations, and the same is true of another reference to an exorcist (whose ethnic and religious affiliations are not specified), in a nasty epigram attributed to Lucian in the *Greek Anthology*:

---

[71] Synagogue: Mk 1.23–26 // Lk 4.33–35. Countryside: Mk 5.1–13 // Mt 8.28–32 // Lk 8.26–33. Disciples: Mk 9.14–29 // Mt 17.14–21 // Lk 9.37–43. For Jesus the exorcist, see Hull 1974, esp. pp. 61–72; Geller 1977; Aune 1980, pp. 1529–33; Sterling 1993, and esp. Twelftree 1993 (with much further bibliography) and Sorensen 2002, pp. 118–67.
[72] Be muzzled: Mk 1.25 // Lk 4.35. Dumb and deaf spirit: Mk 9.25.
[73] bt Meʿila 17b (this is no ordinary exorcism, since it involves a collusion between the demon and the exorcist, but they clearly tried to make it look like one).
[74] And see esp. the exchanges with the demon(s) Legion in Mk 5.8–12 // Mt 8.30–32 // Lk 8.29–32.
[75] bt Pes 112b.
[76] Lucian, *Philops.* 16 (GLAJJ 372). I leave aside the vexed question whether Lucian, who says that πάντες ἴσασι τὸν Σύρον τὸν ἐκ τῆς Παλαιστίνης, refers to Jesus himself or to an exorcist of his own time and place. For another reference to a Jewish exorcist, see *Trag.* 171–73 (GLAJJ 374).

> Many demons were expelled by the bad-breathed exorcist
> Not by his adjurations, but by the smell of shit![77]

Such "outsider" reports not only confirm some conclusions which emerge from the "insider" sources (for example, that the exorcist often got quite close to the demoniac), and supplement others (for example, that some exorcists charged hefty fees), they also remind us of the hostility, and downright mockery, that Jewish exorcists – and especially those who relied on their own innate powers – could expect from some of their contemporary observers. Moreover, such reports might show that by the second century CE Jewish exorcists were quite a common sight in many parts of the eastern Roman empire, not only in Palestine itself.

Exorcisms by means of incantations, implements, and rituals
So far, we have seen two types of exorcistic techniques, and two types of exorcists. On the one hand, we noted the use of exorcistic substances, which work by virtue of their occult properties. On the other, we saw stories of exorcists whose success in exorcizing demons was based not on the occult powers of special substances, but on their own innate powers. To these two types we may now add a third, utilized by those practitioners who assumed that the occult powers of specific substances do not suffice for all exorcisms, but who could not rely on their innate powers to scare the demons away. To achieve their goal, they had to master an elaborate technique, which included the use of special substances, implements, and powerful incantations. These incantations (and perhaps also some instructions on when, where, and how to use them), were often passed down from one practitioner to another *in a written form*, as we now know both from "outsider" and from "insider" evidence. Let us look at each of these and see what they can teach us about the mechanics of this type of exorcism in the Second Temple period.

Exorcisms by means of incantations, implements, and rituals – the "outsider" evidence

By far the earliest "outsider" citation of an exorcistic Jewish prayer is provided by the *Book of Jubilees*, which dates to the second century BCE. Having recounted the story of the Fallen Angels, their copulating with the daughters of men and the bastard progeny they produced, *Jubilees* eventually reaches the generation of Noah, and explains how his children and grandchildren

---
[77] AP 11.427.

were greatly troubled by these demonic spirits. Noah then prayed to God, and *Jubilees* cites this prayer, which runs as follows:

> God of the spirits which are in all flesh, who has acted mercifully with me and saved me and my sons from the water of the Flood ... Let your grace be lifted upon my sons, and do not let the evil spirits rule over them, lest they destroy them from the earth ... Shut them up and take them to the place of judgment ... because they are cruel and were created to destroy ... and do not let them have power over the children of the righteous henceforth and forever.[78]

It is as a result of this prayer that God decides to punish the demons, but ends up letting one tenth of them remain free and pester Noah's children, as noted above. In looking at the exorcistic prayer, we may note how simple it is in form and content – a humble prayer to God to destroy all the cruel demons, devoid of any specifically magical technology or terminology. As such, it may fruitfully be compared with the (more or less contemporary) Delos curses, to which we shall turn below. But Jewish exorcistic hymns were constantly evolving, and more elaborate formulae and techniques soon came to the fore. Our next piece of evidence is found in a book known as *The Antiquities of the Bible*, wrongly attributed in the manuscript tradition to Philo of Alexandria and probably written (in Hebrew?) in the first century CE, but preserved only in a later Latin translation, which was based on a Greek one. In recounting the story of Saul's afflictions (1 Sm 16.14–23), the author describes how the spirit of God left Saul, and how he was afflicted by an evil spirit. David was summoned, and he played a psalm on his lyre by night, whose words ran as follows:

> Darkness and Silence existed before the world came into being; then Silence spoke, and Darkness became visible. Then your name was created ... fastening together of what had been spread out; its upper part was called heaven and the lower earth. The upper part was commanded to bring down rain according to its season, and the lower part was commanded to produce food for all creatures. And after this was the tribe of your spirits created. Now do not be troublesome, since you are a secondary creation. Otherwise, remember Tartarus wherein you walk. Or is it not enough for you to hear that by means of what resounds before you, I sing to many? Or do you not remember that your brood was created from an echo in the abyss? But the new womb, from which I was born, will rebuke you, from which in time one will be born from my loins and will rule over you.

After citing this long exorcistic psalm, the narrator concludes the scene by informing his readers that when David would recite it, the spirit would

---

[78] *Jub.* 10.3–6, tr. by Wintermute in Charlesworth 1985, pp. 75–76. See also Abraham's prayer in *Jub.* 12.20.

leave Saul unharmed.[79] We, however, must note that his composition – obscure and textually corrupt as it certainly is – seems to employ two basic tactics in the exorcism of a troublesome demon. First, the direct address of the demon itself, in the second person, accompanied by taunts (of his lowly birth and miserable abode), threats (of the exorcist (Solomon? Jesus?) who would one day be born to David) and many rhetorical questions. Second, the use of an aetiology of the demon's origins, which goes back to creation itself, and which in this case seems to present the demon as an unintentional or secondary by-product of creation, which therefore should not try to exceed its assigned location.[80] On the other hand, we may also note the complete absence of God, and of God's praises, and even of God's angels, from this exorcistic psalm, in marked contrast with most of the exorcistic texts of the Second Temple period.

The last, but not least, pieces of "outsider" evidence are provided by Josephus in his *Jewish Antiquities*. Having devoted hundreds of pages to describing Jewish history from the creation of the world onwards, mainly for the benefit of his non-Jewish readers, Josephus recounts how the divine spirit had left King Saul and passed on to David, and how

> Saul was beset by some misfortunes and demons, which caused him such suffocations and strangulations, that the physicians could devise no other remedy except for ordering a search for someone who could exorcize and play the harp, and who, whenever the demons might come and torment Saul, would stand over his head and play and recite his hymns.[81]

Josephus goes on to describe how the search soon led to David, son of Jesse, whom Saul then appointed as his armor-bearer,

> for Saul would repeatedly be exorcized by him, and whenever the demons would afflict Saul, David was the only physician against their tormenting, as he would utter his hymns and play the harp and make Saul return to his senses.[82]

In a subsequent passage, Josephus has Jonathan reminding his father Saul of how David had been so helpful in restoring the king's very health, for "when the evil spirit and the demons settled inside you, he drove them out,

---

[79] Ps.-Philo, *LAB* 60. For the Latin text, see Jacobson 1996, p. 82. My translation follows his (pp. 187–88) with some modifications, but much in this text is unclear to me. For different attempts to solve the many difficulties posed by this psalm, see Philonenko 1961; Bogaert 1978; Delcor 1987; Jackson 1996.

[80] For the creation of the demon from an echo, cf. *T.Sol.* 4.8 (p. 20* McCown) with Jackson 1988, pp. 34–37 and Jackson 1996.

[81] Josephus, *Ant.* 6.166 (LCL tr., with modifications). Note that here, some twenty years after writing the *War*, Josephus no longer explains what "demons" are.

[82] Josephus, *Ant.* 6.168.

and granted peace from them to your soul."⁸³ Finally, Josephus recounts that "when the demonic spirit came to Saul once again and disturbed and tortured him," he ordered David "to exorcize him with his harp and his hymns" – and then tried to kill him.⁸⁴

The biblical story of Saul's affliction could, of course, easily be interpreted, and even rationalized, as a case of melancholia relieved by the soothing (or should we say, "enchanting"?) power of music, a power of which ancient writers, including Josephus, were very much aware.⁸⁵ Josephus, however, along with other ancient Jewish writers, clearly preferred to interpret the "evil spirit" afflicting Saul as a demon, and David's harp-playing as part of an exorcistic ritual. In so doing, he reveals his own familiarity with some of the symptoms of demon-possession, and with the details of the exorcistic technique, apparent both in his use of such technical terms as *exaidein* ("to sing out," or "ex-chant," i.e., "to exorcise") or *ekballô* ("to drive away," or "throw out" the demons, a verb commonly found in Greek magical texts), and in his description of the procedure itself. The description of David standing over Saul's head, playing the harp and reciting his exorcistic hymns is Josephus' own addition to the biblical story, and a clear reflection of what he knew of Jewish exorcisms in his own days. But even this description pales in comparison with another passage of the *Antiquities*, embedded in Josephus' account of the great wisdom of King Solomon. This was a favorite topic of the biblical narrators themselves, but one on which Josephus had even more to say. Not only does he repeat the biblical claims that Solomon was wiser than all other men,⁸⁶ and amplify the reports of his voluminous writings and his scientific investigations (as we already noted above), he also devotes a long digression to an entirely non-biblical account of Solomon's expertise in demonic lore. Once again, the passage deserves to be quoted in its entirety:

And God granted him knowledge of the art used against demons for the benefit and healing of men. And he composed incantations by which illnesses are relieved,

---

⁸³ Josephus, *Ant.* 6.211. Cf. 1 Sm 19.4–5, which does not mention David's medical services.
⁸⁴ Josephus, *Ant.* 6.214. Cf. 1 Sm 19.9–10.
⁸⁵ For the enchanting power of music, see Josephus, *Ant.* 9.35 (and cf. 2 Kgs 3.15): A man came to play the harp and Elisha became divinely inspired. For David's musical instruments, see also *Ant.* 7.305–06. For the Greek views of the healing power of music, see Dodds 1951, pp. 78–80 and esp. West 2000.
⁸⁶ Josephus (*Ant.* 8.43) also turns the דרדע of whom Solomon was wiser (1 Kgs 5.11) into Δάρδανος, which many scholars (see Duling 1985, p. 19) saw as a reference to the Dardanus who is sometimes mentioned in the Greek magical literature (see also Chapter 3, n. 88), and in Pliny, *NH* 30.2.9. This is possible, but note that Josephus explicitly identifies this Dardanus as a Jew, and as the son of Hemaon (bibl. מחול), and evinces no familiarity with any additional traditions about him.

Jewish magic in the Second Temple period 101

and left behind modes of exorcisms by which the possessed[87] drive out the demons so that they would never return. And this kind of healing is of very great power among us to this very day, for I have seen myself [88] a certain Eleazar, a fellow-Jew, who in the presence of Vespasian, his sons, military tribunes and a multitude of soldiers, was releasing demon-possessed persons of the demons. And this was the mode of healing: He would bring to the nose of the demoniac the ring which had under its seal one of the roots prescribed by Solomon, and then, as the man smelled it, drew out the demon through his nostrils, and, when the man at once fell down, adjured the demon never to return, while mentioning Solomon's name and reciting the incantations which he (i.e., Solomon) had composed. Then, wishing to convince the bystanders and prove to them that he had this power, Eleazar would place a cup or foot-basin full of water a little way off, and would order the demon to overturn it as it was leaving the person and make known to the spectators that he had left the person. And when this happened, Solomon's intelligence and wisdom were clearly revealed, on account of which we have been induced to speak of these things, so that all men may know the greatness of his nature and how God favored him, and that no one under the sun may be ignorant of the king's surpassing virtue of every kind.[89]

This passage has often been cited in studies of ancient Jewish magic, and our own analysis thereof will therefore be limited to those aspects which are most pertinent to the present enquiry.[90] Unfortunately, Josephus does not tell us when or where this public demonstration of an exorcist in action took place, but the presence there of Vespasian and his sons, Titus and Domitian, as well as numerous Roman commanders and soldiers, may point to the early stages of Vespasian's campaign to quell the Jewish revolt.[91] And we must also note once again Josephus' great pride in the Jewish art of exorcism. If he chose to insert into his dreary paraphrase of the biblical account of Solomon's reign this lively description of an event that took place almost twenty years before the completion of the *Antiquities*, it is because he assumed his non-Jewish readers to share his own excitement about such a glorious manifestation of the supreme wisdom of an ancient

---

[87] The text is uncertain here, and even if we follow the reading *hoi endoumenoi*, favored by Niese, its translation remains problematic – cf. the LSJ s.v., *endeô*, with the LSJ Supplement to the same verb!
[88] Note that ἱστόρησα is used only once more in the *Antiquities*, in *Ant*. 1.203, where Josephus relates how Lot's wife was turned into a pillar of salt, and adds "I have seen it myself, for it remains to this very day."
[89] Josephus, *Ant*. 8.45–49 (LCL tr., with modifications).
[90] See Herrmann 1954–55; Duling 1975, 1985; Förster 2001; Deines 2003, pp. 385–93.
[91] More specifically, I am tempted to locate this event during the twenty days' rest taken by Vespasian in Caesarea Philippi in summer 67 CE (Josephus, *War* 3.443–444), especially since that city boasted quite a few connections to the world of demons and exorcisms (for which see Nickelsburg 1981). Against this hypothesis, one may note that while the presence of Vespasian and Titus in Palestine from early 67 CE is well attested, there is no other evidence that the young Domitian (b. 51 CE) had joined them there.

Jewish king. (Needless to say, he never doubted the attribution of the exorcistic formulae to Solomon, just as he had no doubt that Cyrus had read the prophecies of (Deutero-)Isaiah or that Alexander read Daniel's prophecies).[92] Writing in the early 90s CE, he was especially proud of the fact that this proof of Solomon's wisdom was viewed not only by the late Emperor Vespasian (d. 79), and by his late son Titus (d. 81), but also by Vespasian's other son, the reigning emperor, Domitian. We may also note that Josephus was not the only Oriental who was proud of his own, and his countrymen's, magical abilities – witness, for example, Apion's claim, broached in his public lectures in Rome several decades earlier, that he had raised the ghost of Homer from the dead, to find out once and for all which was his native city.[93] Josephus, who was very sensitive to what non-Jewish writers wrote about Jews and did much to refute the anti-Jewish rhetoric of some pagan authors, certainly found nothing offensive in reports about Jewish exorcisms.[94]

What all this does not tell us, however, is why a high-ranking Roman general, or a Roman emperor (if the scene took place after 69 CE), would want to see a Jewish exorcist in action to begin with. After all, while diviners and magicians could be of some use to a military commander (and in antiquity, military commanders often had such practitioners in their entourages), an exorcist presumably had little to offer that was of any practical value for Vespasian and the Roman army. But the answer to such queries is readily supplied by what we hear in other sources about Greek and Roman curiosity with regards to various exotic customs and peoples. When in Egypt, a visitor or a conqueror was expected, and often wanted, to visit such world-famous *mirabilia* as the tomb of Alexander the Great, the Pyramids, the sacred Apis bull, and dozens of other attractions. He would also want to spend an evening or two discussing the secrets of the universe with Egypt's famed priests, whose hoary wisdom was so admired by Greeks, Romans, Jews, and everyone else in antiquity. Palestine, however, had much less to offer, and apart from the monuments of Jerusalem, all of which were inaccessible to Vespasian in 67 CE and non-existent after 70 CE, or the Dead Sea (to which he indeed went), there was little that a Roman commander would want to see.[95] He could, of course, spend an evening with some Jewish priests, and try to find out why they observe so many

---

[92] For Cyrus reading Isaiah's prophecy about Cyrus (Is 44.28 and 45.1), see *Ant.* 11.5–6. For Alexander reading Daniel's prophecy about Alexander (Dan 8.21), see *Ant.* 11.337 and cf. 10.273.
[93] Apion, FGrH 616 F15 in Pliny, *NH* 30.6.18. For additional examples, see Förster 2001.
[94] As was rightly stressed by Bloch 2003, who also notes Josephus' lengthy re-telling of the Endor episode in *Ant.* 6.327–42.
[95] For the Dead Sea as Palestine's most remarkable natural site, see the list of sources in GLAJJ, vol. III, pp. 116–17. For Vespasian's visit there, see *War* 4.476–82.

strange customs, but the more interesting priestly figures were locked up in Jerusalem and awaiting his onslaught (and mostly dead after 70 CE), and of the less interesting ones he probably had his fill once he had met Josephus. A Jewish exorcist, however, was more of a novelty, and a nice way to pass an evening while looking at what the natives claimed as a local expertise. An interest in such phenomena was in no way alien to the Roman elite, and one could easily adduce such intriguing comparanda as Nero's studies of magic and his initiation into the Magi's rites by the Parthian Tiridates (who came to Rome in 66 CE to be crowned as the king of Armenia), or Hadrian's supposed admiration for the aggressive magical ritual shown to him by the Egyptian priest Pachrates, not to mention the story of how Vespasian himself, during his stay in Alexandria on the way from Palestine to Rome, performed two miraculous healings.[96] It is, moreover, quite possible that Vespasian's own curiosity was also aroused by stories about the Jewish exorcist who had been crucified by Pontius Pilate some thirty years earlier, and whose followers – some of them accomplished exorcists in their own right – were periodically running into trouble with the Roman authorities.

While Vespasian's involvement in this folkloristic event can be reconstructed in spite of Josephus' silence on this score, Eleazar's identity cannot. The name itself, which literally means "God has helped," certainly is a most appropriate name for an exorcist, but need not be construed as a professional name – it was common enough in first-century Judea.[97] As for his religious affiliation, it has often been suggested that he was an Essene, or a Pharisee, or a priest, or even a Judeo-Christian, and all these identifications, and several others beside, indeed are quite plausible.[98] What may be assumed with greater certainty is that he was an experienced, and we might even say professional, exorcist, who had the special implements and texts needed for this kind of ritual, and enough self-confidence to face even a potentially hostile – and certainly very powerful – audience, made up mostly of non-Jews. Such facility comes only with many years of practice. Moreover, whereas in many exorcisms the successful operation served to enhance the operator's reputation, and perhaps also the appeal of his religious convictions, in this case, at least as Josephus tells the story, it served to enhance the reputation of an author who died long ago, and of

---

[96] Nero: Pliny, *NH* 30.5.14–6.17, and cf. Suetonius, *Nero* 34.4. Hadrian: PGM IV.2444 (for Hadrian's supposed interest in magic, see also *Sib. Or.* 8.56 and 12.169). Vespasian: Tacitus, *Hist.* 4.81; Suetonius, *Vesp.* 7; Dio Cassius 65.8.

[97] For such names, note *Tobit* 5.12, where Raphael, disguised as a human, adopts the name Azariah (YHWH has helped), son of Hananiah (YHWH has been gracious).

[98] Note also the suggestion of Herrmann 1954–55, p. 306, that this was the same Eleazar who was captured at Machaerus, right next to where the *ba'aras* root grew (Josephus, *War* 7.196–209).

the Jewish nation as a whole. Little did Vespasian and his legionaries know that such humble exorcists from Judea would one day conquer the mighty Roman Empire from within!

Leaving the exorcist aside, we must examine the exorcistic ritual itself. As described by Josephus, Eleazar's technique – which he apparently demonstrated on several different demoniacs on this single "show" – consisted of two main stages.[99] First, the demon was pulled out through the patient's nostrils, the effect being produced by the root which was brought to his nose.[100] This is the same procedure we already noted in an earlier section, but here the power of the root apparently was not deemed sufficient by itself; for the root to perform its work, it had to be placed in a special ring, under its seal. Unfortunately, Josephus says nothing else about this ring, and one wonders, for example, whether it had anything (such as the Tetragrammaton, written in Paleo-Hebrew letters?) engraved on the seal itself.[101] Similarly, the exact nature of the exorcistic root is left unstated; since Josephus does not refer back to his discussion of the *ba'aras* root in his earlier work (and such cross-references are not uncommon in the *Antiquities*), we may either conclude that he simply forgot that he had once described the root and how it is handled, or that this was a different root altogether. It is even quite possible that Josephus simply could not tell which root Eleazar was using for his exorcisms, and was content to know that it was "one of the roots prescribed by Solomon."

With the demon(s)' departure and the patient's subsequent collapse, stage one of the exorcism was over. To convince the skeptical, however, Eleazar would provide an additional demonstration of the demon(s)' departure.[102] In other exorcisms – and those performed by Jesus readily come to mind here – the demon would be forced to speak up (perhaps even in a voice, or a language, which was not the patient's own), and identify itself or provide other verbal testimony of its departure.[103] But with the audience consisting mostly of Roman spectators, who would be extremely suspicious of a collusion between the Jewish exorcist and his patient, a more "objective"

---

[99] Both the reference to "a cup *or* a wash-basin" and the use of past continuous (and not the aorist) indicate that the "show" included more than one successful exorcism.

[100] In modern Jewish exorcisms, the fear lest the demon would choke the patient or harm some important organ on its way out makes the exorcists pull the demons out through the small toe of the left foot (a practice apparently borrowed by the Jewish exorcists from their Muslim colleagues); evidently, ancient Jewish exorcists had no such fears.

[101] For comparanda, see, e.g., Bonner 1943, pp. 39–40 (a *Kyranides* recipe for an exorcistic ring with an image of Nemesis). In bt Git 68b, Solomon's ring, which helps capture Ashmedai, has the Name engraved upon it.

[102] For what follows, see esp. Bonner 1943.

[103] For a demoniac speaking in a different voice or a different language (so common in later exorcisms, and in Hollywood films such as *The Exorcist*!), see Lucian, *Philops.* 16; Philostratus, *VAT* 3.38.

demonstration of the demon's presence was needed, and so it was made to stir up the water in a small container. Such methods are not unparalleled in other ancient exorcisms, especially when the exorcist was operating outside his home turf – as when Jesus, in action near the large pagan town of Garasa and in the presence of a potentially hostile audience, forced a departing host of demons to enter a group of pigs which then jumped into the Sea of Galilee. In others, the departing demons rattled or toppled adjacent statues, or even appeared to the spectators in the form of a sooty substance.[104] But while the audience, or at least some of it, would thus be satisfied that the demons had left their victims, the victims themselves had to be protected against the demons' return. To achieve this, the second stage of the exorcism consisted of an adjuration of the demon never to return, and a recitation of exorcistic hymns supposedly composed by the great Solomon himself. Josephus does not say this, but we may assume that the hymns in question were composed and recited in Hebrew, and were therefore entirely incomprehensible to Vespasian and his men, a fact which only added to their folkloristic authenticity.

What did Eleazar's hymns look like? Unfortunately, Josephus is extremely vague on this score. That the hymns were attributed to King Solomon is beyond doubt, and his reference to the "modes of exorcisms" left behind by Solomon, and to "one of the roots prescribed by Solomon," might imply Josephus' familiarity with books which contained both the incantations to be uttered and instructions on which roots to use and how to conduct the ritual. And yet, the vague description of how Eleazar "would adjure the demon never to return, while mentioning Solomon's name and reciting the incantations that he (i.e., Solomon) had composed," might make us think that only the exorcistic incantations were read from a written text, while the rest of the ceremony was constructed more freely on an ad hoc basis. Unfortunately, we shall soon see that the examination of the "insider" sources at our disposal does not help decide the issue.

Exorcisms by means of incantations, implements, and rituals – the "insider" evidence

As noted above, exorcisms are the only magical activity performed by Jews in the Second Temple period for which we have "insider" sources to complement the accounts provided by "outsiders." It is now time to look at these intriguing sources – almost all of which are found among the Dead

---

[104] Pigs: Mk 5.11–17 // Mt 8.30–34 // Lk 8.32–37 (and see Twelftree 1993, pp. 74–75, 155, 164–65, for a different explanation of the pigs' fate). Statues: Philostratus, *VAT* 4.20; *Acts of Peter* 11 (see James 1924, p. 315 or Hennecke and Schneemelcher 1965, pp. 293–94). Sooty substance: Lucian, *Philops.* 16. For an illuminating comparandum, see Quesalid's methods as analyzed by Lévi-Strauss 1963.

Sea Scrolls discovered in Qumran half a century ago.¹⁰⁵ Unfortunately, all the Qumran exorcistic texts are in a highly mutilated state, and while some Qumran scholars have spent many hours staring into the lacunae in these tattered fragments until they saw all the missing letters float into their appropriate positions (should we call this form of divination "lacunamancy"?), different scholars ended up offering widely divergent reconstructions of the very same passages. In light of these difficulties, we shall focus in what follows only on those fragments whose exorcistic nature is beyond doubt, and only on those sections of the texts in question which can be reconstructed with some certainty, and leave most textual speculations aside.¹⁰⁶ And, as throughout the present study, we shall not be looking at the physiognomical, astrological, and other Qumran fragments which do not belong in the realm of magic *stricto sensu*.

Before turning to the examination of the texts themselves, a word is in order about the peculiar nature of Qumran demonology. Within the dualistic worldview of this small Jewish sect, the Sons of Light were in a state of constant and mortal struggle against the Sons of Darkness, who were abetted by a host of demons, always trying to lead the Sons of Light astray and tempt them into error, sin, and doubt. This is why, as we noted above, any nonconformist behavior by one of the sect's members (and given its stringent and elaborate rules and regulations, such cases must have been quite common) could be attributed to demonic possession or seduction and judged accordingly. But this also means that whereas all our previous examples dealt with persons whose demonic possession was an individual affair, to be cured by whoever knew what to do, in Qumran the fight against demons was a community affair, encouraged and regulated by its leaders (as it would later be in some of the Christian communities).¹⁰⁷ Thus, the presence of several different *types* of exorcistic texts at Qumran, and especially of all-purpose apotropaic psalms, designed to scare away the demons before they approach their victims, may reflect not only the interest in exorcism displayed by other Second Temple Jews, but also the

---

¹⁰⁵ In what follows, I have made much use of several recent surveys of the Qumran magical texts, including Baumgarten 1991; Nitzan 1994, pp. 227–72; Alexander 1997; Lange 1997; Lyons and Reimer 1998; García Martínez 2002; Eshel 2003; I also profited from an unpublished paper on the Qumran magical texts by Larry Schiffman, which he had kindly sent me.

¹⁰⁶ In what follows, I decided to leave out 4Q184 = 4QWiles of the Wicked Woman, 4Q444 = 4QIncantation, 6Q18 = 6QHymn, and 8Q5 = 8QHymn. For all these texts, a magical interpretation has been put forward, but is either unlikely (4Q444 and especially 4Q184) or impossible to substantiate, given the fragmentary nature of the text.

¹⁰⁷ For the communal nature of the Qumran exorcisms, see esp. Kister 1999. For demonic deceptions, see also Ps.-Philo, *LAB* 53.3. For the Qumranites' elaborate demonology, see Alexander 1999a and Reimer 2000.

Jewish magic in the Second Temple period

Qumranites' special needs, as shaped by their peculiar understanding of what it is that demons actually do.

With all this in mind, let us turn to the actual texts, focusing on three exorcistic scrolls from Qumran, and moving from the "least magical" to the "most magical" texts:

4Q510–511 = 4QSongs of the Sage. The two leather scrolls in question, paleographically dated to the last quarter of the first century BCE, contain either two copies of the same text or copies of two related texts.[108] Unfortunately, the size of the original composition(s) cannot be determined with certainty (but it certainly was large), and much of the text is badly mutilated. The text consists of a long string of religious hymns in Hebrew, whose main feature is the endless praise of God and the constant emphasis on the hymnographer's own worthlessness and humility. Such hymns are quite common among the sectarian compositions from Qumran, and would not be classified as exorcistic but for the recurrence within them of passages which make it clear that one of their functions was to ward off evil spirits. A typical example runs as follows:

> And I, a *maskil*, proclaim the majesty of His splendor, to scare and frighten all spirits of angels of destruction, and spirits of *mamzerim*, demons, lilith, *aḥim* and [ ], and those who strike suddenly to lead astray a spirit of understanding and to destroy their hearts and [ ] in the age of the rule of wickedness.[109]

While much of the text is fragmentary and obscure, this much seems clear: the *maskil*, a sectarian functionary mentioned in other Qumranite texts as well, recites these hymns of praise for God not only in order to glorify his Creator, but also to keep at bay the demonic forces of evil which seek to lead his community members astray.[110] This fight against the forces of evil is part of a wider eschatological war, in this "age of the rule of wickedness" which shall soon culminate in God's intervention and the complete destruction of the forces of evil, including all the demons. Thus, while the exact wording of many individual passages in these two mutilated scrolls is much debated among scholars, the overall nature of the text is not in doubt. It is a collection of sectarian hymns, to be recited by the *maskil*, perhaps on fixed dates or occasions, and intended to protect the Sons of Light from the invisible evil spirits which seek to harm and mislead them.

---

[108] They were edited by Baillet 1982; see also Nitzan 1992 and 1994, pp. 236–71; Alexander 1997, pp. 319–24; Eshel 1999, pp. 309–13.
[109] 4Q510 1 4–7/8 (Baillet, p. 216). Cf. 4Q511 10 1–6.
[110] For the functions of the *maskil*, see Nitzan 1994, p. 237, n. 45.

The power of these hymns seems to derive both from the *maskil*'s *ex officio* authority and the righteousness of those on whose behalf they are recited, and from the power of God's praises to keep all demons cowering in their hideouts and waiting for the pious verbiage to end. These hymns, in other words, are likely to have been used solely by the Qumranites, perhaps even as part of their standard liturgical cycle (and should hardly be classified as "magic"), and may have been entirely unknown to all other contemporary Jews.

11Q11 = 11QApocryphal psalms. Unlike 4Q510 and 4Q511, this leather scroll has been preserved in such a way as to assure us of its original size: it was c. 9.5 cm high and 71 cm wide, and contained only six columns of text, in Hebrew.[111] It is, in other words, a relatively short composition. Unfortunately, none of its columns has survived intact, and – as often happens when scrolls are found in their rolled state – the first columns have suffered the heaviest damage, while the last two columns have been relatively well preserved. Beginning with the last and best-preserved column, we find a version of Psalm 91 that differs somewhat from that found in the Hebrew Bible. This psalm, which assures him who "dwells in the shelter of the Most High, residing under the shadow of the Almighty" that he need fear no night terrors nor arrows, no evil pestilence of noontime or night, since "a thousand will fall on your (left) side, a myriad on your right," is one of the most widely cited biblical passages in later Jewish (and Christian) magic. It is known in rabbinic literature as "the song of the afflicted," i.e., of those afflicted by demons, and the rabbis also insist that this psalm used to be recited in pre-destruction Jerusalem, either as a part of the Temple cult or over the afflicted (or both) – a claim that is at least partly corroborated by our text.[112]

Returning to our scroll, we note that the beginning of this psalm is missing in a lacuna, but its attribution to David, as in its Septuagint version (in the Massoretic text of the Hebrew Bible it is not attributed to any author), seems quite likely. But be this as it may, the penultimate psalm in this collection is explicitly attributed to David and is clearly anti-demonic in nature. At its heart lies a direct taunt of the offensive demon:

---

[111] For the text, see García Martínez *et al.* 1998; for studies thereof, see Delcor 1987; Puech 1990 and 2000; Nitzan 1994, pp. 232–38; Alexander 1997, pp. 325–29; Eshel 1999, pp. 270–83.

[112] See pt Shab 6.2 (8b); Eruv 10.12 (26c); bt Shev 15b, and Chapter 6, below. Note also the appearance of the same word, הפגועים[, right before Psalm 91 of our scroll, as well as in 11QPs[a], cited below. For the magical uses of Psalm 91, see also Benayahu 1985, pp. 65–80. For its use by Christians, see Chapter 3, n. 194.

Jewish magic in the Second Temple period

[When] it comes to you by ni[ght, you shall] say to it: Who are you, (born) [from the seed?] of man and from the seed of the ho[ly one]s? Your face is the face of [nothingne]ss and your horns are the horns of [a dre]am; you are darkness and not light, [injusti?]ce and not righteousness.[113]

This is followed by a description of how "the chief of the army" had bound or imprisoned (or, *will* bind and imprison) the offensive attacker in the dark recesses of the underworld – an explicit or implicit reminder to the evil demon of the events so vividly described in 1 Enoch and in *Jubilees*. The rest of the psalm is too broken to be reconstructed with any certainty, but its overall function seems clear – it is an apotropaic psalm to be recited by any individual when he (or she?) senses the ominous presence of a malevolent demon about to make its attack. And the technique involved apparently is not that of an adjuration, but of a condescending rebuke addressed to the demon itself (making fun of its dubious ancestry, as one of the "bastard" offspring of the Fallen Angels and the daughters of man, and even of its physical features, of which we therefore get a glimpse!), coupled with threatening references to the divine and angelic forces which are ranged against it. Both features are, of course, strongly reminiscent of the exorcistic psalm attributed to David in the Pseudo-Philonic *Biblical Antiquities*.

Given the very different nature of the last two psalms in this scroll, it seems clear that the original scroll contained several different types of hymns, apparently united by their exorcistic focus. Unfortunately, their original number cannot be determined, but judging from the length of the last two psalms, and that of the entire scroll, the total number probably did not exceed about eight such psalms. And while the psalm preceding these two is badly broken, it seems to contain the verb "adjure," and certainly contains another second-person singular address to a malevolent demon, followed by yet another reference to the sending down (in the past, or in the future, or both) of the demon "to the great abyss and the deepest [Sheol]." And the presence in the more heavily damaged sections of this scroll of references to "[the spir]its and the demons," and to "Solomon," supports the assumption that these columns too originally contained exorcistic psalms which were fathered either on David or on his son, whose propensity for such compositions has already been noted above. Finally, the recurrence of sequences of praise for God might induce us to assume that this technique too – already known to us from the *Songs of the Maskil* – was utilized in

---

[113] 11Q11 V 5–8 (García Martínez *et al.* 1998, p. 198). My understanding of the text is based in part on a Genizah parallel, for which see Chapter 5.

some of these exorcistic psalms. And the fact that one long phrase from 11Q11 resurfaces both in the Babylonian incantation bowls and in the Cairo Genizah (see Chapter 5) certainly lends some support to the assumption of a non-sectarian origin, and wide diffusion, of these exorcistic hymns.

To these data we may add one more datum, which is of interest for our inquiry even if its relevance here cannot be proven. In a list of David's compositions which is found in one of the Qumran Psalms scrolls, we learn that David had composed 4,050 pieces, which consisted of 3,600 psalms, 364 songs for the daily sacrifices, 52 songs for the Sabbath sacrifices, 30 songs for other festivals, and 4 "songs to play over the afflicted."[114] Thus, some scholars have plausibly suggested that the present scroll originally contained these four apocryphal exorcistic hymns of David; as the last psalm in our scroll is Psalm 91, it is even possible that the scroll originally had four "apocryphal" exorcistic psalms *in addition* to the well-known biblical psalm. But be that as it may, this catalogue of Davidic compositions is of importance for our inquiry, both because it demonstrates the Qumranites' awareness of the existence of a distinct genre of exorcistic hymns, of the kind also mentioned by Josephus, and because it shows that such "songs" were fathered not only upon Solomon, but upon his father as well. Thus, the presence in the scroll of at least two exorcistic hymns supposedly written by David clearly is no accident. And here too, just as in the case of Josephus, we may note that David's composition of these psalms was taken by the Qumranites as a fact, in marked contrast with our own cultural instincts and our ingrained hermeneutics of suspicion.

We now come to what is perhaps the most intriguing question facing us: is this the kind of composition used by Eleazar in his demonstration before Vespasian? It so happens that the scroll itself has been paleographically dated to between 50 and 75 CE, precisely the time when Eleazar was active, but this coincidence cannot decide the issue for us. Unfortunately, since the beginning of the scroll is badly damaged, it is impossible to know whether the psalms to be recited were supplemented by materials, implements, or ritual actions, such as the rings or roots we encountered in Josephus' description of Eleazar's exorcism. And yet, this string of exorcistic hymns found at Qumran probably is the closest we can now get to anything resembling the kind of exorcistic hymns used by Eleazar in his demonstration of Solomon's great powers. It is quite possible, however, that the careful analysis of all the Pseudo-Davidic and Pseudo-Solomonic exorcistic texts of late antiquity

---

[114] See 11Q5 = 11QPs^a col. XXVII, lines 4–10, in Sanders 1965, p. 92, and see Sanders 1967, p. 136. The Hebrew reads: ושיר לנגן על הפגועים ארבעה.

and the Middle Ages will shed more light on their Second Temple period precursors and models. For it is here, more than in any other type of Jewish magical texts, that some continuity can be demonstrated from the first century BCE all the way to the eleventh century CE and beyond – a point to which we shall return at greater length in Chapter 5.

4Q560 = 4QExorcism ar. By far the most intriguing document at our disposal (and therefore, in line with Murphy's Law, the most severely mutilated!) is 4Q560, a small fragment of what may have been a full-blown manual of exorcistic incantations. Unlike the previous two items, it is written not in Hebrew but in Aramaic, which may mean that its adjurations were not pseudepigraphically ascribed to some biblical authors, and almost certainly means that it was not a sectarian document, but was brought to Qumran from elsewhere. This fragment, paleographically dated to c. 50 BCE, is only 4 cm in height and 16 cm in width, and contains the remains of 6 lines of one column, and the beginnings of six or seven lines of the following column. Thus, the size and scope of the original composition is entirely unknown. The text is difficult not only to read, but also to interpret, as many of the Aramaic technical terms it uses are not attested elsewhere. A rough translation of the better preserved lines of the first column would run as follows:

> And there entered into the flesh male lḥlḥy' and female ḥlḥlyt,
> [into the hear]rt iniquity and sin, fever and chill and the fire of heart,
> [ ] into the tooth male prk and female pkyt, which dig
> [ ] wicked ones.[115]

This is, to put things mildly, quite an obscure text, but it seems quite clear that the pair lḥlḥy' and ḥlḥlyt is intimately connected with the Aramaic root ḥlḥl, "to dig through, perforate," while the pair prk and pkyt derive from the Aramaic root prk, "to break off, crumble, crush." Half a millennium later, both the ḥlḥl- and the prk-demons will reappear in the Babylonian incantation bowls.[116] The whole sequence, it would seem, describes the onslaught of the evil perforators and crushers which enter one's flesh, climb to one's teeth, and begin the kind of digging and crushing that give modern

---

[115] My translation follows the reading of Naveh 1998, which supersedes that of Penney and Wise 1994. (The DJD edition of this text is still forthcoming; for photographs, see Eisenman and Robinson 1991, nos. 640, 1522, and 1549.) In line 4, I reconstruct the first word as בל[בא.

[116] For חלחולא and חלחולי, see Gordon 1937, Bowl H, p. 86. For פרכ(י)א, see Gordon 1941, p. 354, and Sokoloff 2002, p. 933.

dentists a respectable income.¹¹⁷ In the next column of this text, of which only a few half-lines are preserved, we find the telling words "and I, spirit of oath," in one line, and "I adjure you, spirit," in the next. It thus seems quite clear that what we have here are the remains of one or more exorcistic adjurations, at least one of which was intended to drive away the toothache demons. Such dental exorcisms, we may add, are well documented in Babylonian magic as well as in many other magical traditions, and it is to be hoped that a more thorough search for comparanda would aid us in understanding this specific adjuration.¹¹⁸

In commenting on this text, some scholars have suggested that it is a fragment of a magical recipe book, a precursor of the Aramaic magical recipe books of late antiquity.¹¹⁹ If this were true, it would be the only such fragment known to us from the Second Temple period, and in fact the only evidence we have that such Jewish magical recipe-books indeed existed at this early date. It is therefore a suggestion that must be taken with extreme caution, for when we re-examine the text we see that there is no reason to assume that it contained anything but one or more exorcistic hymns, and that one of these hymns included a "case-history," or even a mythological account (*historiola*), of the birth and onslaught of the toothache demons. Such an exorcistic manual is of great interest, but it is still a far cry from the Jewish magical recipe-books of late antiquity and the early Middle Ages, to which we shall turn in the following chapter.

Jewish exorcisms in the Second Temple period – an overview
To sum up our long and detailed discussion of Jewish exorcisms in the Second Temple period, we may note once again how they seem to fall into three distinct types, each with its own technology, explanation of its own success, and distribution of the credit that goes with it. Each, moreover, is very different in terms of the "insider" sources it might produce, and therefore in terms of our chances of ever finding them. First, we have those substances which are assumed to thwart demons naturally. The exorcism in such cases demands the acquisition of the substance (which may be readily available, but may also be quite exotic, and therefore hard to find or dangerous to procure, and probably quite expensive to buy), and a very simple ritual, such as bringing it to the demoniac's nostrils or fumigating it under him or her. In such an exorcism, the act alone, unaccompanied by any verbal activity, often suffices to drive the demon(s) away, and, as far as we

---

¹¹⁷ For מחתורי, here translated as "which dig," note the tooth-related uses of חתר in rabbinic Hebrew (e.g., bt Kidd 24b).
¹¹⁸ For possible Babylonian influences in this text, see Geller 1998, p. 229, n. 23.
¹¹⁹ See Penney and Wise 1994; Naveh 1998; Swartz 2001.

Jewish magic in the Second Temple period

know, the whole procedure could be carried out in complete silence (unless noise too was used to scare the demons away), and in the patient's own home. It is a form of exorcism which must have been widely used by people like Tobias, who had no real interest in magic, demons, or even exorcisms, only in solving his own specific problem. It is, of course, possible that some people specialized in such techniques, by learning how to identify the demons which must be driven away, and which substance is good against which demon. This knowledge may even have been transmitted in a written form, but unfortunately such "insider" sources from the Second Temple period have not come down to us, and we may only speculate about their existence and their possible form and contents. And yet, it is a system in which the successful exorcism does not bring much glory to the exorcist, since the process was considered entirely "natural," and since the special knowledge involved was mostly in the public domain.

The second type of exorcism, that performed by the holy man, is a very different ball game, as it is due entirely to the exorcist's innate powers, and therefore serves to demonstrate these powers. Thus, from exorcism as a mechanical procedure, in which a substance X is known to drive away a demon Y, we move to exorcism as a social drama, in which the exorcist tests his powers against those of the demon(s). In such exorcisms, the social component is crucial, because it is surrounding society which decides whether the exorcism has been successful – either during the exorcism, when the demon demonstrates its departure, or afterwards, when the demoniac's daily behavior proves that the demon indeed has left, at least for a while. The social component also is crucial because each successful exorcism enhances the exorcist's own reputation, and in some cases even helps him acquire a community of followers. And because the exorcist's innate powers are at stake, he employs no exorcistic substances, as in the first type of exorcism, and no pre-existing exorcistic hymns and rituals, as in the third type of exorcism. As a consequence, there is nothing for him to write down, and we can hardly imagine any "insider" documents pertaining to this type of praxis, nor should we be surprised if most of the evidence we have for such exorcisms lies in the reports of the exorcists' own followers or detractors about how the exorcism was carried out.

The third type of exorcism is again very different, and involves the carrying out of rituals, or the recitation of hymns, some of which were supposedly composed in the distant past, preferably by some famous exorcist like King Solomon or King David. In such a ritual, the exorcist may use special substances and implements, as prescribed by his sources, and would also recite long chunks of text, which are often transmitted in written form. Whether he also converses with the demon(s) – and thus diverges from the pre-existing script – is not entirely clear, but here too, the exorcism is first and foremost a social drama, with the audience playing a key role. In this case, however, the success is attributed not so much to the exorcist as to the supposed composer of the exorcistic hymn, or to God's support of the community on whose behalf the exorcism was carried out. It is in this type of exorcism that we would expect the production of detailed "insider" sources, and it thus comes as no surprise to find fragments of such exorcistic hymns among the Dead Sea Scrolls, and some evidence of their circulation even outside Qumran. A great number of such hymns, and of several different types, were composed in this period; some were fathered on such figures as David and Solomon, others were not; some were designed to ward off demons and prevent their attacks, others served to expel demons who had already entered their victims; some were limited to a particular community or sect, others probably circulated more widely; some were designed for recitation by specific persons (the Qumran *maskil*, or professional exorcists like Eleazar), others may have been intended for personal use in daily-life situations; some were written in Hebrew, others in Aramaic, and some, presumably, in Greek.[120] And the techniques utilized by these hymns also seem to have been quite varied: in some cases, the mere praising of the Lord was considered enough to keep the demons at bay; in others, the demon was addressed in the second person and taunted, ridiculed, or threatened into submission; in others, they were simply adjured to depart. Exorcism, in other words, was a highly developed field of activity for Second Temple Jews, and one for which they possessed quite an impressive technology – impressive enough to be presented even to Vespasian and his entire entourage.

Amulets

Of all the artifacts which strike us by their apparent absence from the Jewish society of the Second Temple period, the absence of inscribed Jewish amulets is perhaps the most surprising. Given the presence of two Jewish silver amulets from the sixth century BCE (briefly mentioned in the previous chapter), and of dozens of lead, bronze, silver, and gold amulets from the fourth or fifth to the seventh or eighth century CE (which shall be surveyed in the next chapter), one might be tempted to assume that there was a continuous Jewish tradition of inscribing amulets on thin sheets of metal. This, however, apparently was not the case, as the absence of archeological

---

[120] For Greek exorcistic texts which may be identified as Jewish, see Chapter 3, n. 191.

Jewish magic in the Second Temple period

support for this practice eloquently demonstrates.[121] Since such amulets would have been quite durable, the absence of metal amulets from the Second Temple period – as compared with their ubiquity in a later period – makes it clear that this *argumentum ex absentia* is not to be dismissed. This point is worth stressing, if only for its methodological implications, for here we have a clear demonstration of how misleading it might be to extrapolate backwards from later data or forwards from an earlier period. In this case, both types of extrapolation would have yielded the same result – a strong case for the use of inscribed metal-plate amulets by Jews in the Second Temple period – but both the archeological and the literary evidence fail to substantiate such a hypothesis.

How are we to explain the total lack of evidence for the Jewish use of written amulets over the many centuries of the Second Temple period? One possible explanation would be that Jews made no use of amulets throughout that period. In support of such a thesis one might adduce the paucity of references to the Jewish use of amulets in the "outsider" literature of the time.[122] This silence stands in marked contrast with the numerous references to amulets found in rabbinic literature (to which we shall turn in Chapter 6), and with the repeated claims of some late-antique Christian writers, such as John Chrysostom, concerning the manufacture of amulets by late-antique Jews. But such a thesis, reassuring as it might be for some scholars, stands in marked contrast not only to all we know about human nature, but also to the little evidence we do have for the Second Temple period, as we shall soon see.

A different explanation for the absence of written amulets would be that Jews did use them, but they were written solely on perishable materials and therefore did not survive. If Jews wrote amulets on papyrus and vellum, for example, as they certainly did in late antiquity, we may only expect to find such amulets in arid regions such as the Judean Desert or the sands of Egypt, and so their absence from our archeological record would become much easier to fathom. But the fact that in the Judean Desert quite a few perishable objects managed to survive, including some *tephillin* and

---

[121] Second Temple Jews were, of course, well aware of the technical possibility of writing on metal, as is clearly demonstrated by the inscribed gold plate on the high priest's forehead, or the famous Copper Scroll from Qumran (3Q15), or the rabbinic references to the inscribed golden tablet prepared by Queen Helena (m Yoma 3.10).

[122] I have found no explicit references to amulets in the writings of Josephus or Philo (not even in *Sacr.* 26, where Colson's LCL translation is quite misleading), in the New Testament (pace Bowman 1953–54, who suggests that Mt 23.5 refers to written amulets), in the Dead Sea Scrolls (for 4Q560, sometimes described as an amulet, see above), and in the Apocrypha and Pseudepigrapha, apart from those cited below.

mezuzot and hundreds of written texts from the Second Temple period, as well as texts and documents of somewhat later periods (including one Arabic amulet and one bilingual Greek-Arabic magical text of the tenth century, as well as a magical formulary in Christian Palestinian Aramaic!), and even an amuletic T-shirt (see below), but no written amulets of the Second Temple period seems quite telling.[123] The same is true for the Egyptian papyri, which include dozens of Hellenistic and early-Roman texts identified as Jewish or as having to do with Jews, and not a single Jewish amulet. Moreover, to the lack of any archeological remains we may add several other indications that would argue against the use of written amulets by Jews in the Second Temple period.

As one pertinent example, we may note that in later Jewish magic, as well as in the non-Jewish world, it was not uncommon for an exorcism to be accompanied by the manufacturing of an amulet or a group of amulets to be worn by the recently exorcized person.[124] The logic of this practice is clear to see, and was known to Jews at least as early as the first century, for, as the most famous Jewish exorcist of the time is reputed to have said, when the impure spirit comes out of a man it traverses waterless regions in search of rest, and if it finds none it might return to its former dwelling-place and bring along some newly acquired friends, so that the man will be worse off than he was to begin with.[125] And yet, the evidence we do have for the manner in which exorcisms were performed by Jews at the time – and as we saw, that evidence is quite abundant – seems to indicate that Jewish exorcists did not produce an amulet upon the completion of a successful exorcism. In the book of *Tobit*, once the right fumigation is performed the demon is bound by Raphael in the remotest regions of Egypt, thus assuring the reader that he would never return to haunt Sarah or Tobias again. In Josephus' description of the Solomonic technique of exorcizing demons, he insists that it drives the demons away "so that they would never return," and describes how Eleazar would orally adjure each demon "not to return" into the person whom it had afflicted.[126] And Jesus, too, never prescribes amulets to his newly exorcized patients – or to anyone else, for

---

[123] For the *tephillin* and *mezuzot* found in the Judean Desert, see Schiffman 2000. Note, moreover, that they display no magical "additions," of the type sometimes found in medieval Jewish *mezuzot* and frowned upon by Maimonides. For the Arabic amulet and Greek-Arabic magical text, see DJD II, nos. 157, 171–73; for a Christian Aramaic parchment codex said to have come from Wadi en-Nar, see Baillet 1963.

[124] For modern Jewish examples, see Nigal 1994, pp. 53–54, 63, 65, 104, etc.; Chajes 2003, pp. 70, 88, 90, p. 213, n. 66, etc. For a late-antique example, see PGM IV.1252–64. For a Genizah example, see MTKG III, 65 (T-S K 1.78).

[125] Mt 12.43–45; Lk 11.24–26.   [126] *Tobit* 6.8, 17; 8.3. Josephus, *Ant.* 8.45, 47.

that matter – and instead orders the demon to come out of the demoniac "and no longer enter him."¹²⁷ Thus, while in some later Jewish exorcisms a post-exorcism amulet was deemed necessary, this probably was not yet the case in the Second Temple period.

To the absence of any reference to amulets in exorcistic contexts, we may add the complete absence of amulets among the Qumran texts, in spite of the Qumranites' pervasive fear of demons which might lead them astray, and their documented use of many apotropaic and exorcistic psalms to keep such demons away.¹²⁸ In a similar vein, we may note that the earliest Christians seem to have made no use of written amulets, and that this practice – unlike, for example, the recourse to exorcisms – seems not to have been a part of their "Jewish heritage." In light of all this evidence (most of which is, admittedly, evidence from silence), we should probably conclude that Second Temple period Jews made no use of written amulets. And yet, one possible exception must be mentioned here, namely, the practice of writing God's Name (often in Paleo-Hebrew letters) on various objects, and on the human body itself, as an apotropaic or magical device. The origins of this practice may lie already in the First Temple period, as the marking of apotropaic signs upon the human body appears in such scenes as the Mark of Cain or Ezekiel's visions.¹²⁹ But from a certain point onwards, it seems as if the Tetragrammaton became the apotropaic mark *par excellence*. The evidence for this practice is quite scanty, but it does come from several different sources, and it is a practice for which we are not likely to find much archeological corroboration, as most of the writing surfaces on which the Name would have been written would have perished long ago.

The best known example of the writing of the Name is, of course, the golden plate (*ẓiẓ*) carried by the high priest on his forehead. The importance and uniqueness of this piece of decoration were stressed by numerous ancient Jewish writers, most of whom said nothing about its magical powers or potential uses.¹³⁰ Other sources, however, have more to say about its magical uses, which are so much in line with the biblical precedents for the uses of sacred objects. In rabbinic literature, Hillel's dictum that "Whoever uses the Crown passes away," is understood by some early interpreters as referring to the Crown of Torah, that is, to the misuse of one's

---

¹²⁷ See Mk 9.25, with Twelftree 1993, pp. 95–96.
¹²⁸ And cf. Hogan 1992, p. 166, who is puzzled by the absence of amulets from Qumran.
¹²⁹ See Gn 4.15; Ez 9.4. See also Rv 7.3; 9.4; 14.1; 17.5; 19.12, 16; 20.4; 22.4.
¹³⁰ See, for example, *Let. Arist.* 98; *Wisd. Sol.* 18.24; Philo, *Vita Mosis* 2.114; Josephus, *War* 5.235; *Ant.* 3.178, 8.93, 11.331.

Torah-learning, but others take it as referring to the misuse of the Name.[131] And in several rabbinic retellings of events of the Second Temple period, the *ziz* is assumed to have had great divinatory and magical powers.[132] That this was not some uniquely rabbinic fantasy is made clear by the recurrence of similar stories in other sources too, and by the frequent reference to the *ziz* in Jewish magical texts, in Aramaic and in Greek, in late antiquity.[133] In later periods, this implement continued to fascinate the Jewish imagination, and some Jewish magical and mystical texts of the Middle Ages even prescribed the manufacture of a suitable substitute, which the magician or mystic would subsequently use.[134]

That this cultic object was considered to possess such magical powers seems quite certain, but the practice of writing the Name seems not to have been limited to the high-priestly vestments. One piece of evidence is provided by the rabbis' elaborate description of how Moses inscribed God's name on a gold lamella and threw it in the Nile, in an effort to retrieve Joseph's coffin which the Egyptians had sunk there. The trick worked, the coffin floated, and Moses could begin the Exodus from Egypt. This story, preserved in tannaitic literature but perhaps originating in the writings of Artapanus (on whom more below), probably reflects the use of the Name, written even on metal-plate lamellae, to achieve various magical feats.[135] The same usage is reflected by another rabbinic story, in which David writes the Name on a pottery sherd and seals with it the Abyss, which threatens to flood the earth; in this story, we even find David's counselor, Ahitophel, providing a *halakhic* justification for the practice, by referring to the *sotah* ceremony, in which God's Name is erased into water which is drunk by the suspected adulteress.[136] And the Mishnah, compiled c. 200 CE, explicitly refers to the prohibited practice of tattooing the Name upon oneself, which makes it likely that some Jews indeed favored this practice.[137] Elsewhere,

---

[131] Hillel: m Avot 1.13. Misuse of Torah: m Avot 4.5. Misuse of the Name: AdRN A 12 (p. 56 Schechter). If the second interpretation is correct, this saying might reflect Hillel's explanation of why the high priests at the time were changing at such an alarming rate.

[132] See, for example, bt Kidd 66a; bt Yev 60b.

[133] Non-rabbinic stories: e.g., *Protev. Jacobi* 10. Magical texts: e.g., MSF, A17 ll. 3–6 (in line 6, the reading should be מח[מה]); A27 ll. 1–2; PGM IV.1217.

[134] For a pertinent example, see *Sepher ha-Malbush* in Wandrey 2004, pp. 137 and 169, and Swartz 2000, p. 70.

[135] See *Mekhilta* Be-Shalah p. 78 Horovitz-Rabin (with the *variae lectiones*), with Heinemann 1974, pp. 49–56 and Goldin 1976, pp. 127–129.

[136] See bt Sukk 53b and pt San 10.2 (29a), with Heinemann 1974, pp. 17–26 and Sperber 1994, pp. 47–54; note that this talmudic passage was used by later Jewish practitioners to legitimize the magical use of the Name(s) – e.g., Nigal 1994, p. 108. For the Name as the "active ingredient" in the *sotah* ceremony, see also Josephus, *Ant.* 3.270–72.

[137] See m Mak 3.6 (and Sifra, Kdoshim 6.10), with Bar-Ilan 1987; for religious tattoos, see also Jones 1987, pp. 144–45 and 152.

rabbinic sources contemporary with the Mishnah refer to the writing of the Name on one's body (but without tattooing it) or on furniture and utensils, and numerous rabbinic passages refer to the Name which supposedly was engraved upon Moses' staff and gave it its great power, or upon some of the Israelite weapons at Sinai, or on the ring and chain with which King Solomon had captured Ashmedai.[138] Moreover, it has plausibly been suggested that signs found on several Greek magical texts, and identified in one text as "the Seal of Solomon," represent a slightly garbled rendition of YHWH in Paleo-Hebrew letters.[139] Thus, a unique feature of Jewish religion, namely, the great sanctity surrounding the Tetragrammaton, gave rise to a whole set of ritual practices which utilized its power, including its inscription on different writing surfaces. But for full-blown Jewish textual amulets we would have to wait until the third century CE, and perhaps even later.[140]

If Jews made no use of written amulets, which amulets did they use, beyond the writing of the Name on themselves or on various implements and writing surfaces? As far as we can tell, these amulets consisted of various apotropaic objects and substances, which seem to fall into two distinct types, namely, those with a clearly pagan nature and those which could be considered religiously and culturally neutral. Let us examine each type in greater detail:

Pagan amulets used by Jews in the Second Temple period. As it happens, the earliest evidence for the Jewish use of amulets in the Second Temple period is highly polemical and condemnatory. It is found in 2 Maccabees, which probably dates to the late second century BCE and describes itself as an abridgement of a longer work, written by a certain Jason of Cyrene, of whom nothing else is known. In this glowing account of Judas Maccabeus and his wars against the Seleucid armies, one of the battles is described as less than a major success, resulting in the death of many of Judas' soldiers. And whereas in 1 Maccabees and Josephus the same failure is attributed to the incompetence of the local Jewish commanders and their failure to follow Judas' orders, 2 Maccabees has a different

---

[138] On the body: bt Yoma 8a // Yoma 88a // Shab 120b. On furniture and utensils: bt Shab 61b // bt Arakhin 6a (I owe this reference to Shlomo Naeh, in the name of Yaakov Sussman). On Moses' staff: e.g., PRK 19.6 (p. 308 Mandelbaum). On Israelite weapons: e.g., Lam.R. Petiḥta 24 (p. 24 Buber). On Solomon's ring and chain: bt Gitt 68a.
[139] See Jordan and Kotansky 1997, pp. 54, 64–69.
[140] Another possibly magical practice, the inscription of long stretches of the Hebrew or Greek alphabet on walls, ostraca, and other surfaces, also seems not to have led to the use of written amulets. For this practice, see Bij de Vaate 1994 and Hachlili 2005, pp. 508–11.

explanation of what happened.¹⁴¹ For, he says, when the Jewish warriors went to bury their fallen comrades,

> they found upon each one of the dead, under their garments, sacred images of the idols of Iamneia,¹⁴² which are forbidden to Jews by the Torah. And it became clear to everyone that it was for this reason that they have fallen. So everyone praised the verdict of the Lord, the just judge who makes what is hidden manifest, and they turned to supplication, asking that this sin might be entirely blotted out. And noble Judas exhorted the people to guard themselves against sin, having seen with their own eyes what had happened because of the sin of those who had fallen.¹⁴³

In commenting upon this passage, we may note that it provides not only an ingenious excuse for a military debacle (modeled on such biblical precedents as Joshua 7?), but also an interesting perspective on the amulets used by at least some Jews in the 160s BCE. The apotropaic use of cultic objects – be it statuettes of the pagan gods or any object or emblem connected with their shrines or their worship – was extremely common throughout antiquity, and was well known to the Jews of the time.¹⁴⁴ But the claim that some of Judas' soldiers – not the "Hellenizers," but the "good Jews" of 2 Maccabees' account – had recourse to such pagan amulets from the next-door town of Iamneia is quite striking.¹⁴⁵ The claim itself, of course, would be hard to verify archeologically, for when we find amuletic statuettes of pagan deities from Hellenistic or early-Roman Palestine, it is hardly possible to prove that they were used by Jews, and not by their non-Jewish neighbors.¹⁴⁶ For all we know, quite a few Second Temple Jews may have made amuletic use of pagan objects they picked up in a neighboring shrine or a bustling market; in a later period, we find the rabbis repeatedly railing against the use of such objects by Jews, as we shall see in Chapter 6.

One final point. The author of 2 Maccabees clearly condemns the use of the Iamneian amulets, and it stands to reason that Judas had condemned

---

¹⁴¹ See 1 Mc 5.55–62; Josephus, *Ant.* 12.350–52.
¹⁴² Gr.: ἱερώματα τῶν ἀπὸ Ἰαμνείας εἰδώλων. ἱέρωμα is a rare word whose meaning here cannot be determined with certainty, but note its use by Josephus in *Ant.* 1.322 to describe Laban's *teraphim*. See also *Ant.* 1.119, and the Revised Supplement to the LSJ, s.v.
¹⁴³ 2 Mc 12.39–42.
¹⁴⁴ For an illuminating comparandum, see Ps.-Philo, *LAB* 25–26 (with Hogan 1992, pp. 120–25), on the shining stones of the Amorite idols, which also cured blindness (25.12), and how Kenaz took them, and God destroyed them. For a useful discussion of amuletic statuettes, see Turcan 2003, esp. pp. 414–15, on how Sulla was saved by one in battle.
¹⁴⁵ Goldstein 1983, pp. 448–49 suggests that the objects in question were looted by Judas' soldiers and hidden under their garments, but the objects in questions clearly were amulets, worn even in battle, and not looted property which the soldiers forgot to unpack. Note also Judas' subsequent actions (12.43–45), to expiate the soldiers' sin and grant them a better future in the world to come. See further Goldin 1976, p. 116, and cf. Trachtenberg 1939, p. 147.
¹⁴⁶ For such statuettes found in controlled excavations, see, e.g., Aviam 2004, pp. 7–12.

them as well, but the reason for this condemnation is not the fear that Jews would dabble in magic, but that they are dealing with idolatrous objects. This is also visible from the narrator's insistence that rather than protect their wearers, as they would have hoped, these amulets in fact had the opposite effect. Not only did they hasten their wearers' demise, they also brought upon their entire military unit a disgraceful debacle, making it the interest of any Jewish soldier to make sure that none of his comrades had such forbidden amulets upon him when setting out for battle. The connection between magic and idolatry appears in other Second Temple period sources, such as the colorful story found in the Pseudo-Philonic *Antiquities of the Bible* of how the Midianite magician Aod, active in the days of the Judges, showed the Israelites the sun by night and thus convinced them to worship his gods.[147] And as we noted in the previous chapter, the Jewish attempts to forego pagan magical technologies – not to mention the deliberate destruction of many pagan cults and temples by the Hasmonean armies – may even have encouraged the development of more "kosher" substitutes, and thus contributed to the growth of an independent Jewish magical tradition. This, however, is a process on which the sources currently at our disposal seem to shed very little light.

"Neutral" materials and substances used as amulets by Second Temple period Jews. As we shall see in Chapter 6, the amuletic use of stones, coins, bells, knotted ropes and fibers, the tooth of a fox, a nail from a crucifixion, and numerous other apotropaic objects was well known to, and often accepted by, the Mishnah, compiled c. 200 CE.[148] There is no reason to think that such objects had not been in use for many centuries earlier, and some evidence showing that they were. In the Hebrew Bible, we find several different types of amulets, for humans and for animals, not all of which can be identified with certainty.[149] And in the Second Temple period, the belief that various substances – the entrails of a certain fish, the roots of a known plant, and so on – had anti-demonic powers certainly would have encouraged the development of many different types of amulets. And as the use of amuletic substances was extremely common in all walks of Greek and Roman society (the emperor Augustus, for example, was said to carry on him a piece of seal-skin, as a protection against thunder and lightning), their extensive use among Jews too would hardly be

---

[147] Ps.-Philo, *LAB* 34.
[148] The bibliography on such amulets in antiquity is vast. See, for example, Kropatscheck 1907; Seligman 1927; Papamichael-Koutroubas 1986.
[149] See, e.g., Gn 35.4; Jgs 8.26; Is 3.18–23, and Blau 1901, p. 546.

surprising.[150] A striking confirmation of this is provided by a child's linen T-shirt found by Yigael Yadin in the Cave of Letters, where some Jews took refuge during Bar Kokhba's disastrous revolt. This shirt, preserved for us by the dry air of the Judean Desert, displays several little "pouches" which were created by pushing some materials through the fabric, and then tying a cord around the resulting protrusion. When cut open, these pouches turned out to contain shells, salt crystals, seeds, and some unidentified materials.[151] As Yadin gradually came to realize, these pouches must have served an apotropaic function, not unlike the "knots" mentioned by the Mishnah as apotropaic devices for children, as we shall see in Chapter 6. Luckily, the context in which this amuletic T-shirt was found assures us that it was used by Jews, and even provides an exact date, in the early 130s CE. The T-shirt itself, however, has nothing "Jewish" about it, and the ingredients found in the pouches seem not to have differed from those placed in non-Jewish amulets in antiquity. Moreover, whereas in later periods one finds amuletic garments which are adorned with apotropaic images and/or inscribed with apotropaic texts, in this case the T-shirt seems to display no writing, again illustrating our general claim that Jews did not yet use written amulets at the time.[152]

To this bit of archeological evidence we may add such evidence as the *Testament of Job*, a work probably written by Greek-speaking Jews in the first century BCE or CE (though a later, Christian authorship cannot be ruled out), where we find three cords which God Himself had given to Job when He finally healed him of all his afflictions. Aware of his coming death, Job passes these cords to his three daughters, describing them as protective amulets against the Devil. Girding themselves with the cords, the three daughters are infused with a holy spirit and recite angelic hymns in heavenly dialects; Job himself dies without any pain, yet another effect of the wondrous cord.[153] Such amuletic cords were extremely common throughout antiquity, as in many other times and places.[154]

To sum up. In spite of the existence of two Jewish amulets, inscribed on silver lamellae, from the sixth century BCE, and in spite of the well-attested

---

[150] For such amulets, see Kropatscheck 1907, pp. 20–28; for Augustus, see Suetonius, *Aug.* 90.

[151] See Yadin 1963, pp. 257–58 and pl. 89; Yadin 1971, pp. 79–82 (incl. excellent photographs). I owe this reference to Haggai Misgav, and am grateful to Orit Shamir, of the Israel Antiquities Authority, for access to the original shirt.

[152] For inscribed apotropaic garments, see Goitein 1967–93, vol. IV, pp. 196–99, 417, and Shani 1999. For instructions for making one, see *Sepher ha-Malbush* (e.g., Wandrey 2004, pp. 136–37). See also Trachtenberg 1939, pp. 135–36.

[153] *T. Job* 46–52. Note esp. 47, where the cord is described as a φυλακτήριον of God.

[154] See, e.g., Petronius, *Sat.* 131: "*illa (anicula) de sinu licium protulit varii coloris filis intortum, cervicemque vinxit meam*".

Jewish use of *tephillin* and *mezuzot* in the Second Temple period, there is virtually no evidence for the Jewish use of written amulets throughout that period, even in contexts which in later stages of the Jewish magical tradition would call for the production of a written amulet. There is, however, some evidence for the amuletic use of pagan cultic objects by some Jews, as by their non-Jewish neighbors, and some evidence, and an inherent likelihood, that Jews also used some more neutral objects and substances – such as roots, stones, cords, coins, bells, and so on – as amulets for the protection of persons, animals, or places. For the extensive use of written amulets we must wait for a later period, as we shall see in the following chapter.

Erotic and aggressive magic

Looking at later Jewish magic – as documented not only by the magical recipe-books from the Cairo Genizah, but also by archeological finds from late-antique Palestine – we find abundant evidence for the Jewish recourse to aggressive and erotic magical practices. It thus comes as a surprise to see how little we know about the use of such rituals by the Jews of the Second Temple period. In part, the paucity of the available evidence may be attributed to the reticence of some Jewish authors to deal with such issues. Josephus, for example, is reluctant to talk about such issues even in non-Jewish contexts, as can be seen even from a comparison of his brief remark that Piso had killed Germanicus with a *pharmakon* with Tacitus' colorful description of the same event and of the magical rituals it apparently involved.[155] And when dealing with the aggressive magic practiced by or for Jews, Josephus is even more evasive, as we shall note below. And yet, such reticence cannot serve as the sole explanation for the paucity of our evidence for erotic, agonistic, and aggressive magic over many centuries of Jewish history. Thus, as we examine the available evidence, we must also ask ourselves whether the nature of this evidence might also explain its paucity.

When dealing with aggressive magic, we must first make an important distinction between standard curses, as uttered by an individual or a community, and those kinds of aggressive magical practices for which we must be looking here. Animosity between individuals often leads to one individual cursing another, and the pages of Josephus, for example, are filled with instances in which he had cursed his opponents, or in which his opponents – especially the besieged Jews of Jerusalem who were starving inside

---

[155] Cf. Josephus, *Ant.* 18.54 with Tacitus, *Ann.* 2.69.

the walls as he was encouraging them to surrender to the Romans – heaped many a curse upon his head.[156] Such curses, however, can hardly be classified as "magic," even if we must admit that Josephus describes neither their verbal contents nor the actions which may have accompanied their utterance.[157] In a similar vein, we probably cannot speak of "magic" when the *Letter of Aristeas*, written in the second or first century BCE, describes how once the translation of the Pentateuch into Greek had been completed the Jews of Alexandria gathered together, praised the new translation for its accuracy, and decreed that the Greek text should never be changed or revised. They also placed a curse, "as is their custom," against anyone who would revise the text by adding, transposing, or deleting anything at all.[158] Such curses belong in the realm of a community's sanctions against wayward individuals and other social dangers, a procedure for which numerous non-Jewish comparanda may be adduced.[159] In later periods, we may add, biblical manuscripts often included elaborate curses against whoever might alter the text, or steal the manuscript itself – and not only Rabbanite manuscripts, but Karaite ones as well.[160] This is equally true of the "frightful oaths" which, according to Josephus, a neophyte had to take before becoming a full member of the Essene community, or of the many liturgical curses and cursing-rituals, as well as the many blessings and blessing-rituals, utilized by the Qumranite sectarians as part of their highly dualistic views of their relations, qua Sons of Light, with the Sons of Darkness.[161] Finally, a long range of private curses, from curses written on graves against whoever would violate them to curses against trespassers of private or sacred property, were a common sight throughout the ancient world.[162] All these

---

[156] See, for example, Josephus, *War* 4.361–62: Niger's curses upon those who killed him (that they should suffer from the Romans, and also famine, pestilence, etc.); Josephus, *War* 6.98: Josephus addresses John, who curses (καταρασάμενος) him in return. Cf. Josephus, *Ant*. 18.346: a curse upon Anileus and Asineus by a fellow Jew who was angry at their transgression of their ancestral laws, and whom they have sentenced to death.

[157] And note, for example, *Life* 323, where Josephus describes how the people of Tiberias staged a mock-funeral for him. He presents it as their attempt to deride him, but one wonders whether this was an excommunication ritual, or some aggressive magical procedure.

[158] *Let. Arist*. 311 (and cf. Josephus, *Ant*. 12.108–09, who greatly waters down this passage). The roots of this practice lie in Dt 4.2 and 13.1, and cf. *Ap*. 1.42, for Josephus' pride in the Jews' adherence to this injunction.

[159] See, for example, Herodotus 1.165 (the Phocaeans, deserting their city because of the Persians, lay a curse on anyone who would not join them); Appian, *Pun*. 20.134, 136 (the Romans razed Carthage to the ground, and cursed whoever might live there in the future, so when Augustus refounded it, he changed its location, to avoid the curse); the famous En-Gedi inscription, cursing whoever might disclose the town's secret to strangers, is another example.

[160] For one example out of many, see MSF, G20 (T-S 12.41), with the editors' notes.

[161] Frightful oaths: Josephus, *War* 2.139–42. Qumran curses and blessings: Nitzan 1994, pp. 119–71.

[162] See Hachlili 2005, pp. 494–507.

curses could hardly be classified as "magic," unless they can be shown to employ some distinctly magical technologies.

Leaving such examples aside, we shall focus on five examples of aggressive magic utilized by Jews in the Second Temple period, each coming from a very different context and providing a different perspective on the aggressive magical practices of the time.[163] Beginning with two epitaph-curses from Delos, we shall then turn to the Jewish novelist Artapanus, to the (non-) curse of the holy man Honi and to some priestly curses, and end with a cluster of stories of love-potions and deadly poisons in King Herod's court.

Two curses from Rheneia (Delos). The first item to be examined is the only example known to date of an elaborate Jewish curse dating back to the Second Temple period that was committed to writing. The evidence here consists of two inscribed stones from Rheneia, a small island next to Delos which also served as its cemetery.[164] The better preserved of these stones is c. 42 cm high, 31 cm broad, and 6 cm thick, and is inscribed on both sides. The two inscriptions are virtually identical, and on both sides the inscription is capped by the image of two hands stretched upwards to heaven in prayer. The letter-forms help date these inscriptions in the late second century BCE, and the text runs as follows:

> I invoke and beseech the Most High God, Lord of the spirits and all flesh, against those who treacherously murdered or killed with *pharmaka* the wretched Heraclea, untimely dead, spilling her innocent blood in unjust fashion, so that the same would happen to those who murdered or killed her with *pharmaka* and also to their children. Lord who oversees all things and angels of God, before whom every soul humbles itself in supplication on this present day, may you avenge this innocent blood and seek [justice?] speedily.[165]

A second stone, of similar dimensions but inscribed only on one side, has an identical inscription (though in a much worse state of preservation), except that the name of the hapless victim is Mar[th]in[ê], and the last sentence does not contain the word "seek," which seems to have been misplaced on the first stone.

---

[163] In what follows, I have left out the supposed curse tablets from Tell Sandahannah (Maresha), described by Bliss and Macalister 1902, pp. 156–57 and pl. 86–88 and edited by Wünsch 1902, partly corrected by Ganszyniec 1924 (see also SEG VIII, 245–46), and used by Gager 1992, pp. 203–04. As far as I can see, these limestone tablets are *enteuxeis* (petitions), not *defixiones*, and have nothing to do with magic.

[164] For the removal of all tombs from Delos and the permission of burials only at Rheneia, see Thucydides 1.8.1 and 3.104.1–2.

[165] I. Delos 2532 = CIJ I, 725 = IJO I, Ach 70 and Ach 71. For the Greek text and much useful analysis, see Wilhelm 1901; Deissmann 1927, pp. 413–24 (or. Ger. pub., 1902); Bergmann 1911. See also Gager 1992, pp. 185–87.

In commenting upon this text, which may be taken either as a plea for divine justice or as a curse (and which therefore need not even be classified as a "magical" text), we must note several important points. First, while tomb-curses against whoever might open the tomb for robbery or re-use were common enough in antiquity, here we are dealing with a curse against an unknown offender who had already committed the crime of murder. Apparently, the suspicion that the untimely death of these two victims was due not to natural causes but to foul play, either through poisoning or by witchcraft, could not be turned into a legally convincing indictment, and the "case" was therefore brought before the powers above, to find the culprit and mete out the proper punishment. This, we may note, was a common procedure in Antiquity, and the only unique feature of these specific stones is that they appeal not to Helios, Nemesis, Isis, or the Syrian goddess, but to the Jewish God.[166]

And this leads us to a second point, namely, the obvious Jewish qualities of these curses. This is made clear by the many phrases which can only be seen as reflecting a Jewish usage, and an extensive familiarity with the Greek Bible. An expression like "the Lord of the spirits and all flesh" (for which see Nm 16.22 and 27.16) is simply inconceivable in a pagan Greek text, and finds ample parallels in Noah's exorcistic prayer in the *Book of Jubilees* or in a late-antique amulet which we shall cite in Chapter 5. Similarly, the reference to humbling oneself in supplication on this present day, certainly is biblical (see LXX Lv 23.29).[167] Thus, the person(s) who composed this curse may safely be classified either as a Jew or a Samaritan (the presence of both communities is well attested on the island of Delos), while the clients (presumably, the living relatives of the deceased) may have been Jews or Samaritans as well, but may also have been Gentiles, as the names Heraclea and Marthinê were borne by Jews and non-Jews alike.

Before leaving the Delos curses, we must note the most important feature of the magical praxis they display, namely, the complete absence of any specifically magical vocabulary and techniques. At most, we could say that whoever composed these curses borrowed from the non-Jewish world the image of the two hands stretched upwards to heaven (which, however, also appears on other ancient Jewish epitaphs) and the habit of writing down such a curse and placing it in a visible location. The text itself, however, displays no foreign influences whatsoever. This becomes doubly significant when we recall that Delos was a small island which thrived in the Hellenistic

---

[166] For comparanda, see the two inscriptions cited by Bergman 1911, and the detailed discussion by Versnel 1991a, esp. pp. 70–72.
[167] It might even refer to the celebration of the Day of Atonement, as argued by Deissmann.

period mainly on trade, and was therefore a place where persons coming from all corners of the known world would meet and interact. Moreover, the absence of any non-Jewish elements from these curses is paralleled by the absence of any Jewish elements from the roughly contemporaneous non-Jewish curses found in Delos, and this in spite of the Jewish and Samaritan presence on this island.[168] This, along with much other evidence, clearly shows that the *Verschmelzung* of the magical traditions of various ethnic groups, to which we shall briefly turn in the following chapter, had not yet taken place c. 100 BCE, and that here, as elsewhere, practitioners of different religious and magical technologies could work side by side with each other and yet operate within different cultural traditions and practices.[169]

Moses whispering the Name. Moving from Delos to Ptolemaic Egypt, we now turn to the Jewish writer Artapanus, who probably wrote in the second century BCE and is arguably the most colorful of all Second Temple period Jewish authors. It is therefore extremely unfortunate that only a few abridged fragments of his work – which consisted of the inventive recasting of the biblical stories about the Jewish ancestors – are extant. The longest of these fragments focuses on the career of Moses, and covers such intriguing topics as his establishing of Egyptian zoolatry or his military campaigns in Ethiopia. In one scene, Artapanus has the Egyptian king mockingly ask Moses for the name of the god who had sent him (cf. Ex 5.2). Moses then bends over the king's ear and whispers the Name, but when the king hears it he falls down speechless, and only comes back to life when Moses picks him up.[170]

Simple as this praxis might seem, the aggressive use of the power inherent in God's Name is of extreme importance, because it probably is the oldest and longest-continuing practice in the history of Jewish magic, as we already noted in Chapter 1, and as we shall see throughout the present study. For the time being, we must only note that Moses' action consists solely of reciting the Name, with no apparent need for any rituals or implements to accompany this action or enhance its power.

---

[168] For the non-Jewish curses from Delos, see Jordan 1979 and Versnel 1991a, pp. 66–67.
[169] For a useful comparandum, see the Nabatean magical text published by Naveh 1979. Whatever this text might say, it seems clear that it is not influenced by such Greco-Egyptian elements as shall be studied in Chapter 4.
[170] Artapanus fr. 3 Holladay in Eusebius, *PE* 9.27.24–25. For the rabbis' stories of how Moses had killed the Egyptian (Ex 2.12) by mentioning the Name over him, see, e.g., Blau 1898, p. 50, and Harari 2005c, pp. 298–309.

Honi's "curse". The next episode in our series comes from the writings of Josephus, and describes an event which took place in the spring of 65 BCE, during the Jewish civil war which was soon to lead to Roman intervention and to Pompey's conquest of Palestine. We join the scene when John Hyrcanus II and his followers are besieging his brother Aristobolus II and the priests who supported him in the Temple, which was not just the religious center of all Jews but also the most fortified place in Jerusalem. Fearing that the siege might be long and arduous, Hyrcanus' men decided to employ some extra-military means to defeat their opponents, and turned to Honi – the same Honi who had once convinced God to send rain – and asked him "to place curses upon Aristobolus and his fellow-rebels." Honi, however, refused to play the role of Balaam against fellow-Jews, and when the mob tried to force him, he stood between them and loudly prayed to God. His prayer is given by Josephus thus:

O God, King of the Universe, since those who now stand here are Your people and those who are besieged are Your priests, I beg You neither to assist those there against these here, nor to fulfill what these here ask for against those there.

Incensed at his refusal to cooperate with their desire, says Josephus, the mob simply stoned him to death, there and then.[171] Students of the earliest Christian movement will want to ponder the ease with which Josephus recounts how the Jewish mob had killed its favorite holy man, and especially the ease with which the stoning itself was carried out. Apparently, the fact that the man of God could run into trouble with the authorities, and with fellow Jews, was taken for granted, as was his inability, or unwillingness, to save himself from an ignominious death. And yet, such men were deemed to have great powers, and these powers could be used not only for beneficial purposes such as the production of rain, but for aggressive purposes as well. Having seen, in Chapter 1, how Elijah had caused a prolonged drought and how Elisha brought the bears upon hapless children, we shall not be surprised to find holy men using their powers for aggressive aims in later periods too. Readers familiar with the New Testament will no doubt recall how the hungry Jesus effectively cursed a fig tree or how the angry Paul brought blindness upon Bar-Iesus.[172] They might also recall, however, the story of Jesus' refusal to let his disciples ask for fire from heaven to destroy a Samaritan village in spite of their eagerness to do so.[173] And readers

---

[171] Josephus, *Ant.* 14.22–24. A story in bt Taan 23a relates how the Temple priests (*bnei lishkat ha-gazit*) sent Honi a message in which they quoted Job 22.28–30, but the connection between this story and that told by Josephus seems very tenuous.

[172] Fig tree: Mk 11.12–14 // Mt 21.18–21. Bar-Iesus: Acts 13.9–11.   [173] Lk 9.51–56.

Jewish magic in the Second Temple period

of rabbinic literature will recall not only the many stories about Rabbi Shimeon Bar Yoḥai and others who could "place their eyes upon" someone "and turn him into a heap of bones," but also the story of Baba ben Boṭa's refusal to curse King Herod.[174] Both the use of the holy man's power for aggressive purposes and the reticence to do so recur in all our evidence, and we shall see their later transformations when we turn to the rabbis' use of aggressive rituals in Chapter 6.

Looking at the "non-curse" uttered by Ḥoni, and presumably composed by Josephus or by his source, we may note its general resemblance to Noah's exorcistic prayer in *Jubilees* or to the Delos curses; like them, it consists mainly of a humble appeal to God to execute His justice, and is entirely devoid of any specifically magical technology, of the kind so common in later Jewish magic. This seems to be a recurrent pattern in our sources.[175]

Some priestly curses. Josephus' story of Ḥoni's refusal to curse the besieged priests is quite informative, but his account of what transpired next is even more intriguing, for he claims that God Himself soon punished the Jews for the heinous crime committed against Ḥoni. For when the besiegers next refused to provide the besieged priests with suitable victims for the Passover sacrifices, and even cheated them of large sums of money, "the priests prayed to God to exact justice on their behalf from their fellow Jews." God was quick to respond, sending a mighty wind which blighted the crops of the entire country and led to a steep rise in the price of food.[176] Josephus, to be sure, wants his readers to see this drought as God's response to the murder of the innocent, and God-beloved, Ḥoni, but most contemporary Jews probably saw it as a direct result of the priests' vengeful prayers. As Agamemnon learns at the very beginning of the *Iliad*, the curses of disgruntled priests can be extremely powerful, for they enjoy a certain proximity with a powerful deity.[177] This story, in other words, is an important reminder that not only holy men, but priests as well, had access to divine power; their power was not *ex persona*, as Ḥoni's was, but rather *ex officio*, but it was potent enough nonetheless. When convinced that justice was on their side, all they had to do was raise their hands to

---

[174] "Heap of Bones": see Chapter 6, n. 159. Baba ben Boṭa: bt BB 4a.
[175] For another example, see t San 8.3 (p. 427 Zuckermandel), where Shimeon ben Sheṭaḥ curses a murderer that "the One who knows thoughts, He will punish that man."
[176] Josephus, *Ant.* 14.25–28. For the rabbinic recollections of the same events, see bt Sot 49b // BK 82b // Men 64b.
[177] Homer, *Iliad* 1.8–52; for a similar situation, but narrated from the priests' point of view, see Engelmann 1975, p. 9 (how Sarapis muzzled those who opposed his priest).

heaven while offering their sacrifices and ask for God's vengeance to assert itself. The divine response was sure to follow.

Before leaving this issue, one additional set of sources may be adduced. Among their various recollections of the Second Temple period, the rabbis of late antiquity recall that this period witnessed an incredibly large number of high priests following each other. As the position was supposed to be for life, this was quite unexpected, and one explanation provided by the rabbis is that "some people say that they used to kill each other with *keshaphim*."[178] Josephus, whose information on such subjects is much more reliable, often speaks of the deposition of high priests within their lifetime, and even of their brutal murder, but not of the use of witchcraft in this context; if such rumors had reached him, he chose to keep them to himself.[179] But the rabbis also preserve other traditions which point to the use of aggressive magic by the priests of the Second Temple period, and at least some of these seem to reflect older stereotypes. Thus, when describing the priests' cruel manner of gathering the tithes due to them, the *Tosephta* recites an acerbic poem, which it attributes to Abba Shaul ben Botnit and Abba Yosi ben Yohanan of Jerusalem:

> Woe unto me of the House of Boethus, woe unto me of their stave (or, curse);[180]
> Woe unto me of the House of Cathros, woe unto me of their writing-reed;
> Woe unto me of the House of Elhanan, woe unto me of the house of their whisper;
> Woe unto me of the House of Elisha, woe unto me of their punches;
> Woe unto me of the House of Yishmael ben Phiabi, who are high priests, and their sons are Temple-treasurers, and their sons-in-law are Temple-officers, and their slaves come and pound upon us with sticks.[181]

This nasty song, which sounds quite like the mocking poems composed by the Alexandrians for their Ptolemaic rulers or those sung by Roman soldiers for their commanders ("Caesar f–d the Gauls, but Nicomedes f–d Caesar"), may indeed go back to the period prior to the destruction of the Temple, and the complaints about the high-handed manner in which

---

[178] pt Yoma 1.1 (38c): ויש אומרין שהיו הורגין זה את זה בכשפים. For other discussions of the large number of Second Temple period high priests, see Lev R. 21.8 (pp. 488–89 Margalioth); bt Yoma 9a. For other stories of priests killing each other (but not by witchcraft), see pt Yoma 2.2 (39d) and bt Yoma 23a.
[179] Of Josephus' statements on this score, see *Ant.* 11.299 and 20.224–51, esp. 250.
[180] מאלתן. The word אלה could refer either to a stave (see, e.g., m Shab 6.4) or to a curse (see, e.g., Num 5.21, 23, etc.).
[181] t Men 13.21 (p. 533 Zuckermandel); bt Pes 57a.

some priests gathered the tithes due to them are amply paralleled in the writings of Josephus.[182] Rabbinic literature, in turn, preserves the claim that earthquakes are caused by the failure to pay the priestly tithes, a claim which might reflect a scare-tactic employed by the priests to assure the smooth flow of their income.[183] But as recorded by our "poem," the priestly use of magic for social control apparently went beyond the use of such bugbears to stem disobedient behavior, and included the use of curses and "whispers," to punish wayward individuals and lax taxpayers. In the first line of this poem, we hear of the *'alah* of the House of Boethus, and this word, which can mean both "stave" and "curse," probably was intended here in both meanings. And in the third line, we hear of the *beit leḥishah* of the House of Elḥanan, and this term, which is loosely based on Isaiah 3.20, has clear magical overtones. What these "whispers" sounded like we cannot really say, but it seems clear that the priests, because of their proximity to God and to His holy objects, had much magical power at their disposal; that they used it to assert their prerogatives, and perhaps ask for a few more, would hardly be surprising. In Chapter 6, we shall find late-antique rabbis following the same path.

Erotic magic in Herod's court. Our last set of sources for Jewish aggressive magic centers around the events which transpired in the court of King Herod, the king of Judea from 39 (or 37) BCE to 4 BCE. This king, whose greatness as a ruler, administrator and builder was more than matched by his paranoia and madness – expressed most clearly in the systematic murder of his friends, relatives, and descendants – ran a royal court filled with rumors, suspicions, plots, and intrigues. Luckily, his greatness also expressed itself in his choice of Nicolaus of Damascus, a rich aristocrat who was also a man of letters, as his ambassador for special circumstances, his personal lawyer and adviser, and his court historian. Nicolaus' huge compendium of world history is lost, but as it was freely and extensively plundered by Josephus, it so happens that we are particularly well informed about daily life in Herod's court, including the extensive use of, or accusations about, *pharmaka*. In analyzing these passages, however, we are repeatedly confronted with the difficulty of deciding whether the specific *pharmakon* alluded to in any given case was a poison or a magic potion, since the Greek word carries both meanings.

Focusing on the clearer cases, we may note the accusation leveled by Herod against his own wife, Mariamme. As Josephus tells the story, Herod's

---

[182] Josephus, *Ant.* 20.181, 206–07.   [183] See pt Ber. 9.2 (13c).

sister, Salome, made Herod's wine-pourer tell him that Mariamme had made a philter and asked him to give it to her husband, Herod. Herod wanted to know more about this *pharmakon*, tortured Mariamme's eunuch, and finally brought Mariamme to trial, accusing her of dealing with love-potions and drugs. Herod's cronies (including, presumably, Nicolaus), who served as judges, understood what was required of them and condemned her to death; she was soon executed.[184] Herod also accused his sister-in-law of turning her husband Pheroras, his own brother, against him, "having bound him with *pharmaka*."[185] Here we seem to be diving deeper into the world of erotic magic, and of accusations of its use by the wives of the powerful, including Josephus' claim elsewhere that Antony's infatuation with Cleopatra may have been due not only to the pleasure of her company, but also to her use of *pharmaka* upon him.[186] But the charges against Pheroras' wife led nowhere for the time being, and Pheroras was allowed by Herod to keep her, as he so desperately wished. It was only after his death that the charges resurfaced, when Herod became convinced that Pheroras had been killed by some *pharmaka* which his wife had given him.[187] Josephus goes on to tell his readers that two days earlier, the wife's mother and sister had brought from Arabia a woman who specialized in *pharmaka*, to prepare a love-potion (*philtron*) for Pheroras, but she – instigated by Sylleus, the Arab ruler whose hatred for Herod had long been simmering – provided a deadly poison instead.[188] The search for damning evidence – which, as was common in antiquity, consisted mainly of torturing the slaves and freedmen who may have been in the know concerning what had transpired – soon led to accusations against other members of the royal court, and especially against Antipater, Herod's own son. It was he who once bought a deadly poison prepared by a physician in Alexandria, in order to poison Herod.[189] It was he who had procured another poisonous drug, made of the venom of asps and extracts from other reptiles, in case the first drug proved ineffective.[190] And, at the trial which ensued – presided

[184] Josephus, *Ant.* 15.223–31; cf. the much shorter account in *War* 1.441–44.
[185] Josephus, *War* 1.571 (ἐνδησαμένη φαρμάκοις). The parallel account in *Ant.* 17.46–47 omits this charge.
[186] Josephus, *Ant.* 15.93. For Cleopatra's use of *pharmaka*, see also *Ant.* 15.89 or Plutarch, *Marc. Ant.* 37.4. For queens who "bound" their husbands, cf. the much more colorful stories about Theodora and Justinian in Procopius, *Anecdota* 22.27–32.
[187] Josephus, *War* 1.582: διεφθάρθαι φαρμάκοις. Cf. the similar claim in *Ant.* 17.61–62.
[188] Josephus, *War* 1.583. In *Ant.* 17.62–63, Josephus adds a short note explaining that a *philtron* is a *pharmakon* intended to procure erotic desires, and the more interesting claim that "the women of Arabia are great experts in *pharmaka*."
[189] *Ant.* 17.69 (φάρμακον θανάσιμον), 70, 73. Cf. *War* 1.592 (δηλητήριον φάρμακον), 598.
[190] *War* 1.601. Cf. *Ant.* 17.79.

over by Varus, the Roman governor of Syria – both Herod and Nicolaus of Damascus accused Antipater of plotting against his own father, and Nicolaus did not fail to mention a reference by Antipater's mother to supposed "divinations and sacrifices against the king," a reference which, unfortunately, is never fleshed out in Josephus' account.[191] Wishing to ascertain Antipater's guilt, Varus tried the remains of the *pharmakon* which was adduced by the prosecution as a key piece of evidence on a convicted criminal – who quickly perished.[192] With this sound proof of Antipater's guilt (under the *Lex Cornelia de sicariis et veneficiis*) he was immediately placed in prison; at a later stage, Herod also had him killed.[193]

Useful as such passages might be for the education and edification of Josephus' readers, they pose quite a challenge to students of ancient Jewish magic. On the one hand, they clearly show that members of Herod's court indeed used *pharmaka* against each other, and we may safely assume that these *pharmaka* included not only poisons, but also more magical means for getting rid of kings and rivals. Such claims may fruitfully be compared with the goings-on in the courts of Augustus and his heirs – from the story of how Livia managed to poison her ageing husband in spite of all his precautions to the gruesome death of Germanicus in Piso's house in Antioch. Unfortunately, however, we cannot tell what exactly lay behind the accusations of "divinations and sacrifices directed against" King Herod, a claim which sounds very much like what went on in many other royal courts in antiquity, in which rituals for divining when the present king would die and who would replace him, and sacrifices and magic rituals aimed at speeding up the process, were quite common. Whether Antipater and his Idumean mother were supposed to have offered such nefarious sacrifices in the Jerusalem Temple or in a pagan shrine, or perhaps even in their own private chambers is, unfortunately, a moot point. What is clear, however, is that most, if not all, the poisons and potions which circulated in Herod's court were imported from abroad, and thus tell us relatively little about the erotic magical rituals used by local *Jewish* practitioners at the time.[194]

Summary
We have examined in some detail five different instances of the Jewish use of aggressive magic in the Second Temple period, and in so doing covered virtually all the available evidence on this score. In summarizing

---

[191] *Ant.* 17.121.   [192] *War* 1.639; *Ant.* 17.132.   [193] *War* 1.663–64. *Ant.* 17.187.
[194] In addition to Arabia and Alexandria, mentioned above, see the reference to a *pharmakon* supposedly prepared in Ascalon, in *Ant.* 16.253.

what we have found, we must stress once again the paucity of the available evidence, and the total absence of any hint of many types of aggressive magic. Agonistic magic, for example, such as often accompanied athletic and cultural competitions, is entirely absent from our sources, even for the period after Herod's establishment of such competitions in Jerusalem, Caesarea, and Sebastia.[195] Of magic practiced in the court of law – to harm or silence one's opponents or make the judge(s) take the "right" decision – we only hear a stray remark in rabbinic literature (attributed to the late-first-century Yoḥanan ben Zakai) that "when the whisperers of whispers in the (court of) law became too numerous," the *Shekhina* (Divine Presence) removed itself from the Jewish people.[196] One would love to know what exactly these "whispers" sounded like, but this is just one more example of the silence of our sources on precisely those issues which interest us most. And the same is true of erotic magic, almost unattested in the Second Temple period, but for a few references to love potions procured from abroad or Philo's familiarity with the (non-Jewish?) erotic magic of his home town, Alexandria. Finally, even military magic, of whose existence some Jews clearly were aware (as may be deduced from their suspicion that the men hosted by Josephus were such magicians, sent by the Romans), seems to have left no traces in our sources, in spite of its potential appeal for Hasmonean armies or anti-Roman rebels.

Not only are certain spheres of aggressive magical activity unattested or barely attested in our evidence for the Second Temple period, some aggressive magical techniques are surprisingly absent from the sources at our disposal. This is especially striking with regards to the practice of sending malevolent demons to harm one's opponents, which is so common in later Jewish magic but entirely missing from the earlier sources. In all the cases where we can follow the Jewish recourse to aggressive magic – be it the Delos curses, the curse which Honi was supposed to direct at the besieged priests, the subsequent curse of those priests, or even the cursing of the fig tree by Jesus – the practice seems to involve either the direct cursing of the victim or an appeal to God to harm this victim. Of the adjuration of demons to go and harm an individual, disturb his sleep, make him sick, or "bind" his virility we do not yet find a trace. And in this regard, it is also interesting to note that when Jewish exorcists of the time confronted malevolent demons, there is not even a suspicion that they had been sent

---

[195] For which see Josephus, *Ant.* 15.268 (Jerusalem); 15.341 (Caesarea); 16.137–40 (Sebastia). For agonistic magic, see, e.g., Faraone 1991; Gager 1992, pp. 42–78.

[196] See t Sot. 14.3 (p. 320 Zuckermandel = p. 236 Lieberman), with TK pp. 751–52 and Urbach 1975, p. 97.

by a conniving magician or a disreputable witch. When Ashmedai afflicts Sarah's bedroom in the book of *Tobit*, there is no claim that some evil witch had sent him there,[197] and when Jesus interrogates the demons he is about to expel, he never asks them who had sent them, and does not try to "expose" the witches or magicians whose orders they may have obeyed.[198] As far as we can tell, when contemporary Jews were afflicted by demons, they either assumed these demons to have been sent by God (like the evil spirit which had once haunted King Saul) or to have come of their own volition. This too might indicate that aggressive rituals for sending a demon against one's enemy were not yet in vogue.

Even more striking than the absence of many activities and techniques which will become so common in later Jewish magic, the practices which are attested for the Second Temple period seem to be characterized by their very "soft" (not to say "naive") magical techniques, so innocuous that even their definition as "magic" might in some cases be contested. Moreover, these techniques seem to diverge greatly among themselves. The use of God's powerful Name (as in Artapanus' description of Moses), the writing down of a stylized curse (as in the Delos inscriptions), the use of potions procured from abroad (as in the court of Herod), and the cursing of one's opponents by priests or holy men, all seem to go their own ways, and do not add up to any coherent body of magical praxis. Viewed together, they only strengthen our conclusion that a complex, creative, and professional body of Jewish magical knowledge has not yet come into being. Unlike some of the exorcistic hymns, the aggressive magical practices of Second Temple Jews probably were transmitted orally (if at all) and enacted mostly on an ad hoc basis by holy men, priests, foreigners, and the general public. Of the professional Jewish magician we find not even a trace.

THE JEWISH MAGICAL TRADITION IN THE SECOND TEMPLE PERIOD: AN OVERVIEW

Having devoted some attention to the different Jewish attitudes to magic in the Second Temple period and to some of the Jewish magical activities at the time, we may now draw some broader conclusions about the general features of this early stage in the development of the Jewish magical tradition. In so doing, we shall focus on three basic questions, which would help us arrange

---

[197] And when in some mss of *Tobit* we find the reason for Ashmedai's serial killing of Sarah's husbands, it is because of his own love for her, for which see Ego 2003.

[198] And cf. the story of R. Yehoshua in Rome, cited in Chapter 6, in which the "binding" of a bridegroom is attributed to a witch, who is exposed by Rabbi Yehoshua.

our findings in a coherent manner: (1) Why is there so little evidence for Jewish magic in the Second Temple period? (2) Who were the practitioners of Jewish magic at the time? and (3) What magical technologies did they use?

The paucity of the available evidence

Any study of Jewish magic in the Second Temple period must come to grips with the fact that there is relatively little evidence for the magical activities utilized by Jews at the time, especially in comparison with the abundance of the evidence for subsequent periods.[199] In explaining this anomaly, we may set aside the possibility that Jews simply did not dabble in magic, for the evidence that we do have clearly shows that this was not the case. While there may have been some Second Temple period Jews who made some efforts to shun any magical activities for ideological and theological reasons, most Jews saw nothing wrong with an appeal to magical rituals and practices, at least in some contexts.

Dividing the evidence according to its origins, we may first note that the relative paucity of references to magic in the "outsider" sources is the easier to explain, for these sources may have been disinterested in, or reluctant to talk about, the issue that interests us here. Above, we noted several instances in which Josephus' reluctance to expand upon such themes as aggressive magic can be documented.[200] Returning to Classical literature, we may note that while the poets (Homer, Theocritus, Virgil, Lucan) and (at a later period) the novelists (Antonius Diogenes, Apuleius, Heliodorus) display a great interest in magical rituals and the practitioners who carried them out, ancient historians generally were less interested in such phenomena, or at least less eager to discuss them. Moreover, as we shall see in Chapter 6, rabbinic literature displays a great interest in magic and in stories about it, but is sometimes reticent when it comes to the actual rituals and spells employed by some magicians and rabbis. Thus, the "failure" of earlier Jewish literature to devote much space to magic and magicians may be explained in part as resulting from a general disinclination to talk about such issues. It may also result from the fact that such writers as Artapanus, who apparently showed no such reticence, and such works as the story of the Egyptian priests *Jannes and Jambres* and their encounter with Moses and Aaron,

---

[199] For a similar conclusion regarding Jewish astrological texts, see Leicht 2006, pp. 35–38.

[200] Thus, we may add nascent Jewish magic (and nascent Jewish mysticism?) to Momigliano's famous discussion of "those things which Josephus did not see," or did not wish to talk about (Momigliano 1987).

which may have included some juicy descriptions of magicians in action, are very fragmentarily preserved.[201] Thus, we may also be dealing with the choices made by later (and mostly Christian) readers and copyists, whose own preferences helped determine which ancient Jewish texts would be preserved and which would be irretrievably lost. And yet, such observations certainly would not suffice to explain the absence of "outsider" accounts of Jewish magic, and the feeling one gets after reading all the available evidence is that magic was not really a "hot" topic in the Jewish society of the Second Temple period, at least not among the literate public and the intellectual elite. The lesser-educated in towns and villages may have had a greater interest in such issues, but their views are not well represented by the available sources.

If the paucity of the "outsider" sources may be explained in this manner, the paucity of the "insider" sources calls for a different explanation. One could, of course, argue that this paucity is due to purely technical reasons, and that all the Jewish magical texts of the Second Temple period were written on papyrus and vellum, and simply disintegrated in Palestine's humid soil, never to be seen again. As supporting evidence, we may note that the "outsider" evidence implies the existence of *written* books on the properties of roots and stones, of which there is not yet a trace in the "insider" sources, and that of the exorcistic psalms found at Qumran – even those which are non-sectarian – we would never have known were it not for their preservation in the dry caves of Qumran and their discovery by a Bedouin goat. Against this argument, however, one may point to the growing corpus of Second Temple period Jewish texts unearthed in Egypt and especially in the Judean Desert, and to the extreme paucity of magical texts within that large body of textual evidence. Perhaps more important, we should note that even the little evidence that we do have seems to point to the *oral* nature of much of Second Temple period Jewish magic.

Perhaps the best clue as to the oral nature of Jewish magic at the time is the striking absence of collections of magical recipes, of the type so common in late antiquity. With the possible exception of 4Q560, whose nature is far from clear (but which certainly is an exorcistic text), all the magical texts from Qumran that have come down to us are exorcistic *hymns*, and it is precisely such hymns which Josephus assumes to have been handed down, presumably in written form, from the days of King Solomon himself. And even when we make room for lost pseudepigraphic works on

---

[201] For *Jannes and Jambres*, see Pietersma 1994.

the properties of various substances, we are still far removed from the Jewish magical formularies of late antiquity, with recipes for every conceivable type of magical activity. To this argument from silence we may add another, namely, the absence of any references to writing as part of the Second Temple period magical rituals to which we do have some access. As can be seen from Josephus' description of Eleazar, from Josephus' and Pseudo-Philo's description of David's exorcizing of Saul, from the Qumran exorcistic hymns, and from the many relevant passages in the New Testament, such rituals could entail much verbal activity, and some manipulation of physical objects, but no writing whatsoever. The same seems true of all the other magical practices of which we get a glimpse, and the few exceptions – such as the habit of writing the Name on some objects, or even on one's own body – only prove the general rule. And when we find a written Jewish magical text – such as the Delos curses – there is no sign at all that it was copied from a pre-existing, written recipe, again in marked contrast with some of the Jewish magical artifacts of late antiquity. It thus seems quite clear that most of Second Temple Jewish magic was transmitted orally, and even when it was transmitted in writing, as in the case of some exorcistic hymns, its "performance" normally included an oral recitation but no writing. And in this regard, it is the absence of any evidence for written amulets which is the most surprising, especially when viewed against the Ketef Hinnom amulets on the one hand, the late-antique ones on the other. To these considerations, we may add that in the next chapter, we shall see that the pagan Greek magical texts, while demonstrating many Jewish influences, preserve only a handful of Jewish magical recipes, the earliest apparently dating to the third or fourth century CE. This too might be due, at least in part, to the oral nature of earlier Jewish magic, and to the availability of *written* Jewish magical recipes, in this case in Greek, only from after the destruction of the Jerusalem Temple.

These observations have some disturbing implications for the future study of ancient Jewish magic. In coming years, we are not likely to find too many new "outsider" sources for the study of Jewish magic in the Second Temple period, and its mostly oral nature means that we are not likely to find too many new "insider" sources either, even if large caches of manuscripts are again found somewhere in Palestine or in the Diaspora. We may find more exorcistic hymns, and perhaps even some manuals of rhizotomy, lapidaria, and the occult properties of different substances. And when more late antique and early medieval Jewish magical texts are identified, edited, and studied, we may find there bits of earlier Jewish magic, as shall be noted in Chapter 5. But the ongoing study of later Jewish magical texts would probably create an even wider gap between our extensive knowledge of late antique and medieval Jewish magic and our meager knowledge of the earlier period. As noted at the beginning of this chapter, it is essential that we highlight this gap and learn to accept its implications, rather than pretend it does not exist and extrapolate backwards from the later evidence. History is the art of searching for all the available evidence and trying to make sense of it, but history has its limits; when no evidence exists, history makes way for theology.

The identity of the practitioners

Moving from the evidence for the study of Jewish magic in the Second Temple period to the people lurking behind it, they seem to fall into three distinct types. First and foremost, we find the holy men, who can perform a large repertoire of miracles, including those performed by such biblical men of God as Elijah and Elisha as well as a few never contemplated by these paradigmatic predecessors, such as the exorcizing of demons.[202] Like their biblical models, they also have the power not only to perform many miracles, but also to harm those who stand in their way or offend them, be it a fig tree or a troublesome opponent; but, in some cases at least, they display some reticence about the free use of this power. And like their biblical predecessors, these men of God rarely need anything more complex than a touch of the hand, a few drops of spittle, a few ordinary words, a simple vessel, or a simple ritual (like drawing a circle around themselves) as aides in performing their miracles. Thus, it is not even clear whether we should classify these men and their feats under the rubric "magic" at all, and quite clear that they were not classified as such by most Jews at the time. What is very clear, however, is that such men used no specialized magical technology and needed no written manuals to perform any of their miracles, for the quality of "holiness" was innate, and not acquired. In rare cases, it was passed on by a master to his disciples, as Jesus sometimes tried to do; but in most cases, those who tried to imitate the men of God probably ended up as Peter is said to have done when he tried to walk on water.

[202] In a few rare cases, we also find references to holy women – see *Judith* 8.31, Lk 2.36–38, Philo's description of the female Therapeutai, and the stories of the *ḥasid* and his wife in pt Taan 1.4 (64b) and of Abba Ḥilqiah and his wife in bt Taan 23a–b. For later periods, see Chajes 2003, pp. 97–118 and Chajes 2005.

And even when the transfer of these marvelous abilities was successful, it involved nothing more elaborate than Elijah's throwing of his garment upon Elisha's shoulders.

A second type of wonder-worker was performing great feats not out of some innate qualities (though in some cases they may have had them too), but rather *ex officio*. Looking at the Qumran exorcistic hymns, we noted that some of them were to be recited not by any member of the Qumran community, but by the *maskil*, as part of his religious and administrative duties. More important, we kept on running into priests who performed various rituals and achieved various goals which clearly were not a part of their regular Temple-service. Priests cursing and using other aggressive means to obtain the high priesthood, avenge an injury or keep the populace paying their tithes seem to have been quite common in the Second Temple period. While we have no direct access to the kinds of magical rituals which may have been performed by the priests, or to the manners by which they were transmitted from one generation of priests to the next, it seems quite likely that the use of the sacred objects entrusted to them as part of their Temple service, or a few words of prayer at the right moment, were all they needed to achieve the feats they wished to perform.

The thaumaturgical efforts of holy men and of priests are interesting in their own right, but we are still missing the most important figure, that of the professional magician, or, at the very least, the professional physician with a strong interest in magic. The only professional wonder-workers we seem to meet in the Second Temple period are such exorcists as Eleazar, and the owners and users of such exorcistic handbooks as 11Q11 or 4Q560, while Jewish professionals specializing in other magical rituals are nowhere to be found. It is this factor which is partly responsible for the paucity of "insider" sources for the Jewish magical tradition of the Second Temple period, for it is especially the professional magician who caters to a large clientele with many different demands, and who employs complex rituals and elaborate incantations, who is in greatest need of written magical texts. But with so many holy men and priests offering their services and catering to the needs of the masses, there was little need for professional magicians who mastered their art through study. Herodian princes and princesses made special orders from abroad, but the rest of the population probably relied on the local holy men, the priests, the specialist exorcists, and, perhaps, also the non-Jewish experts, with little incentive for the growth of the all-round Jewish magician. Only in a later period, with the Temple gone and with Jewish holy men on the wane, do we begin to find the tell-tale fingerprints of professional Jewish magicians.

The magical technologies of the Second Temple period

Having seen who practiced magic in the Second Temple period, we must now try to get a general sense of what techniques and rituals they practiced. And perhaps the most striking feature here is the apparent lack of uniformity, or even coherence, between the practices mentioned by many of the individual sources. Jewish exorcisms seem to add up to a coherent whole, but Jewish aggressive and erotic rituals employ a diffuse set of magical techniques, as do Jewish amulets. Much of the activity seems to have been carried out on an ad hoc basis, without any pre-set ritual instructions or incantation formulae, and without the *nomina barbara*, the vowel permutations, the *charactêres*, and the magic signs, all of which will appear in later Jewish magic. This is yet another argument for the lack of an "authoritative tradition," i.e., the lack of professional magicians or of written magical texts in which the technical knowledge was transmitted. As we shall see in the next chapter, when we turn to late-antique Jewish magical texts we find ourselves in a very different world.

In spite of its diffuse nature, and of the paucity of the sources for its study, Second Temple period Jewish magic does seem to contain at least some of the features which would be among its culture-specific hallmarks in later periods. First and foremost, the use of the Name, for which we found ample traces in the Hebrew Bible itself, is very well attested, certainly as an oral "word of power" and probably also as a written one. Similarly, the use of sacred objects, such as the priestly vestments and the high-priestly *ẓiẓ*, for aims and purposes which had little to do with their original cultic functions, builds on the biblical precedents for the uses of the holy and develops them further. A third element, the use of biblical verses, might be a more recent development, but the Ketef Hinnom amulets prove that at least the Priestly Blessing was used in such a manner already in the First Temple period. In the Second Temple period, we find the extensive citation of Psalm 91 in an exorcistic scroll found at Qumran, and the use of biblical phrases in the Delos curses, in Noah's prayer in *Jubilees*, and in the Qumran exorcistic texts.

Two other features of Jewish magic in the Second Temple period magic may have been more recent developments. The appeal to angels, which is echoed in *Tobith* and is apparent in the exorcistic texts, seems to have grown hand in hand with the Jewish demonology and angelology of the last few centuries BCE, but it will remain a permanent fixture of Jewish magic for many centuries to come. Similarly, the attribution of magical lore, and especially magical texts, either to angelic origins (Raphael) or to the biblical heroes (David, Solomon) also is likely to have been a relatively new development, but it too was destined for a long and fruitful existence. Thus, while we cannot perhaps speak of the birth of a Jewish magical tradition until late antiquity, we certainly can say that this tradition had very long roots, going back to the Second Temple period, and in a few instances perhaps even to the First.

CHAPTER 3

Jewish magic in late antiquity – the "insider" evidence

INTRODUCTION

In the previous chapter, we had more than one occasion to note the relative paucity of the sources pertaining to the study of Jewish magic in the Second Temple period. In the next chapters, we move to a later period – roughly from the third to the seventh century CE – a period for which both the "insider" and the "outsider" sources become much more abundant. It is this abundance which makes it possible to separate "insider" from "outsider" evidence, to first study the former on its own (as shall be done in the next two chapters), and then to study the "outsider" accounts and discussions of magic in light of the "insider" evidence (as we shall do in Chapter 6), all of which were simply out of the question in the study of Second Temple period Jewish magic.

Before analyzing the evidence, we must find it. Thus, the present chapter will be devoted to a broad outline of all the "insider" sources, with special emphasis on the relevance and contribution of each type of evidence for the historical analysis of late-antique Jewish magic in Palestine and the Eastern Mediterranean.[1] But before embarking upon our survey, two preliminary notes are in order. First, it is important to recall our suggestion in Chapter 2 that the main reason for the paucity of "insider" evidence for Jewish magical practices in the Second Temple period is that these practices were transmitted mostly orally, and that the magical praxis itself usually did not involve the act of writing. It is with this in mind that we may now note that the most significant characteristic of late-antique Jewish magic – significant especially in terms of our ability to study it – is its *written* nature. This is not to deny, of course, the existence in this period, too, of non-scribal magic (and we shall note some of the evidence for its existence in our survey of

---

[1] For previous surveys, see Alexander 1986; HAITCG, pp. 16–22; Harari 1998, pp. 123–30; Swartz 2006. For what follows, see also Bohak 1996 for a survey of different types of ancient magical texts, accompanied by useful photographs and accessible on the Internet.

the rabbinic sources, in Chapter 6), but such magical practices are almost by definition unattested in the "insider" sources. The spells uttered by the Weird Sisters in Shakespeare's *Macbeth* would leave no archeological remains, and their sizzling cauldron would hardly be recognized as a magical implement by the archeologist who might unearth it. And even when we can securely identify some ancient objects as "magical," we would be hard pressed to demonstrate their Jewish origins. Thus, the sources which we can identify as both "magical" and "Jewish," and which can contribute useful information to our study of Jewish magic, often are those on which a text, or an image, or both, have been inscribed. In the present chapter, we shall survey a wide array of such texts, written on many different materials and displaying great diversity in length, complexity, and quality of execution, but what is common to all of them is that they were committed to writing. We shall have more to say about the possible causes of the scribalization of the Jewish magical tradition in late antiquity in the next chapter. For the time being, we may merely note that were it not for this "literate" aspect of late-antique magic, and for the abundance of "insider" documents, we would have had to focus almost exclusively on the "outsider" sources, and especially the rabbinic corpus, in our reconstruction of late-antique Jewish magic, as was done by Ludwig Blau more than a century ago.

A second important point to remember is that once we distinguish between "outsider" and "insider" evidence, and decide to focus on the latter, a second distinction must be made, this time within the "insider" evidence itself. When looking at the textual remains of ancient magicians whose magical praxis involved much writing, we must distinguish between the recipes which they composed, copied, and used as instructions for carrying out the magical praxis, and between those texts which they produced as a part of the magical praxis itself. We must, in other words, distinguish between recipes, instructions, and blueprints on the one hand, and "finished products," or "applied charms" or "activated spells" on the other. We also must distinguish between different types of "finished products," for even when an amulet and an aggressive spell, for example, look exactly the same in terms of their physical appearance, their contents often make it clear that they were manufactured under different circumstances and used in different manners. Such distinctions are of extreme importance if we are to reconstruct the world in which these "finished products" were in use.

To make this point clearer, let us examine one specific example, by looking at two magical texts from the Cairo Genizah. The first text (on the left, below) is a recipe which is embedded in a large collection of recipes of which a single bifolium survives (apparently the external bifolium, containing the first two and last two pages of the entire booklet), and which has been dated by its editors in the eleventh century. This booklet apparently began with two lists of divine names in acrostics (some of them jumbled), followed by an assorted medley of recipes in Hebrew, Aramaic, and Judeo-Arabic, and ending with a set of recipes entirely consecrated to aggressive magic but clearly stemming from several different sources. It is in this final section that our recipe may be found. The second text (on the right) is found on a strip of vellum from the Cairo Genizah, a strip which contains this text only, written mostly on one side of the page (the other side has the last lines of the text, followed by a blank space). These are, then, two very different *types* of texts, and yet their contents are almost identical, as the following synopsis immediately demonstrates:[2]

<J> To annihilate (someone).
<B, on the margins:> (For) Sickness.
<J> (Take) a sheet of lead and write
on the first hour of the day, and bury it
in a fresh grave:

<A> I adjure you, Anger and Rage and Fury and Wrath and Destroyer, you merciful[3] angels, to destroy all flesh; you, destroy the body of NN from the world, and do not delay him for even one hour.	<A> I adjure you, Anger and Rage, Breaker and Fury and Wrath and Destroyer, you angels who are appointed over destroying all the sons of flesh; you, destroy the body from this world, and do not delay his limbs for (even) one moment.
In the name of GHWDR YH YH WH	In the name of 'BRGTW DDYN YHWH
Sabaot, who created the world in his wisdom and completed the earth in his intelligence, and created the first man from dust, and returned him to dust;	Sabaot, who created the world in his might and completed the earth in his intelligence, and created the first man from dust; he stood and sinned? and returned to dust;
He will give you permission to destroy NN. And the death of NN shall be in this hour of all hours and in this period of all periods. A(men), A(men), S(elah). Hang it.	He will give you permission to destroy the body of this in this hour of all hours and in this period of every period. Amen Amen Selah.

A comparison of the two texts immediately reveals the similarity of their contents, except that the one text begins with ritual instructions, and then

---

[2] See MTKG I, 2 (T-S K 1.56) 2a/6–15 and Mann 1931–35, vol. II, p. 94 (Mosseri VI, 17.2), respectively. Here and throughout, I have used the following signs to mark the linguistic make-up of those Genizah magical texts which use more than one language: <A> = Aramaic; <B> = Arabic; <H> = Hebrew; <J> = Judeo-Arabic.
[3] As was noted by the text's editors, who were unaware of the parallel "finished product," רחמני ("merciful") must be corrected into דממוני ("who are appointed over").

provides the spell to be written, while the other contains only the spell itself. Given what we already noted about the external layout of both texts, it is easy to conclude that the text on the left is a recipe for aggressive magic ("To annihilate"), one of several such recipes in this recipe-book, while the text on the right is a "finished product" aimed against a specific individual, which was executed along the instructions provided by such a recipe. In passing, we may note that at first sight this "finished product" might look like an amulet, but certainly was not one, and was not hung around the client's body as an amulet normally would be; we may also note that this "finished product" clearly was "pre-fabricated," so that all the magician had to do when a curse was needed was to fill the intended victim's name in the appropriate places.[4] But given this assumption, how are we to explain the many differences between the two texts, which also readily emerge from the above synopsis? And how are we to explain the fact that our recipe calls for the engraving of the curse on a *lead* tablet and its burial in a grave, while the curse itself is written on *vellum* and was found in the Cairo Genizah? There are two possible answers to these questions – first, that whoever executed the curse on the right from the recipe on the left was extremely sloppy, or simply took the liberty to alter the text he was copying. This is not impossible, but if this were true, our copyist must have been intelligent enough to detect an error in his recipe, and to correct the entirely inappropriate "merciful angels" into the orthographically similar, and certainly correct, "angels who are in charge of"; such intelligence is not unheard of among medieval Jewish magicians, but is not too common either. Thus, we may opt for a second explanation, namely, that the text on the right indeed was more or less faithfully copied, but not from the recipe on the left; it was copied from a similar recipe, which differed slightly from the one we have here. Whether these differences were the result of some copyists' ignorance and carelessness or of deliberate changes would again be a matter of some speculation, and both types of explanations are quite plausible. Of course, further sifting through other Jewish magical texts, within the Genizah itself as well as outside it, might lead to the discovery of other versions of this recipe, some of which might be closer to the "finished product" on the right; it might also lead to the discovery of other curses based upon our recipe or its textual "relatives." To give just one example from an earlier period and from a non-Jewish context, we may note the case of a recipe for a *defixio* (curse tablet) found in one of the Greek magical

---

[4] As was correctly noted by Mann, 1931–35, vol. II, p. 94, n. 139, who had no knowledge of the parallel recipe.

Jewish magic in late antiquity: "insider" evidence 147

papyri, and to five lead *defixiones* and one inscribed clay pot, all of which show an affinity that clearly proves their interrelations. And yet, no two of the six "finished products" are identical, not even those copied by the same practitioner, for the same client, and in order to obtain the sexual favors of the same victim (!), and none is identical with the text provided by the extant recipe.[5] And when we turn to Jewish examples, we have an ever-growing body of parallel recipes, and of "finished products" which parallel known recipes, all of which provide ample demonstration of the enormous fluidity of the process of copying the magical recipes and producing the "finished products."[6] And once again we must stress that most magicians – ancient and modern, non-Jews and Jews – prove remarkably willing to copy magical texts inaccurately, either through carelessness and ignorance, or through a desire to improve or adapt the materials at their disposal, or both. A prevalent scholarly myth (which is partly based on some late-antique theories of magic) would have us believe that magicians are convinced that for a recipe to work it must be performed accurately, and that they therefore tend to be extremely meticulous in copying their sources. But when we turn from the theory of magic to its actual praxis, as reflected in the magicians' own texts, we cannot help noting that while careful and accurate copying (including even the recording of textual variants in one's parallel sources!) is not unattested, the processes of textual entropy and deliberate adaptations are far more common.[7] Returning to our synopsis, we may note that even the divine name in the spell's very middle is very different in both versions, in spite of the claim of some ancient philosophers and theologians and many modern scholars that the correct pronunciation of such names was the single most important factor determining a spell's success.[8] Many practitioners, it would seem, were much less worried about such issues than we might expect them to have been.

Both the recipe and the curse which we just read deserve much further analysis, and we shall have more to say about them in the present and the subsequent chapter. For the time being, however, let us focus solely on the issue of recipes versus "finished products." Taking our cue from molecular

---

[5] See SM I, 46–51, with an exhaustive treatment in Martinez 1991. See also Jordan 1994a, pp. 123–25 and Gordon 1997, p. 79, n. 61.
[6] For pertinent examples, see Bohak 2005; another example shall be discussed below (the Ḥorvat Rimmon sherds).
[7] This point was stressed by Swartz 1990, pp. 166–67, and HAITCG, pp. 52–53. For copying and editorial mistakes in the PGM, see Brashear 1995, p. 3415; for errors in copying onto "finished products," see SM I, pp. 92, 122, etc., and Faraone 1999, p. 33; for wrong or missing images in illustrated magical texts, see Procopé-Walter 1933, p. 36, n. 4. For Jewish parallels, see below, n. 55.
[8] See esp. Dillon 1985 and Janowitz 2002, pp. 33–43.

biology, we may say that magical recipes are a bit like the DNA of a living organism, containing the information which enables the creation of a new organism, and the mechanism by which to replicate itself. Moreover, just like DNA, some of the longer spells are actually made up of smaller units or "blocks" which could be grouped together in different forms, so that a passage from one recipe or "finished product" bears close resemblance to a passage from another recipe or "finished product," while the remaining parts of the two texts may differ.[9] Finally, just as in biological reproduction, the proliferation of magical recipes and "finished products" is an ideal breeding-ground for mutations, which may occur on two different levels – either when a recipe is deliberately or accidentally altered while being copied in its entirety, or when a recipe is used to produce a "finished object." The end result, just as in the biological sphere, is a potentially endless amount of replication and variation.

With these distinctions in mind, we may turn to a survey of all the "insider" sources at our disposal, that is, all the texts and artifacts produced by the Jewish magicians (for Jewish or non-Jewish clients) in late antiquity, or copied by their intellectual heirs in the Middle Ages, and sometimes even later. We shall survey the actual texts and artifacts produced by Jewish magicians in a chronological and geographical order, beginning with the period before the rise of Islam and looking at the Aramaic and Hebrew magical texts from Palestine and the Eastern Mediterranean and those from Babylonia, and at the Greek magical texts which are likely to be Jewish in origin. We shall then turn to medieval Jewish magical texts – first those preserved in the Cairo Genizah, and then those found in non-Genizah Jewish manuscripts of the medieval and later periods. It must be stressed, however, that in the surveys of both the Babylonian and the medieval magical texts our emphasis will be on what they can teach us about the Jewish magical tradition of late-antique Palestine and the Eastern Mediterranean. It must also be stressed that the following survey is by its very nature incomplete, since it is often difficult to decide which of the sources to leave out of such a survey as too late or as not necessarily Jewish or both, and which to include, and because new sources are being discovered and published all the time.

---

[9] See, e.g., the "finished product" in HAITCG, no. 12 (T-S K 1.152), whose lines 18–32 closely parallel the recipe in MSF, G28 (T-S NS 246.32), p. 4, ll. 7–18 (as was noted by Harari 1998, pp. 197–98); as Ortal Saar told me, this section is partly paralleled by a "finished product," T-S AS 142.256 (unpublished). See also HAITCG, no. 3, where a recipe from K1.24 is almost identical with a section from a curse in K1.42; and see Geller and Levene 1998.

JEWISH MAGICAL TEXTS FROM LATE ANTIQUITY WRITTEN IN ARAMAIC AND HEBREW

When searching for late-antique, i.e., pre-Muslim Jewish magical texts, one encounters at least seven different types of artifacts written in Hebrew or Aramaic – amulets written on metal lamellae, aggressive and erotic spells written on metal lamellae or on clay sherds, magical gems, magical papyri, "literary" books of magic, Babylonian incantation bowls, and inscribed human skulls. Almost all of these texts are "finished products" produced by Jewish magicians, for while the existence of at least some Jewish magical recipe-books in late antiquity is beyond any doubt, these were written mostly on perishable organic materials and therefore disintegrated long ago. Here, as in many other cases, chance factors such as the desire or need to write certain texts on specific materials – some of which happen to be perishable, others quite durable – determined the types of evidence that would survive. However, as the following survey will demonstrate, the quantity and diversity of the extant evidence suffice to give us a good sense of what late-antique Jewish magic looked like, even if the formularies which kept it going are no longer available. Let us, then, closely examine each type of evidence, while focusing especially on their usefulness for a study of late-antique Jewish magic.

Metal amulets

In their groundbreaking study published in 1985, Joseph Naveh and Shaul Shaked edited some fifteen Jewish Aramaic amulets, and noted the existence of six more such texts.[10] But as they soon discovered, the very act of alerting other scholars to the importance of these objects led to an immediate increase in their number. By 1993, the corpus of such amulets grew to more than thirty pieces,[11] and the last decade saw a steady publication of new Jewish Aramaic amulets. The total number of published Jewish amulets from late antiquity now amounts to c. forty specimens, and there are more amulets which are known but have not yet been published.[12] These amulets

---

[10] See AMB, p. 22. All these numbers are, of course, far from exact: A6 is a Syriac amulet, and is not Jewish; A7 has two amulets; A10 is a curse, and not an amulet; MSF, A32 is Christian, and so on.
[11] See MSF, pp. 11–12.
[12] See AMB and MSF; Kotansky 1991a; Kotansky 1991b (republished in Kotansky 1994, no. 56); Kotansky, Naveh, and Shaked 1992; Tsereteli 1996 (republished in Shaked 2006); McCollough and Glazier-McDonald 1996; McCollough 1998; (Naveh 2001 is an aggressive text, discussed below); Naveh 2002b; Müller-Kessler, Mitchell, and Hockey 2007. I am grateful to Joseph Naveh, Shaul Shaked, Ada Yardeni, Zeev Weiss, Steven Fine, Dan Levene, Giuseppe Veltri and David Jordan for information on unpublished amulets.

thus form the largest corpus of late-antique Palestinian Jewish magical texts at our disposal, and a primary source for the study of the Jewish magical praxis of that period and region.[13]

From the perspective of ancient magical praxis, these Aramaic and Hebrew amulets differ little from those amulets which were written by pagans, Christians, and Gnostics. Like them, they were inscribed – usually with a sharp stylus of some sort – on metal *lamellae*, that is, on thin sheets of lead, bronze, silver, or gold, measuring only a few centimeters in width and in length, and usually inscribed on one side of the sheet only (see Figure 3.1).[14] To be used, they were either rolled or (more rarely) folded, placed in a special container (metal tube or box, or a leather/cloth pouch) or wrapped around a cord, and worn around the neck, leg, or some other part of the body (see Figure 3.2).[15] Unfortunately, the few depictions of persons in Jewish art which have survived (Dura Europus, synagogue mosaics, etc.) display no amulet-wearing individuals, but in non-Jewish art (such as the Fayyum mummy portraits) one occasionally sees such amulets worn in the open, and rabbinic literature confirms that in Jewish society, too, an amulet could be worn in public for all to see, and was not considered unlawful or problematic.[16] Thus, the only feature which sets these amulets apart from other amulets at our disposal, and which helps us identify them as stemming from Jewish practitioners, is the fact of their having been written in Aramaic (usually with some Hebrew too) or in Hebrew, and in the square script, which seems to have been used exclusively by Jews.[17] Chronologically, those amulets which were found in controlled excavations seem to date to the fifth and sixth centuries CE, and this gives us a general sense of the likely date of all the amulets whose findspots are unknown (except for those manufactured in our own times by greedy forgers), since they too display no Arabic influence whatsoever. Geographically, those amulets whose provenance is known range all the way from Sicily to Georgia to the Nile Valley, but with a large proportion coming from the Jewish communities in Palestine itself. And as for their archeological contexts, those ancient Jewish amulets whose findspots are known were found either in

---

[13] Note also the gold lamella from Comiso (Sicily) discussed by Calderone 1955; Schmoll 1963; Lacerenza 1998; JIWE I, 156. I have yet to see a sound interpretation of this obscure text, but cannot offer one myself.

[14] For Greek metal amulets, see Kotansky 1991c; Kotansky 1994. For a Mandaic amulet inscribed on *both sides* of a gold lamella (as are all the Mandaic lead tablets as well), see Müller-Kessler 1998a.

[15] For metal amulet-cases, see AMB, pp. 42, 58, 70, and pl. 1, and MSF, pp. 53, 86, and pl. 1.

[16] For mummy portraits of amulet-wearing individuals (which are only a small percentage of all mummy portraits), see the list in Kotansky 1991a, p. 268, n. 5.

[17] Some amulets are written bilingually, partly in Greek and partly in Aramaic or Hebrew, as we shall note at greater length in the following chapter.

Figure 3.1 A bronze amulet, found in Sepphoris. The Aramaic text and the *charactères* are written twice (lines 1–6, 7–12), and as no client name is mentioned in this generic amulet against fever, it may have been "mass produced" in advance. The amulet was photographed from the back, with the photograph flipped over horizontally.

graves (presumably those of their owners), in private homes, or in public spaces; in one case, a cache of amulets was found inside a synagogue – an intriguing find to which we shall return in Chapter 5.[18]

---

[18] For amulets found in tombs, see, e.g., Dahari, Avni, and Kloner 1987, p. 99, and Gudovitch 1996. For the archeological context of amulets in a non-Jewish site, see the illuminating study of Russell 1995.

Figure 3.2 Five of the amulets found in the apse of the synagogue at Ḥorvat Maʿon (near the modern Kibbuẓ Nirim). Note that one has been folded, while the rest have been rolled.

Examining the amulets' actual contents, we may note that virtually all of them were made for what might broadly be called "medical purposes" – either to exorcize demons which were deemed to be afflicting a specific patient, or to prevent any harm from such demons and from the evil eye. The means for securing these goals usually consisted of the adjuration of these malevolent powers to exit the patient's body, or not to enter it at all, and the use of powerful words, signs, and designs, all of which will be discussed in greater detail in the next two chapters. In many cases, it seems clear that a certain amulet was produced from a written formulary, an issue to which we shall return below; some amulets, however, are so short and so simple that they may well have been manufactured from memory, or even on an ad hoc basis. Finally, we may note that while most amulets were made for specific individuals and in order to answer specific needs, some amulets clearly were prefabricated, with the client's name inserted only at the last moment, or without a client's name at all (i.e., a "generic" amulet).[19]

For students of the Jewish magical praxis of late antiquity, these tiny lamellae have one enormous advantage – they form the only substantial body of evidence for late-antique Palestinian Jewish magic which actually

---

[19] For a prefabricated amulet, see, e.g., MSF, A25 (where blank spaces were left in lines 6 and 10 for the insertion of the client's name). For a "generic" amulet (and perhaps even two, which the producer did not separate correctly!), see McCollough and Glazier-McDonald 1996 and McCollough 1998, pp. 270–73 (see Figure 3.1).

stems from late antiquity itself. Thus, any analysis of the activity of Jewish magicians at the time must begin with these contemporary bits of data. It must also be stressed, however, that these amulets suffer from three crippling characteristics, which limit their usefulness for our study. First, many amulets carry a relatively short text, and the texts often are extremely hard to read. Thus, they often deprive us of a sound textual basis, which must be the starting-point for any serious historical enquiry. Second, we must always remember that these amulets give us access to only one type of ancient Jewish magical praxis, namely exorcistic and apotropaic adjurations against demons and the evil eye, and that while this activity certainly was central to the Jewish magical praxis of the time, it was not the only activity practiced by Jewish magicians. Finally, it must be stressed that the amulets at our disposal clearly represent only a small segment even of the amulet-production of late-antique Jews, since most Jewish amulets would have been written on papyrus or on leather. This statement is supported not only by considerations of probability (the latter materials were much cheaper and much easier to write upon) and by comparison with those Greek, Coptic, and Syriac amulets from late antiquity which were written on papyrus or parchment, but also by the explicit statements found in rabbinic literature, to which we shall turn in a subsequent chapter.[20] Unfortunately, those amulets, which would have been much easier to produce and therefore much cheaper to procure, were destroyed long ago by humidity and worms; in some cases, we even find empty amulet-cases, which might indicate that the metal case survived the ravages of time, but the amulet it once contained did not.[21] Thus, it seems quite clear that the amulets which happened to survive represent the "high end" of the ancient market, and the fact that silver and gold foils tend to last longer than those of other metals might have skewed our evidence even further. As far as we know, the amulets written on cheaper (and perishable) materials may have looked quite like those that did survive, but this is something which cannot be taken for granted.

Aggressive and erotic spells

While the defensive and anti-demonic magical practices of late-antique Jews are well represented by the dozens of amulets at our disposal, the more

---

[20] For Greek amulets on papyrus (all preserved by the dry sands of Egypt), see SM. For Syriac amulets on leather (preserved by the metal containers which housed them, and perhaps by having been placed in their owners' tombs), see Gignoux 1987, and Naveh 1997. For Coptic amulets, see Meyer and Smith 1994.
[21] For an empty amulet-case, see Gudovitch 1996 and Saar 2003, pp. 57–58.

aggressive magical practices of these Jews have not fared so well.[22] That they dabbled in aggressive and erotic magic is made clear not only by the numerous recipes found in the Cairo Genizah and displaying much evidence of their late-antique origins, but also by such "outsider" evidence as Epiphanius' detailed story of the young son of Hillel the Patriarch, who, in the days of Constantine, had his friends procure women for him by way of magic rituals and incantations.[23] Unfortunately, Epiphanius does not give an exact description of the rituals involved, but his report of a secret ritual carried out in the cemetery right after sunset sounds very much like what we would expect in such cases. Whether this ritual included the writing down of a text, on a perishable or a non-perishable material, Epiphanius does not say, nor does he hint at the content of the spells and adjurations used, beyond saying that they included the victim's name. Unfortunately, other "outsider" sources are even less helpful on this score.

To learn more about aggressive and erotic Jewish magic, we must turn to the "insider" sources, which are, as we already noted, few and far between. The very fact that such items are so rare is not without significance, especially since it seems to show that Aramaic-speaking magicians did not pick up the habit developed by their Greek colleagues of writing *defixiones*, that is, texts of aggressive magic which were inscribed on thin lead lamellae. This practice, which dates back to Classical Athens, and which can be traced all the way to the sixth or seventh century CE, has assured the survival of many hundreds of Greek curse tablets from every corner of the ancient world, including Palestine itself.[24] It also was adopted by speakers of other languages, as can be seen from the numerous Latin *defixiones* which have survived, and from a handful of Etruscan, Oscan, Celtic, Punic, and Coptic *defixiones*.[25] It is thus interesting to note that at least among the published *defixiones*, even those from Palestine, none are written in Aramaic or in Hebrew, and none are written bilingually, with the Greek text accompanied by at least some Aramaic or Hebrew. While it is no doubt true that the unpublished ones – including some sixty badly mutilated pieces from Caesarea Maritima alone – might prove this generalization wrong, it must

[22] For Jewish aggressive and erotic magic in late antiquity, see esp. Harari 1997b and 2000a.
[23] See Epiphanius, *Panar.* 30.4–8; for this story, see also Rubin 1982; Thornton 1990; Reiner 2004.
[24] For *defixiones*, see esp. Jordan 1985 and 2000; Gager 1992. For published *defixiones* found in Palestine, see Jordan 1985, pp. 191–92 and Gager, nos. 77 and 106; for unpublished *defixiones* found in Palestine, see Jordan 2000, pp. 25–26. I am grateful to Robert Daniel, Yotam Tepper, Yosef Porat, Hannah Cotton, and David Jordan for further information on such *defixiones*. For the supposed curse-tablets from Tell Sandahannah (Maresha), see above, Chapter 2, n. 163.
[25] Punic *defixiones*: Audollent 1904, nos. 213–14 (often republished, see Müller 2000). Celtic ones: Lejeune 1985. Etruscan and Oscan: Dickie 2001, pp. 98, 128–29. Coptic: Meyer and Smith 1994, pp. 202–03.

Jewish magic in late antiquity: "insider" evidence

be noted that among the dozens of published metal lamellae inscribed in Aramaic and Hebrew, only two are not amulets but aggressive magical texts. Moreover, these specific subjugation texts, to which we shall soon return, happen to have been inscribed on bronze, and not on lead. Thus, it seems that although Jews were well aware of the custom of writing aggressive magical texts on lead (as some of the Jewish magical recipes amply demonstrate), they wrote their own curses on other media, mostly of the perishable type, or even recited them orally.[26] Returning to the example with which we opened the present chapter, we may note that there too the recipe calls for incising the curse on a *lead* lamella and burying it in a fresh grave, but the actual specimen which happened to be preserved – and which, it must be stressed, dates to the Middle Ages, not to late antiquity – is written not on lead, but on vellum, and ended up in the Cairo Genizah, and not in the cemetery next door. Why it was that Jewish magicians chose to avoid the manufacturing of lead *defixiones*, even when the recipes at their disposal enjoined this practice, is a vexing question. The answer might lie in a purely technical factor, such as less access to lead, but this seems quite unlikely in light of the presence of Greek *defixiones* on lead from several sites in Palestine. The answer might also lie in some cultural factors which kept Jewish magicians away from this specific practice, but what these factors might be remains an open question.

The first piece of evidence for the aggressive magical practices of the Jews of late antiquity comes from the ancient village of Meroth (in Upper Galilee), in the ruins of an ancient synagogue.[27] At the heart of this intriguing text lies a request to God, that "Just as you have suppressed the sea with your horses and stamped the earth with your shoe," and "just as the sky is suppressed before God, and the earth is suppressed before human beings, and human beings are suppressed before death, and death is suppressed before God, so will the people of this town be suppressed and broken and falling down before Yose son of Zenobia." This is, of course, not an amulet, but the attempt of Yose son of Zenobia to make his fellow townspeople obey his wishes and submit to his desires. The use of magic for social control is something which we repeatedly encounter throughout the present study, and while we cannot say what social circumstances generated this specific

---

[26] For instructions for Jewish *defixiones*, see, e.g., ShR II/63–72 (pp. 84–85 Margalioth): Take a piece of (lead) from the (municipal) cold water-pipe, etc. (see Margalioth's notes to ShR II/63–72, pp. 3–4); see also *Synopse* §617 (*Ḥarba de-Moshe*, shorter version), and *Ḥarba de-Moshe*, p. 44 Harari. Note that the lamella identified by Klein-Franke 1971 as a *tabella devotionis* in fact is just an amulet (below, n. 60).

[27] For the text, see MSF, A16. In addition to the editors' notes there, see Naveh 1985.

appeal, the desire to make an entire community submit to the client's will is easily paralleled in the non-Jewish magical texts of this period.[28] Moreover, the same practice – of writing an aggressive magical text intended to subdue or silence one's opponents within the Jewish community and placing it in a synagogue – seems to be attested by a very fragmentary bronze lamella found in the small synagogue in Bar'am, which adjures the angel Naḥamel ("comfort, console" + -el ending) to "guard the ... of Yudan son of Nonna against the speech of the mouth and the 'singing' (i.e., incantations?) (of) ...".[29] In spite of its fragmentary nature, it seems clear that this too is a text intended to silence one's enemies – and it too was found inside a synagogue. We shall return to the issue of synagogues and magic in Chapter 5, but should already note the possibility that the practice of burying socially aggressive "finished products" in the walls and floors of one's synagogue might partly explain the relative paucity of such finds, both because whenever ancient synagogues were renovated such magical artifacts would have been discovered and discarded and because more such artifacts may still lie buried within the structures of already excavated synagogues. Future research is likely to shed more light on such issues.

An even more intriguing object is presented by a group of five broken pieces of pottery, found in an archeological excavation of the synagogue complex at Ḥorvat Rimmon, in the Northeastern Negev (see Figure 3.3). Stratigraphically dated to the fifth or sixth century CE, these five pieces, when joined together, form a large part of a very interesting erotic spell, which begins by listing six magical names and continues with "You ho[ly...] angels, [I adjure] you, just as [this sherd burns, so shall] the heart of R[achel? daughter of Mar?]in burn after me, I [X son of Y]." The final section is too broken to be reconstructed in its entirety, but the reference to "[shall perform] my desire in this [hour]" is unmistakable. As the attentive reader will note, much of the text of this fragmentary group of sherds has not been preserved, and was supplemented by its modern editors. This reconstruction, however, is made virtually certain by several medieval recipes which parallel the Ḥorvat Rimmon fragments, sometimes almost to the

---

[28] Levine 2000, p. 428, suggests that Yose was a synagogue official seeking to gain the obedience of his congregation, a suggestion which seems to me quite unwarranted.

[29] The text was published by Naveh 2001. On pp. 182–83, Naveh suggests that the root ZMR, which normally means "to sing," here refers to the "evil gaze," a suggestion which was further developed by Ford 2002b, pp. 29–30. However, it is more likely to refer to the words "sung" behind the client's back, and might even be a technical term for magical incantations (cf. the Greek ἐπῳδή or the Latin *incantamentum*, whence English "incantation," still retaining its resemblance to "chant"). Note also the appearance of זמורה in AMB, A1, l. 16, as an apparent parallel with לוחשה, and cf. TK Shabbat, p. 97, with further references.

Figure 3.3 Clay sherds from Ḥorvat Rimmon, with an erotic spell, incised on wet clay which was then thrown into a fire (the right-hand fragment belongs below the other four, at some distance). Recipes for the production of this specific spell have been continuously transmitted from late antiquity to the twentieth century. Note the *charactêres*, and the "cartouches" surrounding the angel-names (lines 1–2).

letter.[30] Such parallels also aid in reconstructing the entire ritual which these fragments represent, in which the erotic spell was inscribed on a piece of unbaked clay which was then burned in a fire or kiln. The sympathetic nature of the ritual is made explicit by the adjuration itself, "just as this sherd burns, so will the heart of NN" – whose name, of course, cannot be reconstructed from the Genizah recipes which parallel this "finished product" – burn in love or desire for the client who ordered this ritual, and whose name too is irretrievably lost. And here, too, we must note how a peculiar feature of our ritual – that the text was incised upon wet clay and then fired, rather than being written upon a potsherd (or a piece of papyrus, vellum, or cloth) with ink, inadvertently assured its preservation and facilitated its identification as a magical text. And given the enormous popularity of this recipe, which is continuously documented for a millennium and a half, it

[30] For the text, see AMB, A10 and MSF, G22 (T-S Misc. 27.4.11), 1/8–16. In addition to the editors' notes there, see Naveh 1996, pp. 454–56. I hope to adduce all the parallel recipes in a forthcoming study.

would not be surprising if more such "finished products" become available in the future.

In addition to these three artifacts, one should also mention a recently published text said to have been found in the vicinity of Nazareth.[31] It is a well-preserved Aramaic inscription, incised onto wet clay which was smeared over a carefully cut potsherd, and contains an interesting counter-spell. In this text, God himself is asked to "upturn the magic spells of Neḥemiah son of Elisheva and of Jonathan son of Elisheva and of every evil magician," a request that is followed by further details concerning the spells which must be annulled. If this artifact is not a modern forgery, it is noteworthy for the unique form of writing on a clay-coated sherd, for the appeal to God Himself to take care of such trivialities, and for the many parallels between this spell and a Geonic-period Babylonian-Jewish magical text known as the *Havdala de-Rabbi Akiva*.[32] If it is a forgery (clearly produced after Scholem's 1981 edition of the *Havdala*-text, and borrowing the name Elisheva-Elisabeth, and several other elements, from the New Testament), its usefulness would lie mainly in reminding us of one more uncertainty pertaining to the study of ancient Jewish magic: the growing interest in such artifacts, and the entry into this market of some very rich private collectors, also spells a stronger incentive for fabricating "ancient" Jewish magical texts.[33] In the study of ancient Jewish magic, we may fully trust texts and artifacts found in controlled excavations carried out by competent and reliable archeologists, and lend much credence to those which have been lying in museums for a long time (i.e., either excavated or acquired at a time when the market value of Aramaic and Hebrew magical texts was too low to encourage forgeries, and when knowledge of such texts was too crude to allow sophisticated forgeries which would still seem authentic today) or which can be shown through other means (such as parallels with unpublished Genizah fragments, which could not have been accessible to any forgers) to be authentic. In all other cases, however, we must exercise extreme caution before taking unprovenanced artifacts as solid evidence for the study of ancient Jewish magic.

Magical gems, rings, and pendants

One of the most widely attested magical activities in late antiquity is the production of magical gems. Although such gems must have been quite

---

[31] Hamilton 1996.
[32] Cf. Scholem 1980/81, pp. 277–78 with lines 6–11 of the Nazareth counter-spell.
[33] For another pertinent example, see Naveh 1982.

Jewish magic in late antiquity: "insider" evidence 159

expensive (even when the stones used were not rare ones, the workmanship must have cost much more than the production of papyrus amulets or even metal ones) and therefore less common than cheaper amuletic devices, the durability of the materials ensured their preservation over the centuries, and it is estimated that around 5,000 late-antique magical gems are extant in dozens of collections worldwide. These gems, which in previous generations were wrongly labeled "Gnostic," usually contain a variety of magic designs and/or *voces magicae* and powerful formulae, and sometimes also a specification of the aim for which they were produced ("For the stomach," "Digest!," "For hip(-pain)s," etc.). In the next section of this chapter, we shall look more closely at some of the pagan Greek magical gems, but for the moment we may focus on those magical gems that can be said to have been manufactured by Jews or according to designs provided by Jewish magicians. And, once again, it turns out that geographic provenance is no indicator of ethnic affiliation. When we examine the magical gems found in Caesarea Maritima, Tel Dor, Maẓubah, and elsewhere in Palestine, we repeatedly realize that these gems are in no way different from those found elsewhere in the late-antique Roman world. Like the *defixiones* found in Palestine, to which we already had occasion to refer, the magical gems found there display the same mixture of Egyptian and Greek deities and symbols, and of Egyptian, Greek, Jewish, and non-linguistic *voces magicae* that characterizes late-antique magical gems as a whole.[34] Such finds certainly raise the possibility that Jews, too, made use of these gems, but they also make the quest for magical gems manufactured by Jews or according to Jewish designs much more difficult.

Looking for Jewish symbols and iconography on ancient magical gems, we find two different types of evidence.[35] On the one hand, we may point to a small group of gems and rings which carry the sign of the Menorah, the seven-branched candelabrum, some of which may securely be identified as amuletic in nature.[36] It is interesting to note, however, that in the thousands of pagan magical gems which are extant the Menorah never appears as a magic symbol, not even on those gems which incorporate Jewish divine and

---

[34] For pertinent examples, see Hamburger 1968 and Manns 1978 (both of which contain some magical gems); Gitler 1990 (gem no. 1); Dauphin 1993; Bohak 1997 and Kotansky 1997; note also the broken gem mis-published by Ovadiah and Mucznik 1996.
[35] Note also Morton Smith's attempts to identify biblical scenes on magical gems (Smith 1981); having examined myself all the gems in question (which are now available in Michel 2001), I am unconvinced by most of his interpretations. Equally problematic is the attempt of Mastrocinque 2002, to connect one magical gem with the Jewish exegetical tradition, especially when a Christian interpretation seems far more convincing.
[36] For such gems, see Goodenough 1953–68, vol. II, pp. 217–22, and Hachlili 2001, pp. 109, 188, 341–47, 433, 435, 436. And cf. the example studied below, n. 46.

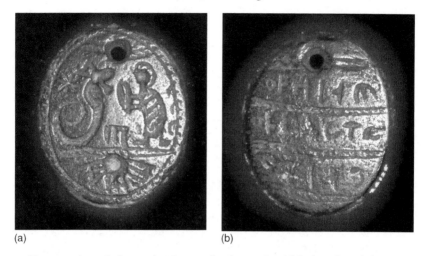

Figure 3.4 A magical gem, showing, on the obverse, Daniel feeding the Babylonian snake-god; on the reverse, a quasi-alphabetic inscription. This is one of a series of similar gems with scenes from the Hebrew Bible, the Apocrypha, and the New Testament, all probably produced by a Christian workshop in late-antique Syria.

angelic names, while the handful of magical gems which display this Jewish symbol sport none of the images which are so common on the pagan magical gems. Thus, even these few pieces highlight the gulf between the Jewish and the pagan magical gems, which shall become even more apparent below. On the other hand, there are several series of ancient magical gems which carry scenes based upon the biblical and apocryphal stories, and especially the binding of Isaac, Solomon mounted on a horse and spearing a prostrate female demon, Daniel in the lions' den, Daniel feeding the Babylonian snake-god (see Figure 3.4), or the maritime adventures of Jonah.[37] It seems, however, that all these gems stem from Christian workshops (which also produced gems with such scenes as the raising of Lazarus or Jesus and the twelve Apostles), and there is not even a single specimen that may securely be identified as Jewish.[38] This, however, is an issue to which we shall return below.

---

[37] Isaac: see esp. Finney 1995 and Michel 2001, nos. 461–62; Solomon: see esp. Walter 1989–90 and Michel 2001, nos. 430–50, with further bibliography; Daniel: Bonner 1950, p. 222 (lions' den) and p. 225 (*Bel and Draco*, which Bonner does not recognize; and cf. Michel 2001, no. 465); Jonah: see esp. Bonner 1948 and 1950, pp. 227–28, with Michel 2001, no. 464. For all these types, see also Goodenough 1953–68, vol. II, pp. 222–35, and Goodnick Westenholz 2000, pp. 58–63 and 124–29.

[38] These gems are discussed in Spier 2007; I am grateful to the author for pre-print copies of some of his work.

One type of magical gem which may securely be identified as Jewish is that displaying Hebrew or Aramaic inscriptions. Unfortunately, a detailed survey of a staggering number of magical gems in dozens of collections recently concluded by Jeffrey Spier resulted in a surprisingly modest list of Hebrew and Aramaic magical gems – no more than a dozen pieces at the most. Thus, one may compare the absence of Aramaic-language *defixiones* with the almost total absence of Aramaic magical gems, an absence whose wider implications shall be discussed in a subsequent chapter. For the time being, we must note one further difficulty in the study of Hebrew magical gems, namely, the popularity of Jewish and pseudo-Jewish exotica among the Christian Hebraists and Kabbalists of the Renaissance and early modern period, a popularity which occasionally led to the manufacture of "authentic" Hebrew antiquities, including some engraved gems.[39] Thus, even the gems which do carry Hebrew or Aramaic inscriptions are not necessarily ancient, and each gem must be closely examined in its own right.[40]

All these difficulties notwithstanding, some magical gems inscribed in Hebrew letters certainly date back to late antiquity and clearly belong in the same magical tradition as the other sources surveyed in the present chapter. Let us look at some examples:

(a) A bilingual gem (cornelian) bought in Smyrna and said to have come from Ephesus sports a long Greek inscription on one side: "O heaven-form, darkness-form, sea-form and all-shape, eternal, leader of myriads, leader of thousands, inconceivable, at whose sides stand myriads of angels, eternally living Adônaios, for you are the One who Is; ET BOS GAR DAK AS OF ZA AS TAN IAN CHAL."[41] In and of itself, this long string of divine epithets certainly would not have marked the gem as necessarily Jewish, even if it so happens that two of these, "heaven-form" and "sea-form," in fact appear in one of the few PGM recipes which may be identified as Jewish (see below), and even if both Adônai(os) and "the One who Is" are evidently Jewish.[42] What follows these epithets, however, is a slightly garbled version of the *atbash* series, the result of writing the Hebrew alphabet in a way parallel to an English series AZBYCXDW, etc.; in this case, each pair of letters was made into a "word" by adding vowels between the consonants,

---

[39] For these Renaissance objects, see, e.g., Schwab 1892; Ahrens 1916.
[40] I note, for example, the curious piece published by Goodenough 1958 and discussed by Kahn *et al.* 1959, which does not seem to fit what we know about ancient Jewish magic.
[41] See Keil 1940, and the brief notes of Scholem 1987, p. 29, n. 48; IJO II, Magica1; Spier 2007, no. 961.
[42] For οὐρανοειδῆ and θαλασσοειδῆ, see PGM IV.3063–64 (as noted already by Keil 1940). Both epithets are not found elsewhere in the PGM.

so as to make the equivalent of AZ BY CeX DoW, and so on. And when we turn the gem over, we find a long inscription in Hebrew letters, including the *Ehyeh Asher Ehyeh* formula (which in the Septuagint was translated into Greek as "the One who Is," which we saw on the Greek side of the gem), the full *atbash* series, a citation of Dt 28.57, the name "Israel," and other words which have yet to be deciphered. While the authenticity of this gem cannot be taken for granted, all the components which have been identified – the *Ehyeh* formula, the *atbash* series, and the use of Dt 28 (a favorite chapter for Jewish magicians of all times) – are well attested in ancient Jewish magic, and the gem certainly deserves a more thorough analysis than had been given it so far.[43]

(b) A gem once in the Reifenberg collection presents seven lines of Hebrew letters and a small depiction of the "hand of God" motif (also known from other Jewish artistic media, such as synagogue mosaics), all enclosed within an *ouroboros*.[44] The inscription is hard to make out, as the letter forms hardly resemble what one normally finds on less difficult writing surfaces. The first two and a half lines, however, clearly add up to a magical formula (here spelled '*GRYT MRTY PLL ZYBH*) which appears on some of the Palestinian amulets, on one ring inscribed in Greek (see Figure 3.5), and in medieval Jewish magical texts, both in the Cairo Genizah and in non-Genizah manuscripts.[45] The gem's authenticity and its connections with the other sources surveyed in this chapter therefore are in no doubt, as no forger would have been familiar with a magic formula which has only recently been identified on other objects produced by Jewish magicians in late antiquity and the early Middle Ages. Unfortunately, the rest of the inscription does not add up to any coherent text, and is not paralleled by any other ancient magical text, but the presence of bizarre and unparalleled "magic words" is so common on ancient magical gems as to cause no surprise. Here too, however, a re-examination of the gem might yield more satisfactory results.

(c) A gem in the British Museum carries a Menorah on one side, a Hebrew inscription on the other, which may tentatively be read as "L'KYM / L'KR- / L'RSY / L'ZZ-"-."[46] When read in this manner, the inscription makes no

---

[43] For the *atbash* sequence, see also MSF, A28, but as this amulet was first published by Montgomery in 1911, it does not prove the authenticity of Keil's gem.

[44] See Reifenberg 1950, p. 143; Goodenough 1953–68, vol. II, p. 219 and vol. III, no. 1024; Spier 2007, no. 956.

[45] For this formula, see Bohak 2001, pp. 126–29, and note its citation (from MS British Museum 752) by Scholem 1963, p. 257 (read by Scholem as ללווּבה מראוּתך נירת או). Its presence on the Reifenberg gem was brought to my attention by Jeffrey Spier.

[46] See Goodenough 1953–68, vol. II, p. 221; Smith 1981, p. 191 and Michel 2001, no. 473 (all of whom fail to read the inscription correctly).

Figure 3.5 A bronze amuletic ring, showing a holy rider spearing a prostate female demon. The Greek inscription surrounding consists solely of "magic words," but the exact same formula appears in some Aramaic and Hebrew magical texts. This amulet is either Christian or Jewish.

sense whatsoever, but when read from left to right (or, in the English transliteration, from right to left), it yields some sense – the first line is "Michael," the third is "Israel," and the other two probably contain angel names, such as Raphael, and perhaps even Azazel or Azael.[47] While the authenticity of this gem is far from certain, it is at least possible that a Jewish magician created the basic design, which a non-Jewish gem-cutter then produced, but incised the letters in reverse order. It also is quite possible that the inscription was deliberately written in a retrograde manner, as this mode of writing is well attested in ancient (Jewish and non-Jewish) magic.[48]

(d) A broken gem found in Caesarea Maritima carries a lion on one side, and a Hebrew inscription, ". . . -LWM / YWN-," on the other.[49] The lion was a common motif in Jewish synagogue art, and even in such

---

[47] And cf. Spier 2007, no. 953, who has independently reached the same reading as that offered here, but reads the last line as L'YRB'G-, i.e., "-Gabriel."
[48] For retrograde writing, see Naveh 1988 and Faraone 1991, pp. 7–8.
[49] See Hamburger 1968, p. 16 and no. 115.

magical texts as *Sepher ha-Razim* (see below), and the first legible word of this inscription could easily be read as *shalom*, "Peace." Thus, it is quite possible that this is a Jewish amulet, but here too no certain conclusions may be reached.[50]

Looking at these four gems, to which a few more could be added, we may note that the overall number of such gems clearly is very small, and that this fact is not due to the decay of the ancient artifacts. Magical gems are engraved on extremely durable surfaces, which is why so many of them have survived. And if a corpus of c. 5,000 ancient magical gems yields only a dozen specimens written in Hebrew or Aramaic, it is a sure sign that practitioners within that linguistic tradition generally avoided producing magical gems (or turning to professional gem-cutters with designs to be executed), and preferred other scribal media instead. Whether they did so as a matter of cultural preferences, or for purely technical reasons, is an issue to which we shall return in Chapter 5.

Before leaving the issue of Aramaic and Hebrew magical gems, two further notes are called for, on one type of amulet that apparently *was* produced by late-antique Jewish magicians and several types that apparently *were not*. Looking at the many glass-paste pendants found in Syria and northern Israel, we note the recurrence of pagan and Christian motifs, but also of some Jewish elements, such as the Menorah, and of elements which *could* be attributed to Jewish artisans, such as lions and stars. And as the amuletic use of some of these pendants is hardly in doubt, it would seem that here too we have some access to amulets manufactured by Jews in late antiquity.[51] But when we turn to the many bronze rings, pendants, and bracelets of various shapes and sizes which display biblical scenes and Greek inscriptions, they seem to be Christian rather than Jewish. We shall return to these objects below, but for the time being we must note the paucity of similar artifacts with Aramaic or Hebrew inscriptions. In a few rare cases, bronze or silver pendants with Hebrew or Aramaic inscriptions do surface up in the antiquities market, but there has been no attempt to gather them together and assess their authenticity; they may be ancient, but they also might belong to a later period, or even to present-day forgers.[52] Similarly, while many Samaritan bronze pendants and rings, as well as one Samaritan

---

[50] And cf. CIJ II, 875 = IJO III, Syr20, for a gem with a bilingual inscription and the image of a man raising his hands.

[51] For the evidence, see Spaer 2001, pp. 170–90, esp. 173–76 (by Dan Barag). I am grateful to Ortal Saar for this reference.

[52] For a pertinent example, see Wolfe and Sternberg 1989, no. 46. See also CIJ II, 874 = IJO III, Syr27, for a bronze pendant with a common magical iconography and a Greek inscription, as well as the Hebrew word *shalom*, "peace."

Jewish magic in late antiquity: "insider" evidence 165

bracelet and one gem have been found, almost all of which contain biblical verses in the Samaritan script and clearly served as amuletic devices, there seem to be no Jewish parallels to these objects.[53] The same seems to apply to oil-lamps with magical inscriptions, for which the Christian and Samaritan specimens are not paralleled by Jewish artifacts.[54] In each of these categories, a more thorough search for evidence certainly would be most welcome, but it does seem as if the Jewish magicians of late antiquity tended to shun some forms of amuletic devices, perhaps because they became firmly associated with the magical practices of rival religious groups, and perhaps for some other reasons, but much further research will be needed before we can reach any definite conclusion on this score.

Aramaic magical papyri

As we already noted, the Aramaic amulets to which we now have access are those which happened to be preserved because of the non-organic materials on which they were inscribed, while those amulets that were written on perishable organic materials had perished long ago. This is all the more so for ancient collections of magical recipes, which, because of their greater length, must have been written especially on such perishable materials as papyrus and vellum. That such Jewish formularies did in fact exist can be inferred not only from a comparison with the finds from Roman and Byzantine Egypt (such as the Greek magical papyri), but also from several pieces of data provided by the "finished products" that did survive. First, the close parallels between some of the "finished products" of late antiquity (and especially the erotic sherds from Ḥorvat Rimmon) and recipes from the Cairo Genizah and elsewhere show the latter recipes to be copies of copies of recipes which are at least as old as the artifacts they parallel. Second, at least one late-antique Jewish amulet seems to contain sections mistakenly copied by its producer from the recipe in front of him, quite a common occurrence in pagan magic as well.[55] Third, some of the magical recipes

---

[53] The Samaritan amulets have repeatedly been collected, the fullest and most recent list being Reich 2002. See also Pummer 1987.
[54] For such oil-lamps, see Naveh 2002c, on pp. 379–81.
[55] See Kotansky, Naveh, and Shaked 1992, pp. 9 and 18, where a section inadvertently copied from the recipe's instructions reads כתוב בפטיקן, i.e., "write on a πιττάκιον" (for this common loanword, see Krauss 1898–99, pp. 441–42). In the Greek section of the same amulet, a section inadvertently copied from the recipe's instructions reads "if possible, on fine linen; if not, on a strip of linen" – Kotansky, Naveh, and Shaked 1992, pp. 9 and 21–22. (Note also that at least in the second case, and probably in both, the instructions demand the use of a perishable material as a writing surface.) For mistakenly copying parts of the recipe unto the "finished product," see also MSF, A30, lines 7–8, with Naveh 1996, p. 457. For non-Jewish examples, see above, n. 7, and cf. n. 171 below.

in the Cairo Genizah can be shown – by virtue of the Greek loanwords, *voces magicae*, magic signs, and other elements they contain – to be copies of copies of late-antique originals. Thus, the existence of Jewish magical recipe-books in late antiquity is virtually secure. Unfortunately, the Judean Desert has not yet produced any late-antique Jewish magical texts (though it did preserve some non-Jewish ones, as well as the Qumran texts, as noted in Chapter 2), and even the dry sands of Egypt, which preserved an abundant supply of Greek and Coptic magical papyri and a fair amount of Demotic ones, have so far produced only a very small number of Aramaic and Hebrew magical papyri.[56] This is hardly surprising, however, given the history of the Jewish communities of Roman Egypt. Crushed in the great revolt of 115–17 CE, the Greek-speaking Jews of Egypt have left few traces in the papyrological remains of the Roman period. Only from around the fourth century CE can we begin to sense the gradual re-emergence of an Egyptian-Jewish community, including the use of Aramaic and Hebrew texts and documents. It is within the small corpus of c. 200 fragments of Aramaic and Hebrew papyri (compared with tens of thousands of Greek papyri for the same period) that we must look for magical texts, a quest that is exacerbated by the abysmal state of preservation of many of these fragments, often too small and too mutilated to allow a certain identification of their contents or nature.[57]

With all these caveats in mind, let us examine three specific instances of Jewish magical papyri, and see what they might contribute to the study of Jewish magic in late antiquity:

(a) A small fragment, found in Oxyrhynchus and containing twelve mutilated lines in Aramaic (the verso is blank).[58] The securely readable portion contains an adjuration of a demon "by the pupil of the eye of your father [She]mhaza? who fell into [ ]" (a reference to the story of the Fallen Angels?),[59] and, two lines later, "for/to a dog that bit someone." Mark Geller, the text's most recent editor, sees it as a fragment of a collection of recipes, the extant portion preserving the end of one recipe (the adjuration), the title of another (for a dog-bite), and perhaps even the beginning of a third recipe.

---

[56] For broad surveys of the Greek, Coptic, and Demotic magical papyri, see Brashear 1995, Pernigotti 1995, and Ritner 1995b, respectively. For the Aramaic ones, see Brashear 1995, p. 3428.

[57] The most comprehensive catalogue of these fragments is Sirat 1985.

[58] Bodleian Heb. d83(P) S. C. 37016. Ed. pr. in Cowley 1915, p. 212 and pl. XXVIII; republ. by Geller 1985 (with a line drawing, but no photograph). See also Sirat 1985, p. 121, and pl. 76.

[59] My reading follows Geller's except for reading his קיחא as [שמ]חזא. For a similar formulation in a Genizah magical text, see T-S NS 322.87 (unpublished): "I adjure you by the name [ ]name of Shemhazai your father." Unfortunately, much of the Genizah page is torn off, so it is hard to reconstruct the missing parts.

Jewish magic in late antiquity: "insider" evidence 167

This is quite possible, but both the format of this fragment and the fold lines it displays argue more for its use as an amulet. And yet, while the exact meaning and function of this text will only be clarified by further study, and especially by the search for parallels in the other Jewish magical texts of late antiquity and the Middle Ages, its importance for the present survey lies in its very existence. Together with one of the Aramaic metal amulets, which is said to have been found in Oxyrhynchus, it provides valuable evidence for the activity there of Aramaic-speaking Jewish magicians sometime in the fifth or sixth centuries CE.[60]

(b) A second set of Aramaic magical fragments – five in all – is of a potentially greater significance. It was found (in an unknown location) as part of a "multilingual magical workshop," containing several fragments of a Coptic magical codex (with some pages remarkably well preserved), thirteen fragments of Greek magical papyri (both recipes and "finished products"), and five Aramaic fragments, most of which may safely be classified as magical.[61] Unfortunately, the Aramaic fragments have been published in an entirely inadequate manner, and the photographs provided by their first and only editor are mostly illegible.[62] But while the exact contents of these small fragments are yet to be established, they may securely be dated to the fifth or early sixth century CE, as were their Coptic and Greek fellow travelers. And when we read on one fragment the Tetragrammaton, YHWH (written, we may note, not in the Paleo-Hebrew script, but in the square script), and on another the abbreviation A(men) A(men) S(elah) at the end of one textual unit, we know for sure that we are dealing with Jewish magical texts, and with the remains of at least one collection of Aramaic Jewish magical recipes from late antiquity. Moreover, as two of the fragments have Aramaic on one side, Greek on the other – including not only Hallelujah, but also *baroch sêmo*, which is a transliteration of the Hebrew for "Blessed be His Name" – we know that some of the Jewish participants in this "international" workshop worked in both languages, an issue to which we shall return in the following chapter. Thus, while the fragments in question are exasperatingly small, they provide hard evidence for the circulation of Jewish magical formularies in late antiquity. More important, perhaps,

---

[60] See Klein-Franke 1971 (republished as AMB, A9). For another amulet which probably was found in Egypt, see Kotansky, Naveh, and Shaked 1992, said to have come from Tell el-Amarna. Such amulets may, of course, have been manufactured elsewhere, and brought to Egypt by their owners.

[61] For the Aramaic fragments (not mentioned in Sirat 1985!), see Marrassini 1979; for the other fragments in this "packet," see Pernigotti 1979 and 1993 and Maltomini 1979. For their possible place of origin, see Pernigotti 1979, pp. 44–46. The Greek fragments have been translated in Betz 1986 as PGM CXXIII–CXXV and re-edited as SM II, 96–98.

[62] I am grateful to Prof. Claudio Gallazzi for sending me good photographs of these fragments.

they provide an interesting perspective on the transfer of pagan, Jewish, and Christian magical technologies across ethnic, religious, and cultural boundaries, an issue to which we shall soon return.

(c) The last fragment to be discussed here is the smallest, but by no means the least intriguing. It is a tiny scrap of papyrus, on whose recto are extant only the broken remains of two lines of Hebrew text – "[char]iots of the Holy One with . . . in the voice of the *ophanim*."[63] In spite of its small dimensions, the general contents of this text are clear enough – it deals with the music and liturgy of the angels and other heavenly servants (including the *ophanim* – originally the wheels of God's chariots as described by Ezekiel, but subsequently conceived as heavenly creatures endowed with attributes of their own) in God's heavenly palaces.[64] As such, this fragment could easily have come from some ancient *piyyut* or from a Hekhalot-type text, the topic being a favorite one in both genres, or, a far more intriguing possibility, from the kind of divine liturgy texts we find among the Dead Sea Scrolls. What is unusual about this fragment, however, is that its verso contains the remains of two lines of *charactêres* and the "frames" in which they were encapsulated. It is, of course, not impossible that the two sides were written by different people and in different cultural contexts, but this seems quite unlikely. Thus, we must consider the intriguing possibility that this description of the divine liturgy was quite like the hymns of praise for God and His angels found in some Genizah magical texts and in *Sepher ha-Razim*. Here too, in other words, a small papyrus fragment from late-antique Egypt might corroborate what we know from the other sources at our disposal.

These, then, are the most significant Aramaic and Hebrew magical papyri which are currently available. They are, of course, extremely few and painfully fragmentary, but their significance lies in their very existence, for they clearly show that not only Palestine, but Egypt too, and presumably many other places where Jews lived, had centers of Jewish magical activity in Aramaic and Hebrew in late antiquity. They also give us some sense of the kinds of cross-cultural cooperation between non-Jewish and Jewish magicians which is one of the hallmarks of late-antique magic, and provide the only direct access we currently have to the actual recipe books used by Jewish magicians at the time. Finally, the chance survival of these fragments leaves much room for hope that new and more substantial pieces will

---

[63] Paris, Louvre, Département des antiquités islamiques E7020, for which see Sirat 1985, p. 106 and Planches 32 and 33. The text reads: ‏[בות קדוש עם | בקול אופנים‎]‏ / . The most likely reconstruction would be ‏מרכבות‎, but other words (‏להבות, ערבות‎) cannot be ruled out.

[64] For the *ophanim*, see Halperin 1988, pp. 45–47 and passim; Olyan 1993, pp. 34–41.

be identified and published. Just as the focus on Aramaic metal amulets led to the identification of more such amulets, so the focus on Aramaic magical papyri might lead to the discovery and publication of more such texts.

"Literary" books of magic

One of the most important types of sources for the study of ancient Jewish magic is what we might call "literary" books of magic, that is, books which give instructions for magical practices but frame them within a larger literary structure. Unlike the many Genizah formularies to which we shall soon turn, in which the magical recipes are simply listed one after the other in an accumulative manner, the following books may indeed be called "books" in the more usual sense of the word. They have a beginning, an end, and a logical inner structure, into which the recipes themselves are somewhat artificially embedded. As we shall soon see, the structure differs from one example to the next, but the decision to enclose the magical instructions in a larger literary framework is common to all these books, and to a few others as well, and sets them apart from the structureless magical formularies.

The "bookish" nature of these texts has some important implications, which must be considered before we examine each work in greater detail. First, it raises complex questions about the authorship and composition of these works, problems which are hardly relevant when it comes to slowly accumulating and ever-changing formularies of the type we shall examine next. Each of these works must have had an original author who thought up the underlying literary structure and arranged the magical materials accordingly. Moreover, this kind of process raises the issue of the sources used by each of these authors, for unless we assume that both the literary frame and the recipes were written *de novo* by a single author – and as we shall see, this is unlikely in each of these cases – we must postulate an author who took existing literary materials, or existing recipes, or both, and refashioned them to suit his own taste and needs. Trying to detect, analyze, and date such processes is a very risky endeavor, as will be readily admitted by any student of other strands of ancient Jewish or Christian literature, from the "books" of Enoch to the apocryphal Gospels and Acts. Second, unlike the formularies, which were owned by individuals, copied haphazardly by others, and often discarded after their owners' deaths, the texts in question here are literary pieces which were often copied by scribes and underwent the same transformations undergone by other pieces of ancient popular literature. Later editors could abridge, expand, or re-arrange such works, and as they were copied in many different locations and in different periods, they survive in manuscripts of different times and places, which often present a great deal of recensional variation. In such circumstances, the quest for each text's "original" version is a difficult, or impossible, undertaking.

Of the handful of books of ancient Jewish magic whose names have come down to us, only two – *Sepher ha-Razim* and *Ḥarba de-Moshe* – are extant in their entirety (though not necessarily in their original versions), and it is to these two texts that we now turn. We shall then turn to the *Testament of Solomon*, a Christian work which is of some importance for the study of late-antique Jewish magic. In a subsequent section of this chapter, we shall have occasion to mention a few more Jewish books of magic, which are either too late to be included in the present chapter or too vaguely known at present to allow a detailed analysis of their contents or their possible origins.

Sepher ha-Razim

"This is one of the books of the mysteries given to Noah, the son of Lamech . . . by the angel Raziel in the year when he entered the ark, before his entry." Thus begins *Sepher ha-Razim* ("The Book of the Mysteries"), an ancient book of Jewish magic which was virtually ignored by students of Jewish culture until it was painstakingly reconstructed from its scattered remains by Mordechai Margalioth.[65] This book is mentioned by the Geonim and the Karaites (see below), but no copy of the text as it existed at that period is extant today. What has survived are a few dozen Genizah fragments of various sections of the book, in its Hebrew original and in Judeo-Arabic, a few dozen medieval and later manuscripts containing parts or all of a much-corrupted version of the Hebrew text, an Arabic translation of unknown date, a late Latin translation, and even a Hebrew version which is partly based on a retranslation from Latin.[66] Confronted with such assorted pieces of data, Margalioth's pioneering edition provided a text as good as was possible with the textual evidence at his disposal. But given the deficiencies of his edition, a Berlin research team headed by Peter Schäfer is currently busy identifying as many additional Genizah fragments and medieval and later manuscripts as possible, in order to provide a more reliable textual basis for further work on the earliest version of this important

---

[65] For the Hebrew text, see Margalioth 1966; for an English translation, see Morgan 1983.
[66] See Margalioth 1966, pp. 47–55. The existence of an Arabic version was brought to my attention by Alexander Fodor, and see now Fodor 2006.

Jewish magic in late antiquity: "insider" evidence

book.⁶⁷ But while the new edition might offer many new insights into the book's textual and editorial history and into the exact readings of many individual passages, the overall structure of the book is likely to remain that reconstructed by Margalioth. Let us therefore begin with this basic structure.

Following a brief preface, which stresses the book's angelic origin and lists the various biblical figures who supposedly used it – and both items certainly served to legitimate the book's contents in the eyes of its Jewish readers – comes a detailed description of the seven heavens.⁶⁸ For each of the heavens, there is a description of its appearance and inner structure, and lists of the angels found in each section of each heaven, together with the "minister" or "overseer" who is in charge of them. As each commanding angel and his group of underlings are in charge of specific tasks, the lists of angel names are invariably followed by recipes with practical instructions on how to make these angels fulfill one's needs in the sphere which is their field of practice. Thus, to give just one example, the first heaven has seven "camps," the fourth of which is commanded by the overseer KLMYYH, who has some forty-four angels serving under him – 'BRYH, 'YMRHY, DMN'Y, 'MNHR, and so on; they are all in charge of entertaining kings and grandees and granting grace and charm to whoever approaches them in purity. Thus, "If you wish to turn the king's mind favorably towards you, or that of the minister of the army . . . or the heart of an important or rich woman, or the heart of a beautiful woman," you must perform an elaborate ritual which includes slaughtering a lion cub with a bronze knife, mixing its blood with wine and aromatics, standing before the planet Venus, mentioning the name of the overseer (i.e., KLMYYH) and all his underlings, and reciting an elaborate adjuration. "And when you finish reciting this adjuration twenty-one times, look upwards and you shall see something like a flame of fire descending into the blood and the wine." This is followed by variants of this recipe for related cases (if you wish to go before the king, you should use the blood and wine in the X manner; if you want to win the public's favor, you should use the lion cub's heart in the Y manner), and by a second recipe, with different ingredients and instructions, intended to win over the heart of a great or rich woman.⁶⁹

---

⁶⁷ For useful discussions of *Sepher ha-Razim*, see Margalioth 1966, pp. 1–62; Niggemeyer 1975; Gruenwald 1980, pp. 225–34; Alexander 1986, pp. 347–50; Janowitz 2002, pp. 85–108; Alexander 2003b.
⁶⁸ For this common technique, see Swartz 1994; see also Montgomery 1913, no. 10, for the seal given by Adam to Seth, used by Noah, and now used by the bowl's producer (a passage pointed out to me by Dan Levene).
⁶⁹ ShR I/107–150 (pp. 72–75 Margalioth).

While the first and second heavens contain many "camps" and "grades" and lists of the angels who dwell therein, and therefore also many recipes with instructions on how to mobilize these angels, the number of heavenly subdivisions and magical usages declines the further up one ascends. By the time one reaches the seventh heaven, at least in the text reconstructed by Margalioth, there are no more subdivisions, overseers, or lists of angel names, and no magical recipes. The seventh heaven is God's abode, and the description thereof contains only an elaborate hymn of praise for the one and only Ruler of the Universe.

Sepher ha-Razim, as the above summary shows, is a complex compilation. Its basic structure, that of the seven heavens and their contents, immediately reminds one of many related discussions in ancient Jewish literature, be it the heavenly voyages of the Jewish apocalypses or of the Merkabah mystics, Paul's enigmatic reference to a visit to the third heaven, or the rabbinic speculations concerning the names and sizes of the seven heavens. The long and tedious lists of angels – undoubtedly corrupted by the book's copyists and therefore impossible to reconstruct accurately – are more problematic; some of these names look like standard Jewish angel names, made up of a Hebrew (or, sometimes, a Greek) verb or word relating to the angel's supposed duties and the standard ending -el.[70] And yet, most of the angel names of *Sepher ha-Razim* have no meaning in any language, and the method by which they were "generated" – if there ever was one – remains obscure. Worse still, only a handful of names borrowed from the world of Greco-Egyptian magic can currently be identified, a sure sign of the carelessness of later copyists in copying names which to them were both meaningless and unfamiliar. That the book itself is heavily influenced by the world of Greco-Egyptian magic is amply demonstrated not only by those Greco-Egyptian *voces magicae* which may still be identified in the lists of angelic names, but also by its magical recipes.[71] As Margalioth correctly noted, the ritual instructions of these recipes evince not only a close resemblance to those of the Greek magical papyri, but also a long line of Greek words and technical terms which could only have come from Greek-speaking magicians.[72] *Sepher ha-Razim*, in other words, is the thoughtful composition of a well-educated Jewish author – his Hebrew

---

[70] As noted by Margalioth 1966, p. 6. For this common Jewish method of generating new angelic names, see Trachtenberg 1939, pp. 260–61; HAITCG, p. 36; Bar-Ilan 1997.

[71] For the Greco-Egyptian *voces magicae* found in *Sepher ha-Razim*, see Margalioth 1966, p. 8, and the examples adduced in Chapter 4, below.

[72] See the detailed discussion by Margalioth 1966, pp. 1–16. His attempts (Margalioth 1966, pp. 17–22) to demonstrate the book's Gnostic affiliations carry little conviction, as has often been noted (e.g., Dan 1968). For the book's Greek vocabulary, see also Sznol 1989.

is extremely rich and his use of biblical idiom is quite sophisticated – who was thoroughly familiar with the vocabulary and techniques of the pagan, and especially Greco-Egyptian, magic of late antiquity. This author, however, decided to impart his knowledge to his Jewish brethren not in the form of a collection of useful recipes, but as a full-fledged "book of mysteries," supposedly written by an angel, given to Noah, and utilized by many Jewish Patriarchs. As we saw in Chapter 2, such claims about the angelic origins of magical technologies were quite popular already in the Second Temple period, and in this respect *Sepher ha-Razim* may be seen as a direct descendant of the magical pseudepigrapha of an earlier period. But unlike the earlier period, the compiler of this work was dealing with a highly elaborate magical technology, and must have edited and reformulated many of the recipes at his disposal in order to make them fit the overall structure he gave to the entire book. Such editorial processes – though perhaps by later editors – are also evident when we examine the place of the magical *charactêres* within the manuscripts (apparently only in a few places, and always at the end of lists of angelic names, quite unlike what we find in pagan magical texts and in Jewish magical formularies) and note the absence of any *voces magicae* within the spells themselves (apparently, because some were omitted while others became angelic names) and the complete absence of any magical iconography accompanying the text.[73]

When and where did this process take place? Unfortunately, we have no real clues with which to answer this question. One of the recipes uses a chronological dating system, the fifteen-year indiction cycle, which had been in use in the late-Roman and Byzantine periods, from the fourth century onwards, and scholars have seized upon this datum as a clue for dating the entire book.[74] But while this casual reference to contemporary realia might help date one specific recipe, it is a very inaccurate date – the indiction system was in use well into the Byzantine period – and it only applies to one specific recipe. Since it stands to reason that the author of *Sepher ha-Razim* used existing recipes as the building blocks for his composition, and then changed them to suit the overall structure and underlying suppositions which shaped it, dating any specific unit will only provide a *post quem* dating for the entire composition. An *ante quem* limit is provided only by the fact that the book shows almost no influence of the Arabic

---

[73] Other features, such as the intrusion of Aramaic words in ShR I/149–150 and I/167 (p. 75 Margalioth), might be attributed either to irregularities in the original composition or to subsequent scribal errors. See also Niggemeyer 1975, pp. 17–62.
[74] See ShR I/27–28, with Margalioth 1966, pp. 23–26 and Alexander 1986, pp. 348–49. For the indiction cycle, see Meimaris 1992, pp. 32–34 and Bagnall and Worp 2004, pp. 7–35.

language or of the Muslim magical tradition, and may thus be dated no later than the seventh century CE.⁷⁵ A more exact dating is, unfortunately, impossible. Similarly, it is extremely difficult to decide where the book might have been written, as neither the ingredients nor the social situations envisaged by its author disclose his exact time and place: spells for winning the chariot races or igniting and quenching the bathhouse fire and instructions to use metal (lead) stolen from the municipal water-pipes fit well in a late-antique urban context, but the references to reinstating kings and to slaughtering lion cubs are highly problematic, as few late-antique Jews had direct access to either species.⁷⁶ Furthermore, *Sepher ha-Razim* repeatedly enjoins the manufacture and use of "finished products" made of materials which happen to be quite durable – especially the engraving of angel-names and other texts on metal lamellae, the manufacture and use of metal rings and seals with images engraved upon them, and the production of bronze or stone apotropaic statues⁷⁷ – and yet the archeological evidence at our disposal includes no artifacts produced according to these instructions.⁷⁸ Arguments from archeological silence are highly problematic, and new finds may easily prove them wrong, but the fact that none of the forty or so published metal lamellae which we have surveyed above conform with any of the lamellae enjoined by the recipes of *Sepher ha-Razim* certainly militates against assuming that this work was widely utilized by the Jewish magicians of late antiquity.⁷⁹ Thus, we must either date the book as late as possible in the pre-Muslim period, or assume that it is an earlier work but was not widely utilized by Jewish practitioners at

---

⁷⁵ The rare Arabic-looking elements – such as the angelic name הוד הוד in II/120 (p. 88 Margalioth), which seems suspiciously close to the Arabic word for "hoopoe" (and see Quran 27.20–45!) (but cf. Morgan 1983, p. 54, n. 40) – probably are due to the book's Muslim-period Jewish copyists rather than to its original author.

⁷⁶ One may note, however, that the rabbis loved to tell stories of Rabbi Judah ha-Nasi's many encounters with king "Antoninus," and that encounters with local Roman governors and generals certainly were not uncommon for some Jews in late-antique Palestine.

⁷⁷ Writing on metal lamellae: I/135 (p. 74 Margalioth) (a lamella, type of metal not specified), I/144 (p. 74) (a tin lamella), I/201 (p. 78) (four bronze lamellae), II/31 (p. 82) (two bronze lamellae), II/54–55 (p. 84) (a silver lamella), II/63–64 (p. 84) (a lead lamella), II/69 (p. 85) (see next note), II/100–01 (p. 87) (a silver lamella), II/111–12 (p. 87) (an iron lamella), II/115–16 (p. 87) (two bronze lamellae), II/125–26 (p. 88) (a gold lamella), II/126–27 (p. 88) (four silver lamellae), II/137–38 (p. 89) (a silver lamella to be placed in a bronze tube), II/151–52 (p. 89) (a bronze lamella), III/37 (p. 94) (a silver lamella), V/20 (p. 102) (twelve gold lamellae), VI/29–31 (p. 105) (a gold lamella).

⁷⁸ Possible exceptions are provided by the instructions to produce a seal-ring with the image of a lion (II/69 (p. 85 Margalioth)) and an iron ring with the image of a man (Hercules?; cf. Bonner 1950, pp. 62–64) and a lion (VI/29–31 (p. 105)). Both images are common on ancient seals, glass pendants, rings and magical gems, and in pagan magical recipes. The same holds true for the apotropaic statues of ShR II/111–16 (p. 87).

⁷⁹ Note, in this regard, that the PGM's instructions for the manufacture of magical gems often are paralleled by actual gems, as was pointed out by Nagy 2002a.

Jewish magic in late antiquity: "insider" evidence 175

the time, or suggest that those practitioners who used it chose to produce the "finished products" based upon it only on perishable materials. Be that as it may, it seems that the evidence currently at our disposal does not allow any definitive claims regarding the date or place of composition of this late-antique Jewish book of magic, which may have been composed in Palestine, Egypt, Syria, or any other region where Hebrew-writing Jews came into contact with Greco-Roman culture and Greco-Egyptian magic.

Before leaving *Sepher ha-Razim*, one additional note is in order. Excited by his epoch-making discovery, Margalioth became convinced that "most of the Palestinian and Egyptian [Jewish] magical literature of the generations immediately following the composition of *Sepher ha-Razim* was to a lesser or greater extent influenced by it, and borrowed from it materials or phrases."[80] While the importance of this work is demonstrated by the many Genizah fragments and non-Genizah manuscripts thereof, by occasional borrowings from it in later Jewish magical texts, and by the many references to it in medieval Jewish literature, there is little doubt that the ongoing publication of dozens of late antique Palestinian Jewish amulets and hundreds of Babylonian incantation bowls, as well as the countless magical texts from the Cairo Genizah, will transform our view of *Sepher ha-Razim*'s place within the Jewish magical tradition. Whether it will give us better access to some of this book's postulated sources is still too early to say, but it certainly will provide numerous examples of magical texts which are roughly contemporaneous with *Sepher ha-Razim* or postdate its postulated date of composition, yet are entirely independent of it. *Sepher ha-Razim* is an important source for the study of ancient Jewish magic, but given the enormous historical and textual uncertainties surrounding it, the other sources at our disposal often provide better starting-points for the historical study of ancient Jewish magic. It is for this reason that in the subsequent chapters *Sepher ha-Razim* will occupy second stage to some of the other Jewish magical texts at our disposal.

Ḥarba de-Moshe

Of all the sources at our disposal, *Ḥarba de-Moshe* ("The Sword of Moses") is perhaps the most exasperating.[81] Extant in at least three different versions, its longest version is attested only in very late manuscripts (none, apparently, earlier than the sixteenth century) all of which are obviously corrupt, while its shorter versions are attested in manuscripts of the fourteenth or fifteenth

---

[80] Margalioth 1966, p. 35, based on his detailed discussion in pp. 29–46.
[81] For the *Sword of Moses*, see the useful discussions by Gaster 1896; Alexander 1986, pp. 350–52; Schäfer 1991, pp. vii–xvii; Harari 1997a; Harari 2005c.

century, but they too do not inspire much faith in the accuracy of the texts they preserve. Worse still, the few Genizah fragments of this work that have been identified and published show a remarkable similarity to the longer version, while other Genizah fragments have yet to be identified and analyzed.[82] Thus, although we possess two modern editions of the longer version of this text, two editions of the shorter one, and one edition of a third and even shorter version, we are far from possessing anything close to a reliable text of this work, on which to base a detailed historical analysis.[83] One thing we do know, however, is that a "Sword of Moses" was already known to Hai Gaon, and that the *incipit* he cites for this work (see below) roughly matches the beginning of the longer version, but not of any of the shorter ones. Whether this should argue for the priority of the longer version, as Gaster quite naively assumed, is a matter of grave doubts.

In its present form, the longest version of the *Sword of Moses* consists of three unequal parts. First comes an introduction (written partly in Hebrew, partly in Aramaic), relating how Moses had acquired this "sword," and what newcomers must do before they even try to use it themselves. This is followed by the "sword" itself – an extremely long list of mostly meaningless "words," in which are embedded a few meaningful Aramaic sentences. This is followed by a list consisting of about 140 recipes, all written in Babylonian Jewish Aramaic with some Hebrew words. Each recipe uses a section of the "sword" as a spell to be recited or written down, the sections usually following each other in the "sword" itself. Thus, the sixth to eighth recipes run as follows: "For a demon, write from H' BŠMHT until Y'WYHW. For fear, from Y'W YHYW to YY YY YY. For diphtheria, say on rose-oil from YY YY YY to 'WNṬW, and place it (i.e., the oil) in his mouth." Each of these "from X-word to Y-word" sequences usually encompasses around ten consecutive "words" of the "sword" itself, but shorter or longer sequences are not uncommon. The entire text, as it currently stands, is characterized not only by the ignorance of its copyists (to which we shall soon return), but also by their carelessness, for there is not even a full agreement between the "words" as spelled in the "from X-word to Y-word" instructions and themselves (cf. Y'WYHW with Y'W YHYW in the above example), and

---

[82] For the published Genizah fragments, see Harari 1997a, pp. 154–56 (four fragments, all from a single codex) and Hopkins 1978, pp. 74–77 (one fragment, from a different codex).

[83] For the longer version, see Gaster's and Harari's editions; for the manuscripts which preserve it, see esp. Benayahu 1972; for the shorter version, see Gaster 1896, Appendix A and *Synopse* §598–622. For the third version, see *Synopse* §640–50. And cf. the *Sword*-related fragments published by Harari 1997a, pp. 139–45.

especially between them and the "words" found in the "sword" itself, only a few pages earlier.

As even this cursory description shows, this is a complex text, and there is little doubt that it underwent several stages of editing.[84] This also explains the existence in one of the manuscripts of the longer version of several citations and excerpts taken from a *Sword of Moses* which differs from that known to us, and which may represent an earlier stage, or earlier stages, in its textual history.[85] But here too, the work of identifying all the excerpts and fragments (including those from the Cairo Genizah) and studying their implications for the textual history of the entire work, is only in its infancy. For the time being, all we have are agonizing demonstrations that the currently available texts are late and unreliable, and some pointers towards the reconstruction of the long history of the different parts of the *Sword of Moses*.

As the introduction to the entire work is somewhat superfluous, and could easily have been added, expanded, abridged, or emended by the book's later editors (it is, we may add, absent from the shorter versions), it is also the hardest section to date. The "sword" and the recipes, on the other hand, go hand in hand, and it stands to reason that a single editor is responsible for both. Locating this editor, however, is again a very tricky business, though it is important to note that unlike the recipes of *Sepher ha-Razim*, which seem to point to an educated urban elite living in a Hellenized social milieu, those of the *Ḥarba de-Moshe* – at least of the longer version – tend to be much simpler and more "rustic" in nature, and display few signs of contact with Hellenic culture.[86] They aim to heal a whole host of diseases (arranged according to the afflicted members of the body, from top to bottom, a common arrangement both in Babylonian and in Greek medicine), to solve various agricultural problems, and to help one in such mundane occurrences as falling into a well or a river or encountering a hostile gang. (Here too, however, one meets some unlikely scenarios, such as "If you wish to grab a lion by its ear.") The materials used for the magical praxis tend to be vegetal oils, palm fibers, water, pottery sherds, and other materials available to any village or small-town dweller, with only a small percentage of the recipes necessitating the use of silver or gold lamellae and

---

[84] For the editorial complexity of this work, see Schäfer 1991, pp. ix–xii, and esp. Harari 1997a, pp. 77–133.
[85] As was convincingly argued by Harari 1997a, pp. 145–49.
[86] Note, however, that this is less true for the shorter version (=*Synopse* §598–622), which does contain race-course recipes (§609–610 (note that קמטון is an error for קמפון = *campus* (see Margalioth 1966, p. x, n. 3, and Krauss 1898–99, p. 510), a *defixio* (§617), and even a recipe whose origins must be Greco-Egyptian (§616). For these recipes, see further discussion in Chapter 5.

none calling for the productions of elaborate rings or engraved gemstones. And when one looks for the kinds of Greek terminology which so abounds in *Sepher ha-Razim* and some Genizah magical texts, one finds that such terminology is almost totally absent from the recipes of the *Sword of Moses*. Instead, one finds many terms and *materia magica* which commonly appear in the medical recipes of the Babylonian Talmud, to which we shall turn in Chapter 6. Even more telling is the fact that magical materials which are typical of the Greco-Roman magical tradition and which appear in *Sepher ha-Razim* or in the shorter *Sword* excerpts in Hebrew transliteration of their Greek names appear in the longest version of the *Sword* in their Aramaic translations – a sure sign of the replacement of Greek terms which were not easily understood in a Greek-less cultural environment by their Aramaic equivalents.[87] Finally, we may note that while the very concept of a magic "sword" of an ancient cultural hero is paralleled in the Greek magical tradition, this does not necessarily argue for the dependence of our "sword" on Greek models.[88] Enough materials within the Jewish exegetical tradition could have spawned the concept of Moses' magical "sword" in a manner that would have been entirely independent of such Greek parallels.[89] Similarly, the fact that quite a few of the *Sword*'s recipes enjoin the production of a written "finished product" (and, as in the case of *Sepher ha-Razim*, the archeological record has provided no such artifacts, even though some of them should have been quite durable), might argue for the late-antique Palestinian origins of at least some of these recipes.[90]

With such data at hand, it would be easy to conclude, as have done most of the few scholars who have paid attention to this work, that it is a Geonic compilation, and therefore too late for the present study, and that it is likely to be a Babylonian compilation, and once again less relevant for our purposes. And yet, when one turns to the "sword" itself, one is surprised to

---

[87] For example, the common magical ingredient ζμυρνομέλαν is given as זמירנה מלינן in ShR I/95–96 (and see Margalioth, p. 2), but as מורא אוכם in HdM recipes no. 56 (p. 41 Harari) and 98 (p. 44 Harari) (see AMB, p. 88; and cf. זמרנא אביא in *Synopse* §599?). Note also how the commonly used plant ἀρτεμισία is given as ארטמוסיס and ארטימוסיה in some *Sword*-related excerpts (Harari 1997a, pp. 140 and 142 respectively; see also *Synopse* §618 and §621), but as שואצרא in recipes no. 2 and 51 of the longer version.

[88] For Greek parallels, see the Ξίφος Δαρδάνου of PGM IV.1716 and 1813; note also the Ομη(ρου) μαντ(ειον) η ακινακης ("Homer's Oracle, or Scimitar") of P.Oxy. LVI, 3831, with the editor's note.

[89] And see Harari 2005c, pp. 298–309.

[90] For writing and writing surfaces, note recipes no. 1 (p. 36 Harari) (a red (bronze?) lamella); 2 (p. 37) (a silver lamella); 3 (a plate?); 4, 5, 6, 7, 14, 15, and 16 (writing surfaces not specified); 31 (p. 39) (papyrus?); 35 (a plate?); 45 (p. 40) (bay leaf); 47 (w.s.n.s.); 48 (red bronze lamella); 48a (w.s.n.s.); 50 (silver lamella); 53 (w.s.n.s.); 55 (p. 41) (a new lamp); 57, 58 (pottery sherds); 59 (a lamella); 60 (the skin of a donkey); 61 (cranial membrane?); 64 (a door); 68 (p. 42) (a voodoo doll); 70 (a silver lamella); 92 (p. 43) (w.s.n.s.); 96 (an egg?); 105 (p. 44) (lead lamella); 106 (papyrus); 107 (papyrus?); 126 (p. 45) (a lead lamella); 128 (an egg); 129 (p. 46) (bay leaf).

find embedded in it a long, and garbled, Greek formula in one section of the "sword," a formula whose Aramaic translation is found in another section of the same text.[91] In the shorter version of the *Sword of Moses*, one finds a similar phenomenon in the "sword" section – but with an entirely different Greek formula.[92] And returning to the longer version, one also finds a whole cluster of *voces magicae* which happen to be very common in the Greek magical texts of late antiquity embedded in the first part of the "sword."[93] Like fossils embedded in a sedimentary rock which had been displaced by age-old tectonic movements, these *voces* provide ample evidence of the antiquity of the textual layer in which they are embedded and of the forces which tossed that layer from an ancient stratum to a much younger one. We shall return to the issue of Greek loanwords and *voces magicae* in Jewish magical texts in the following chapter, but for the moment we must note the significance of these specific examples for our present survey. While the *Sword of Moses* probably is too late, and too Babylonian, to deserve close attention in the present study, there is no doubt that the materials from which it was constructed included some Palestinian Jewish materials of late-antique origins, including complete Greek sentences transliterated in the Hebrew alphabet and a whole line of Greco-Egyptian *voces magicae* which a late editor incorporated into his magical "sword" without ever realizing their ultimate origins or original significance. Thus, even if the *Sword of Moses* might have been excluded from the present survey, one reason for its inclusion is that this specific case amply demonstrates the complexity of classifying some of the Jewish magical texts as "early" or "late," and as "Palestinian" or "Babylonian," and the danger of neglecting those sources which seem to lie outside pre-set chronological or geographical boundaries.

The Testament of Solomon

Unlike *Sepher ha-Razim* and *Ḥarba de-Moshe*, which are Jewish works of magic written in Hebrew and Aramaic, the *Testament of Solomon*, to which we now turn, is written in Greek and is a demonstrably Christian work. Its inclusion in the present chapter therefore is quite anomalous, and yet the

---

[91] As was brilliantly demonstrated by Rohrbacher-Sticker 1996.
[92] Note esp. *Synopse* §603, where "and mention the one hundred holy and powerful names" is immediately followed by אירימנא ... שמא ... אינימטא ... שמא מינלא, i.e., τὰ μεγάλα ... ὀνόματα ... τὰ ... εἰρημένα ("the great ... names ... which are to be spoken"). The entire passage deserves a more thorough analysis.
[93] Note the presence of the following *voces* on p. 31 Harari: אוזרוס אוזרוס (=Osiris?); יאוס (Zeus?; see Sperber 1994, p. 89); סומרשא (=σουμαρθα; Brashear 1995, p. 3599); אבסכס (=Abraxas?); קנמא סמאה קנמאה (=the σημεα κοντευ-formula, discussed in Chapter 4); סא מסולם מסולם (=σεμεσειλαμ, slightly garbled); אבלא נאתה ... לבאתה (=αβλαναθαναλβα, slightly garbled), etc. For the construction of the "sword" from several distinct conglomerates, see Harari 1997a, pp. 115–21.

work bears so much resemblance to some ancient Jewish texts and traditions, both magical and non-magical, as to merit at least a brief discussion here.[94] Its antiquity, or at least the antiquity of one section, is vouchsafed by a papyrus fragment found in Egypt and dated paleographically in the later fifth or early sixth century CE.[95] In its medieval and later manuscripts, the *Testament of Solomon* is found in at least four different Greek recensions (and at least one Arabic translation), which read like strange hybrids of a para-biblical story and a demonological *vademecum*. As a story, the *Testament* relates mainly how King Solomon, when building the great Temple of Jerusalem, used a magical ring he had received from the angel Michael to subdue a whole host of demons and set them to work on the construction of the Temple; the angelic origins of anti-demonic lore is a phenomenon we already encountered often enough in the present study, and the story of Solomon's subjugation of the demons and their assistance in constructing the Temple finds ample parallels elsewhere, including in the Babylonian Talmud.[96] But instead of merely retelling this popular story, the *Testament* weaves into the narrative some very useful demonological lore, for whenever Solomon subdues a demon, he forces that demon to identify his or her name, malicious activities, and the angel by whom, or technique by which, he or she is thwarted. To these essential data, which are provided for each of the fifty-nine evil demons interrogated by Solomon, and which would enable the *Testament*'s readers to identify and subdue the demons troubling them, other information is occasionally added, such as the demon's place of residence, zodiacal sign, physical appearance, origins and genealogy, means of travel, and so on. Thus, to summarize a typical scene, one female demon appears to King Solomon in the shape of a woman with disheveled hair, identifies herself as Obyzouth, confesses that her favorite pastime is strangling newborn babies (but she also causes other painful bodily afflictions), and explains that she is thwarted by the angel Raphael. All one must do, she says, is write her name (why not his?) on a slip of papyrus and place it next to the woman in childbirth, and she shall flee the place and leave the newborn infant unharmed.[97]

Reading such passages, which are strung one after the other on the thin narrative thread, one becomes convinced that this text is sincere when it

---

[94] For useful discussions of the *Testament of Solomon*, see McCown 1922a and 1922b; Duling 1983 and 1988; Alexander 1986, pp. 372–79; Jackson 1988; Greenfield 1995; Torijano 2002; Johnston 2002; Alexander 2003a; Klutz 2003b and 2005.
[95] For the papyrus fragment of *T. Sol.*, see P. Rainer Cent. 39 and van Haelst 1976, no. 570.
[96] See bt Gitt 58a–b, and the Gnostic Nag Hammadi materials discussed by Giversen 1972.
[97] *T. Sol.* 13 (pp. 43*–45* McCown).

Jewish magic in late antiquity: "insider" evidence 181

has Solomon say "I wrote this testament to the sons of Israel and I gave it to them so that they might know the powers of the demons and their forms, as well as the name of the angels by which the demons are thwarted."[98] But like a fruit tree cloaking its seeds in thick layers of juicy tissue for them to achieve their ultimate goal, so our author wrapped his dry catalogue of demons and how to keep them at bay in a juicier literary flesh.[99] Instead of passing on such useful knowledge in the form of magical recipes, as did the authors of *Sepher ha-Razim* and *Ḥarba de-Moshe*, he embedded it into a more amusing tale; in this, he was aided by the fact that the means he employed for thwarting the demons were all quite simple, be it the uttering of an angelic name or a short formula, or the writing down of a very simple name or magic word. Of the elaborate magical practices of the Greek magical papyri or *Sepher ha-Razim* there is hardly a trace in his work.

If the author's aim seems quite clear, his exact identity, and that of his postulated readers, is much less so, especially since as it now stands the text reveals many Christian elements, be it the demons Beelzebul or Legion, known to us from the Gospels, or the many references to how the demons would one day – long after Solomon's own death – be thwarted by Emmanouêl, the son of a virgin who shall be stretched high on a cross, and similar references to Jesus Christ.[100] And yet, much in this work is paralleled in Jewish magical texts, and as the magical rituals recommended by it are all quite simple (they involve very little writing, few *materia magica*, only some very basic ritual activities, and very short spells), and rarely display the influence of the Greco-Egyptian magic of late antiquity, it is tempting to see in this text a distant descendant of the pseudepigraphical books of magic which may have been in circulation in Second Temple period Jewish society (see Chapter 2). Unfortunately, excising all the obviously Christian elements out of the *Testament of Solomon* and pretending that we have thus reached the original Jewish text is no solution; it would be like excising all the obviously American elements out of Walt Disney's "Snow White" in the hope of arriving at the Grimm Brothers' version of this tale. When all we have is the Christian text, and not even a proof that a Jewish original ever existed, we must proceed with great caution before using it in a study of ancient Jewish magic. We may, however, use the *Testament* as evidence for *Christian* demonology and magic in late antiquity, note the parallels with the Jewish texts, and speculate about their possible meanings – as

---

[98] *T. Sol.* 15.14–15 (pp. 47*–48* McCown).
[99] For the claim that the *T. Sol.* is a recipe-book in disguise, see also Torijano 2002, pp. 58–65.
[100] See *T. Sol.* 6.8; 11.6; 12.3; 15.10–11; 17.4; 22.20; etc.

shall be done, for example, in the next chapter, when we discuss a Genizah recipe which is closely paralleled by instructions found in the *Testament of Solomon*.

Summary
We examined two Jewish books of magic and a Christian one, and noted the prospects offered by each for the study of late-antique Jewish magic. To these specific points we may add one more general observation. As we already noted, such "literary" books of magic often reach us in more than one recension, proving that they were subjected to all the editorial processes suffered by pseudepigraphical books in antiquity and the Middle Ages. We may now stress that the transmission history of their magical recipes is quite different from that offered by the other mode of transmitting magical recipes, that of the structureless formulary. For whereas a copyist of an old collection of recipes normally felt free to copy only those recipes which he found useful for his own needs (and in many cases we can see a practitioner copying one recipe from one source, a second from a different source, and so on), the copyists and editors of the "literary" books of magic tended to work on larger textual units, and felt less freedom to omit individual recipes merely because they were no longer useful, or even somewhat offensive. In a way, the "literary" books underwent a certain form of "canonization" or "fossilization," and as a result of this process they sometimes preserve older types of magical aims and technologies which are mostly absent from the "non-literary" formularies. The use of the indiction-cycle in one *Sepher ha-Razim* recipe, or of such technical terms as "*psychrophoros*," the Greek word for the city's water-pipes, are good examples of this process, for such terms were utterly meaningless for the books' medieval copyists, but they copied them nonetheless. In the Genizah formularies, on the other hand, we repeatedly note how old terminology is translated into, or replaced by, terms which would be more meaningful for the recipes' daily users, just as the users and copyists of the *Sword of Moses* replaced Greek technical terms with Aramaic ones. Even more striking, there are recipes for winning the horse and chariot races of late-antique Roman cities in *Sepher ha-Razim*, in *Ḥarba de-Moshe* (or at least in one of its versions), and perhaps even in the *Havdala de-Rabbi Akiva* (on which more below), even though these recipes would not have been of much use for their medieval copyists.[101]

---

[101] See *Sepher ha-Razim* III/35–43 (p. 94 Margalioth) and *Ḥarba de-Moshe* (see above, n. 86); and cf. the *Havdala de-Rabbi Akiva*, p. 277 Scholem, where the overturning of the horse, rider, and chariot might refer not only to Pharaoh and the Egyptians, but also to more contemporary events; see further Harari 2000b, pp. 33–36.

Jewish magic in late antiquity: "insider" evidence 183

Such recipes seem to be unparalleled in the "non-literary" recipe-books from the Cairo Genizah, an absence presumably due to Genizah scribes' lack of interest in recipes that were no longer relevant in their own world. And the same is true for the presence of many "problematic" elements – such as a Greek prayer to Helios – in *Sepher ha-Razim*, for as we shall note in Chapter 5, when practitioners transmitted and copied their magical recipes they not only "updated" their sources (e.g., by translating the ritual instructions, and even the spells themselves, into their new vernacular, Judeo-Arabic), but also censored out those elements which they found too offensive for their, or their clients', religious sensibilities. Such processes, which in some cases probably were quite unconscious, were much less likely to occur when copying a book like *Sepher ha-Razim*, which was not seen as a loose collection of practical recipes, but as a real book. Thus, one more reason why the "literary" books of magic have much to tell us about ancient Jewish magic is that sometimes they preserve old materials which are no longer extant in the more free-floating formularies from the Cairo Genizah and elsewhere.

Babylonian incantation bowls

Of all the different types of textual artifacts which were produced by late-antique Jewish magicians and are directly accessible to us, the so-called "Babylonian incantation bowls" are by far the most numerous, but, at the present stage of research, the hardest to study in a systematic manner.[102] For while the number of published bowls already approaches three hundred, this number is dwarfed by the number of known but still unpublished bowls, which is estimated at more than 1,500 pieces.[103] Thus, while Montgomery's 1913 study of the bowls available to him at the time remains the cornerstone of all scholarly work on such bowls, its general introduction to the field has long been in need of revision in light of texts which have been published since, but cannot be revised before all the bowls whose publication is imminent become available for all to see. In what follows, we shall therefore note not only what these bowls are and what may be deduced from those that

---

[102] For useful introductions to this vast field, see Montgomery 1913, pp. 7–116; Gordon 1957, pp. 160–74; Yamauchi 1965; Isbell 1978; AMB, pp. 19–21; Levene 2002; Morony 2003; Shaked 2005c; Bohak 2005/6. See also Juusola 1999, for a linguistic analysis.

[103] The major publications of Aramaic incantation bowls are Montgomery 1913; Gordon 1934, 1937, 1941; Jeruzalmi 1964; Isbell 1975 (who reprints bowls published up to that date); Geller 1980 and 1986; AMB and MSF; (and cf. the list of the Aramaic bowls published up to 2000 in Sokoloff 2002, pp. 62–66, with 152 entries); Segal 2000; Levene 2003; Müller-Kessler 2005. Many more studies will be cited below. For bowl numbers, cf. Morony 2003, pp. 87 and 93 with Shaked 2005c, p. 10.

have already been published, but also why they will mostly be left out of the present study, and what the ongoing publication of new bowls might contribute to the study of ancient Jewish magic as a whole.

First discovered in the middle of the nineteenth century, the bowls in question are limited to one geographical location, roughly that of present-day Iraq and Western Iran, and to one chronological period, probably from the fifth or sixth to the eighth century CE.[104] Unfortunately, a vast majority of the bowls known to date have surfaced on the antiquities markets as the result of clandestine excavations (and Iraq's recent political history certainly is partly to blame for the paucity of controlled excavations and the recurrence of illegal digging and smuggling of archeological treasures), and this makes the determination of their geographical and chronological contexts much more difficult.[105] However, the number of bowls found in controlled archeological excavations does suffice to formulate some general conception of their geographical and chronological distribution and of the modes in which they were put to use, and the texts and drawings found upon the bowls themselves provide abundant information about the clients who ordered them, about the bowls' aims, and about the cultural world of the scribes who produced them.

When found in controlled excavations, the bowls are most commonly found in upside-down position (a fact which incidentally helped protect the texts and drawings, which are usually written on the bowls' inside) within the premises of a dwelling, or under the thresholds, or in a cemetery, or in large groups of bowls in one location (perhaps the atelier which produced them).[106] Occasionally, two bowls are found which are, or used to be, glued together by bitumen, and even tied together with ropes, the internal space enclosed between them sometimes containing such items as a broken eggshell, with or without an inscription or a scribbling upon it.[107] The bowls themselves are not uniform in shape or size – a typical bowl is c. 16 cm in diameter and c. 5 to 6 cm in depth, and looks like a modern cereal bowl, but other sizes and shapes are not uncommon – and are not different from other

---

[104] For a bowl which has been stratigraphically dated to the eighth century, see Gawlikowski 1988; for bowls which are said to show Arabic influences, see Segal 2000, p. 22. For Arabic bowls, see below, n. 111.

[105] It also raises the question of forgeries, but the low price of most bowls on the market, and the difficulty of forging such long texts, greatly reduce the likelihood of forgeries, except for some crude and easily detectable examples; on the other hand, dealers have been known to "improve" the texts upon some bowls, for which see Shaked 2005c, pp. 6–7.

[106] For bowls found in controlled excavations, see, e.g., Hilprecht 1904, pp. 337, 440, 447–48; Montgomery 1913, pp. 13–14; Waterman 1931, pp. 61–62; Kaufman 1973; Franco 1978–79; Hunter 1995 and 2004.

[107] For the eggshells, see Hilprecht 1904, pp. 447–48.

bowls from Sasanian Mesopotamia. There is no doubt, therefore, that they were not produced by the magicians for the purpose of this specific ritual, but were bought in the marketplace in very large quantities, and then used as a surface on which to inscribe the magical spells.[108] The fact that they were so cheap certainly helps explain their apparent popularity, including the acquisition by some clients of many bowls for a single domicile.

When we turn from external appearances to actual contents, we must note both the texts and the drawings (which are found only on some of the bowls). Looking at the texts, we note five different writing systems: by far the most common is the square Aramaic script, which is found on well over half the bowls, the second most common script being Mandaic (the script of the Gnostic Mandeans).[109] Syriac (both the Estrangelo and the "proto-Manichaean" scripts) is a distant third, and a cursive Pahlavi script is found on a few bowls only, none of which has yet been deciphered.[110] The same is true for a handful of incantation bowls written in Arabic script and displaying Muslim elements, none of which have so far been published.[111] (In later periods, Muslim practitioners, and the Jews who learned from them, often wrote on clay, glass, or metal bowls as part of their magical and divinatory rituals, but neither the ritual practices involved nor the texts they inscribed resemble those of the Babylonian incantation bowls).[112] The texts also are characterized by a great variety of scribal competence, from the sure hand of experienced scribes to the pseudo-script "squiggles," or the endless repetition of a single word or pseudo-word, of practitioners who catered to an illiterate clientele and may even have been only semi-literate themselves (see Figure 3.6). Moreover, both the archeological records and the bowls' contents amply demonstrate that such bowls were produced by many different individuals in a variety of locations; in many cases, a whole group of bowls (for the same clients or for different ones) may safely be attributed to the same scribe or the same atelier, and the presence of many "duplicate" bowls, containing what is essentially the same spell – prepared either for the same clients (each bowl to be deposited in a different room of the house, or in a different corner of the same room) or

---

[108] For the bowls' physical appearance, see Hunter in Segal 2000, pp. 165–70; Morony 2003, pp. 84–94.
[109] For the Mandaic bowls, see esp. Yamauchi 1967; Müller-Kessler 1999a; Ford 2002a.
[110] For the Syriac bowls, see esp. Hamilton 1971; for their two scripts and their significance, see esp. Shaked 2000a. For Pahlavi on the bowls, see Shaked 2005c, p. 6.
[111] For references to Arabic incantation bowls, see, e.g., Hilprecht 1904, p. 337; Montgomery 1913, p. 21. I am grateful to Shaul Shaked and Michael Morony for information on the Arabic incantation bowls known to them.
[112] For Muslim magic bowls, see, e.g., Montgomery 1913, pp. 44–45; Canaan 1936; Harari 2005a; and cf. Hägg 1993 for Christian bowls, and Bos 1994, p. 90 for the mouse-trap bowls used by Ḥayyim Vital.

Figure 3.6 A Babylonian incantation bowl with the image of two bound male demons, surrounded by pseudo-alphabetic "squiggles." Note the demons' beards, their six wings and bound hands, and the shackles surrounding each demon.

for different ones – clearly points to the existence of professional local bowl-writers who worked from pre-set models.[113] Whether these models were transmitted orally or in writing is not entirely clear, but an examination of the "duplicate" bowls tends to argue in favor of a mostly oral transmission, as the differences between pairs of parallel bowl-spells do not seem to display the kinds of errors that stem from copying written *Vorlagen*, and as the producers seem to have used "blocks" of spells whose order they could change at will.[114] The corrupt citation of biblical verses on some of the bowls, which clearly is due to recitation from memory and not from a written

---

[113] For more detailed discussions of this issue, see Hunter 1995; Shaked 1999a, esp. p. 187; Müller-Kessler 1999a; Bohak 2005/6, pp. 256–57.

[114] See, e.g., Levene 2003, pp. 24–30. For a useful synopsis of many parallel passages in different bowls, see Segal 2000, pp. 153–62. Note, however, the "duplicate" bowls with the same magical signs

text, also argues for the oral composition of at least some of the bowls.[115] Moreover, none of the bowls published thus far displays the tell-tale signs of miscopying the instructions from a written formulary (as we saw in one of the Aramaic metal amulets from Egypt); this might indicate that if the practitioners who manufactured the bowls used some written sources, these did not look like the Greek magical papyri or the Cairo Genizah formularies, with their elaborate instructions followed by equally elaborate incantations and leading to some confusion when the actual "finished products" were being made. It seems clear, however, that only a careful weighing of all the available evidence would enable a more conclusive statement on this score.

The actual spells upon most of the bowls are apotropaic, designed to protect a person, a family, or an entire household from various types of evils, especially from sorcery and demons. They were, in other words, mostly domestic and "environmental" or "spatial" phylacteries and were, as their fragile nature makes abundantly clear, fixed amuletic devices rather than mobile ones. Often, the spell includes an explicit reference to "this amulet" or "this press," and to the binding, pressing, overturning (note the bowls' upside-down position when found *in situ*) and averting of the demons and evil spells which beset or might beset the clients, who are almost always named. Occasionally, the outer section of the bowl (which usually remains blank) has brief instructions as to where the bowl should be placed – "in the kitchen," "for the porch," "for the bedroom," and so on – a clear indication of their having been manufactured in an atelier and then moved, often in large groups, to the house where they were placed in their pre-assigned locations.[116] In some cases, the spell makes it clear that the bowl was intended to heal one sick person of one specific disease, in which case we may assume the bowl to have been deposited under the client's bed or in some other location which was deemed potent (which would help explain why the bowl was not discarded after the patient recovered or passed away). Occasionally, the bowls seek not only to avert evil, but also to send the evil eye or the magic of one's enemies against them, with the bowl serving as a sort of "mirror" to reflect all evil back to its perpetrators.[117] And in some cases, the text is not apotropaic at all, but aggressive, and seeks to

---

discussed by Harviainen 1978 or by Levene 2003, pp. 28 and 62 – such non-verbal components would be hard to transmit accurately in an oral fashion.
[115] For a good example, see AMB, B3, with the editors' notes. See also Gordon 1941, p. 350.
[116] For examples, see Shaked 2005c, p. 8.
[117] For examples, see Montgomery 1913, p. 83; MSF, B23; Segal 2000, Bowl 036A. We shall also examine one such bowl, published in Gordon 1941, in the next chapter. For the bowls' references to aggressive magic practiced by the client's opponents, see also Morony 2003, pp. 99–100.

(a)   (b)

Figure 3.7 A Greco-Egyptian magical gem, showing, on the obverse, the cock-headed snake-legged god and numerous "magic words" (including, above the shield, Michaêl, Raphaêl, Gabriêl and Ouriêl, and, below the whip, the *sêmea kenteu*-formula), all surrounded by an *ouroboros*; on the reverse, an eagle-headed deity with six wings.

harm a named individual or (very rarely) to make a named individual love another named individual.[118]

When we turn from the spells to the images which often accompany them (often drawn at the very center of the inside part of the bowl), we note that by far the most common image is that of shackled demons, both male and female (see Figure 3.6),[119] but other figures also make an appearance, which may be interpreted as those of the client or practitioner,[120] of animals whose noxious bite the practitioner apparently seeks to avert,[121] or of the

---

[118] For aggressive bowls, see, e.g., Obermann 1940, pp. 15–29; AMB, B7 and B9; Levene 1999 and Shaked 1999b; Segal 2000, Bowls 039A–043A; for erotic spells on incantation bowls, see Montgomery 1913, nos. 13 and 28; and cf. Gordon 1957, p. 170.

[119] For a shackled female demon, see, e.g., Moussaieff 59 in Levene 2002, p. 22, fig. 7, and see Lesses 2001, pp. 354–59. See also Hunter in Segal 2000, p. 174.

[120] See Montgomery 1913, p. 55; Gordon 1937, p. 98; Morony 2003, p. 98. But cf. Hunter 1998, pp. 100–01 (and ead., in Segal 2000, p. 178), who argues that such figures too are intended to represent demons.

[121] See, e.g., Levene 2002, p. 23, fig. 10, for the image of a scorpion, and Segal 2000, 108M, for another scorpion.

animals the incantation bowl seeks to protect.[122] Additional designs include the occasional appearance of the *ouroboros* or of *charactêres*, both of which will be discussed at greater length in the following chapter, and a host of other designs which have not yet received the attention they deserve, not least because many of the earlier publications of such bowls were not accompanied by reliable photographs.[123]

The peculiar nature of the incantation bowls raises many questions to which no satisfactory answer has yet been given. The reason for their sudden emergence in the fifth or sixth century CE remains obscure, in spite of some attempts to point to "precedents" for the bowls in Mesopotamia itself or elsewhere in the ancient world.[124] Moreover, the practice seems not to have spread outside a limited geographical region, in spite of the fact that the bowls' manufacturers – certainly the Jewish ones – were in close contact with their brethren outside Mesopotamia. Like the so-called Greek "confession inscriptions," a unique type of epigraphical documentation of an individual person's sins, their punishment, and the repentance and forgiveness which followed, which is attested in a small region of Asia Minor and in a "time window" of a few centuries only, the Babylonian incantation bowls provide a startling testimony to the local nature of much of late-antique religiosity.[125] A custom prevalent in one region did not always spread to neighboring regions, even when the language in which it was produced was widely accessible elsewhere, as the Greek of the confession inscriptions and the Aramaic, Mandaic, and Syriac of the incantation bowls certainly were. And as is the case with the confession inscriptions, one wonders whether the sudden appearance of the custom of writing such bowls is not the result of a mere change of scribal medium, that is, whether texts such as are inscribed on the bowls had earlier been inscribed on perishable materials, or even applied in an oral fashion, and therefore vanished from the archeological record. (In a similar fashion, we may note that the sudden appearance of the so-called "Fayyum mummy portraits," yet another example of the local nature of many late-antique religious customs, certainly is due to minor local changes in the age-old Egyptian custom of mummification.) This possibility gains much probability both from the complex and varied nature of the texts inscribed on the

---

[122] See, e.g., the first bowl in Isbell 1976, in which an image of four domestic animals is found within a spell to protect the client's family and property, including his cattle.
[123] For the bowls' iconography, see esp. Montgomery 1913, pp. 53–55; Hunter 1998; Hunter in Segal 2000, pp. 170–88; Wolfson 2001, pp. 106, 115.
[124] See Montgomery 1913, pp. 44–45 and 106–16; Hunter 1996, p. 226; see also Lesses 2001, p. 345, n. 2.
[125] For the Lydian confession inscriptions, see Versnel 1991a, pp. 75–79; Petzl 1994.

bowls, which certainly do not look like *de novo* compositions, and from the possible parallels between some of the magical spells in these texts and older Babylonian materials, magical and non-magical alike.[126] The whole issue, however, still awaits a careful consideration of all the available evidence, including quite a few Mandaic magical texts inscribed on lead, silver, and gold, and a unique lead tablet on which a Babylonian Jewish Aramaic spell was written in ink (but whose authenticity is far from certain).[127] Similarly, while the demise of incantation bowls sometime in the eighth century may probably be attributed to the Muslim conquest and the social and cultural changes it brought about, the re-emergence of some bowl-type incantations in later Jewish magical texts requires more attention than it has hitherto been granted, as it may shed more light on the transmission and adaptation of Jewish magical spells in Sasanian and early-Muslim Babylonia.[128]

Such questions are bound to keep bowl-scholars busy for many years to come. For the purpose of the present study, however, we must focus mainly on the bowls' possible contribution to the study of late-antique Jewish magic. The first point to be noted in this regard is that at least in the bowls published thus far, there seems to be a correlation between the script and dialect used upon each bowl and the cultural identity of its producers (but not necessarily the clients).[129] The bowls written in the square script (and in a dialect, or dialects, whose nature is differently described by different scholars, partly because these very bowls are the best point of departure for the study of the Eastern Aramaic dialects in late antiquity) contain many biblical verses (usually cited in the Hebrew original, but sometimes in an Aramaic Targum) and many specifically Jewish terms, concepts, and stories; a few even cite passages from the rabbis' Mishnah.[130] The bowls written in the Mandaic script use many specifically Mandaic terms which are almost entirely absent from the Aramaic or Syriac bowls. Only the Syriac bowls, which are far fewer than the other two corpora, seem to display a greater variety of cultural and religious influences and origins.[131] Thus, while the practitioners who produced these bowls never identify themselves, they may safely be divided into "Jews," "Mandaeans," "Christian, pagan, or

---

[126] For such continuities – which seem to be surprisingly rare – see Müller-Kessler 2002; Oelsner 2005; Geller 2005.
[127] For the Mandaic lamellae, see Greenfield and Naveh 1985; Müller-Kessler 1998a and 1999a. For the ink-on-lead amulet, see Geller 1997, pp. 331–35, with Naveh 2002b, p. 232.
[128] For the most striking example, see Scholem 1980/81, esp. pp. 262–66.
[129] As was noted, for example, by Harviainen 1995; Shaked 1997; Segal 2000, pp. 25–27.
[130] For Targumic verses on the bowls, see Kaufman 1973; Müller-Kessler 2001; Levene 2003, p. 11. For the Mishnaic passages, see Tan Ami 2001, p. 19; Shaked 2005b.
[131] For this issue, see esp. Juusola 1999b; Shaked 2000a.

Manichean Syriac-speakers," "Zoroastrian Parthian-speakers," and perhaps also "Arabic-speaking Muslims," and we may safely focus mainly on the first group, which is also the largest. Before we do so, however, we must stress that the ethnic and cultural identity of the clients often differed from that of the producers, as may be seen not only from the many patently non-Jewish client-names on many of the "Jewish" bowls, but also from the fact that upon some bowls the spells are written in one language while the brief instructions on the bowls' outside as to where they should be placed are written in another language – presumably, that of the clients who took them home. The fact that bowls written in different scripts and dialects occasionally are found within the same house, or were prepared for the same client(s), lends further support to the claim that clients often procured their bowls from producers of different linguistic and cultural backgrounds.[132]

When read together, the Jewish incantation bowls – that is, those bowls which were manufactured by Jewish practitioners for Jewish and non-Jewish clients – offer some striking contrasts to all the other magical artifacts surveyed in the present chapter, whose origins lie many miles to the west of Babylonia. The comparison between the two corpora is hampered by the different media and genres involved (for the western branch of Jewish magic, we have many different types of magical artifacts, but no incantation bowls, while for the eastern branch we have only the Aramaic incantation bowls), by the fact that most of the incantation bowls have yet to be published, and by the somewhat repetitive and stereotyped nature of many of the bowl-texts, which generally represent only one type of a (mostly apotropaic) magical praxis. And yet, both textual corpora are large enough to allow some general comparative remarks, and a general assessment of the broad gulf separating these two branches of the Jewish magical tradition.[133] First, not only do we lack any Aramaic incantation bowls from Palestine or the Eastern Mediterranean, the many recipes in the Cairo Genizah never enjoin the manufacture of such bowls – a sure sign that at least one magical practice was limited only to one branch of late-antique Jewish magic.[134] Second, whereas the Jewish magical texts from late-antique Palestine, Syria, Egypt, and their vicinity display many elements whose origins lie in the

---

[132] As noted by Levene 2002, p. 35.
[133] For what follows, see also MSF, p. 21: "Palestine and Mesopotamia had two separate traditions (of magic), each with its own style and set of formulae."
[134] The Genizah recipes do enjoin the manufacture of Muslim-type magic bowls – "write in the bowl, erase it with water, etc." (e.g., MSF, G9 (T-S K 1.15) p. 1 ll. 14ff; G14 (T-S K 1.58) p. 4, ll. 8–10) – but such bowls were not necessarily made of clay, were not deposited in one's house, and did not serve as apotropaic devices. See further above, n. 112.

Greco-Egyptian magical tradition (an issue to which the next chapter will be devoted), these elements are almost entirely absent from the Babylonian incantation bowls; a few bowls display some *charactêres*, or the *ouroboros*-design, or such *voces magicae* as Abraxas, but such bowls are few and far between.[135] Even Greek loanwords, so common in the textual remains of the western branch of late-antique Jewish magic, are almost entirely absent from the bowls. Third, the Aramaic, Mandaic, and Syriac bowls display many similarities, and even long parallels (a phenomenon which is partly to be explained by the relative ease with which spells composed in one dialect of Eastern Aramaic could be understood by speakers of another), a sure sign of the cross-fertilization by bowl-practitioners of different cultural milieus.[136] Thus, it is hardly surprising to find that some of the Jewish incantation bowls present interesting Gnostic, Christian, and pagan elements, and that these foreign elements are not the same as those found in the Palestinian sources.[137] Fourth, the Jewish bowls also display a plethora of Persian loanwords, including religious and magical terminology borrowed from a Persian milieu and unattested in the Palestinian magical texts or in the Cairo Genizah.[138] Fifth, some of the Aramaic incantation bowls contain deities, formulae, and spells whose origins go back to older Babylonian magic and religion, and such motifs are again unparalleled in the magical texts from Palestine.[139] Sixth, some of the bowls display their composers' use of distinctly rabbinic materials, including even citations of the Mishnah and of rabbinic prayers, and such materials are virtually absent from the "western" Jewish magical texts of late antiquity.[140] Finally, the iconography of the bowls is quite different from that of the magical gems (or any other artistic medium) of the Greco-Roman world, and seems to reflect older Mesopotamian ways of looking at demons and thwarting them. Even its very presence on the Jewish incantation bowls stands in marked contrast with the generally image-less magical texts of late-antique Palestine and the Cairo Genizah, a subject to which we shall return in Chapter 5.[141]

---

[135] For "Hellenistic" elements in the bowls, see Montgomery 1913, pp. 55–56, 113–15 and Shaked 2002, pp. 71–72. For another well-known example of the movement of a spell from Palestine to Babylonia, see the *smamit* story in AMB, B15, with the editors' detailed notes.

[136] For such inter-dialect parallels, see, e.g., Greenfield and Naveh 1985; Müller-Kessler 1998b; Moriggi 2005, p. 55.

[137] For a striking example, see Levene 1999, with Shaked 1999b.

[138] For Persian elements, see esp. Shaked 1985 and 1997.

[139] For such motifs, see Chapter 4, n. 66.

[140] For pertinent examples, see Shaked 2005b.

[141] The same distinction seems to hold true for Jewish seals – those from the Sasanian empire sometimes displaying iconographic elements, while those from Palestine do not (as noted in Spier 2007).

Jewish magic in late antiquity: "insider" evidence 193

Given the many differences between these two distinct branches of late-antique Jewish magic – which are, no doubt, partly to be explained by the fact that the Jews of Palestine and those of Babylonia dwelled in two different empires, often at war with each other – it seems clear that they should first be studied separately, and within their specific cultural milieus. The western branch should first be studied vis-à-vis the cultural context and magical practices of the Greco-Roman world, as we shall try to do in the next two chapters. The eastern branch, however, calls for the full publication of all the unpublished bowls, and for their study vis-à-vis the earlier Mesopotamian magical practices on the one hand and the Iranian cultural milieu of Sasanian Babylonia on the other. Only with these two separate tasks completed may we embark upon a comparative and synthetic study of ancient Jewish magic as a whole.

In light of all these considerations, it should become clear why in the following chapters we shall be making only a limited use of the Aramaic incantation bowls, in spite of their having been produced by late-antique Jewish magicians and in spite of their abundance. In the study of the Greco-Egyptian influences on late-antique Jewish magic (in Chapter 4), we shall use the bowls mainly in order to see which of these elements traveled as far away as Sasanian Babylonia. And in the analysis of the Jewish elements in the Jewish magical texts of the western branch of Jewish magic (in Chapter 5), we shall use the bowls mainly as a source for the study of those magical techniques and practices which were common to both branches of late-antique Jewish magic. Throughout our study, however, we will keep in mind that the publication of many hundreds of new incantation bowls might soon necessitate a re-evaluation of the relations between the eastern and the western branches of late-antique Jewish magic, and of their mutual exclusivity or resemblance.

Aramaic magical skulls

One more type of late-antique Jewish magical artifact, which is all the more intriguing for its rarity, is a handful of human skulls inscribed in the Aramaic language and the square script, skulls which probably were produced by Jews in late-antique Mesopotamia, and perhaps elsewhere too. Briefly discussed by Montgomery in his study of the magic bowls, such objects lay mostly neglected by subsequent scholars, and are only now beginning to receive the attention they deserve.[142] How much these macabre relics may teach us

---

[142] See Montgomery 1913, pp. 21, 256–57; Levene 2006.

about the magical technologies of those who produced and used them is still unclear, but the custom of inscribing on skulls is quite well attested in other magical traditions, and the very existence of such Aramaic artifacts serves as a powerful reminder that not only new sources, but also new *types* of sources, are emerging all the time in the ever-growing corpus of evidence for the Jewish magic of late antiquity. But as the inscribed skulls have yet to be analyzed – and especially since they might all be Babylonian Jewish artifacts, with no Palestinian parallels – they shall be left out of our analysis of the western branch of Jewish magic in late antiquity.

JEWISH MAGICAL TEXTS FROM LATE ANTIQUITY WRITTEN IN GREEK

Having surveyed a large array of Aramaic and Hebrew magical texts, whose language and script make their identification as Jewish quite certain (at least until such a specimen is found which is demonstrably non-Jewish in origins), we must now turn to the vast quantities of Greek magical texts from late antiquity, some of which may have been produced by Jews or contain elements borrowed from the Jewish magical tradition. That some Jewish practitioners produced magical texts in Greek is made clear by the bilingual and trilingual (Greek-Aramaic-Hebrew) magical texts which we already mentioned, and to which we shall return in the next chapter. And yet, the number of Greek-speaking Jewish magicians certainly was dwarfed by the number of pagan (and, from a certain point onwards, Christian) ones, and so we must develop sound criteria for separating the few Jewish magical texts in Greek from the many non-Jewish ones.

Looking at the Greek magical texts of late antiquity, we may note the rise – around the first century BCE or CE – of a unique magical idiom, which differed both from earlier magical traditions and from other strands of late-antique magic.[143] This new idiom found its expression in several different types of magical texts and objects, and especially in magical papyri (both recipe-books and amulets, curses, and other "finished products" inscribed on papyrus), curse tablets (incised on thin sheets of lead), magical gems (incised on many types of semi-precious stones, and ranging in size from a few millimeters to a few centimeters), metal-plate amulets (incised on thin sheets of gold, silver, or other metals), and other, less common, magical implements (such as elaborate bronze divination-boards). These objects

---

[143] The bibliography on the Greco-Egyptian magic of late antiquity is vast; see the useful basic surveys by Preisendanz 1927; Nock 1929; Ritner 1995b; Brashear 1995; Calvo Martínez 2001.

Jewish magic in late antiquity: "insider" evidence

enjoyed a wide diffusion throughout the Roman empire and beyond, but their survival also depends on the materials upon which they were written or engraved, with magical recipe-books, for example, attested throughout the Roman Mediterranean but preserved only by the dry sands of Egypt.[144]

While a detailed history of this distinctive magical tradition has yet to be written, such a study is out of the question here.[145] Instead, we shall have to do with a brief outline of some of its main features, with special emphasis on those aspects which are of greater significance for our present enquiry. First, we may note that this was a literate, and even scribal, magical idiom, as its complex technical know-how and magical instructions normally were transmitted in written formularies (whose copyists' sometimes even noted the variant readings in their sources!), and as the magical practices which it enjoined often involved the writing down of elaborate texts on many different writing surfaces and with numerous types of writing implements and inks.[146] Writing clearly was a central component of the cultural make-up of this magical idiom, in marked contrast with many other magical traditions of late antiquity, such as the magical recipes preserved in Pliny's *Natural History* or those found in rabbinic literature, which show few signs of such a scribal mentality. And it is the scribal nature of this magical tradition which has assured us the preservation of so many "insider" sources which make its detailed study possible.

A second feature of these magical texts is that in spite of some variation between the different types of magical products (e.g., magical papyri vs. magical gems), they all display a common set of magical techniques, "words of power," and visual designs, images, and symbols, most of which are unique to this specific magical idiom. As we shall encounter these throughout the present section, and again in the next chapter, we need not examine them at this stage, other than to note the ease with which we can identify texts and artifacts as belonging to this magical tradition or as influenced by it. The appearance of "ring letters" *charactêres*, the use of certain "magic words," or even the formula "now, now, quickly, quickly," suffice to tell us that the text in which they appear belongs to, or was influenced by, this magical tradition. Finally, a third feature characterizing this magical idiom is the international, or cosmopolitan, nature of its cultural make-up, and

---

[144] For the wide diffusion of Greco-Egyptian magic, see Brashear 1995, pp. 3417–19.
[145] For the need, and some of the difficulties involved, see Smith 1983. For more recent studies, see Ritner 1993; Graf 1997; Faraone 1999.
[146] This aspect was rightly emphasized by Smith 1995, p. 26. And cf. Frankfurter 1998, pp. 198–264 with Dickie 1999 for different historical explanations of this process.

especially the mixing of Greek, Egyptian, and Oriental elements visible in most of its textual and iconographical manifestations.[147] Among the latter, the Jewish ones predominate, thus raising our hopes that these texts and artifacts might shed much light on the Jewish magical tradition, at least in its Greek-speaking form. Unfortunately, this is not the case. To see why this is so, we shall divide our enquiry in three, beginning with the individual Jewish elements embedded in pagan magical texts, moving to longer Jewish recipes embedded in them, and ending with smaller texts whose identification as "Jewish," "pagan," or "Christian" becomes far more difficult.[148]

Jewish elements in pagan magical texts

Perhaps the best starting-point for the study of the Jewish elements which entered the Greco-Egyptian magical tradition is provided by PDM xiv / PGM XIV, a bilingual Demotic-Greek magical papyrus (Demotic being the cursive version of the Hieroglyphic writing system) which once formed a part of a large cache of late-antique magical and alchemical texts found in Egyptian Thebes. In the lengthy Demotic sections of this formulary – that is, in recipes and spells written in a script which was utilized solely by Egyptian priests – we find numerous Egyptian rituals and myths, as well as elements clearly borrowed from the Greek magical tradition.[149] Moreover, we find here not only occasional references to Iahô or Adônai (on which more below), but also a more explicit reference to the Jewish god and his biblical exploits. It is found in a long recipe intended to secure a god's appearance for the purpose of divination and revelation, a ritual which is entirely Egyptian in form and content, but which at one point commands this god to

Reveal yourself to me here today in the manner of the form of revealing yourself to Moses which you made upon the mountain, before which you had already created darkness and light.[150]

The author of this spell was a Demotic-writing Egyptian priest, who apparently knew something about the (Jewish) god's revelation to Moses upon a

---

[147] For useful surveys of the different ethnic contributions, see Hopfner 1931; Brashear 1995, pp. 3422–29.
[148] For previous surveys, see esp. Hopfner 1931, pp. 336–47; Goodenough 1953–68, vol. II, pp. 190–205; Simon 1986, pp. 340–56; Alexander 1986, pp. 357–59; Fernandez Marcos 1985; Smith 1986/1996; Alexander 1999b.
[149] For a recent analysis of the Demotic magical papyri see Dieleman 2005.
[150] PDM xiv.129–31 (Betz 1986, p. 202, tr. by Janet H. Johnson).

mountain, whose name he may not have known, and even heard some distant echoes of the creation story in Genesis 1, with the separation of light from darkness. Moreover, he saw nothing wrong in incorporating these references too in his elaborate recipe, and apparently assumed that they would only enhance its magical efficacy. In this, he was far from unique, for our evidence shows that numerous pagan magicians throughout the Roman empire gladly incorporated the Jewish god, his names, his angels, his exploits, and his favorite human heroes into their polytheistic magical compositions.

To see this process even more clearly, we may look at another example, this time a beautiful magical gem of an unknown provenance, currently at the Kelsey Museum (see Figure 3.7).[151] On the obverse, we see the *ouroboros* (the serpent swallowing its own tail) enclosing a cock-headed, snake-legged deity dressed in Roman military garb and sporting a whip and a shield; on the reverse, we see an eagle-headed deity with six wings, wearing an apron and carrying Egyptian-style amulets in both hands; on the bevel, we see crocodiles, scarabs, a baboon, and other animals and figures. Moreover, both sides are covered with inscriptions in the Greek alphabet, none of which adds up to "normal" Greek words. Looking at the images, we immediately recognize some elements (the *ouroboros*, the animal-headed deities, the amulets, the scarab, crocodiles, baboon, etc.) as Egyptian, some (and especially the realistic style and the Greek alphabet) as Greek or Greco-Roman, and some (such as the military garb) as Roman. A closer look might reveal other influences as well, but none of the iconography seems to be Jewish in origins.[152] However, this is not the case with the inscriptions, for in addition to standard Greek vowel permutations and the *sêmea kenteu*-formula (to which we shall return in the next chapter) and Egyptian sounding *voces* like *psinôthertherno* (at the bottom of the obverse), we find here some old Phoenician and Syrian deities (Semeseilam, "eternal sun," and perhaps also the gods Sasm and Haduram = "Hadad the Most High") and four of the Jewish angels, Michael, Raphael, Gabriel, and Ouriel, whose names are written right above the shield.

That the four Archangels are indeed Jewish (or Christian) in origin is beyond any doubt, but what exactly is their function here? We could, of

---

[151] The gem is KM 26054, published by Bonner, 1950, no. 172.
[152] There have been repeated attempts (esp. Philonenko 1979 and Nagy 2002b) to find a Jewish "iconographical etymology" for the cock-headed snake-legged god, who appears on hundreds of magical gems. But while the origins of this image remain obscure, the search for a Jewish explanation says more about the ingenuity of modern scholars than about the iconography of ancient Jewish magic.

course, begin to look into Jewish and Christian angelological lore, and come up with some fanciful theories of why these angelic names would have been attached to that specific figure, or why a magician would bother to invoke these four together with the other deities invoked or alluded to in this gem. Such speculations, however, would be based on a grave misunderstanding, for an examination of many hundreds of similar gems reveals the relations between the images and the inscriptions to have been quite fluid. On many gems, the cock-headed snake-legged god is identified as Iaô, but on many others (including this one) he is not, and on yet others the name Iaô is attached to other figures.[153] Thus, it seems quite clear that the names written above, below, or on a figure were not necessarily intended as a tag of identification, but as separate sources of power, complementing that of the image itself. And on countless gems, including this one, the magicians seem to have been bent on piling up as many vowel sequences, *voces magicae*, *charactêres*, and images as possible, with little regard for their actual contents or internal consistency. The magician who designed this gem apparently knew that the four -êl "words" went together, but it is not even clear that he knew where they had come from or what they had originally meant. He added them to his gem because he had heard of their great powers, quite as great as that of the vowel permutations or the cock-headed god.

The entry of the Jewish god and his many angels into the pagan pantheon, and the transformations they underwent in the process, are visible in almost every text and artifact of the Greco-Egyptian magical tradition. Even the most casual reading of these texts cannot fail to note the preponderance there of numerous Jewish names and epithets for God, including the greatest Name, Ia(h)ô (which was widely known to non-Jews in antiquity),[154] and such common epithets as Adônai ("My Lord"), Elôai ("My God"), Sabaôth ("(Lord) of Hosts"), and so on, as well as a plethora of angel names such as Michaêl, Gabriêl, Raphaêl, and even names which in the Jewish tradition were not those of God or his angels, but, for example, of the Patriarchs. It must be stressed, however, that the appeal to the Jewish god entailed no concession to his famous claim for exclusivity. In the

---

[153] Anguipede identified as Iaô: e.g., Michel 2001, nos. 181, 188, 189, 190, etc. (numerous examples). Anguipede not identified as Iaô: e.g., Michel 2001, nos. 187, 202, 213, 216, 223, etc. Other figures identified as Iaô: e.g., Michel 2001, nos. 74, 83, 286, 347, 395, etc.

[154] For Iaô, see Diodorus Siculus 1.94.2 (GLAJJ 58), with Stern's commentary, and cf. Lampe 1961, p. 662, s.v. Ἰαώ, and Philo, *Legatio* 353; see also Aune 1996, for a fuller survey. Unlike Greek, Demotic and Coptic provide for an *h*-sound, hence the possibility of a more correct transliteration of the Name as *IAHO* (e.g., Betz 1986, pp. 196, 205, 208, and cf. PGM IV.92). See also Dieleman 2005, p. 78.

pagan magicians' pantheon, Iaô is just one more deity, sometimes appearing side by side with other deities, sometimes equated with one of them, just as many other pagan gods could easily be equated or conflated with each other (e.g., Hecate-Selene etc.), and sometimes even split up into many different deities. And in many other cases, it seems as if the many names of the Jewish god and his angels became nothing but powerful *voces magicae* for the magicians who invoked them. Thus, one recipe uses the well-worn Egyptian religious and magical technique of claiming to be a god and claims that he is ordering Eros to do his will "since I am the god of all gods, Iaôn Sabaôth Adônai Ab[rasa]x Iarabbai Thouriô Thanakermêph Panchonaps."[155] Another insists that the great god Arsamôs[i] Mouchalinoucha Arpax Adôneai must come to him, since "I am the one whom you met below the holy mountain and to whom you granted the knowledge of your great name, which I shall keep in purity and shall not pass on to any but your fellow-initiates into your holy mysteries."[156] And a third recipe instructs its users to engrave an elaborate image of Aphrodite, Psyche, and Eros on a magnet stone, and write, all around the image, a long series of *voces magicae*, including the intriguing sequence "Adônaie Basma Charakô Iâkôb Iaô," a sequence which re-emerges later in the recipe, embedded between different *voces*.[157] As the sequence contains such names as Adônaios (in the vocative), Jacob, and Iaô, and even the Hebrew word, *be-shem* (or its Aramaic equivalent, *bi-shma*), "in the name of," which appears in almost every Jewish adjuration, there is no doubt that it had some Jewish origins. But the garbled order of the words, the inclusion of Iaô, Adônai, and Jacob as if all three were divine names, and the appearance of the same sequence in other pagan magical texts all demonstrate that here was a garbled Jewish formula, fossilized within the Greco-Egyptian magical tradition and transmitted from one practitioner to the next without a clue as to its correct order or real meaning.[158] In our recipe, this formula is to be engraved on a gem side by side with standard Greek religious iconography, proving once again that the connection between image and inscription was only tenuous. And in other recipes, we find such Hebrew words as *Barouch* ("Blessed is . . .") or *Amên* undergoing similar transformations, and embedded in pagan magical

---

[155] PGM XII.74–75 (pp. 6–7 Daniel).
[156] PGM XII.91–94 (pp. 6–7 Daniel). In line 93, I follow Preisendanz in understanding ουσου as ὀν⟨όματός⟩ σου.
[157] PGM IV.1734–36 and 1799–1801.
[158] See PGM V.133–34; *SM* II, 87 (and cf. Betz 1986, PGM CV, where "Iabok" is silently corrected to "Jacob"!); PGM IV.1376–77; for *basym*, see also Alon 1977. For another example of such processes, see the gem discussed by Robert 1981, pp. 6–27.

texts in contexts which eloquently display their users' ignorance of their original meanings.[159]

In Chapter 6, we shall see that the rabbis were quite aware of the pagan use of God's Name(s), and far from certain about how to relate to it. For the time being, we may cite the words of Origen, who in a famous passage not only reveals his familiarity with this process, but also professes his great disdain towards it. Quoting and then condemning some of the Ophite Gnostics' myths and rituals, Origen notes that

> One must know that those who composed these things neither understood the magical texts nor grasped the meaning of divine Scripture, but mixed everything up. From magic they took "Ialdabaôth" and "Astaphaios" and "Hôraios," while from Hebrew Scripture they took "Iaô" (also called "Ia" by the Hebrews) and "Sabaôth" and "Adônaios" and "Elôaios." Now the Names which they took from Scripture are epithets of the One and Only God, but these enemies of God did not understand this, as they themselves admit, and thought that "Iaô" was one god, "Sabaôth" another, and a third besides this was "Adônaios" (whom Scripture calls Adônai), and yet another was "Elôaios" (whom the Prophets call in Hebrew "Elôai").[160]

Clearly, the "paganization" of the Jewish God was not lost on its ancient Jewish and Christian observers, and to the process noted by Origen, whereby the different Names of the monotheistic God became the names of many different polytheistic ones, we may add other processes of which he was well aware, such as the entry of the formula "the god (of) Abraam, the god (of) Isaac and the god (of) Jacob," into the pagan magicians' formularies, and their complete misunderstanding of the true nature of these names of the Jewish Patriarchs.[161] When powerful formulae moved from one culture to another, and into the hands of people who had no firm grasp of the culture whence they came, such misunderstandings, transformations, and creative reconfigurations were almost bound to happen.

Before ending this brief discussion of the Jewish elements in the Greco-Egyptian pagan magical tradition, one more issue must be addressed, namely, the fictitious Jewish influences invented by modern scholars. One of the favorite pastimes of students of ancient magic is the proposal of

---

[159] For *Barouch*, see PGM IV.363, and esp. PGM V.479–80, where the magician identifies himself as Iaô Sabaôth, as Zagourê Pagourê (the secret names of Seth-Typhon!), and as "Barouch Adônai Elôai Abraam" which is a good transliteration of the Hebrew for "Blessed is the Lord, the God of Abraham." For *Amên*, see PGM IV.857; XII.86 (p. 6 Daniel, with a different division of the "words"); see also PGM VII.271, probably a Jewish recipe.

[160] Origen, *CC* 6.32.

[161] Origen, CC 1.22 and 4.33. For the use of this formula by Jewish exorcists, see also Justin Martyr, *Dial. w. Trypho* 85.3. And see the useful surveys by Rist 1938 and Siker 1987.

Jewish magic in late antiquity: "insider" evidence 201

ingenious, and mostly far-fetched, Hebrew and Aramaic etymologies for virtually every *vox magica* whose origins escape us, and even for some whose origins do not.[162] A full history of the wide-ranging practice of offering "Hebrew" etymologies to every word under the sun – including the sixteenth century claims that the lands of the newly discovered Americas are all there in the Hebrew Bible (Peru, for example, still retained enough of its old name, Ophir, the biblical land of gold), the eighteenth-century claim that all the Homeric heroes had Hebrew names (even "Homer" comes from the Hebrew root *'mr*, "to say"!), or the nineteenth-century claim that the entire English language is in fact derived from Hebrew – would shed much light on Renaissance and modern intellectual mentalities, but is out of the question here.[163] For the purpose of the present study, we must recall that the question is not whether a given "magic word" can be explained by way of Hebrew, for virtually every word in every language can find such an explanation, if only we try hard enough. The question is whether we should look for a Hebrew etymology to begin with, and whether we have any sound criteria with which to judge the plausibility of any attempt to identify unusual words in Greek magical texts as Hebrew or Aramaic in origins.[164] And the same is true for the many scholarly attempts to explain every obscure Gnostic or magical myth, symbol or term as somehow due to "Jewish" influences, without first developing sound criteria with which to test the plausibility or viability of such interpretations.[165] But as long as such self-reflective criticism is absent from this kind of scholarship, students of the Jewish contribution to pagan magic in late antiquity are better served by ignoring the hundreds of supposedly Hebrew and supposedly Jewish words, myths, and symbols strewn throughout the pagan magical texts, and focus instead on the few dozen which can indeed be shown to be taken directly from the Jewish religious or magical tradition.

Jewish recipes in the Greek magical papyri

While the numerous Jewish elements embedded in pagan Greek magical texts prove surprisingly disappointing for the study of ancient Jewish magic (especially as they seem to encompass only the most obvious and

---

[162] The "best" example of this trend remains Schwab 1897, esp. pp. 382ff, but many other examples could be adduced here. Unfortunately, one sad by-product of the unruly erudition of the much-lamented William Brashear is that his own "glossary" of *voces magicae* (Brashear 1995, pp. 3576–603) resuscitates many dubious etymologies which should have been laid to rest long ago.
[163] For Homer, see Adler 1893. For English, see Govett 1869.
[164] For a first attempt to develop such criteria, see Bohak 2003b.
[165] For the most recent example, see Mastrocinque 2005.

widespread elements of the Jewish magical tradition), the quest for whole Jewish recipes embedded in the pagan magical formularies might prove more useful. However, in conducting such a search we must distinguish between what the magical recipes claim and what their actual contents reveal. One typical feature of the Greco-Egyptian magical recipes is that some of them are prefaced not only by a title which explains their aim but also by a specification of their supposed origins. One recipe is said to have been found in a temple library, another is couched in a letter supposedly sent to an ancient king, and a third is said to have been tested in the presence of the emperor Hadrian himself. Within these rubrics, we also find several claims that some recipes and spells are of Jewish origin, such as the identification of one elaborate text as "A holy book called *Monad* or the *Eighth (Book) of Moses*," and the references within that text to a work titled "the *Key of Moses*," one called "the *Archangelic (Book) of Moses*," and even to "Moses' apocryphal *Moon-Book*."[166] To these claims, all taken from PGM XIII, we may add similar claims from the other magical papyri, such as the citation of one invisibility spell "from the *Diadem of Moses*," the attribution of a trance-divination recipe to Solomon, and the labeling of one text as "the Prayer of Jacob."[167] In and of itself, the fathering of magical recipes and procedures on Moses and (far less frequently) Solomon is not insignificant, for it tells us something about their reputation among non-Jewish magicians in antiquity, a reputation which some Jews (like Josephus), and some Christians clearly were glad to enhance. But when we turn from the recipes' rubrics to their actual contents, we find that in most cases there is no correlation whatsoever between the identification of their supposed origins and their actual contents.[168] Thus, in our search for Jewish recipes, we must focus not on their titles, but on their contents. In what follows, we shall look at two specific examples of recipes which may securely be identified as Jewish, while briefly pointing to several others.

(a) The magical formulary known today as PGM XXXVI was bought in the Fayyum by the Norwegian scholar Samson Eitrem, and apparently

---

[166] *Eighth (Book) of Moses*: PGM XIII.3 (p. 32 Daniel), 343 (p. 46), 724 (p. 62), 732 (p. 62), and cf. 1078 (p. 80); *Key of Moses*: ibid., 21 (p. 32), 229 (p. 42), 382–83 (p. 48); *Archangelic (Book) of Moses*: ibid. 971 (p. 74); Moses' apocryphal *Moon-Book*: ibid. 1057 (p. 80). For previous studies of PGM XIII, and of the Jewish elements it contains, see esp. Smith 1984 and 1986; Merkelbach and Totti 1990, pp. 179–222. For works fathered on Moses, see Gager 1972, pp. 146–59 and Gager 1994, and Patai 1994, pp. 30–40.

[167] "Diadem of Moses": PGM VII.619 (nothing Jewish in this or the following recipes); trance-divination of Solomon: PGM IV.851 (a recipe which is very Egyptian, and displays no Jewish elements); "Prayer of Jacob": PGM XXIIb.1 (on which more below, n. 181).

[168] This applies not only to claims regarding Jewish provenance, but to all such claims in the Greek magical papyri; see Betz 1982, and esp. Dieleman 2005, pp. 261–80.

was written in that region sometime in the fourth century CE.[169] It is a magician's working copy, containing nineteen magical recipes, all of which seem to focus on issues of interpersonal relations, from finding grace in the eyes of kings and judges to bringing a desired girl to the practitioner or his client.[170] The owner of this collection may have specialized only in this sort of magical activity (which, given the constant demand, certainly would have been quite lucrative), or he may have had similar collections of recipes for divinatory magic, for healing the sick, and for exorcizing the possessed, which happen to have perished long ago. What seems clear, however, is that he did not compose all of his magical recipes himself, for the collection shows many signs of having been copied, at least in part, from earlier sources. One telling sign is the copyist's many errors – in one recipe (no. 12), he refers to the design which supposedly accompanies the verbal instructions, but apparently forgot to copy the design itself; in another (no. 7) the design accompanying the recipe does not match its description in the recipe itself. As we already noted, such a cavalier attitude to one's magical recipes is far from uncommon in Greek magical recipes and "finished products," and in the Jewish ones as well.[171]

Turning to the recipes themselves, we note that they display a typical mixture of Egyptian and Greek elements. On the Egyptian side, we may note the recurrent return to the cycle of myths about Osiris and his sister-wife Isis, and their struggles with their evil brother Seth-Typhon, by far the most popular set of myths in late-Egyptian magical texts. This cycle provides our recipes with many useful *historiolae* (mythical precedents for the action desired by the magician or his client), with some *voces magicae* (such as Iô Erbêth, Iô Pakerbêth, etc., which are often identified in the magical texts as the secret names of Seth-Typhon), with some of the iconographical motifs of its magical designs (such as the animal-headed deities), and with some ritual specifics (such as writing a spell with the blood of an ass, the animal associated with Seth-Typhon). One recipe (no. 16) even includes a command in the Egyptian language, but written in Greek letters, which is followed by its Greek translation – a sure sign of its composer's bilingual capabilities.[172] On the Greek side, we may note that all the recipes are written

---

[169] For PGM XXXVI, see the excellent edition and commentary by Eitrem 1925; the following discussion is partly based on Bohak 2004. The numbering of the recipes is my own.

[170] Even the fourteenth recipe, "To open a door," is not intended for burglaries, but for the kind of situations envisaged in Song of Songs 5.2 or Theocritus 2.127–8. The only partial exceptions are the tenth recipe, which is aggressive but not erotic, and the thirteenth recipe, in which an amulet for finding grace in the eyes of people is said to be effective for demoniacs too.

[171] For copying and editorial mistakes in the PGM, see above, n. 7. For Jewish parallels, see above, n. 55.

[172] For similar phenomena elsewhere in the PGM, see Dieleman 2005, who does not discuss our passage.

in Greek (rather than Demotic), and that even some of the Egyptian gods' names, and some Egyptian place-names, are given here in their standard Greek, not Egyptian, form. We also find some specifically Greek deities here, such as Hecate (no. 8) the underworld goddess who was the "patron saint" (if we may use that expression here!) of all late-antique magicians, some Greek magical practices, such as the writing of aggressive magical spells on thin sheets of lead, i.e., producing *defixiones* (nos. 1, 7?, 10), a few *voces magicae* which bear ample signs of their Greek origins (e.g., Pyripeganax, etc. in no. 5), such magical formulae as "now now, quickly quickly," and even a touch of Greek literary culture, as seen in the poetic formula "hearken unto me" (*klythi moi*) in one of the recipes (no. 4).

What we have here, in other words, is a Greco-Egyptian amalgamation, perhaps best exemplified by the wish, in recipe no. 14, that "she, NN, will love me forever just as Isis loved Osiris, and remain pure for me like Pelenope for Odysseus." The striking coupling of an Egyptian and a Greek myth is a telling testimony to the recipes' mixed cultural origins, as is the misspelling of Penelope's name. Whoever wrote these recipes had some Greek and some Egyptian background, but certainly was not much of a scholar or a critic. It thus comes as something of a surprise to read the fifteenth recipe of his formulary:

A "bringer," an "inflamer" with unburnt sulfur, in this manner: Take seven lumps of unburnt sulfur, and make a fire from vine branches. Say the following spell over each lump, and throw it into the fire. The spell is this: "The heavens of heavens opened, and the angels of God went down and overturned the five cities – Sodom and Gomora, Adama, Sebouie and Sêgôr. A woman, hearing the voice, became a pillar of salt. You are the sulfur which God rained down in the middle of Sôdom and Gomôra, Adama, Sebouie and Sêgôr! You are the sulfur which served God – just so, serve me, NN (male), with regards to NN (female), and do not let her lie down nor find sleep until she comes and completes the mystery of Aphrodite."

Throw into the fire and say: "If I throw you into the fire, I adjure you by the great Pap Taphe Iaô Sabaôth Arbathiaô Zagourê Pagourê, and by the great Michaêl, Zouriêl Gabriêl Sesengenbarpharangês Istraêl Abraam, bring her, NN (female), to NN (male).[173]

Suddenly, we are in a very different world. We have left the adventures of Isis and Osiris or of Odysseus and Penelope, and are surrounded instead by a very biblical atmosphere. The main *historiola* used by this spell is the well-known Genesis story of Sodom and Gomorrah, of which the spell's composer seems to know all the important details. Not only has he

---

[173] PGM XXXVI.295–311. For previous discussions of this recipe, see Eitrem 1925, pp. 108–10.

accurately mentioned all five cities by name, he also remembered the sad fate of Lot's wife and the importance of sulfur in the act of destruction. Even the language used here displays many clear echoes of the biblical account, including words and idioms (such as "heavens of heavens," or the "raining down" of sulfur), which are entirely biblical in nature, and quite unattested in non-biblical Greek. Whoever composed this recipe must have known his Bible (probably in its Septuagint translation) quite well, and the minor discrepancies with the biblical account – Zoar was not destroyed (see Gn 19.20–23, 30), and Lot's wife did not hear a voice (see Gn 19.26) – might point either to imperfect memory or to a deliberate modification of some details to suit the magician's needs.[174] As we shall see below, and again in subsequent chapters of the present study, both the use of the Sodom and Gomorrah story for magical purposes and its modification in the process were quite common among the Jewish magicians of late antiquity. And while the specific technique used here – creating an identity between the current object and its mythological prototype, so that it would now perform a service analogous to that performed *in illo tempore* – may be non-Jewish in origins (and it was extremely popular in Egyptian and Greco-Egyptian magic), it certainly was common among Jewish practitioners too.[175] In Chapter 5, we shall read a Genizah recipe in which some malodorous liquids are equated with the forces which destroyed Sodom and Gomorrah, and in Chapter 6 we shall find the third-century Rabbi Yoḥanan using exactly the same technique to turn a humble thorn bush into the Burning Bush which was encountered by Moses and use its power to cure a fever. Even the fact that this recipe, unlike many other recipes in PGM XXXVI, is not accompanied by a drawing and does not call for producing one, fits well with the generally aniconic nature of the western branch of ancient Jewish magic, to which we shall return in Chapter 5.

With these observations, we may move from a textual analysis to a possible historical reconstruction of the entry of this recipe into PGM XXXVI. As noted above, the producer and owner of this collection was a bi-cultural, Greco-Egyptian practitioner, and the collection itself is devoted to interpersonal relations, including erotic magic. Apparently, at some point this practitioner received from a colleague an erotic magical recipe which he deemed very useful for his own little collection, even if he had no idea

---

[174] It might also point to its author's familiarity with post-biblical Jewish traditions, as was valiantly argued by Sperber 1994, pp. 110–14. Note, however, that Josephus' version in *War* 4.483–85 is no more faithful to the biblical account than that of our spell.

[175] For Egyptian precedents to this technique, see Podemann Sørensen 1984. For PGM examples, see, e.g., SM II, 72 col. ii (=PGM CXXII), "You are the myrrh with which Isis anointed herself."

where Sodom was or why exactly some unnamed god rained down sulfur in its midst. And it is probably one of the recipes' non-Jewish copyists and users who added the final clause ("Throw into the fire and say," etc.), which is neither consistent with the earlier instructions (which already told you what to say when you throw the sulfur into the fire) nor as purely Jewish as was the first part of the recipe. This pagan scribe invoked Zagourê Pagourê (usually identified as secret names of the Egyptian god Seth, and frequently appearing in the other recipes of PGM XXXVI) and piled up Abraam, Istraêl (sic), and divine and angelic epithets without any regard to their original Jewish meanings, of which he may have been utterly unaware.[176] As we shall see throughout the present study, the addition of new units to existing spells and recipes was far from unusual in all strands of late antique magic. Finally, we may note that this magician's familiarity with one Jewish magical recipe did not make him insert the myth of Sodom and Gomorrah, or any other biblical story, into the other eighteen recipes in his collection.[177]

The fact that the Greek magical papyri do preserve authentically Jewish magical recipes, even if only rarely and in a somewhat altered form, certainly is heartening, and calls for a similar quest outside of PGM XXXVI, a quest which reveals a few more examples of recipes which are likely to be of a Jewish origin. First and foremost, we may note the famous exorcistic ritual of PGM IV.3007–86, the Jewish origins of which have often been noted.[178] The text is labeled "Pibechis' (recipe) for demoniacs," an attribution which, given the spell's obvious Jewish origins, must have been added by a later scribe and proves once again the general mismatch between the recipes' pretended origins and their actual contents. The recipe itself is quite complex, and includes the preparation of *materia magica*, the recitation of an oral spell, and the inscription of an amulet on a tin lamella, whose text consists solely of *voces magicae*. All this is followed by a long adjuration, to be recited over the patient, which is structured as a series of "I adjure (Greek *exorkizô*, whence the Modern English "to exorcize") you (demon), by," followed by numerous references to the Jewish god and

---

[176] For the name Istraêl, see also Astraêlos in the eleventh recipe, and the other appearances of this name in the pagan magical texts, for which see Scholem 1960, p. 95.

[177] Allusions to Sodom and Gomorrah are extremely rare in pagan magical texts, but note the reference to "Sodom's apple" (for which see *Wisd. Sol.* 10.6–7; Josephus, *War* 4.484; Tacitus, *Hist.* 5.7.1 [GLAJJ 281]; Solinus, *Coll. rer. mir.* 35.8 [GLAJJ 449]), in Jordan 1988, pp. 120–26 and 1994a, pp. 323–25. Note also the "Sodom Gomorrah" graffito from Pompeii, in JIWE I, 38.

[178] For earlier discussions of this much-studied text, see Dieterich 1891, pp. 138–48; Blau 1898, pp. 112–17; Gaster 1901; Deissmann 1927, pp. 252–64; Knox 1938; Simon 1986, pp. 349–51; Merkelbach 1996, pp. 29–43; Alexander 1999b, pp. 1073–74; van der Horst 2006.

Jewish magic in late antiquity: "insider" evidence 207

his biblical exploits. Reading these adjurations, so different from most of the magical spells found elsewhere in PGM IV, we find ourselves again in a fully Jewish environment, including the use of such specifically Jewish terms as *dekaplêgon* ("ten plagues") or *chouoplastês* ("fashioned from dust"), and references to the holy city of Jerusalem and its unquenchable lamp (which used to burn there before Titus took it to Rome and destroyed the temple which had housed it).[179] And yet, the many errors found in this recipe, the reference to "Jesus, the God of the Hebrews," and the instruction to keep oneself pure, "for this charm is Hebraic? and is preserved among pure men,"[180] all seem to show that this recipe may have passed through some non-Jewish hands before finally being copied by the pagan owner of PGM IV into his own magical formulary, which was found in the large cache of magical and alchemical Greek and Demotic papyri in Egyptian Thebes a millennium and a half later.[181]

(b) From the Greek magical papyri, we turn to the writings of a sixth-century physician, Alexander of Tralles. Coming from an illustrious family which enjoyed a position of social eminence (one of his brothers was an expert in geometry, mechanics, and architecture, some of whose works are still extant, another was a famous rhetor, to whom the nobles of Constantinople sent their sons for their education, a third was a lawyer, and a fourth was a physician in his native city of Tralles, as had been their father before), Alexander was a well-traveled man, whose writings display his habit of collecting *materia medica* and recipes from all over the Justinianic empire.[182] His clients, as they emerge from his medical writings, seem to have included the rich and the powerful, and as these clients were constantly pushing him to supplement or replace his "methodic" (i.e., medical) treatments with "natural" (i.e., magical) ones, his writings provide many interesting magical recipes, including one found in his section on "natural" remedies for gout:

---

[179] Note, however, that the use of "unquenchable fire (ἄσβεστον πῦρ)" rather than "unquenchable lamp (ἄσβεστος λύχνος)" (as in PGM IV.1219) might be due to the non-Jewish motif of the unquenchable fire which recurs elsewhere in the PGM – e.g., PGM IV.269, PGM LXII.2, 21.

[180] Note, however, that instructions for ritual purity are pervasive in the PGM, and even the abstinence from pork is paralleled in the Egyptian magical rituals, such as PGM I.105 (and see Betz 1986, p. 6, n. 24).

[181] In addition to PGM XXXVI.295–311 and PGM IV.3007–86, I note the following recipes as of possibly Jewish origin: PGM VII.260–71 (discussed in the next chapter); PGM XXIIb.1–26 (the "Prayer of Jacob," displaying many Jewish elements (see also Merkelbach 1996, pp. 105–10), and cf. the Hebrew "Prayer of Jacob" in MTKG II, 22 (T-S K 21.95.T) 2a/1–17 and Leicht 1999)).

[182] For Alexander's family, see Agathias, *Historiae* V.6–9 (pp. 260–68 Costanza). For his travels, see his references to his stay in Rome (vol. I, p. 373 Puschmann, vol. II, p. 541, etc.) and his visits to Tuscia (vol. I, p. 563), Gallia (vol. I, p. 565), Spain (vol. I, p. 565), Cyrene (vol. II, p. 319) and Corfu (vol. I, p. 565).

Another one, for gout and every rheumatic flux:
Dig around the holy plant, that is henbane, when the moon is in Aquarius or Pisces, before sunset, without touching the root. Dig with these two fingers of the left hand – the thumb and the fore-finger – and say: "I tell you, I tell you, holy plant, tomorrow I will call you to the house of NN, so that you will stop the rheumatic flux of the feet and of the hands of this man or that woman. But I adjure you by the great name Iaôth Sabaôth, the god who founded the earth and stopped the sea in spite of the influx of rising rivers, he who dried up Lot's wife and made her salty. Take the spirit of your mother Earth, and her power, and dry up the rheumatic flux of the feet or the hands of this man or that woman." On the next day, before sunrise, take the bone of any dead creature, dig it (the henbane root) up with this bone, take the root and say: "I adjure you by the holy names Iaôth, Sabaôth, Adônai, Elôi." And as you take it, throw on the root some salt and say: "Just like this salt will not grow, let not the illness of this man or that woman (grow)." Then take the tip of the root and tie it around the patient as an amulet – but make sure it does not get wet – and hang the rest (of the root) above the hearth for 360 days.[183]

So biblical did this recipe seem to the text's nineteenth-century editor, that he concluded that Alexander was in fact a Christian, a suggestion which finds no support whatsoever in the ancient evidence about him.[184] But this pagan author clearly used "natural" recipes from many different sources, including a few which bear close resemblance to the magical recipes of the Greek magical papyri, and in this case he seems to have had direct or indirect access to a Jewish magical recipe.[185] For the appearance of Iaô(th), Sabaôth, Adônai, Elôi, and especially the explicit reference to Lot's wife, who turned into a pillar of salt (just as in the PGM XXXVI recipe), and the complete absence of any non-Jewish elements from the entire recipe, point to the Jewish origins of this recipe. In fact, we already noted some Second Temple period claims about the Jewish knowledge of the cutting of roots, and we shall see in Chapter 6 a spell which is quite reminiscent of this recipe and is found in the pages of the Babylonian Talmud and attributed there to a Palestinian rabbi of the third century. In light of all this, we may

---

[183] Alexander Trallianus, vol. II, p. 585 Puschmann. For this recipe, see also Delatte 1961, pp. 126, 129, 159, 173, 180.

[184] Puschmann 1878–89, vol. I, p. 84. For more recent scholarship on Alexander Trallianus, see Duffy 1984, pp. 25–26, and Scarborough 1984, pp. 226–28. I hope to treat his "natural" remedies at greater length elsewhere.

[185] The best example of a PGM-like recipe known to Alexander is found in the previous page (vol. II, p. 583 Puschmann), with a recipe which includes such tell-tale signs as the *vox* Bainchô(ô)ôch (which Puschmann divided in two!) or the magicians' ubiquitous battle-cry, "now now, quickly quickly." See also vol. II, p. 377, for a recipe with an iron ring, a well-known magical formula and a *charactêr*.

conclude that this too is a Jewish magical recipe, borrowed and used by a pagan physician as late as the sixth century CE.

Greek "finished products" likely to be Jewish

In a previous section of this chapter, we noted how the pagan magical texts of late antiquity often borrow many Jewish elements, a fact which makes the identification of magical texts as "Jewish" simply because they contain a reference to Iaô, to Jewish angels, or even to Abraham or Moses utterly untenable. This observation leads to some uncertainties when dealing with shorter Greek magical texts – which means, especially, the numerous "finished products" prepared for individual clients – which contain some Jewish elements, for they may easily have been produced either by Jews or by pagans. Moreover, even when a Greek magical text contains such Jewish elements as to make a pagan authorship unlikely, we must still consider the possibility that it was penned by a Christian, not a Jewish, magician.[186] Faced with such difficulties, we may adopt three different criteria for assessing the likelihood that a Greek magical text was composed by a Jewish magician:

(a) The presence of Hebrew or Aramaic, either in the square script or in Greek transliteration is a sure sign of Jewish authorship. In the next chapter, we shall look at some bilingual (Aramaic/Hebrew-Greek) and trilingual (Aramaic-Hebrew-Greek) magical texts, whose Jewish authorship is hardly in doubt. For the time being, we must focus on the more difficult case of texts written entirely in the Greek alphabet but displaying some transliterations of Hebrew or Aramaic words and phrases. Before classifying such texts as "Jewish," we must always consider what exactly we identify as Hebrew or Aramaic words. On the one hand, we must exclude all the real Hebrew and Aramaic words which have become part and parcel of the Greco-Egyptian magical tradition, and a part of the active vocabulary of at least some pagan magicians. Words such as Adônai, Sabaôth, *be-shem, barouch, amên*, and so on cannot be used to prove a text's Jewish authorship, since they are widely attested even in demonstrably pagan texts. On the other hand, we must also exclude all those *voces magicae* which have been saddled by modern scholars with ingenious Hebrew and Aramaic etymologies. "Words" such as Ablanathanalba, Akrammachammarei, Marmaraôth, Semeseilam, or Sesengen Barpharangês cannot be considered "Jewish" in any way, as the dubious Semitic etymologies offered for them are not supported by any of

---

[186] These difficulties were rightly stressed by Lacerenza 2002, pp. 401–10.

the Hebrew and Aramaic magical texts at our disposal.[187] Finally, we must always bear in mind that some Hebrew words and names were so deeply embedded in the Christian tradition that their presence in a magical text is more likely to point to a Christian authorship than to a Jewish one. *Allelujah*, for example, might appear both in a Jewish and in a Christian magical text, but Emmanuel is not likely to appear in a Jewish text but very likely in a Christian one.

With such precautions in mind, we may look at two examples of Greek magical amulets which are likely to have been produced by Jews. The first is a gold amulet found in Wales in 1827 whose Greek text contains many transliterated Hebrew words and phrases – not just the ubiquitous Adônaie Elôaie Sabaôth, but also accurate transliterations of such biblical and liturgical phrases as *Ehyeh Asher Ehyeh* ("I-am-who-I-am"), *ha-nora ha-gibbor* ("the mighty one, the hero," two of God's commonest epithets), or *hayei 'olam le-'olam*, ("eternal life, forever").[188] The fact that all these Hebrew words do not appear in other Greek magical texts amply proves that they did not become part and parcel of the pagan magical tradition (nor of the Christian one); their presence in this amulet virtually assures us of its Jewish origins. The same seems true of a long bronze amulet found in Sicily, whose Greek text invokes a long list of angels, culminating in the series "ia Chrob[im], ia Seraphim Msôrthôm, i[a] Arphellim, ia Maôn, ia Ra[kia? ia] Zboul." The Cheroubim and Seraphim are not unattested in pagan magical texts, but the words *meshartim*, "servants," and *arphellim*, "clouds, mists," and especially the series *ma'on, raqi'a?*, and *zebul*, three of the seven heavens in some Jewish ouranologies, make the Jewish identification of this text (favored by all previous scholars) quite certain. And the client's name, Ioudas, seems to show that this was an amulet produced by a Jewish magician for a Jewish client.[189]

(b) A second criterion for the identification of texts as Jewish is the presence of extensive biblical scenes, allusions, and citations. Given the general disinterest among the pagan magicians in the Hebrew Bible or its Greek translation, we may be fairly certain that the more specifically biblical elements a text displays, the less likely it is to be a pagan composition. A single allusion to Moses' encounter with a god on a mountain could easily be the work of a pagan magician, even a Demotic-writing Egyptian priest, but the accumulation of such references in a single text is not attested in the demonstrably pagan texts, and is very common in the Jewish ones. Here

---

[187] For these examples, see Brashear 1995, pp. 3577, 3578, 3591–92, 3598, 3598–99, respectively.
[188] For the Wales amulet, see Kotansky 1994, no. 2 with Bohak 2003b, pp. 74–77.
[189] For this amulet, see Sciacca 1982–83; Kotansky 1994, no. 33; JIWE I, 159; and cf. Veltri 1996b.

too, however, caution is called for. On the one hand, we must always bear in mind that not every motif which "sounds" biblical to its modern readers need be interpreted as a biblical allusion. Creation stories, for example, tend to echo each other, and a reference to a god who created the world out of chaos should not be taken as "Jewish" unless we have other reasons for accepting it as such. On the other hand, when a magical text displays a real familiarity with the (Greek translation of) the Hebrew Bible, we should always consider the possibility of a Christian authorship, and search for Christian elements within the text. Their absence does not suffice to prove that a text is not Christian, but the longer the text, and the more biblical elements it displays, the more likely it is to be a Jewish rather than a Christian magical text.

As a case in point, we may take the famous curse tablet from Hadrumetum (North Africa), whose Jewish origins have often been recognized.[190] Here, we find a long series of adjurations, in which the ghost of the person in whose tomb the lead tablet was deposited is asked to go and make Urbanus son of Urbana love the client, Domitiana daughter of Candida. Let us quote the first five of the fifteen adjurations which make up this spell:

> I adjure you, demonic spirit which lies here, by the holy name Aôth Ab[aô]th, by the god of Abaraan, and the Iaô of Iacos, Iaô Aô[th Ab]aôth, the god of Israma. Hear the glorious and [frigh]tful and great name and go out to Urbanus, son of Urbana, etc.
> I adjure you by the great god, the eternal, over-eternal and pantocrator who is above the supernal gods.
> I adjure you by the one who created the heaven and the sea.
> I adjure you by the one who set aside the righteous.
> I adjure you by the one who crossed? his staff in the sea, to bring and bind Urbanus, son of Urbana, etc.

It would, of course, be very hard to argue that this is not a Jewish text, for there are many references here, and throughout the rest of the tablet, that seem to be specifically Jewish. And yet, it also seems that the last copyist of this spell was not really in control of the data mentioned in his text, which is why he did not notice that the names of Abraham, (Isaac?), Jacob and Israêl were corrupt or that the reference to the splitting of the Red Sea by means of Moses' staff was badly garbled. Once again, we see a pagan writer using a magical recipe which originally was composed by a Jewish practitioner, a

---

[190] For the Hadrumetum *defixio*, see Audollent 1904, no. 271. For a recent translation, see Gager 1992, no. 36. For previous discussions see especially Deissmann 1901, pp. 269–300; Blau 1898, pp. 96–112; Merkelbach 1996, pp. 111–22; Alexander 1999b, pp. 1074–75.

process we already noted in PGM XXXVI and PGM IV and in the works of Alexander of Tralles. Unfortunately, this seems to have occurred only rarely, and of the many hundreds of *defixiones* published to date, from all over the Roman Empire, no other example displays such tell-tale signs of having been copied from an originally Jewish magical recipe. Here too, in other words, we see that Jewish magical recipes were available to some pagan magicians in late antiquity, but were far from commonly used by them.[191]

(c) A third criterion for the identification of a Greek-language "finished product" as Jewish is far more problematic, and involves the separation of the Jewish magical texts from the Christian ones.[192] In many cases, a magical text or artifact may easily be identified as Christian by virtue of its contents or iconography, be it Greek magical papyri with citations of or allusions to the New Testament, magical gems, pendants and bracelets with scenes from the life and death of Jesus, or magical texts and artifacts with such Christian symbols as the Cross. But when we encounter pendants with the image of Solomon spearing a prostrate female demon or of the Binding of Isaac (which also figures in synagogue mosaics!), or papyrus amulets with the Septuagint version of Psalm 90 (91 in the MT), we are less sure as to how they should be classified, as their contents could easily be explained both within a Jewish context and within a Christian one. One helpful approach is the identification of series of related artifacts, assuming that those artifacts whose origins are in doubt belong with those whose origins are more readily identifiable. In the case of the magical gems and pendants with the holy-rider iconography (where the rider often is identified as Solomon), the Christian origins of some of the artifacts are made clear by the presence of Crosses and other Christian symbols. Some of these gems and pendants display no such obviously Christian motifs, but none display motifs (such as Hebrew or Aramaic inscriptions, or a Menorah) which would necessitate their identification as Jewish. Thus, while some scholars see those objects which display no Christian motifs (see, for example, Figures 3.5 and 3.8) as the Jewish precursors of the obviously Christian pendants, this is far from certain.[193] The same is true of the long series of papyrus amulets, and

---

[191] In addition to the Hadrumetum tablet, the following artifacts may be identified as Jewish: Kotansky 1994, no. 32 (an amulet/recipe-book, found in Sicily and displaying numerous biblical references and citations); Benoit 1951 = van Haelst 1976, no. 911 (a Greek exorcistic hymn, written on papyrus and displaying some affinity with the Qumran exorcisms); Merkelbach 1996, pp. 44–46 (an exorcistic amulet recalling Solomon's subjugation of the demons).

[192] The problem of separating Jewish from Christian texts appears in other genres too – see, for example, the liturgical fragments discussed by van der Horst 1998.

[193] For different reconstructions of the relative chronologies and possible Jewish origins of the Solomon-rider iconography, see Bonner 1950, pp. 208–12; Walter, 1989–90; Alexander 1999b, pp. 1076–78; Torijano 2002, pp. 129–41; Lässig 2001; Spier 2007.

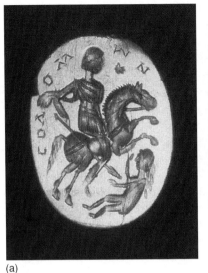 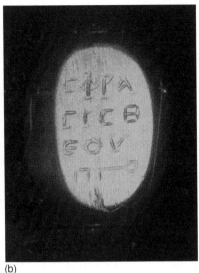

(a) (b)

Figure 3.8 A magical gem, showing, on the obverse, a holy rider (identified as King Solomon) spearing a prostate female demon; on the reverse, a Greek inscription, "The Seal of God," and a key. Such gems might be Jewish, but are more likely to be Christian.

metal medallions, bracelets, rings, and other artifacts on which all or some of the Septuagint Psalm 90 have been inscribed; a recent survey of all the known evidence came up with about eighty such pieces, none of which is demonstrably Jewish, and most of which are demonstrably Christian.[194] This is a very interesting conclusion, since the anti-demonic use of this psalm certainly is a part of the "Jewish heritage" of earliest Christianity; it is not its exorcistic use, but its *writing down* in Greek-language amulets, that the Christians had to develop by themselves, hence the apparent lack of any Jewish specimens. Here too, however, future research might shed more light on such issues, and perhaps even adduce clear evidence that some of these artifacts were, in fact, produced by Jews.

If in the judgment of whole series of similar artifacts, some of which are demonstrably Christian, we may adopt the rule that the burden of proof lies on those who insist that the objects which do not display any Christian signs are in fact Jewish, in the study of individual Greek "finished products" we have no such help. Looking at texts which display both Jewish and Christian elements, we probably may classify them as Christian, in spite of the temptation to ascribe them to the ever-elusive Judeo-Christians of late

---

[194] See Kraus 2005. I am grateful to Thomas Kraus for much information on these artifacts.

antiquity.¹⁹⁵ But when the texts display Jewish elements and no Christian ones, their classification becomes much more difficult, and none of the above criteria prove very helpful; such texts could be interpreted as Jewish, but could easily be interpreted as the work of a pagan magician, and even of a Christian one. For when we read a silver amulet found in Oxyrhynchus, whose text consists of a vowel series followed by "Adônaie Sabaôth, give grace, love, success, charm to the bearer of this amulet," we could easily imagine a Jewish scribe producing this amulet, but could also imagine its production by a pagan scribe (whose next amulet invoked Sarapis in a similar fashion) or by a Christian one.¹⁹⁶ And when an excruciatingly fragmentary papyrus of an unknown provenance contains the remains of an exorcism, written in a very biblical Greek and including a reference to Solomon's imprisonment of the demons in special vessels, a Jewish and a Christian context seem equally plausible.¹⁹⁷ Thus, any study of the Jewish magical tradition in late antiquity must come to terms with the fact that when it comes to magical texts written in Greek, the corpus of the available evidence is not as well defined as when dealing with magical texts written in Hebrew and Aramaic.

MEDIEVAL AND LATER JEWISH MAGICAL TEXTS

In the previous sections of the present chapter, we focused on those Jewish magical texts which may securely be dated to late antiquity, that is, to the period before the Muslim conquest of the Near Eastern world in the seventh century CE. But while such texts provide an obvious starting point for any study of the Jewish magic of the time, sources which date from later periods should not be disqualified from our study solely on the basis of their later dates. Rather, as often is true in the study of any magical tradition, the later texts often preserve much useful evidence for periods earlier than their actual date of copying. Thus, some of the most important sources for the study of late-antique Jewish magic were written after the Muslim conquest,

---

¹⁹⁵ For pertinent examples, see Harrauer and Harrauer 1987; Kotansky 2002. Note also Kotansky 1980, no.1, for a "Jewish" amulet with a Christogram, and Kotansky 1994, no. 52 (to be read with the parallel texts in Gelzer, Lurje, and Schäblin 1999), where a long "Jewish" amulet ends with "One God and His Christ." Such examples will have to be gathered together and analyzed as a group before we can assess their "Jewishness."

¹⁹⁶ The amulet is SM II, 64 = Kotansky 1994, no. 60. And cf. SM I, 7, for a very similar papyrus amulet, but invoking Sarapis. For another Iaô amulet which might be Jewish, see PGM LXXI, re-edited in Jordan 2001, pp. 183–86. For a magic key (to aid in childbirth?) which might be Jewish, see Hamburger 1974, and for an amulet which deserves a closer study see Libertini 1927.

¹⁹⁷ The text is SM I, 24 = van Haelst 1976, no. 753.

but can be shown to contain copies of copies of much earlier texts. These types of sources may broadly be divided in two – magical texts found in the Cairo Genizah, and those found in non-Genizah manuscripts. As each of these two types of texts poses its own unique features and possibilities, we shall examine them separately.

The magical texts from the Cairo Genizah

Of all the sources at our disposal for the study of the Jewish magical practices of late antiquity, especially its western branch, those found in the Cairo Genizah are perhaps the most rewarding.[198] This might seem paradoxical, as the texts in question were found in the storehouse of a medieval synagogue in Cairo, and none of them predates the ninth century CE, a period much beyond the chronological limits of the present study. And yet, this immense treasure (with more than 200,000 fragments!) has already demonstrated its usefulness not only for the study of many aspects of medieval Jewish life, but also for scholars of earlier stages of Jewish history and culture. To students of the Second Temple period it provided a few tantalizing texts, most notably the Hebrew version of Ben Sira and the so-called "Damascus Document," whose identification and publication preceded the discovery of the Dead Sea Scrolls by almost half a century. To rabbinic scholars it provides some of the best textual evidence for the classical works of rabbinic Judaism, such as the Mishnah and the Talmudim. To scholars of late-antique Palestinian Jewish liturgy, hymnography, and even secular poetry it provides thousands of illuminating fragments, mostly of previously unknown texts.[199] To students of late-antique and medieval Jewish magic it offered a similar reward, but its call went unheeded for almost a full century. It was only with Margalioth's 1966 publication of *Sepher ha-Razim* that the importance of the Genizah magical texts was acknowledged, and only from the 1980s that students of Jewish magic embarked on a systematic search for Genizah texts which could shed light on this topic. Their cumulative efforts have so far resulted in the publication of c. 160 Genizah magical texts, which is just a small fraction – and not necessarily a representative sample – of the Genizah magical texts which have already been identified,

---

[198] For previous surveys of the Genizah magical texts see esp. Golb 1967, pp. 12–16; Schäfer 1990; Wasserstrom 1992; Shaked 2000b.
[199] For the Cairo Genizah and its contribution to different branches of Jewish scholarship, see now the excellent survey by Reif 2000. Reif says little about the Genizah magical or mystical texts (see pp. 112, 143, 154–55, and 201–02), and the same is true for the surveys included in Brody 1990, Friedman 1999, and Reif and Reif 2002.

not to mention those that still await identification.²⁰⁰ If in Chapter 2 we noted how the few Jewish magical texts of the Second Temple period are chased by too many scholars, here we may note the opposite process, with an almost endless supply of magical texts whose value has not yet been appreciated by their potential consumers.

When we examine the Genizah magical texts – omitting such occult sciences as alchemy or astrology, and all the more specialized forms of divination (*gorallot* (=*sortes*), geomancy, physiognomy, palmomancy (twitch-divination), brontology (thunder-divination), dream interpretation, and so on) – we find a full range of both "finished products" and magical recipes, mostly written on paper and vellum, in Aramaic, Hebrew, Judeo-Arabic (Arabic written in Hebrew letters), Arabic, or any mixture thereof.²⁰¹ Among the "finished products," we may note hundreds of amulets of every conceivable form and size – from long amulets painstakingly prepared on an "ad hoc" basis for specific individuals in specific circumstances to short, "prefabricated" pieces, designed for a single purpose or for all purposes alike. Numerous curses and subjugation spells also find their rightful place in this rich gallery, as do erotic binding spells, oracular dream requests, and adjurations of angels for such varied tasks as memorizing the Torah or finding hidden treasures.²⁰² Among the recipes, we may note, besides the fragments of more "literary" books of magic (which we already discussed above and to which we shall return below), the presence within the Genizah of any conceivable form of written magical recipes, from the single recipe scribbled on the margins of a non-magical book or a used piece of paper, through the single sheet with a small collection of magical recipes, to full-fledged formularies, some of them dozens of pages long.²⁰³ These usually consist of a seemingly endless series of magical recipes, sometimes arranged in a more or less topical order, with recipes for similar aims often clustered together and the whole collection sometimes preceded by such prefatory materials as a more theoretical treatise or a list of divine or angelic names. In other cases the order of the recipes seems entirely arbitrary, the result

---

[200] For Genizah magical texts, see AMB; HAITCG; MSF; MTKG. See also Shaked 1988a and 1988b, Díaz Esteban 1998, and Bohak 2005. For a list of earlier publications, see MTKG I, pp. 12–13. My knowledge of unpublished Genizah magical texts depends on a list prepared by Prof. Shaul Shaked, which he kindly placed at my disposal, and on my own additions to this list, which I hope to publish in due course. Another useful starting-point is provided by Isaacs 1994.

[201] In some cases, the magical texts were written in special codes; being based on simple substitutions, they pose little difficulty even for the amateur cryptographer, as I hope to demonstrate elsewhere.

[202] For a phenomenological survey of the aims of ancient Jewish magical practices, including many Genizah magical texts, see esp. Harari 1998, pp. 136–226.

[203] The longest formulary published so far is MSF, G18 (T-S K 1.143), of which twenty pages survive, but which is incomplete.

of the gradual accumulation, by a single practitioner or over a few generations, of magical recipes from every conceivable source. Unfortunately, the earlier Genizah collections never specify these sources, in marked contrast with the situation in the Greco-Roman world, in rabbinic literature, or in later Jewish magical texts, where recipes are sometimes attributed to specific tradents.[204]

We shall have more to say about the characteristic structure of these formularies, and about its possible origins, in the following chapter. At present, we must stress that most of these formularies did not reach us intact, for besides the natural deterioration of pages many centuries old, these texts often underwent two additional processes of decomposition. First, as these formularies could be quite long (unlike the "finished products," which often occupy no more than a two-page leaf), the bifolia from which their quires were made often became detached from each other, so that one finds pages and bifolia from the same quire or the same booklet under different shelf-marks and even in different Genizah collections worldwide, without any prior indication as to which fragments should be joined with which. Such a process of dispersal is well known to all Genizah scholars, as it affected all types of manuscripts found there, be they talmudic compendia, piyyutic collections, biblical manuscripts, or philosophical treatises. Less common, however, but quite common with Genizah magical recipe-books, is the deliberate tearing up of many such booklets before they were deposited in the Genizah. This process of cutting the pages – mainly vertically, each page cut into several strips, and sometimes horizontally, in the middle of the page – resulted in the dispersal throughout the Genizah of hundreds of narrow strips of paper with obviously magical contents (see Figure 3.9).[205]

Once all the relevant fragments are identified, reconstructed, and analyzed with all the standard tools of philological analysis (and all these processes have barely begun, and are sure to take many years), these heterogeneous materials can, and should, be studied from many different perspectives. Paleographers and Genizah experts might accurately date some of these fragments, which almost always carry no date (and whose dates can range from the ninth to the nineteenth century!), and perhaps even identify some of the scribes who wrote them, scribes whose non-magical output has

---

[204] For Greco-Egyptian examples, see, e.g., PGM XII.96–143 (p. 6–10 Daniel) (three recipes, attributed to "Himerios," "Agathocles," and "Zminis of Tentyra," attributions whose veracity is impossible to assess). For such attributions in later Jewish magical texts (where they become extremely common), see, e.g., Bos 1994, pp. 61–63. For a Genizah example, see T-S K 1.108 (unpublished).

[205] For a more detailed description of these processes, see Bohak 2005.

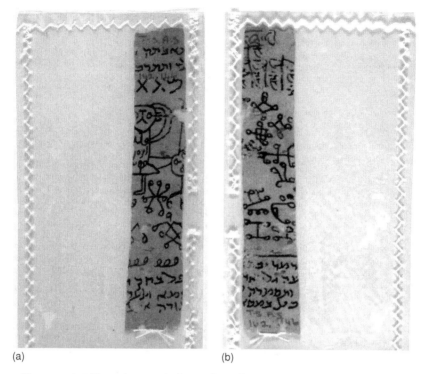

(a) (b)

Figure 3.9 A deliberately-cut strip from a Genizah magical recipe-book. The text is in Judeo-Arabic. Note the anthropomorphic figure (a demon? the client? the victim?) and the numerous *charactêres*. Such images are relatively rare in the Genizah magical texts.

previously been identified in other Genizah fragments.[206] Students of the social world of medieval Jewish magic might wish to focus especially on the "finished products" prepared for (or against) named individuals, as these individuals might already be known to us from other Genizah documents, or to examine such issues as magician–client relations, the modes of production of "finished products," or the public and communal uses of magical rituals for the cursing or excommunication of wayward individuals.[207] They

---

[206] For this kind of identification, see Goldstein and Pingree 1977, p. 124: "Professor S. D. Goitein informed us that this text (a nativity horoscope) is in the hand of Hillel ben Eli, a court clerk who left about 100 documents in the Geniza that date from the period 1066 to 1108, after which time he is not otherwise known to have been active." Goitein later re-identified the scribe as Hillel's son-in-law, Halfon b. Manasse (Goitein 1967–93, vol. V, p. 625, n. 28 [but cf. vol. V, p. 292 and p. 588, n. 98]). For a non-Jewish comparandum, see the amulet written by the well-known sixth-century poet and scholar Dioscorus of Aphrodito (PGM 13a).

[207] For the need for this kind of research, see Wasserstrom 2005.

Jewish magic in late antiquity: "insider" evidence 219

might also wish to look for evidence of Jewish magical activity at the time in the non-magical texts of the Cairo Genizah, be they personal letters, business documents, halakhic discussions and responsa, or book lists and library catalogues.[208] Kabbalah scholars would wish to focus on the Kabbalistic texts preserved in the Cairo Genizah, and students of the occult sciences and their medieval transmission would find a bewildering array of Genizah texts to choose from.[209] Students of Muslim and Arabic magic will find hundreds of fragments of non-Jewish or barely Judaized magical texts, in Arabic and in Judeo-Arabic (and sometimes in Hebrew translations), most of which have never been studied, and an equally large number of Jewish magical texts with strong Arabic and Muslim influences.[210] Even students of the Coptic magical traditions will find a few fragments of Coptic magical texts, and some evidence of the use of such materials by the Jewish magicians of medieval Cairo.[211] Finally, students of medieval and later Jewish magic will find here not only rich deposits of Jewish magical texts from the lands of Islam (including some in Judeo-Persian), but also some whose ultimate origins lie in medieval Ashkenaz or in pre-Expulsion Spain, including some magical texts in Judeo-Spanish (Ladino).[212]

All this will have to be dealt with elsewhere. For the purpose of the present enquiry, we must focus only on those Genizah magical texts that can be shown to preserve pre-Muslim Jewish magical materials. One excellent starting-point, though by no means the only one, is provided by the many Genizah fragments of Hebrew, Aramaic, and Judeo-Arabic collections of magical recipes. Like every other text found in the Cairo Genizah, these recipes too were copied no earlier than the ninth century, and thus stem from a period later than that which lies at the heart of our discussion. However, as we shall have abundant occasion to note in the subsequent chapters, many of the Genizah magical texts can be shown to be copies

---

[208] See, for example, Friedman 1986, pp. 166–68, for a Geonic responsum (T-S G 1.80) discussing the complaint of a man who claims that his inability to perform his marital duties with his present wife is due to a spell cast upon him. See also Allony 2006, for interesting evidence on the diffusion of magical, astrological, oneirocritical, and divinatory texts in medieval Jewish libraries.

[209] For some of the Kabbalistic fragments in the Cairo Genizah, see Benayahu 1980.

[210] The best published example remains Friedländer 1907 (which is, however, a book of divination). For useful points of entry into this material, see Golb 1965; Golb 1967, pp. 12–18; Khan 1986; Baker and Polliack 2001 (whose identification of the magical texts could greatly be improved).

[211] For a published Coptic magical text from the Cairo Genizah (T-S 12.207), see Meyer and Smith 1994, pp. 197–99. A few unpublished Coptic magical texts from the Cairo Genizah are currently being studied by Jacques van der Vliet. For Coptic elements in the Jewish magical texts, see Bohak 1999.

[212] For a Judeo-Persian Genizah magical text, see below, n. 216. For Judeo-Spanish Genizah magical texts, see Gutwirth 1983 and 1989 (the text he mentions on p. 99, n. 28 has now been published as MTKG III, 83 (T-S NS 324.92)).

of copies of texts which actually do go back to late-antique Palestinian models.²¹³ To give just one specific example, we may return to the Jewish Aramaic love-charm from Ḥorvat Rimmon, which is paralleled, with greater or lesser accuracy, by several Genizah magical recipes.²¹⁴ As with the example with which we opened the present chapter, we could print all of these parallels synoptically, although the "finished product" from Palestine predates the recipes from Cairo by half a millennium and more. However, it must also be stressed that the transfer of magical recipes from late-antique Palestine to medieval Cairo also involved several important changes. On the more technical level, we must note the move from papyrus to paper (vellum, on the other hand, seems to have been used continuously) and perhaps also from scroll to codex, changes which apparently left few traces in the Genizah recipe-books.²¹⁵ Far more important are the linguistic and cultural changes, from a world in which the spoken languages were Aramaic and Greek and surrounding culture was either pagan or Christian or both, to an Arabic-speaking, Muslim environment. The effects of these two changes will be seen on almost every Genizah magical recipe-book at our disposal. Thus, if we return to the example with which we began this chapter, and examine only the left-hand column of our synopsis, we may note that the recipe in question might go back to a late-antique model – the instructions are those of a standard *defixio* (to harm someone, you write the curse on a lead lamella, and deposit it in a grave), and the adjuration itself is in Aramaic, although the text around it is in Judeo-Arabic. And yet, when this text passed on from one period to another, the Aramaic instructions which must have accompanied the spell were translated into Judeo-Arabic, the more natural idiom for the recipe-book's Cairoene readers.²¹⁶ A later hand even added an Arabic gloss on the margins, explaining the recipe's aim (and serving as a useful indexing-sign – when you wanted to find specific recipes quickly, you looked only at the Arabic "keywords" on the margins of the page!). Finally, this ancient recipe ended up between many other recipes of different origins and history, including some which were copied, no doubt in medieval Cairo, from a bilingual Coptic-Arabic collection of Christian

---

[213] For the continuity between the late-antique Palestinian magical texts and those of the Cairo Genizah, see also Golb 1965; HAITCG, pp. 22–32. I hope to return to this issue in a forthcoming paper.
[214] See above, n. 30.
[215] I note, however, the existence of magical *rotuli*, some of which clearly date from the earliest days of the Cairo Genizah, but which have not yet received any scholarly attention.
[216] And see Leicht 2005, who pays some attention to these processes, which are also paralleled, for example, in the Demotic-Greek magical papyri (see Dieleman 2005, p. 126). See also Shaked 1988b (instructions in Judeo-Persian and spells in Aramaic).

Jewish magic in late antiquity: "insider" evidence 221

magical recipes.[217] In what follows, we shall have to bear in mind that the Cairo Genizah does not preserve any late-antique Palestinian Jewish magical texts in a "pure" state, but only distant copies of such texts, as copied, translated, re-edited, and "updated" by the Jewish magicians of medieval Cairo.

While the Genizah magical texts have the great disadvantage of being relatively late, and therefore necessitating in each case a detailed examination of the signs of their earlier origins and an awareness of the transformations and corruptions to which they probably were subjected during the process of textual transmission, they have three enormous advantages for our study, which make them in effect a major source for the study of the western branch of late-antique Jewish magic. First, their almost inconceivable abundance. While the late-antique metal amulets currently at our disposal amount to a few dozen pieces, mostly quite short, the Cairo Genizah provides us with thousands of pages of magical texts, ranging all the way from tiny scraps of paper to well-preserved, or at least reconstructible, recipe-books of some twenty pages or more. Second, unlike the texts crudely scratched upon the metal amulets, or those written in ink on the inside of convex baked-clay incantation bowls, the Cairo Genizah texts were written on much more natural writing materials – mainly paper and vellum – and some of them are much easier to read than all the other magical texts at our disposal, and therefore provide a secure textual foundation on which to base our cultural-historical analysis. Third, unlike all the late-antique artifacts, which tend to represent a small number of magical practices and a limited variety of spells and formulae, the Cairo Genizah provides us with ample evidence for virtually every kind of magical praxis known to late-antique and medieval Jews, except perhaps for those practices which were transmitted only orally throughout these periods or which were filtered out of the Jewish magical tradition before the ninth or tenth century.

Medieval and later manuscripts (outside the Cairo Genizah)

Leaving the Cairo Genizah and turning to the vast treasures of medieval and later Jewish manuscripts scattered in dozens of collections worldwide, we are confronted by a bewildering array of Jewish magical texts, most of which have never even been studied.[218] And, as with the late-antique

---

[217] And see Bohak 1999.
[218] In what follows, I leave out the printed books of Jewish magic (for which see Matras 1997 and 2005), which have passed through processes of selection and self-censorship, and are far less useful for the study of ancient Jewish magic.

magical recipes, here too we find two main forms of textual transmission – "literary" books of magic on the one hand, and free-form formularies, or even individual recipes, on the other. Turning to the "literary" books first, we note the continued creation and compilation of new books of Jewish magic, such as *Sepher ha-Yashar*, the *Havdala de-Rabbi Akiva*, *Shimmush Tehillim* (the "Uses of the Psalms"), the *Pishra de-Rabbi Ḥanina ben Dosa* (the "Spell-Loosening of Rabbi Ḥanina ben Dosa"), most of which already are mentioned by the Karaites and/or the Geonim, or *Sepher ha-Malbush*, which is first attested in the thirteenth century, or even *Sepher Raziel*, which was printed in Amsterdam in 1701 and remained popular ever since.[219] All these books may contain some remnants of late-antique Jewish magic, and in some cases such continuity may easily be demonstrated. Unfortunately, the process of identifying, editing, and analyzing the sources of these "literary" magical compositions has only just begun, and their use for the study of late-antique Jewish magic remains somewhat limited, as neither their original contexts nor their transmission histories have hitherto been established.

Worse still is the fate of the Jewish magical formularies and recipes of the medieval and later periods, which have never been catalogued, or even identified, in any systematic manner.[220] Of course, bibliographers of Jewish manuscripts could not entirely ignore such manuscripts, which is why we do find occasional descriptions thereof in the catalogues of Steinschneider, Neubauer, Scholem, and others, but such descriptions often are either disdainful or superficial or both, and no study has ever been devoted to an overall survey of the shapes and contents of such manuscripts. A few manuscripts have been studied, sometimes even quite extensively, but none has been edited from start to finish, or placed in the wider context of the Jewish magical tradition as a whole.[221] In a few other cases, scholars have taken a single theme, or a specific type of magical ritual, and tried to gather together the relevant data from many different magical manuscripts.[222] And in a few other cases, scholars have mined the manuscripts to which they had access for interesting recipes and rituals, often without even specifying

---

[219] For *Sepher ha-Yashar* and *Sepher ha-Malbush*, see Wandrey 2004. *Havdala de-Rabbi Akiva*: see Scholem 1980/81 and Juusola 2004. *Shimmush Tehillim*: see Trachtenberg 1939, p. 109; Fodor 1978; Rebiger 1999; MTKG III, pp. 2–17. *Pishra*: see Tocci 1986 and MTKG II, 22 (T-S K 1.144) 1a/1–1b/9. *Sepher Raziel*: see Trachtenberg 1939, passim, and Leicht 2006, pp. 187–294.

[220] For brief overviews of this vast field, see Scholem 1974, pp. 182–89 and Dan 1972. Unfortunately, these manuscripts are mostly ignored in such surveys as Sirat 2002. The only available tool for their study is the catalogue of the Institute of Microfilmed Hebrew Manuscripts, whose classifications of such materials are not always reliable.

[221] See, for example, Steinschneider 1862; Thompson 1906–07; Benayahu 1972; Barel 1991; Bos 1994; Verman 1999; Petrovsky-Shtern 2004. And see now Buchman and Amar 2006.

[222] See, for example, Daiches 1913.

Jewish magic in late antiquity: "insider" evidence 223

which recipes they found in which manuscripts.[223] And while all these works are not without value, their perusal is hampered by the absence of the most basic research tools, including a basic typology of this type of manuscript, or even a set of guidelines as to how they should be classified and catalogued, beyond the mere listing of recipe titles.

To see the potential contribution of such magical manuscripts to the study of Jewish magic in late antiquity, we may look at a single manuscript, MS Sassoon 56, formerly in the collection of David Sassoon and currently in the New York Public Library (NYPL Heb. 190). This manuscript was written "in a Greek cursive hand," by Moses b. Jacob b. Mordechai b. Jacob b. Moses, between the years 1465 and 1468, and contains a miscellany of Kabbalistic and magical materials. And while some of the Kabbalistic passages have been mined by students of Jewish mysticism, the numerous magical recipes have never been utilized by scholars.[224] In the next chapter, we shall adduce some recipes and practices from this important manuscript, as examples of the continuity of Jewish magic from late antiquity to the fifteenth century and beyond. For the time being, we may note that among its many recipes, one is a direct descendant of the recipe according to which the Ḥorvat Rimmon erotic sherds were produced almost a full millennium earlier.[225] Such parallels clearly prove that much in this late-Byzantine manuscript *could* go back to late-antique sources, but they also highlight the main difficulty involved in the use of such late evidence. When we look in such manuscripts for recipes and spells which we already know to be of late-antique origins, we often find them, in different stages of textual entropy and translated into different vernaculars. But when we look at the late manuscripts in search of other late-antique materials, we run into a great difficulty, for whereas the Genizah magical fragments contain many recipes whose language (Jewish Palestinian Aramaic with many Greek loanwords) and contents (and especially borrowings from the Greco-Egyptian magical tradition) help identify them as late antique in origin, in the non-Genizah manuscripts, which tend to be much later and further removed from late-antique Palestine, such tell-tale signs of an ancient origin are much less common. Thus, without sound criteria for the identification in the later manuscripts of demonstrably early textual units, we are at present reduced to searching within these manuscripts for textual units

---

[223] See, for example, Grunwald 1900, 1906, 1907, and 1923b.
[224] For brief descriptions of this manuscript, see Sassoon 1932, vol. I, pp. 424–25 and Benayahu 1972, p. 200. I am grateful to Michael Terry for bringing this manuscript to my attention and letting me study it.
[225] See Sassoon 56, p. 178, and cf. n. 30 above. The same recipe reappears in a manuscript bought in Mossoul in the early twentieth century (Thompson 1907, p. 166, no. 9).

we already know to be early. Even this, however, is a task which will require much labor, and which has only just begun.

In summary, we may note that the great advantages of the non-Genizah manuscripts are that they are plentiful, and that in many cases they preserve dozens of consecutive pages, unlike the Genizah fragments, which are often tattered and scattered. Their great disadvantage is that they are later than many of the Genizah fragments, and further removed from the magical texts of late-antique Palestine. But their greatest disadvantage is that they remain unpublished, and almost entirely uncharted. In the future, they *may* turn out to contain much that is useful for the study of ancient Jewish magic, but before we reach this stage much hard work remains to be done. It is for this purely technical reason that these sources will go mostly unnoted in the next three chapters.

CONCLUSION

In his oft-quoted responsum to the Jews of Kairouan (ancient Cyrene) to a question on the efficacy and legitimacy of using the divine Name and other magical techniques, Hai Gaon (939–1038), the famous leader of the Yeshivah of Pumbedita, delves at great length into various magical and mystical techniques known to him from contemporary Jewish practice. He also has some interesting words about the books available to him for the study of such traditions:

> And the texts which you saw – He who wishes to do X should do Y – we have many of those here, such as the one called *Sepher ha-Yashar*, and the one called *The Sword of Moses* (which begins with "Four angels are in charge of the sword, for it has exaltations and wonders"),[226] and in the book called *Raza Rabba*, in addition to the selections and the individual (recipes) which are endless and innumerable, and many have labored and spent their years and found no truth in the matter.[227]

Both the questions posed by the Kairouan Jews and Hai's own response provide ample proof of the wide diffusion of Jewish magical texts in the Geonic period, and their circulation among the masses and the rabbinic elite alike; apparently, there was nothing esoteric about such texts, and

---

[226] Most scholars translate the passage as "'Four angels are in charge of the sword,' for it (i.e., the book) has exaltations and wonders," in which case the *incipit* exactly matches that of the longer version of the *Sword of Moses* as extant in the manuscripts. However, it seems that the translation offered here is a more accurate rendering of Hai's text.

[227] My translation follows the newest and best edition of this text, by Emanuel 1995, pp. 131–32; for this passage, see Mann 1931–35, vol. II, pp. 90–91; for its wider context, see Ben-Sasson 1996, pp. 275–78 and Brody 1998, pp. 142–47.

they were not the hidden possessions of a secretive guild of magicians, but available for all to see. And his detailed discussions of different magical practices and technologies could serve as an excellent starting-point for the study of medieval Jewish magic, which lies outside the scope of the present study. For the purpose of the present chapter, we need only note a medieval Jewish leader's very useful typology of Jewish magical texts; he begins with three "literary" books of magic, each with its own title, and to his list we could easily add a few more titles mentioned by other medieval Jewish opponents, observers, and defenders of the Jewish magical tradition. He then turns to the formularies and individual recipes, which are, he says, both endless and innumerable. Searching for medieval Jewish magical texts, in the Cairo Genizah and elsewhere, one finds the *disjecta membra* of the "literary" books of magic mentioned by these "outsiders," as well as an endless variety of "non-literary" formularies and recipes.[228] One also finds, of course, hundreds of "finished products," produced according to the instructions of all these recipes by and for Jews who did not share the Gaon's conviction that there was "no truth in the matter." And while these magical texts, and Hai's responsum, are all medieval and post-Muslim, many of the magical spells and practices they preserve and transmit go back to late-antique Palestine, and are therefore of the utmost importance for the study of Jewish magic in late antiquity.

To end this chapter, and our survey of the "insider" sources, we must stress once again the chance element in the preservation of the evidence for ancient Jewish magic. Those magic rituals which were transmitted orally and which involved no writing have left virtually no trace, and are mostly inaccessible to us (rabbinic literature providing some exceptions, as we shall see in Chapter 6). But even written magical texts are not uniformly preserved; paradoxically, it seems as if for the pre-Islamic period our evidence consists almost exclusively of texts written on non-organic materials (metals and pottery), while for the Genizah period we have hundreds of texts written on organic materials (and especially paper and vellum), but none written on non-organic ones. This is, of course, not an accurate reflection of the writing materials used by Jewish magicians in different periods, but of the different places and conditions under which each body of evidence happened to survive. In fact, one very useful mental exercise, whenever reading a magical recipe or an "outsider" description of a magician in action is to ask ourselves what would a magician performing that ritual

---

[228] And note Margalioth 1966, pp. xv–xvi, the results of whose work on these fragments have, as far as I know, never been published.

have left behind, and what would have survived fifteen centuries later. In addition to giving us some sense of what evidence we might expect to find in the future, such a mental exercise helps us develop a healthy sense of scholarly humility, for it repeatedly demonstrates that most of the evidence for the magical practices of late-antique Jews is irretrievably lost.

So much for the empty half of the glass. When we turn to the full half, however, we must note that while the sources at our disposal represent only a tiny fraction of the magical activities of late-antique Jews, they also happen to be quite numerous, and, what is perhaps more important, extremely varied. If in our search for Jewish magic in the Second Temple period we were repeatedly struck by the paucity of the evidence, the search for late-antique Jewish magic results in an equally surprising variety of Jewish magical texts and artifacts. From late antiquity itself, we have metal lamellae in particular to represent the western branch of ancient Jewish magic, but stray papyrus fragments from Oxyrhynchus and from a "multilingual workshop" in late-antique Egypt assure us that we are on the right track, as do a few contemporary Aramaic magical gems and some Jewish magical texts in Greek. We also have the "literary" books of magic, which contain some materials whose origins clearly lie in late-antique Palestine, numerous Aramaic incantation bowls, and a handful of inscribed skulls, which provide us with abundant evidence for the eastern branch of late-antique Jewish magic. And when we turn to a later period, we see how the Genizah magical texts, and even later Jewish manuscripts, provide ample evidence for the transmission and transformation of the western branch of the Jewish magical tradition into the Middle Ages and beyond. All these "insider" sources, which are the working manuals used by the Jewish magicians and the "finished products" produced by them, have very little to tell us about the magicians' exact identity, about their working habits, fees, and many other important questions. For such data, we will have to turn to the "outsider" sources, as we shall do in Chapter 6. But what these "insider" sources can teach us is about the different services rendered by the Jewish magicians, and about the cultural make-up of their highly specific technology. It is to this last question that the next two chapters shall be devoted. First, we shall focus on all the foreign elements which entered the Jewish magical tradition in late antiquity (Chapter 4), and then we shall consider the "Jewishness" of these magical texts and artifacts, and the kind of "Judaism" they represent (Chapter 5).

CHAPTER 4

Non-Jewish elements in late-antique Jewish magic

INTRODUCTION

Perhaps the most striking feature of late-antique Jewish magic is the extensive and pervasive foreign influences it displays. The phenomenon itself has not been lost on previous scholars, who often found this issue not only fascinating, but also very useful. Jewish scholars of a more apologetic bent used the foreign elements they could detect in the Jewish magical texts known to them as evidence that magic was not really endemic to the Jewish tradition; it was, they said, just a foreign thread in the Jewish cultural fabric, the result of a temporary Jewish loss of nerve which led to the adoption of some superstitious customs and beliefs whose origins lie in the popular culture of an ignorant pagan world.[1] Alternately, some apologetes for rabbinic culture insisted that the foreign elements in the Jewish magical texts are the work of Jewish heretics, a group entirely removed from mainstream Jewish culture as embodied in the rabbinic corpus.[2] Other scholars, however, Jewish and non-Jewish alike, used the magical texts to stress how "paganized" ancient Jews really were, and how open to the culture of their non-Jewish neighbors – a claim which often has important implications for modern Jews and Judaism.[3]

Such were some of the motives which shaped the development of the enquiry. Unfortunately, the enquiry itself was not only biased, it was also based on the wrong kind of sources and on misguided methods of enquiry. Rabbinic literature, which was the first body of literature to capture such scholars' attention, is – as we shall see in a subsequent chapter – not the best set of sources on which to base a meticulous enquiry into the foreign influences on ancient Jewish magic. And many of the other sources available to earlier scholars, such as medieval Hebrew manuscripts or ancient pagan and Christian magical texts, are too far removed from the ancient Jewish

[1] For this claim, see, e.g., Rubin 1887, pp. 12–13.   [2] Margalioth 1966, esp. pp. 13–22.
[3] For an extreme formulation of this argument, see Goodenough 1953–68, esp. vol. II, pp. 153–207.

magical tradition to allow a reliable reconstruction of its cultural makeup. Only over the last few decades, with the systematic publication of many new ancient Jewish magical texts, did we finally acquire the kinds of evidence which enable a thorough analysis of how, and to what extent, late-antique Jewish magic had been influenced by the magical traditions of the non-Jewish world. However, in analyzing these new sources, we must also note our predecessors' grave methodological errors, and especially the constant confusion of early and late texts and traditions, the neglect of basic philological caution in handling corrupt and difficult texts, the insistence on piling up real and imagined parallels and using them as evidence for foreign influence, and the constant recourse to fanciful etymologies of different words and phrases.[4] Thus, the aim of the present chapter is not only to demonstrate and assess the influence of the Greco-Egyptian magical tradition of late antiquity upon the Jewish one, but also to show how such a claim should be demonstrated, and in so doing lay more solid foundations for future study. The subject, as we shall soon see, can hardly be exhausted in a single chapter.

In the previous chapter, we mentioned the Jewish elements which entered the Greco-Egyptian magical tradition of late antiquity, as reflected in the Greek and Demotic magical papyri and in the Greek *defixiones*, amulets, and magical gems from about the first century CE onwards. It is now time to examine how, a few centuries later, that magical idiom penetrated and transformed the Jewish magical tradition as practiced by the Aramaic- and Hebrew-speaking magicians of late-antique Palestine. Before attempting such a survey, however, we must spell out some methodological guidelines which would enable us to avoid most of the errors of our predecessors and make sure that our analysis of the foreign materials in the Jewish magical texts leads to tenable results. At the most basic level, we must note the obvious need to exercise extreme caution in the handling of texts whose state of preservation often is abominable and whose contents are often obscure. When dealing with such materials, we must always focus on those sources whose contents and meaning are clearer, and move to the less secure ones only as a last resort. We should also stress the following points about the kinds of parallels we should be looking for between the Jewish and the non-Jewish magical texts, and the kinds of questions we should ask about them:

---

[4] The most notable exception is Margalioth 1966, pp. 1–16, which remains the best available treatment of the Jewish borrowings from the Greco-Egyptian magic of late antiquity, but is limited solely to *Sepher ha-Razim*.

(1) The first rule to be followed in the search for cross-cultural transfers is that parallels – even convincing parallels – do not always demonstrate influences, especially in the realm of religious and magical beliefs and rituals. As an example, we may note James Frazer's famous generalizations about the logic of homeopathic and contagious magic, a logic which clearly manifests itself independently in many different cultures. Thus, such parallels as the use of yellow things to cure jaundice, or the use of a victim's clothes or fingernails for aggressive magical rituals – and hundreds of other common magical practices – cannot be used as evidence for cultural diffusion, even when they are found in two cultures which are geographically and chronologically connected. Moreover, even when the parallels are specific enough to make influence the most likely explanation of a specific similarity, the direction of the borrowing may be hard to establish; in such cases, assuming that what came earlier must have influenced that which came only later is hardly a solution, since it wrongly presupposes that the evidence which happened to survive is somehow representative. Thus, while much of what late-antique Jewish magicians did and wrote closely resembles what was done by their non-Jewish colleagues, we shall focus here on those parallels that can only be explained as the result of a direct borrowing by Jews of a practice that was demonstrably non-Jewish in origin. In so doing, we shall willfully limit our survey to only a fraction of the parallels between the Jewish and the non-Jewish materials, but in return gain a less equivocal image of the processes of cross-cultural contacts and borrowings.

(2) Once we identify a foreign element which entered the Jewish magical tradition, we must next ask about its status within its new home. Adopting the type of status-classification terminology utilized by Internal Naturalization Services worldwide, we may note how some foreign elements entered the Jewish magical tradition and became fully "naturalized" in their new homeland, a part of the active vocabulary of many Jewish practitioners; some were even "Judaized" retroactively, when their Jewish users explained them as having been entirely Jewish to begin with. Other foreign elements may be classified as "multiple entry" items, which appear in more than one Jewish magical text or artifact; such items may be said to have had some success within the Jewish magical tradition, but not enough popularity to be fully naturalized into it and become part and parcel of the active vocabulary of many Jewish magicians. Finally, we may find cases of "one time entry," that is, a foreign element which appears only once, or very rarely, in the Jewish magical tradition. Such examples would prove that this item too was potentially available to the Jewish practitioners, and would

raise the possibility that its rarity is due not only to technical factors, but to a deliberate choice on the part of most Jewish magicians to leave this item out of their own compositions. For a study of the cultural make-up of Jewish magic, the "naturalized" and "multiple entry" items are of great importance because of their ubiquity within the Jewish magical tradition, but the "one time entries" are also important, precisely because they demonstrate what other foreign elements were available to some late-antique Jewish magicians, but were not commonly adopted by them. Needless to add, all these designations are approximate, and the publication of more ancient Jewish magical texts may well show that some of the "one time entry" items in fact were more common than we now realize. And yet, the currently available corpus is already large enough to make such distinctions meaningful, as we shall see throughout the present chapter.

(3) In studying how elements move from one culture to another, we must always remember the old scholastic maxim that *Quidquid recipitur ad modum recipientis recipitur*, "Whatever is received, is received in the manner of the recipient." A word, an object, a symbol, or a ritual, may have one meaning in one culture, and quite a different meaning in another, even if the second borrowed it directly from the first. Thus, in studying the foreign elements which entered late-antique Jewish magic we must not only count their frequency in their new home, but also check the meanings they acquired in their new cultural context. In the previous chapter, we briefly noted how the Jewish God entered the Greek magical tradition but was entirely "paganized" on the way, becoming just another pagan deity – and often even a whole set of deities, with exotic names like Iaô, Sabaôth, Michaêl, or Abraam. In the present chapter, we shall repeatedly see how elements borrowed by the Jewish practitioners from their Greek-speaking colleagues were often transformed in the process, to fit better the overall structure of Jewish magic and of Jewish culture as a whole. Such processes are of great significance for our study, for it is the overall structure, much more than the individual pieces of evidence, that we wish to elucidate.

(4) As we noted in the previous chapter, much of our evidence for the western branch of late-antique Jewish magic stems from the Genizah magical texts, that is, from sources which postdate the period on which we wish to focus in the present study. It is therefore essential, when we find foreign elements in such texts, to ask not only whence, but also when these elements entered the Jewish magical tradition. Can we be sure that a certain foreign element entered Jewish magic already in late antiquity, or is its appearance in the Cairo Genizah or in other medieval Jewish manuscripts due to influences post-dating the Muslim conquest, and thus belonging more in

a study of medieval Jewish magic? Luckily, in some cases the dating – at least in a rough manner – of the actual borrowing is not so difficult, as we shall note in the course of our enquiry. In others, however, the possibility must at least be left open that some of the foreign elements we shall detect here entered the Jewish magical tradition not in late antiquity, but in the early Middle Ages.

With these methodological caveats in mind, we may turn to the actual evidence. For the sake of clarity, we may begin with the most obvious cases (bilingual and trilingual magical recipes and translations from Greek originals), move to small but evidently foreign elements (Greek words and phrases; foreign deities and demons; and magic words, signs, and designs), turn to the overall structure of the Jewish magical recipes and recipe-books, and end with the larger issues, especially those relating to the aims and techniques of the magical praxis itself.

BILINGUAL AND TRILINGUAL (ARAMAIC-GREEK-HEBREW) MAGICAL TEXTS

Perhaps the best starting-point for the study of the interface between the non-Jewish and the Jewish magical traditions of late antiquity is offered by the few bilingual (Hebrew/Aramaic-Greek) and trilingual (Hebrew-Aramaic-Greek) Jewish magical texts at our disposal. When viewed from the perspective of ancient magic in general, bilingual magical texts are far from unusual – witness the Demotic-Greek and Coptic-Greek magical papyri, or, in a later period, the Coptic-Arabic or Greek-Arabic magical texts. However, when viewed from a Jewish perspective, the Semitic-Greek magical texts offer an interesting test case for the study of the non-Jewish influences on the Jewish magical tradition of late antiquity. At the very least, they offer evidence for Aramaic-speaking Jewish magicians who either knew Greek and could inscribe Greek magical texts, or were interested enough in such materials to ask their Greek-speaking colleagues to collaborate with them in the manufacturing of such texts. Whether these colleagues were Jews themselves is a question worth pondering, especially when we keep in mind our earlier observation that the pagan Greek magical texts of late antiquity display very little interest in Aramaic or Hebrew, and contain not even a single line written in either language. To do so, let us look at several specific examples.

(a) Our first example is a bilingual amulet inscribed on a copper lamella and found in Israel, near Kibbuẓ Evron (Western Galilee), and dated by its editor to the third or fourth century CE.[5] The top five lines are written in Hebrew, and contain little more than divine names, such as *Ehyeh Asher Ehyeh*, YHWH, and Elohim. These are followed by eleven lines of Greek text, which consists of a pious prayer to God that just as He created the universe with His Word, so He, with the same Word, will heal and save Casius son of Metradotion, and that there will be a cessation of the pain and fever which afflict him. The amulet ends with an adjuration by the One who made the heavens and earth and the sea, He who created everything, Iaô Sabaôth. Both the contents and the style of this Greek section point to a Palestinian Jewish authorship – even the Greek syntax certainly is not that of a native speaker – and, with the possible exception of what might be construed as a Christian sign (see below), evince little evidence of any non-Jewish influence. For all we know, both the Hebrew and the Greek sections could have been written by one trilingual scribe, whose mother tongues were Aramaic and Hebrew and who had mastered some Greek, a scribe whose repertory, at least as reflected in this specific amulet, hardly displays any of the non-Jewish influences for which we are presently looking. That this is not an isolated example is made clear by such artifacts as the bilingual magical gem discussed in the previous chapter, which displays the *atbash* series and other Jewish elements both in Hebrew and in Greek, or by the transliterated Greek sentences found in the *Sword of Moses*, to which we shall turn below. In such cases, we see the incorporation of some Greek sections into Aramaic and Hebrew magical texts, but these Greek texts do not seem to contain much that was borrowed from the Greco-Egyptian magical tradition. This, however, was not always the case, as the following example clearly shows.

(b) Of all the ancient Jewish amulets published thus far, the longest, and certainly the most interesting, is a silver lamella said to have come from Tell el-Amarna in Egypt.[6] As we noted in the previous chapter, both its Aramaic section and its Greek one seem to contain phrases inadvertently copied from the recipe from which it was manufactured, and it seems quite likely that they were found in a bilingual, Aramaic-Greek formulary. The existence of such bilingual formularies might also be demonstrated by the Greek-Aramaic papyrus fragments from the "multilingual workshop," also found in Egypt and discussed in the previous chapter. Moreover, as we shall

---

[5] Kotansky 1991b, republished in Kotansky 1994, no. 56.
[6] See Kotansky, Naveh, and Shaked 1992, and cf. the corrections of some readings in Shaked 2000a, p. 70, n. 55. While the provenance of this amulet is uncertain, its authenticity is vouchsafed by having been presented to the Ashmolean Museum, Oxford, in 1921, at a time when knowledge of such objects was too rudimentary to allow for such a complex forgery.

see in the next chapter, the Aramaic section of this amulet seems to cite an apocryphal psalm of David, which itself is of some interest, and which might even date back to the Second Temple period. For our present discussion, this small amulet (12 × 6 cm) provides interesting evidence of the contacts between Jewish and non-Jewish magical traditions in late antiquity. To see this, we must first note its unusual layout – it opens with six lines written in Greek letters and consisting solely of divine Names and *voces magicae*. Below these we find two Greek vowel-triangles which extend some eleven lines downwards, but only occupy a small (and diminishing) space on each of these lines. The Aramaic text, on the other hand, begins on line 7, but "jumps over" the two triangles, a sure sign that the Greek text had been written first. Inversely, when the Aramaic text ends, on line 29, it occupies only a small space on that line; the rest of the space is occupied by the Greek letters which end the amulet, and which add up to ten lines of magic words, magic signs, and a few meaningful Greek phrases. Thus, the very layout of the text makes it clear that the order of writing of this amulet was Greek-Aramaic-Greek, a clear testimony to the close connections between the text's two languages. This impression is strengthened once we note that both the Greek and the Aramaic sections specify the name of the same client, and that the Greek section includes the claim that "this amulet is written in Hebrew." Whether all this implies that the amulet was written by a single bilingual scribe, or by two scribes who worked in close cooperation is not entirely clear, but the recurrence in both sections of a sloppy miscopying of ritual instructions which should not have been copied onto the "finished product" probably argues in favor of the former scenario. But be this as it may, greater significance lies in the closer examination of both parts of this amulet, recalling their intimate interdependence. For when we read the Aramaic section of this amulet, we encounter many features whose Jewish origins are beyond doubt, as shall be noted in greater detail in the following chapter. The Greek sections, however, present a very mixed bag; on the one hand, they contain such Jewish elements as standard divine and angelic names (Sabaôth, Michaêl, Gabriêl, Raphaêl, etc.) and even a long adjuration "by the Name of Adônai Eloue Sabaôth, who sits upon the Throne of Glory and reigns," and by the angels who stand there. But the same Greek sections also contain some patently non-Jewish materials, including *charactêres*, vowel-triangles, and some *voces magicae* which are familiar to any student of the Greco-Egyptian magic of late antiquity. These include some *voces* which are well attested in the Aramaic magical texts, such as Ablanathanalba, Akrammachammarei, Marmaraôth, Semeseilam or Sesengen Barpharangês (on all of which more below), and Soumartha, as well as Arsenophru, Pakerbôth, Phre, and Satraperkmêph, which have yet to surface in the Aramaic and Hebrew magical texts of late antiquity. These last *voces* are particularly interesting, as they clearly stem from an Egyptian religious context: Pakerbêth is one of the secret names of the evil god Seth in many Greco-Egyptian magical texts, Phre is Egyptian for "the Sun-god," Satraperkmêph is one of several compounds of the Egyptian God Knêph, and Arsenophrê also is of Egyptian derivation, though its exact etymology remains contested. Even more surprising, in one line of the bottom Greek part of our amulet the editors read the phrase "Osornôphrês (the) god," a clear reference to Osiris and quite unexpected in a Jewish amulet.[7]

While the specific details of this amulet might be modified in light of subsequent re-examinations of its barely legible text, the overall picture is patently clear. This amulet was produced by a Jewish scribe, perhaps in close cooperation with a second scribe, who was either Jewish or not, and it contains not only many Jewish elements, but many non-Jewish ones as well. If all these materials came from a single bilingual recipe-book, it may have contained many other mixtures of Jewish and non-Jewish elements; but even if they did not, it is abundantly clear that our amulet does not represent an isolated case. Another bilingual amulet, of an unknown provenance, has an Aramaic exorcistic text, in the midst of which are embedded three lines in Greek letters; among these, one can still read the well-known sequence Phtha(ô) phôza, which Egyptologists usually interpret as Egyptian for "Ptah, the healthy one".[8] And in *Sepher ha-Razim*, a transliterated Greek prayer to Helios, embedded into a Hebrew book, may derive from pagan sources, though in this case – as we shall soon see – proving such a claim is far more difficult.

To summarize this section, we may note that the bilingual and trilingual magical texts we examined clearly come from several different places and were produced by different practitioners. They attest to the activity not of a single bilingual magician, or even one idiosyncratic school of such magicians, but of many unrelated individuals, each of whom incorporated some Greek bits into his or her Aramaic and Hebrew magical texts. These practitioners differed from each other in the level of their linguistic competence in the Greek language and in their willingness to incorporate non-Jewish materials into their own compositions. From the above examples, it might

---

[7] For these *voces*, see Brashear 1995, pp. 3580 (αρσενοφρη), 3598 (σατραπερκμηφ), and 3601 (φρε and φρη); for *pakerbêth*, see Betz 1986, p. 334.

[8] AMB, A14, ll. 4–6. The other Greek letters do not seem to add up to any known Greek word or *vox magica*. For *Pephtha phôza* (the common form of these *voces*), see Brashear 1995, p. 3596.

be tempting to conclude that the Egypt-based Jewish magician who produced the el-Amarna amulet was more exposed to pagan or Greco-Egyptian influences, and more flexible in his or her attitudes towards them, than the Galilean magician who produced the Evron amulet, for example, but we must be very cautious in formulating such claims. Given the great mobility of these tiny artifacts, it is far from certain that the provenanced amulets have been produced in the vicinity of their find-spots, and quite possible that they traveled great distances before reaching their final resting place. Moreover, it is also quite possible that the same magician produced many different amulets, some of which were less "Jewish" than others, perhaps even basing his decision in such matters on the perceived or expressed sensibilities of his clients. But be that as it may, the fact that some Jewish magicians had a sound knowledge of Greek, direct access to the Greco-Egyptian magical technology, and a willingness to incorporate some Greek and Greco-Egyptian materials in their own Aramaic and Hebrew magical texts, is amply demonstrated by the Jewish bilingual and trilingual magical texts of late antiquity.

ARAMAIC AND HEBREW RECIPES TRANSLATED FROM GREEK ORIGINALS

In the previous chapter, we noted the need to separate between cases where non-Jewish magicians borrowed Jewish motifs and used them in creating their own recipes, and cases when they borrowed whole spells and recipes from their Jewish colleagues. In the present chapter, however, the issue is somewhat more complicated, for here we are dealing not with the movement of Greek spells and recipes from Greek-speaking Jews to their homophonous non-Jewish neighbors, but with the movement of non-Jewish spells and recipes in Greek into the Aramaic and Hebrew Jewish magical texts of late antiquity. Thus, if Jewish magicians borrowed whole spells and recipes from their non-Jewish colleagues, they had to translate them first, which would have made the process much more cumbersome, and much harder for us to detect.

Looking at all the available evidence, we may note the existence of some late-antique Jewish Aramaic texts which *may* be based on non-Jewish Greek sources, but for which such an origin cannot be proven.[9] We also note several medieval Jewish magical texts which can be shown to be based on

---

[9] The best example for such uncertainty is the *smamit* story of AMB, A15, fully discussed by Naveh and Shaked *ibid.*, pp. 111–22, esp. p. 120.

the translation or adaptation of Greek magical recipes (including some of a demonstrably Christian origin!), but which seem to have been borrowed only in the Middle Byzantine period, and thus lie outside the chronological framework of the present study.[10] In a few other cases, we find intriguing evidence of translation from Greek in texts which have to do more with medicine or with astrology, and these too lie outside the scope of our current enquiry.[11] Thus, the cases in which a Jewish magical text can be shown to have been translated or adapted from a Greek original already in late antiquity are few and far between. Let us look at two such examples:

(1) Our first example comes from a comparison between the Greek *Testament of Solomon*, that late-antique Christian book of magic which we briefly discussed in the previous chapter, and a Genizah magical text in Aramaic. In the *Testament*, King Solomon interrogates the 36 "elements," or astrological Decans, each of whom tells the king what harm he causes and how he is thwarted. Within this tedious catalogue – which probably is based on an earlier, pagan, list of Decans – we find the following passage:

The thirty-third (element) said, "I, King, am called Achôneôth. I cause pain in the throat and tonsils. If anyone writes on ivy leaves, "Lykourgos," in a receding grape-cluster shape, I recede immediately."[12]

With this instruction, whose antiquity is vouchsafed by its presence on the one papyrus fragment of the *Testament* that happened to survive,[13] we may compare a short recipe from the Cairo Genizah, found in a well-preserved formulary and apparently copied from some late-antique model:

For a head(ache) and a migraine: On deer-skin (?) parchment, write [L?]YQWRGWS YQWRGWS QWRGWS WRGWS RGWS GWS WS S.[14]

The identity of the two recipes is virtually incontrovertible; not only is this precisely the same *vox*, appearing once in Greek and once in Aramaic but looking exactly the same, in both cases the practitioner is instructed to write them in a "grape-cluster," or triangular shape, and in both recipes

---

[10] For a pertinent example, see *Synopse* §742, with an amulet for the שמרינא (an error for Greek *hystera*, "womb") which is based on the Greek μελάνη μελανωμένη formula (for which see Spier 1993 and 2006) (as noted by Scholem 1960, 2nd edn, p. 134). For another, see Leicht 2003.

[11] For the astrological texts, see now Leicht 2006, e.g., pp. 71–73.

[12] *T. Sol.* 18.37 (p. 58* McCown). Note that Duling 1983, p. 981 mistranslated the technical term βοτρυδὸν [ἀναχωρίς], as was rightly noted by Jackson 1988, pp. 53–54. For the list of Decans as a pre-*Testament* composition, see, e.g., Klutz 2003b, pp. 221, 242–43.

[13] P. Rainer Cent. 39, frr. c–d, lines 15–18, where the *vox* is written backwards, σο]γρυοκυλ.

[14] MSF, G18 (T-S K 1.143), p. 14, ll. 10–12. Note also the Greek loanword MQRNYH = *hemicranion*, "migraine." For lack of a better solution, I follow the editors in taking the meaningless שרי as טבי, "deer."

the practice is used to heal pains in the head. Moreover, as "Lykourgos" (or, rather, Lycurgus, to use the standard Latin spelling) is a Greek name, and not much in use by Jews or Christians in antiquity, there is no doubt that this recipe originated in the Greek-speaking world of pagan magic, and subsequently entered both the *Testament of Solomon* and the Aramaic magical texts.[15] However, it must be noted that tracing its entry into the Jewish and Christian magical traditions sheds little light on its ultimate origins, and on the question of which Lycurgus was intended by the recipe's original inventors.[16] It is also worth noting that both the above-quoted recipes call for the writing of this specific magical triangle on perishable writing surfaces, so we are not likely to find too many "finished products" bearing it. And yet, we can securely document the transfer of this specific recipe from the non-Jewish world into the Jewish magical tradition, and can probably assume that the process occurred already in late antiquity.

(2) A second example is provided by a much-studied recipe from the Cairo Genizah, which is part of a larger collection of gynecological recipes. The aim of this specific recipe is to make sure the patient's womb does not begin to wander around in her body (a common fear in Greek medicine and magic), and it finds an almost verbatim parallel in a recipe found in one of the longer Greek magical papyri.[17] The parallels between the two recipes suffice to prove their dependence, but the direction of the borrowing is harder to determine. On the one hand, the Greek recipe, although found in a pagan recipe-book, seems quite "Jewish" in contents, invoking only God the Creator and incorporating such phrases as Allêlouia and Amên. On the other hand, the Aramaic recipe bears several clear signs of having been translated or adapted from Greek, including a misunderstanding of the Greek word *anadromê*, "running up" (of the womb), which the Aramaic adaptor turned into a set of *voces magicae* ('DR MNH 'DR MNH etc.) and a transliteration in Hebrew letters of some Greek which he apparently could not translate. Even more striking, where the Greek original uses a Greek pun on the word *kuôn*, which in Greek means both "a dog" and "pregnant," in the Aramaic version we get an entirely meaningless adjuration of the womb not to "inflate like a dog." Finally, and perhaps most revealingly, the

---

[15] That the Lycurgus-triangle enjoyed some popularity in the Jewish magical tradition may be seen from its appearance in one of the many interesting recipes of MS Sassoon 56 = NYPL Heb. 190 (on p. 142), a Byzantine Jewish manuscript of the fifteenth century.

[16] For some speculations about our Lycurgus, see SM I, pp. 4–5.

[17] See MTKG I, 8 (T–S K 1.157) 1a/11–23 with PGM VII.260–71. For previous discussions of this example, see Veltri 1996a, Betz 1997, Bohak 1999 (on which the following discussion is based), and Faraone 2003.

Aramaic recipe is accompanied by a crude rendition of the uterine symbol, which commonly appears on pagan magical gems but is found nowhere else in the Jewish magical texts.[18] Thus, it seems quite clear that the Aramaic recipe is based on (some version of) the Greek one, but the origins of the latter are not as clear. For all we know, it too may have been Jewish to begin with, and may be added to our list of Jewish magical recipes in the Greek magical papyri; but it may also have been composed by a non-Jew, who – like many other pagan magicians – invoked the Jewish God, a fact which made the recipe far easier for an Aramaic-speaking Jewish magician to adopt and translate.

Before leaving the issue of Jewish translation and adaptation of Greek magical recipes, we must note once again that such examples are quite rare. In speculating about the reasons for this paucity of direct translations from non-Jewish sources, especially in light of all the other borrowings which we shall soon see, we may suggest that most pagan magical recipes were just too "pagan" to be borrowed *en bloc*. As we shall see both below and in the next chapter, the Jewish magicians of late antiquity seem to have spent quite some effort in filtering out various elements of the Greco-Egyptian magical tradition which they found too offensive for their own consumption and use. Thus, the wholesale translation of pagan magical texts – certainly the most efficient way to catch up with pagan magical technology – was a road they preferred not to take.

GREEK WORDS AND PHRASES IN JEWISH MAGICAL TEXTS

One of the common features of the Jewish texts of late antiquity – from the extensive rabbinic corpus to such mundane documents as marriage contracts (*ketubot*) and tomb-inscriptions – is the preponderance of Greek, and to a much lesser extent Latin, loanwords. In an earlier period, and at least in some Jewish circles (most notably in the Qumran literature) one finds evidence of an obstinate linguistic purism, expressed by an insistence on writing in Hebrew (rather than Aramaic), and on not letting any "modern" Greek or Latin words enter one's language.[19] This kind of "language policy," which would be well understood by anyone familiar with the current French, German, or Israeli attempts to wipe out the anglicisms from their respective languages, is paralleled elsewhere in the Hellenistic

---

[18] For this symbol, see Bonner 1950, pp. 79–94.
[19] See Qimron 1986, pp. 116–17; the Qumranites' linguistic purism is made even clearer by the presence of some Greek loanwords in the *Copper Scroll* (for which see García Martínez 2003), and by the Qumran Judeo-Greek texts (for which see VanderKam 2001).

period. In Ptolemaic Egypt, for example, some writers of Demotic apparently avoided as much as possible the use of the Greek loanwords whose presence in their language is well documented in other sources.[20] And Pliny the Elder, whose Latin encyclopedia of the universe and all it contains was bound to incorporate both Greek and "barbarian" words, repeatedly apologizes for this grave offence.[21] In late antiquity, however, such sensitivity is almost entirely absent, at least in the Near Eastern languages; both Coptic and Syriac display an impressive array of Greek loanwords, many of which became fully naturalized in these non-Indo-European languages. Similarly, the Jewish texts of late antiquity, in Aramaic and Hebrew alike, sport several thousand such loanwords, many of which have become part and parcel of the Hebrew language to this very day.[22] And the magical texts are no exception – here too one finds a large number of Greek loanwords, and a smaller number of Latin ones, transliterated in Hebrew letters and utilized by the Jewish magicians as part of their regular vocabulary. But given the preponderance of this feature in all types of Jewish texts and documents of the time, the appearance of foreign loanwords in the Jewish magical texts cannot be used as evidence for non-Jewish influences on Jewish magic. When Jewish magicians used words like *parzuph* (Greek *prôsopos*, "face"), or *lisṭim* (Greek *lêistês*, "robber, highwayman"), or *silon* (Greek *sôlên*, "tube, pipe"), they did so because such words were fully naturalized in the Hebrew and Aramaic of their day, as their frequent appearance in rabbinic literature demonstrates. Such magicians may even have been unaware of the Greek origins of the words they used, just as many French-, German-, or Hebrew-speakers today must be reminded of the English origins of some of their daily vocabulary. Even the presence of loanwords which are only seldom attested, or even never attested, in other strands of ancient Jewish literature, often tells us little about the origins of the spells in which such words appear. If a Jewish magician wrote a curse against his client's *antidiki* (the Greek word for "opponents in court"), this is perhaps because this was a common term in the law-courts of late-antique Palestine, and commonly used by many Aramaic-speakers too.[23] If a magical spell was to be written on a *petalon* (the Greek word for a thin sheet of metal), we may conclude that this technical term (which is also used in the Septuagint to describe the gold plate on the high priest's forehead) was commonly used in the Aramaic and Hebrew of late-antique Palestine; as we shall see in

---

[20] See Ray 1994, and esp. Dieleman 2005, pp. 104–09.
[21] For Pliny's apologies, see, e.g., *NH* Pr. 13; 2.13.63; 9.20.52.
[22] For this much-studied issue, see esp. Krauss 1898–99 and Lieberman 1942.
[23] See MSF, G9 (T-S K 1.15), p. 3, l. 2.

Chapter 6, it even appears in rabbinic literature, though its presence there was not detected by previous scholarship.[24] And when a Jewish magician wrote that a certain item should be swallowed *nestiqos* (the Greek word for "on an empty stomach"), or wrote an exorcistic amulet against the spirit of *qefalargia* (the Greek word for "headache"), or against *miqrana* (Greek *hemikranion*, "half-the-head (ache)," whence our "migraine"), or against *tertaia* (Greek *tritaios*, Latin *tertiana*, whence English "tertiary") fever, he probably was using the standard terminology of late-antique Jewish physicians.[25] As we shall see in Chapter 6, rabbinic literature tells us that at least some amulets were produced by such physicians, so that even the use of Greek medical terminology is no sure sign of the foreign origin of the recipe or the praxis in which it is found, but of the Hellenization of Jewish physicians, and the Jewish population as a whole, around the late-antique Mediterranean.[26]

There are, however, several exceptions to this general rule. One exception concerns words which were not really Greek to begin with, but were "words of power" or "magic words," unknown in the standard Greek vocabulary of late antiquity and utilized solely by late-antique magicians and their disciples. We shall soon turn to a more detailed analysis of such *voces magicae* and their extensive borrowing by the Jewish magicians. A second exception involves a group of Greek words which were used by non-magicians, but which acquired new meanings, as specific technical terms, in the Greco-Egyptian magical texts of late antiquity. When we turn to the word *charactêres*, we shall see how a standard Greek word acquired a new meaning in the realm of magic, and was adopted, *with that specifically magical meaning*, by the Jewish magicians as well. The same is true of such technical terms as *koinologia*, "(say/write) the usual words," which end many a Greek magical spell and which, as we shall see below, were borrowed, and subsequently mutilated, by the Jewish magicians of late antiquity.[27] Similarly, when we turn to an analysis of the *materia magica* used by the Jewish magical texts, we shall note many such materials whose

---

[24] See MTKG III, 61 (T-S K 1.162) 1b/13 (פיטלין) and 1a/35 (where the scribe replaced it by the more familiar פלטין); see also Bodleian Heb. a3.31 (unpublished), and cf. Krauss 1898–99, vol. II, p. 441. For the Tosephta passage, see Chapter 6, n. 64.
[25] *Nestiqos*: MSF, G11 (T-S K 1.19), p. 4, l. 9. *Qefalargia*: AMB, A11 (and further discussion below). *Miqrana*: G18 (T-S K 1.143), p. 14, l. 10 (cited above); T-S AS 142.32 (unpublished); see also further discussion below. *Tertaia*: see MSF, A19/2, 25 and MTKG I, 2 (T-S K 1.56), 2a/1, 2, 4. See also the word *trpyh* in MSF, A22, with the editors' notes ad loc. For Greek loanwords in Islamic medicine, see Ullmann 1978, pp. 27–30.
[26] For the importance of medicine in ancient Jewish magic, see also MSF, pp. 31–39.
[27] The same is also true of δοκίμη in ShR II/86 and III/47 (see Margalioth 1966, pp. 4–5), which, however, has yet to surface in the Jewish magical texts outside *Sepher ha-Razim*.

Non-Jewish elements in late-antique Jewish magic 241

very names betray their origins in the Greek-speaking world. But for the time being, let us focus on two other types of examples, those involving larger sequences of Greek words and those involving mistranslations from Greek. We shall then turn to the phenomenon of *calques*, namely, of neologisms in Aramaic or Hebrew which were fashioned after existing words and technical terms in the magicians' Greek idiom.

Greek phrases in Hebrew transliteration

One type of foreign word which clearly demonstrates the foreign origins of a given spell or formula relates to the appearance of longer Greek phrases in Jewish magical texts, rather than only individual words. Just as in Chapter 3 we noted a Greek amulet with several sets of Hebrew formulae, all transliterated in Greek letters, so we may now turn to several examples of long Greek formulae transliterated in the Hebrew alphabet. In one instance, a long sequence of supposedly meaningless *voces magicae* in the "sword" section of the *Sword of Moses* turns out to be transliterated Greek, with a subsequent section of the "sword" containing the Aramaic translation of the same text. The presence of both versions in the same text – which clearly was lost on its copyists and on its earliest modern editor and readers – is ample evidence of the editorial processes undergone by this complex text, an issue to which we briefly alluded in the previous chapter.[28] For the purpose of the present chapter, it is important to note that the availability within the text itself of the Aramaic translation of the transliterated Greek is indispensable for the correct understanding of the much-garbled Greek words. Without it, we would at best be in a position to suspect that some of these *abracadabra* words in fact are the corrupt remains of some transliterated Greek, and offer learned guesses as to their possible original meanings, but would not have been able to provide any reliable reconstruction of the sequence as a whole. Moreover, even with this unexpected textual assistance, the reconstruction of the entire Greek section is far from complete, a sure sign of how badly garbled such transliterated foreign phrases quickly become.

Our next examples are taken from *Sepher ha-Razim*. Certainly the most intriguing passage in this fascinating work is the Greek prayer to Helios which is embedded in one of the recipes of the fourth heaven, a prayer which has proved exceptionally exciting to modern scholars. The nature

---

[28] For a synopsis and analysis of the Aramaic and transliterated Greek, see Rohrbacher-Sticker 1996, pp. 34–45, and cf. the Greek words in Harari 1997a, pp. 140–41, and our list in Chapter 3, n. 93.

of the text is hardly in doubt, as it is found in a long set of recipes which begins with "If you wish to see the sun in the day, sitting in the chariot and rising," and provides a complex ritual to achieve that noble goal, after which comes the complementary recipe, "And if you wish to see the sun by night," with its own complex ritual. "And after you see it (the sun) in this manner," the text continues, "you shall bow down and fall down upon your face and pray this prayer," an instruction which is followed by a sequence of some two dozen Greek words, in Hebrew transliteration, and by a Hebrew prayer, "I, NN, beg you to show me without (causing me) fear and reveal to me without (making me) shudder, and do not hide anything from me, and reveal to me all that I ask." The instructions end with a short formula of dismissal once the sun has revealed all that was asked for and is no longer needed.[29] In this case, there is no doubt that we are dealing with a prayer to the sun – or, more exactly, to the Greek Sun-god Helios, who is mentioned by name in the transliterated section – and that the first part of the prayer is in Greek. The Greek which lurks behind this sequence has been reconstructed by Morton Smith, to the best of his ability and his fertile imagination, and this dubious reconstruction has unfortunately been taken at face value not only by Mordechai Margalioth, but by almost all subsequent scholars.[30] What has not been noted, however, is that in this case the Greek text clearly is not the equivalent of the Hebrew half of the same prayer, or of any other section of *Sepher ha-Razim*, or any other known Jewish magical text. Worse still, the Greek prayer it contains has never been identified – even in approximation – in any of the Greek magical papyri or related texts. Thus, there is no external yardstick with which to measure the plausibility of our reconstruction of the Greek text, and while the forthcoming edition of *Sepher ha-Razim* will at least give us a better sense of the manuscript divergence at this point, it will not alleviate the difficulty of reconstructing an unknown Greek prayer from the garbled remains of its Hebrew transliteration. Some of the Greek words – and especially the name "Helios" – are readily recognizable, but the exact contents of this Greek prayer are likely to remain elusive until a convincing Greek parallel is found in pagan or Christian texts. The same is true of a sequence of some seven transliterated Greek words which apparently serves as a magical formula to dismiss an angelic apparition (the "minister" of a sea or a river?) in the first heaven of *Sepher ha-Razim*. Here, too, there is no doubt that the formula is Greek, but it seems equally certain that the suggested reconstruction of this formula is more imaginative than probative, and that only a detailed

---

[29] ShR IV/25–72 (pp. 97–100 Margalioth).
[30] See Margalioth 1966, pp. 12–13, and note the slightly different reconstructions by Morgan 1983, p. 71, n. 21 and Alexander 2003b, p. 182, n. 35. See also Sperber 1994, pp. 92–94.

Non-Jewish elements in late-antique Jewish magic 243

examination of the textual tradition for this passage, and a meticulous search for similar dismissal-formulae in Greek magical texts, might provide more effective clues for the reconstruction of the original Greek sequence.[31]

Before leaving these examples, we should add one important comment about the nature of the Greek passages in the *Sword of Moses* and in *Sepher ha-Razim*. As the above analysis makes quite clear, in both cases the Greek phrases embedded in the Aramaic or Hebrew texts were intended to serve as meaningful textual units, and not as a sequence of *voces magicae*. In the case of *Sepher ha-Razim*, we see how the Greek prayer flows into the Hebrew one in a seamless manner, demonstrating their original textual unity. In the *Sword of Moses*, we find either the original author or (more likely) a later transmitter providing not only the Greek original of his source, but also an Aramaic translation, for those readers whose Greek was a bit wobbly. And in both cases, we may speak of bilingual magical texts, not very different from those with which we began the present chapter. Moreover, the entry into Jewish magical texts in Aramaic and Hebrew of spells and phrases in Greek seems to have taken place on more than these isolated instances. Unfortunately, such cases are extremely hard to identify, both because the vowel-less Hebrew alphabet is inherently inadequate for the transliteration of Indo-European and other languages (as any reader of the modern Hebrew attempts to transliterate foreign names and phrases correctly can surely testify), and because the magical texts at our disposal are either engraved on thin sheets of metal, which makes them very hard to read accurately, or are copies of copies of earlier magical texts. Thus, when faced with long series of *voces magicae* in the Palestinian Jewish amulets or in the Genizah magical texts, and even in the medieval manuscripts of the Hekhalot literature, one is often tempted to suggest that a certain sequence is in fact a garbled transliteration of a Greek phrase or a Greek sentence.[32] Unfortunately, only rarely can we achieve any certainty that this is indeed the case, and in most cases all we have are strings of meaningless "words" which *might* go back to some Greek origins, but whose original Greek wording can no longer be reconstructed. In such cases, we must always proceed with great caution, keeping in mind that regardless of the claims – raised by some ancient philosophers and theologians and enthusiastically adopted by modern scholars – that magic words and powerful foreign names must be copied with great accuracy lest they lose their potency, such words always follow the basic rule of textual entropy: what is neither meaningful nor familiar will soon be miscopied.

---

[31] ShR I/234–235 (p. 80 Margalioth); Morgan 1983, p. 42, n. 76.
[32] And cf. Levy 1941 with Bohak 2001. For another interesting example, see *Synopse* §357, where Greek-looking *voces* are explicitly identified as Greek.

While the insistence on the enormous difficulties of reconstructing such Greek sequences from their Hebrew transliterations might seem discouraging, it should not blind us to the great importance of the phenomenon itself. The presence of long sequences of transliterated Greek in Jewish magical texts demonstrates a high level of familiarity with the Greek language of at least some Jewish practitioners, who clearly assumed that their readers would know how to pronounce the Greek phrases and would even know what they meant. What they, and all other residents of the late-antique world, failed to divine was the coming of a new prophet, and a new language, from the remote oases of the Arabian desert, and the subsequent demise of Greek as the *lingua franca* of the inhabited world.[33] It was history, and not magic, which turned the Greek sections in their Hebrew and Aramaic spells and recipes into meaningless "magic words" for their post-Islamic, and utterly Greek-less, readers.

Mistranslations of Greek phrases in Jewish magical texts

A second type of linguistic phenomenon which clearly demonstrates the dependence of the Jewish practitioners upon Greek textual sources involves cases where we find them misunderstanding or mistranslating these sources. Above, we noted an Aramaic recipe in which one Greek word was turned into a *vox magica*, and a Greek pun was entirely lost on its Aramaic translator. Similar examples, which are both amusing and illuminating, may be found in Genizah magical formularies. The first of these comes from a recipe we already printed in its entirety, at the beginning of the previous chapter.[34] It is an aggressive recipe, and its instructions begin with "(Take) a sheet of lead and write on the first hour of the day, and bury it in a fresh grave"; next comes the spell to be written, ending with the ubiquitous formula "A(men), A(men), S(elah)." All this is very standard, but the next and final two words, *teli yateih*, "Hang it," seem entirely out of place in an aggressive recipe (though common in recipes for amulets), especially since we have already been told to deposit the "finished product" in a grave. The clue to this crux probably lies in the Jewish practitioner's misunderstanding of a recipe for a *defixio* which he was translating or adapting. The original recipe presumably ended with the Greek phrase *telei auton*, "consecrate it," a common ending of such recipes, but the Aramaic-speaking Jewish practitioner was not sure how to translate the phrase, and so he exchanged

---

[33] And see, e.g., bt Yoma 10a, for the rabbinic debates, so amusing from our perspective, over whether the Persian Empire would finally beat the Romans or vice versa.
[34] See also Bohak 1999, pp. 34–35.

Non-Jewish elements in late-antique Jewish magic

the Greek words *telei auton* for a similar-sounding Aramaic phrase, *teli yateih*, "hang it."[35] That the end result makes little sense is something that he, and the subsequent copiers, apparently never noticed; after all, their formularies were so full of passages of little or no semantic coherence or internal consistency that the contradictory instructions of this recipe would hardly seem unusual.

While the previous example may raise some objections, and perhaps an alternative interpretation or two, our next examples are much simpler, and therefore beyond any doubt. One erotic magical spell, to be written on a piece from the victim's clothes, seems to end with the unusual formula "now, now, now, quickly, quickly, well, well, well, Amen, Amen, Amen, Selah."[36] The phrase "now, now, quickly, quickly" and its many permutations are extremely common in the magical texts of late antiquity, as we shall note at greater length below, and are often found at the spells' very end. But the exclamation "well, well, well" is unique, and makes little sense in such a context; even the spelling, *ṭby*, seems unusual, as the Aramaic word for "well" normally requires no final *yod*. In this case, however, the source of the confusion is plain to see, for rather than reading *ṭby* we should read the word as *ṭky* (*beth* (ב) and *kaph* (כ) are almost indistinguishable in the square Hebrew script), and see it as a transliteration of the Greek word, *tachy*, "quickly."[37] At some point, in other words, a Jewish practitioner not only used the common Aramaic translation of the Greek "now, now, quickly, quickly," formula, but also transliterated the Greek word "quickly" three times. A later scribe, unfamiliar with the Greek word, decided that all is well that ends with "well," and the error went unnoticed even by the spell's modern editors. That this was not a rare occurrence is shown by an unpublished Genizah magical recipe, in which we find the long sequence *'ty 'ty dky dky dky*, a rough transliteration of the Greek *eti eti tachy tachy tachy*, "immediately immediately, quickly quickly quickly."[38] In this case, it is quite possible that whoever transliterated the Greek words knew what they meant, but later copyists probably took the resulting sequence as Aramaic, and understood it as meaning something like "coming, coming, pure, pure, pure." What exactly they made out of such a sequence remains an open question.

---

[35] For *telei*, see Jordan and Kotansky 1997, p. 74.
[36] The text is MTKG III, 66 (T-S NS 246.14), p. 1a/18–19.
[37] From the photograph, it seems as if the scribe actually wrote טבי טכי, but one can hardly be sure.
[38] T-S NS 158.101 (unpublished): אתי דכי דכי דכי, in a frag. whose *charactēres* look like Greek letters with circlets.

Greek-based calques in Hebrew and Aramaic

One more feature, or by-product, of the Jewish magicians' extensive use of Greek magical texts was the formation in Aramaic and Hebrew of new words and technical terms which were modeled after current Greek expressions (what linguists call a *calque*). A full survey of this phenomenon remains a desideratum, but for the time being we may point out a few striking examples.[39] It must be stressed, however, that many of these borrowings need not have taken place among the practitioners of magic, for it would seem that quite a few technical terms, and certainly the medical terms, probably had a wide diffusion among Jewish physicians and other specialists in late antiquity. By way of example, we may note *Sepher ha-Razim*'s recipes for healing "the ache of half the head," or helping "a man who was afflicted, and half of him was withered by a spirit or by *keshaphim*."[40] The first expression is a literal translation of the Greek term *hemikranion*, "half the head (ache)," which, as we already noted above, also entered the magicians' formularies and amulets in a transliterated form, *miqrana*, while the second expression is a literal rendition of the Greek term *hêmixêros*, "half withered."[41] To these two examples, correctly identified for Margalioth by Saul Lieberman, we may add the several references in the same book to *peraḥ lavan*, literally "white flower," which is likely to be a calque from the Greek *leukanthemon*, commonly used by Greek physicians.[42] As we shall see below, in the realm of *materia magica* and *materia medica*, both the transliteration of Greek terms and their translations were quite common. Thus, it is more interesting to note that many of the terms used in the Jewish magical texts for fevers – which were a major way of classifying illnesses in pre-modern medicine – are directly based on the Greek medical system. Above, we already noted the loanword *ṭerṭaia* for tertiary fever. To this, we may now add that semi-tertiary fever appears in the Jewish magical texts both as *ḥemiṭerṭaia*, which is yet another loanword from Greek, *hêmitritaios*, and as *palgut ṭerṭaia*, which is an Aramaic-Greek hybrid – with

---

[39] For one more example, which may be medieval, see the use of the loanword אורא (Greek οὐρά), for the *membrum virile* in MTKG III, 61 (T-S K 1.162) 1c/43, and its calque, זנב, in Gruenwald, 1970–71, p. 318. For calques from Greek in late-antique Jewish Palestinian poetry, see Yahalom 1999, pp. 61–62.

[40] ShR II/181 (p. 90 Margalioth, with the note on p. 91) and II/94–95 (p. 86 Margalioth, with the note on the bottom of the page) respectively.

[41] For migraines, see also MSF, G23 (T-S Ar. 44.44), p. 2, l. 8: באב לשקיקה, literally "A recipe for half the head," שקיקה being an Arabic calque based on the Greek word ἡμικράνιον. For ἡμίξηρος, see Lampe 1961, p. 607.

[42] ShR V/40 (p. 103 Margalioth) (and cf. Margalioth's note ad loc.); see also *Synopse* §612 (ḤdM, shorter version); for *leukanthemon*, see LSJ, s.v.

hêmi correctly translated by Aramaic *palgut*, "half," and *ṭertaia* left in its standard, transliterated form.⁴³ It seems quite likely that many of the other Aramaic terms for fever, such as "fever and shivering," "eternal fever," and so on, are calques from Greek, although this would be hard to prove given the universality of the medical phenomena they describe.⁴⁴ But be these specific cases as they may, we shall have ample occasion to note more such calques – some certain, others less so – in the Jewish magical texts of late antiquity, yet another indication of how deeply their users were influenced by Greek magical technology.

FOREIGN DEITIES AND DEMONS

Certainly the most conspicuous feature of the Greco-Egyptian magic of late antiquity, at least when viewed from a Jewish or Christian perspective, is its polytheistic nature. In the Greek magical papyri, in the Greek *defixiones* and amulets, and on the Greek magical gems, there is a wide range of Greek, Egyptian, and other deities and heavenly or chthonian powers, each with its own name(s), image(s), myths, and rituals. In the Jewish magical tradition, however, the Jewish God and His angels predominate to a point of near exclusivity, and foreign deities make almost no appearance. This is a point to whose significance we shall return in the next chapter, but for the time being we must focus on a few striking exceptions to this general rule, namely, on foreign deities and demons which do make an appearance in the Aramaic and Hebrew magical texts of late antiquity. We examine them in the order of their frequency in the Jewish magical texts, beginning with Abrasax and with the *charactêres*, which seem to have been entirely naturalized, and sometimes even "Judaized," in the Jewish magical tradition of late antiquity, moving to the sun-god Helios, a "multiple entry" into the Jewish magical tradition, and ending with several examples of "one time entry."

Abrasax

Of all the divine figures invoked in the Greco-Egyptian magic of late antiquity, none has captured the popular imagination of later periods more than Abrasax/Abraxas (both forms are attested in the pagan and in the Jewish

---

⁴³ חמיטריטין: MSF, A19/3 (and cf. Arabic *amiṭritawus* in Ullmann 1978, p. 27). פלגות טרטיה: MTKG I, 2 (T-S K 1.56), 2a/2.
⁴⁴ See also Kotansky, Naveh, and Shaked 1992, p. 9, l. 20: "For fever and shivering which attacks every day," with the editors' note, p. 17.

magical texts, but in both corpora the former is far more common). From the neo-Gnostic sermons of Carl Gustav Jung to the New Age discourse of spirituality and from the City of London to the pubs of Tel-Aviv, Abraxas seems to have carved quite a niche for himself, almost becoming a household name in modern Western culture. One reason for his modern popularity, and for the common association of ancient magic with his name, is that he was the most popular of all the new-fangled divine figures in the magical and Gnostic texts of late antiquity. And in spite of many modern attempts to offer a Hebrew or Aramaic etymology of his name, there is little doubt that his appearance in the Jewish magical and mystical texts of late antiquity is due to the influence of the Greco-Egyptian magical tradition, and not to the re-emergence of some age-old Jewish creation.[45] Looking at the Jewish magical texts, in Aramaic, Hebrew, and Judeo-Arabic, we find Abrasax making an appearance in dozens of such texts, both in the Palestinian amulets of late antiquity and in the magical texts of the Cairo Genizah.[46] He also appears quite often in the Babylonian incantation bowls, a sure sign of his reputation even beyond the confines of the Roman empire.[47] He even appears in some of the Merkabah/Hekhalot texts, as we shall see in the next chapter. And he also appears, though less frequently, in later Jewish magical texts, both Oriental and Ashkenazi, a sure sign of his survival even after the triumphs of Christianity and Islam.[48] In the earlier Jewish texts, which are our focus here, his name appears in several different spellings – *'brsks* seems to be the most common, but many other variants are also attested. It is clear, however, that the solar aspect of his name – which in Greek is made up of 7 letters, whose numerical values add up to 365 – was lost in transliteration, for none of the different spellings of his name adds up to 365 in *gematria*, and most do not even contain 7 letters, though this would have been easier to achieve.

The frequent appearance of Abrasax in Jewish magical texts, and under different spellings, eloquently demonstrates that this was not a "one time entry," but a "multiple entry" into the Jewish magical tradition, for it is clear that he was borrowed by different Jewish practitioners from their

---

[45] For "Jewish" etymologies of Abrasax, see, e.g., Brashear 1995, p. 3577.
[46] See, for example, AMB, A1, l. 9 (אברסקופ); A2, l. 3 (אברסכס); A12, l. 2 (אברסכס); MSF, A19, l. 11 (אבראסכס); A24, l. 5 (אברכסיס); AMB, G6 (T-S K 1.73), p. 1, l. 11 (אברסכס); G7 (=HAITCG 8) (T-S K 1.127), l. 29 (אברסכס); MTKG I, 21 (T-S K 1.4), 2b/14 (אברכסה). More examples will be cited below.
[47] E.g., Montgomery 1913, p. 57, and no. 34 (אברכסס מריא תקיפא, "Abrasax, the mighty lord"!); Gordon 1937, p. 86, Bowl H, l. 4 (אברסכס שידא); Shaked 1996, p. 517 (a bowl from the Schøyen collection (no. 1911/1:1) which opens with אברחסיא רבא קדישא מלכא דצלמא). See also Geller 1997, pp. 329 and 331 (but the second text might be a modern forgery); Levene 2003, p. 51; Müller-Kessler 2005, p. 100.
[48] See, e.g., Trachtenberg 1939, p. 100; Margalioth 1966, p. 8.

non-Jewish colleagues on more than one occasion, and that he was so fully naturalized in this new home that some Jewish magicians had no difficulty in adding him to their spells and recipes whenever they saw fit. Moreover, it seems clear that Abrasax was not seen by many of his Jewish users as just another powerful magic word, devoid of any semantic meaning or "signifiée," but as the name of a very powerful angel or celestial power. In one of the Nirim amulets, for example, we find an invocation "in the name of Abrasax, who is in charge o[f . . .], and guards fetuses in the[ir mothers' wombs?]," and in another late-antique amulet, against fevers, demons, and the evil eye, we find an adjuration of Abrasax, "who is appointed over you (sg.), that he will uproot you, fever and sickness," from the patient's body.[49] In *Sepher ha-Razim* we find him as the first in a list of some thirty angels who lead the sun by day (a sure sign that his solar connections were not lost on all ancient Jews), and in the *Sword of Moses* we find an adjuration of "the minister, whose name is Abraxas," who is ordered to reveal to the adjurer all that he or she may want to know.[50] Such examples, we must stress, could easily be multiplied. But not only was Abrasax naturalized into the Jewish magical tradition, in some cases he seems to have been entirely "Judaized" in the process. One striking example is afforded by his appearance in an erotic recipe from the Cairo Genizah, which runs as follows:

<A> Another (recipe), <J> to be written on an unbaked potsherd and thrown in the fire, and this is what should be written: . . . <A> In the name of Nuriel, the great angel who is in appointed over charm and grace . . . In the name of Abrasax, the great angel who overturned Sodom and Gomorrah, so will you (pl.) overturn the heart, the mind, and the kidney of NN after NN. <H> Amen A(men), A(men), A(men), S(elah), H(allelujah).[51]

In this specific case, not only has the Gnostic or pagan Abrasax become a Jewish angel, he was even read back into the biblical story and identified as the angel who had once overturned Sodom and Gomorrah.[52] Having once done so, he should now perform (together with another angel, whose name is made up of the Hebrew word *nur*, "fire" and the angelic ending -el) an analogous service against the recipe's intended victim. We already noted one erotic use of the Sodom and Gomorrah story in Chapter 3, and shall have more to say about its magical uses in Chapters 5 and 6, but,

---

[49] See AMB, A12, ll. 2–3, and MSF, A19, ll. 10–14, respectively.
[50] ShR IV/13 (p. 96 Margalioth). ḤdM, p. 40 Harari; p. 82 Gaster.
[51] AMB, G6 (T-S K 1.73), p. 1, ll. 3–14.
[52] For the angel who destroyed Sodom and Gomorrah, see also Gen. R. 51.4 (p. 536 Theodor-Albeck).

for the time being, we may note that this recipe is not the only example of Abrasax's entry into the midst of the Jewish heavenly host. In another Genizah magical text, the names Siphon, Bizon, and Abarscas (this, at least, is how the scribe vocalized the name!) are given as those of the three "creatures" (*ḥayyot*) which carry God's chariot up on high. The fact that there are only three of them here (instead of the usual four), and that they all seem to carry names of a non-Jewish origin is quite striking, but the appearance of this list in quite a few Jewish magical texts (often in the same recipe, for safe travel) proves its wide circulation.[53] And once again, we see Abrasax being "Judaized," and taking his rightful place in heaven, not far from God Himself. And in a few instances, it seems as if Abrasax became one of the many Names of the Jewish God Himself.[54] If in Chapter 2 we noted how, already in the Second Temple period, an Iranian "demon of wrath" became the Jewish demon Ashmedai, now we find a new-fangled pagan and Gnostic deity turned into an angel, a heavenly companion of Michael, Raphael, Gabriel, and their many colleagues, and one whose name may occasionally even be shared by God.

The charactêres

In a subsequent section, we shall note the pervasive presence in the Jewish magical texts of late antiquity and later periods of the *charactêres*, those "ring-letter" symbols which so fascinated ancient, medieval, and modern students of magic. The origin of these symbols is obscure, but what is certain is that in Greek magical texts they were often treated as divine emblems, and even as divine powers in their own right, to be invoked, appeased, and adjured just like any other divine and semi-divine power in the pagan pantheon.[55] It is therefore quite interesting to note that in the Jewish magical texts too these magical signs are often not only drawn upon the writing surface, but also invoked as independent powers. In one Genizah recipe, we find a series of angel names and 'HWY-combinations followed by a line of crude *charactêres*; these are followed by "You holy

---

[53] See JTS ENA 3780.1 (unpublished), and the parallels in T-S K 1.108 (unpublished); T-S K 1.121 (unpublished); Mosseri VIII.417 (unpublished). And cf. Hyginus, *Fab.* 183 (p. 128 Rose), for the claim that Homer had listed Abraxas as one of the (three?/four?) horses who pull the Sun-god's chariot.

[54] See, for example, the Name אברסכס תרכוסיה in MTKG II, 40 (T-S AS 143.106) 1a/8; MTKG II, 42 (T-S K 1.163) 1a/26–27; and cf. the Name אברסכסוה in MTKG II, 45 (T-S K 1.26) 1a/6, and the Name יהוה אבראקס, for which see Chapter 5, n. 93.

[55] For the invocation of the *charactêres*, see, e.g. SM I, 21, with the editors' notes (p. 59); Jordan and Kotansky 1996, pp. 163 and 165.

angels and exulted *charactêres*, give (pl.) grace and favor to NN," and so on.⁵⁶ In another recipe, to release a "bound" (i.e., impotent) man, two lines of *charactêres* and 'HWY-names are followed by "You (pl.) holy letters and *charactêres*, release and make fit the big 'sinew' of NN," and so on.⁵⁷ To these two examples many more could be added of the coupling of the *charactêres* together with "angels," "names," "letters," and so on (all of which may fruitfully be compared with the uses of *onomata* and *stoicheia* in Greek magical texts), and of the direct appeal to them as powers which could achieve the outcome desired by the recipes' producers and users.⁵⁸ It is not really clear whether the Jewish magicians who invoked them saw these *charactêres* as some angelic figures or as a different kind of potent being, but a careful analysis of all the relevant sources might shed some more light on such issues.

Helios

While Abrasax and the *charactêres* were the creations of magicians or Gnostics, and not found in any of the ethnic pantheons of antiquity, Helios, the Greek Sun-god, was a standard member of the Greek pantheon from Homer onwards, as well as the Greek equivalent of the Egyptian god Ra, the Phoenician Shamash, the Roman Sol, and so on. And given the importance of the sun in many Near Eastern and Mediterranean religions, it is hardly surprising to find Jews too drawn to his cult in various ways. In the First Temple period, there is much evidence for the Yahwists' relentless war against the worship of the solar deity along with, or instead of, the worship of Yahweh.⁵⁹ But whereas in the Second Temple and later periods, when Jewish monotheism was well established, this all-out war lost most of its steam, the threat of solar cults remained quite strong. In the Mishnah, for example, we find specific injunctions that "Whoever finds vessels on which are images of the sun, the moon . . . should lead them to the Dead Sea," i.e., should annihilate them entirely, a sure sign of the rabbis' familiarity with the ubiquity of solar symbols on artifacts of daily life throughout the Roman empire. And when we turn to the archeological evidence, we find the design of Helios, riding in his chariot and surrounded by the Zodiac circle, adorning the mosaic floors of some of the most impressive synagogues

---

[56] MSF, G15 (T-S K 1.80) 2/1–7, with the editors' notes.
[57] MSF, G16 (T-S K 1.91) 3/1–6, with the editors' notes.
[58] See, e.g., AMB, G1 (T-S AS 142.174); MTKG I, 2 (T-S K 1.56), 2a/2–3; MTKG I, 12 (CUL Or. 1080.15.81), 1a/91, etc.
[59] For a useful survey of the evidence, see Taylor 1993.

of late-antique Palestine.⁶⁰ Unfortunately, it is hard to know for sure what exactly the ancient synagogue-goers would have made of this figure; for all we know, his popularity may have been due not only to the great popularity of Sol Invictus (the Invincible Sun) throughout the later Roman empire, but also to a peculiarity of his name which to us might seem entirely accidental. When written in Hebrew letters, HLYWS contains all the letters of God's very Name, YHW(H), and some ancient Jews may have identified the figure of Helios with God's famous promise to send an angel to lead the Israelites to the Promised Land, and His insistence that they must obey this angel and not rebel against him, "for My Name is within him."⁶¹ Accidentally or not, Helios certainly fit the bill, and this may have contributed to his popularity among some synagogue-goers in late-antique Palestine.

Such speculations notwithstanding, the magical texts at our disposal certainly testify to a lively interest in Helios. In *Sepher ha-Razim*, the fourth heaven is entirely devoted to the sun, whose abode this heaven is.⁶² Following the customary lists of angels, where Abrasax and Marmaraoth are the first of the angels who lead the sun by day, we find a recipe which begins with "If you wish to see the sun by day, sitting in the chariot and ascending." This recipe, whose aim is revelation – as the sun travels around the universe and sees everything, he is quite a good figure to interrogate about one's affairs – is followed by another revelatory recipe. "If you wish to see the sun by night," you should follow the ritual instructions, adjure the angels who lead the sun by night, and, once you see the sun, recite the transliterated Greek prayer we already discussed above (including a direct appeal to Helios!) and then a Hebrew request of the sun to tell you all you wish to know. The recipe ends with a brief dismissal formula, which also brings the fourth-heaven section of *Sepher ha-Razim* to a close. And when we turn to the *Sword of Moses*, we find there too a recipe which begins with "If you wish to see the sun," and insists that if you follow the instructions you will see him "like a man dressed in white" who will answer all your questions "and even a woman (you desire) he will bring to you."⁶³ And in the *Testament of Solomon*, Solomon is informed how he may see the heavenly serpents which pull the chariot of the sun, a sure sign that

---

⁶⁰ This is a much-studied issue; see Smith 1982; Foerster 1987; Weiss 2005, pp. 104–41; Wandrey 2004, pp. 82–87, all with further bibliography.

⁶¹ Ex 23.20–21; and cf. PRE 6: החמה, שלוש אותיות של שם כתובים בלבו, "the sun, three letters of the Name are written in its heart." I hope to explore this issue in greater detail elsewhere.

⁶² ShR IV (pp. 96–100 Margalioth). See also ShR I/98 (p. 72): "I adjure you, the sun."

⁶³ HdM recipe 49 (p. 40 Harari = pp. 82–83 Gaster), and cf. the parallel in recipe 144 (p. 140 Harari), with a slightly different ending.

Christian magicians too were interested in such revelations.[64] Such solar recipes seem to reemerge in later Jewish magical texts, but it is quite possible that others were filtered out of the Jewish magical tradition, remaining intact mainly in the codified "literary" books of magic, and mostly absent from the free-form formularies, from which "offensive" recipes were more easily removed.[65] Thus, while the exact extent of the appeal to Helios in ancient Jewish magic is hard to judge, it seems quite clear that at least some practitioners incorporated him in their magical recipes, not as a rival or equal to God, but as one more celestial power, along with the angels and perhaps even as one of them.

Other pagan deities and demons

If Abrasax and the *charactêres* are conspicuous for their many appearances in the Jewish magical texts, and Helios for his occasional presence and for the prayers directed to him in *Sepher ha-Razim*, the other pagan gods are conspicuous mainly for their absence from the Jewish magical texts and artifacts of late antiquity. In the Babylonian incantation bowls, one occasionally finds the old Babylonian planetary-gods – Shamish, Sin, Nabu, Dalibat, Bel, Nirig, and Kiwan – appearing in Aramaic magical texts which clearly were composed by Jews.[66] Even there, however, such bowls are few and far between, and prove not only that the old gods were still available to the Sasanian-period spell writers (as may be seen also from the Mandaic and Syriac bowls), but that most Jewish bowl-writers probably preferred to shun these gods and leave them out of their magic spells.[67] And when we turn to the western branch of Jewish magic, the pagan gods of late-antique Palestine and Egypt hardly make an appearance in the Jewish magical texts.[68] We shall return to this very clear trend in the next chapter, but may now focus on a few possible exceptions. In a few instances, we find the pagan names of the planets (and we still use the Latin names – Mercury, Venus, Mars, etc. – for the same purpose),[69] and in many other instances, we find magic words

---

[64] See *T. Sol.* 6.10 (p. 28* McCown, with the *variae lectiones*), with Jackson 1988, pp. 43–44.
[65] For other examples, see MTKG II, 26 (T-S K 1.35) 1a/29 ("If you wish to speak to the sun"); *Sepher Raziel* with Bodleian Heb. a2.2 (unpublished) ("If you wish to see the sun rising in the chariot"); T-S AS 142.34 (unpublished) (to ask the sun and moon to foretell the future).
[66] See Obermann 1940, pp. 15–29; Segal 2000, Bowls 039A (p. 79) and 047A (p. 90); Müller-Kessler 1999b.
[67] For the Babylonian gods found in Mandaic bowls, see Müller-Kessler and Kessler 1999.
[68] And cf. how in Kotansky 1994, no. 33 (briefly discussed in the previous chapter), Artemis seems to appear as the evil which must be driven away from the client.
[69] See, e.g., ShR I/125–126 (p. 73 Margalioth): Aphrodite as the name of the planet נוגה (i.e., Venus). And note the reference to the "mystery of Aphrodite" in PGM XXXVI.306, discussed in Chapter 3.

or angel names which may have been derived from those of pagan deities. Here, however, we must proceed very cautiously, always recalling that many words and phrases in the Jewish magical texts at our disposal are corrupt, and many had no real semantic meaning to begin with, but were part of the arsenal of powerful *voces magicae* which the Jewish magicians, like their non-Jewish comrades, so fervently employed. This, and the nature of the vowel-less Hebrew alphabet, means that a combination of letters might occasionally appear which looks like the name of a pagan deity, but whose identity as such cannot be demonstrated. Thus, it has often been stated that the Jewish magical texts of late antiquity – both the Palestinian and the Babylonian ones – display a whole host of known pagan deities, including the Greek Hermes, Aphrodite, Apollo, Zeus, and many others; the Egyptian Osiris, Sarapis, Ammon, Thoth, and so on; or the Phoenician Shamash, to name but a few.[70] Looking at such a list, which could easily be extended, one might get the impression that the Jewish magical texts are entirely syncretistic, abounding in deities and incorporating the Jewish God and His pagan counterparts shoulder to shoulder. But when we turn to the actual evidence, the picture which emerges from it is quite different. Beginning with *Sepher ha-Razim*'s endless lists of angels, we may note that some of these names *might* be based on those of pagan deities, such as HRM'Y'L (IV/16), which sounds quite like Hermes, or SRPY'L (I/213), which is suspiciously close to Sarapis, but such suggestions are only tentative at best, given the presence of hundreds of randomly generated angelic names within that work.[71] The same is true of the "sword" section of the *Sword of Moses*, which consists of a long sequence of meaningless "words," including such suspicion-arousing sequences as 'WZRWS 'WZWRWS, which certainly could remind us of Osiris, a favorite deity in the Greco-Egyptian magical tradition.[72] And in later Jewish magical texts, the "Name of twenty-two letters," 'NQTM PSTM PSPSYM DYWNSYM, has often been interpreted by modern scholars as containing the name of the Greek god Dionysus (and those of several other pagan deities).[73] This too is not impossible, but how can we demonstrate that this indeed was the origin of this "word," if the meaning of the entire formula still eludes us, and if we can never be certain that it ever had a real meaning in any human language?

---

[70] For such claims, see, e.g., Montgomery 1913, pp. 70–73, 99–100; Sperber 1994, pp. 96–97; Shaked 2005c, p. 11. For the pagan gods in later Jewish magic, see Grunwald 1923a, p. 18.

[71] And cf. the caution exercised by Margalioth 1966, p. 7 and by Trachtenberg 1939 throughout his book (e.g., p. 102). For Sarapis-names, see also Synopse §581: סרפסיון.

[72] See HdM p. 76 Gaster = p. 31 Harari, and the other instances cited in chapter 3, n. 93.

[73] And see Trachtenberg 1939, pp. 92–93; Sperber 1994, pp. 97–98; Rohrbacher-Sticker 1996, p. 26, n. 10, with further bibliography.

Given these difficulties, we cannot be satisfied with the mere identification in the Jewish magical texts of names which look like those of pagan deities. Rather, we must look for other factors which would strengthen the case for identifying a certain word or phrase as containing the name of a pagan god, and not just a haphazard collection of letters which happens to look like one.[74] As an illustrative example, we may note how in several Genizah amulets against snake- and scorpion-bites one finds the recurrence of a magic triangle, which runs as follows:[75]

'PDYRṬ'
'PDYRṬ
'PDYR
'PDY
'PD
'P
'

The *vox magica* which serves as the basis for this triangle seems suspiciously close to the name of the Greek goddess, Aphrodite (D (ד) and R (ר) are almost indistinguishable in the Hebrew square script), and we would thus be tempted to add this example to those mentioned above. In this specific case, however, there is no need for any hesitation, for the use of Aphrodite-triangles in Greek snake- and scorpion-amulets is well attested in late-antique Egypt.[76] Thus, in this instance we can examine the special use of the name of this Greek goddess in a specific magical context within the Greek magical papyri, and see how the entire practice was borrowed by the Jewish practitioners (perhaps only in the Middle Ages, but probably already in late antiquity) and ended up in our Genizah amulets. Elsewhere in the Genizah, we find similar scorpion-amulets, but this time with three triangles, based on the "words" 'BLYGM', 'PDYRṬ', and 'PYQRWS.[77] The origins of the first "word" are quite elusive, but the second is Aphrodite once again, and the third is likely to be Epicurus, presumably the famous Greek philosopher whose teachings were so disturbing to Josephus and the

---

[74] One doubtful case is ShR I/178, a necromantic adjuration of רוח קריפוריא, which Morton Smith, followed by Margalioth 1966, p. 76 and Alexander 2003b, pp. 174–78, took as Κριοφόρος, the "ram-bearer," which they took as an epithet for Hermes. However, this epithet of Hermes seems to be quite rare, and its presence here is, at best, doubtful.

[75] See, for example, the "mass-produced" scorpion-amulets of T-S AS 143.26, which I hope to publish elsewhere.

[76] See PGM 2 (tr. in Meyer and Smith 1994, pp. 48–49), a Christian scorpion-amulet of the sixth century with an Aphrodite-triangle.

[77] See, for example, JTSL ENA NS 73.12, which I hope to publish elsewhere. In this case, the "tips" of the triangles add up to ',', S, a standard abbreviation in Jewish magical texts for A(men), A(men), S(elah).

rabbis. Why he – who surely denied the efficacy of amulets – was used in such a triangle is far from obvious, but as we already met a Lycurgus-triangle in the Jewish magical texts, the entry of Epicurus is hardly unique. And in passing, we may note that a garbled version of these three *voces magicae* still appears in a Jewish magical manuscript written in Kurdistan in 1896, yet another proof of the remarkable longevity of some of these elements, as well as the corruption they suffered at the hand of their many copyists.[78]

With this last example in mind, we may return to the previous ones. On the one hand, it only strengthens the impression that many of the *voces* in the Jewish magical texts which look like the names of pagan deities may indeed have begun their life in such a manner. On the other hand – and this is the most important point – it reminds us that in all these cases the pagan gods entered the Jewish magical texts not as gods, not even as distinct entities of any sort, but as mere names and "words of power." Hermes, Sarapis, Osiris, Aphrodite, Erechshigal, and their many friends and relatives are not invoked in the Jewish magical texts, they are not even recognized as independent beings, but merely included in long lists of names and *voces magicae*, or, at most, turned into Jewish-sounding angelic names by adding the ending -el to their original names. This is, of course, a far cry from their status within the Greco-Egyptian magic of late antiquity, in which Erechshigal and Semeseilam might be just names, but Aphrodite, Hermes, Osiris, and Ptah are well-known, and well-worshiped, deities. It is quite different even from Abrasax's entry into the Jewish magical texts, not only as a *vox magica*, but also as an independent angelic being, sometimes even fully incorporated into the Jewish angelological system. Similarly, the *charactêres*, which retained their independent status in some Jewish magical texts, and even Helios, who occasionally became a powerful angel and an object of devout prayer, fared much better than all the other gods of antiquity.

By formulating our conclusion in this manner we are, in fact, offering a challenge to future students of ancient Jewish magic. Rather than looking for more examples of pagan gods whose names seem to surface in the Jewish magical texts, we must now search for gods which appear there as gods, or angels, or demons, or show some other sign that they were not seen merely as *voces magicae*. For such occurrences, there is only a small number of possible examples, more exasperating than probative. As noted above, in the Greek sections of the el-Amarna amulet one finds a brief

---

[78] See Meiri 1998, p. 116: אבנה גמה מיחסה איברי רטה אפיקורוס; I am not yet sure what the מיחסה stands for, but the other "words" are easily recognizable as אפדירטה אפיקורוס אבליגמה. The same series appears in Thompson 1907, p. 166 as אבנה ומה מוחסה אברי רנוה אפקורוס.

reference to "Osornôphrês (the) god," which might imply that this was seen as more than a mere *vox magica* by the producer(s) of this amulet. In one Aramaic amulet from late-antique Palestine (an amulet which, unfortunately, is extremely hard to read), we find a list of heavenly rulers and servants which seems to incorporate transliterated Greek words and names, including the eye-catching phrase "the one who rules the sun . . . and his servant you, you TY'WN the great 'MWN'." As *theon* is the Greek for "god" (in the accusative), one could see here a somewhat garbled transliteration cum translation of some Greek phrase like **megan theon Ammôna*, "the great god, Ammon," this Egyptian god being quite conspicuous in the Greco-Egyptian magical texts. And as the next lines in our amulet include garbled renditions of Abrasax and Sesengen Barpharanges as other rulers and servants in this list, the presence of Ammon too would not be that surprising.[79] And yet, even if Ammon did make it into one Jewish magical text, this only serves to highlight his absence from all the others, and the inherent difficulty of "catching" ancient Jewish magicians in the act of invoking pagan gods. They may have been more liberal in their oral spells (and this too is far from certain), but in their written texts made for specific clients they generally avoided such "un-Jewish" behavior, even when producing small metal lamellae which no one but the scholars of a millennium and a half later would bother to unfold and read.

To realize the full significance of this phenomenon, we must compare it with our findings in the previous chapter. There, we saw how the Jewish god entered the pantheon of the pagan magicians and was transformed, and even "paganized," in the process. What we are now seeing is the other side of the coin, namely, what happened to the pagan gods when they entered the Jewish magical texts; in rare cases, they were either invoked as gods or turned into angels, or into Names of the many-Named Jewish God.[80] In most cases, however, they were either ignored or turned from independent and powerful entities with their own myths, rituals, and iconography into mere words of power, as meaningless to their Jewish users as all the other abracadabra words at their disposal. Here, as elsewhere, we see how asymmetric cross-cultural contacts and transmission can often be, with each culture offering to the other much of what it has but receiving only what it can and wants to handle, and thoroughly transforming it in the process.

---

[79] MSF, A22. For a possible parallel, see PGM XII.106 (p. 6 Daniel): σὺ εἶ ὁ μέγας "Αμμων.

[80] For another possible example of this process, see the divine Name אוגוסטוס (clearly based on Augustus, so common in the Roman imperial cult) in B.L. Or. 5557A 66 (unpublished) and T-S NS 317.22 (unpublished). For the rabbis' familiarity with this cultic title, see pt Ber 9.1 (12d), and esp. Ex.R. 23.1.

MAGIC WORDS AND VOWEL PERMUTATIONS, WORD-SHAPES, AND MAGIC SIGNS, SYMBOLS, AND IMAGES

One of the characteristic features of the Greco-Egyptian magic of late antiquity, and of all the magical traditions which were influenced by it, is the preponderance of non-semantic elements in its spells and incantations. These may broadly be divided in five distinct types: magic words, written and pronounced, but devoid of any lexical meaning in the language in which the spell is written; vowel permutations, which were intended either to be pronounced or merely to be written down (or both); word-shapes, constructed through the pictorial manipulation of written words or letters; magic signs and symbols, that is, non-alphabetic signs which recur in many different magical texts; and magic images, which form a part of the iconography which sometimes accompanied the practitioners' scribal productions. Let us examine each of these in detail, and note their entry into the Jewish magical tradition in late antiquity.

Magic words

Among the many striking features of the Greco-Egyptian magical tradition, the proliferation of *voces magicae* certainly is the most conspicuous. The phenomenon of "speaking in tongues" is common enough in many mystical and magical traditions, but in the Greco-Egyptian case it is clear that we are not dealing with some sort of effervescent glossolalia, which would yield an ever-changing variety of combinations of letters and syllables, but with a growing canon of "magic words," which are repeated again and again in Greek magical texts from every corner of the ancient world. It is this unusual combination of "words" and "phrases" which were both meaningless and fixed which makes them such a distinct feature of Greco-Egyptian magic and so tempting for modern scholars to study. In Chapter 3, we already had the occasion to mention some of these *voces magicae*, namely those *voces* for which a Jewish origin has, rightly or wrongly, been postulated. There are, of course, many other *voces magicae* in the Greek magical texts besides those which we already examined – some of which can be identified as coming from some known language (and we already noted such examples as Pephtha Phôza or Semeseilam), some perhaps stemming from lesser-known languages, and some of a demonstrably non-linguistic origin. The latter category testifies to the magicians' fertile imagination, and their fondness of various linguistic games, such as the combination of existing words and word-parts to create new "words," the creation of palindromes, some dozens of letters long, the invention of "words" with special isopsephic values (such as 365, 3,663 or 9,999), or the creation of repetitive yet modular series of syllables such as *phôr bôrphorba phorbabor baphorba*, and so on. So complex, and so standardized, have some of these sequences become, that the magicians' recipes are full of abbreviating references such as "write the iaeô-formula," which indeed is much easier than spelling out the entire palindrome, which is dozens of letters long.

Focusing on the Jewish magical texts, we note that from late antiquity onwards the Jewish magicians too were very much infatuated with such abracadabra words. Their fondness for *voces magicae* may itself be the result of non-Jewish influence – it has no precedents in the Hebrew Bible or those Jewish texts of the Second Temple period to which we have any access – but such claims are a priori impossible to substantiate. The use of such *voces* is well attested in many magical traditions all over the world, including some which certainly were not influenced by the Greco-Egyptian magic of late antiquity.[81] And in antiquity itself, the use of meaningless "words" seems to have been common in many different cultures, be it the enigmatic chants of the Salian priests in Rome, the "mumblings" of the Persian Magi, or the prophetic "speaking in tongues" in some early Christian churches, and perhaps also in the Hekhalot literature.[82] But while the very use of *voces magicae* by Jewish magicians is no clear evidence of Greco-Egyptian influence (and is also evident in the Babylonian incantation bowls, and even in the Babylonian Talmud), some of the actual *voces* used by these magicians eloquently betray their origins in the Greco-Egyptian magic of late antiquity. For our current enquiry, such *voces* are of great importance, since they provide an ideal demonstration of elements whose presence in the Jewish magical tradition can only be explained as the result of a direct borrowing from pagan magicians, and in most cases we can even date the borrowing to the pre-Muslim period, or at least prove that it was not done through Arabic intermediaries. Above, we already noted the entry of some *voces magicae* (such as Pephtha Phôza, Arsenophru, and so on) into the Greek sections of several bilingual Jewish magical texts. We may now turn to the far more abundant evidence for the entry of such *voces* into the Aramaic and Hebrew magical texts themselves. This process, which involved the transliteration of meaningless "words" into an alphabet unsuited for this task, caused many problems to the Jewish practitioners,

---

[81] For the ubiquity of such phenomena in many cultures, see Tambiah 1968; Staal 1989, pp. 191–346.
[82] Salian priests: e.g., Quintillian 1.6.40: *Saliorum carmina vix sacerdotibus suis satis intellecta*. Persian Magi: Greenfield 1974. "Speaking in tongues": 1 Cor. 14; Acts 10.46, 19.6; T. Jb 48–50 (briefly mentioned in Chapter 2); for the Hekhalot literature, see the next chapter.

and especially to those who copied and recopied these meaningless strings of letters, and often corrupted them in the process.[83] And yet, as we shall soon see, it is precisely this textual entropy which provides us with some of the best clues for analyzing the entry of foreign materials into the Jewish magical texts and their subsequent transmission within the Jewish magical tradition itself.

Of dozens of available examples demonstrating these processes, let us examine only a few. We shall ignore those *voces* which are most commonly found in the Jewish magical texts – and especially *ablanathanalba*, *akrammachamari*, *marmaraoth*, and *sesengenbarpharanges* – whose presence in the Jewish magical texts has often been noted, and focus on some lesser-known examples.

(a) (*h*)*yesemmigadôn*:
This *vox magica*, whose origins entirely elude us (though here too a Hebrew etymology has ingeniously been offered!), has entered the Jewish magical tradition on quite a few occasions, each time with a slightly different spelling.[84] One of the metal amulets from the Nirim synagogue opens with "I-am-who-I-am. In the name of Q[ ] HŠNʔRWN ʼRSKYʼL N[. . . / . . .]ʼL MŠNʔYD HŠMGRWN[85] SKSK DWKWN DWKWN," and continues with several angelic names, adjuring them all to uproot the *qefalargia* (the Greek word for headache) from poor Natrun, daughter of Sarah.[86] Looking at the *vox* HŠMGRWN (and perhaps also at HŠNʔRWN), we can easily recognize a transliteration of the Greek *yesemmigadôn*, the D (ד) and the R (ר) being virtually indistinguishable in the square Hebrew script. We also note the name ʼRSKYʼL, which seems suspiciously close to the common "word" *ereschigal*, originally the name of a female Babylonian deity, Ereshkigal, but in the Greco-Egyptian magical texts merely a "word of power." In this case, it seems that a Jewish practitioner, by adding a small squiggle to the letter *gimmel* (ג) and turning it into an *aleph* (א), changed the (to him) meaningless magic word Ereschigal into the name of a nice Jewish angel, Ereschiel. This suggestion, we may add, gains further support

---

[83] In later periods, scribes who feared that they might mispronounce the "words" they had copied in the vowel-less Hebrew alphabet, often provided partial or full vocalizations (and cf. Hai Gaon's discussion of the vocalization of the Name of forty-two letters!), but the vocalization systems known to us were not yet in use in late antiquity.
[84] For this *vox*, see Brashear 1995, p. 3600, who cites the etymology *huʼa semo gadol*, which supposedly means "That is: his name is great" in Hebrew. See also Martinez 1991, pp. 37–40, for the appearance of this *vox* and the difficulty of interpreting it.
[85] My "word"-division differs slightly from that of the editors' MŠNʔYDH ŠMGRWN.
[86] AMB, A11.

from the frequent appearance in the Greek magical texts of a long formula in which *erechsigal* and *yesemmigadôn* appear side by side.[87]

Returning to *yesemmigadôn*, we may note how in *Sepher ha-Razim* 'ŠMYGDWN is one of the angels of the twelfth step in the second heaven, in charge of healing migraines and cataracts.[88] And he also appears in two Genizah magical texts – in one case, we read "In the name (of) HWŠMGDWN (carefully vocalized by the scribe as "Hushmagdon"!) 'PŠWN BS'S 'WSṬDPWS YH God Sabaot," as part of a long adjuration of angels, and in another our *vox* appears three times, once as HWŠMGRWN in a recipe to escape robbers and twice as HŠMGRWN in a recipe for invisibility.[89] Looking at the different appearances of this *vox*, we may conclude that the different spellings (and especially the transliteration of the *ypsilon* both as aspirated [*he*] and as non-aspirated [*aleph*]) suggest that this *vox* entered the Jewish magical tradition on more than one occasion. The fact that in two cases it is connected with headaches might show that in some circles it was seen as connected with that problem, but this might also be a mere coincidence. Future research, and the identification of this *vox* in other Jewish magical texts, will no doubt shed more light on these issues.

Before leaving this example, one more comment is in order, one which applies for the following examples as well. While looking at the *voces magicae* which moved from the Greco-Egyptian magic of late antiquity into the Jewish magical tradition, we must always distinguish between the search for origins and the search for meaning. We can now say for certain that this *vox* reached the Jewish magicians from their Greek-speaking pagan colleagues, but this tells us nothing about its original meaning, if it had any. As with many other features of late-antique magic, tracing the transmission history of this *vox* is quite easy, but the resulting trajectory cannot be used to reconstruct, by way of extrapolation backwards in time, its ultimate origins. Moreover, the fact that *we* know that this was a foreign import into the Jewish magical tradition does not mean that the Jewish practitioners who used it were aware of this fact, or understood this "word" to mean what it meant to their non-Jewish colleagues. To see what it meant to its

---

[87] For this formula (*yessemmigadôn orthô baubô noêre soire soirê sankanthara ereschigal sankistê dôdekakistê akroubore kodêre* and its variants), see Martinez 1991, pp. 37–39; cf. PDM xiv.212 (translated in Betz 1986, p. 207), showing its entry into the Demotic magical spells. Is SKSK DWKWN DWKWN a much-garbled rendition of *sankistê dôdekakistê*?

[88] ShR II/177 (p. 90 Margalioth). Note also, right next to him, the names BWBWKWK (on which more below) and ARṬMYKṬWN, which might be Greek in origin.

[89] See MTKG II, 33 (T-S NS 91.46) 1b/17 and T-S K 1.123 (unpublished), respectively.

Jewish users, we would have to closely examine all its appearances in the Jewish magical texts of late antiquity, and only then compare our findings with what we find in the pagan magical texts.

(b) The *chych bachych*-formula:
Of all the magic "words" and formulae whose entry into the Jewish magical tradition can still be documented, the most conspicuous is the formula which in the Greek magical texts usually appears as *chych bachych bakachych bakaxichych bazabachych bennebechych badêtophôth bainchôôôch*, with some variations.[90] Its great popularity in late antiquity is vouchsafed by its appearance on numerous Greek magical texts, including, for example, a Greek *defixio* from Beth Shean.[91] And while no fully-fledged etymology has ever been offered for this sequence (perhaps it is the generative cough of a Gnostic Demiurge, or a learned parody of Aristophanes' *Frogs*?), one would do well to follow Dornseiff's intuition that this formula resulted from the Greek magicians' love of syllable-series on the one hand, and magical "triangles" and "ladders" on the other, and Winkler's demonstrations that such series are common in many cultures.[92] But regardless of the origins of this sequence, its appearance in several Genizah magical texts is quite striking. Looking at one published fragment, we find it embedded in a recipe for a *defixio*, which displays many signs of its late-antique origins. The aggressive ritual aims to subdue one's *antidiki* (the Greek word for "opponents in court") by the name of "KWYR BKWYR BQH KWR BNYKWYR BNYKWYR" who are identified as "names which sit upon the winds and subdue them so that they would not come out and shake the world."[93] That these names are based on the Greek sequence seems beyond doubt, but, once again, we are a step removed from the actual borrowing. Originally, the Greek sequence must have been transliterated as *KWYK BKWYK BQKWYK BQKSYKWYK BZBKWYK, or some similar sequence (depending also on which version of the Greek sequence each practitioner was transliterating). But later copyists, entirely unfamiliar with this *logos*, miscopied the final *kaph* (ך) of all the "words" as a *resh* (ר), split up

---

[90] For this formula, see SM II, p. 11, and cf. Brashear 1995, p. 3582 (who unwittingly breaks it into several separate *voces*, although they often appear as a series).

[91] Youtie and Bonner 1937, pp. 54 and 57.

[92] See Dornseiff 1922, p. 68; Winkler 1935; Vycichl 1938. It has been suggested, however, that *bachych* (or, if the "words" are differently divided, *chychba*) is based on the Hebrew word *kokhab*, "star," yet another proof that any *vox* can find a Hebrew etymology if only we wish hard enough; for this suggestion, see Hopfner 1931, p. 336, and cf. Brashear 1995, p. 3582, Ritner in Betz 1986, p. 202, n. 76, and Dieleman 2005, p. 101, for the possible Egyptian origins of these *voces*.

[93] MSF, G9 (T-S K 1.15), p. 3, ll. 3–6. Note that in this case, the Aramaic spell is almost fully vocalized (by the Arabic-speaking Jewish copyists!), while the *voces magicae* are not. This is a recipe which I hope to analyze at greater length elsewhere.

the "word" BQKWYK in two, and garbled and duplicated the last "word." Such processes, as we already saw, were almost *de rigeur* in the transmission of *voces magicae* from one magician to the next and from one generation to another, and support for our postulated reconstruction of this process is found in an older (and still unpublished) Genizah fragment, in which our series of *voces* retains its original form.[94] In a later Genizah recipe, a sequence of *voces* appears which may be based on a much greater corruption of our formula, and later corruptions of this sequence seem to survive well into modern Jewish magic.[95] Perhaps most intriguing, it is even possible that one garbled version of the same formula appears in the Babylonian Talmud, as we shall see in Chapter 6.

(c) The *sêmea kanteu*-formula:

One long formula which often appears in the Greek magical texts of late antiquity is *sêmea kanteu kenteu konteu kêrideu darungô lukunx*, with some variations (see Figure 3.7).[96] This formula, or at least its first half, emerges in several Jewish magical and mystical texts. In one instance, it appears as SM'D 'GYNṬWN 'YQWNṬY 'NṬYDYGWN ṬRG?GWN, in which the first three "words" of the *sêmea*-formula may still be recognized.[97] In another, it is embedded in the "sword" section of the *Sword of Moses* as SM'H QNṬ' QNṬ'H QNṬ'W 'WNṬW QWGṬ'W QWGṬWW QWNṬZ, again making us wonder how it had changed its original ending for a new one.[98] Unfortunately, it is not clear what exactly the Jewish practitioners made of this series, and the elucidation of this point will have to wait until further instances of its entry into the Jewish magical tradition are identified and analyzed.

To round off our discussion of this topic, we may note that the above examples hardly exhaust the *voces magicae* borrowed by the Jewish practitioners from their non-Jewish colleagues, and are just the tip of the iceberg. The iceberg itself is one of the best bodies of evidence we have for the close

---

[94] See Bodleian Heb. a3.31 (unpublished), lines 57–59, where "KWYK BKWY[K] BKWYK BZ BYZ BKWYK BRYPWT 'BR[" are identified as "those who are in charge of every word." And note how *badêtophôth* became BRYPWT.

[95] See, e.g., T-S NS 322.19 (unpublished): For grace (now come instructions in Arabic) write in the name of קור בא קור עהור ברקוק (+*charactêres*), you holy angels and praised knots, etc.; and cf. the names חור בר קור and קור בר חור in Zacuto's *Shorshei ha-Shemot*.

[96] For the σημεα-formula, see PGM V.429 and Bonner 1950, pp. 196–97; cf. Brashear 1995, p. 3599. And note its appearance on a *defixio* from Beth Shean (Youtie and Bonner 1937, pp. 55 and 66). For its appearance in a Demotic magical spell, see PDM xiv.214 (translated in Betz 1986, p. 207).

[97] G-F, G19 (Antonin 186), 1b/26–27. For a fuller discussion of this example, see Bohak 2001, pp. 129–30.

[98] HdM p. 31 Harari = p. 76 Gaster. And cf. the "Sword" in *Synopse* §640, with KM'H QNṬ'Y QNṬY'W, and Harari 1997a, p. 140 (ṬYM'H QNS' QNṬ'Y QNṬW) and esp. p. 143 (SM'H QNṬ'H QNṬ'W QYNṬW).

contact between Jewish and pagan magicians in late antiquity, and for all the valuable things which the latter learned from the former. It also is the clearest demonstration of the fact that in late antiquity, as in other times and places, magic was a body of knowledge, a technological corpus to be mastered by those who wished to utilize it. And it is precisely this "sheer gibberish of magical abrakadabra" (to use Scholem's words) which often looks like "the vocabulary of a stuttering visitor from some distant planet" (to use Trachtenberg's colorful simile) which in fact provides the best clues for the study of this cultural-technological transfer.[99] As we shall see in the following sections too, it is often in those sections where the magical texts are least meaningful that they have the most to tell us about their complex transmission history.

Vowel permutations

In addition to the large corpus of *voces magicae*, one finds in the Greco-Egyptian magical texts a great abundance of long sequences of the seven Greek vowels, *a, e, ê, i, o, y,* and *ô*. In some cases, these are placed on the writing surface in such a way as to create various magical designs, as shall be noted below. In many other cases, they are simply strung together in seemingly endless, and certainly structureless, sequences. That this was not merely a scribal phenomenon is made clear not only by the instructions in some of the magical recipes as to the pronunciation of each vowel, but also by such evidence as Ammianus Marcellinus' famous story of a young man who was executed (in 371 CE) after he was caught touching the bath-house marbles and his chest and reciting the seven vowels of the Greek alphabet, all as a remedy for his aching stomach.[100] It is also vouched for by the extensive evidence for the interest in the seven vowels and their mysterious or powerful nature in Gnostic, Neoplatonist, and other intellectual or religious circles in late antiquity, including some Christian Greek magical texts.[101] That interest, we may add, is visible even in the Demotic magical papyri, even though the fascination with vowels made little sense within the Egyptian writing systems, and in spite of their being very poorly equipped to display the seven Greek vowels.[102]

---

[99] And see Scholem 1960, p. 76 and Trachtenberg 1939, p. 82, respectively.
[100] Ammianus 29.2.28.
[101] For broad surveys of this issue, see Dornseiff 1922, pp. 35–60; Cox Miller 1986; Frankfurter 1994; Janowitz 2002, pp. 45–61.
[102] See Dieleman 2005, pp. 64–68.

Non-Jewish elements in late-antique Jewish magic

That the Jewish magicians of late antiquity had access to this Greek magical technology is made clear by such examples as the trilingual Greek-Aramaic-Hebrew amulet from Tell el-Amarna which, as we already noted, contains in its Greek sections several vowel-triangles. And when we turn to the Hebrew and Aramaic magical texts, we find exactly the same phenomenon, with the magical and mystical texts displaying an endless variety of the permutations of the four letters ', H, W, and Y, which come closest to what we might consider "vowels", and which were considered as such in antiquity.[103] In this case, however, the two parallel phenomena need not necessarily imply a process of borrowing, for the pervasiveness of 'HWY-names in the Jewish magical texts may be explained without any recourse to outside influence. As the Names YHWH and 'HYH (*Ehyeh Asher Ehyeh*, "I-am-who-I-am") were extremely popular in Jewish magic of all periods, it is quite possible that it is the combination of these two names which gave some Jewish magicians the idea of creating further permutations of their constituent letters. That they had not yet done so in the Second Temple period (at least as far as we can judge from the Qumran texts surveyed in Chapter 2) might serve as an argument for the suggestion of a late-antique, foreign influence, but this would hardly clinch the case. Moreover, one may speak here of the tendency of cultures to borrow from their neighbors such features as already have a sound basis in the "host" culture, thus creating cultural phenomena whose features make sense within both cultures. The magical use of the vowels in Greek magic, and of the "vowels" in Aramaic and Hebrew magic, might well be the best example of such cultural congruence.[104]

Word-shapes

One more central feature of the Greco-Egyptian magic of late antiquity is the use of words, names, *voces magicae*, and letter-series to produce various geometric shapes. Sometimes, a word was written several times, one below the other, thus creating a rectangle or a square.[105] More often, a word was written several times, each time deleting one letter from its beginning, or

---

[103] For H, W, and Y as "vowels," see, for example, Josephus, *War* 5.236.
[104] For this model and its application, see the illuminating study of Katz 1995. For the claim itself, see Janowitz 2002, p. 60: "The Hebrew name theory and the Greek vowel theory merge when the Hebrew divine name is thought to consist of only vowels."
[105] It must be stressed, however, that the most celebrated example, the SATOR AREPO square, is attested neither in the Greco-Egyptian magic of late antiquity nor in the Jewish magical texts of the time, in spite of its presence in Pompeii prior to 79 CE (for some brave attempts to prove its Jewish origins, see Simon 1986, pp. 352–54, and p. 502, n. 90 and, most recently, Vinel 2006). It

from its end, or from both sides, thus creating different triangular shapes, such as the Aphrodite-triangle we already studied above. The phenomenon itself – using letters and words to create physical shapes on the writing surface – was well known in Greek culture from the Hellenistic period onwards, and was used, for example, by some poets who would write poems whose shape matched their contents, such as a double-wing-shaped poem about the winged Eros.[106] Compared with such ingenuity, the magicians' efforts seem meager indeed, as they limited their "word-shapes" to several basic geometric shapes, to which they gave such telling technical names as "the grape-cluster (shape)" or "the wing (shape)" design.

While the exact reasons for the magicians' predilection for such shapes are far from clear, it has reasonably been suggested that one force behind their emergence and popularity was the desire of many Greek-writing magicians to "imitate" the sacred Hieroglyphic writings (which by late antiquity were properly understood only by a handful of Egyptian priests, and mistaken for a pictorial-symbolic writing system by everyone else), by producing, with the alphabetic signs at their disposal, "words" which would combine the audible with the visible.[107] It has also been noted that in the Demotic magical texts such phenomena are nowhere to be found – which is hardly surprising given the non-alphabetical character of the Egyptian scripts which would have made the production of geometric shapes from letter-sequences almost impossible.[108] In later periods, however, this practice clearly fired the imagination of magicians in many different cultures, and is alive and well in different magical traditions to this very day. Thus, to give just the most famous example, the amuletic usage of the ABRACADABRA triangle is continuously attested from the third century CE to the twentieth century and beyond.[109] (It is not, however, attested in the Greco-Egyptian magic of late antiquity, and enters the Jewish magical tradition only in the Middle Ages).[110]

When we turn from the pagan and Christian magical texts to the Jewish ones, we again find some unmistakable signs of borrowing. Here too word-shapes are very common – the triangle being the Jewish magicians' favorite design – and one can list dozens of examples of words and *voces magicae*

must also be stressed that such word-squares are entirely different from the magic squares with numbers, which only entered the Jewish magical tradition in the Muslim period.
106 For Simias' *Wings of Eros*, see *AP* 15.24 (and cf. 15.21–27 for similar poems).
107 See Frankfurter 1994.   108 See Dielemen 2005, p. 67, n. 55.
109 For the earliest example, see Q. Serenus Sammonicus, *Liber medicinalis* 935ff. For later examples, see Thomas 1971, p. 246 and Levi 1947, pp. 237–38.
110 For *abracadabra* in Jewish magical texts, see, e.g., Levy 1990, no. 118 and p. 90 (an אבראקאסאברא-triangle in a Yiddish formulary).

Non-Jewish elements in late-antique Jewish magic 267

used for the construction of such word-shapes.[111] Sometimes the words used are themselves of a non-Jewish origin (including, as we already saw, Lycurgus, Aphrodite, and Epicurus), and such examples only strengthen our conviction that the emergence of this practice in the Jewish magical texts of late antiquity is not due to some accidental coincidence, but to the direct borrowing of Greco-Egyptian magical technology. However, in other cases the words chosen for manipulation have nothing alien about them, and the habit of producing such word-shapes clearly was fully naturalized in the Jewish magical tradition; it is attested, moreover, not only in the western branch of late-antique Jewish magic, but also – though far more rarely – in the eastern branch.

Of the endless stream of examples that could be adduced here, we may look at only a few, each with its own specific interest beyond the mere presence of the word-shape itself. We begin with one of the famous "Ephesian Letters" which re-emerges, almost intact, in the Cairo Genizah, move to a Genizah recipe in which the copyist utterly garbled what must have been three magic triangles (and one of which is very interesting in its own right), and end with an example taken from the Babylonian incantation bowls, thus demonstrating the wide diffusion of this practice.

(a) Our first example comes from a well-preserved Genizah recipe-book which displays clear signs of the late-antique origins of many of its recipes (including, for example, the Lycurgus-triangle). Embedded in a recipe to heal headaches, we find a nice magical triangle, fully laid out as follows:[112]

'M'N'M'NWS
M'N'M'NWS
'N'M'NWS
N'M'NWS
'MNWS
MNWS
NWS
WS
S

Apart from a minor error (the omission of one *aleph* from the fifth line onwards), our copyist got his triangle entirely correctly. And as with the other triangles we have examined, this one too seems to be based on a Greek *vox magica*, *damnameneus*, of which the initial letter was lost in transmission. This example deserves our attention since *damnameneus* is

---

[111] It must be stressed, however, that the production of calligraphic Hebrew amulets, with their texts written, e.g., in the shape of a Star of David, is a later development, and shall not be treated here.
[112] MSF, G18 (T-S K 1.143), p. 9, ll. 6–14.

the fifth of the "Ephesian Letters," a sequence of six "words" which are first attested in Greek magical practice in the fifth century BCE, and which also entered the Greco-Egyptian magical tradition of late antiquity.[113] In Chapter 6, we shall note the rabbis' possible familiarity with other "words" from this sequence, but for the time being we may note the appearance of one of these "words" in a Jewish magical text a full millennium and a half after their first appearance in Classical Greece.

(b) The second example is again from a magical formulary found in the Cairo Genizah, but this one demonstrates a slightly different process, namely, the gradual corruption of such triangles by subsequent copyists. It is found in a recipe for an exorcistic amulet, whose spell begins with a much-garbled set of three magic triangles, whose nature clearly was lost on the medieval Jewish copyist (but not on the modern editors).[114] When "straightened out," these triangles turn out to be based on three "words" – 'RDZKZ (or 'DRZKZ), 'TRTRWKS, and 'BRSKS. The third of these is our old friend Abrasax, and the first one might be a garbled rendition of the same name.[115] But the second "word," 'TRTRWKS, deserves more attention, for it is nothing but a Hebrew transliteration (with a prosthetic *aleph*) of the Greek adjective, *tartarouchos*, "the holder of Tartarus," one of the commonest epithets of the goddess Hecate in the Greco-Egyptian magical texts.[116] The Greek origins of this triangle are beyond any doubt, and once again we find a pagan goddess, or, in this case, one of her main epithets, turned into a meaningless *vox magica* and making her own modest contribution to the Jewish magical texts of late antiquity and the Middle Ages.

(c) Our third and final example comes from the Babylonian incantation bowls. In these bowls, one rarely finds word-triangles of the type surveyed here, and even when they appear they are not written in a triangular form, which would have been quite difficult on a concave writing surface, but in one straight line. The clearest example appears on at least four different bowls, three of which unfortunately are still unpublished. The published bowl comes from Kish (Iraq), and contains a short spell intended to send the

---

[113] For the *Ephesia Grammata*, see Stickel 1860 (who provides a fanciful Semitic etymology); Wessely 1886 (who also discusses Greek *voces magicae* in general); McCown 1923. For a *damnameneus* triangle on a Greek magical gem, see Névérov 1978, vol. II, p. 848 and pl. CLXXVI (I owe this reference to Chris Faraone).

[114] MTKG II, 36 (T-S NS 153.162), 2a/8–11, with the editors' notes.

[115] The spelling אדרצכץ might display the influence of Arabic, with the Hebrew *Zadi* pronounced like the Arabic *sad*.

[116] For Ταρταροῦχος, see, e.g., PGM IV.2237, 2289; Meyer and Smith 1994, p. 160. For the transcription of final -ος as ס-, see Bohak 1990. For τάρταρος as a loanword, see MTKG II, p. 146 (cited from Oxford Ms. Michael 9): דין דדחלין מיניה טרטרוס דארעא, a calque on such expressions as τάρταρα γαίης (e.g. PGM V.4).

Non-Jewish elements in late-antique Jewish magic 269

afflictions of Akarkoi son of Mama back upon those who sent them. Its first line runs as follows: QPRGYH PRGYH RGYH GYH YH H.[117] That this is a triangle of the kind we are looking for seems quite obvious, and was duly noted by the bowl's editor. Less obvious, however, is the identity of the word itself, QPRGYH, which seems like the Greek word *kefalargia*, "head-ache," which we already discussed above (with l + r assimilated into a single r). And in the other three bowls in which it appears, the "word" which "dwindles" is spelled as QPLRGYH, KPLRGY', and KPLRGYH, perhaps pointing to the oral (rather than written) transmission of this sequence.[118] And as is often the case, it was the name of the illness (sometimes identified with the name of the demon which caused it), which was written in this "dwindling" formation, apparently in order to bring the same effect upon the illness itself.[119] This suggestion gains further support from the appearance of a PLRGYH triangle, right next to a MWQRYN (our "migraine" once again) triangle, in MS Sassoon 56, the Byzantine Jewish grimoire which preserves so many ancient Palestinian Jewish magical recipes and practices.[120]

What we see here, in other words, is how a Greco-Egyptian magical technique enters the western branch of the Jewish magical tradition but reaches even its eastern branch. It does so, however, in an entirely "fossilized" form, with the same triangle used on four different bowls, and in a way that has nothing to do with its original meaning, as none of these bowls seem to be aimed against headaches. In Chapter 6, we shall see a similar process occurring in the Babylonian Talmud, the only differences being that in the Talmudic example the word made to "dwindle" is the Babylonian Aramaic name of the illness (*shabriri*, i.e., night- or day-blindness) and not some Greek name, and that it is used in a recipe against that specific illness. Elsewhere in Chapter 6, we shall also see how the Talmud preserves several examples of the turning of Greek names of illnesses – which were no longer understood in Greek-less Babylonia – into the names of the demons which supposedly caused them.

As noted above, these are just three examples, to which many others could easily be added.[121] But rather than belaboring the obvious, let us merely

---

[117] See Gordon 1941, text 9, pp. 131 and 141.
[118] One of these bowls, MS 2053/13, was brought to my attention by Shaul Shaked, the other two by Dan Levene.
[119] For this interpretation of this practice, see e.g., Trachtenberg 1939, pp. 116–17. For the demonization of illnesses, see, e.g., Montgomery 1913, pp. 89–92.
[120] See MS Sassoon 56 = NYPL Heb. 190, p. 143.
[121] Another common example is the ηριχθονιη-triangle (for which see SM I, 34 (pp. 99 and 101) = Meyer and Smith 1994, p. 37); for its appearance in the Genizah, see, e.g., T-S Ar. 42.122 (unpublished) (WS DKWTYNWS KWTYNWS etc., written in a straight line); for its possible use by Eleazar of Worms, see Trachtenberg 1939, p. 117. For a modern example, see the 'RKTWNYNYM-triangle in Levy 1990, no. 118 (p. 76).

stress that this too is a practice which the Jewish practitioners clearly learned from their non-Jewish colleagues, and it too was fully naturalized into the Jewish magical tradition.[122] So much so, that in later Jewish magic, one even finds biblical verses written as sequences of such triangles, with each word in a given verse used to form one triangle.[123] And in present-day Israel, one Hasidic group has turned one magic triangle, based on the name of the charismatic founder of their sect, who is buried in Uman (the Ukraine), into a veritable slogan to be sprayed, in one continuous line, as graffiti on private and public spaces as "Na Naḥ Naḥma Naḥman of Uman" (in the vowel-less Hebrew alphabet, the number of letters of the name rises from one to four). And with this comforting observation of how a practice which was born in a pagan Greco-Egyptian milieu still enjoys an enduring success among some Orthodox Jews we may turn to other bits of non-Jewish magical technology borrowed by the Jewish practitioners of late antiquity.

Magic signs and symbols

So far, we have focused on what might broadly be termed the alphabetic components of late-antique magical texts, be they meaningful words, meaningless ones, and even non-linguistic sequences of letters and various shapes created from the layout of the letters on the writing surface. In addition to all these, however, there existed in the Greco-Egyptian magic of late antiquity a whole range of non-alphabetic signs and symbols, and these too made their way into the Jewish magical tradition at the time. To examine these, we begin with the *charactêres*, and then turn to other, less frequent, magical signs and symbols.

(a) The *charactêres*:
Of all the magical signs in the magical texts of late antiquity, the *charactêres*, those quasi-alphabetical signs with circlets at their end, are by far the most numerous. In spite of many attempts to reconstruct the origins of these "ring letters," not much is known about how exactly this type of sign came into being.[124] And in spite of numerous attempts to "decipher" these signs and their meanings – attempts whose origins lie deep in the Jewish, Christian, and Muslim Middle Ages and which flourished in the Renaissance and in

---

[122] For its use in modern Jewish magical texts see, for example, Thompson 1907, p. 283, no. 52.
[123] See, for example, the example from *Sepher Raziel* adduced by Schrire 1966, p. 61.
[124] For a brief summary, and much further bibliography, see Brashear 1995, pp. 3440–42.

Early Modern scholarship, but are mostly abandoned today – we have no real clue as to their original meaning, if they ever had any.[125]

Such problems, however, need not detain us here. For our own purpose, we must note several other important features of the *charactêres*. First, we should denounce the old habit, which still persists in some circles, of calling them "Kabbalistic signs," for they predate the rise of Kabbalah by more than a millennium and are demonstrably non-Jewish in origin. It is true that just as these signs entered the magical traditions of all late-antique and medieval peoples, languages, and religions – from Ethiopia to Armenia and from Al-Andalus to Yemen – they also entered the Jewish magical tradition, already in late antiquity, as well as the Hekhalot and *Shi'ur Qomah* texts (discussed in the next chapter), and eventually caught the fancy of some Kabbalists. In no period, however, was their use limited to Kabbalistic circles, or even characteristic thereof. Second, we must note the very scribal nature of these magic signs – impossible in an oral context, they were made possible by the shift from oral to scribal magic which took place in the Greco-Egyptian magical tradition in the first century BCE or CE, and in the Jewish one some time later.

Cataloguing all the occurrences of the *charactêres* in late-antique and medieval Jewish magical texts would be a tedious and superfluous task, since their great abundance makes it clear that they were fully naturalized into the Jewish magical tradition. They are found on numerous late-antique Palestinian Jewish amulets, and even on some of the incantation bowls from Babylonia, yet another demonstration of the move of some elements from the "West" to the "East" in late-antique Jewish magic.[126] They are also found in numerous Genizah magical texts (see, for example, Figure 3.9), in the manuscripts of such "literary" books of magic as *Sepher ha-Razim*, in some mystical texts, and in hundreds of medieval and modern Jewish magical texts. And in at least one case, that of the Ḥorvat Rimmon erotic magical text and its many parallels among medieval and later Jewish magical recipes, we can even see how the *charactêres* were carefully copied out by some of the recipe's copyists for many hundreds of years, but were entirely omitted by others.

In studying the entry of these signs into the Jewish magical tradition, we must note that apart from general arguments about the chronological

---

[125] Cf. Bonner 1950, pp. 12–13: "It is possible that we may yet learn something about the characters if some investigator is patient enough to follow up all the leads, but at present they are still undeciphered." The statement remains true even half a century later.

[126] For *charactêres* on Jewish bowls, see, e.g., Hilprecht 1904, opposite p. 447 (*ouroboros* + *charactêres*); Smelik 1978; AMB, B4; Müller-Kessler 2005, no. 11. For non-Jewish examples, see, e.g., AMB, B1 (Syriac).

precedence of the *charactêres* in the Greco-Egyptian magic of late antiquity, two specific arguments help demonstrate the foreign origins of these signs within the Jewish magical traditions. First, like many novel foreign technologies, they entered the Jewish magicians' world together with their technical title, *charactêres*, or, in Aramaic, *kalaqtiraia*.[127] In many Jewish magical texts they are invoked under this name, in such formulae as "you holy signs and sacred *kalaqtiraya*," which we already examined above. In some cases, however, the strange loanword was split into two meaningful Aramaic words, *kol* ("all") and *qtiraia* ("knots"), a process which was no doubt aided by the many connections between (binding) knots and magic (cf. Dn 5.6, 12, 16), and by the funny "knots" at the tip of the actual *charactêres*. Second, many of the actual *charactêres* in the late-antique and Genizah magical texts actually look suspiciously similar to standard letters of the Greek alphabet, with the mere addition of circles at their tips. In some cases, these Greek letters even add up to meaningful sequences, such as the series of five *charactêres* on one late-antique amulet which looks like a Greek alphabetic series whose English equivalent would be JKLMN.[128] This, too, demonstrates the Greek origin of these signs.

Turning for a minute to medieval and later Jewish magical texts, we may note that in addition to the endless copying of age-old *charactêres* into new Jewish magical texts, one sees several important developments, all of which could help us date specific magical texts and traditions. In the Muslim cultural orbit, one sometimes sees the re-entry of the Greek *charactêres* through Arabic channels of transmission, and with a differently garbled name, *qalafṭeriat*, which is entirely based on the ways by which Arabic writers transliterated the Greek term (sometimes, they were even attributed to an ancient philosopher, Qalafṭerius!).[129] In the Spanish cultural orbit, the same technical term enters the Jewish magical tradition once again, this time with spellings such as *carateras*.[130] Such processes, however, were quite rare, since the Jewish magicians did not need their Arab or Spanish colleagues to teach them about these magical signs, which they found all over their own ancient magical texts. Far more common, and even ubiquitous, was the entry in the Muslim period of Muslim-type "seals" and "line-signs" (see Figure 4.1).[131] These new technological innovations clearly did not replace the older *charactêres*, and often coexisted with them on the same magical

---

[127] For a similar process in the Demotic magical papyri see Dieleman 2005, p. 100. Note that the spelling χαλακτήρες is well attested in the Greek magical texts as well – see, e.g, PGM XIII.1003 (pp. 76–77 Daniel), which was "normalized" by Preisendanz in the PGM edition.

[128] See MSF, A30, for what looks like IKΛMN in "ring letters."

[129] See MSF, G9 (T-S K1.15), p. 3, l. 12, with Naveh 1985, p. 377, n. 14.

[130] For קאראמיראש, see JTSL ENA 2712.49 (unpublished).

[131] For these Muslim magical symbols, see esp. Winkler 1930, pp. 55–56 and passim.

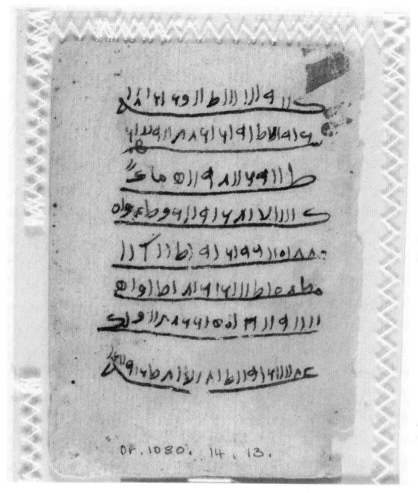

Figure 4.1 A Genizah amulet, consisting entirely of Muslim-Arabic "seals." The verso is blank. This amulet may have been produced by a Jew or by a Muslim, and probably was worn by a Jew.

pages, and still do so in some twentieth-century books of Jewish magic. They are, however, an important reminder of the cumulative nature of the magical tradition, and of the fact that when looking at actual magical texts and artifacts we may sometimes dissect them into "layers" whose ultimate origins lie in entirely different periods. And while new elements were constantly added, some old elements were gradually lost. In the later Genizah fragments, and in medieval Jewish magical texts outside the Cairo

Genizah, the *charactêres* are still around, but their technical name is mostly absent.¹³² In some cases, the name *kalaqtiraia* was garbled into oblivion; in others, it was replaced by the Greek-less Jewish practitioners with names they found more appropriate. Most commonly, these special "seals" were identified as the secret scripts of various angels, be it "the Alphabet of Meṭaṭron," "the font of Gabriel," or some antediluvian writing system – and in this process, we may add, were entirely "Judaized," leaving no real evidence of their ultimate origins in Greco-Egyptian magic. Moreover, many attempts were made, from the Middle Ages onwards, to "decipher" these angelic scripts by ascribing each magic sign an alphabetic value (see Figure 4.2).¹³³ These attempts, by Jews, Christians, and Muslims, to "tame" and "explain" the *charactêres* have yet to receive the comparative scholarly attention they deserve.

So much for some of the later developments of the *charactêres*, a study of which would require, and certainly deserves, an entire monograph. For the time being, let us return to late antiquity, and note how the *charactêres* exemplify the massive entry of technological innovations from the Greco-Egyptian magic of late antiquity into the Jewish magical tradition, and their absorption there; in this case, we see a set of foreign elements which was so fully naturalized in the Jewish magical tradition – and in some medieval cases also fully Judaized – as to assure its survival within that tradition to our very days.

(b) Other magical signs and symbols:
In addition to the ubiquitous *charactêres*, the magical texts of late antiquity are characterized by a long range of signs and symbols, and here too the great overlap between what we find in the non-Jewish and the Jewish magical texts is quite striking. Among the many common signs, we may note various stars (with four, six, eight, or another number of points), lunar crescents, sun-disks with rays, and so on. A full corpus of such designs, in non-Jewish and Jewish magical texts, remains a desideratum, but it probably would not produce any conclusive proofs as to who borrowed what from whom. After all, it does not take much alien wisdom to draw a crude lunar crescent on one's magical text, and even the presence of a swastika – a symbol whose future connotations no ancient magician could divine – cannot prove its borrowing by a Jewish practitioner from his foreign colleagues.¹³⁴ And yet,

---

¹³² See, for example, Trachtenbrg 1939, pp. 140–42 and 150–51.
¹³³ For a pertinent example, see Weinstock 1981, and cf. Trachtenberg 1939, p. 141.
¹³⁴ For a swastika, see MSF, A17, l. 8; for non-Jewish examples, see, e.g., SM I, 21 (a Christian amulet), with the editors' note on p. 59.

Non-Jewish elements in late-antique Jewish magic 275

Figure 4.2 A Genizah fragment, written on a torn piece of used paper (the verso, not shown here, contains the remains of an Arabic documet), and showing an attempt to "decipher" the *charactêres* as letters of the Hebrew alphabet. Such attempts were extremely common in the Middle Ages, among Jews, Christians and Muslims alike.

even in such cases, the parallels must be noted, if only to prevent a purely "Jewish" interpretation of these symbols by modern scholars. Thus, to give just one example, when we find a "fish-bones" design on a late-antique silver amulet which contains some Hekhalot-type materials (discussed in the next chapter), we might be tempted to see this as a crude representation of the Hekhalot mystics' proverbial "ladder of ascent", with which to climb to heaven.[135] This is not impossible, but it must be borne in mind that the "fish-bones" design is extremely common in the non-Jewish magical texts of late antiquity, and is also found in Jewish magical texts which have nothing to do with Hekhalot-type mysticism.[136] In light of such evidence, one should be wary of reading too much Jewish meaning into signs which may have had nothing Jewish about them, and may have been mechanically copied by the Jewish magicians from their non-Jewish sources without any attempt to "Judaize" them in the process.

If the simple signs and symbols on our magical texts can hardly be used as evidence for non-Jewish influence upon the Jewish magical tradition, the more elaborate ones certainly can. Among these, we may include the uterine symbol, to which we already alluded above, and which may be classified as a "one time entry," given its absence from the many Jewish gynecological amulets and recipes of late antiquity and the early Middle Ages.[137] The figure of the *ouroboros* (the snake which swallows its own tail), on the other hand, seems to have fared much better. This Pharaonic symbol frequently appears in the Greco-Egyptian magical texts (and especially the magical gems), and clearly was borrowed by more than one Jewish practitioner in late antiquity. It even traveled all the way to Mesopotamia, where it appears on some Jewish and some non-Jewish incantation bowls.[138] Whether it was fully naturalized into the Jewish magical tradition, or even "Judaized" within it, we cannot yet say, especially since this symbol re-emerges in medieval Jewish texts, and even in non-magical contexts. Whether this was due to its transmission through the Jewish magical tradition, or to the re-entry of this ever-popular symbol from medieval Christian culture, is a question that requires much further research.[139]

---

[135] See MSF, A21, with the editors' note, on p. 72; see also Naveh 1992, p. 169, and Davila 2001, pp. 216–17.

[136] For non-Jewish examples, see, e.g., MSF, A32, l. 7 (Christian Palestinian Aramaic); Naveh 2002, p. 250 (Syriac). For Jewish examples, see MSF, G12 (T-S K 1.42) bottom; G29 (CUL Or. 1080.6.19), p. 2, l. 12; MTKG III, 70 (T-S NS 252.10), 2a/11.

[137] This absence may be explained by the Jews' general avoidance of the manufacturing of magical gems (as noted in the previous chapter), since it is almost exclusively on the Greco-Egyptian uterine gem-amulets (usually hematite) that this symbol is found.

[138] For the *ouroboros*, see Reifenberg 1950, p. 143 (see Chapter 3, n. 44); AMB, A5. For its appearance in Mesopotamia, see, e.g., Hilprecht 1904, opposite p. 447 (*ouroboros* + *charactêres*); Montgomery 1913, no. 15 (Jewish); Gordon 1941, bowl 2 (Jewish); Geller 1976 (one Jewish, one non-Jewish); Segal 2000, bowl 117ES (non-Jewish).

[139] For this Egyptian symbol, see Kákosy 1985; for its "afterlife" in Christian Europe see Preisendanz 1935. In some medieval Ashkenazi manuscripts, Leviathan is depicted as an *ouroboros*, and cf. the discussion of the *teli* in *Sepher Raziel*.

(c) Christian signs and symbols:
In addition to the above signs and symbols, all found in the pagan magical texts and artifacts of late antiquity, we must briefly examine the possibility that the Jewish magical tradition also borrowed some Christian signs and symbols. When we turn to medieval Jewish magic, it is quite easy to demonstrate a recurrent borrowing of Christian elements into Jewish magic, be it the Three Wise Men (i.e., the Magi of Mt 2, often identified as Caspar, Melchior, and Belthazar), the name "Jesus" used for healings, and even monastic Latin ordeals for detecting thieves.[140] It is also easy to demonstrate the entry of Christian elements whose Jewish borrowers did not fully understand, such as a garbled version of the legend of St Eustathius, badly translated from Christian Greek sources, or a Coptic "Jesus Christ, the Lord," inadvertently copied by one Genizah practitioner from a bilingual Coptic-Arabic book of magical recipes which he was mining for powerful recipes.[141] But when we turn to the earlier period, demonstrating such borrowings becomes much more difficult. Reading the Palestinian Jewish amulets, or those Genizah recipes which can be shown to be distant copies of late-antique models, we are struck by the lack of any references to Jesus, to New Testament scenes and figures, or to anything connected with Christian faith or Christian magic. We shall return to this issue in the next chapter, but for the time being let us note a few possible exceptions to this general rule. In the trilingual amulet from Kibbuẓ Evron, which we discussed above, we find a little circle divided in four, with one letter of the Tetragrammaton, YHWH, in each of its quarters; right next to this sign, we see what might be a *Chi-Rho* monogram (a common Christian abbreviation of the name *Christos*, "Christ") but might also be just a six-point star. In another amulet, found in a tomb near Aleppo (Syria), we again see what might be a Christian monogram, but might also be a magic sign not very different from the other magic signs upon the same amulet.[142] In both cases, the absence of any other Christian element on these amulets – both of which date from a time when the Roman empire was being rapidly Christianized – militates against viewing these isolated signs as Christian in origin. The same is true for the numerous appearances of "crosses" in

---

[140] Three Magi: e.g., Steinschneider 1862, p. 13; Grunwald 1900, p. 62, n. 207; Grunwald 1923b, p. 182. Jesus: Trachtenberg 1939, p. 200; monastic ordeal: Bohak 2006.
[141] Eustathius: Leicht 2003. Coptic: Bohak 1999, pp. 35–39.
[142] Evron: Kotansky 1991b, republished in Kotansky 1994, no. 56; the relevant symbol is on line 4, and the Christian reading was suggested by Dauphin 1998, vol. I, p. 220 and Saar 2003, p. 53. Aleppo: AMB, A4, line 8, with the editors' notes. See also Lacerenza 2002, pp. 410–19, esp. the unpublished amulet mentioned on pp. 415–16. For a Chi-Rho monogram on a Jewish synagogue inscription, see IJO III, Syr5.

Genizah magical texts, as the production of a horizontal line crossed by a vertical one is so natural that one need hardly attribute its appearance to Christian influences on the Jewish practitioners.[143]

To see what a borrowing of Christian materials by late-antique Jewish magicians might look like, we have to turn to the Babylonian bowls, and even there such elements are extremely rare.[144] But one bowl, which is aggressive rather than apotropaic, displays not only standard subjugation formulae and adjurations by well-known angels, but also a very unusual closing formula:

In the name of I-am-who-I-am YHWH Sabaot, and in the name of Jesus who conquered the height and the depth with his Cross, and in the name of the Exalted Father, and in the name of the Holy Spirits, for ever and ever, Amen Amen Selah. This press is true and established.[145]

It is in reading such a passage that we realize how the Jewish practitioners of late antiquity could easily have borrowed Christian elements into their magical spells, and how most of them did not. One Jewish practitioner, living in Sasanian Babylonia, apparently saw nothing wrong with incorporating Jesus, the Cross, and a Trinitarian formula – all of which he probably learned from a Syriac-speaking Christian – in his incantation bowl. But even in the large corpus of Babylonian bowls such examples are extremely rare, and the corpus of late-antique Jewish amulets, and of Genizah magical texts which go back to late-antique models, has yet to produce even a single example of the clear incorporation of Christian elements into a Jewish magical text. And while it is possible that future research will uncover more examples of Christian elements which entered the Jewish magical tradition in late antiquity, for the time being we may classify such borrowings as a "one time entry" phenomenon.

Magical images

One more feature of the Greco-Egyptian magic of late antiquity is the abundance of magical images, or (to note the technical term used by some

---

[143] For "crosses", see, e.g., MSF, G23 (T-S Ar. 44.44), p. 2. In my old home-town, Reḥovot, it is said that a pious town-planner tried to avoid building intersections which might be shaped like a cross, a debacle for which exasperated drivers have been paying ever since.

[144] In addition to the example adduced here, see Geller 1977, pp. 149–55 (whose convincing examples are taken from Syriac bowls); Harviainen 1981.

[145] The bowl is M163, published by Levene 1999 (and cf. Shaked 1999b), and republished in Levene 2002, pp. 122–38, whose translation I follow, with minor modifications. I have heard of the recurrence of a similar formula on other bowls, but have not seen them myself.

scholars) *figurae magicae*, that is, pictorial representations with religious or magical significance. These are especially abundant on the magical gems which were so popular in late antiquity, gems in which the magical image usually takes precedence – in terms of the space devoted to it on the gem, and certainly in terms of the amount of work that went into producing it – over the inscribed text, which is necessarily short.[146] But even magical texts which were written on more standard writing surfaces such as papyrus, or on lead, bronze, silver, and gold lamellae, often display not just written texts, but also magical images.[147] The quantity and quality of iconographic materials on different magical texts is far from uniform, and clearly was influenced by technical factors (it is much easier to draw an image on papyrus than incise one into a metal lamella), but also by competence, personal taste, and changing fashions over place and time. Thus, PGM XXXVI, of which we had much to say in the previous chapter, is heavily illustrated, while several other Greek magical papyri have virtually no illustrations at all. That PGM XXXVI was not an isolated case seems clear from the "outsider" evidence, where references to richly illustrated magical texts are not uncommon, and from such "insider" evidence as a cache of *defixiones* from Rome which includes some heavily illustrated pieces, clearly produced from a written formulary.[148]

Looking at the images on Greek magical texts and artifacts, we find that some of them resemble the standard religious iconography of the pagan religions of the Greco-Roman world, though often at a level of execution which is much more crude than that to which most modern museum-goers might be accustomed. There might be images of the triplex Hecate, of the mummy of Osiris, of the emblematic animals of the Egyptian gods (a hawk, a lion, etc.), of religious objects such as altars or of apotropaic images such as the *udjat*-eye. There might also be images of newly fangled deities, apparently the product of the magicians' own imagination, such as the headless god, often with his eyes in his chest, or the snake-legged, cock-headed, shield- and whip-bearing creature who figures so prominently on hundreds of magical gems (see Figure 3.7). There might also be images of the intended victim of the magical ritual, or of the client whose protection the spells are supposed to ensure. And, in many other instances, there are images whose exact nature is not really clear.

[146] See Bonner 1950; Delatte and Derchain 1964; Michel 2001.
[147] For an excellent starting-point, see Horak 1992.
[148] For "outsider" evidence, see, e.g., Zacharia of Mytilene's *Life of Severus*, p. 62 Kugener, for books of magic with "certain images of perverse demons" in fifth-century Beirut. For illustrated *defixiones*, see Wünsch 1898. See also Horak 1992, pp. 150–84 and Nagy 2002a.

280   *Ancient Jewish magic*

Turning to the Jewish magical texts and artifacts, we find ourselves in a very different situation. In the Palestinian Jewish amulets of late antiquity, at least those published so far, there are no images at all.[149] We might excuse this absence by the difficulty of incising complex images into thin metal lamellae, but such excuses are weakened by the presence of quite a few non-Jewish magical texts inscribed on metal and yet accompanied by pictorial representations, and by the demonstrated ability of the producers of these amulets to incise quite elaborate texts, and some magical designs and symbols, upon the very same surfaces. And when we turn to the extensive body of magical texts from the Cairo Genizah, we find there too a general absence of images, although producing them on vellum and paper would have posed no technical difficulties whatsoever. One could perhaps explain this absence by an abhorrence of images among Jews living in a Muslim environment, were it not for the fact that it is precisely in those Judeo-Arabic magical texts which were clearly copied from Arabic-Muslim originals that we find the best examples of magical iconography.[150] It is in the Aramaic magical texts from the Cairo Genizah, and those which can be shown to be Judeo-Arabic translations of earlier Aramaic magical recipes, that we find almost no trace of any pictorial iconography (but see Figure 3.9, for a possible exception).[151] Finally, this absence is even more pronounced when we note that in the Aramaic incantation bowls of late-antique Babylonia, little images, especially of shackled demons, but also of animals, persons, and so on, are far from uncommon.[152] In this, it seems that the western branch of late-antique Jewish magic differed greatly from its eastern contemporary, an issue to which we shall return in the following chapter.[153]

The dearth of magical iconography in the western branch of late-antique Jewish magic may be seen from other evidence too. As an example, we may note how the author of *Sepher ha-Razim* repeatedly enjoins the manufacture of some images, and even of apotropaic statues, as part of the magical ritual. As we noted in Chapter 3, such instructions only highlight the almost complete absence of such artifacts from the archeological records, even though some of them were supposed to be produced on durable materials. Especially important in this connection are the magical gems and metal

---

[149] I have heard of, but have not yet seen, an unpublished Aramaic metal amulet which was found in a controlled excavation and which displays an elaborate image.
[150] For an illuminated, and illuminating, example, see Baker and Polliack 2001, pl. 21.
[151] For other possible exceptions, see MSF, G18 (T-S K 1.143), esp. p. 2.
[152] For these images, see Chapter 3, nn. 119–23.
[153] And note that while the Aramaic magic bowls display a great interest in iconography, the Mandaic ones do not, as was pointed out by Shaked 2005c, p. 5.

pendants, where one finds thousands of pieces with elaborate iconography often accompanied by inscriptions, but these are in Greek, and show no sign of a Jewish origin. On the other hand, one finds a handful of ancient magical gems with Hebrew and Aramaic inscriptions, but these contain hardly any iconography, except for a Menorah or a "hand of God" design, and a larger quantity of glass-paste pendants whose iconography is both crude and extremely repetitive.[154] And even in PGM XXXVI, many of whose recipes are illustrated, the one recipe which we identified as Jewish is accompanied by no images at all. Thus, while there is no doubt that some Jewish practitioners in late-antique Palestine and Egypt did produce some magical images as a part of their magical rituals, they seem to have done so much less often than their pagan and Christian colleagues, and even their Jewish colleagues in far-away Babylonia.

THE STRUCTURE, LAYOUT, AND TECHNICAL VOCABULARY OF JEWISH MAGICAL RECIPES, AND THE SCRIBALIZATION OF THE JEWISH MAGICAL TRADITION

One of the fields in which the Greco-Egyptian and Jewish magical technologies show a marked affinity is in the structure and layout of some of their magical formularies. When we look at books such as *Sepher ha-Razim* or *Ḥarba de-Moshe*, we find books of magic whose overall structure seems to have been determined by "literary" considerations which also shaped the appearance of the individual recipes within these elaborate texts. But when we look at the "free-form" formularies, whose basic structure is that of dozens of recipes following each other in succession, the inner structures they display might tell us something about the models which their producers and copyists had in front of them. At the most basic level, we would expect each recipe to contain a rubric which explains what it is good for, followed by the instructions on what to do (and perhaps also by some indicator that the recipe has ended, before the rubric for the next one); this, for example, is the structure of a long medico-magical *vademecum* found in the Babylonian Talmud to which we shall turn in Chapter 6. But when we turn to many of the Genizah magical formularies, including the earliest ones, we find that they contain a few more elements, all of which seem to have been borrowed from the Greco-Egyptian formularies of late antiquity. In this regard, we may note especially the following features:[155]

---

[154] See the evidence surveyed in Chapter 3.
[155] In what follows, I omit such issues as the marking of *voces magicae* and divine names with special "boxes" and cartouches, or with special lines and dots, or the magicians' preference for writing some

(a) In numerous recipes, the title ("For love," "To catch a thief," etc.) is immediately followed by a boast of the recipe's efficacy, insisting that it is "tried and tested," "tested," "true," "true and clear," and so on.[156] In other recipes, these boasts come at the very end of the recipe, before the title of the next one. These claims, and their location at these specific points in the magical recipes, have since become a permanent fixture of the Jewish magical tradition, and are found in Jewish magical formularies to this very day. It must be stressed, however, that they are not yet there on the (admittedly few) Jewish magical texts from the Second Temple period, nor do they accompany the magical recipes which are scattered throughout rabbinic literature. And as these claims are closely paralleled by what we find in the Greco-Egyptian magical texts, where such boasts are ubiquitous (and often much more elaborate than those in the Jewish texts), it seems quite certain that this is where the Jewish magicians first came across this scribal practice.[157]

(b) Perhaps the most characteristic expression in the Greek magical texts of late antiquity is the demand, found in hundreds of spells, that the practitioner's or client's wishes be carried out "now now, quickly quickly," or even, "now now, quickly quickly, immediately immediately," a battle-cry which tends to appear towards the end of the spell to be recited or inscribed as part of the magical ritual.[158] Above, we already noted how such Greek formulae occasionally were transliterated instead of translated by their Aramaic- and Hebrew-speaking users, and how these transliterations were subsequently garbled in the transmission. However, these were exceptional cases, and in most cases the formulae were correctly translated into Aramaic, Hebrew, and (later) Judeo-Arabic, and are found in dozens of Jewish magical texts from the Cairo Genizah, and those of later periods too.[159] In this case, a foreign expression was translated by the Jewish magicians and was fully "naturalized" in the Jewish magical tradition. Thus, its presence in a specific

---

words backwards, or the use of blank spaces and horizontal lines as separators between recipes. Here too, the pagan and Jewish magical texts display many similarities, but these will have to be charted and analyzed elsewhere.

[156] See, e.g., the list in MTKG I, p. 146, which could be extended almost *ad infinitum*. And cf. Trachtenberg 1939, p. 115; Swartz 1996, p. 139, n. 147; Kanarfogel 2000, p. 99, n. 10, etc.; Idel 2005, p. 105, n. 48.

[157] For these claims in Greek and Demotic magical texts, see Dieleman 2005, pp. 254–76.

[158] For the ubiquitous ἤδη ἤδη ταχὺ ταχύ, see, e.g., PGM I.262; IV.973, and dozens of other examples; see also PDM xiv.282 and 328 (tr. in Betz 1986, pp. 212 and 214); Winkler 1930, p. 29 (Arabic magical texts).

[159] See, for example, MTKG II, p. 73. These expressions seem not to have made it to Babylonia, since in the incantation bowls the practitioners' desire that their demands be carried out at once are usually expressed by "from this day and forever."

text does not suffice to prove that text's antiquity or non-Jewish origins. But the ubiquity of this expression in the Jewish magical texts proves how popular some Greco-Egyptian magical techniques have become among their Jewish (and Christian, and Muslim) users.

(c) Another recurrent feature of Greek magical recipes is that when the ritual instructions contain a spell to be uttered or written, and the spell includes much material that is standard and repetitive, the copyists often omit the redundant materials, and write the word *koinologia*, "common words," or *(ta) koina*, "the common (stuff)," by which they mean "say/write the usual things in such cases." It is thus very interesting to see the Jewish magicians borrowing this technique, and even the exact same technical term, into their recipes. But as the word QYNWLWGYH (or its abbreviated version, QYNW), was misunderstood by later copyists, it often became garbled in the process of textual transmission. Thus, in one Genizah recipe we find a series of *voces magicae*, the last of which is QYNWLGYH, in another a recipe ends with "do my wish in this hour, quickly, immediately, from now and forever, QYNW QYNW Amen Amen Selah Hallelujah," a third has an adjuration formula that ends with QYNW LWGYH, and a fourth ends with "blessed is the Name of the honor of His Kingdom forever QYNW."[160] That some of the copyists and users of these recipes had no idea what the words had originally meant seems quite obvious, but this hardly need surprise us, given the complete absence of Greek from the daily lives of the Jews of medieval Cairo.

Looking at all these examples, to which more could be added, we may conclude that at least some of the scribal technology of the Jewish magicians of late antiquity was based on existing Greco-Egyptian models. This is an important observation, for it might serve as a clue to understanding the very scribalization of the Jewish magical tradition in late antiquity, a process to which we briefly referred in the previous chapter. In a nutshell, our argument could be formulated as follows. In the Greco-Egyptian magical tradition, we have the oft-noted rise, from about the first century BCE or CE onwards, of the very act of writing as a central component of the magician's ritual praxis. The causes of this development have been much discussed, but need not detain us here. For the purpose of our own study, what is of significance is the very process of scribalization, so visible in the Greek magical papyri, in the *defixiones* (which grow much longer in late antiquity than ever before), in the Greek metal amulets (whose quantity and length

---

[160] For these examples, see MSF, G16 (T-S K 1.91) p. 2, l. 16; MSF, G22 (T-S Misc. 27.4.11) p. 1, l. 15; MTKG III, 75 (T-S NS 91.53) 1b/8; MTKG III, 76 (T-S NS 92.20) 1b/8 (all with the editors' notes). There are many more examples in unpublished Genizah magical texts.

rise greatly from some time in the Roman period onwards), in the Greek inscribed magical gems (all of which date from late antiquity), and in the other media of the Greco-Egyptian magic of late antiquity. Since a similar process took place within the Jewish magical tradition as well, apparently beginning some time in the third or fourth century CE, and generating the abundant evidence for Jewish magic in late antiquity, a connection between these two processes seems quite plausible.

The scribalization of the Jewish magical tradition in late antiquity has occasionally been noted by earlier scholars, who sought to explain it as the result of a general rise in Jewish literacy (though it seems to postdate that rise by several centuries!), or to correlate it with a rise of "textual communities" in late-antique Judaism, such as the rabbinic or the early Christian movements, or to somehow connect it with growing demand, by non-Jews, for Jewish magical artifacts.[161] To these suggestions we may add the apparent shift from Temple-based priestly magic, and from the wonder-working holy men, to the services provided by professional magicians whose knowledge was enshrined in written manuscripts.[162] But without downplaying the possible significance of such sociological factors, we must also consider the possibility that the Jewish magicians developed the habit of writing down so many magical recipes and "finished products" as a result of their direct contact with the Greco-Egyptian magical tradition, where this had already become the accepted norm. It is also for this reason that the layout of so many of the magical texts they produced bears such close resemblance to those produced by their non-Jewish colleagues at the time, and is quite different from those produced – and not produced – by their Second Temple period predecessors.

In examining this historical reconstruction, we may note that this is precisely the kind of argument which we refused to accept throughout the present study, an argument which assumes that the occurrence of parallel phenomena in two distinct cultures calls for a diffusionistic explanation, and that the direction of the influence is from the culture in which that phenomenon is first attested to the one in which it appears only later. Both assumptions are problematic, and there is no doubt that the historical reconstruction offered here cannot be proven in any convincing manner, and is bound to remain both hypothetical and subjective. And yet, it must at least be raised, if only because of its great significance for our study, since

---

[161] Literacy: Mock 2001. Textual communities: Seidel 1996, pp. 122–26. Growing demand: Lacerenza 2002, p. 396.
[162] For the shift from temple to home in Greco-Egyptian magic, see Smith 1995, pp. 20–27; for a comparable shift from charisma to scribal authority (in medieval Europe), see Jaeger 1994.

it is first and foremost the shift from mostly oral to mostly written magic which is responsible for the quantum leap in the quantity and quality of the evidence available for the study of late-antique Jewish magic. Moreover, such a hypothesis could help explain one of the major differences between the western branch of late-antique Jewish magic, which was fully scribalized, and the eastern branch, where we find spells which were written down on clay bowls, but apparently were not normally transmitted in written formularies as in the western branch. As we shall see in Chapter 6, rabbinic literature too still reflects especially the older forms of oral magic, and is only partly aware of the scribalization of the Jewish magical tradition which was taking place in the rabbis' own times. Thus, the seemingly trivial similarities in layout and style between the Greco-Egyptian magical texts and the Jewish ones might point to the one borrowing of pagan magical technology which made ancient Jewish magic so much more accessible to its modern students.

THE MAGICAL PRAXIS: AIMS, TECHNIQUES, AND MATERIA MAGICA

In previous scholarship, much has been made of the real and imagined parallels between the aims of the magical practices of different cultures and the rituals and materials employed in order to achieve these aims, in an attempt to demonstrate cross-cultural contacts and borrowings. But as we already noted at the beginning of this chapter, such claims are extremely difficult to substantiate, especially because of the basic phenomenological similarity of the magical traditions of many different people. When we examine the aims of the Jewish magical recipes which can be trusted to date back to late antiquity, we find all the things which practitioners of all cultures are expected to do, such as healing the sick, harming one's opponents, or filling a client's chosen victim with love or sexual desire. Thus, there are very few recipes which could be classified by their aims as specifically non-Jewish in origin (such as recipes for talking to the sun, or winning at the race-courses), and most recipes have nothing distinctly foreign about them, even when non-Jewish parallels could easily be adduced.

When we turn from the recipes' aims to the ritual techniques they employ in order to achieve these aims, we realize once again that phenomenological parallels can hardly prove influence, and even when such influence seems likely, establishing its direction is often impossible.[163] The use of aggressive

---

[163] And cf. Dieleman 2005, p. 20, n. 59: "it is extremely difficult to trace specific cultural or ethnic origins for ritual techniques. Moreover, such an undertaking easily runs the risk of ending up in an essentialistic debate on who was first."

"voodoo" dolls, for example, is attested in Greek magic from very early on, and is attested in Babylonian and Egyptian magic even much earlier; when it emerges in the Jewish magical tradition, as in the *Sword of Moses*, we could interpret this as the entry of a foreign practice into the Jewish magical tradition.[164] But we could also note, and with equal conviction, that this practice is so common in numerous different periods and places that the Jewish magicians need not have borrowed it from their Greek (or Egyptian, or Babylonian) colleagues, and may have developed it themselves. Similarly, when we find both Jewish and non-Jewish magicians and holy men standing within protective "magic circles" they have drawn on the ground, we cannot use the similarity in praxis as a sign of interdependence, and certainly should not use the chronological priority of the sources in which it is first mentioned to prove who was first.[165] The same is true for the practice of identifying a spell's client and victims by their mother's name, a practice which is common to the Greco-Egyptian magical texts, to the Jewish magical texts of late antiquity and the early Middle Ages, and even to the magical recipes in the Babylonian Talmud. There have been many attempts to prove that this habit was borrowed from the Egyptian magical tradition, but as there is nothing specifically Egyptian about this practice, it would be hard to prove that it did not originate elsewhere.[166] And the same is again true for the use of iron against demons, which is well attested in many different cultures, and could hardly be proven to have been adopted by the Jewish practitioners from any of their neighbors, or vice versa.[167] In such cases, and many others beside, it would be wrong to limit our enquiry to the Jewish and the Greco-Egyptian magical traditions, and to assume that the one must have influenced the other. For all we know, such practices may have evolved independently in different ancient cultures, or they may be due to the influence on all traditions of magic in late antiquity of much earlier practices, emanating from Egypt, Mesopotamia, or elsewhere. Moreover, even when the similarities are so close as to make accidental resemblance unlikely, it is often extremely difficult to judge from such resemblances who influenced whom. As one example, we may note

---

164 See HdM 68 (p. 84 Gaster = p. 42 Harari).
165 For "magic circles," see, e.g., Thompson 1908, pp. lviii–lx; Daiches 1913, pp. 32–33; Trachtenberg 1939, p. 121; MTKG I, p. 82.
166 For the use of matronymics in magic, see Jordan 1976; Curbera 1999; Golinkin 2002; and cf. Herodotus 1.173, who claims that the use of matronymics was typical of the Lycians. See also Trachtenberg 1939, pp. 115–16.
167 For iron used against demons, see t Shab. 6.13 (p. 24 Lieberman) and Goldziher 1907. In later Jewish texts, it is stated that iron is so effective because ברזל stands for Jacob's four wives, Bilhah, Rebecca, Zilpah, and Leah (see HAITCG, p. 82 and MSF, p. 157).

how the incising of a spell on unbaked clay and its burning in the fire as part of an erotic magical ritual is attested both in Jewish sources (the Ḥorvat Rimmon sherds, Genizah and non-Genizah magical recipes, etc.) and in the Greek magical papyri. Here, mutual influence seems far more likely, but can we really prove that it was a non-Jewish technique adopted by the Jewish magicians and not the other way around?[168] Similarly, when we find in the Jewish recipe in PGM XXXVI, and again in a Talmudic recipe (discussed in Chapter 6), the technique of saying to an object, "You are the mythological object which performed a service X *in illo tempore* – so go now and perform a similar service for me," we may note that similar rituals have been in use in Egyptian magic, for example, long before, and are well attested in the Greek magical papyri.[169] Does this prove, however, that this technique was simply borrowed by the Jewish practitioners from their Greco-Egyptian colleagues, or perhaps from other non-Jewish colleagues (e.g., in Babylonia)? For all we know, they could easily have developed it themselves, just like the magicians in many other cultures worldwide, who certainly never read the Greek magical papyri (or the works of Mircea Eliade), but developed similar techniques.

In some cases, the resemblance between a Jewish magical practice and a non-Jewish one is so great, and the practice itself is so unusual, as to exclude any possibility other than a direct or indirect borrowing. Even here, however, determining who borrowed from whom often is quite impossible. As one example, we may note the recipes – found in the Greek magical papyri and in medieval Jewish magical texts, both inside the Cairo Genizah and outside it – for catching a thief by means of drawing an eye on the wall and piercing it with a nail, an action which would make the culprit suffer greatly in the eye and turn himself or herself in.[170] While the appearance of this practice in pagan and Jewish sources argues for a diffusionistic explanation, the practice itself is far from culture-specific. It appears in the Greek sources long before its appearance in the Jewish ones, and this could argue in favor of a Jewish adoption of a non-Jewish practice, but would hardly clinch the argument, given the paucity of late-antique Jewish magical recipes at our disposal. And the same goes for the practice of sticking a needle's tip into its eye as a means for "binding" bridegrooms – a

---

[168] For the Ḥorvat Rimmon sherds, see Figure 3.3. For the same technique in Greco-Egyptian magic, see, e.g., PGM XXXVI.187–210; and cf. Harari 2000a.

[169] See Chapter 3, n. 175.

[170] For the eye and nail recipe, see PGM V.70–95, and SM II, 86, with Jacoby 1913 and 1922; Horak and Gastgeber 1995, pp. 205–09. For some Jewish examples, see Trachtenberg 1939, p. 125; T-S NS 322.51 (Judeo-Spanish; briefly discussed by Gutwirth 1989); Benayahu 1972, p. 221, no. 127; Barzilay 1974, pp. 278–79.

technique which is attested from antiquity to our own days, and which is found both in Genizah magical recipes and in non-Jewish magical texts. Here too, the similarity is too great to be accidental, but the popularity of such a practice makes it a priori impossible to trace its ultimate origins and exact lines of transmission.[171]

There are, however, some exceptions to this general rule. First, in the realm of *materia magica* we are on somewhat firmer ground, especially when the materials entered the Jewish practitioners' handbooks with their original Greek names in Hebrew transliteration. In *Sepher ha-Razim*, for example, some of the recipes enjoin writing a divinatory spell with *zmyrnomelan(ion)*, the Greek word for "black myrrh," on a *chartês hieratikos*, that is "hieratic (or, priestly (Egyptian)) papyrus," or engraving an aggressive spell on a thin plate of *psychroforon*, the Greek word for the "(leaden) cold-water pipe" of Roman cities. There, we also find instructions to write an erotic spell on a thin plate of *kassiteron*, the Greek word for "tin" (it's a tin line between love and hate!), or to fumigate *istorqon*, Greek "styrax," in a recipe for grace and charm.[172] In some of these instances, we might imagine that the materials involved were commonly known by their Greek names in the Aramaic and Hebrew of late-antique Palestine, and that their appearance here does not prove a direct borrowing by the Jewish practitioners from the non-Jewish ones, but in other cases this would hardly be convincing. Certainly the theft of "scrapings" from the municipal lead water-pipes, to be hammered into a *lamella* and used for writing an aggressive *defixio*, is a practice which the compiler of *Sepher ha-Razim* could only have borrowed from PGM-like recipe-books and their owners, where this practice indeed is warmly recommended.[173]

A second type of example in which direct borrowing seems irrefutable is when a magical praxis is so culture-specific as to defy any other explanation. As an example of this process, let us look at two short Hebrew recipes found in the shorter version of the *Sword of Moses*:

And if you wish to separate a man from a woman, take meat of a donkey in your mouth and say the sword over both of them; but see to it that you do not tear (?) it with your hand(s).

And if you wish to overturn your enemy, take a lead lamella and (take) from his hair and his clothes, and write the sword and throw it in a ruined building and he will fall.[174]

---

[171] For this practice, see Bodleian Heb. a3.31 (unpublished).
[172] For all these examples, see Margalioth 1966, pp. 1–4, 11.
[173] As was duly noted by Margalioth 1966, pp. 3–4.   [174] *Synopse* §616–17.

Looking at the second recipe first, we may note that the use in an aggressive magical ritual of something which was intimately connected with its intended victim – in this case, his hair and his clothes – is so widespread as to carry no value as a demonstration of any diffusionist interpretation of its cross-cultural manifestations. But the use of lead as the writing surface for such rituals, and its burying in an old ruin, are so close to the specifically Greek (and, in the Roman period, Greco-Egyptian) practice of casting a *defixio* as to make a borrowing by the Jewish practitioners quite likely. But it is in turning to the first recipe, and noting the unsavory (and not very kosher!) meat consumed by the Jewish practitioner that we find irrefutable evidence of a direct borrowing from the Greco-Egyptian magical tradition. Within Jewish culture, one could easily find references to donkeys as stupid, stubborn, and lazy, and even the permission to eat donkey-flesh in order to cure jaundice, but one would be hard pressed to explain why their flesh would be used in a ritual to separate a man from a woman. It is only within an Egyptian context – in which the donkey was the symbol of the evil god Seth, who had separated Osiris from Isis in the Egyptian myth most commonly used in Egyptian and Greco-Egyptian magic – that such a ritual may fully be explained. And looking at the Egyptian magical texts or the Greek magical papyri, we find numerous instances of the use of donkeys and donkey parts for aggressive magical recipes, including those for separating lovers from each other (which are known there as *diakopoi*, "separators").[175] In such cases, when the use of a specific magical substance makes sense only in the context of the Greco-Egyptian magical tradition, we may be fairly certain that this too is something the Jewish magicians had borrowed from their non-Jewish colleagues and mentors, and did not develop it themselves. We shall return to this example in the next chapter, and examine some of its wider implications. For the time being, we may briefly summarize our findings throughout this chapter.

SUMMARY

To end this chapter, we may offer a bird's eye survey of its major findings. From the outset, we took a conservative, minimalist approach, and refused to see every parallel between non-Jewish and Jewish magic in late antiquity as evidence of cultural borrowing. And yet, the amount of evidence we could muster is quite impressive, and while future research might modify

---

[175] See, for example, PDM xii.62–75 (in Betz 1986, pp. 169–70) and xii.76–107 (Betz 1986, p. 170), with Dieleman 2005, pp. 130–38. See also MSF, G9 (T-S K 1.15) p. 1, l. 11.

this point or that, the overall picture seems quite clear. Late-antique Jewish magicians avidly borrowed much from their non-Jewish colleagues, and they did so in many different forms and on numerous occasions. This is hardly surprising, in light of what we know about magicians in general, and late-antique magicians in particular. It is not even so surprising in light of what we know about other strands of late-antique Jewish culture, be it the entry of foreign words, literary motifs, and exegetical techniques into rabbinic literature, or that of foreign images, including the Sun-god Helios, into the synagogues of late-antique Palestine. It is quite possible that the magicians were willing to go a step further than other Jews, or that in the realm of magic some Jews were willing to go further than they did, for example, in their synagogue decorations, but we should not exaggerate the difference. Moreover, we must also stress that the Jewish magical texts of late antiquity are far from being mere translations, adaptations, and imitations of the Greco-Egyptian magical tradition. On the one hand, we noted that there are only a few cases where a direct translation or adaptation of entire recipes can be proven, or even seems very likely. On the other, we noted throughout the present chapter how the Jewish magicians borrowed much pagan magical technology but embedded it in texts and rituals which were entirely their own. This is an issue to which we shall return in the following chapter, when we examine some of the specifically Jewish features of the Jewish magical texts of late antiquity, including the manners by which they absorbed and utilized the foreign elements they so prominently display. For in the study of cross-cultural contacts, we must always ask not just what is borrowed, but also how it is borrowed and used, and how it is transformed in the process into new and distinct cultural amalgams.

CHAPTER 5

How "Jewish" was ancient Jewish magic?

INTRODUCTION

Having surveyed the non-Jewish elements which can be detected in the Jewish magical texts of late-antique Palestine and its vicinity, we may now wrap up our discussion of the "insider" sources by asking one of the most important questions raised in the present study, namely, how "Jewish" was ancient Jewish magic (at least its western branch) and what kind of "Judaism" does it represent? This question has rarely been raised in the past, and when it was, it was answered mostly with vacuous platitudes, such as Montgomery's claim that "all Jewish magic . . . is not Jewish but eclectic," Lieberman's assertion that "the Jewish magi acted in the same manner as their Gentile neighbors," or Margalioth's conviction that *Sepher ha-Razim* was written by a Jewish heretic with Gnostic inclinations.[1] In light of what we have seen throughout the present study, such answers are hardly satisfactory.

The question of the "Jewishness" of ancient Jewish magic could and should be raised from two different perspectives. Viewed from a non-Jewish perspective, the Jewish magical texts which display a strong influence of Greco-Egyptian magic could perhaps be seen as a branch of that magical tradition which happened to have been written down in Hebrew and Aramaic. If this were so – if, that is, the Jewish magical texts are basically the translations or adaptations of non-Jewish models – then they must be studied within the framework of the magic of the Roman empire of late antiquity, and not as a separate cultural entity. Viewed from a Jewish perspective, the question of the "Jewishness" of the Jewish magical texts is important for another reason, namely, that by learning something about the "Jewishness" of these texts we may learn something about the late-antique Jews who lurk behind them. Here, in other words, the answer to the question "how Jewish" could lead to some insights on the kind of "Judaism"

---

[1] Montgomery 1913, p. 9 (and cf. p. 58); Lieberman 1974, p. 25; Margalioth 1966, e.g., p. xv.

that produced the Jewish magical texts of late antiquity, and its possible relations with other types of Jewish cultural productivity from late-antique Palestine.

Before embarking upon this task, we must note the severe methodological problems which must be overcome if our analysis is to be convincing. The first of these involves the difficulty in dating the sources in which our practices are found, in order to ascertain their relevance for a study of *ancient* Jewish magic. The second involves the difficulty of deciding what is "Jewish" in different periods, since "Judaism" is not some frozen, ahistorical entity whose contents remain the same as history passes it by. The third is the ever-nagging question of what exactly to include under the rubric "magic," an issue which is more painful here than in the previous chapter, in which the very provenance of some of the foreign motifs we detected – which only appear in pagan magical texts (some of which even identify themselves as "magical"), and not in the non-magical ones – could help identify the Jewish texts in which they appear as magical texts. Let us examine each of these problems, and its implications, in some detail, before suggesting some more general guidelines on how to proceed with our enquiry.

Dating Jewish magical texts with few non-Jewish elements
One of the most fascinating paradoxes in the study of Jewish magical texts is that the fewer foreign elements a given text displays, the more difficult it is to date it and analyze its transmission history. As noted in the previous chapter, when we find known Greek *voces magicae*, for example, in Genizah magical texts, we can be fairly certain that they were borrowed from the Greek magical tradition, and even offer a rough dating of the process according to the spelling of the borrowed words. It is for this reason that the Cairo Genizah can provide us with much useful evidence concerning the entry of non-Jewish elements into the Jewish magical literature of late antiquity. Similarly, when we encounter Genizah magical recipes which clearly were copied from Coptic-Arabic magical recipe-books, or which contain the Hebrew transliteration of a Latin prayer which can be traced back to Southern Germany in the early thirteenth century, these borrowings again provide us with sound criteria for dating the entry of these recipes into the Jewish magical tradition and even for locating their geographic provenance. But when we turn from such Genizah magical texts to the many texts which display few non-Jewish influences – neither pagan nor Christian nor Muslim – and show no signs of heavy contact with a foreign language – be it Greek or Arabic, or, far more rarely, Coptic or Latin – then

we have no Archimedean point from which to begin dating the given text or reconstructing its transmission history. Thus, while such Genizah texts *may* be copies of copies of late-antique Jewish magical texts, proving this becomes extremely difficult. And given the continuous vigor of the Jewish magical tradition throughout the Middle Ages and beyond, and the constant production of new magical texts and new types of magical practices, one should never assume that any Genizah text must date to long before the time when it was last copied.

As a case in point, let us briefly examine an interesting recipe, found so far in two different Genizah copies (one still incomplete) which were dated by their editors to the eleventh and twelfth centuries, and which includes an "updated" version of the biblical *soṭah* ritual (Nm 5.11–31) discussed in Chapter 1.[2] Leaving aside the complex issues of whether and how the ritual was practiced during the Second Temple period, we may focus only on the Genizah recipe, which explains how the *soṭah*-ordeal should be carried out, "now that we have no priest, and no holy water, and no Temple." The recipe is headed by a title, "The Business (or, Praxis) of the *Soṭah*," and begins with a *Hekhalot*-like doxology of God, recalling God's creation of the universe and of the angels and the spirits and the demons one thousand years before He created man. It next discusses the transmission of God's secret Names to Moses, Elijah, and others, including the Sanhedrin (Great Court) of the Second Temple period, which supposedly used these Names while conducting the *soṭah* ceremony. The text then explains how the biblical verses describing the *soṭah* ceremony must be understood, and how the ritual they describe can be carried out by using God's great Names (many of which again look quite like those found in the Hekhalot texts), and finding substitutes for the biblical ingredients. Instead of holy water, one takes water from a fresh spring, and instead of dust from the Temple one goes to a synagogue and gathers dust from the four corners of the Torah-ark; following an appropriate rite of purification, designed to make one as pure as the officiating priest would have been in the days of the Temple, one may carry out the ritual, which should make the woman, if she indeed was guilty, suffer the very same physical side-effects described by the biblical ritual.

How are we to date such a ritual or determine its place of origins? It certainly dates from after the destruction of the Second Temple, to which it explicitly refers ("now that we have no ... Temple"), and probably postdates

---

[2] See MTKG I, 1 (JTSL ENA 3635.17) and I, 2 (T-S K 1.56), 1b/3–23. The text was first published and discussed by Marmorstein 1925; for more recent discussions, see Veltri 1993; Schäfer 1996; Swartz 2000, pp. 63–66.

that event by at least a few centuries.³ It is written in Hebrew, which could perhaps argue for a Geonic date, since most late-antique Jewish magical texts were written in Aramaic. This, however, is hardly a compelling argument, given the existence of such texts as *Sepher ha-Razim*, written in Hebrew but of a late-antique date, and some late-antique Jewish amulets written mostly or entirely in Hebrew. Thus, while both known Genizah versions of this recipe display much evidence of being corrupt copies of older models, there is no way of telling how old these models may have been. Moreover, while the fact that the text displays no clear Muslim or Arabic influences could perhaps argue for a pre-Muslim date, the fact that it displays no Greek influences, and no Greek loanwords (in marked contrast with *Sepher ha-Razim*, which displays both!), means that we cannot demonstrate such a pre-Muslim origin for the Genizah *soṭah*-recipe. This text, in other words, provides no tell-tale signs of its date or provenance, and it so happens that the best clue for dating it lies in a medieval Jewish chronicle, the *Scroll of Aḥimaaẓ*, written in 1054 by Aḥimaaẓ son of Paltiel.⁴ In this chronicle in verse, which abounds in scenes of miracles and magic, we find detailed descriptions of how Aharon the Babylonian came to Italy in the mid-ninth century. Arriving in Oria (Southern Italy), he met R. Shephatiah and R. Ḥananel, our author's distant ancestors, and settled there for a while. The chronicler's florid account of Aharon's achievements at Oria includes the following description:

> And his wisdom poured forth, and his teaching was implanted,
> And he demonstrated his powers, and the judgment of legal cases,
> As in the times of the Urim and the days of the Sanhedrin.
> And the law of the *soṭah* he there set up and practiced,
> And instead of "dust of ... the earth of the Temple" (Nm 5.17),
> The dust from below the Torah-ark was taken.⁵

One would, of course, hope for a more detailed description of Rabbi Aharon's conduct of the *soṭah* ceremony in ninth-century Oria, and in a source more trustworthy than the colorful *Scroll of Aḥimaaẓ*. And yet, this brief description should suffice to assure us that the Genizah ceremony and the one described here are the same ceremony, or at least related versions of the same ceremony.⁶ This proves that at least by 1054 this ritual

---

³ A similar awareness of the historical distance is displayed by some medieval *gorallot* handbooks, which explain why such divination techniques must be used, "Now that we have no Urim and Thumim" (see, e.g., Swartz 2000, p. 67).
⁴ For the *Scroll* and its historical value, see Bonfil 1987 and 1989; for its many magic-related stories, see Benin 1985 and Yassif 1999a, pp. 200–11.
⁵ *Scroll of Aḥimaaẓ*, p. 15 Klar (entirely mistranslated by Salzman 1924, p. 67).
⁶ As was independently noted by Harari 2006a.

was well known in Southern Italy, and it is quite possible that it had been brought there by Aharon the Babylonian in the mid-ninth century CE, especially since this Aharon is elsewhere described as the major channel of transmission of esoteric lore from Babylonia to Southern and Northern Italy, whence they later traveled northwards across the Alps.[7] Needless to say, a Geonic, and Babylonian, origin for this text would fit nicely with our own conclusions with regard to the *sotah* ceremony's late and Greek-less Hebrew, and would also show that this text actually does not belong in the chronological framework of the present study. Thus, the best clue for dating this specific text is provided by an "outsider" source, and such external clues unfortunately are quite rare in the study of ancient and medieval Jewish magic. Hence the validity of the general rule: the fewer non-Jewish elements a magical text displays, the harder it is to date it or study its transmission history.

Defining what is "Jewish"

A second difficulty besetting the search for the "Jewishness" of the Jewish magical texts is that of deciding what exactly to consider "Jewish." As we noted in Chapter 3, the identification of some magical texts as Jewish hardly poses a problem, since those texts which are written in Hebrew or Aramaic and in the square script may safely be considered Jewish. But the search for those elements within the Jewish magical texts which can only be identified as "Jewish" in the cultural sense is much more complex for several different reasons. At first sight, we might think that anything in these texts which is not demonstrably non-Jewish in origin is in fact "Jewish," which would mean that all we must do is take the Jewish magical texts at our disposal, erase all the non-Jewish elements identified in Chapter 4, and end up with the "Jewish" elements within these texts. Unfortunately, such a naive positivistic method would lead us far astray, both because we must be looking for things which were specifically "Jewish," and were not common to Jews and non-Jews alike and because the contents of the epithet "Jewish" must be allowed to change over time. The label "Jewish," in other words, is both ethnocentric and diachronically flexible. What seems to us "Jewish" might in fact be a common phenomenon which also happens to be attested among Jews, and what is not "Jewish" in one period could easily become "Jewish" in the next. Thus, when we wish to look at the "Jewish"

---

[7] For Abu Aharon, see Harari 2006a, with much further bibliography. For a (far-fetched) attempt to reconstruct the materials he had brought to Europe, see Weinstock 1963 and the quick rebuttal of Scholem 1963.

components of late-antique Jewish magic, we must look for those elements within it that *at that point in time* may be considered *exclusively Jewish*.

One final problem must be touched upon before we may proceed. As we had ample occasion to note in Chapter 3, many elements of Jewish magic – and especially divine and angelic Names – entered the Greco-Egyptian magic of the Roman period and became part and parcel of the pagan magicians' arsenal. Needless to say, there is an even greater presence of Jewish elements – divine and angelic Names, biblical verses, and so on – in the Samaritan and the (far more numerous) Christian magical texts of late antiquity. In all these cases, many elements of Jewish magic can no longer be said to be exclusively Jewish. For the purpose of our present enquiry, however, this issue is of lesser significance, for when we find "Sabaoth," "Adonai," and "Michael," or biblical verses and *historiolae* in Jewish magical texts, our first assumption should be that their appearance there is due to their ubiquitous presence within the Jewish magical tradition. Only in unusual cases – for example, when the name "Iaho" is re-transliterated from the Greek spelling of the Tetragrammaton, "Iaô" – may we conclude that a certain Jewish element re-entered the Jewish magical tradition from the outside.[8] In all other instances, we shall treat the Jewish elements in the Jewish magical tradition as "Jewish" even if they have also entered the world of pagan or Christian magic.

Defining "magic"
One last problem besetting the search for the "Jewish" elements within late-antique Jewish magic is the difficulty of what exactly to include under the rubric "magic" – and what to exclude from it. In the previous chapter, this issue hardly came up, since many of the foreign elements we detected in the Jewish magical texts of late antiquity stemmed directly from the magical technology of the non-Jewish world in antiquity. Abrasax, for example, appears only in the Gnostic and magical texts of late antiquity, or in those patristic texts which polemicize against them. And word-triangles, *charactêres*, numerous *voces magicae*, and even the famous battle-cry "Now now, quickly quickly," are found only in ancient magical texts or in those texts which borrow directly from them. And as these texts sometimes identified themselves as belonging in the realm of "magic," and were often identified as such by "outsiders," their modern classification as magical texts can hardly be faulted. But when we turn to the native Jewish elements found in

---

[8] For יאו, see Margalioth 1966, p. 7; Sperber 1994, pp. 86–91, and Bohak 2000b, pp. 7–8. See also Trachtenberg 1939, pp. 100–01. For similar phenomena in the Demotic magical papyri, see Dieleman 2005, p. 74.

Jewish texts, the distinction between what falls under the rubric of Jewish "magic" and what falls under that of Jewish "religion" can become quite blurred, as we noted in Chapter 1. Returning once again to the Genizah *soṭah* ritual to which we already referred, we may ask whether this reenactment of a disused biblical ritual should be classified as "magic" or as a part of medieval Jewish "religion." Neither the text itself nor the brief reference to this ritual in the *Scroll of Aḥimaaz* necessitates classifying it as "magic," and the *Scroll* even ascribes it to a well-known rabbi. If we could find within this text an adjuration of Abrasax, an invocation of the *charactêres*, or a recitation of the *chych bachych*-formula, we would probably not hesitate to classify it as "magic," since we would be able to document its use of specifically magical technologies. But if it only mentions such common angel-names as Meṭaṭron and Masmeriah, and some Hekhalot-type *voces* such as ẒYẒWẒYH RGMṬYH, classifying it as a magical text becomes much more difficult.

Where, then, does all this leave us? In light of the three problems which we have just examined, we should give precedence in the present chapter to the metal-plate amulets of late antiquity, since they are demonstrably early, demonstrably Jewish, and fall under our definition of "magic," even if not under the ancient Jewish one. But we may supplement this evidence with what we find in *Sepher ha-Razim*, the older versions of the *Sword of Moses*, and the few Aramaic magical gems and magical papyri surveyed in Chapter 3. We may also pay some attention to the Jewish Babylonian incantation bowls, which might help elucidate what is found in the much smaller corpus of Jewish magical texts from Palestine. When some "Jewish" elements appear in both corpora, we may be sure of their wide diffusion in both branches of late-antique Jewish magic, while those which are found only in one region might help us highlight the differences between these two sub-traditions. Finally, we must also pay close attention to evidence provided by the "outsider" sources, and especially the rabbinic literature of late antiquity, which has much to say about the rabbis' familiarity with, and use of, Jewish magical practices (see Chapter 6). And, as with any other historical enquiry, we should place our greatest trust in those phenomena and patterns which recur across these different bodies of evidence.

Analyzing this rich material, we shall focus only on a few detailed probes of some of the specifically Jewish contents and contexts of late-antique Jewish magic. We begin with possible examples of continuity from Second Temple period Jewish magic to its late-antique sequels, as such continuities shed much light on the "Jewishness" of the later Jewish magical texts. We shall then turn to the extensive use of God's Name(s) and of angel-names, and to the equally extensive use of the Hebrew Bible in the Jewish magical texts. We shall then focus on the relations between Jewish magic and three other spheres of Jewish cultural creativity in late antiquity – the synagogues of late-antique Palestine, the Jewish mystical tradition, and rising rabbinic culture, an issue to which we shall return once again, and from a different perspective, in the next chapter. Finally, we shall examine what is perhaps the most "Jewish" aspect of them all, namely, the Jewish magicians' complex attitudes towards the non-Jewish materials they borrowed for their own magical practices. To end this chapter, we shall offer some general conclusions about the overall "Jewishness" of ancient Jewish magic, and the kind of "Judaism" it displays.

CONTINUITIES FROM THE SECOND TEMPLE PERIOD TO LATE-ANTIQUE JEWISH MAGIC

In theory, the best starting-point for any study of the "Jewishness" of the Jewish magical tradition of late antiquity would be a meticulous search for those elements within it which go back to earlier stages in the history of Jewish magic. If we could point to certain elements which were commonly used by the Jewish practitioners of the Second Temple period, and were subsequently used by their late-antique heirs, we could certainly learn much about the inner-Jewish history of ancient Jewish magic. As noted above, this would be true even if these elements originally were of a non-Jewish origin, since their entry at an earlier period would probably mean that by late antiquity they had become fully naturalized within the Jewish magical tradition.

So much for the theory. When we turn to practicing it, however, we are immediately confronted by the sorry state of our evidence for the Jewish magical practices of the Second Temple period, to which we devoted much attention in Chapter 2. Moreover, it seems that this difference between the quantity of available evidence for the earlier periods and for late antiquity is not merely the result of the decay and disappearance of the ancient evidence, but of a fundamental shift within the Jewish magical tradition itself. If our suggestions in the previous chapters are correct, the main difficulty in the search for continuity from an earlier period to late antiquity would be that this search tries to bridge the "scribalization gap" separating the Jewish scribal magical tradition of late antiquity from its non-scribal predecessors. The use of spells to ward off snakes and scorpions, for example, probably goes back to the First Temple period, but only in the Cairo Genizah do we find Jewish magical texts which preserve such spells. The spells they

How "Jewish" was ancient Jewish magic?

preserve may be distant descendants of the spells used for similar purposes a millennium and a half earlier, but they may just as well be entirely unrelated to them, and historical probability tells us that the latter possibility is by far the likelier. Thus, while it is not impossible that the few magical texts of the First or Second Temple period that have come down to us might be illuminated by light from late-antique Jewish magic, this possibility cannot be taken for granted and must first be demonstrated.[9]

In spite of the paucity of the available evidence for the Jewish magical practices of the Second Temple period, certain elements of the later Jewish magical tradition certainly do go back to this earlier period.[10] The use of certain biblical chapters, verses, and themes, or of some specifically Jewish divine, angelic, and demonic Names, certainly goes back to the Second Temple period, and some of it may even go back to the First Temple period. Thus, while the paucity of the evidence often makes it difficult to say whether a specific biblical verse used by late-antique or medieval Jewish magicians was used already in the Second Temple period or became popular only later, the continuous use of some passages and verses – such as Nm 6.24–27 (the Priestly Blessing, attested already on the Ketef Hinnom amulets), Psalm 91 (found, e.g., in 11Q11), Ex 15.26 (for which see the next chapter), Zec 3.2, and so on – is beyond any doubt. The same is true of such biblical phrases as "the God of the spirits for all flesh," and of biblical themes and symbols such as the Rod of Moses, the head-plate of Aaron, or the encounter between these two men of God and Pharaoh's powerful magicians, all of which are amply documented both in tannaitic rabbinic literature and in non-rabbinic sources. Similarly, while we cannot always tell which divine or angelic Names were already used by the Jewish practitioners in the Second Temple period, the fact that they did use such names as YHWH (the Tetragrammaton) or that of the angel Raphael in their exorcisms and other magical rituals hardly is in doubt. And when it comes to demonic beings, at least one malevolent demon, Ashmedai, whose appearance in the book of *Tobith* has been noted in Chapter 2, reappears in numerous "insider" and "outsider" texts, be it the amulets, the *Testament of Solomon*, the Genizah magical texts or the Babylonian Talmud. In a very similar fashion, the evil demoness Lilith, and the class of

---

[9] For a reading of Song of Songs in light of Jewish magical practices of a much later period, see Bar-Ilan 1985. Note also the ongoing attempts to read the Ketef Hinnom amulets in light of Jewish magical texts a millennium younger, for which see Barkay *et al.* 2004. And cf. Parpola 1993 and Gruenwald 1997, for continuities between ancient Assyria and medieval Kabbalah, and Yassif 1988 (and Yassif 1999, pp. 89–106), on Second Temple folkloristic motifs in rabbinic literature.
[10] For an earlier treatment of this question, see Swartz 2001, esp. pp. 190–92.

demons known as male and female *lilin*, or the evil Satan, or Samael and Azazel, or Shemiḥaza, are all continuously attested from the Second Temple literature to late antiquity and beyond. And, as we already noted, the fact that Ashmedai, for example, is of Persian origin, or that Lilith apparently began her demonic career in Babylonia is of lesser relevance here, for both have become part and parcel of Jewish demonology already in the Second Temple period, and have remained there ever since.

To these basic features of early Jewish magic which continued into the later periods, several others could be added. Thus, the tendency to father arcane magical lore on angels (as in *Tobith* or *Jubilees*) or on ancient biblical figures, such as David or Solomon, certainly goes back to the Second Temple period (as we saw, for example, with regards to some of the exorcistic psalms from Qumran and elsewhere). That it continued unabated into late antiquity can be shown from all the "literary" books of magic at our disposal, including, for example, *Sepher ha-Razim*, which provides its readers with a long introduction concerning all the biblical figures who had supposedly used it to their great satisfaction.[11] This practice is, of course, well attested in many other magical traditions from late antiquity onwards – in pagan, Christian, and Muslim texts alike – and is not uncommon in other strands of Jewish culture. And yet, the importance of this technique within the Jewish magical tradition need perhaps not be exaggerated. In the free-standing formularies known to us from the Cairo Genizah, such attributions – not only of whole collections, but even of individual recipes – seem to be quite rare. Thus, while the practice certainly shows an unbroken continuity within the Jewish magical tradition, it never became a central feature of that tradition.

Another sphere in which such continuities may be demonstrated is that of the technical vocabulary utilized by the Jewish magicians of antiquity. Such Hebrew verbs as *ga'ar* ("to rebuke") or *hishbi'a* ("to adjure"), such technical terms as *shir tishboḥot* ("a song of praise," i.e., praises of God, at which the demons shudder), and such phrases as "Amen Amen Selah" at the end of a magical incantation are well attested in the Jewish magical tradition from the Second Temple period – and perhaps even from the First Temple period – to our very days. Even the Aramaic phrase *'ana momi* or *'omi* ("I adjure") is attested both in a Qumran exorcistic fragment (4Q560) and in the Jewish amulets of late antiquity. It is, of course, not surprising that these technical terms – and others which could be added – stem from the realm of exorcism, which is, as we noted in Chapter 2, the

---

[11] For this motif, see Swartz 1994a, and Swartz 1996, pp. 173–205.

one practice in which the Jewish practitioners of the Second Temple period seem to have excelled, and whose spells were consigned to writing at a time when most other magical activities apparently were not. If the Jews indeed moved to a fully scribal magical tradition only in late antiquity, it would be quite natural to find continuity from the Second Temple period into late antiquity and beyond especially in this field in which they seem to have transmitted in a written form from a very early date.[12]

And it is here that we come to what is perhaps the most intriguing aspect of our problem, namely, the possible survival, in one form or another, of some of the exorcistic hymns of the Second Temple period into later periods. One possible example of this intriguing process of cultural transmission is provided by the trilingual Greek-Aramaic-Hebrew amulet from Egypt (apparently Tell el-Amarna), to which we have already devoted much attention in the previous chapter. There, we focused on its Greek section, and on the Greco-Egyptian influences it displays. Here, we focus on its citation of an exorcistic psalm which is attributed to David. This section of the amulet deserves more careful attention than it has so far received, and will have to be re-read in the future, perhaps with the aid of modern imaging technology. For the time being, however, we shall be satisfied with a rough translation of the text, as read by its first and only editors:

<H> These are the words of David, the singing songs that he would recite over King [Saul]:
Redeem me, ****, and save me from all the evil afflictions and all the evil spirits which [ ] ???; recite a song of praises to the glorious King [ ] and mighty, the God who created the spirits. [Amen] Ame[n] [Selah] Hallelujah. May ** rebuke you, He who rebukes the Satan, he who rules the whole [ ] of the eye, who dwells in Jerusalem in holiness.[13]

As this hymn is cited in Hebrew, in the midst of a bilingual Aramaic-Greek text, and as it bears many similarities to some of the apocryphal psalms found in Qumran (including even the use of dots or dashes as substitutes for the Tetragrammaton), it seems quite certain that the passage in question is a citation of a much older text, probably going back to the Second Temple period (without denying, of course, the likelihood of its recurrent corruption and modification along the way). And as other sections of the Aramaic and Greek texts display ample signs of having been copied from a written magical recipe, we may assume that whoever composed this recipe

---

[12] The same would apply to some of the astrological, brontological, or physiognomical texts of the Second Temple period, all of which fall outside the scope of the present study.
[13] Kotansky, Naveh, and Shaked 1992, p. 9, ll. 21–24. Note also the (garbled, or deliberately modified?) citation of Zec 3.2 ("May YHWH rebuke you, Satan," etc.).

had before him a *written* source in which he found the exorcistic psalm of David. Whether the source whence this psalm was taken consisted of a single "Davidic" psalm or included several such psalms of which our author chose the one that suited his fancy we cannot say, but the very fact that such a psalm was still in circulation in late antiquity is of extreme importance for our study. For when its Second Temple author wrote down this psalm, he probably envisaged its recitation as part of an *oral* exorcistic ritual, not unlike that carried out by Eleazar in front of Vespasian and his entourage. Some of its late-antique users, on the other hand, used it in a *scribal* manner, by incorporating it into a spell to be written on an amulet. Thus, by bridging the "scribalization gap" to which we already alluded, this example not only documents some continuity between Second Temple period exorcisms and those of late antiquity, it also helps highlight the main difference between these two subsequent stages of development of a single magical tradition: in the earlier stage, exorcistic hymns were gathered into handbooks, but their use was in a verbal fashion; in the later period, they were used both in a verbal and in a scribal manner.

To highlight the uniqueness of this example, we may stress that, of the more than forty metal-plate Jewish amulets published thus far, this is the only case of the citation of a source fathered upon a biblical ancestor. And when we turn to the Babylonian incantation bowls, we find a similar phenomenon in one of the recently published bowls, where we again find an exorcistic psalm of David, and once again it is cited in Hebrew (and with a short Hebrew introduction) within an otherwise Aramaic spell:

<H> These are th[e words of David?], the first, the last, the last, which he is playing before King Saul: In the name of YHWH Sabaot the God of Israel who sits upon the Cherubim, against all the afflictions against all the demons against every spirit, against all the fever and shivers, against all the (evil) eye; and give glory to the Name of Glory, and may they go away from the place of dwelling of, which is before, Asher daughter of Mama. Blessed are you, YHWH the God of David, who heals the sick.[14]

Even a cursory reading of this text reveals the corrupt state of its textual transmission, and one would do well not to build too much upon such textual foundations. And yet, the reading of yet another psalm supposedly recited by David before the afflicted King Saul makes one wonder whether this was an ad hoc invention of the bowl's producer or a text he had received, in a written form, from elsewhere, a text whose ultimate origins might lie in Second Temple period Palestine.

[14] Levene 2003, bowl M117.

How "Jewish" was ancient Jewish magic? 303

If the attempt to prove the Second Temple origin of late-antique Davidic hymns is based on arguments of similarity, probability, and plausibility, the example to which we now turn provides much sounder proof of direct textual continuity from the exorcistic hymns of the Second Temple period to those of later periods. To see this, we must focus on a badly mutilated Genizah fragment of a medieval recipe-book (whose handwriting probably points to the eleventh century), one section of which may be translated as follows:

> <J> A section for [ ]:
> <A> This amulet is for saving and protecting NN from the evil eye and from a spirit and from . . . and . . . and from all evil spark-demons and harm-demons. In the name of YY Sabaot, YY the God, God, the God of Is(rael), that you (pl.) shall not harm him, NN . . . [one line entirely mutilated] . . . <H> . . . and it c[omes] up[o]n you, whether by day or by night, and say to you (or, it), Who are you, whether from the seed of man or from the seed of cattle? Your face is the face of old age(?) and your horns(?) are (like) a water-current.[15]

Although the text is badly mutilated, it seems clear that the rebuke of the demon, including both the references to its shameful pedigree and to its physical features, is an almost verbatim copy of what we found in one of the Qumran exorcistic texts more than a millennium earlier (11Q11, cited in Chapter 2). That this anti-demonic spell is here quoted in *Hebrew*, in the midst of an entirely *Aramaic* recipe (with Judeo-Arabic recipe-titles, as commonly happens in the Genizah formularies), is hardly surprising, for it seems clear that the scribe who composed this recipe copied the Hebrew sentence from an existing collection, and decided to leave it untranslated.[16] But he – or, more likely, an earlier copyist – apparently did not understand the original text's reference to the demon as "of the seed of man and of the seed of the holy ones" (as in 11Q11), that is, of the miscegenation between humans and the Fallen Angels, and changed the latter word into "cattle." As the Hebrew word for "holy ones" (*qedoshim*) could hardly have been corrupted into "cattle" (*behema*), it would seem that the editor took this idea from the reference to the demon's horns further down the sentence. This process of re-embedding an old Hebrew formula of demonic rebuke into an Aramaic magical recipe probably took place sometimes in late antiquity, and the recipe itself kept on being copied well into Genizah times.[17]

---

[15] T-S K 1.123 (unpublished); I am grateful to Edna Engel for the paleographical analysis. Elsewhere, I hope to provide a fuller edition of this bifolium.

[16] Even the *plene* spelling of the Hebrew is reminiscent of the Second Temple period texts, including the Qumran exorcisms.

[17] In passing, I note a possible parallel in two bowls (M123 and M138) in Levene 2003, pp. 89–90, which contain the puzzling formula, פניו פני שיביל קרניו קרני לון. And as Shaul Shaked has kindly

Before leaving this example, we must stress some of its wider implications. That such exorcistic adjurations as are found in 11Q11 circulated beyond the narrow confines of the Qumran community is suggested by the non-sectarian nature of this collection of exorcistic hymns, as has already been noted by several Qumran scholars. But it now seems quite likely that this collection, or at least some of its hymns, or (at the very least!) this specific anti-demonic rebuke, kept on being transmitted well into late antiquity, passed on from one Jewish exorcist to another in an unbroken chain of transmission. Such a scenario would gain some support from the testimony of Origen (or Pseudo-Origen?), who insists that "Solomonic" exorcisms were still in circulation and use in his own time.[18] If this suggestion proves convincing, it would provide a rare glimpse of channels of textual transmission of "apocryphal" literature from the Second Temple period into later times, channels which are neither Christian nor rabbinic. That such channels did exist has been suggested by some scholars (who noted, for example, the use of *Jubilees* 10, or one of its sources, in *Sepher Asaph ha-Rophe*), but the evidence provided by the Jewish magical texts has never been utilized in this discussion. And here, as elsewhere, we find that a careful study of the Jewish magical tradition may shed some light even on aspects of ancient Jewish history which have nothing to do with magic per se, including the very intriguing question of which Second Temple period texts were irretrievably lost in the aftermath of the great destructions of 70 and 135 CE, and which in fact managed to survive. What other surprises lie waiting among the many thousands of magical fragments from the Cairo Genizah only time, and some very patient scholarship, will tell.

One final point. As a rule of thumb, students of Jewish magic may assume that those Genizah magical texts which are written in Palestinian Jewish Aramaic are likely to be early, while those written in Hebrew (like the *sotah* text with which we began this chapter) are likely to be late, unless their Hebrew is filled with the kinds of Greek loanwords we find, for example, in *Sepher ha-Razim*. To this general rule, however, we must now add the proviso that in some rare cases it is even possible that a Hebrew magical text or formula found in the Genizah is a distant copy of a Second Temple period original. And yet, one should not take the other extreme either, and search for the Second Temple origins of any Hebrew section in the Genizah

---

informed me, some of the unpublished bowls contain a phrase which is much closer to our "Who are you" anti-demonic formula. In a forthcoming study, I discuss all the pertinent evidence and its significance for the study of Jewish magic.

[18] See Origen, *In Matthaeum Commentariorum Series* 111 (PG 13.1757) (=GCS 57, pp. 229–30), with Simon 1986, p. 364 and Perrin 2002, pp. 690–91, n. 88.

magical texts.[19] Even within the same four-page fragment which includes our version of the Qumran spell, one finds not only Aramaic sections, but also many Hebrew phrases and expressions (in addition to the biblical verses, which were always cited in Hebrew anyway), which disclose no sign of such an early origin.

This, then, is what is currently known about those elements of late-antique Jewish magic which may be identified as specifically Jewish by virtue of their attested antiquity within the Jewish magical tradition itself. But as this search has yielded only limited results, we must now turn to other features of late-antique Jewish magic which could only be classified as "Jewish."

JEWISH DIVINE AND ANGELIC NAMES, EPITHETS, AND DESCRIPTIONS

Of all the characteristic features of Jewish magic of all periods, the magical powers attributed to the Name of God are perhaps the longest continuous practice. The sanctity and great powers associated with the Tetragrammaton and with God's many other Names certainly go back deep into the First Temple period, and are already there in the Hebrew Bible itself. They are also well attested in the Second Temple period, and were among the most important contributions of the Jewish magicians to their non-Jewish colleagues. Thus, their use in the Jewish magical texts of late antiquity – and of every subsequent period – hardly is surprising, and certainly should be considered one of the most "Jewish" aspects of Jewish magic of all periods. The exact uses of the Name – pronounced, written (in Paleo-Hebrew letters or in the square script, or in some special manner) on the body or on certain implements, or incorporated into longer magical texts – may have changed from one period to the next, but the basic assumption, that there is power to be derived from God's Name(s), remains remarkably consistent. In fact, we may even speak of a cottage industry of divine Names throughout Jewish history, for whereas the Hebrew Bible knows of YHWH, *Ehyeh Asher Ehyeh*, and a few other Names and epithets of God, later Jews developed many different Names and substitutes for the Tetragrammaton. Similarly, when in the Persian and Hellenistic periods there grew a highly complex Jewish angelology, the names of the angels too came to be evoked for magical purposes, as we had more than one occasion

---

[19] For the danger of hasty identifications of "Second Temple period" materials in the Cairo Genizah, cf., for example, Flusser and Safrai 1982 with Fleischer 1991.

to note throughout the present study. And here too, a cottage industry of angelic names churned out more names than even the most conscientious scholar would ever bother to remember.[20]

A catalogue of all the divine and angelic Names and epithets in the ancient and medieval Jewish magical texts, with pointers to the age of the oldest text in which each name appears for the first time, will no doubt be a major contribution to the study of this topic.[21] The production of such a catalogue, however, is hampered not only by the sorry state of much of the textual evidence (especially that scratched on thin metal lamellae), but also by the difficulty of deciding whether a series of meaningless syllables was seen as a Name of God or one of the angels, or as a series of powerful *voces magicae*; in many cases, it is not even clear where one *vox* or name ends, and where the next one begins. And yet, we may safely include among the divine Names used by late-antique Jewish magicians the endless permutations and variations on the Tetragrammaton (such as Y, YY, YYY, YYYY, or combinations such as YH, YHW, the complete Tetragrammaton (YHWH), the word 'HYH (see below) or long series of permutations of the letters ', H, W, and Y). As we noted in the previous chapter, this last phenomenon might be due to influence from the Greco-Egyptian magical tradition, where vowel permutations were extremely common, but even if it is, there is no doubt that the Jewish magicians' fondness for the letters making up the Tetragrammaton and the Name *Ehyeh* played a part in facilitating the spread of this practice within the Jewish magical tradition. In addition to the Tetragrammaton and its derivatives, we find many of the old epithets of the Jewish God, including Adonai, Sabaot, El, Shaddai, *Ehyeh Asher Ehyeh* ("I-am-who-I-am"), or just *Ehyeh*, Holy Holy Holy, the God of the battle-formations (of Israel), the God of retributions, the One who sits upon the Cherubim, the God of the spirits for all flesh, and many others which are commonly attested in the Palestinian amulets, and are just as common in the roughly contemporary Jewish magical bowls from Mesopotamia. On the other hand, what we do not seem to find in these magical texts are many of the divine Names which in later Jewish magic are extremely popular, and especially the so-called Names of twelve, twenty-two, forty-two, and seventy-two letters. Perhaps most intriguing, the Name of forty-two letters ('BG YTZ QR' STN, etc.), so popular in later Jewish magic, is not yet attested in the late-antique metal amulets or in the Babylonian bowls, nor does it seem to appear among those Genizah

---

[20] For these trends see, for example, Olyan 1993 and Bar-Ilan 1997.
[21] Schwab 1897 is, of course, entirely outdated.

magical texts which are likely to be copies of copies of late-antique magical texts.[22] In the next chapter, we shall discuss the rabbis' reference to such names, and their insistence that this was secret knowledge, passed on only to trustworthy colleagues. For the time being, we may note the absence of these Names from the late-antique Jewish magical texts currently at our disposal.

Even more bewildering than the plethora of divine Names is the virtually endless string of angel names found all over the Jewish magical texts of late antiquity. *Sepher ha-Razim*, in listing some 700 different names of angels, may bring this trend to its absurd climax, but the trend itself is visible in numerous other Jewish magical texts of late antiquity. Moreover, the logic behind the production of new angelic names is not always easy to follow. Some of the angels are those known already from the Hebrew Bible and from Second Temple period Jewish texts, such as Michael, Gabriel, Raphael, and so on. Many others receive their names from the activities they perform, usually with a suffix -el – Kavshiel, for example, appears both in the Palestinian amulets and in the Babylonian bowls and is always associated with the root KBŠ, "to subdue," which clearly gave him his name. Other angels, however, derive their names from different sources. In the previous chapter, we noted how in one magical text Abrasax becomes the angel who had once destroyed Sodom and Gomorrah, and how even Helios is sometimes treated as if he were one of God's many angels. But the entry of foreign names into the Jewish angelological system explains only a handful of angel-names, and most others cannot be explained in this manner. As an example, we may note the reference in the aggressive lamella found in the synagogue of Ḥorvat Meroth to "ḤṬWʿ", the angel who was sent before Israel."[23] As this sounds very much like a reference to the angel whose sending was promised by God to Moses, the one who had God's Name within him (Ex 23.20–21), it is quite possible that his name – which is extremely difficult to pronounce even in Hebrew – was somehow produced with the Tetragrammaton in mind, but how this was done remains a mystery. But be this as it may, ḤṬWʿ is just one of many hundreds of new-fangled angelic names, whose endless proliferation is one of the trademarks of ancient Jewish magic. And as we shall see in the next chapter, traces of this process may occasionally be found even in the magical recipes of the Babylonian Talmud.

---

[22] The only possible exception is the Barʿam lamella, which has the sequence QRʿ QRʿ, which Naveh 2001, p. 184 takes for a part of the Name of forty-two letters. For an attempt to find a forty-two letter name (but not the "right" one) in one of the bowls, see Schiffman 1973.

[23] See MSF, A16, ll. 21–22.

THE USE OF THE HEBREW BIBLE

Perhaps the most important feature of Jewish culture in the Greco-Roman world is the constant presence of a distinct body of ancient sacred texts, available both in the Hebrew/Aramaic originals and in their Greek and Aramaic translations. This large corpus served as the basis of virtually every aspect of Jewish culture, and contributed enormously to setting it apart from the other cultures of the Hellenistic world and the Roman or Sasanian empires. One reason for this differentiating role played by the biblical corpus was that it was – as we already noted in Chapter 3 – only rarely read or utilized by the Jews' pagan neighbors, even when it was available in (an admittedly funny) Greek. Thus, it comes as no surprise that one of the major differences between the Jewish magical texts of late antiquity and the pagan ones is the ubiquitous use of the Bible in the former, and its almost complete absence from the latter texts. When compared with ancient Christian magic, on the other hand, Jewish magic becomes much less distinct in this respect, and there is some overlap between the two magical traditions' use of biblical passages (e.g., Psalm 91), and biblical and para-biblical themes (such as the Seal of Solomon), as we already noted in Chapter 3. And yet, a detailed comparison of the Jewish and Christian magical uses of the Hebrew Bible/Old Testament in late antiquity probably would reveal some interesting differences between these two magical traditions.[24] Similarly, a detailed comparison of the uses of the Hebrew Bible in the Palestinian amulets (and the Genizah texts), as against its uses in the Babylonian incantation bowls, might shed some light on the overlap and differences between these two branches of the Jewish magical tradition in late antiquity. Neither comparison, however, shall be attempted in the present survey, nor shall we offer a systematic survey of all the biblical verses cited in ancient Jewish magical texts, as such surveys have already been offered by others. Our modest aim in the present section is to highlight a few important features of the extensive recourse to the Hebrew Bible in the Jewish magical texts, and especially the modification of biblical verses or parts thereof to suit the magicians' specific needs, and the use of biblical and para-biblical stories as *historiolae*, or magical precedents, in the Jewish magical texts of late antiquity.[25]

---

[24] For useful starting-points, and further bibliography, see Crasta 1979 and Judge 1987.
[25] In passing, I note that the use of biblical verses to generate magical names (e.g., by, צרוף, i.e., joining the first or last letters of the words in a given verse), is not yet attested in the late-antique Jewish magical texts known to me, and seems to be a later development; for this technique, see, e.g., Schrire 1966, pp. 123–35, and HAITCG, p. 78, with further bibliography.

The modification of biblical verses

As we already noted throughout the present study, the Jewish magical texts of late antiquity abound in citations of biblical verses, including all the "usual suspects," such as Ex 15.26, Nm 6.24–27, Ps 91, Zec 3.2, and so on, whose magical uses clearly date to the Second Temple period, and in some cases even to the First Temple period. We must note, however, that there never was some closed corpus of biblical verses to be used for magical purposes, and the choice of which verses to incorporate, and how, also depended on the needs and preferences of individual practitioners and the depth of their familiarity with the Hebrew Bible. Moreover, the corpus of biblical verses used by the magicians seems to have grown enormously with the centuries, and probably keeps on growing to this very day.

A bird's-eye view of the biblical verses utilized by the Jewish magicians of late antiquity reveals two main types of verses which they clearly preferred.[26] In most cases, we find verses which bespeak of God's great powers and past deeds, promise health and salvation, refer to the destruction of evil, and so on. The use of such verses for magical purposes would hardly raise an eyebrow, and is amply paralleled by the magical uses of Scriptures in all other "book religions," and by the extensive use of sacred texts in magical rituals throughout antiquity.[27] In some cases, however, the reason for the use of a specific verse is far less obvious, and is due in part to the magicians' own ingenuity. This tends to be ignored by modern readers, who are so used to the sophisticated manipulation and exegesis of biblical verses in rabbinic literature that they are unimpressed by the magicians' simplistic manipulations of biblical verses.[28] And yet, they too deserve to have their efforts recognized, for whereas the rabbis sought to derive *meaning* from biblical verses (including meanings which they never had in their original biblical contexts), the magicians sought to derive *power* from biblical verses for some very specific goals (even when that power was not really there in the original verses). In what follows, we shall focus on a few specific examples, out of a much larger, and mostly unexplored, body of evidence. We must stress, however, that whereas the Babylonian incantation bowls

---

[26] For useful surveys of the biblical verses used in ancient and medieval Jewish magic, see HAITCG, pp. 37–42 and MSF, pp. 22–31; and cf. Trachtenberg 1939, pp. 104–13 and Schrire 1966, pp. 100–03. Levy 2006 provides an extensive survey of the biblical verses and biblical figures used in all the published Genizah magical texts.

[27] See Judge 1987. For a comparative study of the magical uses of sacred texts in antiquity, see Leipoldt and Morenz 1953, pp. 178–89.

[28] For a brief discussion of the magicians' use of biblical verses, but from a different perspective, see Salzer forthcoming.

often cite biblical verses in a corrupt or approximate manner, apparently as a result of citation from memory, the "western" magical texts to be examined below attest to a different phenomenon. Here, many "errors" in citation are neither aural nor accidental, but deliberate, recurrent, and pregnant with new meanings. Let us look at three specific examples:

(a) One verse which recurs in anti-abortion spells is Psalm 116.6, "God preserves the simpletons; I was brought low and he helped me."[29] The antiquity of this usage is attested by a late-antique bronze amulet which was intended to protect the fetus in the womb of one Surah daughter of Sarah against premature delivery, and which cites the first half of the verse, and perhaps also a part of the second. Its continuous use for such purposes is well attested in several Genizah magical recipes for similar purposes, which cite the verse in its entirety.[30] Cynical readers may wish to comment that God should indeed guard the simpletons who make use of such amulets, and note that "a simpleton will believe anything" (Prv 14.15), has often been cited by rationalist critics of magic and superstition. But the reason for the appearance of this specific verse in anti-abortion amulets lies in the late-antique pronunciation of Hebrew and Aramaic, and especially its weakened gutturals. In late-antique Hebrew, the word for "simpletons" (*pta'im*) and for "openings" (*ptaḥim*) were virtually indistinguishable, and if God guards the "openings," He would also guard that opening of Sarah daughter of Surah from which her fetus might prematurely escape. And so, a verse that had nothing to do with magic, or with miscarriages, became, by virtue of the phonetic resemblance of two unrelated words, a means for expressing the wish (for it certainly is not a command!) that God would save the poor patient's baby.

(b) Moving from anti-abortion rituals to their exact opposite, the desire to aid a woman having trouble in delivery, we find the creative use of Ex 11.8.[31] In the original biblical verse, Moses warns Pharaoh that God is about to kill all the first-born of Egypt, "And all your servants here shall come down to me, and bow to me, and say, Come out you and all the people at your feet, and then I shall come out; and he (Moses) came out from before Pharaoh in great wrath." Needless to say, this verse has much to do with the delivery from Egypt, and nothing to do with the delivery of babies, but the magicians needed only a part of the verse, "come out you and all the people at your feet, and then I shall come out, and he came out," which they now turned upon the dilatory baby. Even the biblical expression "all the

---

[29] For the following example, see the excellent analysis in MSF, p. 105, and Naveh 1996, p. 457.
[30] MSF, A30, l. 4; G18 (T-S K 1.143), p. 17, l. 8, p. 19, ll. 2–3.
[31] See MSF, G9 (T-S K 1.15), 1, 7–10; MTKG I, 7 (T-S NS 322.10) 1a/8 and 1b/29–30.

people at your feet" acquired new meanings when applied to the parturient woman in her birthing position, thus increasing the efficacy of this potent spell. And in some cases, it was thought sufficient merely to cite the verbal forms found in this verse – "come out, I shall come out, and he came out" – for the verse to be effective.[32] And here, too, a verse which acquired a specific connotation at least by Genizah times, and probably already in late antiquity, is used in this context well into modern Jewish magic, and probably to this very day.[33]

(c) In the aggressive magical recipes of the Cairo Genizah, one repeatedly finds a creative use of Lv 6.6, which often appears in Aramaic recipes which seem to be copies of copies of late-antique models.[34] What is interesting in this case is that the original verse – "An eternal fire shall burn upon the altar, it shall not be quenched" – referred to the eternal fire burning in the desert Tabernacle and later in the Temple, and to the priestly obligation to keep it burning. But in the magicians' texts, the word "altar" was replaced by the victim's name, and the wish was uttered that "An eternal fire shall burn upon NN, it shall not be quenched." Altering a single word can go a long way in transforming an innocent biblical injunction into a magically harmful spell, and in some medieval and later Jewish magical texts we find long series of biblical verses mentioning fire or fever, all modified so as to send fire and fever upon a hapless victim. Once the technique was developed, it could be used *ad infinitum et ad absurdum*.[35]

Such examples could easily be multiplied, but at present our main aim is to point to their wider significance. For the Jewish magicians of late antiquity, the Hebrew Bible was not a closed book, nor was it merely a treasure-house of powerful verses to be used in preset contexts. Rather, it was a book to be mined for more and more useful verses, and when all the obvious candidates became too well known and well used, new verses

---

[32] See, for example, MSF, G16 (T-S K 1.91) 2, 2, missed by the editors.

[33] See, for example, the quick-birth amulet T-S NS 172.94 (unpublished), or the recipe in the late magical text JTSL ENA 2699.1 (unpublished), or the *Sepher Raziel* amulets produced by Schrire 1966, pp. 62–63, all of which use this verse (and cf. Trachtenberg 1939, p. 201). As Nissim Hamoi told me, it is still used in a similar recipe in Abraham Hamawi's (nineteenth-century) *Yemalet Naphsho* (printed in the Backal edition of Hamawi's *Abi'ah Hidot*, p. 226; see also p. 166). See also Thompson 1907, p. 168, no. 21h.

[34] See AMB, G6 (T-S K 1.73) p. 3, ll. 1–2; MTKG III, 56 (T-S Ar. 44.26) 1b/5–6 (the same recipe also appears in AS 142.228 + NS 322.53 + AS 142.23, published in Bohak 2005); MTKG III, 60 (T-S K 1.120) 1a/13–14; this verse also appears in aggressive recipes in many unpublished Genizah fragments, including T-S Ar. 14.6, which subjects quite a few biblical verses to such creative transformations for aggressive purposes, and T-S NS 152.83, where it is slightly garbled. It is well attested in modern Jewish magical recipe-books – e.g., Thompson 1906, p. 98, no. 7.

[35] E.g., MTKG III, 60 (T-S K 1.120) 1a/10–18; JTSL ENA 3532.1 (published in Marmorstein 1925); and cf. the previous note.

were added, verses which originally had nothing magical about them, but now acquired some very specific magical uses. These processes tell us much about the Jewish education of at least some of the magical practitioners of late antiquity. And when we note how such creative innovations entered the bloodline of the Jewish magical tradition and survived all the way to the modern period, we realize that it is not just the "Jewishness" of late-antique magic that we are dealing with, but also its professionalization and scribalization, which enabled later generations in all corners of the world to rely on the achievements of their late-antique predecessors.

The use of biblical and parabiblical historiolae

One of the commonest features of many magical traditions is the recurrent use of *historiolae*, that is, of mythical stories and precedents which are narrated or alluded to in order to tap their hidden powers for a specific magical ritual.[36] Ancient Jewish magic also displays a frequent use of this technique, and it is mainly the Hebrew Bible which provides the mythical precedents which the Jewish magicians used in their magical rituals. There are quite a few interesting examples of the use of biblical and parabiblical myths (such as, for example, that of the Fallen Angels), in late-antique and medieval Jewish magic, but in what follows we shall focus on one example only, the extensive use of the biblical story of Sodom and Gomorrah. That this biblical scene, in which God destroys whole cities with fire and sulfur, had much use in Jewish (and Christian) aggressive magic, both "eastern" and "western," hardly is surprising. In the Babylonian incantation bowls, we note such phrases as "I will curse you by the curse which fell on Mt. Ḥermon and on Leviathan the monster and on Sodom and Gomorrah," and frequent adjurations such as "In the name of Gabriel and Michael, you two angels which the Lord sent to overturn Sodom and Gomorrah, you overturn NN."[37] In the "western" sources, we may note the sulfur-based Greek erotic recipe from PGM XXXVI, cited and discussed in Chapter 3, and the Aramaic erotic recipe from the Cairo Genizah which invokes Abrasax, who overturned Sodom and Gomorrah, which we cited in Chapter 4. To these two examples, and to the Talmudic recipe which we shall cite in Chapter 6, many more examples may be added, including a recipe in

---

[36] For useful surveys of this technique, see Podemann Sørensen 1984; Bozóky 1992; Frankfurter 1995.
[37] Montgomery 1913, no. 2 (and cf. no. 27) and Gordon 1941, p. 350. For other examples, see, e.g., Segal 2000, bowls 041A and 044A. And cf. Levene 2003, bowl M156, ll. 10–11, where the demon is threatened that it shall be destroyed "just as mighty cities were destroyed, upon which were sent Nuriel, Raphael and M[ichael]."

Sepher ha-Razim to destroy a fortified wall so that "it shall be overturned like the overturning of Sodom and Gomorrah."[38] And in a Genizah collection of aggressive magical recipes which bears many signs of its late-antique origins, Sodom and Gomorrah appear in two different recipes.[39] In one, an "incantation for (i.e., to send?) an impure spirit" begins with a series of six or seven magic "words" which are followed by

<A> You holy angels whom God had sent in wrath and rage [upon Sodom] and upon Gomorrah and upon Adamah and upon Zeboim [and upon Zoar?] that you shall overturn them, and you overturned them, so shall you over[turn] the hearth (of the victim) as(?) I am standing before the smoke [ ] the hearth, Amen Amen Selah.

Several recipes later, we find Sodom and Gomorrah once again, this time in a much more elaborate recipe. Here the user is instructed to take some cooking-water, a certain root, and the urine of a donkey(?), of a black bull, and of himself, and say over the concoction seven times the following adjuration:

<A> You are the *dynamis* of the great God, you are the spirit of the world (with?) which God overturned Sodom and Gomorrah, Adama and Zeboim, so shall you overturn and uproot and exile NN from his home and from his place.

The long adjuration continues with an invocation of demons of destruction, but for our own enquiry the first part is the important one. How exactly our practitioner came up with the equation of his malodorous liquids with the *dynamis* (the Greek word for "power") of God remains unclear; presumably, he had no access to sulfur, and thought that urine was quite as smelly, and could serve as a proper substitute. But his insistence that the concoction he was manipulating was the same material which God had once rained upon Sodom and Gomorrah, and that it should now perform the same deed against his own victim, sounds very much like what we encountered in PGM XXXVI. Here too, a substance which lies at hand is equated with a mythical substance (or force) and sent on its way, to perform a service analogous to what it had performed in the distant past. And the assumption behind these rituals, namely, that what worked *in illo tempore* could be reactivated now, is manifest in the many other manipulations of biblical stories as magical *historiolae* to be found in late-antique and medieval Jewish magic. These still require a fuller analysis, but this will not

---

[38] See ShR I/75–76 (p. 70 Margalioth). See also MTKG II, 47 (T-S NS 160.18) 2a/3–4, where the victim's name is inserted into Gn 19.24.

[39] See Bodleian Heb. a3.31 (unpublished). I am grateful to the Bodleian Library for excellent photographs of this fragment, which I hope to publish elsewhere.

be carried out here, as we must turn to other aspects of the "Jewishness" of ancient Jewish magic.

MAGIC IN THE SYNAGOGUE

Thus far, we have focused our attention on specific elements within the Jewish magical texts and practices which may clearly be identified as "Jewish," and as stemming from within the magicians' ancestral heritage. It is now time to turn to a somewhat different question concerning the Jewish magical texts, namely, the relations between these texts and other spheres of Jewish cultural activity at the time. The need to ask this question stems from the fact that one of the major problems facing the quest for the "Jewishness" of the Jewish magical tradition is that the period which interests us here – from Bar Kokhba's failed revolt to the Muslim conquest – was a period of great Jewish creativity, which saw the rise or development of many new features of Jewish culture. One such development, namely the emergence of the synagogue – an institution whose roots lie in the Second Temple period – as the central location of Jewish communal worship, raises interesting questions about the possible relations between our magical texts and the synagogues of late antiquity, the subject of the present section. In the following sections, we shall try to examine the relations between the Jewish magical texts and other important strands of late-antique Jewish culture, namely the Jewish mystical tradition(s) of the time and the rabbinic culture of late antiquity.

One of the striking features of late-antique Jewish magic is the apparent connection between some magical practices and the world of the synagogue.[40] In exploring these connections, we shall focus on two clusters of magical activities – the use of the synagogue as a place of healing and a depository for some amulets, and the use of the synagogue for the placing of aggressive (and, presumably, secret) spells against the community by one of its members. Let us look at each of these clusters of magical activities in some detail.

The synagogue as a place of healing

A common feature of the Jewish synagogues of all periods is their use as places of healing, a by-product both of their communal function and of

---

[40] For previous discussions of this issue, see Cohen 1987, p. 168; Naveh 1989, pp. 302–03; Fine 1997, pp. 73–74, 116–17, 145–46; Levine 2000, pp. 274, 383–84, 428, 444–45; Mock 2003.

their religious sanctity. On the one hand, the presence in the synagogue (especially on the Sabbaths) of many Jews and some non-Jews gave much occasion for encounters between the sick and those who would heal them, and for the performing of such healing miracles as are already well attested in the New Testament.[41] That such encounters and healings continued in later periods too seems quite certain, and we may note how John Chrysostom, writing in Antioch in the 380s CE, repeatedly complains that Christians go to the Jewish synagogues in order to be healed by the Jews by means of incantations and amulets.[42] To this type of "outsider" evidence, some "insider" evidence must be added, which may cast additional light on the issue of healing in late-antique synagogues. In one late-antique synagogue, at Ḥorvat Maʿon (near the modern Kibbuẓ Nirim), nineteen metal lamellae were found, either rolled or folded, some still displaying fragments of the fabric in which they were wrapped or the original threads by which they were suspended. All these amulets were excavated in the apse of the synagogue, not far from where the ark of the Torah once stood, and it is possible that they were once stored in a small pit which may still be seen in the floor of the synagogue's apse, and which may have been covered by the wooden ark and the Torah-scrolls it once contained.[43] Of this amuletic hoard – which may have been much larger, given rumors that members of Kibbuẓ Nirim have since found more amulets in the synagogue's ruins – only three items have been opened, deciphered, and published.[44] All three are healing and protective amulets made for named (and apparently unrelated) individuals, and their presence in the synagogue therefore is quite unexpected, as such amulets would normally have been worn around the patients' bodies.[45] In explaining this apparent anomaly, three main types of interpretation are open before us. Taking one of these amulets as our example, we could perhaps argue that when Natrun, the daughter of Sarah, suffered from horrible migraines, an amulet produced to rid her of the demon *kephalargia* (the Greek word for "headache," as noted in Chapter 4) was placed beside, or underneath, the Torah-ark of the local synagogue, in the implicit assumption that this would be a good place in which to invoke the angels Barqiel, Uriel, and Milḥamiel to do the job.[46] Having noted, in

---

[41] E.g., Mk 1.21–34; 3.1–5, etc.
[42] John Chrysostom, *Against the Jews* 8.5.6 (PG 48.935) and 8.8.7–9 (PG 48.940–41).
[43] For the archeological context, see S. Levy *et al.* 1960, p. 7 (S. Levy), and pp. 14–18 (L. Y. Rahmani).
[44] See AMB, A11–13.
[45] Caches of amulets for a single person or a family are not unknown elsewhere (e.g., Müller-Kessler 1999a, p. 198), but caches of amulets for unrelated individuals seem more surprising. For a possible pagan parallel, see Davoli 2004, p. 36.
[46] See AMB, A11.

Chapter 1, how the sacred implements of God's service were utilized in Jewish magical rituals from a very early period, we would hardly be surprised to find late-antique Jews using the inherent power of the Torah, and of the ark in which it was stored, to transmit requests of healing to the Almighty, or to "charge" them with sacred power.[47] As illustrative comparanda, we might note the paper notes with requests, often for specific individuals, placed between the stones of the Wailing Wall in present-day Jerusalem, or those placed near the Torah scroll or Torah-ark of some modern Jewish synagogues (not to mention those placed on the tombs of great Hasidic masters).[48] It must be stressed, however, that such a practice runs counter to everything we know about the use of amulets in antiquity, since these usually were kept next to the patients whom they were supposed to protect and not next to a "source of power."[49] Moreover, this type of explanation would fail to elucidate why the amulet remained in the synagogue after Natrun was healed of her migraines, or after she died, since in both cases the amulet would no longer be needed. Thus, while this line of interpretation cannot be ruled out, it does not seem very plausible.

A second, and more likely, interpretation for the presence of healing and apotropaic amulets in the synagogue would be that such finds reflect the dedicatory practices of those patients who felt that the amulets indeed had done their job and were no longer needed. It was only *after* the migraines disappeared and the amulet went out of use that Natrun brought it to the synagogue, and placed it, by way of some publicly sanctioned dedication ritual, next to the Torah-ark, as a sign of her respect and gratitude.[50] However, it must also be noted that one of the Nirim amulets, made for Esther, daughter of Tatis, was not manufactured in order to alleviate a specific illness, but is a "multi-purpose" apotropaic device.[51] It is therefore hard to imagine when exactly it was deemed to have fulfilled its aim and be no longer needed, unless it was after Esther's death. In such circumstances, it could hardly have been brought to the synagogue as a sign of pride in its great efficacy.

While the possibility that the amulets were placed in the synagogue as part of a post-success dedication certainly seems enticing, another possibility might prove even more likely, namely, that used and no-longer-needed

---

[47] Cf. also Rebecca's action in the Targumim to Gn 25.22 (discussed by Fine 2002, pp. 76–77) with AMB, A12, an amulet to protect the fetus in its mother's belly.
[48] For these comparanda, see Dauphin 1998, vol. I, p. 220, n. 219; Sabar 2000, pp. 175–76.
[49] See, for example, Kropatscheck 1907, pp. 33–35.
[50] For possible pagan parallels, see Valerius Maximus 2.5.6 with Dickie 2001, p. 130; Ammianus 22.13.3 with Turcan 2003, p. 410.
[51] See AMB, A13.

amulets were placed near (or maybe even under?) the Torah-ark not as a dedication, but as a kind of *genizah*, that is, the discarding of texts known to contain divine names and biblical verses in a manner that would not bring about their desecration. In later periods, there is much evidence for the presence of such *genizot* within synagogues, the most famous example being the Cairo Genizah, and much evidence that amulets too were often placed in such *genizot*.[52] Following this line of reasoning, we could suggest that originally the amulets were placed there along with many other texts, such as used biblical scrolls and related writings, but as these were all written on vellum or papyrus they all decayed long ago, and only the amulets – or, rather, only those amulets which were incised on durable metals – happened to survive.[53] This practice, in other words, may have had nothing to do with magic per se or with the effectiveness of amuletic devices, and much to do with the intricacies of the Jews' religious respect for the written word in general, and especially for sacred Names and biblical verses. We should add, however, that this explanation would raise an additional problem, namely, that the apse of the Ma'on synagogue would hardly have had enough space to serve as a long-term *genizah* for the community's used texts, and would have had to be emptied to another location on quite a regular basis. Why the amulets were not removed would remain an open question.

While the choice between these three interpretations, and others besides, must remain tentative, and will have to be re-examined in light of additional evidence (including, of course, those Nirim amulets which have not yet been published), one thing seems certain, namely, that some amulets were placed within the synagogue, and that this probably was a socially accepted custom, at least in some times and places. As historians, we should be grateful for this fact, for it has assured us the preservation of a large cache of amulets from a single location; we should also wonder why similar caches have not turned up in other ancient synagogues – over a hundred of which have been carefully examined by several generations of archeologists – and consider the possibility that the custom lurking behind the Nirim cache was just a local practice.[54] But be this as it may, this practice certainly provides one more confirmation for our contention throughout these chapters that the

---

[52] See Beit-Arié 1996. For amulets and *genizah*-practices, see bt Shab 61b and 115a–b. Students of modern Jewish amulets still search contemporary *genizot* for some of their most interesting sources.

[53] One also wonders whether the placing of used amulets in a *genizah* was only limited to those written on the cheaper metals, while gold and silver amulets were recycled for their metal.

[54] We should also note that while Torah shrines have been a favorite topic of late-antique Jewish art, the dozens of representations of such arks – on mosaics, frescoes, gilded glass, or carved stone – provide no clues as to the presence of any amulets next to these sacred objects.

use of amulets was common and normative among ancient Jews. Many Jews must have worn their amulets in the open (just like many contemporary non-Jews), must have brought them to their synagogue as well, and in some circumstances even left them there in a way that apparently was fully accepted by other members of their congregation.

Before leaving the Nirim synagogue, and to remind ourselves why *we* see amulets as belonging in the realm of magic, we may note that the amulet of Natrun daughter of Sarah happens to be full of those non-Jewish elements which we surveyed in the previous chapter, for the practitioner who inscribed her amulet invoked not only Barqiel and Uriel, but also Erechsiel, Hyessemigadon, and the SKSK DWKWN DWKWN formula. This, then, is how the Babylonian deity Ereshkigal, adopted by the Greco-Egpytian magicians of the Roman Empire as the *vox magica* Erechsigal and borrowed from them by their Jewish colleagues, was slightly Judaized into Erechsiel and found her proper place near the Torah-ark of a sixth-century synagogue in the Northern Negev.

Aggressive magic in the synagogue

While the presence of apotropaic and healing amulets in synagogues may seem quite natural, the use of the synagogues for aggressive magical purposes might seem more jarring. And yet, it so happens that the three provenanced aggressive Jewish magical artifacts from late-antique Palestine published thus far have all been found in or near a synagogue, and that this practice actually is attested in at least one recipe-book as well.[55] As we already noted in Chapter 3, both the Meroth synagogue and the small synagogue in Barʿam produced bronze lamellae with spells intended to "muzzle" the opponents of the clients who procured them.[56] In this case, the choice of the synagogue as the location for depositing the artifacts probably has less to do with the structure's sanctity and more to do with its use as a "community center" – since the whole community gathered there (and also did much of its gossiping, politicking, and brawling there), it was a good place in which to subdue the evil tongues, and perhaps also the evil spells, of one's Jewish opponents. Thus, while the fully preserved lamella from Meroth does not mention the synagogue explicitly, its findspot, "in the fill between the stones underneath the threshold of the eastern entrance," clearly shows that it was buried there on purpose, and in a deliberately clandestine manner.[57] Its major request

---

[55] For what follows, see also Naveh 1985.
[56] The texts are MSF, A16 and Naveh 2001. See Chapter 3, nn. 27 and 29.
[57] See Ilan 1989, p. 29 and Ilan 1998, p. 270.

is that just as God had subdued all of nature by his great powers, "so will *the people of this town* be subdued and broken and fallen before Yose son of Zenobia."[58] Similarly, the Barʿam lamella, found inside the foundations of the synagogue's internal stylobate, "near the threshold" and "under the corner of a large stone," calls for the silencing of all those who speak against Yudan son of Nonna.[59] In both cases, it is clear that the named individuals had turned to a professional magician, who produced a lamella with an aggressive spell to silence and subdue their opponents; the lamella was then buried in a clandestine manner, inside the walls or underneath a threshold in the local synagogue. And that the practice was not limited to Upper Galilee, where these two artifacts happen to have been found, seems clear from a related recipe in the *Sword of Moses*:

> And if you want your fear to be upon people, write on a lead lamella from X to Y and bury it in a synagogue, in the western direction.[60]

In passing, we may note that while the Barʿam lamella was found inside the western stylobate within the synagogue, the Meroth one was found under the synagogue's eastern threshold, and that both synagogue aggressive artifacts were inscribed on bronze, and not on lead. Once again, we see the great fluidity of the magical tradition, with the practitioners sometimes following their recipes quite closely, and at other times changing their recipes or improvising upon them. In this specific instance, we also see how the Greek practice of writing lead *defixiones* and burying them in relevant locations (including the place where the intended victim(s) might be found) is gradually transformed into a Jewish practice of writing aggressive spells on bronze lamellae (and, presumably, other writing surfaces) and burying those which were intended to "muzzle" the entire community inside the community's synagogue. Moreover, this type of magical praxis allows us a glimpse of some of the tensions and rivalries within the Jewish communities of late-antique Palestine, and the clandestine world of magical artifacts and rituals utilized within these contexts. For unlike the amulets, whose deposition near the Torah-ark of the Nirim synagogue clearly was sanctioned by the congregating community, the artifacts we are now dealing with were hidden from the eyes of all but those who buried them in the synagogue's

---

[58] MSF, A16, ll. 17–20. For *ʿama de-hada qarta*, cf. the synagogue's popular appellation as *beit ʿam*, condemned in bt Shab 32a, and such synagogue inscriptions as Naveh 1978, no. *83 (*bene qarta*). In the lamella from Barʿam, the line which should have contained the reference to the community (l. 6) is badly mutilated. Similar expressions appear in T-S K 1.72 (unpublished) and T-S NS 322.19 (unpublished).
[59] For the findspot, see Aviam 2001, p. 163, and Aviam 2002, p. 120.
[60] *Ḥarba de-Moshe* no. 105 (p. 44 Harari = p. 86 Gaster).

walls or underneath its floor. This is also why they are not found in groups – like the nineteen amulets from the Nirim synagogue – but one at a time, and in different locations.

In addition to these two bronze lamellae, one more artifact must be mentioned here, namely, the erotic spell from Ḥorvat Rimmon, also described in Chapter 3.[61] As it was found within the enclosure which encompassed the local synagogue, it is quite possible that its preservation not far from the synagogue attests to the presence there of the magician who produced it, which would certainly corroborate some of John Chrysostom's claims on the proliferation of magical practitioners around the Jewish synagogues. In this case, however, it would be prudent to wait for further evidence, since the later Jewish magical recipes which parallel the Ḥorvat Rimmon "finished product" never mention what must be done with the unbaked clay on which the erotic spell is to be written, apart from the fact that it has to be burned in a fire. And as the Rimmon sherds were found in the close vicinity of two baking ovens, it might well be that it was the ovens, and not the synagogue, which determined their actual location.[62]

Other synagogue-related magical activities?

In addition to these two clusters of magical activities connected with late-antique synagogues, several other isolated pieces of data may be adduced here.[63] Reading the Babylonian incantation bowls, we are struck by some bowls' attempt to "overturn" various curses, including those of "men and women who stand in the open field and in the village and on the mountain and in the temple and in the synagogue," a phrase which may be construed as purely rhetorical and stereotyped, but might also point to the pagan temples and the Jewish synagogues of late-antique Mesopotamia as places where specific individuals might be cursed.[64] In a different mode, we may note how the rabbis of late antiquity develop a ritual for the "amelioration of dreams" – that is, to avert the evil consequences of an ominous dream – a

---

[61] The text is AMB, A10. See above, Chapter 3, n. 30.
[62] For the recipes, see Chapter 3, nn. 30 and 225. For the exact find-spot of the Ḥorvat Rimmon sherds, see Kloner 1989, pp. 46–47.
[63] I have left aside the evidence for the use of synagogues (even by non-Jews) as a place in which to take binding oaths (see, e.g., Levine 2000, p. 274), which probably need not be classified as belonging in the realm of magic.
[64] AMB, B2, ll. 4–5 and Segal 2000, Bowls 001A, l. 5; 002A, l. 6; 066A, l. 2 (and cf. 039A, ll. 2 and 8; 041, l. 11). I leave aside the Christian claims that the Jews cursed Jesus and his followers in their synagogue liturgy, or the Muslim claim that the Jews of Medina cursed Malik b. al-Aglam in their synagogue, which probably belong more in the realm of religion (e.g., *Birkat ha-Minim*) than in the world of magic.

How "Jewish" was ancient Jewish magic? 321

ritual which takes place inside the synagogue at the hour of prayer.[65] Moving to a different region, we find John Chrysostom's bitter complaint that too many Christians go to the synagogue of Daphne (a suburb of Antioch, where a synagogue of great antiquity was still in use in the fourth century CE), including an obscure reference to those who go there for the sake of incubation, near a pit called "Matrona."[66] Whether such a practice indeed was common in Daphne's synagogue, and whether it was practiced in other synagogues as well, is very hard to say, but the availability of a biblical precedent, and the ubiquity of such practices in late-antique temples and churches, make that possibility seem quite likely.[67] Similarly, in a Genizah recipe-book which bears marks of the late origins of some of its recipes, a recipe is found for a ritual to overcome the forgetting of one's knowledge of Torah, which consists of writing an adjuration and burying it in the synagogue, under the Torah-ark.[68] This ritual is probably medieval, and the same is true of the reworked *sotah* ceremony discussed at the beginning of this chapter, which enjoins taking dust from underneath the Torah-ark, or of the instructions in some *goralot* (*Sortes*) handbooks to perform the lot-casting in the synagogue.[69] And yet, the practices reflected in these medieval recipes – to which many more examples could be added – may have been common in earlier periods too. Being the most sacred spot in the entire synagogue, and housing the text with which, as many Jews believed, the world itself had been created by God, the Torah-ark would have been a natural place for tapping the numinous for practical aims.[70] It therefore seems quite likely that further research in this direction would provide other examples of the place of the synagogue in some types of Jewish magical rituals from late antiquity onwards.

The last type of synagogue-related magical activity to be mentioned here is the extensive archeological evidence for the apparent use of various apotropaic signs, symbols, and rituals to protect the synagogue and all those who enter it. Being a place in which large groups of people gathered together,

---

[65] See bt Ber 55b (and note that the ritual offered in pt Ber 5.1 (9a) is much less public).
[66] See John Chrysostom, *Against the Jews* 1.6.2–3 (PG 48.852) and 1.8.1 (PG 48.855), with Levine 2000, p. 384.
[67] Biblical precedents: 1 Kgs 3.5 // 2 Chr 1.7. For incubation in antiquity, see Deubner 1900 (including the claims that Jews too would come for incubation at the martyrium of Cosmas and Damian); pagan temples: Frankfurter 1998, pp. 162–69.
[68] MTKG III, 61 (T-S K 1.162) 1b/40–45; see Naveh 1989, p. 303. See also MSF, G22 (T-S Misc. 27.4.11), p. 2, l. 3, where *arona* probably refers not to a regular "chest" but to *aron ha-qodesh* (and cf. bt Shab 32a). For other examples, see Wandrey 2004, pp. 203 and 222.
[69] See Burkhardt 2003, p. 139. See also JTS ENA 3051.2 (unpublished): "and if you want your friend not to die, write on (i.e., for) his name and hide it in the synagogue," etc.
[70] For the magical use of Torah scrolls and Torah-shrines in later periods, see Sabar 2000.

and therefore were collectively exposed to various dangers, as well as a place which contained sensitive and expensive appurtenances but remained unutilized most nights and some days of the week, synagogues had to be protected against the evil eye, malevolent demons, thieves, earthquakes, lightning, the spells of pernicious sorcerers (including – as we saw – spells placed in the synagogue itself!), and a host of other dangers. The means used to protect the synagogues seem to have been extremely varied, and a full survey of these would require a separate monograph. In Dura Europus, for example, 2 of some 234 tiles which were recovered from the synagogue's ceiling display the "much suffering eye" motif, which was used in Dura and throughout the Roman empire as a protective symbol against the evil eye.[71] In several other synagogues, entrances and other strategic locations were decorated with a "Hercules knot," a symbol much beloved throughout the ancient world and often considered to be endowed with apotropaic value.[72] And in several synagogues throughout Palestine coin hoards have been found which clearly were buried in the synagogue's foundations as a part of the building process, probably for apotropaic reasons. In all these cases, however, we would be hard pressed to draw a clear line between "magic" and "religion," and to classify such symbols and practices in the former category. And yet, a thorough survey of all the scattered evidence might show that here, too, Jews were adopting non-Jewish magical technologies and adapting them to their own specific needs, or replacing them with more "Jewish" substitutes.

JEWISH MAGIC AND JEWISH MYSTICISM IN LATE ANTIQUITY

From the magical texts and practices connected with the late-antique synagogue we turn to what is potentially the most controversial issue confronting the study of ancient Jewish magic, namely the complex relations between Jewish magic and Jewish mysticism in late antiquity. A thorough analysis of this issue may shed much light both on the "Jewishness" of ancient Jewish magic and on the social contexts and contacts of those who practiced it. Moreover, this venue seems especially promising in light of the intuitive assumption that magic and mysticism might somehow be intimately connected, and the observation that in other times and places, including the medieval and early-modern Jewish world, magic and

---

[71] Goodenough 1953–68, vol. II, pp. 238–41; IJO III, Syr128; for this motif, see also Bonner 1950, pp. 97–99 and Engemann 1975.
[72] See, for example, Urman and Flesher 1998, pl. 32b.

mystical traditions sometimes went hand in hand.[73] However, before embarking on this quest we must stress its limited scope, for in raising the question we do not intend to embark on a phenomenological investigation of the relations between mysticism and magic in general, or a comparative study of the relations between mysticism and magic within various cultural traditions in different stages of their history. Our question is culture-specific and period-specific, and the answers to be broached here claim no validity beyond the narrow confines of ancient Jewish culture.

A second point which must be borne in mind is that any serious examination of ancient Jewish mysticism must first confront Gershom Scholem's lasting impact on the study of every aspect of the Jewish mystical tradition. So convinced was the young Scholem that previous generations of scholars have misconstrued and misrepresented Jewish mysticism – and especially its greatest achievement, the Kabbalah – that he devoted his entire academic career to that previously neglected topic. Not only did his efforts produce extensive philological analyses and historical reconstructions of virtually every aspect and manifestation of the Jewish mystical tradition, they also produced a deeply entrenched scholarly paradigm on the centrality of the mystical impulse within Jewish religiosity, and Jewish culture, from antiquity to the present. One sad by-product of the unusual history of this academic field is that whereas nineteenth-century scholars tended to downplay the importance of Jewish mysticism and Jewish magic, Scholem's towering achievement has turned Jewish mysticism into a major field of Jewish Studies, while the study of Jewish magic still lags far behind. The stone rejected by the former builders is now a cornerstone of Jewish Studies, and even those scholars who set out to refute most of Scholem's basic claims often did so from premises and starting-points that were entirely his own.[74] Some students of Jewish mysticism followed his basic assumption, that Jewish magic was a by-product, not to say the ugly step-daughter, of Jewish mysticism.[75] Others broke loose from this paradigm, but still insisted that Jewish magic and Jewish mysticism are closely related phenomena, and examined the place of magic within the mystical tradition without first looking at Jewish magic as an independent, and vibrant, cultural tradition of its own. Even when stressing the need to study Jewish

---

[73] For surveys of previous scholarship on the relations between ancient Jewish mysticism and magic, see esp. Harari 1998, pp. 84–98; Lesses 1998, pp. 24–52. See also Schäfer 1993; Gruenwald 1995, pp. 39–42.

[74] For this common fallacy, see Fischer 1970, p. 28.

[75] For Scholem's attitudes towards Jewish magic, see Schäfer 1993, esp. pp. 59–64, and Bar-Levav 2003, pp. 390–93. For the persistence of such views, see, for example, Kanarfogel 2000, p. 29, on Jewish magic "as an offshoot or an allied field of Jewish mysticism."

magic in its own right, they rarely turned this observation into a concrete program of study.⁷⁶ Thus, only the ongoing publication of ancient Jewish magical texts and artifacts and the study of the Jewish magical tradition in its own right, might enable a fresh examination of the relations between Jewish magic and Jewish mysticism in antiquity from a perspective that does not implicitly assume the temporal or cultural priority of the latter.

But having said that, one more difficulty must be raised here, the gravest one of all. In theory, the study of the relations between Jewish magic and Jewish mysticism in antiquity should be based on a detailed comparison of both corpora of ancient texts. When we set out to practice this theory, however, we soon realize that unlike our knowledge of ancient Jewish magic, our knowledge of ancient Jewish mysticism is entirely dependent on medieval copies and recensions of the older materials, with no "insider" textual evidence dating to late antiquity itself. For whereas the Jewish magicians, at least from late antiquity onwards, produced many written texts and "finished products," some of which happened to be written on durable materials or in dry climates and a small percentage of which thus happened to survive, the Jewish mystics of the time did not produce any written artifacts on durable surfaces, and none of their original writings survived. Thus, all the late-antique Jewish mystical texts to which we now have access are found in medieval manuscripts, edited and copied by medieval scribes and mystics to suit their own needs, and providing no direct access to their late-antique textual ancestors, if they had any.⁷⁷ Similarly, though perhaps for different reasons, while rabbinic literature provides much evidence concerning the magical practices of the rabbinic period, and those used by the rabbis themselves (and both shall be discussed in Chapter 6), it has disturbingly little to say about the mystical traditions and practices of its time. Whether we must interpret this absence as a sign of the paucity of interest in mystical practices in the rabbis' world, or as a deliberate attempt to leave certain things hushed, has been hotly debated among scholars, but makes little difference for our present discussion.⁷⁸ What does matter is that not only do we lack any "insider" evidence for the Jewish mystical tradition of late antiquity, even the "outsider" evidence is scanty and patchy at best. Thus, the comparison of the Jewish magical and mystical traditions in late

---

⁷⁶ See Gruenwald 1980, pp. 225–26; Idel 1995, p. 65, and Idel 1997, pp. 200 and 205.

⁷⁷ This problem has often been noted by students of Jewish mysticism; see, for example, Schäfer 1983; Dan 1986 and 1993b; Herrmann 1993.

⁷⁸ For the rabbinic references to mystical lore, see Scholem 1960; Urbach 1967; Halperin 1980 and 1988; Chernus 1982; Gruenwald 1994.

How "Jewish" was ancient Jewish magic? 325

antiquity is fraught with difficulties, and must be carried out with great caution. Perhaps the greatest difficulty lies in the fact that magical and mystical texts were often copied side by side in the Middle Ages, so that in many of our medieval manuscripts mystical texts and magical recipes sometimes follow each other, or even flow into each other, in seemingly seamless succession.[79] In some cases, especially when dealing with small fragments, it is not even clear whether a certain text should be classified as "mystical," or "magical," or perhaps even both.[80] Moreover, when we leave the "insider" evidence and turn to "outsider" sources, a similar picture seems to emerge. In some cases, such as Agobard's famous letter on the Jews' superstitious beliefs and habits, a discussion of Jewish mystical lore does not seem to enter the issue of Jewish magic at all.[81] In other cases, however, most notably in Hai Gaon's famous responsum, the discussion of Jewish mysticism and Jewish magic goes hand in hand. Asked by the Jews of Kairouan about the effectiveness and permissibility of the use of the Names and other magical techniques, Hai responds by insisting that all the recipes for, and stories about, becoming invisible or stopping robbers or quelling a storm are sheer nonsense, and "the simpleton shall believe anything." He also notes that in Babylonia too, and not just in Kairouan, there are many such books, and lists three specific books of magic and countless nameless formularies (see Chapter 3). He next devotes one sentence to amulets, and an entire passage to the Hekhalot literature and the Merkabah traditions.[82] In his mind, it would seem, the magical texts and the mystical ones belong in different corpora, but these corpora are intimately linked by the use of divine Names and by the (false) promise of accomplishing great feats.

This, then, is where we stand. On the one hand, it seems quite clear that many medieval Jews, and perhaps some of their forefathers as well, tended to read some of the Jewish mystical texts and some of the Jewish magical texts in tandem, as part of a large conglomerate of forbidden, or problematic, or esoteric, or powerful, or dangerous (or all of the above) religious activities. On the other hand, it also seems quite clear that this was a mixing together of cultural activities which could also be entirely unrelated, and which normally were embedded in different types of texts. Thus, rather than focusing on how the two different types of texts were mixed and matched by later scribes and readers, we must try to look for the

---

[79] As was rightly stressed by Schäfer 1986; see also Herrmann and Rohrbacher-Sticker 1989 and 1991/92. For pertinent Genizah fragments, see, e.g., Davila 2001, pp. 228–38.
[80] For a case in point, see the fragment which was discussed in Chapter 3, n. 63.
[81] For Agobard's letter, see PL 104.77–100. For a detailed discussion of its claims, see Bonfil 1986.
[82] See Emanuel 1995, pp. 131–33.

possible connections, in late antiquity itself, between the Jewish magical texts and practices and the mystical ones.

To provide a systematic analysis of the relations between Jewish mysticism and Jewish magic in antiquity, it would perhaps be best to divide the question according to the different strands of late-antique Jewish mysticism currently known to us. We begin with the short and obscure *Sepher Yezira*, which had such a great impact on some strands of medieval Kabbalah and medieval Jewish magic, and then turn to the mystical speculations about the dimensions and names of God's body-parts, known as the *Shi'ur Qomah* texts. From these two strands, which seem to have had little impact upon or connections with late-antique Jewish magic, we turn to the Hekhalot/Merkabah traditions, whose patent relations with the Jewish magical texts are the hardest to describe and define.

Sepher Yezira *and ancient Jewish magic*

By far the most obscure product of ancient Jewish mysticism – so obscure that even its classification as "ancient" and as "mystical" is much contested – is the short and enigmatic "Book of Creation," written in Hebrew and focusing on the materials and methods used by God in the creation of the world, and especially His use of the Hebrew alphabet.[83] Neither the date nor the provenance of this book, which has survived in three different recensions, can be determined with certainty, and a plausible case can be made either for a late-antique Palestinian or Babylonian origin, or for a Muslim-period origin in one of the great urban centers of early Arabic cultural creativity.[84] Thus, it is far from certain that this work, whose original text cannot securely be separated from later interpolations, incretions and revisions, is even contemporaneous with our late-antique Jewish magical texts.[85] And yet, at least one aspect of this text is worth examining here, namely, its description of how, having created the world, God sealed its six extremities – upwards, downwards, eastwards, westwards, southwards, and northwards – with the six permutations of His three-letter Name, YHW (i.e., YHW,

---

[83] For the text, see Gruenwald 1971, and Hayman 2004. For the difficulty, already present among medieval commentators, of classifying *Sepher Yezira*, see Dan 1993a. See also Hayman 1987, who rightly stresses the gulf separating SY from the Hekhalot texts.

[84] For a late-antique date, see, e.g., Scholem 1941, pp. 75–78. For an early-Muslim date, see Wasserstrom 1993 and 2002. A Second Temple period date has recently been suggested by Liebes 2000, esp. pp. 229–37, but his historical arguments leave much to be desired (as was noted by Langermann 2002, esp. 177–89). See also Fleischer 2002.

[85] For the textual difficulties, see Gruenwald 1971, pp. 132–37; Weinstock 1972 (whose own reconstruction of the "original" text is entirely arbitrary); Hayman 2004, esp. pp. 1–8.

YWH, HYW, HWY, WYH, and WHY). The possible relations between this description and ancient Jewish magical practices, as well as some rabbinic discussions of the powers of the letters of the Hebrew alphabet, have often been noted.[86] But given the uncertainty about the relative dates of these sources it would be quite hazardous to base any historical reconstruction upon this patent similarity. On the one hand, we could argue that *Sepher Yezira* is contemporaneous with the magical texts and the rabbinic discussions, and reflects a similar set of assumptions and practices. One could also argue, however, that *Sepher Yezira* is later than the magical and rabbinic texts, and builds upon what its author found in one of them, or in both.

Be that as it may, one statement may be made with certainty, namely, that whereas in medieval Kabbalah and in some kabbalistically influenced magical texts of the Middle Ages and later periods one finds a pervasive influence of *Sepher Yezira*, this certainly is not true of the late-antique Jewish magical texts and practices. Thus, to give just a few examples, the book's description of the 231 possible "couplets" of letters to be created from permutations of the 22 letters of the Hebrew alphabet (the equivalent of an English-alphabet series AB, AC, AD . . . BA, CA, DA, etc.), which so fascinated such medieval Kabbalists as Abraham Abulafia, finds no close parallels in the Jewish magical texts from late antiquity. In a similar vein, the division of the Hebrew alphabet into three distinct sets of three "mothers" (or "primary" letters), seven "double" letters and twelve "simple" ones is unparalleled in the ancient magical texts, and the same is true for the great importance it attributes to the letters *aleph*, *mem*, and *shin*.[87] It is also true for the ten *Sephirot*, which appear in *Sepher Yezira* for the first time (though their meaning there remains obscure) but are entirely absent from ancient Jewish magic. These and other features of this enigmatic text, including its idiosyncratic vocabulary, were put to mystical, theurgical, and even magical uses by some of its Jewish readers from the Middle Ages onwards, but are nowhere to be found in the ancient Jewish magical texts to which we have any access. This absence is doubly significant since a magical use of *Sepher Yezira*'s alphabetic theories and permutations certainly would have encouraged the production of *written* artifacts, yet none of our written magical texts of late antiquity display its characteristic traits. Thus, we may

---

[86] See SY §15 (p. 146 Gruenwald = pp. 89–91 Hayman). For what follows, see esp. Hayman 1989; Gruenwald 1994, esp. pp. 94–98. For speculations about the theurgic-magical background of SY, see Idel 1990a, pp. 9–26 (to be read with Schäfer 1995, pp. 254–61).

[87] I am unconvinced by the attempt of Sed 1971, pp. 300–01, to find parallels for *Sepher Yezira*'s series of 7+12+3 in *Sepher ha-Razim*.

safely leave this work aside and turn to the other major trends of ancient Jewish mysticism and assess their possible relevance for the study of ancient Jewish magic.

The Shi'ur Qomah *and ancient Jewish magic*

If *Sepher Yezira* is the most enigmatic of Jewish mystical texts, the *Shi'ur Qomah* literature is the most bizarre, at least in light of what most people normally think of as "normative Judaism."[88] Preserved in several different recensions, at the heart of the *Shi'ur Qomah* texts (the name may be translated as "the Measure of the Body") lies a long catalogue of God's bodily limbs, each of which is assigned a specific size, a mysterious name, and sometimes other attributes and qualities as well. For example,

> His beard is 11,500 parasangs, HDRQMSY' is its name . . . The black of His right eye is 11,500 parasangs, and the same (is true) for the left (eye); of the right (eye), 'WR HYH 'TTYSWS is its name, and its minister, RHBY'L is his name. And of the left (eye), M'I'T'GRY'MZY' is its name, and the sparks which come out of it – their lights are for all (people).[89]

Such descriptions raise many problems of interpretation and contextualization, and the manuscripts at our disposal certainly are corrupt;[90] note, for example, that in the above-cited excerpts, God's beard is no larger than the pupils of His eyes! Worse still, the date and provenance of this composition, or of the type of speculation which lies behind it, are far from certain, with some scholars opting for a Palestinian Jewish composition of the second century CE (composed as a mystical midrash on the Song of Songs!) and others for an early Geonic composition from Babylonia, postdating the Muslim conquest.[91] Even the exact relations between this type of texts and the Hekhalot literature is far from obvious, and while it seems likely that such speculations were just one more by-product of Merkabah mysticism (on which more below), they might also represent a different strand of late-antique or early medieval Jewish mysticism, incorporated by some of the compilers of the Merkabah materials into their own compilations. But leaving all these issues aside, we may note that the question which interests

---

[88] For earlier work on SQ, see, Scholem 1960, chapter 6 and Appendix D (by Saul Lieberman); Gruenwald 1980, pp. 213–17; Stroumsa 1983; Cohen 1983 and 1985; Wolfson 1992; Janowitz 1992.
[89] See Cohen 1985, pp. 90, 92–93; for Genizah parallels, see, e.g., Schäfer, *G-F*, G9 (Bodleian Heb. c65.6), 6a/16, 22–24.
[90] As has often been noted – e.g., by Scholem 1941, p. 64.
[91] For a tannaitic origin, see Appendix D (by Saul Lieberman), in Scholem 1960; for a Geonic date and a Babylonian provenance, see Cohen 1983, pp. 51–76.

us here, namely, whether such speculations are in any way related to the magical texts and practices of late-antique Jews, seems to yield a clear answer. Neither the sizes of God's limbs nor their secret names and other characteristics were of any use to the late-antique Jewish magicians whose practices are accessible to us. They showed much interest in angelic hierarchies and demonic powers, but little interest in God's physiognomy, and in the detailed reports of those who touched His perfect body with their minds.

A second issue which must be raised here is whether the secret names of God's limbs, as found in the *Shi'ur Qomah* texts, are in any way related to the *voces magicae* and secret names found in the non-Jewish or Jewish magical texts of late antiquity. Here, however, the search for an answer is hampered by the sorry state of our manuscript evidence for the *Shi'ur Qomah* texts, with different manuscripts offering widely divergent names for the same limbs, and none offering names which may be identified with any of the known *voces magicae* of the Greco-Egyptian magical texts. Even the Genizah-fragments, presumably the best textual witnesses we have, have thus far not been very helpful on this score.[92] That some of the names assigned to God's limbs are corrupt versions of *voces magicae* borrowed from the world of late-antique magic is not impossible, but at present there is very little evidence to support such a theory.[93] It is quite possible that the identification and publication of more Genizah fragments of the *Shi'ur Qomah* texts would improve the textual evidence at our disposal and lead to new discoveries, but for the time being we must conclude that there are no perceptible relations between the *Shi'ur Qomah* speculations and the Jewish magical texts of late antiquity.

The Hekhalot/Merkabah texts and ancient Jewish magic

If our analysis of *Sepher Yezira* and the *Shi'ur Qomah* texts led to negative conclusions about the possible relations between these mystical texts and the Jewish magical tradition of late antiquity, the last body of ancient Jewish mystical texts to which we must turn – that known as the Hekhalot or

---

[92] For the published Genizah fragments, see G-F, G4 (T-S K 21.95.I); G9 (Bodleian Heb. c65.6) (=Cohen 1985, pp. 183–86); G10 (T-S K 21.95.H); G11 (T-S K 21.95.J); see also the transcription of Sassoon 522 in Cohen 1985, pp. 188–89.

[93] For a case in point, note the name of God's right thigh, ששנוסת ופרנגסי, i.e., Sesengen Barpharanges (as suggested by Scholem 1960, p. 98) in G-F, G9 6a/9 (and cf. *Synopse* §480 and §948, and G-F, G11, פרנג] (read by Schäfer as [פדנג)). See also Cohen 1985, p. 188, l. 27: יהוה אבראקס (note, however, that this name – which may or may not be related to Abrasax – does not reappear in the other *Shi'ur Qomah* texts). Note also the appearance of the *charactères* in the *Shi'ur Qomah* passages in *Synopse* §468: כל קשורין; §472: כלקטוריך; §728: כל קטורין; §732: כל קיטרין; etc.

Merkabah literature – poses a totally different situation. This disparate body of texts is generally characterized by its unique style (including such features as long hymnic praises of God, long lists of divine and angelic names and epithets, and occasional bursts of what seems like ecstatic glossolalia), by a pseudonymous attribution of many of its statements and traditions to such tannaitic figures as R. Yishmael or R. Akiva, and by its focus both on the mystics' ascent to heaven in the Merkabah (=Chariot) and what they saw, heard, and learned in the Hekhalot (=heavenly Palaces) and on the angels' descent to earth and the secrets they imparted to the mystics who adjured them to descend. This is a relatively large and complex body of literature, which, like the *Shi'ur Qomah* texts, has reached us through two very different channels of transmission. On the one hand, we have medieval Ashkenazi manuscripts, all of which seem to reflect the interest in this literature by Hasidei Ashkenaz, Jewish mystics of medieval Germany, and the extensive editorial activity to which they subjected the texts which had reached them. Thus, for the kinds of questions which interest us here, and which necessitate an access to the texts or oral traditions *as they may have looked in late antiquity*, these Ashkenazi manuscripts are quite exasperating. The most eloquent demonstration of this sad fact is the presence in these manuscripts of some passages which almost certainly contain Greek words and phrases (a possible sign of the late-antique Palestinian origins of at least some of these materials), all of which have been garbled beyond reconstruction.[94] On the other hand, we have about two dozen published fragments from the Cairo Genizah, and a handful of unpublished ones, fragments which have the disadvantage of being fragmentary and often lacunose, but the great advantage of not having gone through the Ashkenazi mystics' editorial mill.[95] It must be stressed, however, that these fragments too were copied in the Middle Ages (the earliest date from around the eleventh century), and provide us with only a shadow of a reflection of what such texts may have looked like in late antiquity. In fact, it is not even clear when exactly such texts as the Hekhalot literature were first written down – the earliest "outsider" evidence of their existence dates to the ninth century[96] – and it is quite possible that the lore contained within them was passed orally for many generations before being first committed to writing. In their present form, these texts sometimes stress the act of writing, but

---

[94] See Levy 1941 and Bohak 2001. A further complication is that some of these texts clearly passed through a Middle Byzantine stage – see the Greek chapter numbers in ms JTS N8128 (§205, §213, §218, §224, §230, §233, §237, §240, §246, §259), or the "Strige" recipe in ms Oxford 1531 (Michael 9) (§742) (for which see Chapter 4, n. 10).

[95] For the published fragments, see esp. G-F.   [96] See Brody 1998, p. 144.

when and how the scribalization of this mystical tradition came about is a question to which no certain answer can be given with the sources currently at our disposal.⁹⁷

Based on such inadequate textual resources, any analysis of this literature and of the mystics who first produced it must remain quite tentative. Moreover, the study of this field has changed dramatically in recent decades, and is beginning to suffer the same inflationary pressures which beset the study of Second Temple period Jewish literature, with too many scholars chasing a limited body of evidence, and often with the wrong questions in mind.⁹⁸ Thus, Scholem's claim that these texts go back to the heart of rabbinic Judaism, and to a time as early as the tannaitic period, has often been challenged, and attempts to find a more suitable historical context for these texts have proliferated. We now have sound arguments for attributing the Hekhalot texts to the *'am ha-'arez*, those non-rabbinic Palestinian Jews whom the rabbis so despised, to a post-rabbinic Babylonian Jewish elite, to a non-rabbinic intellectual elite contemporaneous with the rabbis, to professional scribes, to members of the old priestly families, to descendants of the secessionist priests who had produced the Dead Sea Scrolls, and to a loose guild of Jewish shamans.⁹⁹ As these suggestions cover the entire spectrum of known (and unknown) Jewish groups in late antiquity – with the glaring exception of women, on whom so much of ancient Jewish literature has recently been mothered – it is to be hoped that we shall soon see an end to this exercise in futility. Moreover, the greatest weakness of all these attempts to locate the date, provenance, and social *Sitz im Leben* of the Hekhalot literature lies in their failure to acknowledge the full implications of the deficiency of the available sources. At present, the textual evidence at our disposal simply does not suffice to support any theory concerning the exact date and provenance of this type of Jewish mysticism, and only time will tell whether the identification and publication of additional Genizah fragments of this literature, or of other types of sources, will provide more reliable clues for the reconstruction of their earlier history.

Examining the entire body of the currently available Hekhalot/Merkabah texts, one cannot help noting the obvious relations between some of these

---

⁹⁷ The scribal nature of the Hekhalot texts (as seen, for example, in G-F, G8) has recently been stressed by Arbel 2003, pp. 142–56, but its earlier history remains uncharted, mainly for lack of adequate sources. And cf. Schäfer 1983, on the great fluidity of these texts. Note also the Geonic references to Hekhalot materials as "*mishnayot*," and the use of the root שנה in the Hekhalot texts themselves, a usage which may imply oral transmission.

⁹⁸ For recent studies of the Hekhalot literature, see, e.g., Gruenwald 1980; Schäfer 1988; Halperin 1988; Dan 1992; Lesses 1998; Elior 2004a and 2004b; Boustan 2005, and the following note.

⁹⁹ For useful recent surveys of the relevant scholarship, see Davila 2001, pp. 1–24; Arbel 2003, pp. 7–12.

texts and some of the non-Jewish and Jewish magical texts of late antiquity. Circumscribing these relations, however, and reconstructing the historical processes which generated them, is far from easy.[100] To facilitate our analysis of this issue, we may break it up into two related topics. First, we shall try to see what the Hekhalot/Merkabah texts might tell us about the aims and the social contexts of the practitioners who produced and used them, and compare our findings with what we know about the Jewish magicians and amulet-writers of late antiquity. Next, we shall compare some of the techniques used by the mystics with those utilized by the magicians, in order to see where their techniques overlapped and how such overlaps might be explained.

Mystical and magical aims and social contexts
Scattered throughout the Hekhalot texts – both in the Ashkenazi manuscripts and in the Genizah fragments – are recurrent promises that whoever masters the secret lore provided by these texts will win great and tangible rewards. A typical example runs as follows:

R. Yishmael said, Whoever recites this great secret, his face shines, his bodily stature is fine, his fear lays upon the people, his good name spreads in all the places of (the people) Israel, his dreams are set out for him, and his Torah stays within him and he does not forget words of Torah throughout his days. He is well off in this world, and all right in the world to come, and even the sins of his youth are forgiven him in the coming future. The evil inclination does not rule over him, and he is saved from the spirits and the demons and from robbers, and from all noxious animals, and from a snake and a scorpion, and from all (types of) demons.[101]

Such impressive lists of benefits to be derived from the mastery of Merkabah secrets are not without significance for our present study, for they seem to turn the experienced mystic, once he had mastered all the great secrets, into a kind of holy man, not very different from some of the rabbis whose immunity to magic and other evils will be noted in the next chapter, or from some of the Neoplatonist philosophers or Christian bishops of late antiquity. Interestingly, these passages do not insist that the mystic's great esoteric knowledge would also turn him into a miracle-worker, but if he worked any wonders, he probably had no need for the paltry recipes peddled by the Jewish magicians of his time, given his mastery of much greater powers.

---

[100] For previous scholarship on this complex issue, see – in addition to the studies cited above – Schäfer 1993; Lesses 1998; Davila 2001, pp. 214–56.
[101] *Synopse* §705; for similar passages, see also §7; §81–§92; §311; §377; §500; §940; G-F, G2 (T-S K 21.95.K), G7 (T-S K 21.95.B), G8 (T-S K 21.95.C), etc.

How "Jewish" was ancient Jewish magic?

Moreover, when it comes to more specific aims, the Hekhalot mystics seem to seek either to ascend to the celestial Hekhalot or to bring an angel down to earth, mainly in order to discover divine secrets and master the entire Torah.[102] This is a very limited set of wishes in comparison with the magicians' wide set of recipes for numerous different aims. The magicians, on the other hand, rarely sought the revelation of cosmological or angelological secrets of the type which so interested the Merkabah mystics, and their recipes reveal little interest in self-improvement and self-aggrandizement, and much interest in being of service to (paying) clients with the widest possible range of needs and desires.

The impression of a wide gulf separating the self-oriented mystic from the client-oriented magician is strengthened when we note the repeated stress within the Hekhalot texts on the need to maintain stringent laws of purity before coming into contact with the angels – including, for example, a complete avoidance of any contact with women (one pertinent example will be cited below).[103] That such regulations were taken very seriously, at least in the Middle Ages, is shown by a detailed description in the *Scroll of Ahimaaz* of how Barukh, the grandson of R. Amittai, was studying *Sepher Merkabah*, and a menstruating woman approached it. A plague broke out, and would have caused much devastation were it not for one knowledgeable Jew, who understood what had happened, put the book in a lead vessel, and threw it in the sea.[104] While giving us one more perspective on the paucity of the textual evidence for the Hekhalot literature, this story also highlights the difference between these texts and the magical recipe-books. The same difference emerges in the responsum of Hai Gaon, who describes the magical texts known to him in a matter of fact way (see Chapter 3), but repeatedly stresses that the Hekhalot texts are frightening and terrifying, and must be approached "with purity and fear and trembling."[105] And looking at the magical texts themselves, one occasionally finds a reference to the avoidance of seminal emissions and other polluting substances, but even where such purity regulations appear, they are far more lenient than those of the Hekhalot texts.[106] These texts, moreover, sometimes enjoin the use of menstrual blood, semen, and other materials which the Hekhalot mystics would

---

[102] See Schäfer 1988, pp. 277–95; Lesses 1998, pp. 64–75.
[103] For the Hekhalot purity regulations, see Scholem 1960, pp. 9–13; Lieberman in Gruenwald 1980, pp. 241–44; Swartz 1994b and 1996, pp. 153–72; Lesses 1998, pp. 119–44, esp. 134–44.
[104] *Scroll of Ahimaaz* p. 30 Klar (and cf. p. 147, for a parallel from medieval Ashkenaz).
[105] See Emanuel 1995, pp. 131–33.
[106] For the purity requirements of *Sepher ha-Razim* (which are not necessarily representative of all late-antique Jewish magical recipes), see Margalioth 1966, pp. 8–9.

have found utterly defiling.[107] Moreover, since many of the published metal amulets (and, we may add, of the Babylonian incantation bowls as well) were produced for female clients, and even for non-Jewish ones, it seems certain that the producers of such artifacts saw nothing wrong with coming into direct and repeated contact with potentially polluting customers. And their dabbling in erotic magic – as can be seen from the Ḥorvat Rimmon sherds, from two erotic incantation bowls, and from numerous Genizah recipes – also seems quite distant from what the Merkabah mystics would have done in their spare time.

Seen from this perspective, the mystical and magical texts point to two distinct types of religious personalities and social contexts. On one side stands the Hekhalot mystic, who seeks to acquire esoteric knowledge and mastery of the Torah, and who even expects to benefit from that knowledge in tangible ways, including an elevated social status. There is, however, no sign of his interest in being of service to others – except, perhaps, his close disciples – and much evidence of his avoidance of many types of social contacts as prerequisites for his success in the *via mystica*, and of his observance of stringent laws of purity.[108] His is a male-only universe, in marked distinction, for example, from the world of late-antique Neoplatonism or of early Christian spirituality, where holy women and female mystics were not uncommon. On the other side stands the Jewish magician and amulet-writer, who does not usually seek to master the Torah or converse with angels, and whose very business is to cater to the mundane needs of a very mixed clientele, including men and women of all social and ethnic backgrounds or religious persuasions. This magician, moreover, might even consult with his non-Jewish colleagues and learn from them a powerful magic word, name, or symbol, or a secret magical design, and perhaps even entire magical recipes. In some cases – as in the "multilingual workshop" to which we referred in Chapter 3 – he might even share a studio with these non-Jewish colleagues, writing his Aramaic spells while they wrote theirs in Greek and Coptic. This, too, seems quite different from the master–disciple model assumed by the Hekhalot texts, in which the secret lore is passed on only to those who are worthy of receiving it. Thus, it seems quite clear that these are two different cultural activities; this does not mean that they always were mutually exclusive, but that in most cases they probably were carried out by different people, and in different social contexts.

---

[107] For some uses of menstrual blood, see already Chapter 2; for semen, see AMB, G2 (T-S AS 142.174) p. 1, l. 3; for the use of menstrual stains for erotic magic, see also Chapter 6.

[108] For the Hekhalot mystics as a small elitist group, see already Dan 1995.

Mystical and magical techniques

While the aims and social contexts of mystics and magicians differed greatly, the techniques they employed show at least some degree of overlap. This is hardly surprising, as both groups relied on esoteric lore, and often strove for contacts with God or His angels. Common to both types of practices were especially the use of adjurations (which often were accompanied by complex rituals) and the focus on powerful divine and angelic Names, epithets, and descriptions, and of incomprehensible *abracadabra* words. Looking at the Hekhalot adjuration rituals, we find that although their ritual instructions are far more complex and demanding than anything found in the Jewish magical texts of late antiquity, one can easily illustrate specific components of these rituals with the help of parallels taken from the non-Jewish and the Jewish magical texts of the time.[109] Thus, to give just one example, when a Hekhalot ritual enjoins the mystic to observe complete purity for forty days by avoiding any contact with twins, lepers, or women (he must even bake his own bread, so as to avoid anything touched by a woman!), by eating no meat or fish or onion or garlic or any garden vegetable, and drinking no wine or beer, and by avoiding any contact with semen (even an involuntary ejaculation on the thirty-ninth day means he has to start all over again!), and by bathing in the river (which river?) once a day, and on the last days twice a day, we may easily adduce many parallels to some of these regulations from the religious and magical practices of late antiquity.[110] But other components of this list, such as the prohibition of seeing twins, cannot easily be paralleled from ancient sources,[111] and the entire quest for parallels as a means for contextualizing ancient rituals is – as we noted in Chapter 4 – a priori doomed to failure. To find more conclusive evidence, we must once again leave the rituals aside and focus on the "sheer gibberish of magical abrakadabra" which had provided us in the previous chapter with so many useful clues for the analysis of the Jewish magical texts.

Looking at the non-semantic sections of the Hekhalot literature, we find not only Greek loanwords, but also some of the *voces magicae*, magical technical terms, and scribal habits whose entry into the Jewish magical tradition has been analyzed in Chapter 4.[112] As a case in point, we may take a two-page Genizah fragment, paleographically dated by its editor to the eleventh century but clearly copying a much older Hekhalot-type text, for which the Ashkenazi manuscripts provide no parallels. In this text, we find

---

[109] For what follows, cf. Lesses 1998, esp. pp. 117–60.   [110] See *Synopse* §489.   [111] See Baines 1985.
[112] For this aspect of the Hekhalot literature, see esp. Bohak 2001. Note also the appearance of two mystical names in "boxes," in G-F, G2 (T-S K 21.95.K) 2b/18 (which might, however, reflect the medieval scribe's habits in transcribing other texts).

not only garbled renditions of Abrasax and Sesengenbarpharanges, but also the *semea konteu* sequence in a relatively good state of textual preservation.¹¹³ In such cases, it seems quite clear that the movement of these *voces magicae* was from the non-Jewish magicians to (the Jewish ones, and from them to?) the Jewish mystics. Dating that movement would be quite difficult, but the fact that some of the *voces* had been badly garbled might argue for an early date, perhaps already in late antiquity, and perhaps even at a stage when this literature was transmitted mostly in an oral fashion. But be this as it may, the fact that some mystics borrowed some *voces magicae* and technical terms from the contemporary magical arsenal seems irrefutable. To understand why they would have done so, we need only look at such illuminating comparanda as the adoption of some magical techniques by the pagan Neoplatonist theurgists or the study of magic by Muslim, Christian, and Jewish mystics of later periods.¹¹⁴ In all these cases, members of mystical circles felt that the study of magical technologies would provide them with techniques useful for their own aims as well. And yet, the search for familiar *voces magicae* in the Hekhalot texts also serves to highlight the difference between them and the magical texts, for whereas the Genizah magical texts include numerous occurrences of *voces magicae* whose origins lie in Greco-Egyptian magic (including dozens of appearances by Abrasax alone), in the contemporaneous Genizah Hekhalot fragments, such occurrences are few and far between. Apparently, this is not only because the Hekhalot textual witnesses are fewer and far more corrupt, but also because the original texts simply contained few such non-Jewish *voces magicae* to begin with.

So much for the mystics' borrowings from the magicians. This however, is only one side of the coin, for we must also note that many of the divine and angelic names which are so common in the Hekhalot literature – names such as Adiriron, Yephephiah, Zoharariel, Zavodiel, Ta'zash Tag'az, Akatriel, Azbogah, Sandalphon, and Meṭaṭron – also appear in some of the magical and *piyyutic* texts of late antiquity, and sometimes even in rabbinic literature itself.¹¹⁵ Cataloging and dating all their appearances in the different textual corpora will no doubt shed much light on their archaic history, and will probably strengthen the likelihood that the origins of (some of) these special names do lie within the Jewish mystical tradition, and are

---

¹¹³ The text is G-F, G19 (Antonin 186). For a detailed analysis, see Bohak 2001, pp. 129–30. For Abrasax in a Hekhalot text, see also Schäfer 1988, p. 112 (Sassoon 522 p. 2), l. 28: אברסקס (and cf. above, n. 93).

¹¹⁴ See, e.g., Dodds 1951, p. 291: "Whereas vulgar magic used names and formulae of religious origins to profane ends, theurgy used the procedures of vulgar magic primarily to a religious end." For theurgy, see also Chapter 6, n. 31. For the Renaissance mystics' interest in magic, see Idel 1989.

¹¹⁵ For the appearances of Merkabah elements in the *piyyut*, see Rabinovitz 1965, pp. 62–64; Gruenwald 1967; Bar-Ilan 1987b.

the result of the mystics' visions of and speculations about God and His angelic host. This is especially true of Sandalphon, whose name seems to be the Greek word *synadelphos/n*, "fellow-brother," and of Meṭaṭron, whose name may be derived from Greek *meta thronon*, "(the one who is) behind/beside the Throne." Such angelic titles – which are not derived from the nomenclature of the Roman or Early Byzantine imperial court[116] – are nowhere to be found in the Greek magical texts of late antiquity, and while *synadelphos* appears in some of the Christological debates in Patristic literature, *meta thronon* is not found even there.[117] Thus, it seems that these angelic names were not borrowed by the Jewish mystics, magicians, and rabbis from the pagan magicians of late antiquity, and as the issue of angelic names and hierarchies was of utmost importance for the Merkabah mystics, it seems quite likely that it is they who first adopted these Greek terms as angelic appellations. If this indeed is the case, we would have a set of names and appellations which the Jewish magicians took from their mystically minded coreligionists in order to enhance the power of their own magical rituals. And here too, illustrative comparanda will not be hard to come by, with the influence of some Kabbalistic doctrines and practices on some strands of medieval and modern Jewish magic providing some of the best examples of the ease with which active magicians can adopt the esoteric lore produced by the mystically minded seekers of God's deepest secrets.

The impact of this Hekhalot terminology on the Jewish magical tradition is visible in many of the Genizah magical texts, which often display Hekhalot-like prayers and adjurations. But when we turn to the earlier evidence we find a far greater incidence of such elements in the Babylonian incantation bowls than in the metal-plate amulets of late-antique Palestine and its vicinity.[118] This might tell us something about the origins of the Merkabah speculations, but it must be stressed that even the Palestinian amulets occasionally display names and expressions which seem to have been borrowed from the Hekhalot materials. As an example, let us look at one specific amulet, to protect Marian daughter of Sarah and the fetus in her womb from every affliction and every demon:[119]

---

[116] And I am grateful to Noel Lenski for confirming this point.
[117] For *synadelphos*, see Lampe 1961, s.v. (p. 1296). For this etymology of Meṭaṭron, see, for example, Schwab 1897, p. 3 and 170; Scholem 1941, p. 69; Lieberman in Gruenwald 1980, pp. 235–41.
[118] For Babylonian examples, see esp. Shaked 1995; Lesses 1998, pp. 351–62; Davila 2001, pp. 217–28; Levene 2003, pp. 14–17.
[119] MSF, A28; note that A27 was made for the same client. For another amulet with a large concentration of Hekhalot-type names, see AMB, A3 (written for "Rabbi Eleazar son of Esther, the servant of the God of heaven"!). For the "ladder of ascent" seen by some scholars in MSF, A21, see Chapter 4, n. 135.

Holy, Holy, Holy . . . the God of the gods of spirits[120] for all flesh, the King of Kings of Kings . . . YYY Sabaot is His name. Holy, awesome, calling near, YH, YḤWŠ, 'ḤWŠ, HSWNH, HSWNH, YH YH YH, ḤZQ, 'ḤWŠ, YḤWŠ, ŠWWY, ŠWY, ŠWY, *Ehyeh Asher Ehyeh*, God, God, God, YH YH YH YH YH YH YH YH YH YH YH YH YH, 'T BŠ GR DQ HẒ WP Z' HS TN YM KL YH HWYH Shaddai, hero, DY'S? . . . Jerusalem, El-ot, who sits upon his throne before the two Cherubim, 'YYY 'WT T, 'NT'L, KNPY'L, YH YH YH, KN'W, the holy name of God which was revealed to Moses from within the (burning) bush, YHWH YHW, his name is blessed, I-am-who-I-am, YHWH Sabaot, YHWH God, YHWH (is) One . . . the name,""""".[121]

Looking at such a hymnic praise of God and the recitation of His Names, which seems to cross the line from human language to divine glossolalia, one cannot avoid feeling that both in contents and in style it could easily fit within the Hekhalot texts. A closer examination of each of God's epithets reveals that some of them – such as the expression "the God of the spirits for all flesh," or "King of Kings of Kings", or the *Ehyeh* formula – are of biblical origins, and are therefore attested in many branches of post-biblical Jewish literature. Similarly, both the speculations about the name revealed to Moses in the Burning Bush and the use of the *atbash* series are quite common in many strands of late-antique Jewish culture.[122] But some of the names which are used here are unattested in earlier Jewish literature, but are found both in the Babylonian incantation bowls and in the Hekhalot texts. YḤWŠ and 'ḤWŠ, for example, are quite common in the Genizah fragments of the Hekhalot texts (but much less so in the European manuscripts thereof), and occasionally appear in the Babylonian bowls.[123] And as these are unattested among the *voces magicae* of the Greco-Egyptian magical texts, and are unlikely to have been derived from Greek (which has neither the *ḥet* sound nor the *shin*), it is quite possible that this large concentration of Hekhalot-type mystical names was borrowed by the magicians from the mystics, and not the other way around. Once again, however, we must note that the absence of late-antique Hekhalot texts or fragments makes the final judgment of such examples quite tentative.

[120] In line 10, it seems from the line drawing that the editors' reading should be emended to הרוחות; the phrase is based upon Nm 16.22 and 27.16, and we already met it in Chapter 2.
[121] MSF, A28 ll. 7–29. I have not tried to offer my own readings for the lines which the editors could not read.
[122] For the Burning Bush, see, e.g., G-F, G21 (T-S K 21.95.A) 2a/24, and Rabbi Yoḥanan's recipe, discussed in the next chapter. For the *atbash*-series, see MSF, A28 and Keil 1940.
[123] Montgomery 1913, p. 60, suggested that names like YḤWŠ 'ḤWŠ were derived from the "now, now, quickly, quickly" of Greco-Egyptian magical texts (and formed with ḤWŠ, "to hurry"). This is not impossible, but note that these words are used as if they were mystical names, and not as injunctions, a far cry from the Aramaic equivalents of this formula which we studied in Chapter 4.

Summary

In summarizing our findings, we may note that there seems to be no real connection between late-antique Jewish magic and some strands of early Jewish mysticism, such as *Sepher Yezira* and *Shi'ur Qomah*, but there are some points of contact between the Jewish magical texts and the Hekhalot literature. In circumscribing these contacts, we certainly should not assume that Jewish magic and Jewish mysticism flowed from the same source or that one was a by-product of the other. It seems quite clear that these were independent activities, with different aims and methods and often performed by different people. On the other hand, there clearly are cases where non-Jewish magical technology, which is so visible in the Jewish magical texts, also entered the Hekhalot literature, and there seems to have been some transfer of esoteric knowledge from the Jewish mystics to the Jewish magicians as well. Future research, and especially the study of hitherto unpublished Jewish magical and mystical texts, will no doubt shed more light on these processes, but for the time being we may conclude that although late-antique Jewish magic and mysticism did not stem from the same social circles, and did not share the same body of knowledge, they did not hesitate to borrow each other's technical innovations when these were deemed useful for their own aims and needs.

RABBINIC ELEMENTS IN ANCIENT JEWISH MAGIC

One of the most interesting questions to be asked regarding the "Jewishness" of the Jewish magical tradition of late antiquity is the nature of its relations with rabbinic Judaism at the time. In the next chapter, we shall survey what may be learned from rabbinic literature about the Jewish magic of late antiquity and compare what we find there with what we find in the contemporary "insider" sources. For the moment, we must ask a more modest question, namely, what do the "insider" sources themselves tell us about the possible connections between the Jews who produced them and rabbinic culture of the time? To answer this question correctly, we must be very clear about what it is that we are looking for – not just superficial similarities between the two bodies of texts, which might be due to the fact that both reflect late-antique Jewish cultural sensibilities, but specifically rabbinic elements which may or may not be found in the magical texts of late-antique Palestine. Thus, if we find a biblical verse like Ex 15.26 used for similar apotropaic purposes in rabbinic literature and in our late-antique amulets, this in no way shows the influence of rabbinic culture on the

Jewish magical texts, for the rabbinic texts themselves make it clear that the magical use of this verse is pre-rabbinic and non-rabbinic in origin, as we shall see in the next chapter. Similarly, references to the 248 limbs of the human body are found both in rabbinic texts and in the amulets, but the origin of this concept is Greek, and its presence in two corpora of Jewish texts tells us nothing about the contacts between them.[124] If, on the other hand, we could point to elements within our magical texts which are uniquely rabbinic, and which could only have come from rabbinic circles, we could confidently state that rabbinic Judaism too contributed something to the cultural brew apparent in the Jewish magical texts of late antiquity.

As an intriguing comparandum, we may look at the Babylonian incantation bowls. Surveying this large corpus of texts, one finds quite a few references to Yehoshua ben Perahiah and several more to Hanina ben Dosa, two Second Temple period holy men known to us from rabbinic sources; one also finds citations from Targum Onqelos, a late antique Aramaic version of the Hebrew Bible which is closely associated with the rabbinic movement. Even more telling, one finds entire passages from the Mishnah (cited either directly from the Mishnah or from the rabbinic prayers which use these passages) inscribed on several such bowls, so that here there is no question at all as to who influenced whom, and we can safely say that the Babylonian incantation bowls display at least some rabbinic elements.[125] With such examples in mind, we may note that the western Jewish magical texts currently at our disposal do not really display any such specifically rabbinic elements. This asymmetry may be due solely to the different sizes of the textual corpora available for study, with the much larger body of Babylonian incantation bowls providing a few concrete examples of rabbinic influences, while the small body of Palestinian Jewish texts – many of which are in a sorry state of preservation – has yet to produce any clear examples of such elements. But the complete absence of rabbinic terms and concepts from *Sepher ha-Razim* certainly demonstrates that some late-antique Jewish magicians could manage very well without any recourse to rabbinic materials.

Having said that, we should now make two additional points. First, that while the known Palestinian magical texts include no references to rabbinic figures, no citations of or allusions to rabbinic texts, and no clear instances of the use of rabbinic *midrash*, they do contain some elements

---

124 For the 248 limbs, cf. AMB, A4 ll. 16–17 and A9 l. 3 with Preuss 1993, pp. 60–62.
125 For useful surveys of the evidence, see Chapter 3, n. 130.

How "Jewish" was ancient Jewish magic?

which may perhaps be construed as originating in rabbinic culture. Thus, to give one clear example, the term *Shekhina* for God's "presence" may have been a rabbinic innovation, and this term does appear in several late-antique amulets.[126] Similarly, God's description as "the King of Kings of Kings," which is first attested in rabbinic literature, appears quite often in the Palestinian amulets.[127] But be this as it may, it seems quite clear that unlike the eastern branch of late-antique Jewish magic, the western branch does not display any close contacts with rabbinic Judaism. Moreover, this asymmetry does not seem to be due to chronological differences, as both corpora of texts seem to be roughly contemporaneous.

We shall return to the relations between the Jewish magic of late-antique Palestine and the world of rabbinic Judaism in the next chapter, but must already stress that even if the Jewish magical texts of late antiquity display no specifically rabbinic elements at all, this would tell us little about the actual relations between the rabbis and these magical texts. In the Geonic period, it is very clear that such texts as the *Sword of Moses*, for example, or even *Sepher ha-Razim*, were owned and used by rabbis, and yet, there is very little that is "rabbinic" about the contents of these texts. And as we shall see in the next chapter, when we closely examine the spells transmitted by the rabbis themselves, we find that a few of these spells display specifically rabbinic motifs and features, but most others do not. Thus, the analysis of the cultural make-up of Jewish magical texts can tell us much about the identity of the people who produced them, but we must focus more on the elements which they actively used, and less on those they did not – unless, of course, we can show why they consciously avoided some elements, as we shall see in the following section.

PHILTERS AND FILTERS: THE LIMITS OF CULTURAL RECEPTIVITY

In Chapter 3, we noted how the polytheistic Greco-Egyptian magical tradition, with its open-ended, flexible pantheon, easily incorporated Iaô, Sabaôth, Michaêl, and sometimes even Abraham, into its ever-expanding roster of powerful deities. It also saw nothing wrong with affixing some pictorial representations to the Jewish god/s, and since Iaô had no image to begin with, his name could be affixed to quite a few different images. But we also noted that in line with the general pagan disinterest in the Hebrew

---

[126] For *Shekhina*, see Urbach 1975, pp. 37–65. For its appearance in the amulets, see, e.g., AMB, A1 l. 3; A14, l. 8.
[127] See AMB, A1 l. 24; A12 l. 20; MSF, A28 l. 11.

Bible, magical recipes and rituals based on biblical scenes and verses were quite a rarity in the Greek magical papyri. Greco-Egyptian magicians certainly had access to much Jewish magical technology, but borrowed from it only those things which their cultural conditioning enabled them to accept.

When we turn to the other side of the equation, namely, the Jews' borrowing of non-Jewish materials into their own magical tradition, the issue of cultural receptivity becomes even more problematic. Unlike most pagan magicians of antiquity, whose cultures did not usually condemn mere contact with foreigners, the Jews' ancestral heritage repeatedly warned them against talking to strangers, and especially against "walking in their ways." It is this age-old Jewish anxiety of foreign influence – an anxiety which, we may recall, was the major justification for the Torah's prohibition of magic in the first place – that makes the magicians' attitudes towards pagan magical technology one of the best yardsticks for measuring the "Jewishness" of their activities and self-perception. At first sight, the very presence of all the foreign elements whose entry into the Jewish magical tradition we traced in the previous chapter could taint the entire enterprise as quite syncretistic and very "un-Jewish." A closer look, however, reveals some interesting methods adopted by the magicians for dealing with the non-Jewish magical materials they borrowed. The first is the "naturalization" and even full "Judaization" of some non-Jewish magical elements, a process to which we repeatedly referred in Chapter 4. To our notes there, we may add that it is especially such elements as Abrasax or the *charactêres* which underwent the greatest degree of naturalization and Judaization, because – unlike Isis, Osiris, and Apollo – they were not part and parcel of the age-old pantheons of any pagan religion. Helios was half-heartedly admitted by some Jewish practitioners, but Aphrodite and Sarapis apparently were too hot to handle, except as *voces magicae*. A second process may be seen in a work like *Sepher ha-Razim*, where it seems quite clear that the book's lengthy introduction, and its entire literary structure, were intended to make it more "kosher" in Jewish eyes, so as to forego "Judaizing" every offensive bit which the compiler has let slip into the book while making the entire collection much easier to swallow.

To these two processes, which are the more visible and better studied mechanisms of dealing with foreign elements by the Jewish magicians of late antiquity, we may now add a third, which is by far the most significant of the three, namely, the conscious decision not to borrow many elements from late-antique pagan and Christian magic, in spite of their easy availability, simply because they were considered too "un-Jewish" to handle. To see this process more clearly, we may look at the late-antique Jewish magical texts currently at our disposal, compare them with the pagan magical texts of the time, and ask not only what the Jewish practitioners borrowed from their non-Jewish colleagues, but also what they did not. In some cases, the absence of a certain feature which is prominent in Greco-Egyptian magic from the Jewish magical texts might result from the paucity and poor preservation of our sources, or even from purely technical reasons. Thus, the almost complete absence of Aramaic and Hebrew magical gems, an issue to which we turned in Chapter 3, may reflect a cultural choice, and may perhaps be connected with a certain abhorrence of iconography on the part of some Jewish magicians. But it could just as plausibly be attributed to such technical issues as the lack of qualified gem cutters who would know enough Aramaic not to mess up the models they might receive from the Aramaic-speaking magicians. Similarly, the fact that the Jewish magicians repeatedly avoided producing lead *defixiones* – even when this is what their recipes demanded – may be due to some cultural inhibition, but it would be difficult to see why writing aggressive magical texts on bronze or clay was acceptable, while writing them on lead was somehow judged to be unacceptable. However, in many other cases, the avoidance of specific ritual techniques – in spite of the obvious temptation to borrow whatever is deemed to work – can only be attributed to deliberate cultural choices. Thus, to our categories of "naturalization," "multiple entry," and "one time entry," we may now add a fourth classification, that of "entry denied." And by checking which non-Jewish elements appear in none of the Jewish magical texts of late antiquity, we shall learn something about the "hidden hand," or cultural matrix, which shaped its growth and set its borders.

Before turning to some specific examples, we must note that the "insider" sources at our disposal for the study of the western branch of late-antique Jewish magic are extremely diverse in terms of their times and places of origin. Even if we limit ourselves solely to the metal amulets of late antiquity, we see them coming from a wide range of sites, from Turkey and Syria to Egypt, with a large number coming from different sites in Palestine itself. They are, in other words, not the product of a single practitioner, a single workshop or even a small cluster of such workshops, but were produced by different Jewish amulet-writers, living in a wide geographical area over a period of several centuries. And since there was no central clearing house of Jewish magical texts, in which they were all collated, approved, and disseminated to the local practitioners, what we see are the works of numerous independent practitioners, often learning from each other but never bound by any centralized code.[128] Thus, if certain patterns seem to emerge when we examine all their products at once, these patterns could tell us something about a whole group of people, people who shared certain cultural preferences and sensibilities in spite of the lack of any social mechanism to enforce these preferences or even promulgate them.

A second point to be noted here is that most of these sources were produced by practitioners but were not really intended for others to read. When reading magical recipe-books, we must always recall the possibility that there was some self-censorship involved in copying and re-copying them, for fear of the prying eyes of the local religious or political authorities. But when reading amulets, which were rolled up on the patient's body and were not meant to be opened, or those aggressive spells which were buried in the synagogue's walls, we are reading texts whose producers probably feared little censorship.[129] In such texts, we may expect to find out how far the Jewish practitioners were willing to go in their search of power, that power which would help them achieve their clients' wishes – and their own. The final products, in other words, probably reflect their producers' cultural sensitivities, and where they thought that the lines between "permitted" and "forbidden" should lie.

What, then, did the Aramaic- and Hebrew-speaking Jewish magicians choose not to borrow from their non-Jewish colleagues? First and foremost, we may note the complete or near-complete absence from our Jewish magical texts of the western branch of any Christian elements, and this in spite of the availability of a wide range of Christian magical techniques and practices in late-antique Palestine (not to mention the multilingual workshop from late-antique Egypt, where a Jewish and a Coptic Christian practitioner shared the same atelier!), and in spite of the attraction of some Jews to healings "in the name of Jesus," of which the rabbis were so well aware (see next chapter). In vain shall we look in the Jewish amulets and curses for references to Jesus and his many miracles, to the Crucifixion, to Trinitarian formulae or the Credo, to Alphas and Omegas, to Mary or the Virgin Birth, to Christian saints and their miracles, to the Pater Noster prayer, Gospel *incipit*s or any other New Testament verses or stories. In one or two amulets, a symbol appears which may or may not be reminiscent of a Christian symbol, but such resemblance could be quite accidental, and is not backed up by any other Christian elements within these texts

---

[128] In this, they differ greatly from the magical recipes and knowledge transmitted by rabbinic literature, which clearly passed some editorial processes which reduced their usefulness for our study, as shall be noted in the following chapter.

[129] And as we shall see in the following chapter, even the rabbis of late antiquity never made it a habit to pry open rolled amulets and screen their contents for offensive materials.

(see Chapter 4). This stands in line with the rabbis' sensitivity on this score (see next chapter), and in contrast with the medieval Jewish attitude to Christian magic, which was sometimes more lenient, as can be seen from the entry of Christian elements into medieval Jewish magic.[130]

While the Jewish magicians apparently shunned any borrowings from their Christian colleagues, they clearly showed no such reticence when it came to their pagan colleagues, from whom they borrowed quite a few magical techniques and practices. And yet, our detailed survey of the many elements they borrowed should not blind us to the fact that there were even more things which they apparently did not borrow, even though these were part and parcel of the Greco-Egyptian magical tradition of their time. First and foremost, the pagan gods are absent from the Jewish magical texts, except in those cases where they entered as mere *voces magicae* (see Chapter 4). In the Palestinian amulets, and in the Genizah magical texts, there are no rituals to summon Apollo or Hecate, no references to the myths of Isis, Osiris, and Horus, no instructions to draw up an image of any of these gods and no references to the sacred animals of the Egyptian gods (baboons may have been harder to procure in Palestine, but of dung-beetles there was no shortage!).

But not only the pagan gods are absent from the Jewish magical texts, for it seems that some of the basic techniques of Greco-Egyptian magic were not borrowed by the Jewish magicians. Perhaps the best examples are provided by the common practice in Demotic and Greek magical texts of threatening the gods into submission by means of a whole host of ingenious ruses. One common method was the "I am X" formula, whereby the magician would "pretend" to be a powerful god or human, and to possess the necessary means for compelling a disobedient deity into complying with his own desires.[131] In the Jewish magical texts, on the other hand, angels and demons are often compelled to obey the practitioner, who may recall God's power to adjure them into action. Impersonating God or His angels, or threatening and coercing God Himself into action, is something which the Jewish magicians preferred not to try.[132] It is in light of this general feature of late-antique Jewish magic that we must re-read the story of Honi the Circle Maker (cited in Chapter 1), and note how the Jewish holy man occasionally allows himself actions which even the Jewish magician would rather avoid.

---

[130] For which see Chapter 4, n. 140.

[131] For the Egyptian origins of this technique (which even many Greek and Roman observers found quite unacceptable), see, e.g., Dieleman 2005, p. 82, and esp. 153–55.

[132] This point was rightly stressed (at least with regards to the *Sword of Moses*), by Harari 1997a, pp. 69–70. In the incantation bowls, one occasionally finds such claims as "I am the earth . . . I am the heaven," which seem to go back to Babylonian precedents – see Segal 2000, bowl 049A, with Müller-Kessler and Kwasman 2000 and Morgenstern 2004.

We must also read the rabbis' many boasts of how what God decrees a righteous person (or a rabbi) may annul to realize that the Jewish magicians of their time shied away from all such language.[133] Monotheistic magic has its own limits.

But blatantly pagan gods and rituals were not the only features which the Jewish magicians of late antiquity seem to have avoided. When we look at the magicians' very attitude to "magic," an interesting asymmetry emerges between the Greco-Egyptian magical texts and the Jewish ones. In the former, one can easily see the ambivalence of *mageia* and related Greek terms, with many Greek magical recipes tactfully avoiding that term, with all its evil (and illegal) connotations, while others use the aura of mystification and efficacy surrounding that term to boast of their "holy magic."[134] In the Jewish magical texts, on the other hand, *kishuph*-related terms (or their Aramaic equivalent, *ḥarashin*) appear quite often, but always as one of the things which the recipe is intended to counteract. "If you want to heal a man who is half withered by a demon or by *keshaphim*"; "and no *qesem* or *kishuph* will have any effect upon them"; "annul all the evil *ḥarashin* from NN"; "and all their *ḥarashin* will be annulled", and so on, in dozens of Jewish amulets, bowls and magical recipes.[135] Of a positive reference to *keshaphim*, or a self-identification as a *mekhasheph*, there is hardly a trace, in spite of the useful precedents offered by the Greco-Egyptian magicians.[136] Moreover, this feature of ancient Jewish magic is all the more interesting when we note that the rabbis of late antiquity saw nothing wrong with admitting that they occasionally dabbled in *keshpahim*, and explaining why their kind of praxis actually was permitted, and even desirable (see Chapter 6). Jewish magicians, it would seem, could not subvert the biblical legislation in such a manifest manner, and, like *Macbeth*'s witches, preferred to handle their own art as "a deed without a name."[137]

---

[133] For such rabbinic claims, see Chapter 6, n. 164.

[134] For the self-referential uses of *mageia*-related words in the PGM, see, PGM I.127, 331; IV.210, 243, 2074, etc.; see also Betz 1986, p. 216, for the Demotic epithet "great of magic." For positive references to magic in the "outsider" sources, see, e.g., Apuleius, *Metam.* 3.19, where Lucius describes it as *divina disciplina*, or Thessalus 13 (p. 49 Friedrich), where Thessalus asks the Egyptian priests εἴ τι τῆς μαγικῆς ἐνεργείας σώζεται; and cf. Porphyry, *VP* 33.

[135] For these examples, see ShR II/95 (p. 86 Margalioth); III/42 (p. 94); MTKG II, 29 (T-S NS 322.50) 1a/11; MSF, G15 (T-S K 1.80) p. 1 ll. 9–10, respectively.

[136] The only partial exception of which I am aware is ShR I/176 (p. 76 Margalioth): "And if you wish לשאול באוב," using precisely the word which is prohibited in Dt 18.11 and elsewhere. Note, however, that even the rabbis seem to have been more lenient when it came to necromancy, as can be seen, e.g., from bt Git. 56a (how Onqelos, before his conversion, raised the ghosts of Titus, Balaam, and Jesus) or bt BM 107b (cited in the next chapter).

[137] In later periods, substitute terms were invented – such as *segullot*, or "practical Kabbalah" – in order to avoid the dirty word *keshaphim*, and these terms remain in vogue among Jewish magicians to this very day.

If the magicians' attitude to "magic" seems more conservative than that of some contemporary rabbis, their general avoidance of iconography – which we have highlighted in the previous chapter – is even more so. Unlike the Greco-Egyptian magicians, for whom iconographical representation often was as important or even more important than the magical texts, the Jewish magicians of late-antique Palestine and Egypt seem to have preferred to avoid such iconography as much as possible. This is, of course, not a new phenomenon in Jewish history, for (as we noted in Chapter 2), extreme iconophobia was one of the hallmarks of Second Temple Jewish culture. Thus, whereas the Babylonian Jewish practitioners of late antiquity often saw nothing wrong with illustrating their incantation bowls with demonic, human, and animal figures, and whereas the rabbis of late antiquity could find some excuses for permitting iconographic representation and for using figurative implements and objects, some Jewish magicians adhered more closely to the old-fashioned understanding of the Second Commandment, and avoided the use of magical iconography even if this meant foregoing the use of some powerful magical technologies.

So far, we have offered a bird's-eye view of the differences between the pagan and Jewish magical traditions, but such differences are visible also on the level of the individual spell. To see this, we may note how in Chapter 3 we met pagan magical recipes in which the practitioner adjured Iaô directly, or used the "I am X" formula to claim that he was Iaô himself, or that he was Moses, to whom the god had once revealed all his secrets. Looking for such claims in the Jewish magical texts, we find no adjurations of the Jewish god, and some recipes in which sulfur is addressed as that sulfur which once rained upon Sodom and Gomorrah (see Chapter 3), or a bush addressed as the Burning Bush once encountered by Moses (see Chapter 6). But of the claim that the practitioner himself had sent the sulfur or had met the bush *in illo tempore* there is not even a trace. In such cases, we see both how the pagan magicians had no trouble incorporating Iaô too into their pantheon and using upon him all their magical techniques and how the Jewish practitioners felt that such magical techniques were simply inappropriate for their own use.

Another spell in which the Jewish magicians' cultural sensitivities is readily visible is the separation ritual which we already discussed in the previous chapter, and which involves the use of a donkey's flesh. As noted there, there is no doubt that the origins of this specific technique lie in the Egyptian and Greco-Egyptian magical tradition. What we did not stress there, however, is that in the Greek magical papyri such a ritual would normally be accompanied by a long *historiola* about how the evil Sêth-Typhon had separated Isis from Osiris, by a list of Sêth's secret names (Iô Erbêth, etc.), and perhaps even by a nice asinine design, while in the Jewish version of this recipe all but the basic ritual action have disappeared. Apparently, the Jewish user(s) of this spell felt that separating a man from a woman or eating a donkey's flesh were still acceptable, but delving deeper into Egyptian mythology and ritual was too much for them, or for their clients, to stomach. And with this observation, we probably have one explanation for the paucity of Jewish magical recipes translated directly from pagan Greek originals, as noted at the beginning of the previous chapter. In most cases, it would seem, the Jewish borrowing of pagan magical recipes was not a matter of translation but of adaptation, of taking what the Jewish magician found acceptable and leaving the rest aside. The pagan philters had to pass through some very Jewish filters before they were fit for use by the Jewish magicians.

SUMMARY

We began this chapter with a two-fold question – how "Jewish" was ancient Jewish magic, at least its western branch, and what kind of "Judaism" does it represent? Before providing a tentative answer to this question, we must stress once again that our late-antique Jewish magicians did not belong to some cohesive social group with central mechanisms for unification, purification, and canonization of their magical lore. It is quite likely that different practitioners placed the border between "permitted" and "forbidden" and between "Jewish" and "non-Jewish" in different places. Should we take the existence of "purely Jewish" magical texts (e.g., AMB, A9, or the Evron amulet) as an implied criticism of the proliferation of non-Jewish elements in other magical texts? Are the Nirim amulets more open to foreign influences than some of the other amulets? Is it only a coincidence that the amulet which displays the most wide-ranging Greco-Egyptian influences (the el-Amarna amulet) was found in Egypt, and not in Palestine? Is *Sepher ha-Razim* the most extreme example of the penetration of pagan elements into the Jewish magical tradition, and therefore makes such great efforts to sweeten the bitter pill by providing it with a very Jewish capsule? We are not yet in a position to answer such questions, but merely raising them certainly is a useful mental exercise, in an attempt to learn more about the general characteristics of the entire corpus and the possible variations within it. We may even speculate about the possibility that tomorrow a late-antique Jewish magical text might be found that is written in Aramaic or Hebrew and displays the Jewish identity of its producers, but also contains some fully pagan magical spells, with Isis and Osiris, or Apollo and Hecate, or some of the juicier *historiolae* and magical iconography of the Greek magical papyri. This would be an extremely important find, for it would show that at least some Jewish practitioners were willing to go further than many of their more tradition-bound colleagues. But it would also highlight once again the reluctance of other ancient Jewish magicians to walk down that path. Were we to opt for the now-popular model of "a marketplace of religions," which is sometimes applied to the ancient world, we would claim that as the Jewish magicians walked by the stalls of this marketplace of magical technologies, they were very careful about which technologies they chose to buy, which to reconfigure, and which to leave on the counter. It is in this choice, more than in any other aspect of their magical activities, that they demonstrate their own cultural sensitivities, so different from those of their non-Jewish colleagues.[138] What we are seeing here, in other words, is the "hidden hand" of the marketplace of ideas, which governs the choices made by numerous individuals over long periods of time and thus determines the shape of their cumulative cultural production.

The Jewish magicians' refusal to adopt the Greco-Egyptian magical tradition in its entirety was greatly facilitated by their ability to provide many original Jewish elements in their magical spells and rituals. In some cases, they still had direct or indirect access to Second Temple period Jewish magical technology. In many other cases, they tapped the rich Jewish thaumaturgical tradition and developed it much further, by utilizing God's many powerful Names and developing a highly complex angelology (two features of Jewish magic which even the pagan magicians found extremely enticing). They also used the Hebrew Bible – which some of them clearly knew quite well – as a storehouse of powerful verses and potent *historiolae*. And in some cases, they learned a secret Name or two from their mystically minded coreligionists, or from their own dabbling in mystical adjurations and heavenly visions. Moreover, they also made much use of local realia to develop their own Jewish versions of well-accepted Greco-Egyptian magical techniques (such as burying aggressive magical spells in public spaces, that is, in the local synagogue) and perhaps also some specifically Jewish ones (such as placing amulets under the Torah-ark). Thus, while the Jewish magicians had a professional interest in learning all the recent innovations and "hot" technologies of their non-Jewish colleagues, their decision to forego some of these was compensated by other factors. To their Jewish clients, they could promise that their magic was more "kosher" than that of

---

[138] And cf. Altmann 1992, p. 71 (on Jewish mysticism): "The basic trait of positive, creative assimilation peculiar to Judaism has proved successful also in this area of its intellectual history." While I am not sure that this feature indeed is "peculiar to Judaism," I would argue that it applies to ancient Jewish magic as well.

pagan magicians, and in so doing assure them that they were following the biblical notion of providing Jewish substitutes for forbidden pagan practitioners. And to their non-Jewish clients, and the Jewish ones as well, they could promise that in their arsenal they had some powerful techniques, Names, and *historiolae* which were uniquely Jewish, and which their pagan competitors had never even heard of. And as the archeological evidence amply demonstrates, quite a few people were convinced that the resulting mixture was, indeed, extremely effective.

Looking at the evidence in its entirety, we may now conclude that the Jewish magicians of late antiquity were far less syncretistic, and far more "Jewish," than previous scholars were willing to admit. And while their "Judaism" probably does not merit its own separate label (such as "magical Judaism"), we may be quite sure that it was neither Gnostic nor heretical, neither mystical nor rabbinic. For all we know, it may have been the "Judaism" intuitively shared by most Jews in late antiquity. But before reaching a final verdict on this issue, we must examine the biggest body of "outsider" Jewish evidence on ancient Jewish magic, and see what it may teach us about the Jewish magicians of late antiquity, and about the place of magic and magicians in the rabbis' world. This shall be done in the following chapter.

CHAPTER 6

Magic and magicians in rabbinic literature

INTRODUCTION

Unlike the previous chapters, in which we examined many sources which have only recently been published, or have not yet been published at all, the texts to which we now turn have been studied by scholars for more than a century and a half. Ever since the early days of the new "Science of Judaism" (*Wissenschaft des Judenthums*), the question of the place and role of magic in rabbinic literature has been a much debated issue.[1] Scholar after scholar sought to collect and analyze the magic-related passages in rabbinic literature, both those passages which were judged to be "magical" by modern standards and those that contained the rabbis' own discussions of and references to magic.[2] As may be expected, most of the scholarly work on such issues was clouded not only by fuzzy or derogatory definitions of "magic," but also by deep-seated prejudices and preconceptions with regard to rabbinic literature. Some scholars sought to "expose" rabbinic literature – and especially the Babylonian Talmud, upon which all forms of Orthodox Judaism ultimately are based – as full of magic and superstition and therefore as opposed to the rationalism upon which modern Judaism must be based. These scholars, moreover, could rely not only on the earlier Karaite critique of rabbinic magic, but also on Maimonides' total condemnation of all magical practices, a sound peg upon which to hang any such critique. Most scholars, however, felt quite embarrassed by many of the rabbinic attitudes to, stories about, and recipes smacking of magic, but sought to vindicate the rabbis of the charges of irrationality and superstition. Some

---

[1] For useful surveys of previous scholarship on this topic, see Harari 1998, pp. 59–83; Veltri 1997, pp. 3–18; Stein 2004, pp. 175–83.
[2] Among the most important "classical" works, one may note Brecher 1850, pp. 123–233; Joël 1881–83; Rubin 1887; and esp. Blau 1898. Among the more recent works, see Lieberman 1942, pp. 100–14; Urbach 1975, pp. 97–183 (with Sussmann 1993, pp. 73–4, n. 148); Goldin 1976; Fishbane 1979; Herr 1980; Lightstone 1985; Yassif 1999a, pp. 144–66; Harari 2006; Geller 2006; Levinson 2006. Many additional studies will be mentioned below.

insisted that magic does indeed make an appearance in rabbinic culture, but merely as a topic for lightweight amusement, or as a base foreign import, which never really struck roots within the rabbis' world. Others claimed that magic was the domain of the lower classes, who really took it seriously, with the enlightened rabbis sometimes forced to make room for such popular practices. And others admitted that the rabbis did indulge in magic, but insisted that so did everyone else at the time, from the Roman and Byzantine emperors through the late-antique philosophers to the humblest of slaves. It must be stressed, however, that while the perspectives of many of these scholars were not unbiased, their cumulative efforts produced several reliable surveys of the evidence, to which more recent scholarship has very little to add.

Given this situation, it should be clear that the present chapter does not aim to provide yet another survey of magic in rabbinic literature, but a new – and admittedly narrow – perspective from which to view these rich materials. Its novelty lies in that it seeks to re-examine the rabbinic evidence in light of the "insider" sources, produced by the Jewish magicians who were the rabbis' own contemporaries, which were surveyed in the previous chapters.[3] Simply put, the question we ask here is how does what we find in rabbinic literature tally with what we now know ancient non-Jewish and Jewish magic to have looked like? This question may be subdivided into several more specific questions – (1) What was the rabbis' attitude to magic and what did they include under this rubric? (2) Were the rabbis aware of the (Jewish and non-Jewish) magicians' activities, and if so, what can they tell us about them? (3) Did the magic practiced by the rabbis themselves resemble what we find in the archeological remains of ancient Jewish magic, and in what ways? It must be stressed, however, that the following inquiry is mostly limited to texts from the "classical" rabbinic period (first/second to sixth/seventh centuries CE), that is, to the Mishnah, Tosephta, Talmudim, and the earlier Midrashim. Later rabbinic literature, such as the late Midrashic compilations or the Geonic and later responsa, as well as the Karaite attacks upon rabbinic magic or the discussions of rabbinic magic by medieval philosophers and Kabbalists lie outside the chronological framework of the present study. It is important to note, however, that for these later periods there is much evidence that the kinds of magical texts known to us from the Cairo Genizah, for example, often came from the very heart of the rabbinic establishment, even if some rabbis

---

[3] The only attempt known to me to read rabbinic literature in light of the archeological evidence from Palestine is Misgav 1999, pp. 136–68, which leaves much to be desired.

(such as Maimonides) vehemently objected to the practices they represent.[4] The question, then, is whether in the earlier periods too the rabbis studied, transmitted, and practiced the kinds of magical activities surveyed in the previous chapters, or whether their deep involvement with it came only in the Geonic period.

Unfortunately, rabbinic literature is not the best place in which to look for answers to such questions. As in any other issue, the rabbinic discussions of magic are neither systematic nor consistent; the relevant materials are spread throughout the vast rabbinic corpus, and the different statements, stories, and interpretations do not always add up to one coherent whole. Such problems, as well as the difficulty of accurately dating many rabbinic dicta and stories, or even separating those which originated in Palestine from those whose origins are Babylonian, not to mention the corrupt state of most of the rabbinic texts at our disposal, are well known to all students of rabbinic literature, and are in no way unique to the study of rabbinic attitudes to and knowledge and practice of magic. But the study of this specific issue raises a few additional problems, as shall become apparent throughout the present chapter. Thus, our basic procedure in the following discussion will be to analyze rabbinic literature with the actual artifacts and magical texts in mind: where both corpora present a similar picture, we shall assume them to corroborate each other; where they do not, we shall have to explain why that might be so; and when the comparison simply leads nowhere, we shall try to explain what it is in the nature of both corpora which makes the comparison between them so exasperating.

In order to answer the questions posed here, we shall divide our enquiry into several sub-sections. First, we shall look at the *halakhic* discussions of magic and magicians; these will give us a sense of what the rabbis viewed as forbidden and what they did not, and some hints regarding the Jewish magical practices with which they were familiar. We shall then ask how familiar the rabbis were with the non-Jewish magical practices of their time, and how they related to them. Next, we shall turn to some colorful stories of rabbis who encountered magicians and contended with them, and then to less amusing stories in which rabbis demonstrate their own magical powers. From there, we shall turn to an examination of some rabbinic magical recipes, and end this chapter with a general assessment of our results and with some thoughts on how the "insider" evidence studied in the previous chapters and the "outsider" rabbinic sources

---

[4] For the magical learning and activities of medieval rabbis, see, e.g., Trachtenberg 1939; Zimmels 1952; Kanarfogel 2000.

studied here can complement each other in the study of ancient Jewish magic.

Before embarking upon this quest, let us delimit it further. First, it must be stressed that, as in our analysis of the magical artifacts in Chapters 4 and 5, we are more interested in pointing out the main phenomena and assessing their significance than in offering a detailed analysis of every possible source. Second, in line with our policy throughout the present book, we shall have little to say about all the divinatory sciences, such as astrology, dream-interpretation, physiognomy, divination from omens, and so on. This is not because the rabbis had little to say about such issues – the opposite is true – but in order to focus only on those issues which overlap with the issues raised throughout the previous chapters. Similarly, we shall have little to say about rabbinic demonology or angelology, about the rabbis' understanding of how and why magic actually works, or about its place within their theological worldview; some of these issues have been touched upon in Chapter 1, and others have been, and will be, dealt with elsewhere. Third, it must once again be stressed that we are less interested in the Babylonian Jewish materials and more interested in those that came, or are likely to have come, from the rabbis of Palestine (regardless of whether they are embedded in Palestinian or Babylonian compilations). A detailed comparison of the magical practices and spells revealed by the Babylonian incantation bowls written in Jewish Aramaic with what emerges from Babylonian rabbinic materials certainly would be most rewarding – but it will not be carried out here.[5] It must also be noted, however, that the age-old claim that the Babylonian rabbis were more prone to magical beliefs and activities than their Palestinian contemporaries seems to be quite unwarranted, for while there may have been some differences between the rabbis of Palestine and Babylonia in matters of demonology, the evil eye, the fear of even numbers, or the use of aggressive magic by rabbis, we shall see that both the Palestinian rabbinic compilations and the Babylonian Talmud preserve much evidence for the great interest in magic, and the practice thereof, among the sages of late-antique Palestine.[6]

A fourth self-imposed limitation has to do less with the choice of texts to be analyzed and more with the wider historical questions involved, and especially those relating to the status of the rabbinic class and its *halakhic* legislation in late-antique Palestinian Jewish society. Unlike the situation

---

[5] For some first steps in this direction, see Lesses 2001; Tan Ami 2001; Levene 2003, esp. pp. 10–14, 73–74; Shaked 2005c, pp. 9–11 and 2005b; Bohak 2005/6, pp. 258–59.

[6] As was forcefully argued by Lieberman 1942, pp. 110–14, but denied by Urbach 1986, pp. 17–21.

pertaining to Second Temple Jewish cultural history, where Josephus' narratives provide a useful starting-point and a basic skeleton, to be augmented and improved with the help of other sources (as noted in Chapter 2), the post-70 CE period has no historian, and no basic historical narrative, from which to begin our construction of Jewish history at the time. What we do have is a large corpus of rabbinic literature, a literature which displays a strong sense of itself as the only natural carrier of the Jewish religious tradition, and little interest in other Jewish groups or traditions. It thus used to be taken as evidence for the triumph of Pharisaic-rabbinic Judaism in post-Destruction Judea. But ever since the discovery of the late-antique Palestinian synagogues, with their lovely floor-mosaics – which include such blatantly pagan images as the signs of the zodiac encircling the figure of the Sun-god Helios riding his chariot with its four steeds – a debate has been raging among scholars over the significance of such finds. Some used them to reconstruct the "Reformed" or even "paganized" Jews of late antiquity, or to speculate on the many "Judaisms" in late-antique Palestine, just like the many inner-Jewish divisions in the Second Temple period. According to this model, rabbinic Judaism indeed triumphed in the end, but only after a long struggle against many alternative forms of Judaism, or against the religious indifference of the Jewish masses.[7] Other scholars, however, deny such claims, and try to accommodate the archeological finds within the framework of what one might expect in light of rabbinic literature. The rabbis, according to this model, were quite tolerant of some customs of which they disapproved but which were popular among the masses, including perhaps even the adoption of some pagan symbols. Thus, the archeological finds need not be taken as evidence for the existence of non-rabbinic "Judaisms" in late-antique Palestine, but for the complexity and inclusiveness of the socio-cultural structure built by the rabbis themselves.[8] This is, of course, a debate which is not unrelated to the ongoing turmoil within the Jewish world of our own day, with different religious and cultural interpretations of "Judaism" vying for supremacy, and each new archeological find – a *halakhic* inscription from a late-antique synagogue near Beth-Shean, legal documents from the Dead Sea region from the early second century CE, the mosaics of a newly discovered synagogue at Sepphoris, and so on – is utilized by scholars as evidence for the rabbis' influence on Jewish society at the time, or for the lack thereof. Unfortunately, the magical texts of late antiquity, with the partial exception of *Sepher ha-Razim*, have yet to be

---

[7] For a recent formulation of this model, see Schwartz 2002.
[8] For a classic formulation of this model, see Urbach 1975.

fully utilized within the framework of this debate, and this in spite of the fact that qua *texts*, they are in many ways much easier to interpret than the pictorial representations of the synagogue mosaics or other architectural decorations, whose very meaning and intention is itself a subject of much debate. It must be stressed, however, that while the following analyses might shed some light on the intriguing issue of the rabbis' own position in late-antique Palestinian Jewish society, this is not their main aim. We seek to learn whether and how rabbinic literature might help us in the study of ancient Jewish magic. What the magical texts might teach us about rabbinic literature and rabbinic history is a question that will have to be dealt with elsewhere.

MAGIC IN RABBINIC *HALAKHA*

In Chapter 2, we examined the Jewish discourse of magic in the Second Temple period, and noted especially the relative disinterest in this issue displayed by most Jewish thinkers and groups at the time. Turning to the rabbinic corpus, we face a very different situation, with an abundance of discussions of magic and related issues. Perhaps the most difficult problem in the study of these rich materials is the need to remember the difference between the rabbis' (emic) definition of magic and that of a modern observer (an etic definition), and to avoid forcing the latter upon the former. Moreover, we must also avoid assuming that a definition of magic valid in one ancient culture (be it the Greek, the Roman, the Egyptian, the Babylonian, or the Hittite) would necessarily be valid for rabbinic literature as well.⁹ Thus, to give just one example, we already noted in Chapter 2 that in Greek culture the very term "magic" (*mageia*) was born as part of the Greek encounter with Persia and its priests, the Magi, while in the Jewish world there was no real overlap between *Magus* and *mekhasheph*. And when we turn to rabbinic literature, we find a clear distinction between two terms; a *mekhasheph* is what we might translate as "magician," and the figure on which we shall have much more to say below. Besides him, however, we must place the *amgusha* – the Zoroastrian *Magus* – who (naturally enough) appears quite often in the Babylonian Talmud but never in the Palestinian Talmud, and who is normally *not* equated with a *mekhasheph*.¹⁰

---

⁹ And cf. Ritner 1995a, who stresses that neither the modern nor the Greco-Roman definitions of "magic" should be imposed on the ancient Egyptian view of magic.

¹⁰ Note, in this regard, the great difference between the entry "אמגושא" in Jastrow 1903, p. 75, and the same entry in Sokoloff 2002, p. 138. And cf. Lampe 1961, p. 819, s.v. μαγουσαῖος. The one passage where an *amgusha* is identified, by one Babylonian rabbi, as a magician, is bt Shab 65a. See also bt

Magic and magicians in rabbinic literature

The rabbis had some interesting things to say about these *amgushim*, but their statements on this score do not belong in the present enquiry, but in a discussion of what the rabbis knew about, and how they reacted to, the Zoroastrian religion and its officials.[11] Moreover, while the rabbis shared the Greco-Roman view of Egypt as the land of magic *par excellence*, they did not attribute any unique magical expertise to Persia and its inhabitants, in marked contrast with the Greek and Roman stereotypes of that land. In this respect, as in many others, the rabbinic terms for "magic" differ not only from our own, but also from those of their non-Jewish contemporaries.

With such caveats in mind, we may turn to the rabbinic discussions of magic; first, we shall try to examine the rabbis' own definition of magic, their prohibition of magical actions, and their own exceptions to that general rule. Next, we shall turn to practices which the rabbis do not discuss under their rubric of "magic," but which we might see as belonging in this category, and see how the rabbis accepted some such practices as legitimate, while frowning upon several others. In all these cases, we shall also note whether and how the evidence provided by the rabbis with regards to specific practices converges with what we find in the "insider" sources, as surveyed and analyzed in the previous chapters.

Defining magic – the prohibition and the exemptions

Of all the activities undertaken by members of the rabbinic movement in the first centuries CE, by far the most significant – from their own perspective, as well as that of a modern historian – was the development of their own *halakha*, the way in which a Jew must walk from the cradle to the grave and the rules he or she should follow throughout their lives. As the laws of the Hebrew Bible, and the rabbinic interpretation thereof, had a major impact on the development of rabbinic *halakha*, it comes as no surprise that "magic" – whose place in the biblical legislation was briefly examined in Chapter 1 – was an important category in the rabbis' legal discourse.[12] It also comes as no surprise that magic was forbidden by the rabbis, as it had been repeatedly forbidden by the Pentateuch. When we look more closely, however, the image becomes much more complicated, just as it does in the case of the biblical legislation, though in somewhat different ways.

MoK 18a, and Targum Pseudo-Jonathan to Ex 7.15, and the entry "חברא" in Sokoloff 2002, p. 429, with de Jong 1997, pp. 404–13.

[11] And see the excellent foundations for such a study laid by Greenfield 1974.

[12] For the status of magic in rabbinic *halakha*, see Seidel 1995 and 1996, pp. 157–221; Kern-Ulmer 1996; Veltri 1997, esp. pp. 26–72; Bar-Ilan 2002; Alexander 2005.

When we examine the Mishnah, the basic legal compendium of rabbinic Judaism which was edited c. 200 CE, we find the *mekhasheph* in the list of those criminals who must be executed by stoning.[13] This much is hardly surprising, in light of the biblical legislation which we examined in Chapter 1, but the Mishnah quickly introduces a limiting clause, of a type entirely unknown to the Hebrew Bible –

> The *mekhasheph* – he who performs a deed is liable (to death by stoning), but not he who creates an optical illusion. Rabbi Akiva says in the name of Rabbi Yehoshua, Two men gather cucumbers, one gathers and is exempt, while the other gathers and is liable: He who performs a deed is liable, but he who creates an optical illusion is exempt.[14]

A *mekhasheph*, says the Mishnah, is only to be stoned if he actually performed a real act; if his "act" consisted solely of a sleight of hand or some other kind of optical illusion, he is not liable to the death penalty. This is, no doubt, a sensible distinction, as there was no need for the rabbis to take offence with the many tricksters who crowded the cities and fairs of ancient cities and villages. Thus, to cite an example offered by the Babylonian Talmud, an Arab who dazzled his audience by cutting his camel with his sword and then striking his tambourine as a sign for the camel to get up whole and sound did nothing that was to be condemned as "magic" in the strict sense of the word.[15] Here, then, we see the first exception to the blanket prohibition of all magical activities, when the rabbis admit that some types of magic should arouse no objection. And the example chosen by Rabbi Akiva, the instantaneous production of agricultural produce, was, as we shall soon see, a common type of magical practice at the time.

Taking this emic definition of "magic" as our starting-point, we would quickly conclude that most of the magical recipe-books preserved in the Cairo Genizah and in other medieval and later Jewish manuscripts indeed fall squarely in the rabbis' own category of magic, for although recipes for creating optical illusions are not entirely absent from some late formularies, they certainly are the exception, not the rule.[16] Ancient Jewish magicians,

---

[13] See m San. 6.4.
[14] See m San. 6.7, 11. For Rabbi Akiva's dictum, see also Sifre Dt 171 (p. 219 Horovitz); t San 11.5 (p. 431 Zuckermandel); pt San 7.11 (25d).
[15] bt San 67b. See also bt Hull 56b–57a, on a man who fell from the roof and his intestines were poured out of his belly, but it was all an optical illusion. For street-jugglers in the Greco-Roman world, see Dickie 2001, pp. 224–29; and see also t AZ 2.6 (p. 462 Zuckermandel) and pt AZ 1.7 (40a), for the performers and tricksters in the theatres of Roman Palestine.
[16] For recipes for אחיזת עיניים, see, e.g., MTKG III, 64 (T-S Misc. 9.57); HdM recipe 2 (p. 37 Harari; p. 80 Gaster); Benayahu 1972, pp. 232, 242–43; Harari 1998, pp. 218–19. See also the theoretical discussion of this rabbinic concept in MTKG I, 3–5, and our discussion of magic and fraud in Chapter 1.

like magicians everywhere, certainly sought to change reality and "perform deeds," and not just dazzle an audience for a penny or a song. As the recipe titles of the Jewish magical collections amply show, their owners often sought to heal the sick, harm the healthy, make a woman love a man, make a newly wed man impotent or release him from such impotence, and perform other real changes in the world around them. (And the fact that *we* think that the means they employed would have failed to achieve these goals is quite irrelevant here.) Thus, their actions would fall squarely under the rabbinic category of "magic," and they would be liable to stoning under rabbinic *halakha*; this, however, was not really the case, as we shall see when we turn to some of the more significant exceptions added by the rabbis to their own *halakhic* rule.

The study of magic

The most important exception to the prohibition on dealing with magic appears in the Babylonian Talmud in conjunction with a story of the death of Rabbi Eliezer, the great sage of late-first- and early-second-century Palestine. Sitting before the rabbis who came to visit him on the occasion of his approaching death – the same rabbis who had excommunicated him for disobeying their majority rulings, and thus avoided his company for many years – he bemoans all his *halakhic* erudition that will now go to waste, since he never got the chance to impart it to his colleagues:

Moreover, I know three hundred rulings – and some say, three thousand rulings – concerning the planting of cucumbers, and no man had ever asked me about it, except for Akiva ben Yoseph: On one occasion, I and he were walking down the road; he said to me, Master, teach me about the planting of cucumbers. I said one thing, and the whole field was filled with cucumbers. He said, Master, you have taught me how to plant them, now teach me how to uproot them. I said one thing, and they were all gathered in one place.

In commenting upon this story, the Babylonian Talmud immediately asks

But how could he do this, when the Mishnah says "He who performs a deed is liable (to death by stoning)"? Well, to learn it is a different issue, for it says "You shall not learn to do [like the abominations of those nations]" (Dt 18.9) – to do you may not learn, but you may learn to understand and to teach.[17]

In analyzing this passage, we may note that the Babylonian rabbis had no doubt that R. Eliezer's deed falls squarely under the rubric "magic." This is clear from the story's location within the *sugiya* (talmudic discussion

---

[17] bt San. 68a; for Rabbi Eliezer and the cucumbers, see also Avot de-Rabbi Nathan A 25 (p. 41 Schechter).

unit) analyzing the mishnaic ruling concerning the execution of magicians, and from the explicit statement of the Talmudic editor, who was puzzled by R. Eliezer's performance of deeds liable to death by stoning. It becomes even clearer when we read an instructive parallel in the pseudo-Clementine *Recognitiones*, where Simon Magus boasts to his friends that he can become invisible, dig through mountains and rocks, jump from a mountain unscathed, release himself from bonds and from prison, render statues animate, so they seem like real men (on which more below), throw himself into a fire and emerge unharmed, change his appearance, change into animal-form, make little boys grow a beard, fly through the air, and many similar feats. He can also make new trees suddenly spring up and produce sprouts at once, and he proudly insists that he had once made a sickle reap the crops all by itself, and that he "produced many new sprouts from the earth, and made them bear leaves and produce fruit in a moment."[18] For ancient onlookers, Rabbi Eliezer's "planting of cucumbers" would have been seen as yet another magical feat in a long list of the magicians' favorite accomplishments.

Returning to the Babylonian Talmud, we might be tempted to suggest that the final statement, that while one may not practice magic, one may learn it and teach it (including hands-on experimentation), is just an ad hoc invention intended to save R. Eliezer from the grievous charges, or just a Babylonian add-on to earlier Palestinian traditions. This, however, clearly is not the case, for the assumption that magic is a body of knowledge which requires detailed study, and the claim that one indeed may (or even, must) study it, are central components of the rabbinic view of this subject from very early times, and are attested both in Palestine and in Babylonia.[19] Elsewhere in the Babylonian Talmud, Rabbi Yoḥanan, a Palestinian rabbi of the mid-third century, goes even further, insisting that knowledge of magic is a prerequisite for sitting in the *sanhedrin*, the "supreme court" of the rabbinic legal system, a claim whose origins lie already in early-second-century Palestine.[20] That judges must be *au courant* with the magical practices of their time and place hardly is surprising. Reading the "I-am-not-a-magician"

---

[18] Ps.-Clemens, *Recognitiones* 2.9.
[19] See Sifre Dt 170 (p. 217 Finkelstein) and Midrash Tannaim to Dt 18.9 (p. 109 Hoffmann), for the same exegesis of Dt 18.9. And contrast the prohibition to learn anything from an *amgusha* (for whom see n. 10 above) in bt Shab 75a.
[20] bt San 17a and Men 65a. In Midrash Tannaim to Dt 18.9 (p. 109 Hoffmann), Rabbi Yehoshua deduces from this verse that one may study magic, "in order to serve as a judge." For the rabbis' knowledge of magic, see also bt Ḥag 13a, where R. Ammi (a disciple of Rabbi Yoḥanan) says that one may transmit the secrets of Torah only to one who fulfills all five qualities listed in Is 3.3, including "wise in *ḥarashim* and an expert in *laḥash*."

defense speech of Apuleius, who lived a century earlier than Rabbi Yoḥanan and who was accused in court of practicing erotic magic, one notes two pertinent claims made by this defendant. First, he insists that most of the activities which were attributed to him, and which served as circumstantial evidence for the charge of magic – like the procuring and dissecting of some rare fish whose names happen to recall the (Greek or Latin) words for the female and male pudenda – indeed were practiced by him, but had nothing to do with magic and much to do with a philosopher's interest in natural history. To evaluate such a claim, a judge would have needed quite a detailed knowledge of which practices indeed could be considered innocent and which could only be interpreted as the smoking gun which proved the defendant's guilt. Second, and more important, Apuleius avers that had his accusers really believed him to be such a powerful magician, they would never have brought him to court, for fear of his powerful revenge. In a society where magic is assumed to have great powers, only a powerful magician can serve as a judge in trials of witchcraft, for only he would not fear the defendant's sorceries.[21] Finally, we may note that knowledge of magic could always prove useful in other cases too, for ancient Jewish magic, like the magic of many other cultures, provided many rituals for the detection of thieves, the exposure of liars, and the discovery of hidden guilt and buried treasures. As we already noted in Chapter 2, the rabbis were well aware of the potential uses of "whispers" in court; and as we shall soon see, they were not entirely averse to the use of magic as a means for social control. Thus, while rabbinic literature does not usually portray famous rabbis as boasting of their magical learning (as did, for example, Roman-period Egyptian literature with regards to Egyptian priests), it does make it clear that when the need arose, some rabbis had a secret ritual or two up their sleeves, and that such learning was in no way considered illegitimate for a respectable rabbi.

Magic, then, was nominally forbidden to anyone who followed rabbinic *halakha*, but the study of magic was not. In some cases it was accepted, in others it was even encouraged; and here we may note that it was not only as judges that the rabbis had to have some working knowledge of magic, but as legislators and leaders as well. For example, they state that when purging one's house of all leavened food in preparation for Passover, one who shares a wall in common with the apartment of a non-Jew may forego examining the holes in that wall for wayward crumbs, lest his Gentile neighbor

---

[21] For the first line of defense, see Apuleius, *Apol.* passim; for the second, see *ibid.* 26, and cf. the illuminating story in Apuleius, *Met.* 1.10. See also Rashi's comments on the talmudic passages cited in the previous note.

would fear he was performing a magic ritual.[22] Here, an awareness of the common practice, among non-Jews and Jews alike, of burying aggressive magical spells and objects in the victim's home helps the rabbis shape their *halakhic* regulations so as to avoid innocent Jews running into trouble. This awareness, of what might be suspected as a magical act, reemerges elsewhere in rabbinic literature, both in Palestine and in Babylonia, and determines what one may and may not do, for example, when giving food to someone else's children.[23] And magic-related issues come up in other contexts too – as, for example, when the rabbis debate whether a man may exculpate himself of the charge of adultery by claiming that it was forced upon him by erotic magic, and when they allow certain changes in normal *halakha* because of the danger of *keshaphim*.[24] In light of such discussions, the fact that will emerge from the rest of this chapter – that the rabbis often knew what they were talking about when it came to magic and magicians, and that in some cases they even consulted with professional magicians and witches – should come as no surprise. It is, in other words, not a process that occurred in spite of rabbinic legislation, but in line with it, and in marked contrast with some of the Roman and Christian attempts to forbid not only the practice of magic, but also its study.[25] Moreover, the permission to study magic was not the only exception to the rabbis' anti-magic legislation.

The magic of creation

A second exception to the prohibition of dealing with magic seems to have been less significant for late-antique Jewish society, but was of some importance in later periods in Jewish history. It involves the claim that some rabbis had the power to create living creatures, or to imbue inanimate objects with a soul. First, we may note a statement and a pair of

---

[22] See bt Pes 8b (top), with Rashi ad loc.
[23] See bt Shab 10b // Beza 16a: Whoever gives a slice of bread to a small child should notify the child's mother by putting oil on the child's forehead and blue paint around his eyes. But now, that we are fearful of magic (והעידנא דחיישינן לכשפים), one should smear on him of the same kind (of food). See also pt Demai 3.3 (23c) // pt AZ 1.9 (40a) // Lev R. 37.3 (p. 862 Margalioth) and bt Eruv 64b (and cf. bt BM 23a): One who finds food on the wayside may not ignore it; this was the original ruling, but now it is permitted to ignore it because of *keshaphim*.
[24] Fornication: in pt Nazir 8.1 (57a), Resh Laqish says, A man can claim, I was forced (into adultery) by the *keshaphim* she did to me, while in bt Yev 53b Rava insists that no male can be coerced to have an erection and participate in a sexual union; see also Lieberman 1942, p. 110. Danger: e.g., pt Ket 1.1 (24d): one may not marry a virgin on a Monday, but if this becomes necessary because of (erotic?) *keshaphim* – it is permitted.
[25] See, e.g., Pauli Sententiae 5.23.18: . . . *non tantum huius artis professio, sed etiam scientia prohibita est*; for Christian legislation against clerics consulting magicians, see Flint 1991, pp. 66–67.

Magic and magicians in rabbinic literature

stories embedded side by side in the Babylonian Talmud, in a *sugiya* on necromancy:

> Rava said, If the righteous ones wished to, they could create a world, for it is said, "For only your iniquities have separated between you and your God" (Isa 59.2).
>
> Rava created a man, and sent him to Rabbi Zera; he would converse with him, but he did not respond; he said to him, You are from the Magi[26] – return to your dust!
>
> Rav Ḥanina and Rav Oshayah would sit every Friday and study the Book of Creation, and create for themselves a one-third[27] calf, and eat it.[28]

A few pages later, in the context of the talmudic discussion of the *mekhasheph*, The Babylonian Abaye, a contemporary and close friend of Rava, turns these isolated incidents into a general rule, by concluding that some types of *keshaphim* are liable to death by stoning, some – like the creation of calves with the help of "the rules of creation" – are forbidden but exempt from the death penalty, and some – like creating optical illusions – are entirely permitted.[29] These two passages – the earliest references to the practices which would later be associated with the *Golem*, the artificial anthropoid – have been the subject of numerous studies, which sought to identify the text studied by the creation-hungry rabbis (which is differently labeled in each of the above passages, and even in different manuscripts thereof, and whose relations with the *Sepher Yezira* known to us from medieval Jewish manuscripts and commentaries and discussed in the previous chapter has been much debated) and to assess the place of such creative activities in the rabbis' world.[30] Such questions, important as they are, need not detain us here; for the purpose of the current enquiry, we must note that here is yet another rabbinic exception to the blanket condemnation of magic and to the rule that magicians must be stoned. Contrary to what we may have expected, the Babylonian rabbis make no attempt to "whitewash" their behavior or legitimize it by giving it a less offensive label (as did, for example, some of their Neoplatonist contemporaries, who dabbled in magic but called it "theurgy").[31] Nor do they try to portray the act as a case of an optical illusion, whose permissibility was already noted, for by telling their readers that the rabbis actually ate the

---

[26] For the correct meaning of חברא, see Sokoloff 2002, p. 429. Note, however, the rabbis' own play on *ḥabbarim/ḥaverim* in bt BB 75a (on Jb 40.30).
[27] It is not clear whether עיגלא תילתא refers to "a calf a third of the normal size", or to "a three years old calf," but this makes little difference for the present discussion; the expression itself is based on Gn 15.9.
[28] bt San 65b.   [29] bt San 67b.   [30] See esp. Scholem 1953; Idel 1990, pp. 27–43; Schäfer 1995.
[31] For Neoplatonic theurgy and its foundations in ancient magic, see Dodds 1951, pp. 283–311.

calf they had produced they make it clear that this was a real deed which they had performed, not a mere sleight of hand.[32] Thus, instead of depicting such rabbinic activities as non-magical, the rabbis simply add another exception to the general prohibition of practicing magic. This move is all the more striking when we recall that similar stories about Jesus – how, as a young boy, he used to make images of birds, animate them, and let them fly around – were used by some Jews in late antiquity to accuse Jesus and his followers of practicing magic, and that apocryphal Christian literature tells many such stories about the likes of Simon Magus, including the passage mentioned above.[33] Apparently, the rabbis were not really worried lest their penchant for the creation of calves and men be seen as a blatant transgression of the biblical laws against magic.

Magic and medicine
A third exception to the prohibition of magic, and the one which was destined to have the greatest impact on the relations between magic and *halakha*, is embedded in the rabbinic discussion of "the Ways of the Amorites," those forbidden practices to which we shall turn at greater length below. At present, we must note the rule found in both Talmudim, and attributed to some of the greatest rabbinic authorities of late-antique Palestine and Babylonia, that "Anything which heals is not of 'the Ways of the Amorites'."[34] This ruling is paralleled in contemporary Roman law,[35] but should also be seen within the wider context of the rabbis' insistence on the sanctity of life, evident in many other *halakhic* discussions. To save a mortally sick person, or even someone whose illness *might* be fatal, one may delay, or even forego, a child's circumcision, desecrate the holy Sabbath, eat on the Day of Atonement, and consume various non-kosher substances, even pork, as long as they are known to be good for his or her condition.[36] In the same vein, and for the same reason, the rabbis were willing to adopt

---

[32] And cf. pt San 7.11 (25d): "If you ate from it, it is a real deed."
[33] For Jesus' animation of statues, cf. the *Infancy Gospel of Thomas* 2 (Hennecke and Schneemelcher 1963–65, vol. I, pp. 392–93) with the *Toledoth Yeshu* traditions (e.g., Krauss 1902, pp. 119, 147, and Deutsch 2000, p. 184), and see also Quran 3.45; 5.110. And see pt San 7.19 (25d) for similar stories about *minim*, and for R. Yehoshua's boasts of his own expertise in this field. For pagan references to the animation of statues, see, e.g., Dodds 1947, pp. 62–65.
[34] See bt Shab 67a and bt Hull 77b, where this dictum is attributed to Abaye and Rava, and pt Shab 6.10 (8c), where it is attributed to Rabbi Yoḥanan.
[35] For the Roman parallels, see Apuleius, *Apol.* 40: *nihil enim, quod salutis ferendae gratia fit, criminosum est*; *CT* 9.16.3 (aggressive and erotic magic must be punished, but medical and apotropaic-agricultural magic are acceptable). See also Flint 1991, pp. 25–28, and Dickie 2001, pp. 251–57.
[36] See, e.g., m Yoma 8.5–7 (eating on Yom Kippur and desecrating the Sabbath to save lives); t Shab 9.22 (p. 40 Lieberman) and 15.11–17 (pp. 72–75 Lieberman) (all the things you may do on a Sabbath in cases of mortal danger).

and utilize quite a few foreign customs, including some that we would certainly classify as "magic," as long as they were deemed to have medical value. This rabbinic openness to medical magic can be seen in numerous instances, including the dozens of medico-magical recipes found in rabbinic literature, to which we shall return below.[37] For the time being, we need only note that the acceptance of beneficial medical magic by the rabbis is probably the widest door they left open for the entry of magical recipes and practices into the very heart of rabbinic Judaism. For while the rabbis do not say this explicitly, the permission to use magic in order to save lives could implicitly legitimize apotropaic ("white") magic of all types, including, for example, spells to save one from robbers, rituals for quelling a storm at sea, and recipes for keeping evil beasts or the evil eye away from one's town or home, all of which are abundantly represented in the "insider" sources for late-antique Jewish magic, and some of which may be found even in rabbinic literature itself.

The use of magic against magic and magicians

In addition to the rabbis' explicit exceptions to the general prohibition on magic, we must now turn to two exceptions which are never explicitly stated in rabbinic literature, but which seem to underlie many rabbinic laws, stories, and sayings. The first of these is the notion that to fight magic and magicians, one may resort to magic, so as to beat the opponents at their own game. As we noted in Chapter 1, this notion is already implicit in the biblical stories of Moses and Aaron's encounters with the Egyptian *ḥarṭumim*, stories to which the rabbis themselves had much to add. Among their many accounts of Moses' conflicts with magicians, we should perhaps pay special attention to the wonderful story of how, in order to beat the magician Amaleq and his astrological calculations, Moses temporarily disarranged all the constellations. Such feats were commonly attributed to ancient magicians – witness Nectanebo's very similar exploits in the *Alexander Romance* – and such stories clearly point to the rabbis' conviction that there was nothing wrong in Moses' use of magic to beat pagan magicians.[38] This conviction, moreover, appears not only in their retellings of the Moses stories, but in many other instances as well. As we shall see below, they also had no qualms about stories in which even a sage like Rabbi Yehoshua, in the early second century CE, resorts to magical practices in order to fight a pernicious Roman witch. Rather than watering down the

---

[37] For its later ramifications, see also Trachtenberg 1939, pp. 193–207.
[38] Cf. pt RH 3.8 (59a) with Ps.-Callisthenes, *Alexander Romance* 1.12. And cf. PRE 52, for the claim that Joshua had stopped the sun and moon (Jos 10.12–13) for a similar reason.

magical aspects of his peculiar praxis – by saying, as they do in other cases, that "he did what he did" and providing no specific details – the talmudic narrators are proud of Rabbi Yehoshua's ability to use magical techniques more powerful than those of a powerful witch, and clearly see his behavior as perfectly legitimate, even desirable. This lenient attitude towards the use of magic against magic and magicians is evident in many other instances, such as when throwing a piece of iron into the cemetery and crying "Hada" ("One"?) is forbidden as one of "the Ways of the Amorites," but if it is done "because of *keshaphim*," it is permitted, or when a Babylonian rabbi quotes the anti-witchcraft spell he had received from a real witch.[39] We shall turn to a few such examples in greater detail below, but should already note how they add up to one more exception to the general rule that magic is forbidden. To fight magicians, you may sometimes resort to magic.

Magic as a means for social control
In addition to the implicit permission to use magic against magic and magicians, we must also note the rabbis' apparent intuition that resort to magic was permissible even in other cases where social control – or, to put it bluntly, the rabbis' own authority – was at stake. In searching for evidence for this elusive concept, we may focus on two different issues. First, and less significant, is an almost endless series of warnings that persons who fail to do certain things correctly might be vulnerable to demons or to magic. If you eat peeled garlic you run a great risk, since demons are likely to dwell upon it, and the same is true of a drink which was poured out in the evening but only drunk in the morning. Failing to wash your hands in the morning exposes you to the dangers of the demon Shibbeta which lurks on the bread you eat. Sitting under a water-drain will expose you to demons, and eating vegetables directly from the bundle bound by the gardener or vendor will expose you to *keshaphim*.[40] Peeing between a palm tree and a wall might leave the demon who resides there no choice but to attack you, and if you sleep alone in the house, Lilith will seize you. If after going to the toilet you have sex without first outpacing the toilet-demon, you will sire epileptic children, and wiping your rectum in the wrong manner will make you vulnerable to *keshaphim* coming from as far away as Spain.[41] Often,

[39] For "Hada," see t Shab. 6.12 (p. 24 Lieberman), with TK p. 88. For the anti-witchcraft spell, see bt Pes. 110a–b, cited and discussed below. See also bt Pes 111a, for a spell against two women who are sitting at a crossroads and are presumed to be dabbling in magic.
[40] Peeled garlic and poured water: bt Nid 17a. Shibbeta: bt Yoma 77b and Hull 107b. Drains and bundled vegetables: bt Hull 105b.
[41] Peeing on demons: bt Pes 111a. Sleeping alone: bt Shab 151b. Toilet-demon: bt Gitt 70a. Wiping: bt Ber 62a.

such claims are accompanied by illustrative exempla, such as the sad fate of a man who rode over a puddle of poured water: even though he was riding a donkey and wearing shoes, which normally would have protected him, the fact that *keshaphim* were involved rendered these defensive measures useless, and soon his shoes shrunk and his feet withered away. In another story, we learn how two rabbis were not harmed by the spells of a woman whom they had offended; exasperated, she tells them that because they never wipe their rectums with pottery sherds, never kill the lice on their clothes, and never eat vegetables directly from the bundle bound by the gardener, they are simply immune to all her *keshaphim*.[42] And in many cases such warnings are even followed by instructions on what to do when one mistakenly did the dangerous action, or had no choice but to do it. To give just one example, we may note how two Palestinian rabbis list three actions which expose one to a whole cohort of angels of destruction, or even to the Angel of Death himself. As one of these dangers – meeting women on their way back from a house where someone had died – is very hard to avoid, Rabbi Yehoshua ben Levi advises whoever finds himself in this predicament to take a different route, and if he cannot, to recite Zec 3.2, "May the Lord rebuke you, Satan," a verse whose popularity among the Jewish practitioners was already noted in Chapter 5.[43] This last example also demonstrates that such fears were in no way unique to the Jews of Babylonia, even if their incidence there may have been higher than in late-antique Palestine. In a similar vein, we may note the rabbis' conviction that certain practices (such as having a decent breakfast!) and materials could keep magic and demons away, including such well-known Greco-Roman antidotes as *oinogarum* (a mixture of wine and the Romans' favorite sauce) and the celebrated theriac.[44] And here, too, we are dealing with a Palestinian rabbi who is recommending materials commonly used throughout the Roman empire, but much harder to procure in the Sasanian empire.

The list of things which one must do or avoid so as not to be too exposed to demons and magic is almost endless (and we shall see more examples below), and much of it is not specifically Jewish or intrinsically rabbinic. Thus, it mainly demonstrates the rabbis' interest in such issues, and their attempts to position themselves as fully in the know about demonology and

---

[42] Withered feet: bt Pes 111a. Immune rabbis: bt Shab 81b–82a and Hull 105b. See also Chapter 1, n. 117, for the immunity to magic of other holy men and sages in late antiquity.

[43] bt Ber 51a; for other examples, see, e.g., bt Ber 62a, for a spell to avert *keshaphim* in case one wiped one's rectum incorrectly.

[44] Breakfast: bt BM 107b (a good breakfast saves you from many things, including the *mazikin*). Materials: bt Shab 109b (Rabbi Ḥanina said, forty-days-old urine is good . . . even against *keshaphim*. Rabbi Yoḥanan said, אנינרון אבנגר ותירייקה are good . . . against *keshaphim*).

magic. But it may also demonstrate their occasional attempts to regulate, by means of such threats, the behavior of ordinary Jews in contexts – such as toilet habits and sexual mores – which usually were not exposed to the public, or rabbinic, eye. Moreover, the rabbis' willingness to use demons and magic as bugbears with which to control the behavior of their flock is made clear by a series of explicit promises they make concerning the boons to be derived from observing their own *halakha*. Reciting the *shemaʿ* on the bed before going to sleep keeps the demons away (at a time when they are most active and you are most vulnerable!), and if you see a frightening apparition you should recite the *shemaʿ* (just as a Christian would use the Pater Noster, or the sign of the Cross) – unless you are in an impure place, in which case the rabbis provide a useful incantation instead.[45] Saying your daily prayer in a certain order will keep you from harm's way for the whole day, satiating yourself with Torah will prevent you from receiving bad tidings in your dreams, and the apotropaic value of the *mezuzah* and the *tefillin* are repeatedly stressed by the rabbis.[46] Perhaps more than anything else, it is the Torah itself, and Torah study, which assure one longevity, prosperity, and health, and are simply the ultimate panacea. For, as R. Yehoshua ben Levi put it, "If one ... has a throat-ache, let him study Torah ... if his belly aches, let him study Torah ... if his bones ache, let him study Torah ... if his whole body aches, let him study Torah" – each of these remedies substantiated with a suitable midrash on a biblical verse, the result of many years of studying Torah![47]

Reading such claims, we should not imagine some enlightened rabbis using the superstitious mindset of the ignorant masses to impose their *halakhot* upon them, but see the rabbis and the rest of the population as sharing the same assumptions about the dangers of demons and of *keshaphim*, and as honestly convinced that their rules of religious conduct promised the best protection against such dangers. In this, the rabbis of late antiquity were no different from many other religious leaders throughout history, who taught their followers that observing the religious rituals – such as baptism or the recitation of the Quran, to give just two obvious

---

[45] *Shemaʿ* on the bed: pt Ber 1.1 (2d); bt Ber 5a. *Shemaʿ* against apparitions: bt Meg 3a.
[46] Saying your daily prayer: pt Ber 1.1 (2d); bt Ber 9b. Satiating yourself with Torah: bt Ber 14a. *Mezuzot* and *tefillin*: e.g., pt Peah 1.1, 15d (Rabbi sent Artaban a *mezuzah* and explained that it will protect him); bt AZ 11a (Onqelos explains to Roman soldiers that the *mezuzah* is (or, symbolizes) God's protection of his servants); and see Jansson 1998. For *tefillin* to protect you against demons in the toilet, see bt Ber. 23a-b, with Rashi ad loc., s.v., משום; cf. bt Men 44a (whoever puts on *tefillin* makes his own life longer).
[47] See bt Eruv 54a. See also Num R. 12.3, with many claims that the Torah protects one against demons. For the whole issue, see also Trachtenberg 1939, pp. 153–57.

examples – would preserve them from demons and witchcraft. We should also recall that this is just a small part of a much wider biblical and rabbinic discourse stressing all the boons which accrue from the correct observance of God's commandments and all the horrible things which happen when they are neglected, certainly one of the deepest convictions of the monotheistic enterprise as a whole.[48]

A second issue in which the rabbis' use of magic as a means for social control clearly emerges is the many stories about the use of magic to harm opponents and offenders. As we shall see below, the rabbis repeatedly insist that learned rabbis are men of great power, and therefore not to be treated lightly. But while the claim that a rabbi's curse, for example, is dangerous even if it is unjustly uttered does not really amount to the use of magic, for it only involves the rabbi's innate powers, some rabbis clearly were willing to go a step further when all else failed. In a series of stories, which we shall examine below, prominent rabbis are described as using elaborate magical rituals to harm sectarian opponents, bullies, and other problematic individuals. These stories sometimes express a certain ambivalence about the use of such aggressive rituals, a sure sign that some narrators, and some rabbis, were wary of the use of aggressive magic to settle ideological or personal scores. Others, however, clearly found this acceptable, and could rely on the biblical precedents to which we referred in Chapter 1, and on the pressing need to make sure that various troublemakers are put out of the way as efficiently and as forcefully as possible. And once the rabbis embarked on the extensive study of magic, its use to subdue their opponents was almost inevitable.

To sum up what we have seen thus far, we may note that rabbinic *halakha*, like its biblical predecessor, prohibits its Jewish followers from practicing magic. This prohibition, however, is mitigated by several important exceptions: optical illusions are acceptable, as is the occasional creation of new life by means of "the laws of Creation." The study of magic is permitted, and sometimes even encouraged, and the use of magic for medical purposes also is entirely acceptable. Finally, although the rabbis never say so explicitly, it is repeatedly implied that using magic in order to defeat magicians and witches is acceptable, and perhaps even desirable, and that even the use of magic against non-magicians who pose a threat to rabbinic authority is quite conceivable. Thus, not only the study of magic is endorsed by the rabbis, but even its occasional use. In what follows, we

---

[48] See, e.g., m Shab 2.6 and bt Shab 32a-b: why women, *'am ha-'arez* and others die because of various *halakhic* transgressions; bt Taan 7b: all the sins which cause drought.

shall see how these explicit and implicit *halakhic* attitudes to magic shaped both the rabbis' familiarity with many magical techniques and practices and their own uses of this powerful technology.

Other permitted and forbidden practices

In the previous section, we focused on the rabbinic definition of magic, on the prohibition of magical activities, and on the exceptions to this general rule. It is now time to turn to a few additional practices, practices which *we* might classify as "magic" but which were differently classified by the rabbis themselves. We shall focus on four specific issues: first, the manufacture and use of amulets, which the rabbis clearly saw as entirely acceptable, but did not try to monopolize or even regulate; second, the use of the divine Name, which the rabbis did try to monopolize, at least in part; third, the rabbis' half-hearted condemnations of several Jewish practices which they found quite hard to swallow, but did not refer to them as "magic" and did not really forbid them outright. Finally, we shall note the emergence of a new category, "the Ways of the Amorites," which the rabbis introduced into their *halakhic* discussions, and which served as a "bag" into which they could throw various contemporary non-Jewish activities which they found unacceptable and which they wished to prevent Jews from adopting.

Amulets

Contrary to our own instinctive assumption that amulets are a magical implement, the rabbis saw amulets as a standard constituent of a person's daily garments.[49] Thus, their many references to amulets have nothing to do with their discussions of magic, and do not even raise the question whether their use is forbidden or permitted, a question which their Christian contemporaries found so vexing, and so worthy of their pious fulminations.[50] What does require discussion, from the rabbis' perspective, is such questions as whether amulets may be carried around outdoors on the Sabbath, when one may carry one's essential clothes, but no extra luggage. The Mishnah's ruling is that one may not carry an amulet outdoors on the Sabbath, "unless it is (*min ha-*) *mumḥe.*" This last expression may be translated either as "unless it is made by an approved person," or as "unless it is approved," and both meanings are analyzed in the talmudic

---

[49] For previous discussions of rabbis and amulets, see Blau 1898, pp. 86–96; Preuss 1993, pp. 144–50; Hezser 2001, pp. 221–26.
[50] See, e.g., m Sheq 1.2; Kelim 23.1; Miq 10.2, etc. For the Christian attitude(s) to amulets, see Leclercq 1924, pp. 1784–88, and Dickie 2001, pp. 304–11.

discussions of this ruling.⁵¹ Reading these discussions, one finds the rabbis taking as their basic guideline that an "approved" amulet is one that healed three times, regardless of how many times the same amulet *did not* prove helpful and of the possibility that a given person would have been healed even without it.⁵² Like the efficacious relics and icons of many Christian saints, amulets to which successes were attributed, and the people who produced them, enjoyed some reputation, and this sufficed to make them "approved" in rabbinic eyes. And as we shall see in a wonderful story to which we shall soon turn, when an amulet failed to achieve the goal for which it was procured, it was simply replaced by another.

The rabbis' acceptance of amulets fits well with their notion, to which we already alluded, that if something is good for one's health it cannot be forbidden. One also finds that in spite of the obvious occasion to do so, the rabbis do not try to monopolize the production of amulets, and clearly accept the presence of professional amulet-producers. The Palestinian Talmud even quotes Rabbi Abbahu, in the name of Rabbi Yoḥanan, as saying that "A physician may be trusted if he says, this amulet is approved – I healed with it once and twice and three times."⁵³ The question, in other words, is not a religious question but a medical one, and – as they often did in questions involving technical expertise – the rabbis here willingly step aside and let the experts, in this case the professional physicians, decide which amulets are "approved," and may therefore be carried outdoors on the Sabbath.⁵⁴ In passing, we may note that while some Greek physicians (most notably Galen) were highly skeptical of the use of amulets – though even they admitted that some amulets actually do work – others saw nothing wrong with prescribing every conceivable type of amulet to the patients who sought their aid, and that a similar picture emerges from the study of

---

⁵¹ m Shab 6.2, discussed in bt Shab 61b–62a; pt Shab 6.2 (8b); t Shab 4.9 (p. 18 Lieberman). It must be stressed, however, that the term *mumḥe* is extremely common in rabbinic literature (e.g., m Bekh 4.4–5; m San 3.1; t San 5.1 [p. 422 Zuckermandel]), and clearly has nothing to do with the claims found in the magical recipe books that a certain recipe is *baduk u-menuseh*, and the similar expressions for "tried and tested" which we analyzed in Chapter 4.

⁵² And cf. Galen's famous demonstration of the efficacy of peony-root, worn around one's neck as an amulet, in keeping epilepsy at bay (see Chapter 1, n. 69), or of the uselessness of adding magical symbols to medical gems (*De simp. med.* 10.19 (Kühn XII, p. 207)). While such experiments would not satisfy the modern scientist, both their method and their underlying assumptions differ greatly from those of the rabbis.

⁵³ pt Shab 6.2 (8b). And note the parable in Lev R. 26.5 (pp. 596–97 Margalioth) of a physician who gave an approved amulet to two Jewish epileptics.

⁵⁴ For letting the experts make the decision even when it had *halakhic* implications, see, e.g., m Yoma 8.5 (a sick person may be given food on Yom Kippur if knowledgeable persons (בקיאין) recommend this); pt Shab 18.3 (16c) (go ask a midwife whether the umbilical cord should be cut on the Sabbath), etc.

Islamic medicine.⁵⁵ We may also recall our observation in Chapter 4, that some of the Jewish magical texts of late antiquity display their producers' familiarity with Greek medical terminology. Finally, we may note that the Hebrew Oath of Asaph the physician and Yoḥanan ben Zabda – which has been dated anywhere between the fifth and the ninth century CE – explicitly commands physicians to avoid all magical practices (including, we may note, erotic magic!).⁵⁶ Apparently, medicine and magic often went hand in hand in late-antique Jewish society, a fact which was not lost on the rabbis.

The rabbis' decision to let the professional amulet-makers decide which amulets were "approved" is of great importance for our study. First, it highlights the fact that the many Jewish amulets from late-antique Palestine need not be attributed to "heretical" or even non-rabbinic Jews, for the rabbis saw nothing wrong with the production and use of amulets.⁵⁷ Second, it sheds new light on the proliferation of patently non-Jewish elements in some of these amulets – including, for example, the presence of Abrasax, Erechsigal/-el, and Iyessemigadôn on amulets found in the synagogue at Nirim – for it seems quite clear that even the rabbis never tried to regulate or standardize the *contents* of written amulets, and they readily accepted the fact that amulets were produced and distributed by professionals who were not necessarily of the rabbinic class. If an amulet healed three times, there could be nothing wrong with it, and its contents, subversive as they might be, remained unknown, rolled up or folded and tucked neatly in a tube or a pouch. Thus, while the rabbis explicitly forbid the use of "idolatrous" objects of the Jews' pagan neighbors for healing purposes (and we already saw, in Chapter 2, how such objects could be used by Jews as amulets), and explicitly prohibit being healed by *minim* (on whom much more below), there is no evidence in rabbinic literature for the unfolding or unrolling of a "suspicious" amulet to examine its contents.⁵⁸ This "Don't ask, don't tell" policy stands in marked contrast with what would occur in some later periods of Jewish history, as when Jacob Emden "exposed" the Sabbatean

---

⁵⁵ See the references to Galen, above n. 52, and cf. the many amulets recommended by Alexander Trallianus (e.g., on vol. I, p. 557–75 Puschmann, on "natural" remedies and amulets against epilepsy). For amulets and magic in Islamic medicine, see Ullmann 1978, pp. 107–11.

⁵⁶ See Pines 1976, pp. 258 (text) and 223–24 (notes), and Lieber 1983, p. 88: *Ve-al telkhu beḥuqot ha-mekhashphim le-ḥaber u-le-naḥesh u-le-khasheph u-le-hafrid ish me-eshet ḥeiqo o isha me-aluph ne'ureiha* (v.l., *le-hafrid ish me-ishto o isha mi-ba'alah*).

⁵⁷ And as we briefly noted in Chapter 5, n. 119, at least one amulet was produced for a client identified as "Rabbi Eleazar son of Esther, the servant of the God of heaven," who may have been a member of the rabbinic class.

⁵⁸ Prohibition of being healed through idolatry: e.g., pt Shab. 14.4 (14d); bt Pes 25a, etc., and cf. the Oath of Asaph (Lieber 1983, p. 88): *ve-lo le-hit'azer be-khol 'avodat' elilim lerape' ba-hem*, etc. By *minim*: e.g., pt Shab. 14.4 (14d); bt AZ 27b, etc.

contents of the amulets produced by Jonathan Eibeschütz, or when the Baal Shem-Tov's opponents opened the amulets he had produced in order to convict him of using God's Names for mundane trivialities. Moreover, while the rabbis avoided the writing down of oral Torah, and forbade the writing of "benedictions," they never objected to the writing down of amulets. And while they developed meticulous regulations for the writing of *tefillin* and *mezuzot*, they apparently made no attempt to regulate the shape and contents of non-written amulets, or the contents, layout, or even writing surfaces of written amulets.[59] This fits well with a third feature of the late-antique Jewish amulets, namely their great textual and scribal diversity. There was only one "correct" way, at least in rabbinic *halakha*, to write *tefillin* or *mezuzot*, but the writing of amulets was an open field, both in terms of who wrote them and in terms of how they were written and what they contained. Finally, we may note that while the rabbis forbade the selling of Torah scrolls and other objects to Gentiles, and discussed even such issues as selling cattle to Gentiles, there is no discussion in rabbinic literature of the permissibility of producing amulets for non-Jews, and in one story – which we shall cite below – this possibility seems to be taken for granted. If, as the evidence seems to suggest, some of the Aramaic metal amulets were produced by Jewish practitioners for non-Jewish clients, these practitioners were in no way ignoring rabbinic *halakha*, since rabbinic *halakha* never forbade such commerce.[60]

The rabbis' decision to make no attempt at monopolizing, controlling, or even regulating the production of amulets has one negative implication for the source-thirsty historian. While rabbinic literature has much to say about the aims for which amulets were worn (against the evil eye, against demons, against pirates and highway robbers, against barrenness or abortions or epilepsy),[61] about different types of amulets ("amulets of roots," "amulets of herbs," "amulets of writing," a "preserving stone," and so on),[62] about the different materials of their containers and their different

---

[59] Avoidance of writing down oral Torah: Sussmann 2005; prohibition to write ברכות: t Shab 13.4 (p. 58 Lieberman), with TK pp. 205–06 and Sussmann 2005, pp. 376–77. Regulating *tefillin* and *mezuzot*: e.g., m Meg 1.8; bt Men 32b, etc.

[60] In later periods, objections to producing amulets for Gentiles are not uncommon – e.g., *Midrash Ha-Tappuaḥ ba-ʿAtzei ha-Yaʿar* 16 (p. 283 Wertheimer): *veha-kotev shemot be-qamiʿa bishvil goyim* (listed among those punished in Hell!).

[61] Evil eye: Num R. 12.4 (and see Ulmer 1994, pp. 158–65). Demons: bt Pes 111b (cited below). Pirates and robbers: Lev R. 25.1 (p. 567 Margalioth). Barrenness: Gen R. 45.2 (p. 448 Theodor-Albeck, with Theodor's comments *ad loc.*). Abortions: see the following note. Epilepsy: Lev R. 26.5 (pp. 596–7 Margalioth).

[62] Roots (קמיע של עיקרין): e.g., t Shab 4.9; bt Shab 61a; herbs (של עשבים): e.g., pt Shab 6.2 (8b); writing (של כתב or בכתב): all previously cited passages. A "preserving stone" against abortions (אבן תקומה): bt Shab 66b (and Rubin 1995, pp. 52–61). See also t Kidd 5.17 (p. 299 Lieberman) (with TK pp. 985–86) and bt BB 16b, for the miraculous stone owned by Abraham, which would heal all who saw it.

shapes (a leather pouch, a metal ring, tube, bracelet or necklace, a hollow wooden cane),[63] about the different surfaces on which written amulets were inscribed (including thin sheets of metal),[64] about who wore them (men, women, little children, and even cattle),[65] about the manner in which they were carried (hung on the arm, on the neck, etc.),[66] and sometimes even about who produced them (professional amulet-makers, physicians, and rabbinic disciples),[67] it has precious little to say about the actual *contents* of written amulets. This is much to be regretted, since a detailed discussion of the contents of written amulets would have been very useful for the sake of comparison with the archeological evidence of what actual amulets really looked like.

What rabbinic literature does tell us about the contents of written amulets is that they may be assumed to contain sacred Names and biblical verses,[68] and that for an amulet to work it must contain the correct name(s) of the demon(s) whom the amulet is supposed to drive away. Thus, when the rabbis of Babylonia ask about the meaning of the illness called *kordiakos* which is mentioned in the Mishnah, they explain this word – which in fact is a loanword from Greek, and akin to English "cardiac (condition)" – as the name of the demon which causes that illness. And why would the Mishnah mention a demon's name? "for (the writing of) an amulet," is the response of the Talmudic editor – i.e., so that in writing an amulet against this illness you would know the exact name of the demon which must be thwarted.[69] A similar discussion develops when the Babylonian Talmud deals with the Mishnaic ordinance that on Passover eve one should drink at

---

[63] A leather pouch: m Shab 8.3: עור כדי לעשות קמיע; t Kel BM 1.12 (p. 579 Zuckermandel); bt Shab 62a: מחופה עור. A metal ring (טבעת): pt Shab 6.2 (8b). A tube (סילונה, i.e., σωλήν, a common loanword in Jewish magical recipes (e.g., ShR II, 125, 137, etc.)): ibid. A bracelet (שיר): ibid. A necklace (מומייקה, i.e., μανιάκης): ibid. A wooden cane: Lev R. 25.1 (p. 567 Margalioth): he took a cane (מקל), bore a hole in it (וחקקו) and placed an amulet inside it (such instructions being quite common in Genizah recipes for a safe journey).
[64] Metal: t Kel BM 1.11 (p. 579 Zuckermandel) (קמיע של מתכות). A lamella: t Kel BM 1.12 (p. 579 Zuckermandel) (פסלין is an error for פטלין = πέταλον, a common technical term in Greek magical texts (e.g., MTKG III, 61 (T-S K 1.162) 1b/13 and 1a/35, and cf. LXX Ex 28.36)). I am still puzzled by the word אפטט in the same passage, which baffled all previous commentators. Note also the reference to טס in pt Shab 6.6 (8c), a common designation for a metal *lamella* in Jewish magical texts.
[65] Men: m Shab 6.2. Women: Num R. 12, and cf. Gen R. 45.2 (p. 448 Theodor-Albeck, with Theodor's comments ad loc.). Children: m Shab 6.9; bt Kidd 73b. (For amulets as something usually worn by women and children, note bt BB 75a, where *vetiksherenu le-na'arotekha* (Job 40.29) is understood as referring to producing amulets.) Cattle: pt Shab 5.4 (7c); bt Shab 53b; t Shab. 4.5 (p. 17 Lieberman).
[66] On the arm: See the metaphorical use of "like an amulet hung upon one's arm" in pt Ḥag 2.1 (77a) and bt San 21b–22a. On the neck: pt Shab 6.6 (8c) and cf. the recipes in bt Shab 66b and 67a.
[67] See above, n. 53, and below, n. 71.   [68] See bt Shab 61b and 115b.
[69] bt Gitt 67b, commenting on m Gitt 7.1. For קורדיקוס = καρδιακός, see Krauss 1898–99, p. 519, and Luz 1989, p. 50.

Magic and magicians in rabbinic literature

least four cups of wine. The Talmud notes that drinking an even number of cups is very dangerous (but adds that this is a typically Babylonian fear, for "In the West [i.e., in Palestine] they do not fear even numbers"), and the discussion soon meanders to related issues, such as the many different types of demons.[70] Within this unit, one finds a list of the different demons who dwell in the shades of different shrubs and trees, and when the Talmudic editor asks what is the practical importance of naming all these demons, the response is "for an amulet," or "for writing an amulet." In one case, a story is added which illustrates this point by relating how a certain city official (who probably was not even Jewish) stood by a sorb-bush and was attacked by sixty demons. He went to one of the rabbinic disciples who did not know that a sorb-bush has sixty demons, and thus wrote him an amulet for one demon only. This only made the demons laugh at his expense, so he went to another rabbinic disciple, who knew that a sorb-bush has sixty demons and wrote him the correct amulet, which made the demons flee at once.[71] Reading such a story, we may note that an event which in the Second Temple period would have called for an exorcism (of the types we surveyed in Chapter 2) is here treated with the help of newer technology, that of the written exorcistic amulet. This process must have been quite common in late antiquity, as may be seen both from the recurrence of exorcistic bowls and amulets and from the decline in the occurrence of recorded exorcisms or the appearance of powerful exorcists.[72] And in this case, we find direct evidence that at least in Babylonia, but perhaps in Palestine as well, amulets were written not only by physicians and professional amulet-makers, but also by members of the rabbinic class.[73] We may also note that if an amulet failed to alleviate the affliction, it was assumed that something was wrong with this specific amulet, and perhaps also with the person who produced it, so that one could simply turn to another amulet-writer, who may have a more accurate knowledge of what needed to be written in the amulet.[74] Thus, one lesson to be drawn from this story is that when you go to a

---

[70] For the possible Zoroastrian and Babylonian contexts of some of these beliefs, see Gafni 1990, pp. 167–72, with further bibliography. For the fear of even numbers, see also Trachtenberg 1939, pp. 118–19.

[71] bt Pes 111b.

[72] And note the general absence of exorcism stories from rabbinic literature, in spite of a few famous exceptions (surveyed in Bar-Ilan 1995).

[73] In later periods, we have abundant evidence of rabbis – such as Hayyim Vital, Leo (Judah Aryeh) Modena, Jonathan Eibeschütz, and many others – who often wrote amulets for members of their congregation, and sometimes for non-Jews as well.

[74] Replacing a failed amulet with a more successful one (which thus proves the capacities of its producer, as against the failure of the earlier practitioner) is, of course, extremely common in stories about healing magic. For one illuminating example, see Segev 2001, pp. 47–49.

rabbinic disciple in search of an amulet you better ascertain that he did not miss any of the demonology classes in the core curriculum, for if he did, he might write you the wrong amulet. Finally, we may note the data provided by this story concerning the *contents* of the actual amulet (though not, unfortunately, about the *material* on which it was inscribed, or the price paid for it). As both the story and the discussion around it make abundantly clear, for an amulet to be effective it had to be directed against the specific demon(s) that caused the affliction for which the amulet was needed, an assumption which is borne out by the "insider" evidence at our disposal. Both the Palestinian Jewish amulets and the Babylonian incantation bowls (as well as many other Jewish and non-Jewish magical texts) expend a great deal of effort on identifying the demon(s) whom they wish to thwart, or – when the demon's identity was unknown – on covering all possibilities by providing as detailed a list of demons as was humanly possible. In this case, too, what we find in rabbinic literature fits well with what we know from the magical artifacts themselves, and it is worth noting once again how the successful application of magical technology requires its detailed study, a study which the rabbis openly permitted, and often encouraged.

The magical uses of the Name

Throughout the present study, we had many occasions to note the pervasiveness and importance of the uses of God's Name(s) in the Jewish magical tradition. In Chapter 1, we noted how the Bible prescribes the death penalty for whoever *noqevs* the Name, but also depicts such figures as Elisha as using the Name for aggressive or medicinal purposes. In Chapter 2, we noted how early rabbinic accounts of the uses of the Name corroborate what we find in some passages of Second Temple period literature and support the conclusion that in the Second Temple period the Name was not only uttered, but also written down – on the body, on utensils, and perhaps also on metal lamellae – in order to use the great powers inherent in it. We also noted, in Chapter 3 (and shall note again below) that the use of the Name was soon borrowed by non-Jews, who incorporated it into their own magical spells and recipes, and elaborated (in Chapter 5) on the many uses of God's Names in the late-antique Jewish magical texts. At present, we may note that the rabbis were very well aware of the apotropaic and magical uses of the Name, and raised no objections to such practices.[75] They had no qualms about describing biblical heroes using the Name to

---

[75] For the rabbis' views of the Name and its powers, see Blau 1898, pp. 117–46; Urbach 1975, pp. 124–34; Becker 2002.

perform magical feats, and when discussing the Name which was written on vessels, or on one's own body, the problem they were bothered by was how one may get rid of such vessels when they are no longer needed, or how one may wash oneself, without desecrating the inscribed Name; that writing it was permissible seems quite obvious.[76] Similarly, the rabbis note that written amulets often contain divine Names, but the one question that bothers them in this regard is whether they must therefore be saved from a fire on the Sabbath, or may be left to burn together with the Names they contain.[77] They also report that some (Jewish?) sailors calm storms at sea with the help of clubs on which is engraved "*Ehyeh Asher Ehyeh*, YH YHWH Sabaot, Amen, Amen, Selah," and even enjoin writing a very similar formula on the skin of a hyena to cure rabies.[78] The last two examples stem from Babylonian rabbis, but their Palestinian brethren probably were equally lenient on this score.

While the writing of the Name was quite acceptable, its pronunciation was quite a different matter, and was seen by the rabbis – as already by many Second Temple Jews – as strictly forbidden. In the past, the rabbis said, it used to be recited only in the Temple, and only on such special occasions as the Day of Atonement, when it was uttered ten times by the high priest.[79] But apart from that instance, it was forbidden to utter the Name; whoever cursed his friend by the Name was liable to flogging, and whoever cursed the Name itself was liable to death by stoning.[80] Moreover, to Rabbi Akiva's famous dictum that whoever whispers on a wound and recites Ex 15.26 has no share in the world to come, Abba Shaul adds that "even one who pronounces the Name by its letters (i.e., letter by letter?)" suffers from a similar fate.[81]

The prohibition on the uttering of the Name, and the desire to use the great powers inherent in it, resulted in the proliferation of powerful

---

[76] Using the Name: to the examples adduced in Chapter 2, add bt San 95a (Avishai said the Name, and stopped David in midair ... he said the Name again, and brought David down); Targum Ps.-Jonathan to Num 20.8: "And you shall both adjure the rock by the great and explicit Name (ותימון תריכון ית כיפא בשמא רבא ומפרשא) ... and it shall give its water." And see Shinan 1992, pp. 134–38.
[77] See above, n. 68.
[78] Sailors: bt BB 73a (with interesting variants between the different manuscripts). Hyena: bt Yoma 84a (quoted and discussed below).
[79] See, e.g., m Yoma 6.2 (the high priest reciting the Name in the Temple on the Day of Atonement); m Sota 7.6 // Tamid 7.2 (in the Temple the Name was recited, but outside it, only a circumlocution); Mekhilta de-RY Yithro 11 (p. 243 Horovitz-Rabin); Sifre Num 39 (p. 43 Horovitz) and 43 (p. 48).
[80] Cursing by the Name (המקלל את חברו בשם): t Makk 5.10 (p. 444 Zuckermandel) // bt Makk 16a. Cursing the Name (המגדף): m San 7.4, 5 and Ker 1.1; pt San 7.5 (25a).
[81] See m San 10.1, and cf. Avot de-Rabbi Nathan A 12 (p. 56 Schechter) (whoever uses the *shem mephorash* has no share in the world to come) and bt AZ 17b–18a (R. Hanina ben Teradion was punished, because he used to "pronounce the Name by its letters").

substitutes. In the rabbinic case, there arose a set of special Names, described as the Names of four, twelve, forty-two, and seventy-two letters. These were seen by the rabbis as closely held secrets of their own class, to be passed on only to select individuals who would preserve them in purity and never misuse them.[82] Unfortunately, this secrecy was strictly kept by the editors of rabbinic literature, which therefore provides us no real clues as to the exact nature of these Names.[83] Only in Geonic literature do we find detailed discussions of (some of) these Names, such as the Name of forty-two letters.[84] And as we noted in the previous chapter, these Names are not found in the currently known Jewish magical texts of late antiquity; they seem to have entered the Jewish magical tradition only in the Geonic period, when Jewish magic was undergoing a process of partial rabbinization whose unfolding lies outside the chronological framework of the present study.

Jewish magical practices which the rabbis found problematic
One interesting feature of the rabbinic references to magical practices is that several specific practices were frowned upon by the rabbis, or at least by some of them, but were not included under the rubric of "magic." From our perspective, however, these practices would easily be classified as such, and they seem to have been popular among the practitioners who produced the magical texts and artifacts surveyed and analyzed in the previous chapters. Let us examine several such practices and the rabbinic discussions thereof.

(a) The (mis-)use of biblical verses:
In a celebrated passage in the Mishnah, the rabbinic claim that "All Jews have a share in the world to come," is followed by several specific cases of Jews whose deeds are so horrible as to deprive them of their share in spite of their Jewish pedigree. Among these exceptions, one is of great interest for students of Jewish magic:

And these are the ones who have no share in the world to come . . . Rabbi Akiva says, Also the one who reads in the external books, and the one who whispers over a wound and says "All the disease which I sent upon Egypt I will not send upon you, for I am the Lord your healer" (Ex 15.26).[85]

The first type of person mentioned by Rabbi Akiva, the type who reads unauthorized books, has been the subject of much speculation, but this need not detain us here, for there is no reason to think that books of magic

---

[82] Cf. pt Yoma 3.8 (40d) and Eccl. R. 3.11 (on passing on the Name) with bt Kidd 71a (on the Names of four, twelve, and forty-two letters). For the Name of seventy-two letters, see Gen R. 44.19 (p. 442 Theodor-Albeck) and AdRN A 13 (p. 57 Schechter).
[83] For some unsupported speculations on these Names, see Blau 1898, pp. 144–45, followed by Urbach 1975, p. 131, and cf. Eisler 1926.
[84] For which see Trachtenberg 1939, pp. 94–95; Schiffman 1973 and Idel 1993. [85] m San 10.1.

are what he had in mind. His second category, however, involves healing by "whispering over a wound" and reciting a biblical verse whose appeal for Jewish healers can hardly be in doubt. The practice of whispering spells over wounds is one of the commonest practices in the magical traditions of many different cultures, and in the Greco-Roman world, for example, it is well documented from Homer to the end of antiquity (when Homer's own verses sometimes were used for this purpose!).[86] But Akiva's ire apparently was not aimed against the mere whispering of incantations, which – as we shall repeatedly see – was not uncommon among the rabbis of his own generation as well as those of later periods. What he objected to was the use of biblical verses as spells, a use which, as we already noted throughout the present study, was extremely common in the Jewish magical praxis of all ages. Even the specific verse mentioned by R. Akiva is well attested not only on Samaritan amuletic pendants and rings, but also on the Jewish amulets of late antiquity, including one found in the Nirim synagogue.[87] Thus, not only was Akiva's objection ignored by subsequent Jewish practitioners, even the very verse he chose as an example went on being utilized by them. In passing, we may note that this is yet another example of the shift from oral to written Jewish magic in late antiquity, for a verse which by the time of R. Akiva and/or the editors of the Mishnah was still used as an *oral* spell, whispered over a wound, was used a few centuries later as a *written* spell and inscribed on metal-plate amulets.

Seeing how the Jewish amulet writers failed to heed Rabbi Akiva's warning might lead us to some conclusions about their attitudes to rabbinic *halakha*, were it not for the problematic status of his injunction even within the rabbis' own world. In one passage, the Babylonian Talmud quotes a saying of Rabbi Yehoshua ben Levi (early third-century Palestine) that "One may not be healed with biblical verses," but quickly adds that the same rabbi used to recite Psalm 91 (whose anti-demonic properties we already noted in Chapters 2 and 5) before going to sleep. The *sugiya* then solves the apparent contradiction between Yehoshua ben Levi's views and his deeds by stating that using biblical passages *in an apotropaic manner* is not prohibited. It then refers to Akiva's famous dictum on losing one's share in the world to come, but quickly adds the claim of Rabbi Yohanan (a Palestinian rabbi of a generation later than Rabbi Yehoshua ben Levi) that Akiva's harsh words

---

[86] For medical incantations, see, e.g., Homer, *Od.* 19.455–458; Pindar, *Pyth.* 3.51; Sophocles, *Ajax* 581–2; Plato, *Rep.* 4.426b; Pliny, *NH* 28.4.21 (referring to several additional examples); Apuleius, *Apol.* 40; Porphyry, *VP* 30; Iamblichus, *VP* 29.164; Ammianus Marcelinus 16.8.2. For the use of Homeric verses as incantations, see Reuss 1856 and Heim 1892, pp. 514–19.

[87] For the use of Ex 15.26 on Samaritan amulets, see Reich 2002, p. 306. For the Nirim amulet, see AMB A13, ll. 19–22. See also MSF, pp. 22–23.

applied only to those healers who *spit* and recite Ex 15.26, for one may not recite the Divine Name over spittle.[88] Elsewhere, the Babylonian Talmud cites the statement of the Babylonian Rav that even citing Lv 13.9 (a verse which deals with healing, but does not mention God's Name) in such a context is forbidden, while Ḥanina adds that even Lv 1.1 (which mentions God's Name, but has nothing to do with healing) may not be recited in such a context.[89] The permissibility of using biblical verses in healing rituals clearly was much debated among the rabbis of Palestine and Babylonia over the generations, and no consensus on this score was ever achieved. Moreover, side by side with such debates we must place those passages of the Babylonian Talmud which make use of numerous biblical verses in a long range of apotropaic and healing rituals, some of which shall be discussed below.[90] And in the Palestinian Talmud, one finds several limitations on the use of biblical verses for healing, such as

One may not read a biblical verse over a wound on the Sabbath; and one who reads (a verse) over a mandrake – it is forbidden. "Come and read this verse over my son, since he has fright," "Put a (Torah-)book on him," "Put a *tefillin* on him so he can (fall a)sleep," – (it is) forbidden.[91]

These are very clear prohibitions, but the Palestinian Talmud quickly adds the contradictory tradition that "they used to recite the Song of the Afflicted in (pre-destruction) Jerusalem," and concludes that all these prohibitions apply before the patient or child was afflicted, but once someone is afflicted, one may resort to all these forbidden actions. As we already saw in Chapters 2 and 5, the "Song of the Afflicted" was a common appellation of Psalm 91 already in the Second Temple period, and its uses for apotropaic and healing purposes are amply documented at least from 11Q11 and to our own days.[92] And the permissibility in a medical context of a practice that would otherwise be forbidden is a recurrent feature of rabbinic *halakha*, as we already noted.

---

[88] bt Shev 15b, and cf. bt San 101a, pt San 10.1 (28b) and t San 12.10 (p. 433 Zuckermandel). For spitting and whispering spells to cure eye-disease, see also the story in pt Sot. 1.4 (16d), Lev R. 9.9 (pp. 191–193 Margalioth) and parallels, on the woman who spat into R. Meir's eyes. And cf. bt BB 126b (the healing spittle of the firstborn son) and Mk 8.23; John 9.6.

[89] bt San 101a, and cf. pt San 10.1 (28b). For the actual use of Lev 1.1 in Genizah magical texts, see MTKG I, 15 (T-S AS 142.12) 1a/62–65. And cf. Trachtenberg 1939, p. 110.

[90] See, e.g., bt Ber 51a (Zech 3.2 recited to ward off the Angel of Death); bt Ber 55b (biblical verses used in a "dream improvement" ritual); bt Shab 67a (Rabbi Yoḥanan's recipe, discussed below); bt Pes 111a (two examples), and the examples adduced by Blau 1898, pp. 68–71.

[91] pt Shab 6.2 (8b); Eruv 10.12 (26c).

[92] bt Shev 15b; pt Shab 6.2 (8b); Eruv 10.12 (26c). See 11Q11, discussed in Chapter 2.

The rabbis, as we repeatedly see, were far from unanimous in their condemnation of the use of biblical verses in magical rituals; they were, moreover, very well aware of the practice itself, and their discussions therefore provide us with useful evidence concerning the wide diffusion of such practices, including not only the reciting of biblical verses over wounds and over frightened children and those who had trouble sleeping, but also over a mandrake. This plant (Aram. *yavruḥa*) may be the same as the *ba'aras*-root mentioned by Josephus, but as the rabbis elsewhere equate the *yavruḥa* with the biblical *duda'im*, used for erotic magic in Gn 30.14–16, it seems quite clear that here we have an oblique reference to the use of biblical verses in the process of uprooting or preparing the mandragoras-plant, to be used as an aphrodisiac in an erotic magical context.

(b) The (mis-)use of sacred objects:
If the prohibition of using biblical verses was observed mostly in the breach, the prohibition of using sacred objects for magical protection seems to have aroused fewer difficulties. In the passage we just quoted from the Palestinian Talmud, we also find the prohibition against laying a Torah-scroll or *tefillin* next to a crying child to pacify him or her into sleep. Reading such prohibitions, we must note the extensive use of similar practices in the Greco-Roman world, such as the recommendation of one third-century author to place the fourth book of the *Iliad* under a patient suffering from quartan fever.[93] But we must also stress that the use of sacred objects to achieve concrete goals by tapping their great powers is a practice whose roots go back to the Hebrew Bible itself, and whose implications often proved quite problematic. In this context, we may note the Tosephta's ruling that one may not place agricultural produce or coins which were consecrated for the second tithe on a gouty limb, or use them as an amulet, a ruling that probably goes back to the Second Temple period and reflects a popular custom at the time.[94] And with God's Temple gone, the one sacred object still possessed by the Jews was God's Torah, and the urge to tap its magical powers must have been quite strong. In later periods, we find ample evidence that it proved too strong to resist.[95]

(c) The adjuration of angels:
As we noted throughout the present study, one of the commonest Jewish magical practices of late antiquity was the adjuration of angels. It thus is of

---

[93] See Serenus Sammonicus, *Liber Medic.* 907 (on quartan fevers): *Maeoniae Iliados quartum suppone timenti.* (Is the use of this specific book due to its description of Machaon and his *pharmaka*, or to the use of the *fourth* book for *quartan* fever?)
[94] See t MS 1.3 (p. 243 Lieberman), with TK p. 715.
[95] For the magical uses of Torah-scrolls in later periods, see Sabar 2000.

some interest to note the rabbis' unease with excessive contact with angels, as against praying to God Himself, and their own ambivalence on this score too. We already cited in Chapter 1 Rabbi Yoḥanan's inventive etymology of the word *mekhashphim* ("they contradict/weaken the angelic host"), by which he admits that magic actually works, but probably also explains one reason why *keshaphim* are forbidden in the first place. Such qualms about forcing angels to do one's will may be paralleled by the rabbis' insistence that the worship of angels is just another form of idolatry, and that when one is in need of help one should turn not to an angel, but to God Himself, and cry for help.[96] But perhaps the most interesting attempt they made to stem the appeal to angels was the claim of the same Rabbi Yoḥanan that "Whoever asks for his needs in Aramaic – the angels of service do not heed him, since the angels of service do not know Aramaic." As most of the Jewish magical texts of late antiquity were written in that language, and as they frequently invoke or adjure angels, it would be difficult not to take this dictum as aimed at least in part against such (scribal or oral) magical practices. And here too, an incisive dictum is immediately undermined by the Talmudic *sugiyot* – in one case, by proving that angels do in fact communicate in Aramaic and in another by claiming that sick persons have God's Presence (*Shekhina*) right next to them, which is why one may pray in Aramaic on their behalf.[97] More significant for our discussion, we shall note below how Rabbi Yehoshua decrees upon the Minister of the Sea to fulfill his commands, showing that the rabbis knew very well how to adjure angels, and that they were not too shy about it. We shall also note, however, how in the recipes offered by the rabbis themselves the technique of adjuring angels and demons is entirely absent, yet another sign of the rabbis' own ambivalence on this score and their preference to avoid the adjuration of angels as much as was humanly possible.[98]

Before turning to these issues, however, we must note yet another novel category developed by the rabbis, that of "the Ways of the Amorites."

"The Ways of the Amorites"

Above, we already had the occasion to discuss the Mishnaic rulings concerning what may be carried around on the Sabbath. Within this framework,

---

[96] Angel-worship forbidden: t Hull 2.18 (p. 503 Zuckermandel) // bt AZ 42b // bt Hull 40a (prohibition of slaughtering to heavenly bodies, to Michael, etc.); bt Hull 41b (do not slaughter into the sea (m Hull 2.9) – lest you seem to be slaughtering to the Minister of the Sea). Turning to God and not to angels: pt Ber 9.1 (13a). See also Urbach 1975, pp. 182–83.
[97] See bt Sota 33a and bt Shab 12b, respectively. See also Brody 1998, p. 142, n. 15.
[98] And cf. Lam. R. 2 (pp. 109–10 Buber), on how the Jews in Jeremiah's time trusted in their ability to force the Ministers of Fire, Water, and Iron to build protective walls around Jerusalem, so God switched the angels around, to confound their magic plans.

Magic and magicians in rabbinic literature 383

one finds not only amulets (to which we already referred), but also other apotropaic implements worn by various people in antiquity. Thus, it is allowed to set out on the Sabbath with a coin placed over a gouty limb and *children* may set out with apotropaic knots and bells.[99] As we have already discussed (in Chapter 2) the amuletic T-shirt discovered in the Judean Desert and worn by a Jewish child in the 130s CE, we may now turn to the use of coins to heal gout, a practice well attested throughout the ancient world. In many cases the coin would be one of Alexander the Great, and in this regard it is interesting to note how the rabbis admit that it is also the *image* upon the coin – and not, for example, only the metal of which the coin was made – which was considered efficacious, but tactfully avoid delving into the nature of that image.[100] But while such practices were deemed acceptable, other apotropaic items were more problematic:

> One may set out (on the Sabbath) with the egg of a locust, or the tooth of a fox, or a nail from a crucified convict – for the sake of healing; (these are) the words of Rabbi Meir. But the sages say, Even on weekdays this is forbidden, because of "the Ways of the Amorites."[101]

In commenting upon this passage, we may note the obvious disagreement with regards to the three practices listed here, with one early-second-century authority seeing them as not any different from the wearing of amulets or other apotropaic devices which one may carry around on the Sabbath, while the majority insists that these three practices are forbidden to Jews in any case, and not only on the Sabbath. The debate, in other words, is not about Sabbath laws, but about the very permissibility of wearing these three types of objects, whose use as *apotropaea* was extremely common in antiquity, and is attested both by literary parallels and by the archeological evidence.[102] Those who object to them, however, do so neither because these customs are "superstitious" or "irrational" (in fact, the rabbis are virtually unaware of such a category), nor because they are deemed "magical." Rather than affixing to these practices the label *keshaphim*, the rabbis develop a whole new category of forbidden practices, "the Ways of the Amorites." Whether they invented this category, or used a pre-rabbinic term, is a vexed question; but regardless of the origin of this name, it is clear that they saw this category

---

[99] m Shab 6.6, 9. Note that *Sepher ha-Ma'asim*, a Palestinian *halakhic* compendium of the Geonic period, says that children may go out with knots until they are nine years old; from that age onwards, it is forbidden (text publ. by Levin in *Tarbiz* 1, p. 97 (Heb.)).
[100] See bt Shab 65a. For the use of Alexander-coins to heal gout, see John Chrysostom, *Ad Illuminandos Catecheses* 2.5 (PG 49.240). For coins used as amulets, see Leclercq 1924, pp. 1790–91 and Fulghum 2001. For a later period, see Maguire 1997.
[101] m Shab 6.10.
[102] See Veltri 1997, pp. 95–96 and Saar 2003, pp. 59 and 66 (predators' teeth used as amulets).

as continuing and refining the biblical prohibition against "walking in the ways of the Gentiles."[103] Moreover, such a category had one great advantage, as it could serve as a repository for all those contemporary Gentile practices which could not easily be subsumed under the category of "idolatry" (to which the rabbis devoted much attention elsewhere), since they were not directly related to any specific idol, temple, or pagan cultic activity,[104] but which they did not wish their Jewish followers to adopt. An additional advantage was that while perpetrators of *keshaphim* were supposed to be stoned to death, users of "Amorite ways" could be left to God's judgment; thus, the rabbis never made any real effort to eradicate all these practices from their midst, nor are they likely to have succeeded had they tried.[105]

Looking at the long list of customs which came to be included under this rubric,[106] one cannot help noting that while many of these practices would be included by us under the rubric of "magic" or "divination," others certainly would not.[107] But viewed by a historian of Jewish magic, this rabbinic category is significant for several reasons. First, because the list of such practices amply demonstrates how familiar the rabbis were with many pagan magical practices of their time, an issue to which we shall return below. Second, because with the development of this new category the rabbis took a path never taken by the biblical legislators, that of providing not only a general and vague list of *practitioners* which Jews must not consult, but also of *practices* forbidden to Jews. One important implication of this new development is that those Jews – in late antiquity or in later periods – who followed rabbinic *halakha* either tried to avoid these specific customs, or were forced to find good *halakhic* excuses for not avoiding them. Another, and perhaps more significant implication of this new approach was that while a few dozen practices were forbidden, many others apparently were not. Moreover, once the rabbis declared that "anything which heals is not of 'the Ways of the Amorites'," they opened a

---

[103] See Veltri 1997, pp. 93–94. For Amorite practices, and even Amorite books, see already Ps.-Philo, *LAB* 25–26.

[104] Note that a few spells subsumed under the heading of "Amorite ways" are etymologized by Rav Yehudah as connected with pagan deities, such as Gad (=Tyche) or Dagon – see t Shab. 7.2–3 (pp. 25–26 Lieberman); bt Shab 67b; pt Shab 6.10 (8c). This, however, is an exception, and perhaps also a minority view.

[105] For an illuminating comparandum, see Rowlands 1996; for a modern Jewish example, see Furst 1998.

[106] See also m Hull 4.7, and esp. t Shab 6–7 (pp. 22–29 Lieberman) and bt Shab 67a–b. Cf. pt Shab 6.10 (8c–d).

[107] Only in t Shab 7.13–14 (p. 27 Lieberman) are specific "Ways of the Amorites" equated with the biblical categories of *me'onen* and *menahesh* or with the rabbinic category of *'ahizat 'einayim*. Other "Amorite ways" are not identified as related to magic. And note that even unacceptable hairstyles are included in the list – see t Shab 6.1 (p. 22 Lieberman) and TK pp. 80–81; Veltri 1997, pp. 97–103.

wide door for the entry of numerous foreign customs, as long as they were deemed by knowledgeable experts, or by the rabbis themselves, to have real medical value.

Summary: the status of magic in rabbinic halakha

Let us sum up what we have seen thus far. On the one hand, we saw that "magic" is a common, "emic" term within the rabbinic legal discourse, and that its definition seems quite straightforward. We also noted that, following the biblical legislation, the rabbis condemned the magician to death by stoning, while adding a minor clause exempting practitioners of mere tricks and optical illusions. On the other hand, we saw how the rabbis developed a strong differentiation between the practice of magic (which is forbidden), and its study and teaching (which are allowed, and sometimes even encouraged), and how they explicitly stated that dealing with the magic of "the laws of Creation" was permitted, and that "anything which heals" cannot really be forbidden. We also saw how they implicitly made similar concessions to the use of magic for fighting magic and magicians, and sometimes even as a more general means for social control. Rather than claiming that what they did was not magic, and that only "others" practiced magic, the rabbis developed a discourse of licit and illicit magic, and explained which magical practices were permitted within their religious legislation, and which were not. Moreover, in other cases – such as the apotropaic and medical uses of biblical verses or sacred objects – they condemned certain ritual practices, but without labeling them as "magic" and without establishing any unified policy towards them; in some cases, prominent rabbis even utilized these practices themselves. Finally, we saw how the rabbis developed a special category of forbidden pagan practices, "the Ways of the Amorites," a bag in which a few dozen pagan practices were lumped together, with many more such practices left outside the bag. Thus, just as the biblical laws not only forbade magic but also left many loopholes and explicit paradigms which made Jewish magic possible, and perhaps even inevitable, so in rabbinic *halakha* the blanket condemnation of magic and magicians was mitigated by many other elements in the rabbis' own legislation on this score. By making the study and teaching of magic permissible, and in some cases even desirable, by making some magical practices (especially those with medicinal value) entirely acceptable and implying that others were acceptable in specific social circumstances, by objecting to central constituents of contemporary Jewish magic, such as the use of biblical verses, in a way that was weak-kneed and inconsistent, and which was ignored even by many of the rabbis themselves, and by telling so many stories about prominent rabbis who were deeply involved with magical practices, the rabbis had mostly undermined their own anti-magic legislation.[108] In this manner rabbinic literature, once codified and canonized, shaped the medieval attitudes to, and practice of, Jewish magic; coupled with the Christian discourse of magic as heretical and diabolical, it gave rise to the stereotype of the Jewish magician, the Devil's own henchman.[109] And when some medieval Jewish philosophers objected that magic was "superstitious" and "irrational," and therefore also un-Jewish, their Jewish opponents could expose the latter claim as demonstrably false, and adduce a plethora of talmudic passages to support their claim.[110] Needless to say, it was their side which won the debate, and the Jewish magical tradition proudly sailed on.

RABBINIC FAMILIARITY WITH NON-JEWISH MAGICAL PRACTICES

In the previous section, we examined the rabbinic concept of "magic" and their legislation with regard to that concept, and noted several examples of the rabbis' familiarity with, and even use of, some of the Jewish magical practices at the time. We now turn to a somewhat different question, namely, the rabbis' familiarity with the magical traditions and practices of the pagan population among whom they lived, some of which have been examined in Chapter 4.[111] Certainly the easiest place in which to look for such familiarity is in the long list of practices included by them under the rubric "the Ways of the Amorites," which included foreign customs which the rabbis did not wish their followers to adopt, many of which *we* would surely classify as having to do with "magic." Thus, a detailed examination of every custom included under this rubric might shed interesting light on the rabbis' familiarity with the popular customs of surrounding pagan society. It must be stressed, however, that after more than a century and a half of research, and in spite of some remarkable efforts by previous scholars to elucidate the practices mentioned by the rabbis with the help of parallels from non-Jewish sources, there is much in the list which remains obscure,

---

[108] And cf. also the partial parallels provided by the Christian attitudes towards magic, as analyzed in Flint 1991, pp. 75–84.
[109] For which see esp. Trachtenberg 1943.
[110] And see, for example, Trachtenberg 1939, pp. 19–22, for the status of magic in medieval *halakhah*.
[111] I leave aside the rabbinic debate – in t AZ 8.6 (p. 473 Zuckermandel); Gen.R. 34.8 (p. 317 Theodor-Albeck); bt San 56b, etc. – over whether magic is one of the seven biblical prohibitions which are supposedly binding even upon non-Jews, an issue which makes little difference for the present discussion.

Magic and magicians in rabbinic literature 387

and many references to practices whose exact meaning or original context still elude us.[112]

Looking at the list in its entirety, we may divide the magical practices it contains into three main categories: (1) Forbidden *actions*, such as tying a red string on one's finger, counting pebbles while throwing them into the sea or a river, or tying a bar of iron to the bed of a parturient woman. (2) Forbidden verbal utterances in specific situations, such as saying "Cry" or "Go back" to a crowing crow, or asking one's colleagues not to sit on the plow lest the plowing will (subsequently) become more difficult. (3) Forbidden spells and *voces magicae*, such as YMY' WBYZY',[113] or DNY DNW,[114] or GD GDY WSYNWQ L' 'ŠKY WBWŠKY.[115] But what is common to all these types of forbidden customs is that they seem to reflect the everyday actions of ordinary people, not those of savvy professional magicians. The actions are simple and call for simple ingredients and no special techniques, and the pithy spells and formulae would hardly require a handbook to be remembered. Thus, it should come as no surprise that while points of contact with the Greco-Egyptian magic of late antiquity have often been suggested, none demonstrates a direct affinity between the "Amorite ways" and the scribal magic of the Greek magical papyri and related magical texts. Some (such as the tying of red strings around body parts) are so common in many cultures, ancient and modern, as to preclude the necessity of direct contact between the rabbinic evidence and the Greek magical tradition. Others, and especially the specific spells, could provide interesting clues, if only we could securely identify the spells handed dowm by the rabbis (and now found in often corrupt manuscripts and editions) as stemming from Greek sources. As we shall see again in our analysis of the rabbis' own magical recipes, such quests often prove more exasperating than rewarding.

When we leave "the Ways of the Amorites" aside and turn to other pagan practices mentioned by the rabbis, we find a long range of practices which are known to us from the magical texts and artifacts of late antiquity, and

---

[112] For previous discussions of "the Ways of the Amorites," see esp. Lewy 1893; Avishur 1979; TK Shabbat pp. 79–105; Veltri 1997, pp. 93–220.

[113] t Shab 7.1 (p. 25 Lieberman), with TK pp. 91–92; Veltri 1997, pp. 135–36.

[114] t Shab 7.3 (pp. 25–26 Lieberman); bt Shab 67b; pt Shab 6.10 (8c). Note Lieberman's suggestion (TK pp. 92–93) that דני דנו might be δέν(υ)ω [τὸν] δεῖνα, with his own qualification that "obviously all this is no more than a conjecture." See also Lieberman 1974, pp. 26–28; Lewy 1893, p. 130 and Veltri 1997, pp. 137–38.

[115] bt Shab 67b. Lewy 1893, p. 131, followed by Urbach 1975, p. 725, n. 8, and Veltri 1997, p. 179, compare the last two "words" of this formula (גד גדי וסינוק לא אושכי ובושכי) with the first two "words" of the *Ephesia Grammata* sequence, ἄσκιον κατάσκιον, etc. For the entry of δαμναμενεύς (another "word" of the *Eph. Gr.*) into Jewish magical texts see Chapter 4, n. 112.

were well known to the rabbis as well. Of the many examples which could be adduced here, we shall focus only on a select few, and on the contexts within rabbinic literature in which they appear:

(a) One context in which pagan magical practices naturally appear is in the rabbinic discussions of "idolatry." However, when searching for such evidence, we must always keep in mind that many pagan rituals and objects had both "magical" and "religious" contexts, a distinction which was of little importance to the rabbis themselves but is of great importance for us. Thus, when the rabbis show much awareness of the "idolatrous" uses of white cocks, or of Nicolaus dates (named after Nicolaus of Damascus), pinecones, and figs, we could easily point to the use of these ingredients in pagan magical texts of late antiquity, and even in a Jewish magical text like *Sepher ha-Razim*.[116] It must be stressed, however, that these ingredients were commonly used in many pagan rites in antiquity, and the rabbinic discussions thereof show no awareness of a specifically magical usage thereof. To avoid such dangers, we must focus on those instances which could only refer to pagan *magical* rituals and practices the rabbis had come across. As an illustrative example, we may note the Mishnaic ruling that "Whoever finds utensils with the figure of the sun or the moon, or the figure of the Deraqon upon them, must take them to the Dead Sea." As "Deraqon" is merely the Hebrew transliteration of the Greek word for "serpent" (*drakôn*), both the Tosephta and the Palestinian Talmud explain that the forbidden symbol is not just any snake-figure, but one "which has rays coming out of its neck."[117] This figure of a serpent with solar rays is extremely common on Greco-Egyptian magical gems (where it often goes by the name of Chnoubis or Chnoumis), and was well known to Galen and Origen. Its prevalence in Palestine is demonstrated not only by the many Chnoubis gems found in Caesarea, Tel Dor, and elsewhere, but also by an illuminating story of Rabbi Eleazar ha-Kappar (early third century CE) who found a ring with a Deraqon image and forced an adult pagan to "nullify" it and thus make it usable for Jews.[118] What we would see as a "magic" ring, a late-antique Palestinian rabbi saw as an "idolatrous" object, to be neutralized and then

---

[116] For the prohibition to sell these ingredients to Gentiles, see m AZ 1.5 etc.; for their uses in magical rituals, see, e.g., PGM I.232–47 (making myrrh-ink with Nicolaus dates, pine cones, and figs) and ShR I/95–96 (pp. 71–72 Margalioth) (write with myrrh-ink, etc.). See further Lieberman 1945–47, pp. 47–52. For white cocks, see below, n. 167.

[117] See m AZ 3.3, with t AZ 5.2 (p. 468 Zuckermandel) and pt AZ 3.3 (42d). For what follows, see Bohak 1997 and Kotansky 1997, both with further bibliography. For a different analysis of the Deraqon image, see Schlüter 1982, esp. pp. 121–23.

[118] See bt AZ 43a. The parallel story in pt AZ 4.4 (44a) does not specify which pagan image was engraved upon the ring.

used as a secular object. One wonders, however, why the rabbis never mention the cock-headed, snake-legged figure, which often was identified as Iaô on the magical gems, and which is far more common than the Chnoubis gems in museum collections and archeological excavations. Once again, we find the rabbis telling us some useful things about late-antique magic, while hiding, or ignoring, many others.

(b) Related to the rabbinic discussions of pagan "idolatry" is their frequent discussions of the pagan uses of God's Name(s). In Chapter 3, we noted the extensive entry of Jewish divine and angelic Names into pagan magical texts in late antiquity; we also noted Origen's familiarity with this phenomenon and his great disdain towards it. We may now add that the rabbis were equally aware of this development – and equally unhappy about it. Already in the second century CE, we hear Rabbi Shimeon bar Yoḥai claiming that whoever includes God's Name in his "idolatrous" rituals deserves to perish. Later, we find Rabbi Ḥiyya ruling that whoever hears the Name being uttered by a Gentile need not tear his garment (as the rule once was), since such instances had become far too common.[119] And while such rulings may refer to the "paganization" of the Jewish god in non-magical contexts as well, other references clearly refer to the magical uses of the Name. Samuel, active in Babylonia in the early third century CE, heard a Persian man cursing his son by the Name, and the son died.[120] The rabbi deduced from this that the Persian must have passed by when the Name was discussed or pronounced, and heard what he heard, and both story and conclusion are incorporated into a *sugiya* of the Palestinian Talmud which explains why one must be very careful with the transmission of the Name. To this, we may add the surprising claim, found in the Babylonian Talmud and attributed to a Babylonian rabbi, that Abraham passed on to his non-Jewish descendants some "Names of impurity," an expression which rabbinic literature does not really explain but which became very popular in the later Jewish discourse of magic and in post-rabbinic Jewish magical texts.[121]

(c) A different context in which to find the rabbis' familiarity with the pagan magical practices of their own times is in their re-telling of many biblical stories. We already saw that the re-telling of biblical stories provided

---

[119] RASHBY: Mekhilta de-RY, Mishpatim 17 (p. 310 Horovitz-Rabin). Not tearing the garment: bt San 60a. For tearing the garment when hearing the Name blasphemed, see m San. 7.5; pt San. 7.5 (25a–b) (including משרבו הגודפנים פסקו מלקרוע); bt MoK 26a, etc. For blasphemy and tearing the garments, see Mk 14.61–62 and pars.
[120] Samuel: pt Yoma 3.8 (40d), and cf. Eccl. R. 3.11.
[121] Names of impurity: bt San 91a. See also Ginzberg 1909–38, vol. V, p. 265, n. 313.

some Second Temple period writers the opportunity to describe pagan magicians in action, and that the rabbis incorporated *Jewish* magical practices into their stories of Moses, David, and other biblical protagonists. We may now complement this picture by noting how they often attributed to the Gentile protagonists of the biblical stories magical activities of which they must have been aware from their own time and place. Among the many interesting examples, we may note the description of how the Jebusites (the biblical dwellers of Jerusalem), fearing the onslaught of David's army, placed apotropaic bronze statues in Jerusalem, which prevented David's army from storming the city; only after their removal by David's general Yoav was the city taken. Such practices are, of course, extremely well documented for late antiquity (as for other periods), and not only in the non-Jewish world; *Sepher ha-Razim* provides recipes for the manufacture of such apotropaic statues, showing that Jews too occasionally dabbled in such practices.[122] We may also note the rabbis' description of how, when Esther was first taken to the court of the Persian king, Mordechai was worried lest her menstrual stains would fall into the wrong hands, and be used to perform *keshaphim* upon her.[123] Finally, we may note how the rabbinic discussions of the *teraphim* (a divinatory implement whose nature is not really clear from the biblical accounts) disclose much familiarity with the magical and divinatory rituals of their own world, including the use of specially prepared talking skulls with inscribed lamellae placed in their mouths to make them speak.[124] In all these cases, and many others besides, the rabbis demonstrate their close familiarity with many aspects of the pagan magical traditions of their time and place.

(d) In some cases, rabbinic claims about the magical practices known to them appear without any concrete context. As a case in point, we may cite a passage which appears in two different places in the Babylonian Talmud, but in both cases is merely cited as one of a series of unrelated statements by Rabbi Yoḥanan:

R. Yoḥanan said, (Better) a cup of sorcerers than a cup of sorcery-dissolvers.[125] But this applies only to metal vessels, and does not apply to clay vessels; and in

---

[122] See PRE 36 with Stein 2004, pp. 247–48. For such statues in Jewish magic, see ShR II/110–117 (p. 87 Margalioth).

[123] See Esth.R. 6.8 to Esth. 2.11. In this context, I am tempted to connect the rabbinic claim that *ketem le-reqem* ("A menstrual stain to Petra") was one ancient equivalent of our "coals to Newcastle" (see Lieberman 1942, p. 102, n. 51) with Josephus' stories about the women of Arabia and their involvement in erotic magic, for which see Chapter 2, n. 188.

[124] For the *teraphim* and the stories about them, see Dan 1978, pp. 99–100; Shinan 1992, p. 147; Sperber 1994, pp. 115–18; Veltri 1997, pp. 74–75.

[125] כסא דחרשין ולא כסא דפושרין. For פשר, "to dissolve a spell," see Sokoloff 2002, p. 945, and the Geonic text known as the *Pishra of Rabbi Ḥanina ben Dosa* (see Chapter 3, n. 219).

metal vessels too it applies only if he had not thrown firewood into it, but if he had thrown firewood, it does not apply; and if he did not throw firewood into it, it applies only when it did not hiss (upon boiling?), but if it hissed, it does not apply.[126]

What are we to make of such an obscure passage? At first sight, this might seem like a rabbinic reference to the Babylonian incantation bowls, whose contents we briefly surveyed in Chapter 3.[127] A closer look, however, reveals this to be highly unlikely, for R. Yoḥanan is a Palestinian sage of the third century and the bowls are found only in Babylonia and only from the fifth or sixth centuries onwards. Moreover, the passage seems to discuss the ritual involved in preparing such cups, and this differs greatly from what we find on the Babylonian incantation bowls, which were inscribed with (real or bogus) texts. In fact, the statement here probably refers to some concoctions prepared by sorcerers and sorcery-dissolvers, concoctions which the client probably was made to drink.[128] But the exact nature of the ritual remains obscure, as is the identity of the practitioners who used it; these may have been Jewish spell-busters, but they may also have been non-Jewish ones. Hopefully, further research – and a diligent search for comparanda outside rabbinic literature – might shed more light on this difficult passage. Until this happens, however, we may once again stress how many of the rabbinic discussions of and allusions to the magical practices of their own times still elude us.[129]

Summarizing the above examples, to which many more could be added, we may note that there is little doubt that in the realm of magic, as in many other spheres, the rabbis were keenly aware of goings-on in the world around them. Not only did they need a detailed knowledge of pagan magical praxis in order to shape their own *halakha* so as to contain it, they also utilized this knowledge in their retelling of biblical stories and interpretations of biblical verses, in their sermons and stories, and in their everyday dealings with the non-Jews around them. From our own perspective, this is quite encouraging, since it means that rabbinic literature has much to tell us about the diffusion of magical practices in the pagan world of late antiquity, and the familiarity with them even of those who found them quite repulsive. These rabbinic discussions, in other words, provide us with many excellent "outsider" sources for the study of late-antique magic.

---

[126] bt Hull 84b; bt BM 29b.
[127] And see Montgomery 1913, p. 43, n. 19; Lieberman 1942, pp. 112–13.
[128] For an illuminating comparandum, see the ritual described in Scholem 1980/81, p. 281.
[129] For another difficult passage, see pt San 9.11 (27b), where המקלל בקוסם (m San 9.6) is explained as כגון אילין נפתאי דמקללין לקנייך קנייך קנויך; see Blau 1898, p. 52, n. 1 and MSF, p. 205.

RABBIS AND MAGICIANS

Ever since Evans-Pritchard's groundbreaking study of the role of magic among the Azande, it has become a commonplace that magic and witchcraft often serve as explanations of otherwise inexplicable misfortunes. It has also become a commonplace to study not only a group's claims about magic, but also which persons within or outside the group tend to be accused of magical activities once such activities are suspected or detected. And as anthropologists and historians have repeatedly demonstrated, it is often "the other" who is accused of magical activities, the accusation being both a symptom of the cleavage between "us" and "them" and a means for maintaining and enhancing it.[130]

When read from this perspective, rabbinic literature reveals some familiarity with the attribution of misfortune to such evil forces. In one famous story, we are told that the Babylonian Rav went to the cemetery, *did what he did*, and found out that ninety-nine percent of all the people buried there were killed by the evil eye, and only one percent died of natural causes.[131] In many other cases, the rabbis explain that certain illnesses are the result of *keshaphim* – in some cases, the ultimate source of these evils is identified as women who dabble in *keshaphim*, while in others it is left unidentified.[132] And when we look for more specific accusations of witchcraft and sorcery, we find two distinct clusters of explicit magic accusations. First and foremost, it is women, that "internal other" in the rabbis' male-only religious and cultural elite, who are constantly suspected and accused of magical activities. Second, it is the *minim*, those "Bible-reading heretics", who are the subject of such accusations. Thus, it is in these two contexts that we find the rabbinic stories of rabbis who had to confront powerful magicians – either female witches or male *minim*. Before turning to each class of stories, however, we may note the lack of rabbinic accusations of magic against other social or ethnic groups. Like their non-Jewish contemporaries, the rabbis too saw Egypt as the land of magic *par excellence*, but there are very few references in rabbinic literature to actual Egyptian magicians, in marked contrast with the obsession with them in Greek and Latin

---

[130] For a celebrated use of this model see Brown 1970.
[131] bt BM 107b; Rashi ad loc. explains that Rav knew how to whisper on the graves and fathom for each grave whether the person died in his appointed time or through the evil eye. For this theme, see also Ulmer 1994, pp. 24–27.
[132] See, for example, bt Yoma 83b and pt Yoma 8.6 (45b): Mad dogs might be the "work" of female witches; bt Shab 33a: There are three types of הידרוקן (dropsy) . . . that caused by *keshaphim* is thin.

literature.¹³³ And while the rabbis had some nasty things to say about the Samaritans, and about various groups of "idolatrous" Gentiles, accusations of magical activities, and encounters with Samaritan or pagan magicians, do not loom large in these diatribes, in marked contrast with what we find in the Christian literature of the time. Thus, if we wish to use rabbinic stories about their conflicts with magicians as sources for the study of what magicians and rabbis actually did, it is on the stories of female witches and male *minim* that we must focus. Moreover, while in no way taking such stories as factual accounts of actual events, we may feel safe in avoiding the other extreme, of assuming such stories to be entirely artificial constructs, made up by the rabbis for polemical or rhetorical needs, for otherwise we would expect such stories to be told about Samaritans, pagans, and all the other "others" in the rabbis' world, and not just about these two specific groups.

Rabbis and witches

"Most women engage in sorcery." This incisive dictum is just one of many rabbinic statements on this score, a florilegium of which would make even the staunchest male chauvinist blush with embarrassment. But as the issue has already attracted much scholarly attention and generated several detailed analyses of the roles of such accusations in maintaining male hegemony in rabbinic society, we may safely leave such issues aside.¹³⁴ In passing, we may note that rabbinic literature itself provides much evidence that magic was practiced by men and women alike, and that this is true of Classical and Christian literatures as well. We may also stress that the "insider" sources with which we have dealt in the previous chapters are far more likely to have been produced by men than by women, whose much lower level of literacy in ancient Jewish society means that their magical practices probably involved much less writing than those of their male colleagues and competitors. But while the rabbinic insistence that magic was a female disease should not be taken at face value, the rabbinic stories about encounters with powerful witches might yet tell us something useful about ancient Jewish magic. Let us therefore look at several such stories.

---

¹³³ For Egypt as the land of magic in rabbinic literature, see Bohak 2000a, pp. 220–21. For actual (but anonymous) magicians, see bt San 67b (Ze'iri in Alexandria). For Egyptian magicians in Greco-Roman literature, see Dickie 2001, pp. 229–31 and Dieleman 2005, pp. 239–54.

¹³⁴ For women and magic in rabbinic literature, see Seidel 1992; Bar-Ilan 1993; Fishbane 1993; Veltri 1997, pp. 66–72; Aubin 1998; Lesses 2001; Mock 2001; Janowitz 2001, pp. 86–96. For the biblical and Mesopotamian roots of this stereotype, see Sefati and Klein 2004. For Roman comparanda, see Monaco 1984.

(a) Certainly the most famous of all the rabbinic stories about rabbis who had to deal with dangerous witches is the story of Shimeon ben Sheṭaḥ – who is said to have lived c. 100 BCE, and about whom even the rabbis' own recollections are quite hazy – and the eighty witches of Ashkelon. The story is alluded to in tannaitic sources, and is given in its entirety in two different locations in the Palestinian Talmud; in one instance, it is embedded in a discussion of the Mishnaic passage in which it was briefly mentioned; in the other, it forms part of a series of recollections of the most ancient rabbis and their glorious achievements.[135] The two versions differ in some minor details, none of which, however, is of consequence for the present discussion. The gist of the story is that having decided to exterminate these witches, who lived all together in a cave, Shimeon devised a fabulously complex plot. Setting out on a rainy day, he chose eighty young men to whom he gave clean garments in clay pots as well as detailed instructions – upon his first whistle, they should all put on the fresh garments they brought with them; upon his second whistle, they should all enter the cave, and each man should take one witch, lift her up in the air (whereupon she would lose all her magical powers), and carry her to the gallows. This is how the story continues:

He went and stood at the door of the cave. He said to it, Oyam! Oyam!,[136] open for me, for I am one of yours. They said to him, How did you get here on this (rainy) day? He said to them, I was walking between the drops. They said to him, And what did you come to do here? He said, To learn and to teach; let whoever comes perform what he knows best. So each one of them said what she said, and brought forth bread . . . meat . . . cooked food . . . wine. They said to him, And you, what can you do? He said to them, If you want me to, I will whistle twice and bring you eighty chosen youths, and they will have pleasure with you and bring you pleasure. They said to him, We want that! He whistled once, and they (the eighty young men) put their (fresh) clothes on. He whistled a second time, and they all entered at once. He said, Whoever comes should recognize his partner. So they lifted them up and went and had them crucified.[137]

This fantastic story has often been analyzed – not only by students of Jewish folklore, but also by students of Jewish history, who sometimes even tried to find the historical kernel supposedly embedded in it.[138] But even a purely

---

[135] See the allusions in m San 6.4 and Sifre Dt 221 (p. 253 Finkelstein), and the stories in pt Ḥag 2.2 (77d–78a) and pt San. 6.9 (23c).
[136] For this obscure expression, see Jastrow 1903, p. 24; Sokoloff 1990, p. 38.
[137] pt Ḥag 2.2 (77d–78a); the parallel in pt San. 6.9 (23c), has some minor differences.
[138] See Efron 1990; Hengel 1984; Ilan 2001.

fictional story could tell us much about the assumptions and beliefs of those who invented and promulgated it. Unfortunately, it is on the issues which would interest us most that the story becomes most elusive. The production *de nihilo* of food and even entire meals was commonly attributed to ancient magicians and holy men (be it Pases of Egypt, Jesus of Nazareth, or Rabbi Eliezer), and the idea that witches derived their power from the earth, and that by lifting them up you would annul their power, is so common in so many different cultures that is adds very little to our knowledge of ancient Jewish magic.[139] But the story is particularly silent when it comes to the magical praxis employed by the witches – they use verbal spells, whose actual contents are not even hinted at – and does not even use the opportunity to provide some bloodcurdling descriptions of the witches' gory rituals, of the type so favored by the Roman poets or the Christian heresiologists, demonologists, and inquisitors. No child-sacrifice here, no dancing around a satanic figure and kissing its mouth and rectum, no mad orgies, no flights of fancy, just the most banal of magical acts conducted in a friendly atmosphere. And Shimeon ben Sheṭaḥ uses no magic at all, not even the kinds of miracles used by Elijah in his duel with the priests of Baal, or by Moses and Aaron in Egypt. Rather than beating the witches at their own game, he simply cheats them with a deceitful ruse.

The story of Shimeon ben Sheṭaḥ, with all its colorful exuberance, is virtually useless for students of ancient Jewish magic. Were it the only story concerning rabbinic encounters with witches we might even have deduced that the rabbis always used their scheming ingenuity in such confrontations, and never resorted to more drastic measures or to their own magical expertise. This, however, certainly was not the case, as the following stories demonstrate.

(b) A less-celebrated, but potentially more informative story is found in the Palestinian Talmud's discussion of the Mishnaic laws governing the execution of magicians, laws to which we already devoted much attention. Within this framework, two stories are told of the encounters of Rabbi Yehoshua – who lived towards the end of the first century CE and the beginning of the second – and pernicious practitioners of witchcraft and sorcery. The first of these involves a showdown in Tiberias with a devious male *min*, and shall be dealt with below. The second takes place in distant Rome, and involves a female witch. It begins with three sages – Rabbi Eliezer, Rabbi Yehoshua, and Rabban Gamliel – who are on a visit to Rome

---

[139] Producing food *de nihilo*: Apion FGrH 616 F23 in Suda s.v., Πάσης (vol. IV, p. 65 Adler). Witches and earth: see Patai 1942–43, vol. II, pp. 113–19, and Hengel 1984, pp. 19–21.

and encounter an old Jewish man who is badly in need of their help; he wants them to pray for his son, who had fathered no children. Although neither the cause of this barrenness nor the means thus far taken to alleviate it are specified by the old man, the rabbis are quick to act, and in a way quite different from that requested by the old man:

> R. Eliezer said to R. Yehoshua, What?, Yehoshua ben Hananiah, see what you can do. He said to them, Bring me a seed of flax. And they brought him a seed of flax. They saw him sowing it on the table; they saw him sprinkle water over it; they saw it sprout; they saw him tearing it out, until he pulled up a certain woman by the plaits of her hair. He said to her, Loosen what you have done! She said to him, I cannot loosen it. He said to her, If you do not, I will expose you in public. She said to him, I cannot, for they were thrown in the sea. So Yehoshua commanded the Minister of the Sea, and he spat them out. And they prayed upon him (the barren man), and he was merited with the birth of R. Judah ben Bateira. They (the three sages) said, If we had only come here to raise this righteous person, it would have been enough.[140]

Contrary to the story of Shimeon ben Shetah and the eighty witches, in this story the rabbi employs what can only be seen as a magical ritual. Sowing a seed of flax, he makes it grow instantaneously (quite like the "planting of cucumbers," in which some of R. Yehoshua's contemporaries so excelled), uproots it, and with it uproots the pernicious witch who had "bound" (this is the technical term used by "insider" and "outsider" sources alike for the causing of male impotence) the miserable lad whose father the sages had met.[141] Once the witch is out, he orders her to annul her spells, out of the natural and oft-recurring assumption that s/he who cast a spell is best equipped to dissolve it. The woman refuses, however, insisting that the "finished products" she had produced for this specific spell were thrown by her in the sea, no doubt as part of the magical ritual, and Rabbi Yehoshua forces the Minister of the Sea to spit out these magical artifacts. This, we are made to believe, is enough to dissolve the spell, and now – with the magic-induced impediment to conception removed by the appropriate means – the rabbis fulfill the old man's initial request and pray for his son. Their prayer soon bears its fruit, and, in a manner typical of rabbinic stories, we are told that the offspring was a great sage and that the three rabbis saw this great successs as justifying their entire visit to Rome (and perhaps also

---

[140] See pt San 7.11 (25d).
[141] The "binding" of brides and bridegrooms is explicitly mentioned in Targum Ps-Jonathan to Dt 24.6 and apparently alluded to in pt Ket. 1.1 (24b). See Shinan 1992, p. 148, and Lieberman 1942, p. 110, both with further bibliography. For some relevant recipes, see, e.g., MSF, G16 (T-S K 1.91) p. 3/1–7 (a recipe to loosen a "bound" man) and Bodleian Heb. a3.31 (unpublished) (several recipes to "bind" a man).

as yet another justification for R. Yehoshua's use of such a ritual in the first place). The witch, we may assume, went on with her praxis, but made sure to leave town whenever the sages from Palestine were on a visit to Rome. In any case, it is interesting to see the talmudic narrator apparently letting her live, in spite of the biblical injunction that "a *mekhashepha* you shall not let live" (Ex 22.17), and in a story which is embedded in the talmudic *sugiya* devoted to the execution of magicians!

Read from our perspective, the story sheds some interesting light on the rabbinic views of magic and on their practice thereof. The witch's preparation of a "finished product" which was thrown in the sea certainly fits well with what we know about ancient magical rituals, and a *defixio*, with or without a "voodoo" doll, immediately comes to mind. The pulling of the witch by her hair certainly is common enough, and even the image of a witch lurking under the roots of a plant might bring to mind the various traditions about the *mandragoras* plant and its human-like roots.[142] We must also note how R. Yehoshua "commanded the Minister of the Sea" to produce the magical artifacts. Both the verb used here for "commanded" (*gazar 'al*) and the notion that different forces of nature have a ministering angel (*sar*) who is in charge of their smooth functioning, and who may be adjured by the magician to perform his will, are well attested in the "insider" sources for ancient Jewish magic. Thus, all these clues should lead us to the conclusion that the original narrators of this story were not unaware of the practices and vocabulary associated with contemporary magical activities. They are also a heart-breaking reminder of how these narrators, or the editors who embedded this story into the Palestinian Talmud, chose to remain silent on most of the mechanics of the rituals and the contents of the spells which accompanied the "binding" of men and the loosening of such spells. As we shall see time and again, rabbinic stories of magical praxis often differ from similar stories in pagan and Christian literature in their reluctance to indulge in all the technical details involved.[143] Thus, it is precisely on those details that we need for any comparison of the "outsider" evidence with the "insider" data that such stories fail us most.

(c) In addition to these two stories, the rabbis' assumption that most women engage in sorcery made for many more stories in which rabbis

---

[142] For the parallels, see Lieberman 1942, p. 112 and Gordon 1957, p. 168, as well as the images which accompany PGM XXXVI (e.g., Betz 1986, p. 275).

[143] Such reluctance, however, is not unparalleled in the non-Jewish world. Note, for example, Pliny, *NH* 28.5.29: *carmina* (against hailstorms, diseases, and burns) *quidem extant . . . sed prodendo obstat ingens verecundia in tanta animorum varietate*; *NH* 17.47.267: (A *carmen* against hailstorms) *cuius verba inserere non equidem serio ausim*.

confront a woman who knows a magic trick or two and overcome her.[144] In one such story, a certain woman tries to force herself upon the Babylonian Rav Ḥanina bar Papi; wishing to avoid her, "he said a word, and filled his body with boils and sores." Wishing to overcome his ruse, "she did a thing and he was healed." He then hides in a demon-infested bathhouse, and is miraculously protected against their onslaught.[145] In another story, Yannai runs into trouble with a female innkeeper – and such ladies were notorious for their magical practices throughout the ancient world – but ultimately prevails by turning her into an ass and riding upon her in the market.[146] Such stories, which could easily have been lifted out of the wittiest pieces of Ptolemy Chennus, Lucian, or Apuleius (not to mention Voltaire or Freud!), actually tell us very little about the kinds of practices performed by these women, or of the rituals employed by the rabbis to counteract their spells. They all said something and did something, but what exactly they may have said or done we would never know.

Rabbis, minim, and magic

The term *min* (pl. *minim*) is a pejorative adjective reserved by the rabbis for some of their severest opponents. As neither the etymology nor the meaning of this term are clear, and as it is sometimes used of people who clearly were followers of Jesus, it has aroused an enormous scholarly interest and was the subject of many studies.[147] For the purpose of our current enquiry, however, there is no need to delve into the entire question of whom exactly the rabbis included under this umbrella category or what the rabbis said about them. Our interest in these *minim* lies solely in the fact that one of the charges hurled at them by the rabbis is that of their magical practices and that some of the stories about them are directly related to magic. Examining the charges, we may note the explicit claim that "the books of *minim* are books of magicians" – an excellent (and rare!) example of the rabbis' use of the label "magic" to denigrate "the other," for regardless of who these *minim* may have been, it is clear that they were not an association of magicians, but

---

[144] In addition to the examples discussed below, see also the story of Rava's troubles with a woman who cursed him in bt BB 153a. On the other hand, see the story in bt San 101a of how Rav Yiẓḥaq bar Shemuel got into trouble in an inn, and was saved by a woman who saw him in the market.
[145] bt Kidd 39b–40a. For filling oneself with boils and sores, note bt Kidd 81a–b, where Satan, disguised as a poor man, performs the same trick.
[146] bt San 67b. For an interesting parallel, see Flint 1991, pp. 63 and 78.
[147] For a detailed discussion of magic and *minim* in rabbinic literature, and references to earlier scholarship, see Bohak 2003a.

Magic and magicians in rabbinic literature

members of a rival religious group, or perhaps several such groups.[148] By calling all their books "books of magic," the rabbis were affixing a pejorative label to works which certainly would not have been seen as such by the *minim* themselves. And yet, even here we should note how the rabbis avoid using the more loaded term, *keshaphim*, and use a term (*qosmin*) which indeed is pejorative, but which some rabbis could even use to make fun of other rabbis.[149]

Turning from general accusations to the rabbis' many stories about their actual encounters with *minim*, we note that while the central issue around which such encounters revolved was the conflicting interpretations of Scripture, one more issue had to do with the *minim*'s healings, miracles, and magic. In some rabbinic stories, such *minim* are depicted as successfully healing Jewish patients "in the name of Jesus son of Pandera" (the rabbis' pejorative appellation for Jesus, whom they depicted as the bastard child of a Roman soldier, and as a magician in his own right). This is something the rabbis apparently found so dangerous that they repeatedly express their preference that such patients die rather than be healed in this manner, in marked contrast with their general rule that anything which heals should not really be forbidden.[150] Needless to add, the Christian use of miraculous healings in the name of Jesus as a means to gain new converts is well attested in Christian sources from the New Testament onwards, and it was the fear of such phenomena which made the rabbis so sensitive on this score. Unfortunately, such rabbinic stories shed little light on the kinds of magical procedures we find in the "insider" sources surveyed in the previous chapters. Nor are the rabbinic stories concerning the magical activities of Jesus himself of great help here, as they have very little to say about the magic techniques he supposedly employed, beyond his use of the Name.[151]

A second type of rabbinic story is much more colorful, for it involves not a simple healing performed by an obnoxious *min*, but a real duel between a *min* who uses his magical powers and a rabbi who manages to defeat him. Let us look at one famous example, found in the Palestinian Talmud right

---

[148] For the "books of *minim*" as "*sifrei qosmin*," see t Hull. 2.20 (p. 503 Zuckermandel).

[149] And note how in pt Ma'as 3.10 (51a) R. Zeira teases R. Abba bar Kahana and R. Levy, the masters of aggadah, and calls out to them, "Scribes of *qesamim*" (סיפרי קיסמי). And cf. above, nn. 20 and 26, for similar puns.

[150] For such stories, see, e.g., t Hull. 2.23; pt AZ 2.2 (40d) // pt Shab. 14.4 (14d) // Eccl. R. 10.5, and cf. Reiner 2004, pp. 366–71. Note, however, that Christian writers too often insisted that it was better to die than be healed by a Jew – see, for example, Wilken 1983, pp. 83–88.

[151] For Jesus as a magician, see bt San 43a and 107b (in both cases, the relevant sections were omitted by censorship from the printed editions): *Yeshu . . . kisheph* etc., and the *Toledoth Yeshu* materials (Krauss 1902, pp. 192–93 and passim; Deutsch 2000, pp. 183–85). And cf. Smith 1978.

before the story of R. Yehoshua and the witch in Rome and sharing many similarities with it:

A story: R. Eliezer and R. Yehoshua and R. Akiva went up to bathe in the public bath-house in Tiberias. They saw a certain *min*. He said what he said, and the vault caught them. R. Eliezer said to R. Yehoshua, What?, Yehoshua ben Ḥananiah, see what you can do. When this *min* came out, R. Yehoshua said what he said, and the door caught him, and whoever went in would bang him with the door-knocker, and whoever went out would bang him by forcing the door open. He said to them, Annul what you have done. They said to him, You annul (what you have done), and we will annul (what we have done). Both sides annulled (what they had done). When they came out, R. Yehoshua said to that *min*, Is this how wise you are? He said, Let us go down to the sea. When they went down to the sea, the *min* said what he said, and the sea was split asunder. He said to them, Did not Moses your master do just that to the sea? They said to him, But don't you admit that Moses our master (also) walked in it? He said to them, Yes; they said to him, So walk in it. He walked in it. R. Yehoshua commanded the Minister of the Sea, and he swallowed him up.[152]

As this story has been the subject of several recent studies, we may forego a detailed analysis of its many features.[153] For the purpose of our current enquiry, we must stress that while the story is extremely detailed in some respects, and even provides such details as where exactly it all took place or in which part of the bath-house each protagonist got caught, it is extremely reticent when it comes to the magical praxis utilized by each side.[154] Both the *min* and Rabbi Yehoshua are described as using magic spells ("he said what he said"), but the *contents* of these spells are not revealed. The only hint provided by the narrator is that in the last round R. Yehoshua "commanded" (*gazar 'al*) "the Minister of the Sea" to swallow the *min* up, and since we already met this expression in the other R. Yehoshua story, we cannot help concluding that it was used in a somewhat stereotyped manner by narrators or editors of such stories. In fact, a closer comparison of the two stories clearly shows that the verbal similarities between them reflect the editorial activities of whoever decided to place them side by side, an editor who clearly did not have our own historical needs in mind. And yet, it is interesting to note that whereas the female witch remains alive at the end of one story, the male *min* is killed at the end of the

---

[152] pt San 7.19 (25d). For comparanda, see the story in the *Apostolic History of Abdias* (James 1924, p. 463) of how Hermogenes binds Philetus to his place by magic, but James sends Philetus a handkerchief which releases him.
[153] See Veltri 1997, pp. 31–33; Jacobs 1998, pp. 298–303.
[154] For an "insider" perspective, see the recipes in MTKG III, 69 (T-S AS 142.13 + NS 317.18) (with Bohak 2005, pp. 15–16), for stopping people in the bath-house.

other, apparently reflecting the rabbis' much greater fear of *minim* than of witches.

To sum up. Whereas the analysis of what the rabbis knew about the magical practices of their Jewish and non-Jewish contemporaries repeatedly reveals their familiarity with the kinds of practices known to us from the "insider" sources for late-antique magic, the analysis of the rabbis' own stories of their encounters with witches and magicians is far more disappointing. The spells and rituals utilized by the magicians receive no description, and even the rabbis' actions and words are described in a brief and mostly stereotyped manner. And yet, it is interesting to note that rather than telling us that the rabbi involved merely raised his hands to heaven or uttered a standard prayer (such as the special curse against the *minim* incorporated by the rabbis into the daily liturgy!) and won the duel, the narrators of these stories describe rabbis utilizing extra-*halakhic* means to gain victory over their opponents. For these narrators, it would seem, "magic" was not a frightful label to be avoided at all cost, and the use of magic against its most powerful practitioners was a perfectly legitimate practice. Below, we shall find rabbis who were using even more elaborate magical techniques, and not only against potential practitioners of magic.

RABBIS AS MAGICIANS

One more type of rabbinic text in which magic looms large is the many discussions and descriptions of the wonder-workers of their own times, and especially the charismatic holy man and the powerful rabbinic sage. Among the former, we may note a diffuse group of "men of deeds" (to use the rabbis' own expression), whose life-spans fall in the Second Temple period and in the early rabbinic period, including such figures as Honi the Circle Maker (some of whose exploits were noted in Chapters 1 and 2) and Hanina ben Dosa, whose exploits included healing the sick, fighting demons, and inadvertently demonstrating his own immunity to noxious reptiles.[155] Such figures usually are not credited with any *halakhic* rulings or exegetical expertise, and even rabbinic literature does not try to portray them as members of the rabbinic class or as bound by its specific understanding of Torah. They are, in many ways, the direct heirs of Elijah and Elisha, following their example in healing the sick, working miracles, and

---

[155] See m Sot 9.15: "When Hanina ben Dosa died men of deed came to an end." These figures have aroused a great deal of scholarly interest, e.g., Sarfatti 1956/57; Safrai 1965; Vermes 1972–73; Green 1979; Lightstone 1985; Bokser 1985; Blenkinsopp 1999.

earning the admiration and fear of the population – and of the rabbis themselves. And their miracles, like those of their biblical predecessors, involved the use of the simplest implements and the plainest of words, and were seen as derived solely from their innate powers (what we would call charisma) and their proximity to God.

There is, however, a second type of wonder-worker to be found in rabbinic literature, men whose life-spans cover the time from the destruction of the Temple to the very end of the rabbinic period and whose wonder-working powers go hand in hand with their mastery of Torah and their membership in the rabbinic class. Looking at a figure like Rabbi Shimeon bar Yoḥai, active in the mid-second century CE, we find him not only transmitting many *halakhic* rulings and aggadic statements, but also performing many powerful deeds, such as producing gold coins *ex nihilo*, colluding with a demon in the staging of an exorcism, making corpses float out of their burial places, and killing his detractors with a word or a gaze.[156] And while his miraculous achievements clearly outdid those of most rabbis, the great thaumaturgical power accumulated by masters of Torah are a topic on which rabbinic literature is always glad to elaborate. "Warm yourself against the sages' fire," says an early rabbinic dictum,

> but beware of their burning coal lest you burn yourself, for their bite is the bite of a fox, and their sting is the sting of a scorpion, and their whisper is the whisper of a serpent and all their words are like coals of fire.[157]

Like the men of God of biblical times, rabbis were not to be messed around with, and this point is driven home in a long series of warnings, attributed both to Palestinian and to Babylonian rabbis. "The curse of a sage is fulfilled even when unmerited (by the victim's deeds)"; "a serpent of (i.e., sent by, or on behalf of) the sages is one for whose bite there is no healing"; "every place upon which the sages cast their eyes – (you find there) either death or poverty."[158] And the message is amplified by an endless series of stories of sages who "cast their eyes" upon their opponent(s) and "turned him/them into a heap of bones," as well as stories of rabbis who successfully cursed numerous individuals who had offended them, including other

---

[156] Gold coins: pt Ber 9.2 (13d) and Gen R. 35.2 (p. 329 Theodor-Albeck) (and note how both sources cite RASHBY's actual words, rather than insisting that "he said what he said"; cf. bt Men 37a and Ber 48b, for Ḥanina's words to the roof-beams); exorcism: bt Meʿila 17a–b; floating corpses: pt Shevi 9.1 (38d) and Gen R. 79.6 (pp. 943–44 Theodor-Albeck); killing: last two sources and bt Shab 33b. For a recent survey of RASHBY's exploits, see Rosenfeld 1999.

[157] m Avot 2.10.

[158] Curse: bt Ber 56a; bt San 90b; bt Mak 11a. Serpent: bt Shab 110a; bt AZ 27b; and cf. pt Shevi 9.1 (38d). Every place: bt MoK 17b; bt Ḥag 5b; bt Ned 7b; bt Sot 46b.

rabbis.¹⁵⁹ Many of these stories deal with Babylonian rabbis, and therefore are less relevant for the present study, but Palestinian rabbis did not shy away from such aggression, which they too needed in order to maintain social control over their followers and ward off some of their opponents.¹⁶⁰ And like Elijah and Elisha, the rabbis used their powers not only for aggressive purposes, but for beneficial aims as well. In some cases, they even tried to monopolize many of the services which in an earlier period would have been provided by the holy men, and especially those having to do with healing and protection. Numerous rabbinic stories tell of people who were sick, but when a rabbi, or the rabbis, prayed for them, they regained their health, and in one story we even find the Roman governor (or emperor) Antoninus asking Rabbi Judah the Prince to pray for his health.¹⁶¹ Of one rabbi we learn that his prayer destroys demons, and another insists that "Whoever has a sick person in his home should go to a sage and ask for mercy over the patient." Of one rabbi we learn that when a house was about to collapse he sent one of his righteous disciples to sit there, until the house could be emptied of its contents; when this was done and the disciple left, the house collapsed.¹⁶² Of another rabbi we hear that he entered a bath-house which soon collapsed, but a miracle happened, one pillar was left standing, and it saved 101 men, including, of course, the rabbi.¹⁶³ And, perhaps most striking, the rabbis are convinced that whatever God decrees a righteous man, and especially a righteous rabbi, can annul.¹⁶⁴

The combination of learning and thaumaturgy was far from unusual in antiquity, as may be seen, for example, from the many stories about the magical exploits of Greek philosophers, from Empedocles to Plotinus and beyond. But the rabbis' constant insistence that their mastery of Torah grants them great powers is also directly linked to the age-old Jewish notion

---

[159] Cast their eyes: bt BB 75a // San 100a (he cast his eyes on him and turned him into a heap of bones); bt BB 14a (the rabbis cast their eyes upon him, and he died). For many more examples, see Ulmer 1994, pp. 83–104. Curses: bt Ber 56a (Rava curses a dream-interpreter); bt Meg 5b (Rav cursed a man who sowed on Purim) (did he use Dt 29.22, so popular in Jewish aggressive magic?); bt BB 22a (R. Joseph admits that he had cursed R. Adda); see also bt MoK 27b (a woman mourned too much for her dead son, so Rav Huna told her that her other children would also die – and they did; then she too died).

[160] This aspect of rabbinic culture is highlighted by Neusner 1966–67 and 1987, and by Harari 2006.

[161] Prayers and healings: e.g., bt Ḥag 3a (Rabbi prays for two mute disciples, and they start speaking); bt Ber 6a (Rav Bibi bar Abaye managed to see the demons, but was harmed; the rabbis prayed for him and he was healed). Antoninus and Rabbi: pt San 10.5 (29c) and Lev.R 16.8 (p. 364 Margalioth).

[162] Prayer against demons: bt Kidd 29b. Go to a sage: bt BB 116a. Collapsing houses: pt Taan 3.9 (67a).

[163] bt Ber 60a.

[164] For this statement, see, e.g., pt Taan 3.8 (67a): God annuls His decree because of that of a righteous man; bt Taan 23a: you decreed from below, and God does it up above; bt MoK 16b: I rule men, and who rules me? The righteous person, for I decree a decree, and he annuls it.

(which we examined in Chapter 1), of the great powers inherent in God's sacred objects. With the Temple gone, and with God's sacred objects either destroyed or taken to Rome, God's secret Names and the Torah He had written remained the most sacred divine objects possessed by the Jews. And while the Torah-scroll itself could be used for various magical rituals (such as pacifying a crying child), the rabbis were convinced, and tried to convince all other Jews, that it was the internalization of the text and all its different meanings and implications – which is what the rabbis spent their entire lives doing – that would tap its powers in the most effective way. The rabbi, in other words, became a new type of holy man (and, once again, only men were allowed into the club), and rabbinic literature does much to present him as more than an adequate substitute for the non-rabbinic holy men of old. And yet, what is more surprising in this respect is that rabbinic literature also describes some rabbis whose mastery of Torah apparently did not suffice to work the miracles of which they were in need, and who therefore had to resort to other, more technical means.[165] Above, we noted Rabbi Yehoshua's magical handling of a dangerous witch and an impertinent *min*, to which we may now add two other intriguing rabbinic stories. The first is found in three different places in the Babylonian Talmud, always embedded in a longer unit, whose exact contents vary slightly from one text to the next. The basic story runs as follows:

Our Sages taught: "And God rages every day" (Ps 7.12) and how long is his rage? A moment. And how long is a moment? One of 56,888 of one hour, that is one moment. And no creature can aim for that time except for the wicked Balaam, of whom it is written, "and he knows the mind of the Most High" (Nm 24.16) . . . And when is He angry? Abaye said, In the first three hours (of the day), when the comb of the cock is white . . . R. Yehoshua ben Levi had this *min* in his neighborhood, and he (the *min*) would annoy him with biblical verses. He took a cock, and went and tied it to the feet of his bed, and examined it; he thought, When that hour comes, I will curse him. When that hour came, he fell asleep. He said, Learn from this that it is not a proper thing to do, for it is written "Even for the righteous it is not good to punish" (Prv 17.26).[166]

Above, we already had a chance to look at several stories of magical duels between rabbis and *minim*, in which the rabbis got the upper hand. In this story, however, only one side, the rabbi, resorts to magic, having failed to

---

[165] The rabbis themselves were not unaware of this difference. Note, for example, the complaints of later Babylonian rabbis that while Rav Yehudah would take his shoe off and it would start to rain, their own efforts produce no rain (bt Taan 24a–b; bt Ber 20a; bt San 106b).

[166] bt AZ 4a–b; see the parallels in Ber 7a, San 105b, and the fuller analysis of this passage in Bohak 2003a. Prv 17.26 really means "It is not good to punish the righteous," but is interpreted here as "Even for the righteous it is not good to punish."

face the *min*'s Scriptural challenges. Apparently unable to match the *min*'s exegetical acumen, Rabbi Yehoshua ben Levi – a leading Palestinian rabbi of the early third century CE – opts for an elaborate ritual intended to detect the exact moment of God's blind rage and deflect it upon the triumphant *min*. Looking at this ritual, we may note both the lack of any known contemporary parallels to this use of cocks as detectors of God's moment of wrath (itself an interesting theological concept!), and their common use in other types of aggressive magical rituals.[167] Further research is likely to clarify whether this is a specifically rabbinic ritual, or a slight transformation of a widespread magical technique, but the use of God's numinous wrath does seem quite different from what we find in the "insider" sources for late-antique Jewish magic, which generally avoid involving God in their magical practices. As noted in the previous chapter, such comparisons might make us think that in some respects the Jewish magicians of late-antique Palestine were more conservative and less daring than some contemporary rabbis.

Even more intriguing than the ritual itself is the fact that it ends in a miserable, and even comic, failure, and Rabbi Yehoshua ben Levi concludes that it was God Himself who intervened, since it is not for the righteous rabbis, but for God, to punish the wicked. This is, of course, quite in line with what we saw in Chapter 2, when we noted Honi's refusal to curse the besieged priests or Jesus' refusal to let his disciples curse a Samaritan village, and with the rabbis' own displeasure with Elisha's rough handling of the boys who made fun of him.[168] Such reticence, however, was not always the norm, as can be deduced from a second story involving a rabbi's resort to an aggressive ritual against an opponent. This time, the story is set in Babylonia, and is embedded in a lengthy *sugiya* on the use of excommunication as the ultimate punishment meted out by the Palestinian Patriarch, by the Jewish courts, and by individual rabbis against wayward individuals who refused to abide by the rules laid out by these Jewish leaders. In one case, a certain bully used to bother one of the rabbinic disciples, and when the latter came to Rav Yoseph, the rabbi recommended an excommunication. The disciple, however, was afraid lest the bully retaliate, and so Rav Yoseph recommended that he write a deed of excommunication, "place it in a jar, place it (the jar) in a cemetery, and blow into it a thousand *shofar* blows in

---

[167] For the use of (white) cocks in aggressive magical rituals, see, e.g., PGM II.73; III.693–701; IV.35–58; Levene 1999 = Levene 2003, pp. 120–38, l. 6; Bodleian Heb. a3.31 (unpublished); and cf. ShR I/160–169 (pp. 75–76 Margalioth). For later Jewish traditions about cocks and God's rage, clearly influenced by this passage, see Trachtenberg 1939, pp. 211–12.
[168] For which see bt Sot 46b–47a.

forty days." The disciple followed these instructions, and eventually the jar burst asunder and the bully died.[169] Reading this story (which provides an interesting perspective on some of the aggressive incantation bowls, especially those designated "for the cemetery"!), one is struck by this blatant recourse to aggressive magic as a means for settling the score with a disobedient individual, who clearly was a fellow Jew. Gone are the qualms about the punishment of sinners at the hands of cunning rabbis rather than by God, or about the use of such elaborate, and decidedly non-*halakhic*, rituals to achieve this goal. To maintain their social control, some rabbis (and especially the Babylonian rabbis?) clearly were willing to go the extra mile separating the use of innate personal powers or standard *halakhic* procedure from the use of powerful technologies of preternatural annihilation.

Before leaving this last example, we may note how the rabbinic disciple does not produce a lead *defixio* or some other specifically magical text, but a standard rabbinic text – a written deed of excommunication against a named individual – which is placed at the heart of a complex magical ritual. Such "magicalization" of rabbinic texts and rituals will become a recurrent feature of post-rabbinic Jewish magic, but its roots clearly lie in the rabbinic period itself.[170] We may also note how in this case the magical praxis does involve the act of writing – albeit of a non-magical text – but such a text would have been written on a perishable writing surface, and would have disintegrated long ago. And with this sad thought in mind, we must leave aside the stories of rabbis who behaved like magicians and turn to one more aspect of this broad topic, namely, the magical recipes which fill the pages of rabbinic literature.

RABBINIC MAGICAL RECIPES

Perhaps the most obvious starting-point for a detailed comparison of the magical praxis of the rabbis and that of the "insider" sources is provided by the many magical rituals and practices warmly recommended by the rabbis themselves. In quite a few places in the Babylonian Talmud (and in a handful of passages elsewhere in rabbinic literature), recipes and instructions are found which we might classify as "magic" (though the rabbis certainly did not), most of which are for healing and medicinal purposes, or for gaining immunity from various evils, including magic and witchcraft. Having discussed the rabbinic claims that fulfilling God's commandments would

---

[169] bt MoK 17a–b. For the rabbis' פיתדא, see Sokoloff 2002, p. 947.
[170] For the magical uses of rabbinic texts and rituals, see, e.g., Scholem 1980/81; Schäfer 1996.

Magic and magicians in rabbinic literature 407

protect you from all evil, and that the study of Torah, for example, is an excellent panacea against all types of bodily pain, we may now note how the same rabbis complemented this pious talk with more specific means to fight such evils. We may also note how in rabbinic literature, just as in the "insider" magical texts, the magical recipes never enter such theological issues as whether the patient's illness was sent by God as a punishment for his transgressions and should not be alleviated at all. Elsewhere, the rabbis devote a great deal of attention to such issues, but their recipes are goal-oriented and very specific, leaving no room for moralizing discussions of sins and their punishments or merits and their rewards. But rather than focus on the theological or philosophical implications of this paradox – so typical of the rabbis' attitude to magic – let us focus on the actual instructions they provide.

A detailed survey of all the magical recipes in rabbinic literature – or even a general typology of their forms, aims, and contents, and of their possible classification as "magic", "popular religion," or "folk medicine" – remains a desideratum, but will not be carried out here.[171] For our own purpose, it is important to note what some of the more magical recipes generally look like, and how they compare with the "insider" evidence we have surveyed in the previous chapters. Before attempting such a comparison, however, we must note that the very nature of these recipes limits our ability to compare them with, say, those Genizah recipes which probably reflect the magical practices of late-antique Palestine. For unlike the latter recipes, which cover practices for every imaginable magical aim, the recipes quoted in rabbinic literature are almost entirely limited to healing and apotropaic purposes.[172] As we already noted, rabbinic stories make it quite clear that some rabbis also dabbled in aggressive magic, and provide some examples of the rituals they used for such aims, but erotic magic, for example, is never attributed to rabbinic figures. Whether this means that the rabbis of late antiquity (unlike some of their contemporary Christian monks, for example, and some latter-day rabbis) shied away from all such practices is an open question.[173] But be that as it may, we must note that the absence of such recipes from rabbinic literature means that it cannot be the *aims* of

---

[171] For a useful first step, see Veltri 1997, pp. 222–66. For earlier studies, see Brecher 1850, pp. 187–233 and Blau 1898, pp. 68–86.
[172] This, however, is not very different from what we find in those Greek and Roman authors – Cato, Pliny the Elder, Alexander Trallianus – who provide their readers with useful magical spells and procedures, but usually avoid aggressive magical practices.
[173] As a comparandum, one may note that contemporary Coptic monks did not shy away from such practices; see, for example, Frankfurter 1998, pp. 258–60; Meyer and Smith 1994, pp. 147–81.

individual recipes that we seek to compare with the "insider" sources, but only the recipes' external appearance and the magical praxis they enjoin.

Searching for rabbinic magical recipes, one finds them transmitted in several different forms – as stories of actions taken by different authorities (often with an indication whether the action proved helpful, or with didactic instructions embedded in the story itself), as general suggestions and advice embedded in discussions of a long range of issues, as individual recipes ("For X, do Y"), and even as large clusters of recipes appearing together.[174] In the largest and most comprehensive of these clusters, a long set of over forty medical recipes is topically arranged according to the afflicted part of the body. First comes a recipe "For the blood of the head," then "For migraine" then "For a cataract," then "For night-blindness," "For day-blindness," "For blood coming out of the nostrils," going down to the heart and internal organs, and ending with various fevers.[175] Only two of these recipes are attributed to specific sages, while all the others are transmitted anonymously as part of the wider collection. This, and the fact that the entire unit seems to have been "pasted" after the end of another unit (that dealing with Solomon's adventures with demons), might indicate that the editor of this talmudic *sugiya* used a pre-existing, non-rabbinic, and probably even non-Jewish florilegium of medical recipes, which might even go back to Akkadian medical lore.[176] But be that as it may, when we examine the medical procedures demanded by these recipes we find a whole range of *materia medica* and several interesting rituals and spells – most of which evince no specifically Jewish components, and none of which bears much resemblance to what we find in the "insider" sources of the western branch of the Jewish magical tradition. In passing, we may add that these recipes bear little resemblance to what we find in the Babylonian incantation bowls as well, and that only one set of three recipes demands the use of writing (on an unspecified surface) as part of the magical ritual.[177]

---

[174] For stories of actions, see the previous section. For didactic stories, see, e.g., bt Hull 105b. For single recipes or isolated suggestions, see, e.g., bt Ber 6a (two suggestions for detecting or seeing demons); bt Ber 55b (a ritual for averting the consequences of an ill-omened dream), etc. For clusters of recipes, see, e.g., bt Shab 110a (suggestions for dealing with snakes); bt Shab. 110a–b (recipes against vaginal flows and jaundice), etc.

[175] bt Git 68b–70b; for a translation and comments, see Veltri 1997, pp. 239–49, and for detailed analyses see Freeman 1998–99 and Geller 2000.

[176] And cf. the likelihood of a pre-existing source for the oneirological materials of bt Ber 55a–57b, as argued by Alexander 1995. For the wider phenomenon of pre-existing textual units inserted into the Babylonian Talmud, see Weiss 1962, pp. 251–94. For the possible Akkadian origins of this specific unit, see Geller 2000 (and cf. Geller 1991). See also Freeman 1998–99.

[177] bt Git 69a, "For blood which comes out of the nostril," three alternative spells to be written. Since the first of these involved asking a Jewish priest named Levi to write "Levi" backwards, it certainly was not a part of the supposed Akkadian *Vorlage* of the entire collection.

Thus, while this *vademecum* provides valuable information on the use in Babylonian rabbinic medicine of rituals which we would classify as "magic," and which probably reflect local Mesopotamian practices, it displays no real overlap with the kind of magical rituals we have been studying throughout the present study.

An even clearer proof of the Babylonian rabbis' familiarity with the magical practices of their time and place is provided by the spell for protecting oneself against witches, which is attributed by Amemar (late fourth/early fifth century) to the head of a coven of witches. By now, we should not be surprised to find an important rabbi citing a *mekhashepha*, who was not even necessarily Jewish, especially as what he cites is an anti-witchcraft spell.[178] Why the witch agreed to share her trade-secrets with a Jewish rabbi we may only speculate (did he teach her some powerful Jewish Names or some rabbinic magical recipes in return?), but we should note that in this case, unlike some of those we noted in Chapters 3 and 4, the transfer of magical technology seems to have been entirely oral, with no recipe-books to copy from and no written manuals. What is more interesting, however, is that the spell itself finds close parallels in some of the Babylonian incantation bowls, thus proving that Amemar did not simply invent his own spell and then attributed it to a witch, but quoted an authentic spell which apparently circulated quite widely in late-antique Mesopotamia.[179] Once again, we find clear evidence of the rabbis' familiarity with the magical practices of non-rabbinic persons, both Jews and Gentiles, and a careful comparison of all the incantation bowls with the rabbis' own spells would certainly reveal more such parallels.[180] But such examples would shed light mainly on the eastern branch of late-antique Jewish magic, which lies outside the scope of the present study. In this regard, it is important to note that the spell cited here does not appear in any of the Palestinian Jewish amulets or Genizah magical texts, yet another example of the apparent gulf separating the western and the eastern branches of the Jewish magical tradition in late antiquity.

If the longest talmudic collection of medico-magical recipes and the direct citation of an expert witch prove quite disappointing for the purpose of the present study, other recipes found in the Babylonian Talmud turn out

---

[178] See bt Pes. 110a–b. For learning recipes from Gentiles, see also bt AZ 29a (a medical recipe learned from an Arab); pt AZ 2.2 (40d) // pt Shab 14.4 (14d) // bt AZ 28a // Yoma 84a, with Valler 2000, pp. 172–77 (R. Yoḥanan and the daughter of Domitianus of Tiberias).

[179] For the parallels, see Montgomery 1913, no. 1, pp. 117 and 119–20 (with Epstein 1921, pp. 29–30), and esp. Gordon 1934, pp. 326–28, bowl C, ll. 3–4 and Segal 2000, bowl 035A, p. 74.

[180] And see Müller-Kessler 2005, p. 45, and Bohak 2005/6, pp. 258–59, for other examples. Elsewhere, I hope to provide a fuller discussion of this issue.

to be much more rewarding. Examining such recipes, and comparing them with the recipes found in the Cairo Genizah, we note several interesting features. First, unlike the recipes in most of the Genizah formularies, most of the talmudic recipes are attributed to named authorities, in line with standard talmudic modes of citation and attribution. In some instances, the attribution is to a named rabbi, thus making the recipe look exactly like any other rabbinic dictum in talmudic literature – Rabbi X said Y – and demonstrating how the editors had no qualms about attributing such recipes to great *halakhic* figures. In other cases, however, the recipes are attributed to specific practitioners and non-rabbinic experts, and especially to women. We already noted the recipe attributed by Amemar to an actual witch, and many other recipes – some of a strictly medical nature, others much more magical – are attributed by Abaye, one of the greatest scholars of fourth-century Babylonia, to his mother.[181] In passing, we may note that here rabbinic literature seems to offer us a rare glimpse of the world of women's magic in late antiquity, a world which hardly is represented by the "insider" sources – pagan, Christian, or Jewish. Such issues, however, will have to be dealt with elsewhere, for at present we must note another corollary of this feature, namely, that most of the attributed recipes in the Babylonian Talmud are attributed to (Jewish, and perhaps also non-Jewish) Babylonian tradents, and are potentially less useful as comparanda for the "insider" sources of the western branch of ancient Jewish magic.[182]

A second feature to be noted with regard to rabbinic recipes is that they lack the basic components which characterize the magical recipes whose structure we analyzed in Chapter 4. In vain shall we look in rabbinic literature for the claim that a certain recipe is "tried and tested," for the magicians' battle cry of "now, now, quickly, quickly," or for the *charactêres*[183] which are so prominent in the Jewish magical texts of late antiquity and the early Middle Ages. The presence of such elements would have facilitated the

---

[181] For Abaye's mother (actually, his wet-nurse – see bt Kidd 31b) and her magical recipes, see Veltri 1997, pp. 230–38; Lesses 2001, pp. 362–64. For her medical recipes, see Valler 2000, pp. 161–72.

[182] A related, and much debated, issue is whether such attributions may be trusted at all. As we shall see throughout the present section, recipes attributed to Palestinian figures indeed display a much greater resemblance to the western branch of ancient Jewish magic than those attributed to Babylonian figures.

[183] Whether the rabbis mention the *charactêres* or not is a vexed question, depending on one's interpretation of נלטורי בעלמא in bt Shab 103b. Rashi ad loc., and Winkler 1930, p. 162, identify it as *charactêres*, while Sperber 1994, pp. 71–80, derives it from the late-Latin term *ligatura*, "amulet." I find neither interpretation persuasive, but am unable to offer a better one. See also Sperber 1994, p. 92, n. 2, who understands כלקטירים in Pesikta de-Rav Kahana, p. 107 Mandelbaum, as *charactêres*; but the suggestion of Mandelbaum and Lieberman ad loc., that the word is a corrupt transliteration of φυλακτήρια, seems more persuasive.

comparison with the "insider" evidence, but their absence may just as well be attributed to processes of editorial censorship and textual entropy as to the rabbis' actual avoidance of Greco-Egyptian magical techniques. However, looking at the contents of individual recipes we see that – just as with the long *vademecum* to which we already alluded – their instructions demand the use and manipulation of various *materia magica* and the recitation of various spells, some of which include *voces magicae*, but only rarely demand an act of writing. This last observation is true not only for the recipes attributed to female tradents – none of which even mentions the act of writing – but also, and perhaps less expectedly, to those which are attributed to male tradents, or are not attributed at all. We shall return to this issue below, but may already stress that we are not likely to find too much archeological evidence confirming the actual use of the recipes transmitted and used by the rabbis.

To see what these recipes often look like, and to get a sense of how they might be compared with the "insider" evidence of the western branch of ancient Jewish magic, let us look at several specific examples from a single cluster of magical recipes. Embedded in the talmudic *sugiya* on the Mishnaic dictum that "Boys (may) go out in knots" on the Sabbath – clearly, because such apotropaic knots were a part of the boy's standard clothing, as in the apotropaic T-shirt discovered by Yadin in the Cave of Letters – are many interesting discussions of the uses of such knots. As the talmudic *sugiya* unfolds, more specific medico-magical recipes are cited. First come three recipes of Abaye's mother, against quotidian fever, recommending the use of a white *zuz*-coin hung around the neck as an amulet, the "transferring" of the illness to a hapless ant and then sealing it in a bronze tube, and the "transferring" of the disease to river-water which then flows downstream.[184] These recipes are followed by a recipe attributed to Rav Huna (a Babylonian rabbi of the third century), against tertian fever, calling for the production of an amulet from a long range of *materia magica*, all in groups of seven, and reminding us, for example, of the assorted contents of the "knots" in the Second Temple period amuletic T-shirt discovered by Yadin. This recipe is followed by a recipe attributed to the Palestinian Rabbi Yoḥanan, for inflammatory fever, which is worth quoting in its entirety:

[184] For the "transfer" of illnesses to hapless animals, see, e.g., Pliny, *NH* 28.23.86 (the Magi say that you should cut all your nails, throw the parings near an ant hole, catch the first ant that takes a paring away, tie it around your neck and it will cure your disease); *NH* 28.42.155 (if a scorpion stings you, you should relate the event in the ears of an ass, and the evil will be transferred into the ass); *NH* 30.14.42–43, 30.20.62, 30.50.144, etc.; Marcellus Empiricus 20.66. For a Babylonian ritual to transfer the disease to the river, see Thompson 1908, p. 42, and especially Scurlock 2002, pp. 217–19.

R. Yoḥanan said, For an inflammatory fever, let one take an all-iron knife, go to a place where there is a thorn bush, and tie a thread of white hair to it. On the first day he should slightly notch it and say, "And the angel of the Lord appeared to him, etc." (Ex 3.2). On the following day, he should slightly notch it and say "And Moses said, I will turn aside and see" (Ex 3.3). On the following day he should slightly notch it and say, "And when the Lord saw that he turned to see, etc." (Ex 3.4).

R. Aha son of Rava said to Rav Ashi, But he should say "And he said, Do not come here!" (Ex 3.5). So, on the first day he should say, "And the angel of the Lord appeared to him, etc. And Moses said, etc." (Ex 3.2–3). On the following day he should say "And when the Lord saw that he turned to see" (Ex 3.4). And on the following day he should say "And He said, Do not come here!" (Ex 3.5).

And when he breaks it (the bush) he should push it down and break it and say, O thorn bush, O thorn bush, it is not because you are taller than all the other trees that the Holy One, blessed be He, caused His *Shekhina* to dwell upon you, but because you are more humble than all the trees the Holy One, blessed be He, caused His *Shekhina* to dwell upon you. And just as the fire saw Ḥananiah, Mishael and Azariah and fled from before them, so shall the fire (i.e., fever) of NN leave and flee from him.[185]

Before turning to a detailed analysis of the ritual itself, we may note one feature of its talmudic setting. Pushed right in the middle of the recipe are the suggestions of a fifth-century Babylonian rabbi who "improves" the recipe by offering a slightly different set of biblical verses to be recited on each day. As we had many occasions to note throughout the present study, ancient magicians, non-Jewish and Jewish alike, often saw nothing wrong with editing the recipes they received rather than slavishly copying and executing them. Here, and elsewhere in rabbinic literature, we find the rabbis doing precisely the same thing, when a Babylonian rabbi offers alterations and modifications to a recipe that is said to have come from a Palestinian colleague who lived a century and a half earlier.[186] Leaving his alterations aside for the time being, we may note that Rabbi Yoḥanan's original recipe involves an elaborate ritual by which a simple thorn-bush is turned into the Burning Bush in which God revealed himself to Moses in the desert (Ex 3.2–6). At the end of a two-day ritual aimed at achieving this

---

[185] bt Shab 67a. See Blau 1898, pp. 69–70; Goldin 1976, pp. 124–25. And cf. bt AZ 28a, where R. Yoḥanan says that to cure inflammatory fever, one may desecrate the Sabbath, and where the Talmud adds that R. Yoḥanan was an approved physician.

[186] This is a common occurrence in rabbinic literature, as can be seen even on the previous page of the Babylonian Talmud (bt Shab 66b), where a recipe of Abaye's mother to "transfer" a daily fever to an ant is cited and "improved" by the same fifth-century tradents. In our own recipe, the "improvement" clearly seeks to end with "do not come here" so as to keep the fever at bay, but this distorts the original logic of the *historiola*, since this command originally was addressed to Moses, not to the fire!

goal, the practitioner is supposed to address the bush in the second person, and, by mentioning a second biblical event, and breaking off a branch of the bush, secure the fleeing of the fever from the suffering patient (who, we may assume, had waited patiently all the while). Unfortunately, the recipe does not seem to be complete, and it is not really clear whether breaking off the branch is supposed to "break off" the disease by way of analogy, or whether the broken piece would now serve as an amulet, to be tied around the patient.[187] But as "a thread of white hair" is normally used in rabbinic recipes for the tying of amulets, we may be quite certain that the second interpretation is the correct one, and that once the thorn bush has turned into the Burning Bush, which burns in the fire but is not consumed (Ex 3.2), the piece broken off it (along the notches incised in the bush throughout the ritual?) will keep the patient from being consumed by his or her own fever. In passing, we may note that we have seen a very similar usage in a Jewish magical recipe borrowed by Alexander of Tralles, in which a specific root was adjured, dug out, and its tip was then tied around the patient as an amulet. We shall return to that recipe in a moment.

In analyzing R. Yoḥanan's complex ritual, we may note the different functions of the two *historiolae* utilized here. The second *historiola*, that of the three youths in the fiery furnace, is used here by way of analogy – "just as the fire fled from them *in illo tempore*, so shall it flee from the patient here and now." Such usage of biblical stories, including this specific story, is extremely common in Jewish magical texts, and in Christian ones as well.[188] The first *historiola*, on the other hand, involves not an analogy, but the "actualization" of a mythical object; an absolutely ordinary bush becomes, after a complex ritual, that magical bush which burned but was not consumed, a property which the magician will then use for healing his patient. Such transubstantiations are quite common in religious and magical rituals, and are well attested in ancient Jewish magical texts, such as the erotic Jewish magical spell from PGM XXXVI (see Chapter 3) in which the practitioner addresses the sulfur in his hands as if it were the sulfur which burned Sodom and Gomorrah, and orders it to burn the heart of the victim in love for himself. Rabbi Yoḥanan's recipe, in other words, fits extremely well with what we know about the use of biblical precedents and biblical *historiolae* in the "insider" evidence of Jewish magic

---

[187] A third suggestion (Patai 1942–43, vol. I, pp. 241–42), that the ritual is intended to "transfer" the fever from the patient to the bush, and that cutting the bush symbolizes its death in lieu of the patient, seems to me much less plausible.

[188] For the magical uses of biblical *historiolae*, see Chapter 5. See also bt Ned 41a, for the claim that the miracle of the healing of a fever is greater than that which happened to Ḥananiah, Mishael, and Azariah.

in late antiquity. In passing, we may note that the spirit of the *Shekhina* which was revealed to Moses in the Burning Bush also seems to make an appearance on the bilingual Jewish-Greek amulet from Egypt which has been discussed in the previous two chapters, though the magical context there is a different one.[189]

Rereading this recipe, we notice that it is an entirely "Jewish" recipe, and would squarely belong with the materials discussed in Chapter 5. Moreover, and more interestingly, it is a specifically rabbinic recipe, in that it uses a famous tannaitic midrash on how God deliberately chose the simplest bush (and not, for example, some mighty cedar) in which to reveal His *Shekhina* to Moses.[190] This datum joins what we noted above, concerning Rav Yoseph's use of a rabbinic deed of excommunication as part of his magical ritual, and highlights the significance of our observation in the previous chapter, that the "insider" sources of late-antique Jewish magic – at least its western branch – display no distinctly rabbinic elements. If our spell indeed goes back to Rabbi Yohanan, the foremost Palestinian rabbi of the mid-third century CE, it would show that by that time some rabbis were already using distinct rabbinic motifs in composing their own spells, whereas the late-antique amulets currently at our disposal apparently contain no such motifs.

Interesting as Rabbi Yohanan's fever recipe is, the next recipe provided by our *sugiya* is at least as intriguing, and worthy of a very close analysis. It is transmitted anonymously, but given the talmudic manner of citations, it is possible, though far from certain, that it too is supposed to go back to the Palestinian Rabbi Yohanan.[191] But even if it is not, it certainly would repay a close comparison with the "insider" sources discussed in the previous chapters.

For a furuncle one should say thus, BZ BZYYH MS MSYY' KS KSYYH ŠRL'Y and 'MRL'Y, these are the angels who were sent from the land of Sodom to heal boils and sores. BZK BZYK BZBZYK MSMSYK KMWN KMYK, your eyes are within you, your eyes are within you, your place is within you, your seed like Sodom and a *qalut*,[192] and like a mule that does not multiply and increase, so will you not multiply and increase in the body of NN.[193]

---

[189] See Kotansky, Naveh, and Shaked 1992, p. 9, l. 18, where the text seems to run "And I recall (ומדכרנא) upon you the Spirit of the *Shekhina* (רוחה שכינה) which was revealed to Moses in the Burning Bush." The editors' reconstruction, שׁוכלה, seems to me unwarranted.

[190] See Mekhilta de-RASHBY to Ex 3 (p. 1 Epstein-Melamed).

[191] As was tentatively suggested by Blau 1898, p. 74. And cf. a different recipe for *simta* in bt AZ 28a, and the *simta* recipe in MTKG III, 61 (T-S K 1.162) 1b/13.

[192] See MS Munich 95: כסדום וכקלוט. The printed edition omits Sodom here.

[193] bt Shab 67a. For a previous discussion of this recipe, see Blau 1898, pp. 74–75.

How are we to analyze this elaborate spell? To begin, we may note that the illness is here analogously compared not only to an infertile mule (an analogy which finds ample parallels in non-Jewish and Jewish magical texts of late antiquity),[194] but also to the ruined city of Sodom and to "a *qaluṭ*."[195] The word *qaluṭ*, which is normally used in biblical and rabbinic Hebrew to describe a defect in animals which makes them unfit for certain sacrifices (see Lv 22.23), was explained here by Rashi as "one whose sperm was trapped in his belly's muscles, so he shall not give birth."[196] However, it seems quite likely that the word is simply due to a copyist's error – older than Rashi and the oldest talmudic manuscripts we now have – when a reference to "the wife of Lot" was misunderstood and turned into a *qaluṭ*, which does not really fit in this context.[197] The original recipe would have referred not only to the ruined city of Sodom, but also to the wife of Lot, who looked back and was turned into an immobile pillar of salt. This last event may also help explain the strange exclamations "your eyes are within you" and "your place is within you," as the hapless woman's curious gaze is what made her become so static. Like the ruined city, the crystalized woman, and an infertile mule, so shall the illness not be able to multiply, or grow, or move about the patient's body – this apparently is what the original spell tried to say. And here we may stress that both the analogical use of a biblical story and the choice of the story of Sodom and Gomorrah (including the sad fate of Lot's wife) for such *historiolae* are, as we already noted, quite common in the "insider" sources for ancient Jewish magic, and are no less common in Christian magical texts as well.[198] Especially noteworthy in this regard is the Jewish recipe used by Alexander of Tralles, and quoted in its entirety in Chapter 3, in which a henbane plant is adjured "by the great name Iaôth Sabaôth . . . he who dried up Lot's wife and made her salty" to "dry up the rheumatic flux of the feet or the hands of this man or that woman." There, the plant is even sprinkled with salt, and the magician insists that "Just like this salt will not grow, let not the illness of this man or that woman (grow)" – all

---

[194] See, for example, Marcellus Empiricus 8.191 (against a *varulus* in the right eye): "*Nec mula parit* nec lapis lana fert / nec huic morbo caput crescat aut, si creverit, tabescat." See also the Hadrumetum tablet (see Chapter 3, n. 190), "I adjure you by the one who made the mule sterile," with Blau 1898, pp. 108–09.

[195] The printed editions of the Talmud omit the reference to Sodom here, but do include the reference to Sodom earlier in the recipe.

[196] Rashi ad loc.; Preuss 1993, p. 144 translates it as "*contractus*," while Kottek 1989, p. 652, opts for "your seed shall be locked up."

[197] I.e., לוט (וא(שה) כסדום* was miscopied as כסדום וכקלוט.

[198] For Sodom as a paradigm, see Chapter 5, nn. 37–39. For Christian examples, see Meyer and Smith 1994, pp. 191, 204, etc.

quite close to what we find here, and clearly displaying the same set of magical techniques.[199]

With such parallels in mind, we may return to the spell's very beginning, and the identification of the five *voces magicae* with which it opens as the names of "the angels who were sent from the land of Sodom to heal boils and sores." Where exactly the author of our spell got the idea that some angels were sent there with this mission is not clear, but a comparison with a Genizah spell we cited in Chapter 4, in which Abrasax is identified as "the great angel who overturned Sodom and Gomorrah," might make us think that our recipe had something similar in mind (with five angels, for the five cities of the Pentapolis?).[200] But be our interpretation of this reference as it may, one thing is clear – unlike the Burning Bush recipe, this one is not based on some rabbinic midrash, but on non-rabbinic materials, quite like those found in the "insider" sources discussed in the previous chapters. And looking at the list of angelic names, and especially at the *voces magicae* which begin with BZK BZYK BZBZYK, one may be reminded of the *chych bachych bakachych* formula, for when the two series are written in Hebrew letters they are graphically quite close.[201] Is this indeed the same magic formula – and the irrefutable proof that Greco-Egyptian *voces magicae* were known to, and utilized by, the rabbis themselves? Unfortunately, the issue is not so simple, for once we leave the printed edition and examine the more reliable manuscripts of the Babylonian Talmud, our neat series of BZK BZYK BZBZYK quickly crumbles, with different manuscripts preserving different "words" and no way to establish the original text in a convincing manner.[202] We could, of course, scour the Talmudic manuscripts in search for that reading which is closest to *chych bachych bakachych* and then pronounce it the most trustworthy textual witness, but such a procedure would lead us into a fully circular argument, in which the identification of our formula helps us privilege the textual evidence which would prove

---

[199] See Alexander Trallianus, vol. II, p. 585 Puschmann.

[200] And note how in JTSL ENA 2873.7–8 (unpublished), five angels are invoked in an aggressive recipe as those who destroyed Sodom and Gomorrah.

[201] I.e., כיך בכיך בקכיך* as compared with בוך בוזך בוזביך. Note already Blau's suggestion (1898, p. 75), that the בוזיך formula might be connected with the popularity of the letter *chi* in the magical words of the Greek magical papyri.

[202] See, for example, MS Oxford Oppenheimer Add. fol. 23 (Neubauer 366) and Vatican 108: BZK BZYK BZYK BZK (such forward-backward series of *voces* being quite common in rabbinic recipes and in the Babylonian incantation bowls); MS Munich 95: BZ BZYK MSMSYYK KSKSYYK BZK, etc. Here and below, I have used the CD-ROM version of the Sol and Evelyn Henkind Talmud Text Database, produced by the Lieberman Institute of the Jewish Theological Seminary.

this identification correct.²⁰³ If we had many instances of the appearance of Greco-Egyptian *voces magicae* in rabbinic literature, we could adduce them as further support for our initial identification in this case too; but with this as the only example, we must hesitate to walk down that path.

And here, in a nutshell, is the entire problem of comparing the magical passages in rabbinic literature with the "insider" evidence. Generally speaking, there are many obvious similarities between the magical practices and techniques found in both bodies of evidence, but these parallels often are too vague or too general to allow a conclusion that the two sets of sources *must* reflect the same magical tradition. And when we turn to a meticulous philological analysis of such items as could only be the result of a direct connection – a method which has served us so well in the quest for the non-Jewish elements in late-antique Jewish magical texts in Chapter 4 – we find that the rabbinic texts cannot bear the weight of such a scrutiny. Whereas the Genizah magical recipes preserved the *chych bachych* formula – and many other *voces magicae* known to us from the Greek magical papyri and related texts – in a manner which is still accurate enough to be securely identified, the talmudic manuscripts are later, and far less reliable than the Genizah magical texts – especially when it comes to the accurate transcription of "words" which were entirely alien to the copyists and editors of Talmudic manuscripts. Thus, while the fact that the rabbis too used *voces magicae* in their own magical recipes is not without significance – clearly, their prohibition of some *voces* as "Ways of the Amorites" did not prevent them from using others – it would be very difficult to identify the *voces* they provide on the basis of the late and faulty manuscripts at our disposal. To the self-censorship evident in the rabbinic sources' reticence with regards to the mechanics of some magical rituals must now be added the even more exasperating fact that even when the rabbis design to provide us with specific recipes, the rabbinic manuscripts at our disposal often prove too corrupt and unreliable to provide us with direct access to the original spells, as transmitted by the rabbis themselves.

Examples of the difficulties inherent in the study of rabbinic magic and its relation to the "insider" sources of the western branch of late-antique Jewish magic are plenty. Note, for example, this elaborate recipe, embedded in a talmudic discussion of mad dogs and rabies:

---

²⁰³ The danger of selectively choosing manuscript readings on an ad hoc basis has often been noted – e.g., by Rosenthal 1991, pp. 329 and 352. Note, moreover, that the copyists of the Genizah magical texts could, in theory at least, have been influenced by the Talmudic spell itself.

What it the cure (for one bitten by a mad dog)? Abaye said, Let him take the hide of a male hyena and write upon it, I, NN, am writing on the hide of a male hyena on you KNTY KNTY QLYRWS – and some say, QNDY QNDY QLWRWS – YH YH YHWH Sabaot Amen Amen Selah, and take his clothes off and bury them in a cemetery for twelve months, and take them out and burn them in an oven, and spread the ashes on a crossroads. And throughout these twelve months, when he drinks water he should drink it only through a bronze tube, lest he see the reflection of the demon and be endangered.[204]

In analyzing this recipe, attributed to the Babylonian Abaye, we must note that most elements of the ritual – the writing on hyena-skin, the burying of the clothes for twelve months, the burning and the spreading of the ashes on a crossroads – probably are not specific enough or unique enough to be identified as belonging squarely in one, and only one, magical tradition.[205] More important, in this regard, is the spell, which may easily be divided in two parts. Its final section, "YH YH YHWH Sabaot Amen Amen Selah" is – as we already noted in our discussion of the sailors' spell above – extremely common in late-antique Jewish magic, whence it was also borrowed by many pagan and Christian magicians in late antiquity. More intriguing is the first part, given as KNTY KNTY QLYRWS or QNDY QNDY QLWRWS. The first thing to be noted here is that the adducing of variants in any given spell is a common editorial practice in both Greek and Jewish magical texts of late antiquity. It must also be stressed, however, that the noting of variants is an extremely common practice in the Babylonian Talmud too – even in one of the passages quoted above we read that R. Eliezer knew three hundred (and some say, three thousand) rulings concerning the planting of cucumbers – and its presence here hardly calls for a specifically magical explanation. Here, in other words, the talmudic editors and the editors of magical texts were following the same practice, of recording at least some variants of the textual transmission when two different copies of the same (oral or written) text became available. More importantly, when we look at both variants of the magic formula, we cannot help noting their apparent Greek flavor – and yet, all previous attempts to identify the Greek phrase supposedly lurking behind this formula have

---

[204] bt Yoma 84a (and note pt Yoma 8.5 (45b), insisting that the bite of a mad dog cannot be cured, and ends in certain death); for previous discussions of this recipe, see Blau 1898, pp. 80–82 and Sperber 1994, p. 98.

[205] For the magical qualities of hyenas, and the magical uses of hyena parts, see, e.g., Pliny, *NH* 8.44.105–06, and 28.27.92–106 (esp. 28.27.100 (cf. 29.32.99) and 28.27.104–05), etc. See also Scribonius Largus 171 and 172 (pp. 81–82 Sconocchia) (using hyena parts against hydrophobia, resulting from the bite of a mad dog). For recipes against the bites of a mad dog, see also HdM, recipe 60 (p. 41 Harari = p. 83 Gaster), with instructions to write a section of the "sword" on the skin of a donkey, smear the patient's body with oil, change his clothes and let him carry the amulet.

Magic and magicians in rabbinic literature 419

been inconclusive, and given the great differences between the spelling of these "words" in the different manuscripts of this talmudic passage, any text-critical attempt to reconstruct the spelling of the "original" formula is likely to be misguided.[206] In fact, the only hope of demonstrating its dependence upon Greek sources lies in the identification of a Greek formula for mad-dog bites that will be close enough to Abaye's spell, as transmitted by the talmudic manuscripts, to allow a secure identification of the formula at hand. Unfortunately, this is not very likely to happen.[207]

To end our analysis of rabbinic medico-magical recipes on a more optimistic note, let us look at one final example, where the affinities of rabbinic magic with the "insider" sources for Palestinian Jewish magic stand out much more clearly. It is found in two places in the Babylonian Talmud, in two clusters of recipes dealing with what one must do if one drank water at night and therefore ran into trouble with demons.[208] In the longer cluster, we are first informed that one should not drink water on Wednesday and Saturday nights, because of the danger of an evil spirit. If one is thirsty, one should recite Psalm 29 and then drink. And if not, one should say "LWL ŠPN ANYGRWN ANYRDPYN, between the stars I sit, between lean and fat people I walk." Here too, the *voces magicae* look suspiciously Greek, and there have been several attempts to find the Greek phrase supposedly lurking behind them.[209] Once again, however, our only hope for certainty on this score lies in the identification of the actual spell in the Greek magical texts at our disposal, or even in the Jewish magical texts of late antiquity, and this has not yet occurred. But the cluster of recipes continues, and after three short alternative recipes comes an additional tradition, also found in the second cluster of recipes, and involving the recitation of the following spell: "NN, your mother warned you to watch out against ŠBRYRY BRYRY RYRY YRY RY in white cups."[210] The name "Shabriri," applied to night-blindness (*nyctalopia*) or day-blindness (*hemerolopia*), is of Akkadian origins, and is common enough in the Babylonian Talmud.[211] But the

---

[206] See, e.g., MS Munich 95: QNGY QNTY QLYRYS, and some say QNTY QNTY QLYRYS; MS British Library Harley 5508: QNGY QNGYH QLYRWS, and some say QNTY QNTY QLYRWS; MS JTS Rabb. 1623: QNGY QNTQLYGYS, and some say [.

[207] And note also the partial similarity of QNTY QNTY to the SM'H QNT' QNT'H formula, discussed in Chapter 4 – a similarity which may, however, be purely coincidental.

[208] For the possible Zoroastrian background of this fear, see Gafni 1990, p. 171, but such fears are well attested in other cultures too.

[209] See bt Pes 112a with Blau 1898, pp. 78–79 and Geller 1991, p. 111.

[210] See bt Pes 112a and AZ 12b (with minor differences between the two), with Blau 1898, p. 79 and Trachtenberg 1939, pp. 116–17.

[211] For the Akkadian origins of this term, see Geller 1991, p. 107. And note the very Babylonian shabriri-recipe(s) in bt Git 69a (a part of the *vademecum* discussed above), as analyzed by Stol 1986.

recital of a word – and especially the name of the illness to be averted – in a "dwindling" fashion is part and parcel of the Greco-Egyptian magic of late antiquity, and probably does not reflect old Akkadian practices.[212] And as we noted in Chapter 4, this magical technique is quite common in the "western" Jewish magical texts, and much less common in the Babylonian incantation bowls; in the one example we examined there, we found it applied to the Greek word for "headache," yet another sign of the Greco-Egyptian origin of the practice itself. In the Babylonian Talmud, in other words, we find the technique being adopted by the rabbis, and adapted to a Babylonian Aramaic illness of their own world. And in contrast with all the previous examples, here we are not dealing with a set of easily garbled *voces magicae*, but with a formula which virtually assures the accuracy of its own textual transmission. It is for this reason that the original "triangle" reached us safe and sound, and may still be recognized for what it is even after many centuries of oral and scribal transmission.[213]

It is now time to wrap up our discussion of the magical recipes transmitted by the rabbis themselves. As we noted throughout the present section, when it comes to comparing the aims of rabbinic recipes with those of the "insider" sources, we must admit that rabbinic recipes are devoted almost entirely to apotropaic and healing rituals, a fact which precludes any comprehensive comparison on this score and raises interesting questions about the causes of this anomaly. Did the rabbis abstain from the use of elaborate magical procedures and spells for other aims, or did the talmudic narrators and editors make sure that such stories would never reach us? When it comes to the magical praxis – the mechanics of the rituals and the contents of the incantations – we note that the rabbinic recipes seem to prescribe a mostly verbal type of magic, and not the scribal type which lies behind all our "finished products," especially those of the western branch of late-antique Jewish magic. Even when they do enjoin the writing of a spell, it is never written on a metal lamella (even though the rabbis were aware of the practice of writing amulets on such lamellae), or on pottery sherds. This not only makes the study of rabbinic magic much more difficult, since it is not likely to have left us too many archeological remains, it also highlights one essential difference between the magical technology evinced by the "insider" evidence and that utilized by the rabbis of late antiquity. A second difference, which we have not yet noted, is that the adjuration of angels and demons – perhaps the most characteristic feature

---

[212] Note, however, the Akkadian comparanda adduced by Thompson 1908, pp. lxii–lxiii.
[213] In later Jewish magical texts, and as a result of talmudic influence, the *shabriri*-triangle is utilized for other illnesses too – see, e.g., Barel 1991 p. 223 and n. 157.

Magic and magicians in rabbinic literature

of the "insider" sources surveyed in the previous chapters – is virtually absent from the rabbis' own recipes. Even when their incantations refer to angels (as in the case of the Sodom and Gomorrah recipe) or to demons (as in the case of the shabriri-demon), it does not seem as if these angels or demons were adjured by the users of these incantations, and this in spite of the fact that the rabbinic stories sometimes depict a rabbi commanding a heavenly "minister" to perform this or that service. Such observations must be qualified, since we do not know what was deleted from the original recipes by the Talmud's many editors and copyists, and since we do not know, for example, what was written in the amulet against one demon and the one against sixty demons produced by rabbinic disciples for a certain city official, but the discrepancy between the rabbinic spells and recipes on the one hand and the "insider" sources on the other remains striking even when allowance is made for such factors.

While highlighting the differences between the two corpora, we should not forget the similarities. Not only are some of the main features of late-antique Jewish magical texts utilized by the rabbis, in some cases we find a perfect overlap between the "insider" and the "outsider" sources. The magical use of biblical verses, for example, was frowned upon by some of the rabbis some of the time, but utilized by many others most of the time; often, it is the very same verses that are used, including Psalm 91, Zec 3.2, Ex 15.26, and most of the other "usual suspects," whose use probably goes back to remotest antiquity. Moreover, even the use of biblical stories as *historiolae* is a technique frequently used by the rabbis, and here too there is an overlap not only in the practice itself, but also in some of the specific details, such as the use of the Sodom and Gomorrah story, of the scene of the Burning Bush, or of the three youths in the fiery furnace. Occasionally, a rabbinic recipe will contain some specifically rabbinic *midrash* on a biblical verse or a biblical scene, but such occasions – which, as we saw in the previous chapter, have yet to surface in the late-antique "insider" sources from Palestine – are rare even in the rabbis' own magical recipes. And, what is perhaps most revealing, we saw that just as the Jewish magicians of late antiquity clearly had access to pagan magical technology and many contacts with its practitioners, the rabbis too did not shy away from adopting the magical technologies offered by professional magicians. In one instance, we saw a rabbi citing an entire incantation he had learned from the head of a coven of witches; in a few others, we saw that even some of the techniques borrowed by the Jewish magicians of late antiquity from their pagan neighbors apparently were not only known to, but also utilized by, some rabbis. The use of *voces magicae*, still unattested in the Jewish magical texts of the Second Temple period and quite common in rabbinic recipes, is too universal to prove foreign influence, and when we examine the actual *voces* found in rabbinic recipes we might feel that some of them "smell" like garbled Greek phrases or Greco-Egyptian *voces* but this cannot be proven. But the use of the word-triangle technique in one rabbinic magical recipe seems to provide conclusive evidence for the adoption of some Greco-Egyptian magical techniques not only by some Babylonian Jewish producers of incantation bowls, but also by some Babylonian rabbis. This may not be much, but given all the difficulties involved in the comparison of these two very different textual corpora, it might be the most we may expect.

SUMMARY: THE USES OF RABBINIC LITERATURE IN THE STUDY OF ANCIENT JEWISH MAGIC

We now come to the end of our chapter, but not to the end of our enquiry. For if there is one thing that we can say for certain about the relations between the "insider" sources at our disposal and the data provided by rabbinic literature, it is that much plowing remains to be done in this virtually virgin territory. In some areas, such as the study of the attitudes towards magic in rabbinic *halakha*, the above discussion is likely to be more or less complete. But in other areas, such as the rabbis' familiarity with non-Jewish and Jewish magical practices, or the magical recipes provided and utilized by the rabbis themselves, further study is bound to adduce many new examples and insights. For the time being, we may only offer a provisional summary of what the present enquiry has shown, and a few notes on where it might be headed in the future. To do so, we may revert to the question with which we began, namely, how does what we find in rabbinic literature tally with what we now know ancient non-Jewish and Jewish magic to have looked like? In trying to answer this question, and the sub-questions into which we divided it, we may make the following points:

(1) Looking at the rabbinic discourse of magic, we find them forbidding all types of *keshaphim*, in line with the biblical prohibition, but also leaving many loopholes which enabled their entry into the heart of rabbinic Judaism. We also find them convinced that amulets, exorcisms, and other activities should not be subsumed under the category of *keshaphim*, and reserving their ire for the recourse by Jews to pagan, and especially Christian, healings and magic. Moreover, the rabbis often employed magical practices themselves, were not too shy about it, and even saw the study and occasional practice of magic as quite desirable. Finally, while some

of the magical recipes offered by rabbinic literature are non-rabbinic, and perhaps even non-Jewish, in origin, others are distinctly Jewish and even specifically rabbinic, thus providing yet another confirmation of the rabbis' deep interest and involvement in such activities. In all this, the rabbis of late antiquity followed a path which sought neither to uproot all magical activities by Jews nor to monopolize them in rabbinic hands, but to master some magical techniques, denounce others, and ignore all the rest, and in so doing paved the way for the flourishing of a Jewish magical tradition even among the strictest observers of rabbinic *halakha*. And while the roots of this easy coexistence between magic and Jewish religious law lie deep in the Hebrew Bible (as noted in Chapter 1), it is the rabbis of late antiquity who gave it its most characteristic and enduring features.

(2) The rabbis were well aware of the magical activities taking place all around them, both among non-Jews and among Jews, and rabbinic literature is extremely useful for the study of many aspects of the Jewish magical tradition in late antiquity. Rabbinic sources have much to say about the social contexts of Jewish magic, about who practiced it, about how amulets were worn and by whom, and even about the magical recipes handed down by some women. These are issues on which the "insider" sources – by their very nature – shed less light, and any additional evidence is most welcome. Moreover, in those cases where the "insider" and the "outsider" evidence overlap, there seems to be a welcome degree of congruity between the data provided by these two very different bodies of evidence. Thus, when we find amulets or incantation bowls which were written by Jewish practitioners for non-Jewish clients, we may recall not only John Chrysostom's objection to the fact that Christians went to Jewish practitioners for amulets, but also the talmudic story of the city official who turned to rabbinic disciples for his amulets. When we learn of a multilingual magical workshop whose existence in late-antique Egypt is documented by the Coptic, Greek, and Aramaic magical texts which its members produced, we may recall Amemar's consulting with a local witch and learning her magic spells, including one which re-emerges in some of the Babylonian incantation bowls. When we find the rabbis referring to amulets produced, or approved, by physicians, we may recall the occurrence of Greek medical terminology in some Aramaic amulets from late-antique Palestine and some Genizah magical recipes, and the "No magic, please" rhetoric of the *Book of Asaph the Physician*. And when we run into an obscure passage in the Tosephta we realize that its discussion of amulets may be elucidated by the Greek technical terminology found in the Jewish magical texts of late antiquity. This is, in other words, a two-way street,

with the rabbinic sources casting more light on the magical ones and vice versa.

Even here, however, we must also stress the limitations of the rabbinic sources. In many cases, the rabbis censor out some of the technical details, and simply inform us that a certain practitioner "did what s/he did" or "said what s/he said."²¹⁴ In many other cases, their discussions of magic focus on those things which *they* found most significant, and leave out those things which *we* would find more important. Looking at the rabbinic evidence as a whole, we note the absence of any references to the placing of amulets in the synagogues of late-antique Palestine, or the burying of aggressive spells within their walls and under their floors. We also note the complete absence of any discussion of "heretical" or problematic amulets, whose contents the rabbis may have found offensive, or even of such questions as how much different amulets may have cost. There are no clear references to the Babylonian incantation bowls in rabbinic literature, and even when the rabbis refer, for example, to the Greco-Egyptian Chnoubis-gems, they do not refer to gems with the snake-legged, cock-headed god, although the latter seem to have been far more popular than the former. And, perhaps most exasperating, there are many rabbinic references to and discussions of magical practices which we simply do not yet understand. Rabbinic literature has much to teach us about ancient non-Jewish and Jewish magic, but some of its lessons still defy our modest comprehension.

(3) Rabbinic literature is less helpful when it comes to comparing the magical practices practiced by the rabbis themselves with those known to us from the "insider" sources for the western branch of ancient Jewish magic. In some cases, it avoids describing a rabbi's magical praxis, and simply tells us that "he did what he did" or "said what he said," or that a certain rabbinic disciple wrote an amulet for one demon and another wrote an amulet for sixty. In many other cases, it provides the wording of spells and incantations, but when we examine these closely we find that the textual evidence of the talmudic manuscripts is not reliable enough to allow for the kind of philological analysis we carried out in the last two chapters. And yet, even when allowance is made for such factors, a detailed examination of the rabbis' own magical recipes reveals that while overlaps

---

[214] In some cases, the talmudic editors seem to have censored out of their texts entire magic-related stories, such as the story of the witch Yoḥni bat Retivi, merely alluded to in bt Sota 22a, but well known to Nissim Gaon (see Lewin, *Ozar ha-Geonim*, vol. XI, pp. 241–42), to Rashi (ad loc.), and to Nathan ben Yeḥiel (*Arukh*, s.v., יוחני, vol. IV, p. 117 Kohut). Note that later Jewish descriptions of magical rituals (e.g., those collected in Nigal 1994) often are less parsimonious with regard to the technical details.

between the magical technologies of the "insider" sources and those of the rabbis are not uncommon, the magical practices utilized by the rabbis often are of a different *type* than those known to us from the "insider" sources, especially as they reflect a magical tradition where writing is not (yet!) a central component of the magical praxis and as they are quite opposed to the adjuration of angels. These features of rabbinic magic could be seen as preserving older Jewish magical traditions, as reflecting Akkadian or Zoroastrian magical practices (or at least the absence of extensive Greco-Egyptian influence), or even as reflecting the rabbis' general objection to the writing down of oral Torah and their heightened sensitivity to angelolatry. But regardless of their origins, they certainly join our conclusion in Chapter 5, that the "insider" evidence of the western branch of late-antique Jewish magic displays few rabbinic elements or none at all, in highlighting the differences between the magic of the Jewish magicians of late antiquity and that of the rabbis.

Turning from such phenomenological observations to their possible socio-historical implications, we may conclude that both the claim that the Jewish magical texts we have examined belong to heretical Jews and the claim that they belong at the heart of rabbinic Judaism seem false.[215] There is no doubt that the rabbis had direct access to magical technologies, including some which bore a great resemblance to what we examined in the previous chapters. There also is no doubt, however, that their magic often differed from that practiced by other Jews at the time. Clearly, any attempt to posit either "magicians" or "rabbis" as a closed group and to examine their social relations with the other group in terms of complete identity, total separation, or partial overlap does not do justice to the complexity of the questions involved. There is no doubt that some, and perhaps even most, of the practitioners whose remains have reached us did not see themselves as members of the rabbinic class, and perhaps not even as bound by the rabbis' *halakha*, but not necessarily as ranged against it or trying to subvert it. And there is no doubt that most rabbis had at least some access to the magical texts and technologies employed by these practitioners, but did not always employ the same techniques themselves, and certainly did not start an all out war against these practitioners.

---

[215] For the former view, see Margalioth 1966, pp. xv–xvi; for the latter, Alexander 1986, p. 349: "there is good evidence to suggest that such material circulated at the very heart of rabbinic society."

Epilogue

We now come to the end of our study, but this "end" is only the beginning, in at least two different ways. On the one hand, there is no doubt that much remains to be done before we have a clearer picture of ancient Jewish magic. The ongoing publication of more "insider" evidence, and especially the hundreds of unpublished Babylonian incantation bowls and the abundant Genizah materials (not to mention the archeological finds which constantly come to light in Israel and elsewhere) is bound to provide a much sounder foundation on which to build a history of this field. Moreover, the absence of some basic research tools – such as a survey of ancient Christian and Muslim references to Jewish magic, or a catalogue of *voces magicae* and non-linguistic signs, symbols, and images in Jewish magical texts – and of reliable and comprehensive histories of Greco-Egyptian, Christian, or Muslim magic, renders the study of ancient Jewish magic much more difficult. On the other hand, it must be borne in mind that the present study deals only with the first stage in the development of the Jewish magical tradition, and focuses only on its western branch. A thorough study of the non-Jewish and Jewish incantation bowls, and further studies of the later history of the Jewish magical tradition – from the Muslim conquest onwards – are bound to raise new questions and shed new light on the earliest stages of Jewish magic, including those covered here. It is especially when we examine how much of late-antique Jewish magic survived into the Middle Ages and beyond, which parts thereof were mostly neglected by the wayside, and which new materials were added to the mix, that we shall be able better to appreciate the contours of ancient Jewish magic as a formative stage in the development of the Jewish magical tradition.

All this, however, still lies in store. For the time being, we must be satisfied with a brief outline of the history of ancient Jewish magic, as it emerges throughout the present study, with some general observations on the Jewish magical tradition, and with some methodological guidelines for its future study. Beginning with some concrete conclusions, we may reiterate our claim, in Chapter 1, that the discourse of magic in the Hebrew Bible not only enabled the growth of a Jewish magical tradition, but also predetermined some of its most characteristic features, both by insisting that some things may not be done by Jews and by implying that others surely may. Turning to the Second Temple period, in Chapter 2, we noted the paucity of the available sources and the very diffuse set of magical practices they seem to display, the one major exception being the Jewish praxis of exorcism, which seems to have undergone a remarkable degree of professionalization already in the last two centuries BCE. We then turned to late-antique Jewish magic, and noted (Chapter 3) the marked change in the quantity and quality of sources for the study of late-antique Jewish magic; the main reason for this change seems to be the scribalization of Jewish magic, a process which – as we suggested in Chapter 4 – may have been due to the impact of the Greco-Egyptian magical tradition, but also was connected with a sociological shift within Jewish society from the thaumaturgy of holy men and priests to the services of professional magicians and amulet-makers. In Chapter 4, we also saw numerous other elements of Greco-Egyptian magic which certainly entered the Jewish magical tradition sometime in late antiquity, and which often were entirely "naturalized" within that magical tradition. But we also noted, in Chapter 5, that there is much in the Jewish magical texts and practices of late antiquity which makes them uniquely Jewish, and justifies the study of ancient Jewish magic not as a mere offshoot of the Greco-Egyptian magical tradition, but as an independent magical idiom with many distinctive features of its own. Finally, turning from the "insider" sources to the "outsider" evidence (Chapter 6), we saw how a survey of the extensive rabbinic discussions of magic helps explain the prevalence of Jewish magic even in *halakhically* minded Jewish circles, and how what the rabbis tell us about magic and magicians often tallies with, and helps complement, the evidence supplied by the "insider" sources. We also noted how the rabbis' own testimony supports the conclusion which emerges from the "insider" sources themselves about the identity of their producers – some of them may have belonged to the rabbinic class, but most probably did not, and while their "Judaism" was not heretical or antinomian, it was not identical with rabbinic Judaism. At a later stage, not covered in the present study, one may see the gradual "rabbinization" of the Jewish magical tradition, but one also sees some non-rabbinic and pre-rabbinic elements surviving in the Jewish magical texts and practices into the Middle Ages and beyond.

To this brief historical outline of the development of Jewish magic in antiquity, several broader conclusions may be added. First, we may note what is perhaps the greatest paradox in the history of Jewish magic of all ages, namely, the ways in which the biblical prohibition of magic shaped its future development. As we already noted in Chapter 1, magic was not forbidden by the Hebrew Bible because it was "superstitious," and certainly not because it did not work; what was forbidden was the consulting of foreign experts. But the prohibition of consulting foreign practitioners, coupled with a promise that the Jewish religious system would provide suitable substitutes for the services provided by pagan magicians and diviners, virtually assured the growth of a Jewish magical tradition. It also shaped the ways in which Jewish practitioners often turned to non-Jewish ones in order to learn the latest magical technologies, but then adopted and adapted them – or replaced them with "kosher" substitutes – in ways that made the final result acceptable to other Jews. And since the Hebrew Bible is not really clear on what is included under the rubric of "magic," the Jewish practitioners tended to assume that everything was acceptable, unless it touched on some other sensitive taboo, such as idolatry, Christianity, or the adjuration of God Himself. It was within these parameters that the Jewish magical tradition flourished – and continues to do so to this very day.

And this brings us to a second point of great importance. In the Jewish world, and not only in antiquity, magic was not some socially deviant set of practices and beliefs condemned by heresiologists and punished by the authorities, nor was it a set of silly superstitions practiced solely by the ignorant masses. Rather, it was a technology mastered by many specialists and lay persons and accepted, and even utilized, by the religious establishment itself. Throughout the present study we had ample opportunity to note the recurrent use of magic as a means for social control – first by Moses, then by the priests, and finally by the rabbis. This would remain a central feature of Jewish magic in subsequent generations as well, and it goes a long way towards explaining the pervasiveness and longevity of the Jewish magical tradition, and the horror with which many Jewish leaders viewed the medieval attacks on magic by the Karaites or by Maimonides.[1] Jewish magic, however, was not just, and not even primarily, an affair of the religious establishment, but of the many laymen and professionals who catered to the needs of Jewish and non-Jewish clients, needs which apparently were not answered by the religious systems available to them.

Given the centrality of magical practices at all levels of Jewish society, it would hardly be surprising to see that – contrary to some ancient societies – in the Jewish world "magic" was only rarely used as a polemical

---

[1] In passing, we may note that in the shaping of Jewish modernity, the decline of the belief in the powers of demons and magic and the collapse of the rabbis' social control over Jewish society seem to have gone hand in hand.

label affixed to the religious practices of one's opponents. Moreover, in a religious system which strongly believes in Divine Providence, afflictions and misfortunes will lead not to a quest for who is the witch, but for a search for one's sin, or those of one's neighbors. Thus, while ancient and medieval Jews often explained misfortune as the result of demonic intervention, they rarely attributed that intervention to the magical activities of human agents. And while ancient and medieval Jews often castigated other people's religious beliefs and customs, they had a whole plethora of labels to affix to these "other" religions – apostasy, idolatry, heresy (*minuth*), and so on – and rarely used the label "magic" for such purposes in spite of its availability within their native discourse. Moreover, as we saw in Chapter 6, the rabbis of late antiquity saw nothing wrong with admitting that they too practiced magic, and warmly recommended its study and its occasional use. Rather than insisting that "magic" is what other people do, they adopted a more flexible definition of magic, and developed a discourse of "licit magic," that is, of magic whose practice was inoffensive, and sometimes even desirable.

A fourth point that bears stressing once again is that unlike most pagan magicians, who had few theological difficulties with incorporating foreign magical technologies, the Jewish magicians were very much aware of the fact that (as the rabbis put it) "Ten measures of *keshaphim* went into the world; nine were taken by Egypt, and the rest was shared by the rest of the world," but also knew that much of the Greco-Egyptian magical technology was too "un-Jewish" for Jews to handle. It is this urge to borrow and the need to be selective about what one borrows, coupled with the antiquity of some Jewish magical practices and the vitality of Jewish culture in late antiquity as a whole, which gave late-antique Jewish magic its unique flavor. Moreover, this peculiar make-up of Jewish magic will remain characteristic of the Jewish magical tradition in later periods too. Looking at medieval or modern Jewish magical texts, one can easily see the transmission and gradual transformation of older Jewish magic (including some elements which had been borrowed from foreign cultures, but were "naturalized" at an earlier stage), the entry of new magical technologies from the non-Jewish world, carefully stripped of all that the Jews of that time and place found offensive (and the exact details of this cultural sensitivity often changed from one period or region to the next), and the development of entirely new forms of Jewish magic.[2] Always influenced by the outside world and

---

[2] One can also see how when the mixture moved from one cultural context to the next, it often was the foreign influences, once borrowed from a no-longer-familiar culture, which suffered the greatest textual entropy, simply because they were far less likely to be understood correctly than the more "Jewish" elements.

always worried by such influences, the Jews developed a magical tradition which was both quite like those of their neighbors and uniquely their own.

Finally, we may raise one more point, which has only emerged here and there in the previous chapters, and whose wider implications may now be emphasized. As we noted in Chapter 2, in the Second Temple period, at a time when Jewish literary culture was thriving – at least in quantity, if not always in quality – Jewish magic was mostly transmitted and performed in an oral manner. The magical texts of the time thus add only a little to what we already know from other sources about Jewish history as a whole. But in late antiquity, at a time when rabbinic culture was mostly oral, and when non-rabbinic Jews were either not producing many written texts or producing texts that we no longer have, the Jewish magical tradition underwent a process of scribalization, which assured us a wide range of written Jewish magical texts and artifacts from late antiquity. It is for this reason that the magical texts of late antiquity may teach us much not only about Jewish magic, but about many other aspects of late-antique Jewish society, including economic and social conditions, the languages spoken by Jews, their contacts with non-Jews, their understanding and observance of *halakha*, their attitudes towards God, and even their views of women and gender. In the present study, we did not try to highlight all these aspects of the Jewish magical texts, though some of them did emerge; but we must stress that the "non-magical" data provided by the Jewish magical texts should make them a useful set of sources for all students of ancient Jewish history and culture, even those who still refuse to acknowledge the existence or importance of the Jewish magical tradition.

Throughout the present study, we have sought to reconstruct the history of ancient Jewish magic. Many specific elements of this reconstruction can, and should, be challenged, either with new sources or with different interpretations of the same sources. But while specific details will be corroborated, improved, or refuted by others, the main underlying claim – that a history of Jewish magic, as a distinct sphere of Jewish culture, can and should be written – will remain valid even after the present book is digested, criticized and superseded by future studies. But for this to happen, two popular myths must be exposed and discarded, myths which may pass for phenomenological generalizations or harmless platitudes, but often serve to justify intellectual laziness and ahistorical thinking. In their stead, we must adopt sound methodological guidelines which would enable the study of Jewish magic to develop and flourish.

The first misleading generalization which we must learn to do without is the claim that magic is universal and generally uniform across all human cultures. This claim is not entirely baseless, and when we look at Frazer's famous discussion of homeopathic magic and the magic of contagion, we find that ancient Jews too used both types of magical reasoning, as when they prepared voodoo dolls and attached to them something belonging to the intended victim. It also is this similarity which enables us to use such terms as "voodoo dolls" when speaking of Jewish magic, or to utilize the category of *historiola* in our analysis of how the Jewish magicians "applied" the biblical stories in their newfangled magical rituals, or to speak of *voces magicae* when Jewish magicians and mystics employ meaningless "words" as part of their special rituals. And yet, we must always remember that such general similarities, which clearly attest to some basic proclivities of the human mind, only appear when we take the bird's-eye view, or the combination of breadth and superficiality which is so characteristic of Frazer's anthropology and Eliade's *History of Religion*. When we look a bit more closely, we find numerous differences between different magical traditions, including those which were, or are, in close contact with each other. Looking at ancient Jewish magic, one is struck not only by its close contacts with the Greco-Roman magical tradition, but also by the many differences between the two traditions. This is not to say, of course, that the borderlines between different magical traditions are always clear-cut; a magical text in Greek, for example, can occasionally be identified as "Jewish," "Christian," or "pagan," and we cannot be sure to which of these magical traditions to attribute it (especially if it is short, or badly preserved). And yet, in most cases when we see a magical text we can easily identify its cultural affiliations, and when we examine large groups of texts belonging to one magical tradition we immediately see the differences between these traditions. Moreover, when we examine the foreign elements which entered each of these magical traditions, we note that there are certain rules governing the entry of foreign elements, and that these rules differ from one culture to the next. Thus, rather than thinking of ancient Mediterranean magic as a huge syncretistic soup in which everything got mixed up, we should think of it as a complex system of independent magical traditions with numerous contacts, borrowings, and influences, whose final appearances are determined not only by what is borrowed, but also by who does the borrowing, and into which cultural framework. In the study of Jewish magic, we must always avoid the "tunnel vision" so characteristic of Jewish Studies as a whole, and the a priori assumption that everything that Jews do is somehow unique; but we also must avoid the equally problematic assumption that when it comes to magic all people are alike, so that Jewish magic could be no different from that of other ethnic or religious groups.

As we saw throughout the present study, both assumptions are equally unwarranted.

The second dangerous platitude that we must learn to avoid is that magic is somehow "timeless" and immune to changes. Looking at the aims of Jewish magical recipes, we note that not much has changed over the years. It is true that the first Jewish magical recipe for winning the lottery dates to the late eighteenth century, and thus post-dates the rise of that august institution, and that amulets for cars and buses are an even more recent development.[3] But these are the exceptions, and as a rule one may note that the aims of most Jewish magical recipes – to heal, to kill, to impose one's will – have changed relatively little over the past fifteen centuries. And looking at the techniques used by the magicians to achieve these aims, we might be tempted into thinking that here too not much has changed, since the manipulation of *materia magica*, the use of incantations, or the adjuration of angels are continuously attested in the Jewish magical tradition for at least fifteen centuries, and in some cases for much longer. But while the general methods show a remarkable stability over the centuries, the specifics of the rituals show a great deal of variety over time. Abrasax and the *charactêres* only entered the Jewish magical tradition in late antiquity, and while Abrasax's enormous popularity gradually diminished after the rise of Islam, the *charactêres* are alive and well in some branches of Jewish magic to this very day. Magic squares (of the mathematical type, not the SATOR AREPO-type) only entered the Jewish magical tradition under Muslim influence, *sephirotic* speculations began making an impact on the Jewish magical tradition only after the rise and spread of Kabbalah, and streptomycin was not used by Jewish magicians prior to its discovery in 1943.[4] To this small sample, many more examples could be added, of phenomena which appear in the Jewish magical tradition only from a certain period onwards, and even of phenomena which more or less die out and disappear from the tradition from a certain point in time, such as recipes for winning the chariot races. Magic, in other words, is neither timeless nor ageless, and a Jewish magical text often provides quite a few indications as to the time(s) and place(s) of its composition and transmission, if only we pay close attention to all these hints. Moreover, the use of "parallels" as the basis for dating or locating magical texts and traditions or for assessing cross-cultural contacts and borrowings is an extremely hazardous procedure,

---

[3] Lottery: Verman 1999, p. 234. Cars: Abramowitch and Epstein 1988.

[4] For the magical uses of streptomycin, see Keter 1990, e.g., p. 148 (I am grateful to Yuval Harari for referring me to this wonderful book). For the magicians' use of modern medical technology, see also Barel 1991, p. 223.

and should be carried out with great care; only real parallels should be admitted, and only those which can be shown to be specific enough to necessitate a diffusionistic explanation. And the use of late texts to elucidate earlier ones is equally dangerous, as is any attempt to bridge over gaps in our evidence for one time and place by borrowing evidence from other times and places.

What we need, then, is a cultural history which is neither entirely synchronic and static (as "thick" descriptions, and all types of Durkheimian analysis, often are), nor parochial in its diachronic perspectives (as "Jewish History" often is). It must utilize the insights offered by phenomenology and comparative religion, but not mistake these for historical analysis. It must make use of comparative anthropological and sociological research, without ever assuming that what is true of one society or culture must be true of another. And, most of all, it must remain close to the available sources, and in constant search for new ones. For, as we saw throughout the present study, it is not the questions we bring to the texts, but the texts to which we bring them, which determine our ability to provide the answers to the questions which interest us most. History is not the art of forcing our perspectives, opinions, and worries upon the dead, but of trying to listen to theirs.

"Nonsense is nonsense, but the history of nonsense is science." This is how, according to a widely circulating story, the great talmudic scholar Saul Lieberman once introduced the great Kabbalah scholar Gershom Scholem to an audience gathered to hear Scholem present the fruits of his academic endeavor. We need not subscribe to the opinion that magic is nonsense, but even if the thousands of Jews who composed, studied, transmitted, borrowed, translated, edited, copied, and utilized magical spells, hymns, adjurations, incantations, and recipes over the last two millennia and more were merely wasting their talents and their clients' time and money, the scholars who study the texts and artifacts these practitioners have left behind would not be wasting their own time in the process. For the abundant remains of the Jewish magical tradition deserve a careful and attentive reading by competent scholars, a reading that would tease out of them all that they have to tell us about the changing features of Jewish magic, and about many other aspects of Jewish history, society, and culture in different periods and different regions of the world. The present book is an attempt to provide a basic outline of the history of the western branch of ancient Jewish magic, but this is just a first step towards treating this important topic, which most previous students of Jewish history and culture simply preferred to ignore.

Epilogue

Almost two centuries ago, a small group of Jewish intellectuals set out to study Jewish culture and religion from a historical-philological perspective, and with all the tools developed by non-Jewish scholars for the study of Classical, European, and "exotic" cultures. Marginalized both by the religious establishment within the Jewish community and by the academic establishments of the European countries in which they lived, these pioneering scholars established a hitherto uncharted academic field, the Science of Judaism. Two centuries later, this field has been immensely transformed, both in terms of the knowledge accumulated and the conceptual and sociological frameworks within which it is studied. From the heroic efforts of a few brave men trying to put some basic order into a chaotic mass of raw, and mostly unexplored, data, we have moved to a world in which thousands of men and women, working from the heart of the academic establishment in Israel, the United States, and – to a growing degree – Europe, are chasing a limited, and by now mostly charted, body of sources. Seen from this perspective, the study of Jewish magic may be seen as the final frontier, the last stretch of *terra incognita* on our ever-more-detailed maps of Jewish history and culture through the ages. Much progress will have to be made before students of Jewish magic will have caught up with those of all other branches of Jewish Studies, and before other scholars learn to incorporate Jewish magic in their accounts of Judaism as a whole. So much remains to be done, so many sources to be identified and studied, so many discoveries to be made and insights to be gained, so many broader syntheses to be conceived and produced. Now, now, slowly, slowly.

Bibliography

ABBREVIATIONS OF JOURNALS, SERIES, ETC.

AGAJU   Arbeiten zur Geschichte des Antiken Judentums und des Urchristentums
ANRW   Aufstieg und Niedergang der Römischen Welt
AO   Archiv Orientální
AP   Anthologia Palatina
ARG   Archiv für Religionsgeschichte
ARW   Archiv für Religionswissenschaft
BASOR   Bulletin of the American Schools of Oriental Research
BASP   Bulletin of the American Society of Papyrologists
BCH   Bulletin de Correspondance Hellénique
BJRL   Bulletin of the John Rylands Library
BO   Bibliotheca Orientalis
BSOAS   Bulletin of the School of Oriental and African Studies
CBQ   Catholic Biblical Quarterly
CC   Corpus Christianorum
CRAIBL   Comptes Rendus de l'Academie des Inscriptions et Belles-Lettres
DJD   Discoveries in the Judean Desert
DOP   Dumbarton Oaks Papers
DSD   Dead Sea Discoveries
EPRO   Études Préliminaires aux Religions Orientales dans l'Émpire Romain
FJB   Frankfurter Judaistische Beiträge
GQ   Ginzei Qedem
GRBS   Greek Roman and Byzantine Studies
HTR   Harvard Theological Review
HUCA   Hebrew Union College Annual
IEJ   Israel Exploration Journal
IOS   Israel Oriental Studies
JAC   Jahrbuch für Antike und Christentum
JAGNES   Journal of the Association of Graduates in Near Eastern Studies
JAOS   Journal of the American Oriental Society
JBL   Journal of Biblical Literature
JEA   Journal of Egyptian Archaeology
JJS   Journal of Jewish Studies

JJTP Journal of Jewish Thought and Philosophy
JJV   Jahrbuch der Jüdischen Volkskunde
JNES Journal of Near Eastern Studies
JPOS Journal of the Palestine Oriental Society
JQR   Jewish Quarterly Review
JRAS Journal of the Royal Asiatic Society
JRS   Journal of Roman Studies
JSAI Jerusalem Studies in Arabic and Islam
JSJ   Journal for the Study of Judaism in the Persian, Hellenistic and Roman Periods
JSJT Jerusalem Studies in Jewish Thought
JSOT Journal for the Study of the Old Testament
JSP   Journal for the Study of the Pseudepigrapha
JSQ   Jewish Studies Quarterly
JSS   Journal of Semitic Studies
LA   Liber Annuus
MGJV Mitteilungen der Gesellschaft für Jüdische Volkskunde
PEQ   Palestine Exploration Quarterly
PL   Patrologia Latina
RB   Revue Biblique
REJ   Revue des Études Juives
RGRW Religions in the Graeco-Roman World
RQ   Revue de Qumran
SAOC Studies in Ancient Oriental Civilizations
SBL   Society of Biblical Literature
SCO   Studi Classici e Orientali
SEG   Supplementum Epigraphicum Graecum
SO   Studia Orientalia
TAPA Transactions and Proceedings of the American Philological Association
TSAJ Texts and Studies in Ancient Judaism
TSMEMJ Texts and Studies in Medieval and Early Modern Judaism
VC   Vigiliae Christianae
VT   Vetus Testamentum
WUNT Wissenschaftliche Untersuchungen zum Neuen Testament
ZDMG Zeitschrift der Deutschen Morgenlandischen Gesellschaft
ZPE   Zeitschrift für Papyrologie und Epigraphik

FREQUENTLY CITED WORKS

AMB Joseph Naveh and Shaul Shaked, *Amulets and Magic Bowls: Aramaic Incantations of Late Antiquity*, Jerusalem: Magnes, 1985

CIJ J.-B. Frey, *Corpus Inscriptionum Judaicarum*, 2 vols., Rome: Pontifico Istituto di Archeologia Cristiana, 1936–52 (vol. I rev. by B. Lifshitz, New York: Ktav, 1975)

FGrH Felix Jacoby, *Die Fragmente der Griechischer Historiker*, Berlin: Weidmann, 1923–

G-F P. Schäfer, *Geniza-Fragmente zur Hekhalot-Literatur*, TSAJ 6, Tübingen: Mohr, 1984
GLAJJ Menahem Stern, *Greek and Latin Authors on Jews and Judaism*, Jerusalem: Israel Academy of Sciences and Humanities, 3 vols., 1976–84
HAITCG Lawrence H. Schiffman and Michael D. Swartz, *Hebrew and Aramaic Incantation Texts from the Cairo Genizah*, Semitic Texts and Studies 1, Sheffield: Sheffield Academic Press, 1992
IJO David Noy, Alexander Panayotov and Hanswulf Bloedhorn, *Inscriptiones Judaicae Orientis Volume I: Eastern Europe*, TSAJ 101, Tübingen: Mohr Siebeck, 2004; Walter Ameling, *Inscriptiones Judaicae Orientis Volume II: Kleinasien*, TSAJ 99, Tübingen: Mohr Siebeck, 2004; David Noy and Hanswulf Bloedhorn, *Inscriptiones Judaicae Orientis Volume III: Syria and Cyprus*, TSAJ 102, Tübingen: Mohr Siebeck, 2004
JIWE David Noy, *Jewish Inscriptions of Western Europe*, Cambridge: Cambridge University Press, vol. I, 1993, vol. II, 1995
LCL Loeb Classical Library
MSF Joseph Naveh and Shaul Shaked, *Magic Spells and Formulae: Aramaic Incantations of Late Antiquity*, Jerusalem: Magnes, 1993
MTKG Peter Schäfer and Shaul Shaked, *Magische Texte aus der Kairoer Geniza*, TSAJ 42, 64, 72, Tübingen: J. C. B. Mohr (Paul Siebeck), vol. I, 1994, vol. II, 1997, vol. III, 1999, vol. IV, forthcoming
PGM Karl Preisendanz, *Papyri Graecae Magicae*, Leipzig: Teubner, 2 vols., 1928–31 (rev. by A. Heinrichs, Stuttgart: Teubner, 1973–74)
SM R. W. Daniel and F. Maltomini, *Supplementum Magicum*, Papyrologica Coloniensia 16, Opladen: Westdeutscher Verlag, vol. I, 1990, vol. II, 1992
Synopse Peter Schäfer, *Synopse zur Hekhalot-Literatur*, TSAJ 2, Tübingen: Mohr, 1981
TK Saul Liberman, *Tosephta ki-Fshutah: A Comprehensive Commentary on the Tosefta*, New York: Jewish Theological Seminary of America, 1955–88 (Heb.)

BIBLIOGRAPHY

Abramowitch, Henry and Shifra Epstein 1988 "Driving Amulets in Jerusalem," *The Mankind Quarterly* 29, pp. 161–64
Abusch, Tzvi and Karel van der Toorn (eds.) 1999 *Mesopotamian Magic: Textual, Historical, and Interpretative Perspectives*, Ancient Magic and Divination, I, Groningen: Styx
Adler, Michael 1893 "Was Homer Acquainted with the Bible?" *JQR* 5, pp. 170–74
Ahn, Gregor 2003 "Dualismen im Kontext von Gegenweltvorstellungen: Die rituelle Abwehr der Dämonen im altiranischen Zoroastrismus," in Lange, Lichtenberger, and Römheld 2003, pp. 122–34
Ahrens, W. 1916 *Hebräische Amulette mit magischen Zahlenquadraten*, Berlin: Louis Lamm

Alexander, P. S. 1986 "Incantations and Books of Magic," in E. Schürer, *The History of the Jewish People in the Age of Jesus Christ*, (revised and edited by G. Vermes, F. Millar, and M. Goodman), vol. III/I, Edinburgh: T&T Clark, pp. 342–79
　1995 "Bavli Berakhot 55a–57b: The Talmudic Dreambook in Context," *JJS* 46, pp. 230–48
　1997 "'Wrestling Against Wickedness in High Places': Magic in the Worldview of the Qumran Community," in Stanley E. Porter and Craig A. Evans (eds.), *The Scrolls and the Scriptures: Qumran Fifty Years After*, JSP Suppl. 26, Sheffield: Sheffield Academic Press, pp. 318–37
　1999a "The Demonology of the Dead Sea Scrolls," in Peter W. Flint and James C. VanderKam (eds.), *The Dead Sea Scrolls After Fifty Years: A Comprehensive Assessment*, 2 vols., Leiden: Brill, vol. II, pp. 331–53
　1999b "Jewish Elements in Gnosticism and Magic, c. CE 70–c. CE 270," in W. Horbury et al. (eds.), *The Cambridge History of Judaism*, vol. III, Cambridge: Cambridge University Press, pp. 1052–78
　2000 "Magic and Magical Texts," in L. H. Schiffman and J. C. VanderKam (eds.), *Encyclopedia of the Dead Sea Scrolls*, Oxford: Oxford University Press, pp. 502–04
　2003a "Contextualizing the Demonology of the Testament of Solomon," in Lange, Lichtenberger, and Römheld 2003, pp. 613–35
　2003b "*Sepher ha-Razim* and the Problem of Black Magic in Early Judaism," in Klutz 2003a, pp. 170–90
　2005 "The Talmudic Concept of Conjuring ('*Aḥizat 'Einayim*) and the Problem of the Definition of Magic (*Kishuf*)," in Elior and Schäfer 2005, pp. 7–26
Allony, Nehemiah 2006 *The Jewish Library in the Middle Ages: Book Lists from the Cairo Genizah*, (ed. by Miriam Frenkel and Haggai Ben-Shammai), Oriens Judaicus I, III, Jerusalem: Ben-Zvi (Heb.)
Alon, G. 1977 "By the (Expressed) Name," in *id.*, *Jews, Judaism and the Classical World: Studies in Jewish History in the Times of the Second Temple and Talmud*, (tr. by I. Abrahams), Jerusalem: Magnes, 1977, pp. 235–51 (first published in *Tarbiz* 21 (1950), pp. 30–39 [Heb.])
Altmann, Alexander 1992 *The Meaning of Jewish Existence: Theological Essays 1930–1939*, (ed. by Alfred Ivry), Hanover, MA: University Press of New England
Aptowitzer, V. 1910–13 "Les noms de Dieu et des anges dans la Mezouza," *REJ* 60, pp. 39–52 and 65, pp. 54–60
Arbel, V. D. 2003 *Beholders of Divine Secrets: Mysticism and Myth in the Hekhalot and Merkavah Literature*, Albany, NY: SUNY Press
Aubin, Melissa M. 1998 *Gendering Magic in Late Antique Judaism*, Unpubl. Ph.D. diss., Duke University
Audollent, A. 1904 *Defixionum Tabellae quotquot innotuerunt tam in Graecis Orientis quam in totius Occidentis partibus praeter Atticas in Corpore Inscriptionum Atticarum editas*, Paris: Albert Fontenmoing
Aune, David E. 1980 "Magic in Early Christianity," *ANRW* II.23.2, pp. 1507–57
　1996 "Iaô," in Ernat Dassmann (ed.), *Reallexikon für Antike und Christentum*, Stuttgart: Anton Hiersemann, vol. XVII, coll. 1–12

Aviam, M. 2001 "The Ancient Synagogues at Bar'am," in A. J. Avery-Peck and J. Neusner (eds.), *Judaism in Late Antiquity* pt III, vol. IV, Handbook of Oriental Studies I, 55, Leiden: Brill, 2001, pp. 155–71
  2002 "The Ancient Synagogues of Bar'am," *Qadmoniyot* 35, pp. 118–25 (Heb.)
  2004 "First century Jewish Galilee: an archaeological perspective," in Douglas R. Edwards (ed.), *Religion and Society in Roman Palestine. Old Questions, New Approaches*, London/New York: Routledge, pp. 7–27
Avishur, Y. 1979 "The Ways of the Emorite," in Ch. Rabin *et al.* (eds.), *Sepher Meir Valenstein*, Jerusalem: Kiriat Sepher, pp. 17–47 (Heb.)
Bagnall, R. S. and K. A. Worp 2004 *The Chronological Systems of Byzantine Egypt*, 2nd edn, Leiden: Brill
Baillet, M. 1963 "Un livret magique en Christo-Palestinien à l'Université de Louvain," *Le Muséon* 76, pp. 375–401
  1982 "510–511. Cantiques du Sage," in *Qumrân Grotte 4 / III*, DJD VII, Oxford: Clarendon Press, pp. 215–62
Baines, J. 1985 "Twins in Egypt," *Orientalia* 54, pp. 461–82
Baker, Colin F. and Meira Polliack 2001 *Arabic and Judaeo-Arabic Manuscripts in the Cambridge Genizah Collections: Arabic Old Series (T-S Ar. 1a-54)*, Cambridge: Cambridge University Press
Bar-Ilan, Meir 1985 "Text Criticism, Erotica and Magic in the Song of Songs," *Shnaton Le-Mikra* 9, pp. 31–53 (Heb.)
  1987a "Magic Seals on the Body among Jews in the First Centuries C. E.," *Tarbiz* 57, pp. 37–50 (Heb.)
  1987b *The Mysteries of Jewish Prayer and Hekhalot*, Ramat Gan: Bar-Ilan University Press (Heb.)
  1993 "Witches in the Bible and in the Talmud," in H. W. Basser and S. Fishbane (eds.), *Approaches to Ancient Judaism* n.s. 5: *Historical, Literary, and Religious Studies*, Atlanta: Scholars Press, pp. 7–32
  1995 "Exorcisms Performed by Rabbis: Something on the Talmudic Sages' Dealings with Magic," *Daat* 34, pp. 17–31 (Heb.)
  1997 "The Names of Angels," in A. Demsky, J. A. Reif, and J. Tabory (eds.), *These Are the Names: Studies in Jewish Onomastics*, Ramat Gan: Bar-Ilan University Press, pp. 33–48 (Heb.)
  2002 "Between Magic and Religion: Sympathetic Magic in the World of the Sages of the Mishnah and Talmud," *Review of Rabbinic Judaism* 5, pp. 383–99
Bar-Levav, Avriel 2002 "Death and the (Blurred) Boundaries of Magic: Strategies of Coexistence," *Kabbalah* 7, pp. 51–64
  2003 "Magic in the Mussar Literature," *Tarbiz* 72, pp. 389–414 (Heb.)
Barclay, John M. G. 1998 "Who Was Considered an Apostate in the Jewish Diaspora?" in Graham N. Stanton and Guy G. Stroumsa (eds.), *Tolerance and Intolerance in Early Judaism and Christianity*, Cambridge: Cambridge University Press, pp. 80–98
Barel, Gabriel 1991 "Rav-Pe'alim – un manuel de médicine populaire de Maroc," in Issachar Ben-Ami (ed.), *Recherches sur la culture des juifs d'Afrique du nord*, Jerusalem: Communauté Israelite Nord-Africaine, pp. 211–32 (Heb.)

Barkay, Gabriel 1992 "The Priestly Benediction on Silver Plaques from Ketef Hinnom in Jerusalem," *Tel Aviv* 19, pp. 139–92

Barkay, Gabriel, Marilyn J. Lundberg, Andrew G. Vaughin, and Bruce Zuckerman 2004 "The Amulets from Ketef Hinnom: A New Edition and Evaluation," *BASOR* 334, pp. 41–71

Barzilay, Isaac 1974 *Yoseph Shlomo Delmedigo (Yashar of Candia): His Life and Works*, Leiden: Brill

Baumgarten, J. M. 1991 "On the Nature of the Seductress in 4Q184," *RQ* 15/57, pp. 133–43

Becker, Hans-Jürgen 2002 "The Magic of the Name and Palestinian Rabbinic Literature," in Peter Schäfer (ed.), *The Talmud Yerushalmi and Graeco-Roman Culture*, vol. III, TSAJ 93, Tübingen: Mohr, pp. 391–407

Beit-Arié, M. 1996 "Genizot: Depositories of Consumed Books as Disposing Procedure in Jewish Society," *Scriptorium* 50, pp. 407–14

Benayahu, Meir 1972 "The Book 'Shoshan Yesod ha-Olam' by Rabbi Yoseph Tirshom," *Temirin* 1, pp. 187–269 (Heb.)

1980 "The Significance of the Geniza Documents of the Sixteenth-Eighteenth Centuries," in M. A. Friedman (ed.), *Cairo Geniza Studies* [*Te'uda 1*], Tel Aviv University, pp. 161–68 (Heb.)

1985 *Ma'amadot and Moshavot* [=*Studies in Memory of the Rishon Le-Zion R. Yitzhak Nissim*, vol. VI], Jerusalem (Heb.)

Benin, Stephen D. 1985 "The Chronicle of Ahimaaz and Its Place in Byzantine Literature," *JSJT* 4, pp. 237–50 (Heb.)

Benoit, Pierre 1951 "Fragments d'une prière contre les esprits impurs?" *RB* 58, pp. 549–65

Ben-Sasson, M. 1996 *The Emergence of the Local Jewish Community in the Muslim World (Qayrawan, 800–1057)*, Jerusalem: Magnes (Heb.)

Bergmann, J. 1911 "Die Rachegebete von Rheneia," *Philologus* 70, pp. 503–10

Betz, Hans Dieter 1982 "The Formation of Authoritative Tradition in the Greek Magical Papyri," in E. P. Sanders et al. (eds.), *Jewish and Christian Self-Definition*, Philadelphia: Fortress Press, vol. III, pp. 161–70

1986 *The Greek Magical Papyri in Translation, Including the Demotic Spells*, Chicago: University of Chicago Press (2nd edn, 1992)

1997 "Jewish Magic in the Greek Magical Papyri (PGM VII.260–71)," in Schäfer and Kippenberg 1997, pp. 45–63 (repr. in Betz, *Antike und Christentum: Gesammelte Aufsätze*, IV, Tübingen: Mohr Siebeck, 1998, pp. 187–205)

Bij de Vaate, Alice 1994 "Alphabet-Inscriptions from Jewish Graves," in J. W. van Henten and P. W. van der Horst (eds.), *Studies in Early Jewish Epigraphy*, AGAJU 21, Leiden, Brill, pp. 148–61

Bilu, Yoram and Eliezer Witztum 1994 "'He Peeped and Was Harmed': On Mystical Beliefs and Practices among Those who Turn to Psychological Therapy and their Application During Treatment," *Alpayim* 9, pp. 21–43 (Heb.)

Blau, Ludwig 1898 *Das altjüdische Zauberwesen*, Strassbourg: Trubner (2nd edn, Berlin: Verlag von Louis Lamm, 1914)

1901 "Amulet," in Isidore Singer (ed.), *The Jewish Encyclopedia*, New York: Funk & Wagnalls, vol. I, pp. 546–550

Blenkinsopp, Joseph 1999 "Miracles: Elisha and Ḥanina ben Dosa," in John C. Cavadini (ed.), *Miracles in Jewish and Christian Antiquity*, Notre Dame, IN: Notre Dame University Press, pp. 57–81

Bliss, F. J. and R. A. S. Macalister 1902 *Excavation in Palestine during the Years 1898–1900*, London: Harris & Sons

Bloch, René 1999 "Mose und die Scharlatane: Zum Vorwurf *goês kai apateôn* in 'Contra Apionem' 2: 145.161," in Jürgen U. Kalms and Folker Siegert (eds.), *Internationales Josephus-Kolloquium Brüssel 1998*, Münster: LIT, pp. 142–57

2003 "Au-delà d'un discourse apologétique: Flavius Josèphe et les magiciens," in Nicole Belayche (ed.), *Les communautés religieuses dans le monde gréco-romain*, Paris: Brepols, pp. 243–57

Bogaert, P.-M. 1978 "Les *Antiquités Bibliques* du Pseudo-Philon à la lumière des découvertes de Qumrân," in M. Delcor (ed.), *Qumrân: Sa Piété, sa Théologie, et son Milieu*, Paris: Duculot, pp. 313–31

Bohak, Gideon 1990 "Greek-Hebrew Gematrias in 3 Baruch and Revelation," *JSP* 7, pp. 119–21

1996 "Traditions of Magic in Late Antiquity," Exhibition Catalogue, University of Michigan (also available on-line: www.lib.umich.edu/pap/magic)

1997 "A Note on the Chnoubis Gem from Tel Dor," *IEJ* 47, pp. 255–56

1999 "Greek, Coptic, and Jewish Magic in the Cairo Genizah," *BASP* 36, pp. 27–44

2000a "Rabbinic Perspectives on Egyptian Religion," *ARG* 2, pp. 215–31

2000b "The Impact of Jewish Monotheism on the Greco-Roman World," *JSQ* 7, pp. 1–21

2000c "Ethnic Stereotypes in the Greco-Roman World: Egyptians, Phoenicians, and Jews," *Proceedings of the Twelfth World Congress of Jewish Studies*, Jerusalem, Division B, pp. 7*–15*

2001 "Remains of Greek Words and Magical Formulae in Hekhalot Literature," *Kabbalah* 6, pp. 121–34

2002 "Ethnic Continuity in the Jewish Diaspora in Antiquity," in John R. Bartlett (ed.), *Jews in the Hellenistic and Roman Cities*, London and New York: Routledge, pp. 175–92

2003a "Magical Means for Dealing with *Minim* in Rabbinic Literature," in Peter J. Tomson and Doris Lambers-Petry (eds.), *The Image of the Judaeo-Christians in Ancient Jewish and Christian Literature*, Tübingen: Mohr Siebeck, pp. 267–79

2003b "Hebrew, Hebrew Everywhere?: Notes on the Interpretation of *Voces Magicae*," in Noegel, Walker, and Wheeler 2003, pp. 69–82

2004 "Jewish Myth in Pagan Magic in Antiquity," in I. Gruenwald and M. Idel (eds.), *Myths in Judaism: History, Thought, Literature*, Jerusalem: Shazar, pp. 97–122 (Heb.)

2005 "Reconstructing Jewish Magical Recipe Books from the Cairo Genizah," *GQ* 1, pp. 9*–29*

2005/6 "Babylonian Incantation Bowls – Past, Present and Future (on *A Corpus of Magic Bowls: Incantation Bowls in Jewish Aramaic from Late Antiquity*, by Dan Levene)," *Pe'amim* 105–06, pp. 253–65 (Heb.)

2006 "Catching a Thief: The Jewish Trials of a Christian Ordeal," *JSQ* 13, pp. 1–19

Bokser, Baruch M. 1985 "Wonder-Working and the Rabbinic Tradition: The Case of Ḥanina Ben Dosa," *JSJ* 16, pp. 42–92

Bonfil, R. 1986 "The Cultural and Religious Traditions of French Jewry in the Ninth Century, as Reflected in the Writings of Agobard of Lyons," in J. Dan and J. Hacker (eds.), *Studies in Jewish Mysticism, Philosophy, and Ethical Literature Presented to Isaiah Tishby on His Seventy-Fifth Birthday*, Jerusalem: Magnes, pp. 327–48 (Heb.)

1987 "Between Eretz Israel and Babylonia," *Shalem* 5, pp. 1–30 (Heb.)

1989 "Myth, Rhetoric, History?: A Study in the Chronicle of Aḥimaaz," in M. Ben-Sasson et al. (eds.), *Culture and Society in Medieval Jewry: Studies Dedicated to the Memory of Haim Hillel Ben-Sasson*, Jerusalem: Shazar, pp. 99–135 (Heb.)

Bonner, Campbell 1943 "The Technique of Exorcism," *HTR* 36, pp. 39–49 (with a supplement in *HTR* 37 (1944), pp. 334–36)

1948 "The Story of Jonah on a Magical Amulet," *HTR* 41, pp. 31–37

1950 *Studies in Magical Amulets, Chiefly Graeco-Egyptian*, Ann Arbor: University of Michigan Press

1951 "Amulets Chiefly in the British Museum: A Supplementary Article," *Hesperia* 20, pp. 301–45

Bos, Gerrit 1994 "Hayyim Vital's 'Practical Kabbalah and Alchemy': A 17th Century Book of Secrets," *JJTP* 4, pp. 55–112

Boustan, Ra'anan S. 2005 *From Martyr to Mystic: Rabbinic Martyrology and the Making of Merkavah Mysticism*, TSAJ 112, Tübingen: Mohr

Bowman, John 1953–54 "Phylacteries," *Transactions of the Glasgow University Oriental Society* 15, pp. 54–55

Bozóky, Edina 1992 "Mythic Mediation in Healing Incantations," in S. Campbell et al. (eds.), *Health, Disease and Healing in Medieval Culture*, New York: St. Martin's Press, pp. 84–92

Brashear, William M. 1995 "The Greek Magical Papyri: An Introduction and Survey; Annotated Bibliography (1928–1994)," *ANRW* II.18.5, pp. 3380–684

Brecher, G. 1850 *Das Transcendentale, Magie und magische Heilarten im Talmud*, Vienna: Ulrich Klopf

Bremmer, Jan 1999 "The Birth of the Term 'Magic'," *ZPE* 126, pp. 1–12

Bremmer, Jan N. and Jan R. Veenstra (eds.) 2002 *The Metamorphosis of Magic from Late Antiquity to the Early Modern Period*, Leuven: Peeters

Brody, Robert 1990 "The Cairo Genizah," in B. Richler (ed.), *Hebrew Manuscripts: A Treasured Legacy*, Cleveland and Jerusalem: Ofeq Institute, pp. 112–33

1998 *The Geonim of Babylonia and the Shaping of Medieval Jewish Culture*, New Haven: Yale University Press

Brooke, George J. 2003 "Deuteronomy 18.9–14 in the Qumran Scrolls," in Klutz 2003a, pp. 66–84
Brown, Peter 1970 "Sorcery, Demons, and the Rise of Christianity from Late Antiquity into the Middle Ages," in Douglas 1970, pp. 17–45 (repr. in Brown, *Religion and Society in the Age of Saint Augustine*, London: Faber & Faber, 1972, pp. 119–46)
Buchman, Yael 2001 "Rabbi Ḥayyim Vital's Notebook of Practical Advice," *Cathedra* 99, pp. 37–64 (Heb.)
Buchman, Yael and Zohar Amar 2006 *The Practical Medicine of R. Ḥayyim Vital*, Ramat-Gan: Bar-Ilan University Press (Heb.)
Burkhardt, Evelyn 2003 "Hebräische Losbuchhandschriften: Zur Typologie einer jüdischen Divinationsmethode," in Herrmann, Schlüter, and Veltri 2003, pp. 95–148
Burnett, Charles and W. F. Ryan (eds.) 2006 *Magic and the Classical Tradition*, Warburg Institute Colloquia 7, London: The Warburg Institute
Calderone, S. 1955 "Per la storia dell' elemento giudaico nella Sicilia imperiale," *Rendiconti dell'Accademia Nazionale dei Lincei (Scienze Morali, Storiche e Filologiche)*, ser. 8, vol. X, pp. 489–502
Calvo Martínez, J. L. 2001 "Cien años de investigación sobre la magia antigua," *MHNH* 1, pp. 7–60
Canaan, T. 1936 "Arabic Magic Bowls," *JPOS* 16, pp. 79–127
Chajes, Jeffrey Howard 1999 "Jewish Magic and Divination," in Paul F. Grendler (ed.), *Encyclopedia of the Renaissance*, 6 vols., New York: Charles Scribner's Sons, vol. IV, pp. 22–24
— 2003 *Between Worlds: Dybbuks, Exorcists, and Early Modern Judaism*, Philadelphia: University of Pennsylvania Press
— 2005 "He Said She Said: Hearing the Voices of Pneumatic Early Modern Jewish Women," *Nashim* 10, pp. 99–125
Charlesworth, James H. (ed.) 1983 and 1985 *The Old Testament Pseudepigrapha*, Garden City, New York: Doubleday, vols. I and II
— 1987 "Jewish Interest in Astrology during the Hellenistic and Roman Period," *ANRW* II.20.2, pp. 926–50
Chernus, Ira 1982 *Mysticism in Rabbinic Judaism: Studies on the History of Midrash*, Studia Judaica 11, Berlin: De Gruyter
Cogan, Mordechai 1995 "The Road to En-Dor," in David P. Wright, David Noel Freedman, and Avi Hurvitz (eds.), *Pomegranates and Golden Bells: Studies... In Honor of Jacob Milgrom*, Winona Lake, IN: Eisenbrauns, pp. 319–26
Cohen, Mark R. 2006 "Goitein, Magic, and the Geniza," *JSQ* 13, pp. 294–304
Cohen, Martin Samuel 1983 *The Shi'ur Qomah: Liturgy and Theurgy in Pre-Kabbalistic Jewish Mysticism*, Lanham-New York-London: University Press of America
— 1985 *The Shi'ur Qomah: Texts and Recensions*, Tübingen: Mohr
Cohen, Shaye J. D. 1987 "Pagan and Christian Evidence on the Ancient Synagogue," in Lee I. Levine (ed.), *The Synagogue in Late Antiquity*, Philadelphia: ASOR, pp. 159–81

Cohn, Norman 1970 "The Myth of Satan and His Servants," in Douglas 1970, 103–28

Collins, John J. 1996 "242. 4QPrayer of Nabonidus ar," in *Qumran Cave 4 / XVII*, DJD XXII, Oxford: Clarendon Press, pp. 83–93

Cowley, A. E. 1915 "Notes on Hebrew Papyrus Fragments from Oxyrhynchus," *JEA* 2, pp. 209–13

Cox Miller, Patricia 1986 "In Praise of Nonsense," in A. H. Armstrong (ed.), *Classical Mediterranean Spirituality: Egyptian, Greek, Roman*, World Spirituality, vol. XV, New York: Crossroad, pp. 481–505

Crasta, P. 1979 "Graeco-Christian Magical Papyri," *Studia Papyrologica* 18, pp. 31–40

Curbera, Jaime B. 1999 "Maternal Lineage in Greek Magical Texts," in Jordan, Montgomery, and Thomassen 1999, pp. 195–203

Dahari, U., G. Avni, and A. Kloner 1987 "The Jewish Necropolis of Beth-Govrin," *Qadmoniot* 20 (79–80), pp. 97–101 (Heb.)

Daiches, Samuel 1913 *Babylonian Oil Magic in the Talmud and in the Later Jewish Literature*, London: Jews' College

Dan, Joseph 1968 "Review of Margalioth, *Sepher ha-Razim*," *Tarbiz* 37, pp. 208–14 (Heb.)

—— 1972 "Magic" *Encyclopaedia Judaica*, vol. XI, cols. 703–15

—— 1978 "Teraphim: From Popular Belief to a Folktale," in Joseph Heinemann and Shmuel Verses (eds.), *Studies in Hebrew Narrative Art*, Scripta Hierosolomytana 27, Jerusalem: Magnes, pp. 99–106

—— 1986 "Periodization of the History of Jewish Mysticism," in *Ninth World Congress of Jewish Studies*, Jerusalem: World Union of Jewish Studies, Division C, pp. 93–100 (Heb.)

—— 1992 "The Revelation of the Secret of the World: The Beginning of Jewish Mysticism in Late Antiquity," Brown University Program in Judaic Studies, Occasional Papers Number 2, Providence, Rhode Island

—— 1993a "The Religious Meaning of *Sepher Yezira*," *JSJT* 11, pp. 1–29 (Heb.)

—— 1993b "The Ancient Heikhalot Mystical Texts in the Middle Ages: Tradition, Source, Inspiration," *BJRL* 75, pp. 83–96

—— 1995 "The Mystical 'Descenders to the Chariot' in Historical Context," *Zion* 60, pp. 179–99 (Heb.)

Daniel, R. W. 1991 *Two Greek Magical Papyri in the National Museum of Antiquities in Leiden: A Photographic Edition of J 384 and J 395 (=PGM XII and XIII)*, Papyrologica Coloniensia 19, Opladen: Westdeutscher Verlag

Dauphin, Claudine 1993 "A Graeco-Egyptian Magical Amulet from Mazzuvah," *'Atiqot* 22, pp. 145–47

—— 1998 *La Palestine byzantine: peuplement et populations*, BAR International Series 726, 3 vols., Oxford: Archaeopress

Davies, T. Witton 1898 *Magic, Divination and Demonology among the Hebrews and their Neighbors*, Nottingham

Davila, James R. 2001 *Descenders to the Chariot: The People Behind the Hekhalot Literature*, Leiden: Brill

Davoli, Paola 2004 "Excavations at Soknopaiou Nesos (Dime)," *Egyptian Archaeology* 25, pp. 34–36
de Jong, Albert 1997 *Traditions of the Magi: Zoroastrianism in Greek and Latin Literature*, RGRW 133, Leiden: Brill
Deines, Roland 2003 "Josephus, Salomo und die von Gott verliehene τέχνη gegen die Dämonen," in Lange, Lichtenberger, and Römheld 2003, pp. 365–94
Deissmann, Adolf 1901 *Bible Studies*, (tr. by A. Grieve), Edinburgh: T&T Clark (or. Ger. edn, 1895)
  1927 *Light from the Ancient East*, 2nd edn, London: Hodder and Stoughton
Delatte, Armand 1961 *Herbarius: Recherches sur le cérémonial usité chez les anciens pour la cueillette des simples et des plantes magiques*, 3rd edn, Bruxelles: Académie Royale de Belgique
Delatte, Armand and Ph. Derchain 1964 *Les intailles magiques gréco-égyptiennes*, Paris: Bibliothèque Nationale
Delcor, M. 1987 "L'utilization des psaumes contre les mauvais esprits à Qumran," in *La vie de la parole . . . études . . . offerts a Pierre Grelot*, Paris: Desclée, pp. 61–70
Deubner, Ludovicus 1900 *De incubatione capita quattuor*, Leipzig: Teubner
Deutsch, Yaacov 2000 "New Evidence of Early Versions of *Toldot Yeshu*," *Tarbiz* 69, pp. 177–97 (Heb.)
Díaz Esteban, Fernando 1998 "A Charm for a Traveller," in U. Haxen *et al.* (eds.), *Jewish Studies in a New Europe*, Copenhagen: C. A. Reitzel, pp. 184–98
Dickie, Matthew W. 1999 "The Learned Magician and the Collection and Transmission of Magical Lore," in Jordan, Montgomery, and Thomassen 1999, pp. 163–93
  2001 *Magic and Magicians in the Greco-Roman World*, London: Routledge
Dieleman, Jacco 2005 *Priests, Tongues, and Rites: The London-Leiden Magical Manuscripts and Translation in Egyptian Ritual (100–300 CE)*, RGRW 153, Leiden: Brill
Dieterich, Albrecht 1891 *Abraxas: Studien zur Religionsgeschichte des späteren Altertums*, Leipzig: Teubner
Dillon, John 1985 "The Magical Power of Names in Origen and Later Platonism," in R. Hanson and H. Crouzel (eds.), *Origeniana Tertia*, Rome: Edizioni dell'Ateneo, pp. 203–16 (repr. in Dillon, *The Golden Chain: Studies in the Development of Platonism and Christianity*, Aldershot: Variorum, 1990)
Dion, Paul-Eugène 1976 "Raphael l'exorciste," *Biblica* 57, pp. 399–413
Dodds, E. R. 1947 "Theurgy and Its Relationship to Neoplatonism," *JRS* 37, pp. 55–69
  1951 *The Greeks and the Irrational*, Berkeley: University of California Press
Dornseiff, Franz 1922 *Das Alphabet in Mystik und Magie*, Stoicheia, 7, Leipzig: Teubner (2nd edn, 1925)
Douglas, Mary (ed.) 1970 *Witchcraft Confessions and Accusations*, London: Tavistock
Duffy, J. 1984 "Byzantine Medicine in the Sixth and Seventh Centuries: Aspects of Teaching and Practice," *DOP* 38, pp. 21–27

Duling, D.C. 1975 "Solomon, Exorcism and the Son of David," *HTR* 68, pp. 235–52
  1983 "The *Testament of Solomon* – a new translation and introduction," in Charlesworth 1983, pp. 935–87
  1985 "The Eleazar Miracle and Solomon's Magical Wisdom in Flavius Josephus's *Antiquitates Judaicae* 8.42–49," *HTR* 78, pp. 1–25
  1988 "The *Testament of Solomon*: Retrospective and Prospect," *JSP* 2, pp. 87–112
Dupont-Sommer, A. 1960 "Exorcismes et guérisons dans les écrits de Qoumrân," in *Congress Volume: Oxford 1959, VT* Suppl. 7, Leiden: Brill, pp. 246–61
Edelstein, Ludwig 1937 "Greek Medicine in its Relation to Religion and Magic," *Bulletin of the Institute of the History of Medicine* 5, pp. 201–46 (repr. in O. and C. L. Temkin (eds.), *Ancient Medicine: Selected Papers of Ludwig Edelstein*, Baltimore: Johns Hopkins, 1967, pp. 205–46)
Efron, J. 1990 "The Deed of Simeon ben Shataḥ in Ascalon," an appendix in A. Kasher, *Jews and Hellenistic Cities in Eretz-Israel*, TSAJ 21, Tübingen: Mohr, pp. 318–41
Ego, Beate 2003 "'Denn er liebt sie' (Tob 6.15 Ms. 319): Zur Rolle des Dämons Asmodäus in der Tobit-Erzählung," in Lange, Lichtenberger, and Römheld 2003, pp. 309–17
Eisenman, Robert H. and James Robinson 1991 *A Facsimile Edition of the Dead Sea Scrolls*, Washington, DC: Biblical Archaeological Society
Eisler, Robert 1926 "Le Mystère du Schem Hammephorasch," *REJ* 82, pp. 157–59
Eitrem, Samson 1925 *Papyri Osloenses I: Magical papyri*, Oslo
Elior, Rachel 2004a *The Three Temples: On the Emergence of Jewish Mysticism*, Oxford: Littman
  2004b *Hekhalot Literature and Merkabah Tradition*, Tel Aviv: Yediot Acharonot (Heb.)
Elior, Rachel and Peter Schäfer (eds.) 2005 *Creation and Re-Creation in Jewish Thought: Festschrift in Honor of Joseph Dan on the Occasion of his Seventieth Birthday*, Tübingen: Mohr
Emanuel, Simcha 1995 *Newly Discovered Geonic Responsa*, Jerusalem and Cleveland: Ofeq Institute, Friedberg Library (Heb.)
Engelmann, Helmut 1975 *The Delian Aretalogy of Sarapis*, EPRO 44, Leiden: Brill
Engemann, J. 1975 "Zur Verbreitung magischer Übelabwehr in der nichtchristlichen und christlichen Spätantike," *JAC* 18, pp. 22–48
Epstein, J. N. 1921 and 1922 "Glosses Babylo-Araméennes," *REJ* 73, pp. 27–58, and 74, pp. 40–72
Eshel, Esther 1999 *Demonology in Palestine during the Second Temple Period*, unpubl. Ph.D. diss., Jerusalem (Heb.)
  2003 "Genres of Magical Texts in the Dead Sea Scrolls," in Lange, Lichtenberger, and Römheld 2003, pp. 395–415
Etkes, I. 1995 "The Role of Magic and *Ba'alei Shem* in Ashkenazic Society in the Late Seventeenth and Early Eighteenth Centuries," *Zion* 60, pp. 69–104 (Heb.)
Fahd, T. 1987 "Magic in Islam," in Mircea Eliade (ed.), *Encyclopedia of Religion*, New York: MacMillan, vol. IX, pp. 104–09

Faraone, Christopher A. 1991 "The Agonistic Context of Early Greek Binding Spells," in Faraone and Obbink 1991, pp. 3–33
  1999 *Ancient Greek Love Magic*, Cambridge, MA: Harvard University Press
  2003 "New Light on Ancient Greek Exorcisms of the Wandering Womb," *ZPE* 144, pp. 189–97
Faraone, Christopher A. and Dirk Obbink (eds.) 1991 *Magika Hiera: Ancient Greek Magic and Religion*, Oxford: Oxford University Press
Favret-Saada, Jeanne 1980 *Deadly Words: Witchcraft in the Bocage* (tr. by C. Cullen), Cambridge: Cambridge University Press
Fernandez Marcos, N. 1985 "Motivos Judíos en los papiros mágicos griegos," in *Religión, Superstición y Magia en el Mundo Romano*, Cadiz, pp. 101–27
Fine, Steven 1997 *This Holy Place: On the Sanctity of the Synagogue During the Greco-Roman Period*, Notre Dame, IN: University of Notre Dame Press
  2002 "'Their Faces Shine with the Brightness of the Firmament': Study Houses and Synagogues in the Targumim to the Pentateuch," in F. W. Knobloch (ed.), *Biblical Translation in Context*, Bethesda, MD: University Press of Maryland, pp. 63–92
Finney, Paul Corby 1995 "Abraham and Isaac Iconography on Late-Antique Amulets and Seals: The Western Evidence," *JAC* 38, pp. 140–66
Fisch, M. 1997 *Rational Rabbis: Science and Talmudic Culture*, Bloomington: Indiana University Press
Fischer, David H. 1970 *Historians' Fallacies: Toward a Logic of Historical Thought*, New York: Harper Torchbooks
Fishbane, Michael 1971 *Studies in Biblical Magic: Origins, Uses and Transformations of Terminology and Literary Form*, unpubl. Ph.D. diss., Brandeis
  1974 "Accusations of Adultery: A Study of Law and Scribal Practice in Numbers 5:11–31," *HUCA* 45, pp. 25–45
  1979 "Aspects of Jewish Magic in the Ancient Rabbinic Period," in N. Stampfer (ed.), *Perspectives in Jewish Learning*, The Solomon Goldman Lectures 2, Chicago: Spertus College of Judaica Press, pp. 29–38
  2003 *Biblical Myth and Rabbinic Mythmaking*, Oxford: Oxford University Press
Fishbane, Simcha 1993 "Most Women Engage in Sorcery: An Analysis of Female Sorceresses in the Babylonian Talmud," in H. W. Basser and S. Fishbane (eds.), *Approaches to Ancient Judaism n.s. 5: Historical, Literary, and Religious Studies*, Atlanta: Scholars Press, pp. 143–65 (also published in *Jewish History* 7 [1993], pp. 27–42)
Fitzmyer, Joseph A. 2003 *Tobit*, Commentaries on Early Jewish Literature, Berlin: de Gruyter
  2004 *The Genesis Apocryphon of Qumran Cave 1 (1Q20): A Commentary*, 3rd edn, Rome: Pontifical Biblical Institute (1st edn, 1966)
Fleischer, Ezra 1991 "Medieval Hebrew Poems in Biblical Style," in Mordechai A. Friedman (ed.), *Studies in Judaica*, Te'uda 7, Tel-Aviv, pp. 201–48 (Heb.)
  2002 "On the Antiquity of *Sepher Yezira*: The Qilirian Testimony Revisited," *Tarbiz* 71, pp. 405–32 (Heb.)

Flint, Valerie I. J. 1991 *The Rise of Magic in Early Medieval Europe*, Princeton: Princeton University Press

Flusser, David 1957 "Healing Through the Laying-on of Hands in a Dead Sea Scroll," *IEJ* 7, pp. 107–08 (repr. in *id.*, *Judaism and the Origins of Christianity*, Jerusalem: Magnes, 1988, pp. 21–22)

Flusser, David and Shmuel Safrai 1982 "A Fragment of the Songs of David and Qumran," in Benjamin Uffenheimer (ed.), *Bible Studies Y. M. Grintz in Memoriam*, Te'uda 2, Tel-Aviv: Tel Aviv University, pp. 83–109 (Heb.)

Fodor, A. 1978 "The Use of Psalms in Jewish and Christian Arabic Magic," in É. Apor (ed.), *Jubilee Volume of the Oriental Collection, 1951–1976: Papers Presented on the Occasion of the 25th Anniversary of the Oriental Collection of the Library of the Hungarian Academy of Sciences*, Budapest: Hungarian Academy of Sciences, pp. 67–71

— 2006 "An Arabic Version of *Sefer Ha-Razim*," *JSQ* 13, pp. 412–27

Foerster, G. 1987 "The Zodiac in Ancient Synagogues and Its Place in Jewish Thought and Literature," *Eretz-Israel* 19, pp. 225–34 (Heb.)

Ford, James Nathan 2002a "Review of J. B. Segal, *Catalogue of the Aramaic and Mandaic Incantation Bowls in the British Museum*," *JSAI* 26, pp. 237–72

— 2002b "Two Syriac Terms Relating to Ophthalmology and their Cognates," *JSS* 47, pp. 23–38

Förster, N. 2001 "Der Exorzist Elazar: Salomo, Josephus und das alte Ägypten," in J. U. Kalms (ed.), *Internationales Josephus-Kolloquium Amsterdam 2000*, Münsteraner Judaistische Studien 10, Münster: LIT, pp. 205–21

Franco, F. 1978–79 "Five Aramaic Incantation Bowls from Tell Baruda (Choche)," *Mesopotamia* 13–14, pp. 233–49

Frankfurter, David 1994 "The Magic of Writing and the Writing of Magic: The Power of the Word in Egyptian and Greek Traditions," *Helios* 21, 189–221

— 1995 "Narrating Power: The Theory and Practice of the Magical *Historiola* in Ritual Spells," in Meyer and Mirecki 1995, pp. 457–76

— 1998 *Religion in Roman Egypt: Assimilation and Resistance*, Princeton: Princeton University Press

Frazer, James G. 1918 *Folk-lore in the Old Testament: Studies in Comparative Religion, Legend, and Law*, 3 vols., London: MacMillan

Freeman, David L. 1998–99 "The Gittin 'Book of Remedies'," *Korot* 13, pp. 151–64

Frenkel, Miriam 2002 "Writing the History of the Jews of the Lands of Islam in the Middle Ages: Milestones and Prospects," *Pe'amim* 92, pp. 23–61 (Heb.)

Friedländer, I. 1907 "A Muhammedan Book on Augury in Hebrew Characters," *JQR* 19, pp. 84–103

Friedman, Mordechai Akiva 1986 *Jewish Polygyny in the Middle Ages: New Documents from the Cairo Geniza*, Jerusalem: Bialik (Heb.)

— (ed.) 1999, *A Century of Geniza Research*, Te'uda 15, Tel Aviv: Tel Aviv University (Heb.)

Fulghum, Mary Margaret (Molly) 2001 "Coins Used as Amulets in Late Antiquity," in Sulochana R. Asirvatham, Corinne Ondine Pache, and John Watrous (eds.), *Between Magic and Religion: Interdisciplinary Studies in Ancient Mediterranean Religion and Society*, Lanham: Rowman & Littlefield, pp. 139–47

Furst, Rachel 1998 "Red Strings: A Modern Case of Amulets and Charms," in Micah D. Halpern and Chana Safrai (eds.), *Jewish Legal Writings by Women*, Jerusalem: Urim, pp. 259–77

Gafni, Isaiah M. 1990 *The Jews of Babylonia in the Talmudic Era: A Social and Cultural History*, Jerusalem: Shazar (Heb.)

Gager, John G. 1972 *Moses in Greco-Roman Paganism*, SBLMS 16, Nashville and New York: Abingdon Press

   1992 *Curse Tablets and Binding Spells from the Ancient World*, Oxford: Oxford University Press

   1994 "Moses the Magician: Hero of an Ancient Counter-culture?" *Helios* 21, 179–88

Ganschinietz (=Ganszyniec), R. 1913 *Hippolytos' Capitel gegen die Magier (Refut. Haer. IV 28–42)*, Texte und Untersuchungen 39/2, Leipzig: Hinrichs

   1924 "Sur deux tablettes de Tell Sandahannah," *BCH* 48, pp. 516–521

García Martínez, Florentino 2002 "Magic in the Dead Sea Scrolls," in Bremmer and Veenstra 2002, pp. 13–33

   2003 "Greek Loanwords in the *Copper Scroll*," in Florentino García Martínez and Gerard P. Luttikhuizen (eds.), *Jerusalem, Alexandria, Rome: Studies in Ancient Cultural Interaction in Honour of A. Hilhorst*, JSJ Suppl. 82, Leiden: Brill, pp. 119–45

García Martínez, Florentino *et al.* 1998 "11. 11QapocryphaI Psalms," *Qumran Cave 11 / II*, DJD XXIII, Oxford: Clarendon, pp. 181–205

Garrett, Susan R. "Light on a Dark Subject and Vice Versa: Magic and Miracles in the New Testament," in Neusner, Frerichs, and Flesher 1989, pp. 142–65

Gaster, Moses 1896 *The Sword of Moses*, London: Nutt (also published in *JRAS* 1896, pp. 149–98) (repr. in *id.*, *Studies and Texts in Folklore, Magic, Medieval Romance, Hebrew Apocrypha and Samaritan Archaeology*, 3 vols., London: Maggs Brothers, 1928 [repr. New York: Ktav, 1971], vol. I, pp. 288–337 and vol. III, pp. 69–103)

   1901 "The Logos Ebraikos in the Magical Papyrus of Paris, and the Book of Enoch," *JRAS* 1901, pp. 109–17 (repr. in *Studies and Texts*, vol. I, pp. 356–64)

Gawlikowski, M. 1988 "Une coupe magique araméenne," *Semitica* 38, pp. 137–43

Geller, Markham J. 1976 "Two Incantation Bowls Inscribed in Syriac and Aramaic," *BSOAS* 39, pp. 422–27

   1977 "Jesus' Theurgic Powers," *JJS* 28, pp. 141–55

   1980 "Four Aramaic Incantation Bowls," in Gary Rendsburg, Ruth Adler, Milton Arfa, and Nathan H. Winter (eds.), *The Bible World: Essays in Honor of Cyrus H. Gordon*, New York: Ktav, pp. 47–60

   1985 "An Aramaic Incantation from Oxyrhynchus," *ZPE* 58, pp. 96–98

   1986 "Eight Incantation Bowls," *Orientalia Lovaniensia Periodica* 17, pp. 101–17

   1991 "Akkadian Medicine in the Babylonian Talmud," in Dan Cohn-Sherbok (ed.), *A Traditional Quest: Essays in Honour of Louis Jacobs*, JSOT Suppl. 114, Sheffield: Sheffield Academic Press, pp. 102–12

1997 "More Magic Spells and Formulae," *BSOAS* 60, pp. 327–35

1998 "New Documents from the Dead Sea: Babylonian Science in Aramaic," in M. Lubetski, C. Gottlieb, and Sh. Keller (eds.), *Boundaries of the Ancient Near Eastern World: A Tribute to Cyrus H. Gordon, JSOT* Suppl. 273, Sheffield: Sheffield Academic Press, pp. 224–29

2000 "An Akkadian Vademecum in the Babylonian Talmud," in S. Kottek et al. (eds.), *From Athens to Jerusalem: Medicine in Hellenized Jewish Lore and in Early Christian Literature*, Rotterdam: Erasmus, pp. 13–32

2005 "Tablets and Magic Bowls," in Shaked 2005a, pp. 53–72

2006 "Deconstructing Talmudic Magic," in Burnett and Ryan 2006, pp. 1–18

Geller, M. J., J. C. Greenfield, and M. P. Weitzman (eds.) 1995 *Studia Aramaica: New Sources and New Approaches (Papers Delivered at the London Conference of the Institute of Jewish Studies, University College, London, 26th–28th June 1991)*, *JSS* Suppl. 5, Oxford: Oxford University Press

Geller, M. J. and Dan Levene 1998 "Magical Texts from the Genizah (with a New Duplicate)," *JJS* 49, pp. 334–40

Gelzer, Thomas, Michael Lurje, and Christoph Schäblin 1999 *Lamella Bernensis: Ein spätantikes Goldamulett mit christlichem Exorzismus und verwandte Texte*, Beiträge zur Altertumskunde 124, Stuttgart and Leipzig: Teubner

Ghosh, Amitav 1992 *In an Antique Land*, London: Granta

Gignoux, Philippe 1987 *Incantations magiques syriaques*, Louvain: Peeters

Ginzberg, L. 1909–38 *Legends of the Jews*, 7 vols., Philadelphia: Jewish Publication Society

Gitler, Haim 1990 "Four Magical and Christian Amulets," *LA* 40, pp. 365–74

Giversen, Søren 1972 "Solomon und die Dämonen," in Martin Krause (ed.), *Essays on the Nag Hammadi Texts in Honor of Alexander Böhlig*, Nag Hammadi Studies 3, Leiden: Brill, pp. 16–21

Glucklich, Ariel 1997 *The End of Magic*, New York: Oxford University Press

Goitein, Shlomo Dov 1967–93 *A Mediterranean Society: The Jewish Communities of the Arab World as Portrayed in the Documents of the Cairo Geniza*, 6 vols., Berkeley: University of California Press

Golb, Norman 1965 "The Esoteric Practices of the Jews of Fatimid Egypt," *American Philosophical Society Yearbook* 1965, pp. 533–35

1967 "Aspects of the Historical Background of Jewish Life in Medieval Egypt," in A. Altmann (ed.), *Jewish Medieval and Renaissance Studies*, Cambridge, MA: Harvard University Press, pp. 1–18

Goldin, Judah 1976 "The Magic of Magic and Superstition," in E. Schussler Fiorenza (ed.), *Aspects of Religious Propaganda in Judaism and Early Christianity*, Notre Dame, IN: University of Notre Dame Press, pp. 115–47

Goldstein, Bernard R. and David Pingree 1977 "Horoscopes from the Cairo Geniza," *JNES* 36, pp. 113–44

Goldstein, Jonathan A. 1983 *II Maccabees*, Anchor Bible 41A, Garden City, NY: Doubleday

Goldziher, Ignaz 1907 "Eisen als Schutz gegen Dämonen," *ARW* 10, pp. 41–46

Golinkin, David 2002 "The Use of Matronymics in Prayers for the Sick," in Aharon Demsky (ed.), *These Are the Names: Studies in Jewish Onomastics*, vol. III, Ramat-Gan: Bar-Ilan, pp. 59–72

Goodenough, Erwin R. 1953–68 *Jewish Symbols in the Greco-Roman Period*, 13 vols., New York: Pantheon

 1958 "A Jewish-Gnostic Amulet of the Roman Period," *GRBS* 1, pp. 71–80

Goodnick Westenholz, Joan (ed.) 2000 *Images of Inspiration: The Old Testament in Early Christian Art*, Jerusalem: Bible Lands Museum

Gordon, Cyrus H. 1934 "Aramaic Magical Bowls in the Istanbul and Baghdad Museums," *AO* 6, pp. 319–34

 1937 "Aramaic and Mandaic Magical Bowls," *AO* 9, pp. 84–106

 1941 "Aramaic Incantation Bowls," *Orientalia* 10, pp. 116–41, 272–76, 278–89, 339–60

 1957 *Adventures in the Nearest East*, London: Phoenix House

Gordon, Richard 1997 "Reporting the Marvellous: Private Divination in the Greek Magical Papyri," in Schäfer and Kippenberg 1997, pp. 65–92

Govett, Robert 1869 *English Derived from Hebrew, with Glances at Greek and Latin*, London: S. W. Partridge (repr. Boston: Longwood, 1977)

Graf, Fritz 1997 *Magic in the Ancient World*, (Eng. tr. by Franklin Philip), Cambridge, MA: Harvard University Press (or. Fr. edn, 1994)

Green, Peter 2004 "Magic and the Principle of Apparent Causality in Pliny's Natural History," in *id., From Ikaria to the Stars: Classical Mythification, Ancient and Modern*, Austin: University of Texas Press, pp. 264–80

Green, William Scott 1979 "Palestinian Holy Men: Charismatic Leadership and Rabbinic Tradition," *ANRW* II.19.2, 619–47

Greenfield, Jonas C. 1974 "רטין מגושא," in S. B. Hoenig and L. D. Stitskin (eds.), *Joshua Finkel Festschrift*, New York: Yeshiva University Press, pp. 63–69

Greenfield, J. C. and J. Naveh 1985, "A Mandaic Lead Amulet with Four Incantations," *Eretz-Israel* 18 [=*Nahman Avigad Volume*], pp. 97–107 (Heb.)

Greenfield, Richard P. H. 1995 "A Contribution to the Study of Palaeologan Magic," in Maguire 1995, pp. 117–53

Gruenwald, Ithamar 1967 "The Liturgical Poetry of Yanai and Merkabah Literature," *Tarbiz* 36, pp. 257–77 (Heb.)

 1970–71 "Further Jewish Physiognomic and Chiromantic Fragments," *Tarbiz* 40, pp. 301–19 (Heb.)

 1971 "A Preliminary Critical Edition of *Sepher Yezira*," *IOS* 1, pp. 132–77

 1980 *Apocalyptic and Merkavah Mysticism*, AGAJU 14, Leiden: Brill

 1994 "The Letters, the Writing, and the Shem Mephorash: Magic, Spirituality and Mysticism," in Michal Oron and Amos Goldreich (eds.), *Masu'ot: Studies in Kabbalistic Literature and Jewish Philosophy in Memory of Prof. E. Gottlieb*, Jerusalem: Bialik, pp. 75–98 (Heb.)

 1995 "Major Issues in the Study and Understanding of Jewish Mysticism," in J. Neusner (ed.), *Judaism in Late Antiquity, Part Two: Historical Syntheses*, Handbuch der Orientalistik, 17/2, Leiden: Brill, pp. 1–49

1996 "Magic and Myth: Scholarship and Historical Reality," in Havivah Pedayah (ed.), *Myth in Judaism, Eshel Beer-Sheba* 4, Beer-Sheba: Ben-Gurion University, pp. 15–28 (Heb.)

1997 "'How Much Qabbalah in Ancient Assyria?': Methodological Reflections on the Study of a Cross-Cultural Phenomenon," in S. Parpola and R. M. Whiting (eds.), *Assyria 1995: Proceedings of the 10th Annual Symposium of the Neo-Assyrian Text Corpus Project, Helsinki, September 7–11, 1995*, Helsinki: Neo-Assyrian Text Corpus Project, pp. 115–27

2003 *Rituals and Ritual Theory in Ancient Israel*, Brill Reference Library of Ancient Judaism, 10, Leiden: Brill

Grunwald, Max 1900 "Aus Hausapotheke und Hexenküche," *MGJV* 5, pp. 1–87

1906 and 1907 "Aus Hausapotheke und Hexenküche II," *MGJV* 19 [n.s. 2], pp. 96–120 and 24 [n.s. 3], pp. 118–45

1923a "Fünfundzwanzig Jahre jüdische Volkskunde," *JJV* 25, pp. 1–22

1923b "Aus Hausapotheke und Hexenküche III," *JJV* 25, pp. 178–226

Gudovitch, Sh. 1996 "A Late Roman Burial Cave at Moza 'Illit," *'Atiqot* 29, pp. 63*–70* (Heb.)

Gutwirth, E. 1983 "Judeo-Spanish Fragments from Cairo," *Anuario de Filología* 9, pp. 219–23

1989 "Casta, Classe y Màgia: Bruixes y Amulets entre els Jueus Espanyols del Segle XV," in R. Barkai et al. (eds.), *La Càbala*, Barcelona: Fondació Caixa de Pensions, pp. 85–99

Hachlili, Rachel (ed.) 1989 *Ancient Synagogues in Israel: Third-Seventh Century C.E.*, BAR International Series 499, Oxford: B.A.R.

2001 *Menorah, the Ancient Seven-Armed Candelabrum: Origin, Form and Significance*, Leiden: Brill

2005 *Jewish Funerary Customs: Practices and Rites in the Second Temple Period*, JSJ Suppl. 94, Leiden: Brill

Hägg, T. 1993 "Magic Bowls Inscribed with an Apostles-and-Disciples Catalogue from the Christian Settlement of Hambukol (Upper Nubia)," *Orientalia* 62, pp. 376–99

Halbertal, Moshe 1997 *People of the Book: Canon, Meaning, and Authority*, Cambridge, MA: Harvard University Press

Halperin, David J. 1980 *The Merkabah in Rabbinic Literature*, American Oriental Series 62, New Haven, CT: American Oriental Society

1988 *The Faces of the Chariot: Early Jewish Responses to Ezekiel's Vision*, TSAJ 16, Tübingen: Mohr Siebeck

Hamburger, A. 1968 "Gems from Caesarea Maritima," *'Atiqot* (Eng. series) VIII

1974 "A Key-Amulet from Caesarea," *'Atiqot* (Heb. series) 7, p. 98 (Heb.)

Hamilton, G. J. 1996 "A New Hebrew-Aramaic Incantation Text from Galilee: 'Rebuking the Sea'," *JSS* 41, pp. 215–49

Hamilton, V. P. 1971 *Syriac Incantation Bowls*, Ph.D. Brandeis University

Hansen, Bert 1978 "Science and Magic," in David C. Lindberg (ed.), *Science in the Middle Ages*, Chicago: Chicago University Press, pp. 483–506

Harari, Yuval 1997a, *Harba de-Moshe (The Sword of Moses): A New Edition and a Study*, Jerusalem: Academon (Heb.)
— 1997b "'If You Wish to Kill A Man: Aggressive Magic and the Defense Against it in Ancient Jewish Magic," *Jewish Studies* 37, pp. 111–42 (Heb.)
— 1998 *Early Jewish Magic: Methodological and Phenomenological Studies*, unpubl. Ph.D. diss., Jerusalem (Heb.)
— 2000a "'For a Woman to Follow You': Love Charms in Ancient Jewish Magic," *Kabbalah* 5, pp. 247–64 (Heb.)
— 2000b "Power and Money: Economic Aspects of the Use of Magic by Jews in Ancient Times and the Early Middle Ages," *Pe'amim* 85, pp. 14–42 (Heb.)
— 2004 "'To Open the Heart': Magical Practices for Gaining Knowledge, Understanding and Memory in Judaism in Antiquity and the Early Middle Ages," in Z. Gries, H. Kreisel, and B. Huss (eds.), *Shefa 'Tal: Festschrift for Bracha Zak*, Beer-Sheba: Ben Gurion University Press, pp. 303–47 (Heb.)
— 2005a "On the Trail of the Magical Plate from the Yeruḥam Cemetery: Incantation Bowls from the Ancient World and in Islam," *Pe'amim* 103, pp. 55–90 (Heb.)
— 2005b "What is a Magical Text?: Methodological Reflections Aimed at Redefining Early Jewish Magic," in Shaked 2005a, pp. 91–124
— 2005c "Sword, Moses, and *The Sword of Moses*: Between Rabbinical and Magical Traditions," *JSQ* 12, pp. 293–329
— 2006 "The Sages and the Occult," in Shmuel Safrai, Zeev Safrai, Joshua Schwartz, and Peter J. Tomson (eds.), *The Literature of the Sages*, Part II, Assen: Van Gorcum, pp. 521–64
— 2006a "The *Scroll of Aḥimaaẓ* and the Jewish Magical Culture: A Note on the *Soṭah* Ordeal," *Tarbiz* 75, pp. 185–202 (Heb.)
Harrauer, Chr. and H. Harrauer 1987 "Ein jüdisch-christlisches Amulett," *Wiener Studien* 100, pp. 185–99
Harvey, W. Z. 1992 "Rabbinic Attitudes towards Philosophy," in H. Blumberg et al. (eds.), *"Open Thou Mine Eyes . . .": Essays on Aggadah and Judaica Presented to Rabbi W. G. Braude*, Hoboken, NJ: Ktav, pp. 83–101
Harviainen, Tapani 1978 "A Syriac Incantation Bowl in the Finnish National Museum, Helsinki: A Specimen of Eastern Aramaic 'Koiné,'" *SO* 51/1, pp. 3–29
— 1981 "An Aramaic Incantation Bowl from Borsippa: Another Specimen of Eastern Aramaic 'Koiné,'" *SO* 51/14, pp. 3–28
— 1995 "Pagan Incantations in Aramaic Magic Bowls," in Geller, Greenfield, and Weitzman 1995, pp. 53–60
Hayman, A. Peter 1987 "Sepher Yeẓira and the Hekhalot Literature," *JSJT* 6 [=*Proceedings of the First International Conference on the History of Jewish Mysticism*], pp. 71–87
— 1989 "Was God a Magician?: Sepher Yeẓira and Jewish Magic," *JJS* 40, pp. 225–37
— 1991 "Monotheism – A Misused Word in Jewish Studies?" *JJS* 42, pp. 1–15
— 2004 *Sepher Yeẓira: Edition, Translation and Text-Critical Commentary*, TSAJ 104, Tübingen: Mohr Siebeck

Heim, Ricardus 1892 *Incantamenta Magica Graeca Latina*, Leipzig: Teubner
Heinemann, Isaak 1932 *Philons Griechische und Lateinische Bildung*, Breslau: M. & H. Marcus
Heinemann, Joseph 1974 *Aggadah and Its Development*, Jerusalem: Keter (Heb.)
Hengel, M. 1984 "Rabbinische Legende und frühpharisäische Geschichte: Schimeon b. Schetach und die achtzig Hexen von Ashkelon," *Abhandlungen der Heidelberger Akademie der Wissenchaften (phil.-hist. Klasse)*, Heidelberg
Hennecke, Edgar and Wilhelm Schneemelcher 1963 and 1965 *New Testament Apocrypha* (tr. by R. McL. Wilson), 2 vols., Philadelphia: Westminster Press
Herr, Moshe-David 1980 "Matters of Palestinian Halakha During the Sixth and Seventh Centuries C.E.," *Tarbiz* 49, pp. 62–80 (Heb.)
Herrmann, Klaus 1993 "Re-Written Mystical Texts: The Transmission of the Heikhalot Literature in the Middle Ages," *BJRL* 75, pp. 97–116
Herrmann, Klaus and Claudia Rohrbacher-Sticker 1989 "Magische Traditionen der New Yorker *Hekhalot*-Handschrift JTS 8128 im Kontext ihrer Gesamtredaktion," *FJB* 17, pp. 101–49
—— 1991/92 "Magische Traditionen der Oxforder *Hekhalot*-Handschrift Michael 9 in ihrem Verhältnis zu MS New York JTS 8128," *FJB* 19, pp. 169–83
Herrmann, Klaus, Margarete Schlüter, and Giuseppe Veltri (eds.) 2003 *Jewish Studies Between the Disciplines / Judaistik Zwischen den Disziplinen: Papers in Honor of Peter Schäfer on the Occasion of his 60th Birthday*, Leiden: Brill
Herrmann, Léon 1954–55 "Les Premiers exorcismes juifs et judéo-chrétiens," *Revue de l'Université de Bruxelles* n.s. 7, pp. 305–08
Hezser, C. 2001 *Jewish Literacy in Roman Palestine*, TSAJ 81, Tübingen: Mohr Siebeck
Hilprecht, H. V. 1904 *The Excavations in Assyria and Babylonia*, Philadelphia: A. J. Holman
Hoffman, C. A. 2002 "Fiat Magia," in Mirecki and Meyer 2002, pp. 179–94
Hogan, Larry P. 1992 *Healing in the Second Temple Period*, Novum Testamentum et Orbis Antiquus 21, Freiburg: Universitätsverlag and Göttingen: Vandenhoeck & Ruprecht
Holland, Bart K. (ed.) 1996 *Prospecting for Drugs in Ancient and Medieval European Texts: A Scientific Approach*, Amsterdam: Harwood
Hopfner, Th. 1921–24 *Griechisch-ägyptischer Offenbarungszauber*, 2 vols., Leipzig: Haessel (repr. Amsterdam: Hakkert, 1974–90)
—— 1931 "Orientalisch-Religionsgeschichtliches aus den Griechischen Zauberpapyri," *AO* 3, pp. 119–55, 327–58
Hopkins, S. 1978 *A Miscellany of Literary Pieces from the Cambridge Genizah Collections*, Cambridge: Cambridge University Library
Horak, Ulrike 1992 *Illuminierte Papyri, Pergamente und Papiere I*, Pegasus Oriens 1, Vienna: Holzhausen
Horak, Ulrike and Christian Gastgeber 1995, "Zwei Beispiele angewandter Bildmagie: Ein griechischer Diebzauber und ein 'verknotetes' Sator-Quadrat," *Biblos* 44, pp. 197–225

Horst, Pieter W. van der 1978 *The Sentences of Pseudo-Phocylides With Introduction and Commentary*, (Studia in Veteris Testamenti Pseudepigrapha 4), Leiden: Brill

    1998 "Papyrus Egerton 5: Christian or Jewish?," *ZPE* 121, pp. 173–82

    2002 "The Tombs of the Prophets in Early Judaism," in *id., Japheth in the Tents of Shem: Studies on Jewish Hellenism in Antiquity*, Contributions to Biblical Exegesis and Theology 32, Leuven: Peeters, pp. 119–37

    2006 "The Great Magical Papyrus of Paris (PGM IV) and the Bible," in *id., Jews and Christians in their Graeco-Roman Context: Selected Essays on Early Judaism, Samaritanism, Hellenism, and Christianity*, WUNT 196, Tübingen: Mohr Siebeck, pp. 269–79

Hull, John M. 1974 *Hellenistic Magic and the Synoptic Tradition*, (Studies in Biblical Theology, 2nd ser., 28), London: SCM Press

Hunter, Erica C. D. 1995 "Combat and Conflict in Incantation Bowls: Studies on Two Aramaic Specimens from Nippur," in Geller, Greenfield, and Weitzman 1995, pp. 61–75

    1996 "Incantation Bowls: A Mesopotamian Phenomenon?" *Orientalia* 65, pp. 220–33

    1998 "Who Are the Demons? The Iconography of Incantations Bowls," in S. Ribichini (ed.), *Magic in the Ancient Near East*, Studi Epigrafici e Linguistici sul Vicino Oriente Antico 15, Verona: Essedue, pp. 95–116

    2004 "Nippur and Aramaic Incantation Texts," in Juusola, Laulainen, and Palva 2004, pp. 69–82

Idel, Moshe 1989 "Jewish Magic from the Renaissance Period to Early Hasidism," in Neusner, Frerichs, and Flesher 1989, pp. 82–117

    1990a, *Golem: Jewish Magical and Mystical Traditions on the Artificial Anthropoid*, Albany, NY: SUNY Press

    1990b "Maimonides and Kabbalah," in Isadore Twersky (ed.), *Studies in Maimonides*, Cambridge, MA: Harvard University Press, pp. 31–81

    1993 "Defining Kabbalah: The Kabbalah of the Divine Names," R. A. Herrera (ed.), *Mystics of the Book*, New York: Peter Lang, pp. 97–122

    1995 *Hasidism Between Ecstasy and Magic*, Albany, NY: SUNY Press, 1995

    1997 "On Judaism, Jewish Mysticism and Magic," in Schäfer and Kippenberg 1997, pp. 195–214 (also published as "On Magic and Judaism," in Sorin Antohi [ed.], *Religion, Fiction and History: Essays in Memory of Ioan Petru Culianu*, 2 vols., Bucharest: Nemira, 2001, vol. II, pp. 13–40)

    2005 "On Sheelat Ḥalom in Hasidei Ashkenaz: Sources and Influences," *Materia Giudaica* 10, pp. 99–109

Ilan, Tal 2001 "A Witch-Hunt in Ashkelon," in A. Sasson, Z. Safrai, and N. Sagiv (eds.), *Ashkelon: A City on the Seashore*, Ashkelon Academic College, pp. 135–46 (Heb.).

Ilan, Zvi 1989 "The Synagogue and *Beth Midrash* of Meroth," in Hachlili 1989, pp. 21–41

    1998 "The Synagogue and Study House at Meroth," in Urman and Flesher 1998, pp. 256–88

Isaacs, Haskell D. 1994 *Medical and Para-Medical Manuscripts in the Cambridge Genizah Collections*, Cambridge: Cambridge University Press

Isbell, C. D. 1975 *Corpus of the Aramaic Incantation Bowls*, SBLDS 17, Missoula, Montana: Scholars Press

    1976 "Two New Aramaic Incantation Bowls," *BASOR* 223, pp. 15–23

    1978 "The Story of the Aramaic Magical Incantation Bowls," *Biblical Archeologist* 41, pp. 5–16

Jackson, Howard M. 1988 "Notes on the Testament of Solomon," *JSJ* 19, pp. 19–60

    1989 "The Origin in Ancient Incantatory *Voces magicae* of Some Names in the Sethian Gnostic System," *VC* 43, pp. 69–79

    1996 "Echoes and Demons in the Pseudo-Philonic *Liber Antiquitatum Biblicarum*," *JSJ* 27, pp. 1–20

Jacobs, Martin 1998 "Römische Thermenkultur im Spiegel des Talmud Yerushalmi," in Peter Schäfer (ed.), *The Talmud Yerushalmi and Graeco-Roman Culture*, vol. I, TSAJ 71, Tübingen: Mohr, pp. 219–311

Jacobson, Howard 1996 *A Commentary on Pseudo-Philo's Liber Antiquitatum Biblicarum*, AGAJU 31, 2 vols., Leiden: Brill

Jacoby, Adolf 1913 "Ein hellenistisches Ordal," *ARW* 16, pp. 122–26

    1922 "Weiteres zu dem Diebszauber Archiv XVI 122ff," *ARW* 21, pp. 485–91

Jaeger, C. Stephen 1994 *The Envy of Angels: Cathedral Schools and Social Ideals in Medieval Europe, 950–1200*, Philadelphia: University of Pennsylvania Press

James, Montague Rhodes 1924 *The Apocryphal New Testament*, Oxford: Clarendon Press

Janowitz, Naomi 1992 "God's Body: Theological and Ritual Roles of Shi'ur Komah," in Howard Eilberg-Schwartz (ed.), *People of the Body: Jews and Judaism from an Embodied Perspective*, Albany: SUNY Press, pp. 183–201

    2001 *Magic in the Roman World: Pagans, Jews and Christians*, Religion in the First Christian Centuries, London and New York: Routledge

    2002 *Icons of Power: Ritual Practices in Late Antiquity*, Magic in History, University Park, PA: Penn State University Press

Jansson, Eva-Maria 1998 "The Magic of the *Mezuzah* in Rabbinic Literature," in U. Haxen *et al.* (eds.), *Jewish Studies in a New Europe*, Copenhagen: C.A. Reitzel, pp. 415–25

Jarvie, I. C. and J. Agassi 1970 "The Problem of the Rationality of Magic," in B. R. Wilson (ed.), *Rationality*, Oxford: Blackwell, pp. 172–93

Jastrow, Marcus 1903 *A Dictionary of the Targumim, The Talmud Babli and Yerushalmi, and the Midrashic Literature*, 2 vols., London: Luzac

Jeffers, Ann 1996 *Magic and Divination in Ancient Palestine and Syria*, Studies in the History and Culture of the Ancient Near East VIII, Leiden: Brill

Jellinek, Adolph 1853–78 *Bet ha-Midrash*, 6 vols., Vienna: Winter (repr. Jerusalem: Bamberger and Wahrman, 1938)

Jeremias, Joachim 1958 *Heiligengräber in Jesu Umwelt (Mt. 23,29; Lk. 11,47): Eine Untersuchung zur Volksreligion der Zeit Jesu*, Göttingen: Vandenhoeck & Ruprecht

Jeruzalmi, Isak 1964 *Les Coupes magiques araméennes de Mésopotamie*, Paris: The Sorbonne

Joël, David 1881–83 *Der Aberglaube und die Stellung des Judenthums zu demselben*, Jahresbericht des jüdisch-theologischen Seminars "Fraenckel'scher Stiftung", 2 vols., Breslau

Johnston, Sarah Iles 2002 "The Testament of Solomon from Late Antiquity to the Renaissance," in Bremmer and Veenstra 2002, pp. 35–49

Jones, C. P. 1987 "Stigma: Tattooing and Branding in Graeco-Roman Antiquity," *JRS* 77, pp. 139–55

Jordan, David R. 1976 "CIL VIII 19525(b).2: QPVVLVA = q(uem) p(eperit) vulva," *Philologus* 120, pp. 127–32

1979 "An Appeal to the Sun for Vengeance (*Inscriptions de Délos* 2533)," *BCH* 103, pp. 521–25

1985 "A survey of Greek Defixiones not Included in the Special Corpora," *GRBS* 26, pp. 151–97

1988 "New Defixiones from Carthage," in J. H. Humphrey (ed.), *The Circus and a Byzantine Cemetery at Carthage*, vol. I, Ann Arbor, MI: University of Michigan Press, pp. 117–34

1994a "Inscribed Lead Tablets from the Games in the Sanctuary of Poseidon," *Hesperia* 63, pp. 111–26

1994b "Magica Graeca Parvula," *ZPE* 100, pp. 321–35

2000 "New Greek Curse Tablets (1985–2000)," *GRBS* 41, pp. 5–46

2001 "Notes on Two Michigan Magical Papyri," *ZPE* 136, pp. 183–93

Jordan, David R. and R. D. Kotansky 1996 "Two Phylacteries from Xanthos," *Revue Archéologique* 21, pp. 161–74

1997 "A Salomonic Exorcism (Inv. T 3)," in M. Gronewald *et al.* (eds.), *Kölner Papyri* 8, Opladen: Westdeutscher Verlag, pp. 53–69 (=P. Köln VIII, 338) and iid., "A Spell for Aching Feet (Inv. T 33)," *ibid.*, pp. 70–81 (=P. Köln VIII, 339)

Jordan, David R., Hugo Montgomery, and Einar Thomassen (eds.) 1999, *The World of Ancient Magic: Papers from the first International Samson Eitrem Seminar at the Norwegian Institute at Athens 4–8 May 1997*, Papers of the Norwegian Institute at Athens 4, Bergen: The Norwegian Institute at Athens

Judge, E. A. 1987 "The Magical Use of Scripture in the Papyri," in E. Conrad and E. Newing (eds.), *Perspectives on Language and Text: Essays and Poems in Honor of Francis I. Andersen's Sixtieth Birthday*, Winona Lake, IN: Eisenbrauns, pp. 339–49

Juusola, Hannu 1999a *Linguistic Peculiarities in the Aramaic Magic Bowl Texts*, Helsinki: Finnish Oriental Society

1999b "Who Wrote the Syriac Incantation Bowls," *SO* 85, pp. 75–92

2004 "Notes on the Aramaic Sections of the Havdalah de-Rabbi Aqiba," in Juusola, Laulainen, and Palva 2004, pp. 106–19

Juusola, Hannu, Juha Laulainen, and Heikki Palva (eds.) 2004 *Verbum et Calamus: Semitic and Related Studies in Honour of the Sixtieth Birthday of Professor Tapani Harviainen*, [=*SO* 99], Helsinki: Finnish Oriental Society

Kahn, C. H., D. E. Gershenson, and M. Smith 1959 "Further Notes on 'A Jewish-Gnostic Amulet of the Roman Period'," *GRBS* 2, pp. 73–81

Kákosy, L. 1985 "Uroboros," *Lexikon der Ägyptologie* VI, cols. 886–93

Kanarfogel, Ephraim 2000 *"Peering Through the Lattices": Mystical, Magical and Pietistic Dimensions in the Tosafist Period*, Detroit: Wayne State University Press

Katz, Nathan 1995 "The Judaisms of Kaifeng and Cochin: Parallel and Divergent Styles of Religious Acculturation," *Numen* 42, pp. 118–40

Kaufman, Stephen A. 1973 "A Unique Magic Bowl from Nippur," *JNES* 32, pp. 170–74

Kaufmann, Yehezkel 1937–63 *The History of Israelite Faith*, 4 vols., Tel Aviv: Dvir (Heb.)

Keil, J. 1940 "Ein rätselhafter Amulett," *Wiener Jahreshefte* 32, pp. 79–84

Kern-Ulmer, Brigitte (Rivka) 1996 "The Depiction of Magic in Rabbinic Texts: The Rabbinic and the Greek Concept of Magic," *JSJ* 27, pp. 289–303

Keter, Shalom Ben Abraham 1990 *Sepher Naḥash ha-Neḥoshet: Being a Book of Segullot, Remedies and Lots, in Which are Explained Geomancy, Chiromancy, Lot-Casting, Amulets, and the Properties of Herbs and Medicinal Plants*, Jerusalem: n.p. (Heb.)

Khan, G. A. 1986 "The Arabic Fragments in the Cambridge Genizah Collections," *Manuscripts of the Middle East* 1, pp. 54–60

Kieckhefer, R. 1994 "The Specific Rationality of Medieval Magic," *The American Historical Review* 99, pp. 813–36

Kister, Menahem 1999 "Demons, Theology and Abraham's Covenant: CD 16:4–6 and Related Texts," in Robert A. Kugler and Eileen M. Schuller (eds.), *The Dead Sea Scrolls at Fifty: Proceedings of the 1997 Society of Biblical Literature Qumran Section Meeting*, Atlanta: Scholars Press, pp. 167–84

Klein-Franke, Felix 1971 "Eine aramäische *Tabella devotionis*," *ZPE* 7, pp. 47–52

Kloner, Amos 1989 "The Synagogues of Ḥorvat Rimmon," in Hachlili 1989, pp. 43–48

Klutz, Todd (ed.) 2003a *Magic in the Biblical World: From the Rod of Aaron to the Ring of Solomon*, (JSNT Suppl. 245), London: T&T Clark

— 2003b "The Archer and the Cross: Chorographic Astrology and Literary Design in the *Testament of Solomon*," in Klutz 2003a, pp. 219–44

— 2005 *Rewriting the Testament of Solomon: Tradition, Conflict, and Identity in a Late Antique Pseudepigraphon*, Library of Second Temple Studies 53, London: T&T Clark

Knox, W. L. 1938 "Jewish Liturgical Exorcism," *HTR* 31, pp. 191–203

Kollmann, Bernd 1994 "Göttliche Offenbarung magisch-pharmakologischer Heilkunst im Buch Tobit," *Zeitschrift für Alttestamentliche Wissenschaft* 106, pp. 289–99

Kotansky, Roy 1980 "Two Amulets in the Getty Museum," *Paul Getty Museum Journal* 8, pp. 181–88

— 1991a "Two Inscribed Jewish Aramaic Amulets from Syria," *IEJ* 41, pp. 267–81

— 1991b "An Inscribed Copper Amulet from 'Evron," *'Atiqot* 20, pp. 81–87

1991c "Incantations and Prayers for Salvation on Inscribed Greek Amulets," in Faraone and Obbink 1991, pp. 107–37
1994 *Greek Magical Amulets: The Inscribed Gold, Silver, Copper, and Bronze Lamellae. Part I: Published Texts of known Provenance*, Papyrologica Coloniensia 22/1, Opladen: Westdeutscher Verlag
1995 "Greek Exorcistic Amulets," in Meyer and Mirecki 1995, pp. 243–77
1997 "The Chnoubis Gem from Tel Dor," *IEJ* 47, pp. 257–260
2002 "An Early Christian Gold Lamella for Headache," in Mirecki and Meyer 2002, pp. 37–46
Kotansky, Roy, Joseph Naveh, and Shaul Shaked 1992, "A Greek-Aramaic Silver Amulet from Egypt in the Ashmolean Museum," *Le Muséon* 105, pp. 5–26
Kottek, Samuel S. 1989 "Remarks on Talmudic Medical Terminology," *Koroth* 9/9–10, pp. 650–63
1993 "Medicinal Drugs in Flavius Josephus," in I. and W. Jacob (eds.), *The Healing Past*, Leiden: Brill, pp. 95–105
2000 "Magic and Healing in Hellenistic Jewish Writings," *FJB* 27, pp. 1–16
Kraus, Thomas J. 2005 "Septuaginta-Psalm 90 in apotropäischer Verwendung: Vorüberlegungen für eine kritische Edition und (bisheriges) Datenmaterial," *Biblische Notizen* 125, pp. 39–73
Krauss, Samuel 1898–99 *Griechische und lateinische Lehnwörter im Talmud, Midrasch und Targum*, 2 vols., Berlin (repr. Hildesheim: Georg Olms, 1964)
1902 *Das Leben Jesu nach jüdischen Quellen*, Berlin: S. Calvary
Kreisel, Howard 1984 "Miracles in Medieval Jewish Philosophy," *JQR* 75, pp. 99–133
Kropatscheck, Gerhardus 1907 *De amuletorum aput antiquos usu capita duo*, diss. Münster, Greifswald: Iulius Abel
Kuemmerlin-McLean, J. K. 1986 *Divination and Magic in the Religion of Ancient Israel: A Study in Perspectives and Methodology*, unpubl. Ph.D. diss., Nashville, Tennessee
Lacerenza, Giancarlo 1998 "Magia giudaica nella Sicilia tardoantica," in N. Bucaria (ed.), *Gli Ebrei in Sicilia dal Tardoantico al Medioevo: Studi in Onore di Mons. Benedetto Rocco*, Palermo: Flaccovio, pp. 293–310
2002 "Jewish Magicians and Christian Clients in Late Antiquity: The Testimony of Amulets and Inscriptions," in Leonard V. Rutgers (ed.), *What Athens Has to Do with Jerusalem: Essays on Classical, Jewish and Christian Art and Archaeology in Honor of Gideon Foerster*, Interdisciplinary Studies in Ancient Culture and Religion 1, Leuven: Peeters, pp. 393–419
Lampe, G. W. H. 1961 *A Patristic Greek Lexicon*, Oxford: Clarendon Press
Lange, Armin 1997 "The Essene Position on Magic and Divination," in Moshe Bernstein, Florentino García Martínez, and John Campen (eds.), *Legal Texts and Legal Issues: Proceedings of the Second Meeting of the Int. Org. for Qumran Studies, Cambridge 1995*, (Studies on the Texts of the Desert of Judah 23), Leiden: Brill, pp. 377–435
Lange, Armin, Hermann Lichtenberger, and K. F. Diethard Römheld (eds.) 2003 *Die Dämonen – Demons: Die Dämonologie der israelitisch-jüdischen und frühchristlichen Literatur im Kontext ihrer Umwelt. The Demonology of*

Israelite-Jewish and Early Christian Literature in Context of their Environment, Tübingen: Mohr Siebeck

Langermann, Y. Tzvi 2002 "On the Beginnings of Hebrew Scientific Literature and on Studying History Through 'Maqbiloṭ' (Parallels)," *Aleph* 2, pp. 169–89

Lässig, Elisabeth 2001 "Ein Amulett mit Reiterdarstellung und Opferung des Isaak: Papyrussammlung der Österreichischen Nationalbibliothek, Privatsammlung Tamerit, M 63," in Ulrike Horak (ed.), *Realia Coptica: Festgabe zum 60. Geburtstag von Hermann Harrauer,* Vienna: Holzhausen, pp. 55–64 and pl. 30–32

Lecker, M. 1992 "The Bewitching of the Prophet Muhammad by the Jews: A Note a propos 'Abd al-Malik b. Habib's *Mukhtasar fi l-tibb,*" *al-Qantara* 13, 561–69 (repr. in *id., Jews and Arabs in Pre- and Early Islamic Arabia,* Aldershot: Variorum 1998, no. XII)

Leclercq, H. 1924 "Amulettes," in *Dictionnaire d'Archéologie Chrétienne et de Liturgie,* vol. I/2, Paris, cols. 1784–860

Leicht, Reimund 1999 "*Qedushah* and Prayer to Helios: A New Hebrew Version of an Apocryphal Prayer of Jacob," *JSQ* 6, pp. 140–76

— 2003 "The Legend of St. Eustachius (Eustathius) as Found in the Cairo Genizah," in Herrmann, Schlüter, and Veltri 2003, pp. 325–30

— 2005 "Some Observations on the Diffusion of Jewish Magical Texts from Late Antiquity and the Early Middle Ages in Manuscripts from the Cairo Genizah and Ashkenaz," in Shaked 2005a, pp. 213–31

— 2006 *Astrologumena Judaica: Untersuchungen zur Geschichte der Astrologischen Literatur der Juden,* TSMEMJ 21, Tübingen: Mohr Siebeck

Leipoldt, J. and S. Morenz 1953 *Heilige Schriften: Betrachtungen zur Religionsgeschichte der antiken Mittelmeerwelt,* Leipzig: Harrassowitz

Lejeune, M. 1985 *Le plomb magique du Larzac et les sourcières gaulois,* Paris: CNRS

Lesses, Rebecca Macy 1998 *Ritual Practices to Gain Power: Angels, Incantations, and Revelation in Early Jewish Mysticism,* Harvard Theological Studies 44, Harrisburg, PA: Trinity Press

— 2001 "Exe(o)rcising Power: Women as Sorceresses, Exorcists, and Demonesses in Babylonian Jewish Society of Late Antiquity," *Journal of the American Academy of Religion* 69, pp. 343–75

Levene, Dan 1999 "'. . . and by the name of Jesus . . .': An Unpublished Magic Bowl in Jewish Aramaic," *JSQ* 6, pp. 283–308

— 2002 *Curse or Blessing, What's in the Magical Bowl?,* The Ian Karten Lecture, 2002 = Parkes Institute Pamphlet No. 2, University of Southampton (also available in www.parkes.soton.ac.uk/articles/levene.pdf)

— 2003 *A Corpus of Magic Bowls: Incantation Texts in Jewish Aramaic from Late Antiquity,* The Kegan Paul Library of Jewish Studies, London: Kegan Paul

— 2006 "Calvariae Magicae: The Berlin, Philadelphia and Moussaieff Skulls," *Orientalia* 75, pp 359–79

Levi, Carlo 1947 *Christ Stopped at Eboli* (tr. by Frances Frenaye), New York: Farrar, Straus and Co.

Lévi-Strauss, Claude 1963 "The Sorcerer and his Magic," in *id.*, *Structural Anthropology*, (tr. by Claire Jacobson and Brooke Grundfest Schoepf), New York: Basic Books, pp. 167–85

Levine, B. A. 1970 "The Language of the Magical Bowls," in J. Neusner, *The History of the Jews in Babylonia*, vol. V, Leiden: Brill, pp. 343–73

Levine, Lee I. 2000 *The Ancient Synagogue: The First Thousand Years*, New Haven: Yale University Press

Levinson, Joshua 2006 "Boundaries and Witches: Stories of Conflicts between Rabbis and Magicians in Rabbinic Literature," *Tarbiz* 75, pp. 295–328 (Heb.)

Levy, B. Barry 1990 *Planets, Potions and Parchments: Scientifica Hebraica from the Dead Sea Scrolls to the Eighteenth Century*, Catalogue of an Exhibition, Montreal and Kingston: McGill-Queen's University Press

Levy, Jochanan (Hans) 1941 "Remains of Greek Sentences and Names in the Book 'Hekhalot Rabbati'," *Tarbiz* 12, pp. 163–67 (Heb.) (repr. in *id.*, *Olamot Niphgashim*, Jerusalem: Bialik, 1969, pp. 259–65)

Levy, S. et al. 1960 "The Ancient Synagogue of Maʿon," in *Bulletin (L. M. Rabinowitz Fund for the Exploration of Ancient Synagogues)* 3, pp. 6–40

Levy, Shani 2006 *The Uses of Biblical Verses and Biblical Figures in Magical Texts from the Cairo Genizah*, unpubl. MA thesis, Tel-Aviv University (Heb.)

Lewis, S. 1905 "Maimonides on Superstition," *JQR* 17, pp. 475–88

Lewy, Heinrich 1893 "Morgenländischer Aberglaube in der römischen Kaiserzeit," *Zeitschrift des Vereins für Volkskunde* 3, pp. 23–40, 130–43, 238

Libertini, G. 1927 "Laminetta plumbea iscritta da S. Giovanni Galerno (Catania)," *Rivista Indo-Greco-Italica* 11, pp. 105–09

Lieber, Elinor 1983 "The Covenant which Asaf son of Berakhyahu and Yoḥanan son of Zebda Made with the Pupils: Text and Translation," in Joshua O. Leibowitz (ed.), *Memorial Volume in Honor of Professor S. Muntner*, Jerusalem: Israel Institute of the History of Medicine, pp. 83–94

Lieberman, Saul 1942 *Greek in Jewish Palestine*, New York: Jewish Theological Seminary of America (2nd edn, 1965)

 1945–47 "Palestine in the Third and Fourth Centuries," *JQR* 36, pp. 329–70, and 37, pp. 31–54

 1974 "Some Notes on Adjurations in Israel," in *id.*, *Texts and Studies*, New York: Ktav, pp. 21–28 (or. pub. in Heb., in *Tarbiz* 27 (1958), pp. 183–89)

Liebes, Yehuda 1993 "De Natura Dei: On the Development of the Jewish Myth," in *id.*, *Studies in Jewish Myth and Jewish Messianism*, (tr. by Batya Stein), Albany, NY: SUNY Press, pp. 1–64

 2000 *Ars Poetica in Sepher Yetsira*, Jerusalem: Schocken (Heb.)

Lightstone, Jack N. 1984 *The Commerce of the Sacred: Mediation of the Divine among Jews in the Graeco-Roman Diaspora*, Brown Judaic Studies 59, Chico, CA: Scholars Press

 1985 "Magicians, Holy Men and Rabbis: Patterns of the Sacred in Late Antique Judaism," in W. Scott Green (ed.), *Approaches to Ancient Judaism*, vol. V, Brown Judaic Studies 32, Atlanta: Scholars Press, pp. 133–48

Lloyd, G. E. R. 1979 *Magic, Reason, and Experience: Studies in the Origin and Development of Greek Science*, Cambridge: Cambridge University Press

Lorberbaum, Yair 2004 *Image of God: Halakhah and Aggadah*, Tel Aviv: Schocken (Heb.)
Löw, I. 1881 *Aramäische Pflanzennamen*, Leipzig: Wilhelm Engelmann
Lust, Johan 1974 "On Wizards and Prophets," (VT editors) (eds.), *Studies on Prophecy*, VT Suppl. 26, Leiden: Brill, pp. 135–42
Luz, M. 1989 "A Description of the Greek Cynic in the Jerusalem Talmud," *JSJ* 20, pp. 49–60
Lyons, W. J. and A. M. Reimer 1998 "The Demonic Virus and Qumran Studies: Some Preventative Measures," *DSD* 5, pp. 16–32
Mack, Hananel 1998 "The Unique Character of the Zippori Synagogue Mosaic and Eretz Israel Midrashim," *Cathedra* 88, pp. 39–56 (Heb.)
Maguire, Henry (ed.) 1995 *Byzantine Magic*, Washington, DC: Dumbarton Oaks
— 1997 "Magic and Money in the Early Middle Ages," *Speculum* 72, pp. 1037–54
Malinowski, Bronislaw 1925 "Magic, Science and Religion," in J. A. Needham (ed.), *Science, Religion and Reality*, London: Sheldon Press, pp. 19–84
Maltomini, Franco 1979 "I papiri greci," *SCO* 29, pp. 55–124
— 1995 "P.Lond. 121 (=PGM VII), 1–221: Homeromanteion," *ZPE* 106, pp. 107–22
Mann, J. 1931–35 *Texts and Studies in Jewish History and Literature*, vol. I, Cincinnati: Hebrew Union College Press, vol. II, Philadelphia: Jewish Publication Society (repr. of both volumes, New York: Ktav, 1972)
Manns, F. 1978 "Gemmes de l'époque Gréco-Romaine provenant de Palestine," *LA* 28, pp. 147–70
Marcus, Ivan G. 1996 *Rituals of Childhood: Jewish Acculturation in Medieval Europe*, New Haven: Yale University Press
Margalioth, Mordechai 1966 *Sepher Ha-Razim: A Newly Recovered Book of Magic from the Talmudic Period*, Tel Aviv: Yediot Acharonot (Heb.)
Marmorstein, A. 1925 "Beiträge zur Religionsgeschichte und Volkskunde. II," *JJV* 27, pp. 283–344
Marrassini, Paolo 1979 "I frammenti aramaici," *SCO* 29, pp. 125–30
Martin, Dale B. 2004 *Inventing Superstition: From the Hippocratics to the Christians*, Cambridge, MA: Harvard University Press
Martinez, David G. 1991 *A Greek Love Charm from Egypt (P. Mich. 757)*, P. Michigan XVI = ASP 30, Atlanta, GA: Scholars Press
Mastrocinque, Attilio 2002 "Studies in Gnostic Gems: The Gem of Judah," *JSJ* 33, pp. 164–70
— 2005 *From Jewish Magic to Gnosticism*, Studien und Texte zu Antike und Christentum 24, Tübingen: Mohr Siebeck
Matras, Hagit 1997 *Hebrew Charm Books: Contents and Origins (Based on Books Printed in Europe During the 18th Century)*, unpubl. Ph.D. diss., Jerusalem (Heb.)
— 2005 "Creation and Re-Creation: A Study in Charm Books," in Elior and Schäfer 2005, pp. 147*–164* (Heb.)
McCollough, C. T. and B. Glazier-McDonald 1996 "An Aramaic Amulet from Sepphoris," *'Atiqot* 28, pp. 161–65

McCollough, C. T. 1998 "Social Magic and Social Realities in Late Roman and Early Byzantine Galilee," in Eric M. Meyers (ed.), *Galilee Through the Centuries: Confluence of Cultures*, Duke Judaic Studies 1, Winona Lake, IN: Eisenbrauns, pp. 269–80

McCown, C. C. 1922a *The Testament of Solomon*, Leipzig: J. C. Hinrichs
  1922b "The Christian Tradition as to the Magical Wisdom of Solomon," *JPOS* 2, pp. 1–24
  1923 "The Ephesia Grammata in Popular Belief," *TAPA* 54, pp. 128–40

Meimaris, Yiannis E. 1992 *Chronological Systems in Roman-Byzantine Palestine and Arabia: The Evidence of the Dated Greek Inscriptions*, Meletêmata 17, Athens: Research Center for Greek and Roman Antiquity

Meiri, David 1998 *Kabbalah Maasit, Teruphot ve-Segullot bi-Ktav Yado shel ḥakham Meir ben Ezri (Ezra), ZAẒAL, Asher Nikhtav be-Erekh bi-Shnat 1896*, Rishon Le-Ẓiyon: n.p. (Heb.)

Merkelbach, Reinhold and Maria Totti 1990–2001 *Abrasax: Ausgewählte Papyri Religiösen und Magischen Inhalts*, Papyrologica Coloniensia 17, Opladen: Westdeutscher Verlag, vol. I, 1990, vol. II, 1991, vol. III (by Merkelbach), 1992, vol. IV (by Merkelbach), 1996, vol. V (by Merkelbach), 2001

Meyer, Marvin and Paul Mirecki (eds.) 1995 *Ancient Magic and Ritual Power*, RGRW 129, Leiden: Brill

Meyer, Marvin and Richard Smith 1994 *Ancient Christian Magic: Coptic Texts of Ritual Power*, San Francisco: HarperSanFrancisco

Michel, Simone 2001 *Die Magischen Gemmen im Britischen Museum*, (herausgegeben von Peter und Hilde Zazoff), 2 vols., London: British Museum Press

Milik, J. T. 1976 *The Books of Enoch: Aramaic Fragments of Qumrân Cave 4*, Oxford: Clarendon Press

Mirecki, Paul and Marvin Meyer (eds.) 2002 *Magic and Ritual in the Ancient World*, RGRW 141, Leiden: Brill

Misgav, Haggai 1999 *The Epigraphic Sources (Hebrew and Aramaic) in Comparison with the Tradition Reflected in the Talmudic Literature*, unpubl. Ph.D. diss., Jerusalem (Heb.)

Mock, Leo 2001 "Were the Rabbis Troubled by Witches?" *Zutot* 1, pp. 33–43
  2003 "The Synagogue as a Stage for Magic," *Zutot* 3, pp. 8–14

Momigliano, Arnaldo 1987 "What Josephus Did Not See," in *id., On Pagans, Jews and Christians*, Middletown, CT: Wesleyan University Press, pp. 108–19 and 318–19

Monaco, Lucia 1984 "*Veneficia matronarum*: Magia, medicina e repressione," in *Sodalitas: Scritti in onore di Antonio Guarino*, 6 vols., Napoli: Jovene, vol. IV, pp. 2013–24

Montgomery, James A. 1913 *Aramaic Incantation Texts from Nippur*, Philadelphia University Museum, Publications of the Babylonian Section 3, Philadelphia: University Museum

Moore, C. A. 1996 *Tobit*, Anchor Bible, 40A, New York

Moore, G. F. 1921 "Christian Writers on Judaism," *HTR* 14, pp. 197–254

Morgan, Michael A. (tr.) 1983, *Sepher Ha-Razim: The Book of the Mysteries*, Chico, CA: Scholars Press

Morgenstern, Matthew 2004 "Notes on a Recently Published Magic Bowl," *Aramaic Studies* 2, pp. 207–22

Moriggi, Marco 2005 "Two New Incantation Bowls from Rome (Italy)," *Aramaic Studies* 3, pp. 43–58

Morony, Michael G. 1984 *Iraq after the Muslim Conquest*, Princeton: Princeton University Press

— 2003 "Magic and Society in Late Sasanian Iraq," in Noegel, Walker, and Wheeler 2003, pp. 83–107

Müller, Hans-Peter 2000 "Die tabella defixionis KAI 89 und die Magie des Fluches," *Orientalia* 69, pp. 393–406

Müller-Kessler, Christa 1998a "A Mandaic Gold Amulet in the British Museum," *BASOR* 311, pp. 83–88

— 1998b "Aramäische Koine: Ein Beschwörungsformular aus Mesopotamien," *Baghdader Mitteilungen* 29, pp. 331–48

— 1999a "Interrelations between Mandaic Lead Rolls and Incantation Bowls," in Abusch and van der Toorn 1999, pp. 197–209

— 1999b "Puzzling Words and Spellings in Babylonian Aramaic Magic Bowls," *BSOAS* 62, pp. 111–14

— 2001 "The Earliest Evidence for Targum Onqelos from Mesopotamia," *Journal for the Aramaic Bible* 3, pp. 181–98

— 2002 "Die aramäische Beschwörung und ihre Rezeption in den mandäisch-magischen Texten am Beispiel ausgewählter aramäischer Beschwörungsformulare," in R. Gyselen (ed.), *Charmes et Sortilèges, Magie et Magiciens*, Res Orientales XIV, Louvain: Peeters, pp. 193–208

— 2005 *Die Zauberschalentexte in der Hilprecht-Sammlung Jena*, Wiesbaden: Harrassowitz

Müller-Kessler, C. and K. Kessler 1999 "Spätbabylonische Gottheiten in spätantiken mandäischen Texten," *Zeitschrift für Assyriologie* 89, pp. 65–87

Müller-Kessler, C. and T. Kwasman 2000 "A Unique Talmudic Aramaic Incantation Bowl," *JAOS* 120, pp. 159–65

Müller-Kessler, C., T. C. Mitchell, and M. I. Hockey 2007 "An Inscribed Silver Amulet from Samaria," *PEQ* 139, pp. 5–19

Muntner, S. 1957 *Introduction to the Book of Assaph the Physician*, Jerusalem: Geniza (Heb.)

Nagy, Árpád M. 2002a "*Gemmae magicae selectae*: Sept notes sur l'interprétation des gemmes magiques," in A. Mastrocinque (ed.), *Gemme gnostiche e cultura ellenistica*, Verona: Pàtron, pp. 153–79

— 2002b "Figuring Out the Anguipede ("Snake-Legged God") and His Relation to Judaism," *Journal of Roman Archaeology* 15, pp. 159–72

Naveh, Joseph 1978 *On Stone and Mosaic: The Aramaic and Hebrew Inscriptions from Ancient Synagogues*, Jerusalem: Karta (Heb.)

— 1979 "A Nabatean Incantation Text," *IEJ* 29, pp. 111–19

— 1982 "An Ancient Amulet or a Modern Forgery?" *CBQ* 44, pp. 282–84

1985 "'A Good Subduing, There is None Like It': An Amulet from Ḥorvat Marish in the Galilee," *Tarbiz* 54, pp. 367–82 (Heb.)
1988 "Lamp Inscriptions and Inverted Writing," *IEJ* 38, pp. 36–43
1989 "The Aramaic and Hebrew Inscriptions from Ancient Synagogues," *Eretz-Israel* 20, pp. 302–10 (Heb.)
1992 *On Sherd and Papyrus: Aramaic and Hebrew Inscriptions from the Second Temple, Mishnaic and Talmudic Period*, Jerusalem: Magnes (Heb.)
1996 "On Ancient Jewish Magical Recipe Books," in A. Oppenheimer, I. Gafni, and D. Schwartz (eds.), *The Jews in the Hellenistic and Roman World*, Menahem Stern Memorial Volume, Jerusalem: Shazar, pp. 453–65 (Heb.)
1997 "A Syriac Amulet on Leather," *JSS* 42, pp. 33–38
1998 "Fragments of an Aramaic Magic Book From Qumran," *IEJ* 48, pp. 252–61
2001 "An Aramaic Amulet from Bar'am," in A. J. Avery-Peck and J. Neusner (eds.), *Judaism in Late Antiquity* pt 3, vol. IV, Handbook of Oriental Studies I, 55, Leiden: Brill, pp. 179–85
2002a "Epigraphic Miscellanea," *IEJ* 52, pp. 240–53
2002b "Some New Jewish Palestinian Aramaic Amulets," *JSAI* 26, pp. 231–36
2002c "Script and Inscriptions in Ancient Samaria," in E. Stern and H. Eshel (eds.), *The Samaritans*, Jerusalem: Ben-Zvi, pp. 372–81

Neusner, Jacob 1966–67 "Rabbi and Magus in Third-Century Sasanian Babylonia," *HR* 6, pp. 169–78 (repr. in his *Talmudic Judaism in Sasanian Babylonia*, Studies in Judaism in Late Antiquity 14, Leiden: Brill, 1976, pp. 78–86)
1987 *Wonder-Working Lawyers of Talmudic Babylonia*, Lanham, MD: University Press of America
1989 "Science and Magic, Miracle and Magic in Formative Judaism: The System and the Difference," in Neusner, Frerichs, and Flesher 1989, pp. 61–81

Neusner, Jacob, Ernest S. Frerichs, and Paul V. M. Flesher (eds.) 1989 *Religion, Science, and Magic In Concert and In Conflict*, New York and Oxford: Oxford University Press

Névérov, O. Ya. 1978 "Gemmes, bagues et amulettes magiques du sud de l'URSS," in Margreet B. de Boer and T. A. Edridge (eds.), *Hommages à Maarten J. Vermaseren*, EPRO 78, 2 vols., Leiden: Brill, vol. II, pp. 833–48 and pl. CLXVII–CLXXVI

Nickelsburg, George W. E. 1981 "Enoch, Levi, and Peter: Recipients of Revelation in Upper Galilee," *JBL* 100, pp. 575–600

Nigal, Gedalyah 1994 *"Dybbuk" Tales in Jewish Literature*, 2nd edn, Jerusalem: Rubin Mass (Heb.)

Niggemeyer, Jens-Heinrich 1975 *Beschwörungsformeln aus dem "Buch der Geheimnisse" (Sefär ha-Razim): Zur Topologie der magischen Rede*, Judäistische Texte und Studien 3, Hildesheim: Olms

Nitzan, Bilhah 1992 "Hymns from Qumran – 4Q510–4Q511," in D. Dimant and U. Rappaport (eds.), *The Dead Sea Scrolls: Forty Years*, Leiden: Brill, pp. 53–63
1994 *Qumran Prayer and Religious Poetry*, (tr. from the Hebrew by Jonathan Chipman), Studies on the Texts of the Desert of Judah 12, Leiden: Brill

Nock, A. D. 1929 "Greek Magical Papyri," *JEA* 15, pp. 219–35 (repr. in *Essays in Religion and the Ancient World* (ed. Z. Stewart), Cambridge, MA: Harvard University Press, 1972, vol. I, pp. 176–88)

Noegel, Scott B., Joel Walker, and Brannon M. Wheeler (eds.) 2003 *Prayer, Magic, and the Stars in the Ancient and Late Antique World*, Magic in History Series, Pennsylvania State University Press

Obermann, Julian 1940 "Two Magic Bowls: New Incantation Texts from Mesopotamia," *American Journal of Semitic Languages and Literatures* 57, pp. 1–31

Oelsner, Joachim 2005 "Incantations in Southern Mesopotamia – From Clay Tablets to Magical Bowls (Thoughts on the Decline of the Babylonian Culture)," in Shaked 2005a, pp. 31–51

Olyan, Saul M. 1993 *A Thousand Thousands Served Him: Exegesis and the Naming of Angels in Ancient Judaism*, TSAJ 36, Tübingen: Mohr

Ovadiah, A. and S. Mucznik 1996 "A Fragmentary Roman Zodiac and Horoscope from Caesarea Maritima," *LA* 46, pp. 375–80

Papamichael-Koutroubas, Anna J. 1986 "Jewish Sources of Greek Amulets and Charms," *Proceedings of the Ninth World Congress of Jewish Studies*, Jerusalem: World Union of Jewish Studies, Division D, vol. II, pp. 167–74

Papayannopoulos, Ioannis, J. Laskaratos, and S. Marketos 1985 "Remarks on Tobit's Blindness," *Koroth* 9, 1/2, pp. 181–87

Parpola, Simo 1993 "The Assyrian Tree of Life: Tracing the Origins of Jewish Monotheism and Greek Philosophy," *JNES* 52, pp. 161–209

Patai, Raphael 1942–43 *Man and Earth in Hebrew Custom, Belief and Legend: A Study in Comparative Religion*, 2 vols., Jerusalem: Hebrew University (Heb.)

1994 *The Jewish Alchemists: A History and Source Book*, Princeton: Princeton University Press

Penner, Hans H. 1989 "Rationality, Ritual, and Science," in Neusner, Frerichs, and Flesher 1989, pp. 11–24

Penney, Douglas L. and Michael O. Wise 1994 "By the Power of Beelzebub: An Aramaic Incantation Formula from Qumran (4Q560)," *JBL* 113, pp. 627–50

Pernigotti, Sergio 1979 "Il codice copto," *SCO* 29, pp. 19–53

1993 "Una Rilettura del P.Mil. Vogl. Copto 16," *Aegyptus* 73, pp. 93–125

1995 "La magia copta: I testi," *ANRW* II.18.5, pp. 3685–730

Perrin, Michel-Yves 2002 "'Rendre un culte aux anges à la manière des Juifs': Quelques observations nouvelles d'ordre historiographique et historique," *Mélanges de l'École Française de Rome: Moyen Âge* 114, pp. 669–700

Petrovsky-Shtern, Yohanan 2004 "The Master of the Evil Name: Hillel Ba'al Shem and His *Sepher ha-Heshek*," *AJS Review* 28, pp. 217–48

Petzl, Georg 1994 *Die Beichtinschriften Westkleinasiens*, [=*Epigraphica Anatolica* 22 (1994)], Bonn: Rudolph Habelt

Phillips, Charles Robert 1986 "The Sociology of Religious Knowledge in the Roman Empire to A.D. 284," *ANRW* II.16.3, pp. 2677–773

Philonenko, Marc 1961 "Remarques sur un hymne Essénien de caractère gnostique," *Semitica* 11, pp. 43–54

1979 "L'anguipède alectorocéphale et le dieu Iaô," *CRAIBL* 1979, pp. 297–304

Pietersma, A. 1994 *The Apocryphon of Jannes and Jambres the Magicians*, RGRW 119, Leiden: Brill

Pinch, Geraldine 1994 *Magic in Ancient Egypt*, London: British Museum Press

Pines, Shlomo 1976 "The Oath of Asaph the Physician and Yohanan ben Zabda – Its Relation to the Hippocratic Oath and the *Doctrina Duarum Viarum* of the Didachê," *Proceedings of the Israel Academy of Sciences and Humanities* 5, pp. 223–64

Plotkin, Mark J. 1993 *Tales of a Shaman's Apprentice : An Ethnobotanist Searches for New Medicines in the Rain Forest*, New York: Viking

Podemann Sørensen, Jørgen 1984 "The Argument in Ancient Egyptian Magical Formulae," *Acta Orientalia* 45, pp. 5–19

Preisendanz, Karl 1927 "Die griechischen Zauberpapyri," *Archiv für Papyrusforschung* 8, pp. 104–67

1935 "Ein altes Ewigkeitssymbol als Signet und Druckmarke," *Gutenberg-Jahrbuch 1935*, pp. 143–49

Preuss, Julius 1993 *Biblical and Talmudic Medicine*, (tr. and ed. by Fred Rosner), Northvale, NJ: Jason Aronson (1st Eng. edn, 1978; 1st Ger. edn, 1911)

Procopé-Walter, A. 1933 "Iao und Set (zu den *figurae magicae* in den Zauberpapyri)," *ARW* 30, pp. 34–69

Puech, E. 1990 "11QPsAp^a: Un rituel d'exorcismes: Essai de reconstruction," *RQ* 55, pp. 377–408

2000 "Les Psaumes davidiques du rituel d'éxorcisme (11Q11)," in Daniel K. Falk et al. (eds.), *Sapiential, Liturgical and Poetical Texts from Qumran*, Leiden: Brill, pp. 160–81

Pummer, R. 1987 "Samaritan Amulets from the Roman-Byzantine Period and their Wearers," *RB* 94, pp. 251–63

Puschmann, Th. 1878–89 *Alexander von Tralles*, 2 vols., Vienna: Wilhelm Braumüller

Qimron, Elisha 1986 *The Hebrew of the Dead Sea Scrolls*, Harvard Semitic Studies, Atlanta: Scholars Press

Rabinovitz, Zvi Meir 1965 *Halakha and Aggada in the Liturgical Poetry of Yannai*, New York and Tel-Aviv: Alexander Kohut Fund (Heb.)

Ravitzky, A. 2002 "Maimonides and His Disciples on Linguistic Magic and "the Madness of the Writers of Amulets," in A. Sagi and N. Ilan (eds.), *Jewish Culture in the Eye of the Storm: A Jubilee Book in Honor of Yosef Ahituv*, Tel-Aviv: Hakibbutz Hameuchad, pp. 431–58 (Heb.)

Ray, John 1994 "How Demotic is Demotic?" in *Acta Demotica: Acts of the Fifth International Conference for Demotists, (Pisa, 4th-8th September 1993)*, Egitto e Vicino Oriente 17 (1994), Pisa: Giardini, pp. 251–64

Rebiger, Bill 1999 "Bildung magischer Namen im *Sepher Shimmush Tehillim*," *FJB* 26, pp. 7–24

Reed, Annette Yoshiko 2004 "Abraham as Chaldean Scientist and Father of the Jews: Josephus, *Ant.* 1.154–68, and the Greco-Roman Discourse about Astronomy / Astrology," *JSJ* 35, pp. 119–58

2005 *Fallen Angels and the History of Judaism and Christianity: The Reception of Enochic Literature*, Cambridge: Cambridge University Press

Reich, R. 2002 "Samaritan Amulets from the Late Roman and Byzantine Periods," in E. Stern and H. Eshel (eds.), *The Samaritans*, Jerusalem: Ben-Zvi, pp. 289–309 (Heb.)

Reif, Stefan C. 2000 *A Jewish Archive from Old Cairo: The History of Cambridge University's Genizah Collection*, Richmond, Surrey: Curzon Press

Reif, Stefan C. and Shulamit Reif (eds.) 2002 *The Cambridge Genizah Collections: Their Contents and Significance*, Cambridge: Cambridge University Press

Reifenberg, A. 1950 *Ancient Hebrew Arts*, New York: Schoken

Reimer, Andy M. 2000 "Rescuing the Fallen Angels: The Case of the Disappearing Angels at Qumran," *DSD* 7, pp. 334–53

Reiner, Elhanan 2004 "Joseph the Comes of Tiberias and the Jewish-Christian Dialogue in Fourth-Century Galilee," in Lee I. Levine (ed.), *Continuity and Renewal: Jews and Judaism in Byzantine-Christian Palestine*, Jerusalem: Ben-Zvi and New York: JTSA, pp. 355–86 (Heb.)

Reuss 1856 "Über den Gebrauch homerischer und anderer griechischer Verse bei therapeutischen Besprechungen, und Anbeitung einer Sammlung von Materialien hierüber," *Serapeum* 17, pp. 351–52

Rist, Martin 1938 "The God of Abraham, Isaac, and Jacob: A Liturgical and Magical Formula," *JBL* 57, pp. 289–303

Ritner, Robert K. 1993 *The Mechanics of Ancient Egyptian Magical Practice*, SAOC 54, Chicago: Oriental Institute

1995a "The Religious, Social, and Legal Parameters of Traditional Egyptian Magic," in Meyer and Mirecki 1995, pp. 43–60

1995b "Egyptian Magical Practice under the Roman Empire: the Demotic Spells and their Religious Context," *ANRW* II.18.5, pp. 3333–79

Robert, Louis 1981 "Amulettes grecques," *Journal des Savants* 1981, pp. 3–44

Robinson, Ira 1983 "Jacob al-Kirkisani on the Reality of Magic and the Nature of the Miraculous: A Study in Tenth-Century Karaite Rationalism," in H. Joseph, J. N. Lightstone, and M. D. Oppenheim (eds.), *Truth and Compassion: Essays on Judaism and Religion in Memory of Rabbi Dr. Solomon Frank*, Waterloo, Ontario, Canada: Wilfrid Laurier University Press, pp. 41–55

Rohrbacher-Sticker, Claudia 1996 "From Sense to Nonsense, From Incantation Prayer to Magical Spell," *JSQ* 3, pp. 24–46

Rosenfeld, Ben-Zion 1999 "R. Simeon Bar Yohai: Wonder Worker and Magician, Scholar, *Saddiq* and *Hasid*," *REJ* 158, pp. 349–84

Rosenthal, Eliezer Shimshon 1991 "Ba'ra," *Tarbiz* 60, pp. 325–53 (Heb.)

Roth, N. (ed.) 2003 *Medieval Jewish Civilization: An Encyclopedia*, London: Routledge

Rowlands, Alison 1996 "Witchcraft and Popular Religion in Early Modern Rothenburg ob der Tauber," in Bob Scribner and Trevor Johnson (eds.), *Popular Religion in Germany and Central Europe, 1400–1800*, London: Macmillan, pp. 101–18 and 245–49

Rubin, Nissan 1995 *The Beginning of Life: Rites of Birth, Circumcision and Redemption of the First-born in the Talmud and Midrash*, Tel-Aviv: Hakkibutz Hameuchad (Heb.)

Rubin, S. 1887 *Geschichte des Aberglaubens bei allen Völkern, mit Besonderen Hinblicke auf das Jüdische Volk*, Vienna: Georg Brög (Heb.)

Rubin, Zeev 1982 "Joseph the Comes and the Attempts to Convert the Galilee to Christianity in the Fourth Century C.E.," *Cathedra* 26, pp. 105–16 (Heb.)

Russell, James 1995 "The Archaeological Context of Magic in the Early Byzantine Period," in Maguire 1995, pp. 35–50

Saar, Ortal 2003 *Superstitions in Israel during the Roman and Early-Byzantine Periods*, unpubl. MA thesis, Tel-Aviv University (Heb.)

Sabar, Shalom 2000 "Torah and Magic: the Torah Scroll and Its Accessories in Jewish Culture in Europe and in Muslim Countries," *Pe'amim* 85, pp. 149–79 (Heb.)

Safrai, S. 1965 "Teachings of Pietists in Mishnaic Literature," *JJS* 16, pp. 15–33

Sagan, Carl 1996 *The Demon-Haunted World: Science as a Candle in the Dark*, New York: Ballantine Books

Salzer, Dorothea forthcoming "Biblische Anspielungen als Konstitutionsmerkmal jüdischer magischer Texte aus der Kairoer Geniza," in Stefan Schorch and Ludwig Morenz (eds.), *Was ist ein Text?: Alttestamentliche, Ägyptologische, altorientalistische und judaistische Perspektiven*, Berlin: De Gruyter

Salzman, Marcus 1924 *The Chronicle of Ahimaaz*, New York: Columbia University Press (repr. New York: AMS, 1966)

Sanders, J. A. 1965 *The Psalms Scroll of Qumrân Cave 11 (11QPs ᵃ)*, DJD IV, Oxford: Clarendon Press

   1967 *The Dead Sea Psalms Scroll*, Ithaca, NY: Cornell University Press

Sarfatti, G. Ben-Ami 1956/57 "Pious Men, Men of Deeds, and the Early Prophets," *Tarbiz* 26, pp. 126–53 (Heb.)

Sassoon, David Solomon 1932 *Ohel David: Descriptive Catalogue of the Hebrew and Samaritan Manuscripts*, 2 vols., Oxford: Oxford University Press, and London: Humphrey Milford

Scarborough, John 1984 "Early Byzantine Pharmacology," *DOP* 38, pp. 213–32

Schäfer, Peter 1983 "Tradition and Redaction in Hekhalot Literature," *JSJ* 14, pp. 172–81 (repr. in Schäfer 1988, pp. 8–16)

   1986 "The Delimitation of Hekhalot Literature," in *Ninth World Congress of Jewish Studies*, Jerusalem: World Union of Jewish Studies, Division C, pp. 87–92 (Heb.)

   1988 *Hekhalot-Studien*, TSAJ 19, Tübingen: Mohr

   1990 "Jewish Magic Literature in Late Antiquity and the Early Middle Ages," *JJS* 41, pp. 75–91

   1991 *Übersetzung der Hekhalot-Literatur, vol. 4 (§598–985)*, TSAJ 29, Tübingen: Mohr

   1993 "Merkavah Mysticism and Magic," in P. Schäfer and J. Dan (eds.), *Gershom Scholem's Major Trends in Jewish Mysticism 50 Years After*, Tübingen: Mohr, pp. 59–78

1995 "The Magic of the Golem: The Early Development of the Golem Legend," *JJS* 46, pp. 249–61

1996 "Jewish Liturgy and Magic," in Hubert Cancik, Herman Lichtenberger, and Peter Schäfer (eds.), *Geschichte-Tradition-Reflexion: Festschrift für Martin Hengel zum 70. Geburtstag*, 3 vols., Tübingen: Mohr Siebeck, vol. I, pp. 541–56

1997 "Magic and Religion in Ancient Judaism," in Schäfer and Kippenberg 1997, pp. 19–43

Schäfer, Peter and Hans G. Kippenberg (eds.) 1997 *Envisioning Magic: A Princeton Seminar and Symposium*, Studies in the History of Religions 75, Leiden: Brill

Schiffman, Lawrence H. 1973 "A Forty-Two Letter Divine Name in the Aramaic Magic Bowls," *Bulletin of the Institute of Jewish Studies* 1, pp. 97–102

2000 "Phylacteries and Mezuzot," in Lawrence H. Schiffman and James C. VanderKam (eds.), *Encyclopedia of the Dead Sea Scrolls*, 2 vols., Oxford: Oxford University Press, vol. II, pp. 675–77

Schlüter, Margarete 1982 *"Deraqôn" und Götzendienst*, Judentum und Umwelt 4, Frankfurt a/Mein: Peter Lang

Schmitt, Rüdiger 2004 *Magie im Alten Testament*, Alter Orient und Altes Testament 313, Münster: Ugarit-Verlag

Schmoll, U. 1963 "Die hebräische Inschrift des Goldsplättchens von Comiso," *ZDMG* 113, pp. 512–14

Scholem, Gershom G. 1941 *Major Trends in Jewish Mysticism*, New York: Schocken

1953 "Die Vorstellung vom Golem in ihren tellurischen und magischen Beziehungen," *Eranos-Jahrbücher* 20, pp. 235–89 (repr. in *Zur Kabbalah und ihrer Symbolik*, Zürich: Rhein-Verlag, 1960, pp. 209–59) (Eng. tr. in Scholem 1965, pp. 158–204)

1960 *Jewish Gnosticism, Merkabah Mysticism and Talmudic Tradition*, New York: Jewish Theological Seminary (2nd edn, 1965)

1963 "Has A Legacy been Discovered of Mystic Writings Left by Abu Aharon of Baghdad?" *Tarbiz* 32, pp. 252–65 (Heb.)

1965 *On the Kabbalah and Its Symbolism*, New York: Schoken

1974 *Kabbalah*, Jerusalem: Keter

1980/81 "Havdala de-Rabbi Aqiva – A Source for the Tradition of Jewish Magic During the Geonic Period," *Tarbiz* 50, pp. 243–81 (Heb.) (repr. in Esther Liebes (ed.), *Demons, Ghosts and Souls: Studies in Demonology by Gershom Scholem*, Jerusalem: Ben-Zvi, 2004, pp. 145–82 (Heb.))

1987 *Origins of the Kabbalah*, (ed. by R. J. Zwi Werblowsky; Eng. tr. by Allan Arkush), Philadelphia: Jewish Publication Society (repr. Princeton, 1990)

Schrire, T. 1966 *Hebrew Amulets: Their Decipherment and Interpretation*, London: Routledge & Kegan Paul

Schürer, E. 1973–87 *The History of the Jewish People in the Age of Jesus Christ* (rev. and ed. by G. Vermes, F. Millar, and M. Goodman), 3 vols., Edinburgh: T&T Clark

Schwab, Moïse 1892 "Médailles et amulettes à légendes hébraiques," *Revue Numismatique*, ser. 3, vol. X, pp. 241–58

1897 *Vocabulaire de l'Angélologie d'après les manuscrits hébreux de la Bibliothèque Nationale*, Paris: Klinsieck

Schwartz, Dov 1999 *Astral Magic in Medieval Jewish Thought*, Ramat Gan: Bar-Ilan University Press (Heb.)

Schwartz, Seth 2002 *Imperialism and Jewish Society, 200 B.C.E. to 640 C.E.*, Princeton and Oxford: Princeton University Press

Sciacca, Sergio 1982–83 "Phylakterion con iscrizione magica Graeco-Ebraica proveniente dalla Sicilia sud-occidentale," *Kokalos* 28–29, pp. 87–104

Scurlock, JoAnn 2002 "Translating Transfers in Ancient Mesopotamia," in Mirecki and Meyer 2002, pp. 209–23

Sed, N. 1971 "Le Sepher-Ha-Razim et la méthode de 'combinaison des lettres'," *REJ* 130, pp. 295–304

Sefati, Yitschak and Jacob Klein 2004 "The Law of the Sorceress (Exodus 22:17[18]) in the Light of Biblical and Mesopotamian Parallels," in Chaim Cohen, Avi Hurvitz, and Shalom M. Paul (eds.), *Sepher Moshe: The Moshe Weinfeld Jubilee Volume*, Winona Lake, IN: Eisenbrauns, pp. 171–90

Segal, Alan F. 1981 "Hellenistic Magic: Some Questions of Definitions," in R. van den Broek and M. J. Vermasseren (eds.), *Studies in Gnosticism and Hellenistic Religions*, EPRO 91, Leiden: Brill, pp. 349–75 (repr. in Segal, *The Other Judaisms of Late Antiquity*, Atlanta: Scholars Press, Brown Judaic Studies 127 [1987], pp. 79–108)

Segal, J. B. 2000 *Catalogue of the Aramaic and Mandaic Incantation Bowls in the British Museum*, London: British Museum Press

Segev, Dror 2001 *Medieval Magic and Magicians – in Norway and Elsewhere: Based upon 12th–15th Centuries Manuscript and Runic Evidence*, Centre for Viking and Medieval Studies, Occasional Papers 2, Oslo: Centre for Viking and Medieval Studies

Seidel, Jonathan 1992 "'Release Us and We Will Release You': Rabbinic Encounters with Witches and Witchcraft," *JAGNES* 3, pp. 45–61

— 1995 "Charming Criminals: Classification of Magic in the Babylonian Talmud," in Meyer and Mirecki 1995, pp. 145–66

— 1996 *Studies in Ancient Jewish Magic*, unpubl. Ph.D. diss., University of California Berkeley

Seland, Torrey 2006 "Philo, Magic and Balaam: Neglected Aspects of Philo's Exposition of the Balaam Story," in John Fotopoulos (ed.), *The New Testament and Early Christian Literature in Greco-Roman Context: Studies in Honor of David E. Aune*, Suppl. to Novum Testamentum 122, Leiden: Brill, pp. 336–46

Seligman, Siegfried 1927 *Die magischen Heil- und Schutzmittel aus der unbelebten Natur, mit besonderer Berücksichtigung der Mittel gegen den bösen Blick: Eine Geschichte des Amulettwesens*, Stuttgart: Strecker and Schröder

Shaked, Shaul 1985 "Bagdâna, King of the Demons, and Other Iranian Terms in Babylonian Aramaic Magic," in *Papers in Honour of Professor Mary Boyce, Acta Iranica* 25 = Hommages et Opera Minora 11, Leiden: Brill, pp. 511–25

1988a "An Early Magic Fragment from the Cairo Geniza," in *Occident and Orient: A Tribute to the Memory of A. Scheiber*, Budapest: Akademiai Kiado pp. 361–71

1988b "An Early Geniza Fragment in an Unknown Iranian Dialect," in *A Green Leaf: Papers in Honour of Professor Jes P. Asmussen, Acta Iranica* 28 = Hommages et Opera Minora 12, Leiden: Brill, pp. 219–35

1994 "The Zoroastrian Demon of Wrath," in Christoph Elsas *et al.* (eds.), *Tradition und Translation: Zum Problem der interkulturellen Übersetzbarkeit religiöser Phänomene, Festschrift für Carsten Colpe zum 65. Geburtstag*, Berlin: De Gruyter, pp. 285–91

1995 "'Peace be Upon You, Exalted Angels': On Hekhalot, Liturgy and Incantation Bowls," *JSQ* 2, pp. 197–219

1996 "Review of D. Sperber, Magic and Folklore in Rabbinic Literature," *BO* 53, pp. 516–19

1997 "Popular Religion in Sasanian Babylonia," *JSAI* 21, pp. 103–17

1999a "The Poetics of Spells: Language and Structure in Aramaic Incantations of Late Antiquity 1: The Divorce Formula and Its Ramifications," in Abusch and van der Toorn 1999, pp. 173–95

1999b "Jesus in the Magic Bowls: Apropos Dan Levene's ' . . . and by the name of Jesus . . . '," *JSQ* 6, pp. 309–19

2000a "Manichaean Incantation Bowls in Syriac," *JSAI* 24, pp. 58–92

2000b "Medieval Jewish Magic in Relation to Islam: Theoretical Attitudes and Genres," in B. H. Hary, J. L. Hayes, and F. Astern (eds.), *Judaism and Islam: Boundaries, Communication and Interaction (Essays in Honor of William M. Brinner)*, Leiden: Brill, pp. 97–109

2002 "Jews, Christians and Pagans in the Aramaic Incantation Bowls of the Sasanian Period," in Adriana Destro and Mauro Pesce (eds.), *Religions and Cultures: First International Conference of Mediterraneum*, Binghamton University, pp. 61–89

(ed.) 2005a *Officina Magica: Essays on the Practice of Magic in Antiquity*, Institute of Jewish Studies, Studies in Judaica 4, Leiden: Brill

2005b "Form and Purpose in Aramaic Spells: Some Jewish Themes (The Poetics of Magic Texts)," in Shaked 2005a, pp. 1–30

2005c "Magical Bowls and Incantation Texts: How to Get Rid of Demons and Pests," *Qadmoniot* 129 (2005), pp. 2–13 (Heb.)

2006 "Notes on Some Jewish Aramaic Inscriptions from Georgia," *JSAI* 32, pp. 503–10

Shani, R. 1999 "A Judeo-Persian Talismanic Textile," *Irano-Judaica* 4, pp. 251–73

Sharot, Stephen 1982 *Messianism, Mysticism, and Magic: A Sociological Analysis of Jewish Religious Movements*, Chapel Hill: University of North Carolina Press

Shinan, Avigdor 1992 *The Embroidered Targum: The Aggadah in Targum Pseudo-Jonathan of the Pentateuch*, Jerusalem: Magnes (Heb.)

Siker, Jeffrey S. 1987 "Abraham in Graeco-Roman Paganism," *JSJ* 18, pp. 188–208

Simon, M. 1986 *Verus Israel: A Study of the Relations Between Christians and Jews in the Roman Empire (135–425)*, (Eng. tr. by H. McKeating), Oxford: Oxford University Press (or. French edn, Paris: Boccard, 1964)

Sirat, Colette 1985 *Les papyrus en caractères hébraïques trouvés en Égypte*, Paris: CNRS
  2002 *Hebrew Manuscripts of the Middle Ages* (ed. and tr. by N. de Lange), Cambridge: Cambridge University Press

Smelik, K. A. D. 1977 "The Witch of Endor: I Samuel 28 in Rabbinic and Christian Exegesis till 800 A.D.," *VC* 33, pp. 160–79
  1978 "An Aramaic Incantation Bowl in the Allard Pierson Museum," *BO* 35, pp. 175–77

Smith, Jonathan Z. 1995 "Trading Places," in Meyer and Mirecki 1995, pp. 13–27
  2002 "Great Scott! Thought and Action One More Time," in Mirecki and Meyer 2002, pp. 73–91

Smith, Morton 1978 *Jesus the Magician*, New York: Harper & Row
  1981 "Old Testament Motifs in the Iconography of the British Museum's Magical Gems," in Lionel Casson and Martin Price (eds.), *Coins, Culture and History in the Ancient World: Numismatic and Other Studies in Honor of Bluma L. Trell*, Detroit: Wayne State University Press, pp. 187–94
  1982 "Helios in Palestine," *Eretz-Israel* 16, pp. 199–214
  1983 "On the Lack of a History of Greco-Roman Magic," in H. Heinen (ed.), *Althistorische Studien (Hermann Bengtson Festschrift)*, Historia Einzelschriften 40, Wiesbaden: Franz Steiner, pp. 251–57
  1984 "The Eighth Book of Moses and how it Grew (PLeid. J 395)," in *Atti del XVII congresso internazionale di papirologia*, Napoli: Centro int. per lo studio dei papiri ercolanesi, vol. I, pp. 683–93
  1986 "P Leid J 395 (PGM XIII) and Its Creation Legend," in A. Caquot *et al.* (eds.), *Hellenica et Judaica: Valentin Nikoprowetsky Festschrift*, Leuven: Peeters, pp. 491–98 (repr. in *id.*, *Studies in the Cult of Yahweh*, RGRW 130, Leiden: Brill, 2 vols., 1996, vol. II, pp. 227–34)
  1986/1996 "The Jewish Elements in the Magical Papyri," *SBL Seminar Papers* 1986, pp. 455–62 (repr. with major improvements in *id.*, *Studies*, vol. II, pp. 242–56)
  1987 "The Occult in Josephus," in Louis H. Feldman and Gohei Hata (eds.), *Josephus, Judaism, and Christianity*, Detroit: Wayne State University Press, pp. 236–56

Smith, Wilfred Cantwell 1993 *What is Scripture?: A Comparative Approach*, Minneapolis: Fortress Press, and London: SCM Press

Smith, William Robertson 1884–85 "On the Forms of Divination and Magic Enumerated in Dt xviii.10, 11," *Journal of Philology* 13, pp. 273–87, and 14, pp. 113–28

Sokoloff, Michael 1990 *A Dictionary of Jewish Palestinian Aramaic of the Byzantine Period*, Bar-Ilan: Bar-Ilan University Press (2nd edn, 2002)
  2002 *A Dictionary of Jewish Babylonian Aramaic of the Talmudic and Geonic Periods*, Bar-Ilan: Bar-Ilan University Press

Sorensen, Eric 2002 *Possession and Exorcism in the New Testament and Early Christianity*, WUNT 2/157, Tübingen: Mohr Siebeck

Spaer, Maud 2001 *Ancient Glass in the Israel Museum: Beads and Other Small Objects*, Jerusalem: Israel Museum

Sperber, Daniel 1994 *Magic and Folklore in Rabbinic Literature*, Ramat Gan: Bar-Ilan University Press

Spier, Jeffrey 1993 "Medieval Byzantine Magical Amulets and their Tradition," *Journal of the Warburg and Courtauld Institutes* 56, pp. 25–62

— 2006 "A Revival of Antique Magical Practice in Tenth-Century Constantinople," in Burnett and Ryan 2006, pp. 29–36

— 2007 *Late Antique and Early Christian Gems*, Wiesbaden: Reichert Verlag

Staal, Frits 1989 *Rules Without Meaning: Ritual, Mantras and the Human Sciences*, New York: Peter Lang

Stein, Dina 2004 *Maxims Magic Myth: A Folkloristic Perspective of Pirkei de-Rabbi Eliezer*, Jerusalem: Magnes (Heb.)

Steinschneider, M. 1862 *Zur pseudepigraphischen Literatur des Mittelalters, insbesondere der geheimen Wissenschaften, aus hebräischen und arabischen Quellen*, Berlin (repr. Amsterdam: Philo Press, 1965)

Sterling, G. E. 1993 "Jesus as Exorcist: An Analysis of Matthew 17:14–20; Mark 9:14–29; Luke 9:37–43," *CBQ* 55, pp. 467–93

Stickel, Johann Gustav 1860 *De Ephesiis litteris linguae Semitarum vindicandis*, Universitätsprogramm Jena

Stol, M. 1986 "Blindness and Night-Blindness in Akkadian," *JNES* 45, pp. 295–99

Stoller, Paul and Cheryl Olkes 1987 *In Sorcery's Shadow: A Memoir of Apprenticeship among the Songhay of Niger*, Chicago and London: University of Chicago Press

Stroumsa, Gedalyahu G. 1983 "Form(s) of God: Some Notes on Meṭaṭron and Christ," *HTR* 76, pp. 269–88

Stuckenbruck, Loren T. 2002 "The Book of Tobit and the Problem of Magic," in Hermann Lichtenberger and Gerbern S. Oegema (eds.), *Jüdische Schriften in ihrem Antik-Jüdischen und Urchristlichen Kontext*, Gütersloh: Gütersloher Verlaghaus, pp. 258–69

Styers, Randall G. 2004 *Making Magic: Religion, Magic, and Science in the Modern World*, American Academy of Religion, Reflection and Theory in the Study of Religion Series, Oxford: Oxford University Press

Sussmann, Yaakov 1993 "The Scholarly Oeuvre of Professor E. E. Urbach," in *Ephraim Elimelech Urbach – A Bio-Bibliography*, Jerusalem, pp. 7–116 (Heb.)

— 2005 "Oral Torah – Indeed," in *Talmudic Studies Dedicated to the Memory of Professor Ephraim E. Urbach, Meḥqerqi Talmud* 3, 2 vols., Jerusalem: Magnes, pp. 209–384 (Heb.)

Swartz, Michael D. 1990 "Scribal Magic and Its Rhetoric: Formal Patterns in Hebrew and Aramaic Incantation Texts from the Cairo Genizah," *HTR* 83, pp. 163–80

— 1994a "Book and Traditions in Hekhalot and Magical Literature," *JJTP* 3, pp. 189–229

1994b "'Like the Ministering Angels': Ritual and Purity in Early Jewish Mysticism and Magic," *AJS Review* 19, pp. 135–67

1996 *Scholastic Magic: Ritual and Revelation in Early Jewish Mysticism*, Princeton: Princeton University Press

2000 "Temple Ritual in Jewish Magical Literature," *Pe'amim* 85, pp. 43–61 (Heb.)

2001 "The Dead Sea Scrolls and Later Jewish Magic and Mysticism," *DSD* 8, pp. 182–93

2006 "Jewish Magic in Late Antiquity," in Steven T. Katz (ed.), *The Cambridge History of Judaism*, vol. IV: *The Late Roman-Rabbinic Period*, Cambridge: Cambridge University Press, pp. 699–720

Sznol, Shifra 1989 "Sepher Ha-Razim – El Libro de los Secretos: Introduccion y Comentario al Vocabulario Griego," *Erytheia* 10, pp. 265–88

Tambiah, Stanley J. 1968 "The Magical Power of Words," *Man* 3, pp. 175–208

1990 *Magic, Science, Religion and the Scope of Rationality*, Cambridge: Cambridge University Press

Tan Ami, Alon 2001 *Rabbinic Motifs in Magic Incantation Bowls from Sasanian Babylonia*, unpubl. MA thesis, Jerusalem (Heb.)

Taylor, J. Glen 1993 *Yahweh and the Sun: Biblical and Archaeological Evidence for Sun Worship in Ancient Israel*, JSOT Suppl. 111, Sheffield

Thomas, Keith 1971 *Religion and the Decline of Magic*, London: Weidenfeld & Nicolson (repr. London: Penguin, 1991)

Thompson, R. Campbell 1906–07 "The Folklore of Mossoul," *Proceedings of the Society of Biblical Archaeology* 1906, pp. 76–86, 97–109, and 1907, pp. 165–74, 282–88, 323–31

1908 *Semitic Magic: Its Origins and Development*, London: Luzac and Co. (repr. New York: Ktav, 1971)

Thornton, T. C. G. 1990 "The Stories of Joseph of Tiberias," *VC* 44, pp. 54–63

Tocci, Franco Michelini 1986 "Note e documenti di letterature religiosa e parareligiosa giudaica," *Annali dell'Istituto Universitario Orientale di Napoli* 46, pp. 101–08

Torijano, Pablo A. 2002 *Solomon the Esoteric King: From King to Magus, Development of a Tradition*, JSJ Suppl. 73, Leiden: Brill

Trachtenberg, Joshua 1939 *Jewish Magic and Superstition: A Study in Folk Religion*, New York: Behrman's Jewish Book House (repr. Philadelphia: University of Pennsylvania Press, 2004, with an Introduction by Moshe Idel)

1943 *The Devil and the Jews: The Medieval Conception of the Jew and Its Relation to Modern Anti-Semitism*, New Haven: Yale University Press

Tsereteli, Konstantin 1996 "An Aramaic Amulet from Mtskheta," *Ancient Civilizations from Scythia to Siberia* 3, pp. 218–40

Turcan, Robert 2003 "Note sur les dieux 'portables'," in François Chausson and Étienne Wolff (eds.), *Consuetudinis amor: Fragments d'histoire romaine (IIe-VIe siècles) offerts à Jean-Pierre Callu*, Saggi di Storia Antica 19, Roma: "L'Erma" di Bretschneider, pp. 409–17

Twelftree, Graham H. 1993 *Jesus the Exorcist: A Contribution to the Study of the Historical Jesus*, WUNT 2/54, Tübingen: Mohr

Ullmann, Manfred 1978 *Islamic Medicine*, Edinburgh: Edinburgh University Press
Ulmer, Rivka 1994 *The Evil Eye in the Bible and in Rabbinic Literature*, Hoboken, NJ: Ktav
Urbach, Ephraim E. 1967 "The Traditions about Merkabah Mysticism in the Tannaitic Period," in E. E. Urbach, R. J. Zwi Werblowsky, and Ch. Wirszubski (eds.), *Studies in Mysticism and Religion Presented to Gershom G. Scholem on His Seventieth Birthday*, Jerusalem: Magnes, pp. 1–28 (Heb.) (repr. in *id.*, *The World of the Sages: Collected Studies*, Jerusalem: Magnes, 1988, pp. 486–513)
— 1975 *The Sages: Their Concepts and Beliefs*, (tr. by Israel Abrahams), 2 vols., Jerusalem: Magnes
— 1986 "Jewish Studies: Impressions and Reflections," in Moshe Bar-Asher (ed.), *Studies in Judaica: Collected Papers of the Symposium in Honour of the Sixtieth Anniversary of the Institute of Jewish Studies (December 1984)*, Jerusalem: Hebrew University, pp. 12–25 (Heb.) (repr. in *id.*, *Studies in Judaica*, (ed. by Moshe D. Herr and Jonah Frenkel), 2 vols., Jerusalem: Magnes, 1998, vol. II, pp. 806–15)
Urman, Dan and Paul V. M. Flesher (eds.) 1998 *Ancient Synagogues: Historical Analysis and Archaeological Discovery*, Studia Post-Biblica 47, Leiden: Brill
Valler, Shulamit 2000 *Women in Jewish Society in the Talmudic Period*, Tel-Aviv: Hakibbutz Hameuchad (Heb.)
Van Dam, Cornelis 1997 *The Urim and Thumim: A Means of Revelation in Ancient Israel*, Winona Lake, IN: Eisenbrauns
van Haelst, Joseph 1976 *Catalogue des papyrus littéraires juifs et chrétiens*, Paris: The Sorbonne
VanderKam, James C. 2001 "Greek at Qumran," in John J. Collins and Gregory E. Sterling (eds.), *Hellenism in the Land of Israel*, Christianity and Judaism in Antiquity, 13, Notre Dame, IN: Notre Dame University Press, pp. 175–81
van der Vliet, Jacques 1995 "Satan's Fall in Coptic Magic," in Meyer and Mirecki 1995, pp. 401–18
Varol, Marie-Christine 2002 "Recipes of Magic-Religious Medicine as Expressed Linguistically," in Avigdor Levy (ed.), *Jews, Turks, Ottomans: A Shared History, Fifteenth through the Twentieth Century*, Syracuse, NY: Syracuse University Press, pp. 260–71
Veltri, Giuseppe 1993 "*'Inyan Soṭa*: Halakhische Voraussetzungen für einen magischen Akt nach einer theoretischen Abhandlung aus der Kairoer Geniza," *FJB* 20, pp. 23–48
— 1996a "Zur Überlieferung medizinisch-magischer Traditionen: Das μήτρα-Motiv in den *Papyri Magicae* und der Kairoer Geniza," *Henoch* 18, pp. 157–75
— 1996b "Jewish Traditions in Greek Amulets," *Bulletin of Judaeo-Greek Studies* 18, pp. 33–47
— 1997 *Magie und Halakha: Ansätze zu einem empirischen Wissenschaftsbegriff im spätantiken und frühmittelalterichen Judentum*, TSAJ 62, Tübingen: Mohr
Verman, Mark 1999 "Signor Tranquillo's Magic Notebook," in Joseph Dan and Klaus Herrmann (eds.), *Studies in Jewish Manuscripts*, TSMEMJ 14, Tübingen: Mohr Siebeck, pp. 231–37

Verman, Mark and Shulamit H. Adler 1993/94 "Path Jumping in the Jewish Magical Tradition," *JSQ* 1, pp. 131–48
Vermes, Geza 1972–73 "Hanina ben Dosa: A Controversial Galilean Saint from the First Century of the Christian Era," *JJS* 23, pp. 28–50, and 24, pp. 51–64
Versnel, H. S. 1991a "Beyond Cursing: The Appeal to Justice in Judicial Prayers," in Faraone and Obbink 1991, pp. 60–106
    1991b "Some Reflections on the Relationship Magic-Religion," *Numen* 38, pp. 177–97
Vinel, Nicolas 2006 "Le judaïsme caché du carré SATOR de Pompéi," *Revue de l'Histoire des Religions* 223, pp. 173–94
von Rad, G. 1962 *Old Testament Theology*, 2 vols., Edinburgh and London: Oliver and Boyd (original German edn, 1957)
von Soden, W. 1966 "Fischgalle als Heilmittel für Augen," *Archiv für Orientsforschung* 21, pp. 81–82
Vycichl, Werner 1938 "Die Aleph-Beth Regel im Demotichen und Koptischen: Eine Untersuchung an ägyptischen und koptischen Zaubersprüchen," *Archiv für Ägyptische Archäologie* 1, pp. 224–26
Vyse, Stuart A. 1997 *Believing in Magic: The Psychology of Superstition*, Oxford: Oxford University Press
Walter, Christopher 1989–90 "The Intaglio of Solomon in the Benaki Museum and the Origins of the Iconography of Warrior Saints," ΔΕΛΤΙΟΝ ΤΗΣ ΧΡΙΣΤΙΑΝΙΚΗΣ ΑΡΧΑΙΟΛΟΓΙΚΗΣ ΕΤΑΙΡΕΙΑΣ 15, pp. 33–42
Wandrey, Irina 2004 *"Das Buch des Gewandes" und "Das Buch des Aufrechten": Dokumente eines magischen spätantiken Rituals, ediert, kommentiert und übersetzt*, TSAJ 96, Tübingen: Mohr Siebeck
Wasserstrom, Steven M. 1992 "The Magical Texts in the Cairo Genizah," in Joshua Blau and Stefan C. Reif (eds.), *Genizah Research after Ninety Years: The Case of Judaeo-Arabic*, Cambridge: Cambridge University Press, pp. 160–66
    1993 "Sepher Yeẓira and Early Islam: A Reappraisal," *JJTP* 3, pp. 1–30
    2002 "Further Thoughts on the Origins of Sepher Yeẓirah," *Aleph* 2, pp. 201–21
    2005 "The Unwritten Chapter: Notes Towards a Social and Religious History of Geniza Magic," in Shaked 2005a, pp. 269–93
Waterman, Leroy 1931 *Preliminary Report upon the Excavations at Tel Umar, Iraq*, Ann Arbor: University of Michigan Press
Weber, Max 1952 *Ancient Judaism*, (tr. by Hans H. Gerth and Don Martindale), Glencoe, IL: Free Press (or. Ger. edn, 1917–19)
Weinstock, I. 1963 "Discovered Legacy of Mystic Writings Left by Abu Aharon of Baghdad," *Tarbiz* 32, pp. 153–59 (Heb.)
    1972 "Towards Clarifying the Text of Sepher Yeẓira," *Ṭemirin* 1, pp. 9–61 (Heb.)
    1981 "The Alphabet of Meṭaṭron and Its Interpretation," *Ṭemirin* 2, pp. 51–76 (Heb.)
Weiss, Abraham 1962 *Studies in the Literature of the Amoraim*, New York: Horeb Yeshiva University (Heb.)

Weiss, Zeev 2005 *The Sepphoris Synagogue: Deciphering an Ancient Message through Its Archaeological and Socio-Historical Contexts*, Jerusalem: Israel Exploration Society

Wendland, E. R. 1992 "Elijah and Elisha: Sorcerers or Witch Doctors?" *Bible Translator* 43, pp. 213–23

Wessely, Karl 1886 *Ephesia Grammata aus Papyrusrollen, Inschriften, Gemmen, etc., Gesammelt*, 12. Jahresbericht des Franz-Joseph-Gymnasiums in Wien, Vienna: A. Pichlers

West, Martin 2000 "Music Therapy in Antiquity," in Peregrine Horden (ed.), *Music as Medicine: The History of Music Therapy Since Antiquity*, Aldershot: Ashgate, pp. 51–68

Wilhelm, Adolf 1901 "Zwei Fluchinschriften," *Jahreshefte des Österreichischen Archäologischen Instituts* 4, Beiblatt, col. 9–18

Wilken, Robert L. 1983 *John Chrysostom and the Jews: Rhetoric and Reality in the Late 4th Century*, The Transformation of the Classical Heritage IV, Berkeley: University of California Press

Winkler, Hans Alexander 1930 *Siegel und Charaktere in der Muhammedanischen Zauberei*, Berlin and Leipzig: De Gruyter

  1935 "Die Aleph-Beth-Regel: Eine Beobachtung an sinnlosen Wörtern im Kinderversen, Zaubersprüchen und Verwandtem," in R. Paret (ed.), *Orientalische Studien Enno Littmann zu seinem 60. Geburtstag*, Leiden: Brill, pp. 1–24

Winkler, John J. 1991 "The Constraints of Eros," in Faraone and Obbink 1991, pp. 214–43

Winston, David 1979 *The Wisdom of Solomon*, Anchor Bible, 43, Garden City, NY: Doubleday & Co.

Wolfe, Lenny and F. Sternberg 1989 *Objects with Semitic Inscriptions 1100 BC–AD 700: Jewish, Early Christian and Byzantine Antiquities*, Zürich: F. Sternberg

Wolfson, Elliot R. 1992 "Images of God's Feet: Some Observations on the Divine Body in Judaism," in Howard Eilberg-Schwartz (ed.), *People of the Body: Jews and Judaism from an Embodied Perspective*, Albany: SUNY Press, pp. 143–81

  2001 "Phantasmagoria: The Image of the Image in Jewish Magic from Late Antiquity to the Early Middle Ages," *Review of Rabbinic Judaism* 4, pp. 78–120

Wright, Archie T. 2005 *The Origin of Evil Spirits: The Reception of Genesis 6.1–4 in Early Jewish Literature*, WUNT 2/198, Tübingen: Mohr

Wünsch, Richard 1898 *Sethianische Verfluchungstafeln aus Rom*, Leipzig: Teubner

  1902 "The Limestone Inscriptions of Tell Sandahannah," in Bliss and Macalister 1902, pp. 158–87

Yadin, Yigael 1963 *The Finds from the Bar-Kokhba Period in the Cave of Letters*, Jerusalem: Israel Exploration Society

  1971 *Bar-Kokhba*, London: Weidenfeld & Nicolson, 1971

Yahalom, J. 1999 *Poetry and Society in Jewish Galilee of Late Antiquity*, Tel Aviv: Hakibbutz Hameuchad, and Jerusalem: Yad Ben Zvi (Heb.)

Yamauchi, Edwin M. 1965 "Aramaic Magic Bowls," *JAOS* 85, pp. 511–23

1967 *Mandaic Incantation Texts*, American Oriental Series 49, New Haven: American Oriental Society

1983 "Magic in the Biblical World," *Tyndale Bulletin* 34, pp. 169–200

Yardeni, Ada 1991 "Remarks on the Priestly Blessing on Two Ancient Amulets from Jerusalem," *VT* 41, pp. 176–85

Yassif, Eli 1988 "Traces of Folk Traditions of the Second Temple Period in Rabbinic Literature," *JJS* 39, pp. 212–33

1999a *The Hebrew Folktale: History, Genre, Meaning* (tr. by Jacqueline S. Teitelbaum), Bloomington, IN: Indiana University Press

1999b "Legend and History: Historians Reading Hebrew Legends of the Middle Ages," *Zion* 64, pp. 187–220 (Heb.)

Youtie, H. C. and Campbell Bonner 1937, "Two Curse Tablets from Beisan," *TAPA* 68, pp. 43–77 and 128

Yuval, Israel J. 2006 *Two Nations in Your Womb: Perceptions of Jews and Christians in Late Antiquity and the Middle Ages* (tr. by Barbara Harshav and Jonathan Chipman), Berkeley: University of California Press

Zimmels, H. J. 1952 *Theologians and Doctors: Studies in Folk-Medicine and Folk-Lore as Reflected in the Rabbinical Responsa (12th–19th Centuries)*, London: Edward Goldston & Son

Index

Ablanathanalba 209, 233, 260
abracadabra 266
Abraham 77, 95, 204, 206, 211, 389
Abrasax/Abraxas 199, 247–50, 252, 256, 257, 268, 296, 307, 312, 336, 342, 372, 416, 432
Abu Aharon the Babylonian 294–95
adjurations 29, 46, 105, 112, 166, 171, 206, 208, 232, 233, 249, 300, 313, 335, 381–82, 420–21
Agrath bat Maḥlat 96
Akrammachammarei 209, 233, 260
Alexander Trallianus 207–09, 413, 415
Alexandria 80, 103, 124, 132, 134
Ammon 254, 257
amulets 30, 41–42, 44, 65, 114–23, 138, 149–53, 159, 162, 164, 165, 167, 187, 206, 208, 210, 214, 216, 231–34, 249, 255–56, 257, 260, 265, 268, 271, 275, 277, 280, 283, 294, 297, 301–02, 303, 310, 334, 337, 343–44, 370–76, 411, 414
amulets, pagan 120–21
angels 46, 58, 168, 171–72, 173, 180, 197–98, 242, 274, 305–06, 307, 381–82, 416
Aphrodite 199, 204, 254, 255, 256, 266, 267, 342
Apollo 254, 345
apotropaic statues 174, 279, 280, 390
Aramaic 89, 111, 150, 158, 161, 166–67, 169, 178, 185, 209, 382
Aramaic magical papyri 165–69
Arsenophru 234
Artapanus 118, 127, 136
Asmodaeus/Ashmedai 89–90, 135, 299, 300
astrology 77, 365
atbash 161–62, 232, 338
Azazel 163, 300

ba'aras root 90–92, 104, 381
Balaam 15, 55, 80, 404
Bar'am, Kibbuẓ, aggressive spell from 156, 318, 319

biblical verses, magical uses of 17, 66, 186, 190, 270, 299, 308–12, 339–40, 374, 378, 385, 412–14, 421
bilingual and trilingual magical texts 167, 231–38, 241, 242, 243, 301–02, 303, 414
Book of Jubilees 82, 93, 97–98, 109
Book of Watchers, see 1 Enoch
Burning Bush 205, 338, 347, 412, 413

catching thieves, rituals for 277, 287
charactêres (ring-letters, magical signs) 168, 173, 189, 198, 233, 240, 250–51, 256, 270–74, 342, 410, 432
Chnoubis (or Chnoumis) 388–89
Christianity, Christian magic, Christian influences 72, 160, 179, 181, 210, 211, 212–14, 232, 252–53, 276, 277–78, 308, 342, 344–45, 399, 415
Chych Bachych-formula 262–63, 416–17
circles, used in magical rituals (*see also* Ḥoni) 286
cock-headed, snake-legged god 197, 198, 279, 389
confession inscriptions 189
Coptic 167, 219, 239
cross-cultural borrowings 12, 65, 126–27, 154, 168, 178, 192, 198, 238, 259–81, 282–83, 284–85, 287, 289–90, 292–93, 296, 342–48, 429–30, 431–32
curse tablets/*Defixiones* 146–47, 154–55, 161, 204, 211–12, 220, 244, 262, 279, 283, 288, 319, 343

Damnameneus 267–68
Daniel 160
David 98–100, 108, 109, 110, 113, 118, 233, 300, 301–02, 390
Decans, astrological 236
Delos, Jewish curses from 125–27, 129, 138
demons 58, 82, 83, 88, 89, 90, 91, 92, 96–97, 98–101, 106, 107, 109, 166, 180, 188, 214, 303, 366, 367–68, 374, 375, 376, 418, 419
Deraqon, see Chnoubis

480

Index

donkey-parts, used in aggressive magic 288, 289, 347
dream requests 43
Dybbuk 92

Egypt 166, 168, 180, 195, 196–97, 232, 234, 239, 357, 392
Ehyeh Asher Ehyeh 210, 232, 265, 305, 306, 338, 377
Eleazar the exorcist 100–01, 103, 104, 105, 110, 116, 140, 302
Elijah 20–21, 23, 24, 26, 33, 128, 293, 395, 401
Elisha 18, 20–23, 24, 26, 31, 33, 49, 128, 376, 401, 405
1 Enoch (*Book of the Watchers*) 81, 109
Ephesian Letters 267–69
Ephesus, magical gem from 161–62
Epicurus 255, 267
Ereschigal 256, 260–61, 318, 372
Evron, Kibbuẓ, amulet from 231, 235, 277, 348
excuses for magical failures 49–50
exorcisms 42, 88–90, 94–114, 116–17, 134, 153, 206–07, 214, 234, 268, 375, 427
exorcistic hymns 107, 108, 109–10, 113–14, 301–04

Fallen Angels 81, 87, 92, 97, 109, 166, 303, 312
Fayyum mummy portraits 150, 189
figurae magicae 279–81

Galen 41, 388
gemaṭria, isopsephy 248, 259
gems, magical 158–65, 197–98, 212, 232, 279, 280–81, 284, 343, 388, 389
Genizah magical texts 8, 9, 66, 110, 144–46, 165, 166, 182, 183, 191, 205, 215–21, 223, 236–38, 244–45, 248, 249, 250–51, 255–56, 261, 262–63, 267–68, 271, 277, 280, 281, 292–95, 303, 310, 311, 312, 313, 321, 352
glossolalia, speaking in tongues 258, 259, 330, 338
God 10, 14, 17, 28, 30–31, 51, 52–58, 95, 98, 99, 107, 126, 129, 172, 196, 198–99, 250, 252, 328, 329
golem 363–64
Greco-Egyptian magic 71, 80, 172–73, 181, 192, 198, 199, 202, 203–04, 234, 240, 247–48, 254, 256, 258–59, 260, 261–62, 264–65, 266, 268, 269, 270–76, 278–79, 281–85, 291, 306, 341–42, 343, 345–47, 387, 388, 416, 417, 420, 422, 427, 429
Greco-Roman magic 70–71, 72, 178, 279
Greek loanwords in Aramaic and Hebrew 172, 178, 179, 182, 192, 236–37, 238–43, 246–47, 272, 294, 304, 374

Greek magical papyri 40, 161, 167, 196–200, 208, 237–38, 279, 281, 283, 287, 289, 312, 347, 387, 413

Hadrumetum, *defixio* from 211–12
Hai Gaon 176, 224–25, 325, 333
halakha, magic and 356–86, 422
Hanina ben Dosa 96, 340, 401
Ḥarba de-Moshe (*Sword of Moses*) 170, 175–79, 224, 232, 241, 243, 249, 252, 254, 263, 281, 286, 288–89, 319, 341
Hasmoneans 38–39, 59, 74
Havdala de-Rabbi Akiva 158, 222
Hebrew 161, 209, 326
Hebrew Bible, (prohibitions of) magic in 10, 11, 13–19, 34–35, 55, 67, 77, 83–84, 121, 427, 428
Hecate 39–40, 199, 204, 268, 279, 345
Hekhalot/Merkabah literature 168, 248, 259, 271, 275, 328, 329–39
Helios 183, 234, 241–42, 251–53, 256, 290, 307, 342, 355
Hermes 254, 256
Herod 131–33
historiola (mythical event used as a magical precedent) 112, 203, 204–05, 296, 308, 312–14, 347, 413–14, 415–16, 421
holy men/men of God 13, 18, 20–27, 31, 33, 67, 94–97, 100–02, 113, 128–30, 139–40, 210, 332, 395, 401–04
holy water 29, 85
Honi the Circle Maker 45, 53, 128, 129, 345, 401, 405
Ḥorvat Ma'on, *see* Nirim
Ḥorvat Meroth, aggressive spell from 155, 307, 318, 319
Ḥorvat Rimmon, erotic spell from 220, 223, 271, 287, 320
Hyesemmigadôn 260–62, 318, 372

Ia(h)ô 196, 198, 199, 208, 211, 232, 296, 347, 389, 415
iconography, magical 159–60, 188–89, 192, 197, 203, 212, 279–81, 347
incantation bowls, Babylonian 65, 110, 111, 183–93, 248, 253, 268–69, 271, 276, 278, 280, 297, 302, 309, 312, 320, 334, 337, 338, 340, 347, 391, 409
iron, used against demons 286, 366, 387
Isaac 160, 212
Isaiah 16
Isis 203, 204, 289, 345, 347

Jacob 199, 202, 211
Jannes and Jambres 136
Jerusalem 207

Jesus 76, 80, 94, 96, 103, 104, 105, 116–17, 128, 135, 181, 207, 209, 277, 278, 344, 364, 399, 405
Josephus 4, 36, 44–45, 74, 75, 79–80, 83–85, 87, 90–92, 93, 99–102, 104, 105, 116, 119, 123–24, 128, 129–30, 131–33, 134, 136, 138

Kabbalah 223, 271, 323, 327
Koinologia 240, 283

Lilith 299, 300, 366
Lot's wife 204, 205, 208, 415
Lycurgus 236–37, 256, 267

mad dogs 417–19
Mageia 79, 346, 356
magic
  aggressive 55–56, 80, 123–35, 145–47, 154–58, 187–88, 244–45, 262, 269, 278, 285, 288–89, 307, 311, 312–13, 318–20, 347–48, 369, 404–06, 407
  and law 82–83, 134
  and politics 24–25, 33, 155–56, 366–69, 406, 428
  and religion 32, 57, 63–67, 297, 322, 388
  and science 43
  apotropaic 64, 109, 122, 153, 187, 316, 321–22, 365, 376, 379–80, 383, 407, 409, 411
  difficulties in defining 3–4, 85, 296–98
  erotic 43, 55, 80, 123, 131–33, 134, 154–58, 185, 220, 223, 245, 249, 287, 289, 312, 320, 334, 381, 396–97, 407–08, 413
  fraudulent 39–40
  Jewish 2, 9–40, 58–61, 66–69
  medical 57, 76–77, 82, 152, 187, 232, 236–37, 246–47, 260, 261, 267, 269, 302, 314–18, 364–65, 371–72, 374, 379–80, 384, 407, 408–09, 411–20
  origins of 81, 82
  squares 432
  study of Jewish 5, 6, 9, 71–73
magical techniques 26, 27, 53, 88, 89, 90, 95, 96, 97, 101, 104–05, 109, 112–13, 114, 135, 141, 173, 193–94, 195, 224, 335–38, 343, 345–46, 349–50, 370–82, 393–422, 432
Magus, Magi 79–80, 84, 277, 356–57
Maimonides 37, 41–42, 43, 64–65, 351
Mandaic 185, 190
Marmaraôth 209, 233, 252, 260
Masṭema 82
medicine, (magic and), *see* magic, medical
Meṭaṭron 274, 336, 337
Mezuzah, Mezuzoth 66–67, 116, 368, 373
Michael 180, 233, 296, 307
migraines, spells against 236–37, 240, 315
Minim 12, 372, 392, 398–401, 404–05

mistranslations from Greek 237, 244–45
monotheism 10, 51–61, 68
Moses 13, 17, 20, 21, 23, 24, 25, 29, 30, 32, 34, 66, 78, 79, 84, 118, 119, 127, 176, 196, 202, 211, 293, 299, 307, 310, 338, 347, 365, 390, 395, 400, 412, 414
mysticism, magic and 322–39

Name(s), the (of God) 17, 18, 19, 22, 29, 32, 117–19, 127, 141, 293, 305–07, 329, 335, 374, 376–78, 389, 404
names of angels 171–72, 198, 233, 299, 305–06, 307, 335, 336–37
names of twelve, twenty-two, forty-two, seventy-two letters 254, 306–07, 374, 378
Naqav/Noqev the Name 17–18, 32, 376
necromancy 38, 363
New Testament, magic in 75–76, 80, 94, 105, 128, 138, 315
Nirim, Kibbuẓ, amulets from 249, 260, 315–17, 318, 319–20, 348, 372, 379
Noah 82, 97–98, 126, 129, 170

occult sciences, the 4–5
Oria (Southern Italy) 294–95
Origen 200, 304, 388, 389
Osiris 203, 204, 234, 254, 256, 279, 289, 345, 347
ouroboros 162, 189, 197, 276
Oxyrhynchus 166–67, 214, 226

Pakerbêth 234
path jumping 45–46
pendants, amuletic 164–65, 212, 281
Pephtha Phôza 258
Pharaoh 310
pharmakon/a 77, 78, 84, 85, 123, 125
Philo 78–79, 80, 87, 134
Phre, the Egyptian sun-god 234
physicians and amulets 370–72
Pishra de-Rabbi Ḥanina ben Dosa 222
planting of cucumbers 359–60, 418
power(s), sources of 23, 28–34, 108, 305–22
practitioners, identity of 14–19, 36, 139–40, 334, 348, 391, 428
  Ba'alat 'ov/ yide'oni 14, 15, 16, 38
  Mekhasheph(a) 15, 19, 346, 356, 358, 363, 382, 397, 409
  Me'onen 14, 15
  Menahesh 14, 15
  Qosem 14, 15, 16, 17, 19
Priestly Blessing (Nm 6.22-27) 30, 141, 299, 309
priests, the/High Priest 28–29, 30–31, 33, 59, 60, 86, 117, 129–31, 140

Index

Psalm 91 (90 LXX) 108, 110, 212, 213, 299, 309, 379, 380, 421
Ptah 234, 256

Qumran 4, 36, 82–83, 87, 95, 124, 137, 138, 140, 238, 301, 303
Qumran, Dead Sea Scrolls 75, 82, 105–12, 114, 117, 168
   4Q510-511 (4Q Songs of the Sage) 107
   4Q560 (4QExorcism ar) 111–12, 300
   11Q11 (11Q Apocryphal psalms) 108–11, 299, 301, 303, 304, 380

rabbinic literature 12, 57, 77, 86, 90, 96, 117–19, 129, 130–31, 150, 190, 192, 227, 240, 251, 263, 269, 287, 297, 351–425
recipes, magical, and recipe-books 112, 144–46, 147–48, 165–66, 169, 171–72, 173, 176, 182–83, 196–97, 199–200, 202–09, 216–17, 219–21, 222, 223, 225, 236–38, 242, 249, 250–51, 252, 253, 262–63, 281–83, 285, 287, 288–89, 293–94, 303, 312, 313, 319, 321, 344, 406–22, 432
rings, magical 101, 104, 119, 159, 162, 164, 180, 388

Sabaôth 198, 199, 204, 208, 209, 210, 214, 232, 233, 296, 306, 338, 377, 415, 418
sacred objects, manipulation and use of 28–34, 117–18, 141, 381
sacrifices 29, 133
Samael, *see* Satan
Samaritan magic 393
Sandalphon 336, 337
Sarapis 254, 256, 342
Satan 76, 300
Satraperkmêph 234
Saul 14, 26, 98–100, 302
scribalization of Jewish magic 36, 60, 185–87, 190, 195, 283–85, 301, 427, 430
Scroll of Aḥimaaẓ 294–95, 297, 333
Sêmea Kenteu-formula 197, 263, 336
Semeseilam 197, 209, 233, 256, 258
Sepher ha-Malbush 222
Sepher ha-Razim 66, 163, 170–75, 215, 234, 241–43, 246, 249, 252, 254, 261, 271, 280, 281, 288, 291, 294, 300, 307, 313, 340, 341, 342, 348, 388, 390
Sepher ha-Yashar 222, 224
Sepher Raziel 222
Sepher Yezira 326–28, 339, 363
Sesengen Barpharangês 209, 233, 257, 260, 336
Seth-Typhon 203, 206, 234, 289, 347
Shamash 251, 254
Shemiḥaza 300

Shimeon ben Sheṭaḥ 53, 86, 394–95
Shimmush Tehillim 222
Shi'ur Qomah 271, 328–29, 339
signs and symbols used in Jewish magic 159–60, 162, 163, 164, 188–89, 270–81
skulls, magical 193–94, 390
Sodom and Gomorrah 204–05, 206, 249, 307, 312–13, 347, 413, 414, 415–16
Solomon 93, 100–02, 105, 109, 113, 119, 160, 180–81, 202, 212, 214, 236, 252–53, 300, 304, 408
Soṭah 28–30, 118, 293–95, 297, 321
Soumartha 233
Sword of Moses, *see Ḥarba de-Moshe*
synagogue, magic and the 155, 156, 314–22
Syriac magical texts 185, 190, 277

T-shirt, amuletic 122, 383, 411
Tefillin 115, 368, 373, 380, 381
Tell el-Amarna, amulet from 232, 235, 256, 265, 301, 348
Temple, the 28, 29, 32, 59, 74, 75, 128, 180, 377
Teraphim, the 390
Testament of Job 122
Testament of Solomon 170, 179–82, 236–37, 252–53
Tetragrammaton, the 117–19, 167, 277, 299, 305, 306
Thoth 254
threatening and coercing God or gods 345–46
Torah, Torah-scrolls and Torah-ark 293, 294, 315, 316, 317, 321, 368, 373, 381, 404
triangles, made of words and letters 233, 236, 255–56, 262, 265, 266–70, 419, 422

voces magicae 159, 173, 179, 198, 199, 203, 204, 206, 209–10, 233, 237, 240, 243, 255, 256, 258–64, 266, 267, 292, 335, 336, 387, 416–17, 419, 421–22
vowels and vowel-permutations 233, 250, 251, 264–65, 326

Wales, amulet from 210
"Ways of the Amorites," the 364, 366, 382–85, 386–87, 417
whisper (*laḥash*) 16, 17, 361, 377, 378, 379
wombs and uterine magic 237–38, 276, 310–11, 337
women and magic 15, 24, 81, 334, 367, 392, 393–98, 410

Yehoshua ben Peraḥiah 340

Zeus 254
Ẓiẓ, of the high priest 239

apotropaic • 30

Made in the USA
San Bernardino, CA
05 October 2015